Connections

Editorial Board

Connections

A Lectionary Commentary for Preaching and Worship

Joel B. Green

Thomas G. Long

Luke A. Powery

Cynthia L. Rigby

General Editors

WESTMINSTER
JOHN KNOX PRESS
LOUISVILLE · KENTUCKY

© 2018 Westminster John Knox Press

First edition
Published by Westminster John Knox Press
Louisville, Kentucky

18 19 20 21 22 23 24 25 26 27—10 9 8 7 6 5 4 3 2 1

Unless otherwise indicated, Scripture quotations are from the New Revised Standard Version of the Bible, copyright © 1989 by the Division of Christian Education of the National Council of the Churches of Christ in the U.S.A., and are used by permission.

Scripture quotations marked CEB are from the Common English Bible, © 2011 Common English Bible, and are used by permission. Scripture quotations marked ESV are from the *The Holy Bible, English Standard Version,* © 2001 by Crossway Bibles, a publishing ministry of Good News Publishers. Used by permission. All rights reserved. Scripture quotations marked JUB are taken from the Jubilee Bible, copyright © 2000, 2001, 2010, 2013 by Life Sentence Publishing, Inc. Used by permission of Life Sentence Publishing, Inc., Abbotsford, Wisconsin. All rights reserved. Scripture quotations marked NIV are from *The Holy Bible, New International Version.* Copyright © 1973, 1978, 1984, 2011 by Biblica, Inc.® Used by permission. All rights reserved worldwide. Scripture quotations marked NKJV are from The New King James Version. Copyright © 1979, 1980, 1982, Thomas Nelson Inc., Publishers and are used by permission.

Excerpt from "The Time of the End Is the Time of No Room," by Thomas Merton, from *Raids of the Unspeakable,* copyright © 1966 by The Abbey of Gethsemani, Inc. Reprinted by permission of New Directions Publishing Corp.

Excerpt from Brian K. Blount, "Pick a Fight" (unpublished sermon). Reprinted by permission.

Book and cover design by Allison Taylor

Library of Congress Cataloging-in-Publication Data
Names: Long, Thomas G., 1946- editor.
Title: Connections : a lectionary commentary for preaching and worship / Joel
  B. Green, Thomas G. Long, Luke A. Powery, Cynthia L. Rigby, general
  editors.
Description: Louisville, Kentucky : Westminster John Knox Press, 2018- |
  Includes index. |
Identifiers: LCCN 2018006372 (print) | LCCN 2018012579 (ebook) | ISBN
  9781611648874 (ebk.) | ISBN 9780664262433 (volume 1 : hbk. : alk. paper)
Subjects: LCSH: Lectionary preaching. | Bible--Meditations. | Common
  lectionary (1992) | Lectionaries.
Classification: LCC BV4235.L43 (ebook) | LCC BV4235.L43 C66 2018 (print) |
  DDC 251/.6--dc23
LC record available at https://lccn.loc.gov/2018006372

PRINTED IN THE UNITED STATES OF AMERICA

♾ The paper used in this publication meets the minimum requirements of the American National Standard
for Information Sciences—Permanence of Paper for Printed Library Materials, ANSI Z39.48-1992.

Westminster John Knox Press advocates the responsible use of our natural resources.
The text paper of this book is made from 30% postconsumer waste.

Most Westminster John Knox Press books are available at special quantity discounts when purchased in bulk by corporations, organizations, and special-interest groups. For more information, please e-mail SpecialSales@wjkbooks.com.

Contents

Publisher's Note

"The preaching of the Word of God is the Word of God," says the Second Helvetic Confession. While that might sound like an exalted estimation of the homiletical task, it comes with an implicit warning: "A lot is riding on this business of preaching. Get it right!"

Believing that much does indeed depend on the church's proclamation, we offer Connections: A Lectionary Commentary for Preaching and Worship. Connections embodies two complementary convictions about the study of Scripture in preparation for preaching and worship. First, to best understand an individual passage of Scripture, we should put it in conversation with the rest of the Bible. Second, since all truth is God's truth, we should bring as many "lenses" as possible to the study of Scripture, drawn from as many sources as we can find. Our prayer is that this unique combination of approaches will illumine your study and preparation, facilitating the weekly task of bringing the Word of God to the people of God.

We at Westminster John Knox Press want to thank the superb editorial team that came together to make Connections possible. At the heart of that team are our general editors: Joel B. Green, Thomas G. Long, Luke A. Powery, and Cynthia L. Rigby. These four gifted scholars and preachers have poured countless hours into brainstorming, planning, reading, editing, and supporting the project. Their passion for authentic preaching and transformative worship shows up on every page. They pushed the writers and their fellow editors, they pushed us at the press, and most especially they pushed themselves to focus always on what you, the users of this resource, genuinely need. We are grateful to Kimberly Bracken Long for her innovative vision of what commentary on the Psalm readings could accomplish and for recruiting a talented group of liturgists and preachers to implement that vision. Bo Adams has shown creativity and insight in exploring an array of sources to provide the sidebars that accompany each worship day's commentaries. At the forefront of the work have been the members of our editorial board, who helped us identify writers, assign passages, and most especially carefully edit each commentary. They have cheerfully allowed the project to intrude on their schedules in order to make possible this contribution to the life of the church. Most especially we thank our writers, drawn from a broad diversity of backgrounds, vocations, and perspectives. The distinctive character of our commentaries required much from our writers. Their passion for the preaching ministry of the church proved them worthy of the challenge.

A project of this size does not come together without the work of excellent support staff. Above all we are indebted to project manager Joan Murchison. Joan's fingerprints are all over the book you hold in your hands; her gentle, yet unconquerable, persistence always kept it moving forward in good shape and on time.

Finally, our sincere thanks to the administration, faculty, and staff of Austin Presbyterian Theological Seminary, our institutional partner in producing Connections. President Theodore J. Wardlaw and Dean David H. Jensen have been steadfast friends of the project, enthusiastically agreeing to our partnership, carefully overseeing their faculty and staff's work on it, graciously hosting our meetings, and enthusiastically using their platform to promote Connections among their students, alumni, and friends.

It is with much joy that we commend Connections to you, our readers. May God use this resource to deepen and enrich your ministry of preaching and worship.

WESTMINSTER JOHN KNOX PRESS

Introducing Connections

Connections is a resource designed to help preachers generate sermons that are theologically deeper, liturgically richer, and culturally more pertinent. Based on the Revised Common Lectionary (RCL), which has wide ecumenical use, the hundreds of essays on the full array of biblical passages in the three-year cycle can be used effectively by preachers who follow the RCL, by those who follow other lectionaries, and by nonlectionary preachers alike.

The essential idea of Connections is that biblical texts display their power most fully when they are allowed to interact with a number of contexts, that is, when many connections are made between a biblical text and realities outside that text. Like the two poles of a battery, when the pole of the biblical text is connected to a different pole (another aspect of Scripture or a dimension of life outside Scripture), creative sparks fly and energy surges from pole to pole.

Two major interpretive essays, called Commentary 1 and Commentary 2, address every scriptural reading in the RCL. Commentary 1 explores preaching connections between a lectionary reading and other texts and themes within Scripture, and Commentary 2 makes preaching connections between the lectionary texts and themes in the larger culture outside of Scripture. These essays have been written by pastors, biblical scholars, theologians, and others, all of whom have a commitment to lively biblical preaching.

The writers of Commentary 1 surveyed five possible connections for their texts: the immediate literary context (the passages right around the text), the larger literary context (for example, the cycle of David stories or the passion narrative), the thematic context (such as other feeding stories, other parables, or other passages on the theme of hope), the lectionary context (the other readings for the day in the RCL), and the canonical context (other places in the whole of the Bible that display harmony, or perhaps tension, with the text at hand).

The writers of Commentary 2 surveyed six possible connections for their texts: the liturgical context (such as Advent or Easter), the ecclesial context (the life and mission of the church), the social and ethical context (justice and social responsibility), the cultural context (such as art, music, and literature), the larger expanse of human knowledge (such as science, history, and psychology), and the personal context (the life and faith of individuals).

In each essay, the writers selected from this array of possible connections, emphasizing those connections they saw as most promising for preaching. It is important to note that, even though Commentary 1 makes connections inside the Bible and Commentary 2 makes connections outside the Bible, this does not represent a division between "what the text *meant* in biblical times versus what the text *means* now." *Every* connection made with the text, whether that connection is made within the Bible or out in the larger culture, is seen as generative for preaching, and each author provokes the imagination of the preacher to see in these connections preaching possibilities for today. Connections is not a substitute for traditional scriptural commentaries, concordances, Bible dictionaries, and other interpretive tools. Rather, Connections begins with solid biblical scholarship and then goes on to focus on the act of preaching and on the ultimate goal of allowing the biblical text to come alive in the sermon.

Connections addresses every biblical text in the RCL, and it takes seriously the architecture of the RCL. During the seasons of the Christian year (Advent through Epiphany and Lent through Pentecost), the RCL provides three readings and a psalm for each Sunday and feast day: (1) a first reading, usually from the Old Testament; (2) a psalm, chosen to respond to the first reading; (3) a second reading, usually from one of the New Testament epistles; and (4) a Gospel reading. The first and second readings are chosen as complements to the Gospel reading for the day.

During the time between Pentecost and Advent, however, the RCL includes an additional first reading for every Sunday. There is the usual complementary reading, chosen in relation to the Gospel reading, but there is also a "semicontinuous" reading. These semicontinuous first readings move through the books of the Old Testament more or less continuously in narrative sequence, offering the stories of the patriarchs (Year A), the kings of Israel (Year B), and the prophets (Year C). Connections covers both the complementary and the semicontinuous readings.

The architects of the RCL understand the psalms and canticles to be prayers, and they selected the psalms for each Sunday and feast as prayerful responses to the first reading for the day. Thus, the Connections essays on the psalms are different from the other essays, and they have two goals, one homiletical and the other liturgical. First, they comment on ways the psalm might offer insight into preaching the first reading. Second, they describe how the tone and content of the psalm or canticle might inform the day's worship, suggesting ways the psalm or canticle may be read, sung, or prayed.

Preachers will find in Connections many ideas and approaches to sustain lively and provocative preaching for years to come. But beyond the deep reservoir of preaching connections found in these pages, preachers will also find here a habit of mind, a way of thinking about biblical preaching. Being guided by the essays in Connections to see many connections between biblical texts and their various contexts, preachers will be stimulated to make other connections for themselves. Connections is an abundant collection of creative preaching ideas, and it is also a spur to continued creativity.

JOEL B. GREEN
THOMAS G. LONG
LUKE A. POWERY
CYNTHIA L. RIGBY
General Editors

Introducing the Revised Common Lectionary

To derive the greatest benefit from Connections, it will help to understand the structure and purpose of the Revised Common Lectionary (RCL), around which this resource is built. The RCL is a three-year guide to Scripture readings for the Christian Sunday gathering for worship. "Lectionary" simply means a selection of texts for reading and preaching. The RCL is an adaptation of the Roman Lectionary (of 1969, slightly revised in 1981), which itself was a reworking of the medieval Western-church one-year cycle of readings. The RCL resulted from six years of consultations that included representatives from nineteen churches or denominational agencies. Every preacher uses a lectionary—whether it comes from a specific denomination or is the preacher's own choice—but the RCL is unique in that it positions the preacher's homiletical work within a web of specific, ongoing connections.

The RCL has its roots in Jewish lectionary systems and early Christian ways of reading texts to illumine the biblical meaning of a feast day or time in the church calendar. Among our earliest lectionaries are the lists of readings for Holy Week and Easter in fourth-century Jerusalem.

One of the RCL's central connections is intertextuality; multiple texts are listed for each day. This lectionary's way of reading Scripture is based on Scripture's own pattern: texts interpreting texts. In the RCL, every Sunday of the year and each special or festival day is assigned a group of texts, normally three readings and a psalm. For most of the year, the first reading is an Old Testament text, followed by a psalm, a reading from one of the epistles, and a reading from one of the Gospel accounts.

The RCL's three-year cycle centers Year A in Matthew, Year B in Mark, and Year C in Luke. It is less clear how the Gospel according to John fits in, but when preachers learn about the RCL's arrangement of the Gospels, it makes sense. John gets a place of privilege because John's Gospel account, with its high Christology, is assigned for the great feasts. Texts from John's account are also assigned for Lent, Sundays of Easter, and summer Sundays. The second-century bishop Irenaeus's insistence on four Gospels is evident in this lectionary system: John and the Synoptics are in conversation with each other. However, because the RCL pattern contains variations, an extended introduction to the RCL can help the preacher learn the reasons for texts being set next to other texts.

The Gospel reading governs each day's selections. Even though the ancient order of reading texts in the Sunday gathering positions the Gospel reading last, the preacher should know that the RCL receives the Gospel reading as the hermeneutical key.

At certain times in the calendar year, the connections between the texts are less obvious. The RCL offers two tracks for readings in the time after Pentecost (Ordinary Time/standard Sundays): the complementary and the semicontinuous. Complementary texts relate to the church year and its seasons; semicontinuous emphasis is on preaching through a biblical book. Both approaches are historic ways of choosing texts for Sunday. This commentary series includes both the complementary and the semicontinuous readings.

In the complementary track, the Old Testament reading provides an intentional tension, a deeper understanding, or a background reference for another text of the day. The Psalm is the congregation's response to the first reading, following its themes. The Epistle functions as the horizon of the church: we learn about the faith and struggles of early Christian communities. The Gospel tells us where we are in the church's time and is enlivened, as are all the texts, by these intertextual interactions. Because the semicontinuous track prioritizes the narratives of specific books, the intertextual connections are not as apparent. Connections still exist, however. Year A pairs Matthew's account with Old Testament readings from the first five books; Year B pairs Mark's account with stories of anointed kings; Year C pairs Luke's account with the prophetic books.

Historically, lectionaries came into being because they were the church's beloved texts, like the scriptural canon. Choices had to be made regarding readings in the assembly, given the limit of fifty-two Sundays and a handful of festival days. The RCL presupposes that everyone (preachers and congregants) can read these texts—even along with the daily RCL readings that are paired with the Sunday readings.

Another central connection found in the RCL is the connection between texts and church seasons or the church's year. The complementary texts make these connections most clear. The intention of the RCL is that the texts of each Sunday or feast day bring biblical meaning to where we are in time. The texts at Christmas announce the incarnation. Texts in Lent renew us to follow Christ, and texts for the fifty days of Easter proclaim God's power over death and sin and our new life in Christ. The entire church's year is a hermeneutical key for using the RCL.

Let it be clear that the connection to the church year is a connection for present-tense proclamation. We read, not to recall history, but to know how those events are true for us today. Now is the time of the Spirit of the risen Christ; now we beseech God in the face of sin and death; now we live baptized into Jesus' life and ministry. To read texts in time does not mean we remind ourselves of Jesus' biography for half of the year and then the mission of the church for the other half. Rather, we follow each Gospel's narrative order to be brought again to the meaning of Jesus' death and resurrection and his risen presence in our midst. The RCL positions the texts as our lens on our life and the life of the world in our time: who we are in Christ now, for the sake of the world.

The RCL intends to be a way of reading texts to bring us again to faith, for these texts to be how we see our lives and our gospel witness in the world. Through these connections, the preacher can find faithful, relevant ways to preach year after year.

JENNIFER L. LORD
Connections Editorial Board Member

Connections

First Sunday of Advent

Jeremiah 33:14–16 *HB 1133*
Psalm 25:1–10 *HB 795*

1 Thessalonians 3:9–13 *NT 342*
Luke 21:25–36 *NT 138*

12-2-18

10-21

Jeremiah 33:14–16 *HB 1133*

¹⁴The days are surely coming, says the LORD, when I will fulfill the promise I made to the house of Israel and the house of Judah. ¹⁵In those days and at that time I will cause a righteous Branch to spring up for David; and he shall execute justice and righteousness in the land. ¹⁶In those days Judah will be saved and Jerusalem will live in safety. And this is the name by which it will be called: "The LORD is our righteousness."

Commentary 1: Connecting the Reading with Scripture

This brief passage consists of three pronouncements, each of which begins by announcing a future that will come to pass and is already on its way. The phrase "the days are surely coming" is distinctive of Jeremiah. It introduces short declarations that articulate the prophet's eschatological vision, which encompasses judgment (7:32–34; 9:25–26; 19:6–9; 51:47), return (16:14–15; 23:7–8), and restoration (23:5–6; 30:3; 31:27–28, 31–32, 38–40). In this instance, the formula introduces a unit that speaks of a restored monarchy and priesthood and of the Lord's determination to fulfill divine promises (vv. 14–26). The unit concludes a collection of messages, generally referred to as the Book of Comfort (30:1–33:27), that looks forward to God's restoration of the people and land.

The passage speaks of a Branch that the Lord will cause to spring up for David. The epithet evokes Isaiah's image of the Branch that sprouts from the stump of Jesse. Isaiah envisions an ideal Davidic king who will reign with wisdom, understanding, and righteousness and preside over a renewed earth that knows no violence or destruction (Isa. 11:1–9). Jeremiah names righteousness as the salient attribute of this king and the land he rules. Righteousness in this context may be understood as the right ordering of the world necessary for life to flourish, specifically as this right ordering is manifested in the Torah by God's ordering of Israel

through commandments, laws, and rituals. As a righteous king, the Branch rules in accord with the divine order. In contrast to the disordering kings of Jeremiah's time, the Branch extends the Lord's righteousness by executing justice.

Divine justice entails the maintenance of social and cosmic equilibrium that emanates from right ordering. Israel's kings were charged with executing justice and righteousness as a necessary condition for the blessing of the land and people (1 Kgs. 10:9; Pss. 72:1–3; 89:14). The king, in short, was to implement the Lord's mandate for justice among the people (Ps. 99:4; cf. Pss. 33:5; 89:14). Jeremiah echoes these sentiments elsewhere by calling the powerful to recognize that the Lord practices "steadfast love, justice, and righteousness in the earth" (9:24) and admonishing Jerusalem's kings to do the same (22:3, 15). Although Judah's kings failed in their mandate, the Branch's reign will unite the people (the house of Israel and the house of Judah) and the land (Judah and Jerusalem) within the sphere of the Lord's beneficial order, so that the land itself may be called "The LORD is our righteousness."

As a whole, the vision of restorative righteousness looks back to and reiterates a prophetic pronouncement that occurs earlier in the book (23:5–6), the "promise" that the Lord confirms will be fulfilled, but with a significant change. In the first instance, the prophet declares that the

Branch will be named "The LORD is our righteousness." In this second utterance, the name is bestowed on the land rather than the king. Here Judah and Jerusalem are given the name. The change shifts the focus, from the character of the Branch (in the first case) to the result of the Branch's reign, that is, the righteous ruling that renders salvation and safety for the land.

The shift in emphasis toward the land becomes clearer when it is recognized that the passage stands between pronouncements of devastation and restoration set in Jeremiah's time (33:1–13), and emphatic declarations that the Lord will bring about every promise of healing and restoration in an unspecified future (33:17–26). The preceding passage presents a terrifying description of the destruction to come at the hands of the Chaldeans (vv. 4–5), abruptly shifts to promises that the Lord will bring restoration, healing, security, and forgiveness (vv. 6–9), and concludes by calling the doomed people to look beyond their devastated land and envision a landscape once again filled with merriment and grazing flocks (vv. 10–13).

The lection then pivots from the near historical horizon to the eschatological fulfillment of the Lord's covenant with Abraham, Isaac, Jacob, and the establishment of salvation and security through the Branch (vv. 17–26). The historical particularity of the Chaldean invasion thus accentuates the failure of Israel's kings to bring salvation, providing the basis for the vision's emphatic declarations that the Lord will unilaterally accomplish this end through the righteous Branch.

The Book of Comfort as a whole strikes a note of hope against the pall of disaster, despair, and divine wrath that pervades much of Jeremiah. The oracles and messages within it declare that destruction and wrath, no matter how utter and complete, are not the Lord's last word concerning Israel. Rather, the catastrophic present must be seen as a pulling down and plucking up necessary for a building up and planting that will remake the landscape (1:10; 24:6–7; 31:28). Jeremiah 33:14–16 declares that the remaking will be the Lord's work through the Lord's king, a new and permanent king who will replace the impotent kings held captive by the moment. The vision of a future beyond the contemporary horizon, therefore, calls the people of God to look beyond the present moment, with its violence, disintegration, and failed leadership, to the restorative end toward which the Lord is moving, and so to orient faith and decision making within the context of God's ultimate power and purposes, rather than the clamoring demands of a paralyzed present. This is but one of many such visions in the prophetic literature that speak of the Lord's determination to renew the creation once and for all (e.g., Isa. 25–27; Ezek. 47:1–12; Hos. 14:4–7; Joel 2:23–32; Amos 9:11–15; Mic. 4:1–5).

The other three lections respond to the promise of eschatological justice with supplication and anticipation. Psalm 25:1–10 can be read as the human response to the promise whose fulfillment is announced by this passage. The psalm is, first of all, a declaration of trust and, second, a plea that the Lord ensure that a waiting people not be put to shame (vv. 1–2). The psalmist responds to the declaration that the Branch will execute justice and righteousness by asking the Lord for instruction in the ways and paths that reflect God's righteousness in the world (vv. 3–10).

The New Testament lections share a sense of expectancy. First Thessalonians 3:9–13 expresses Paul's eagerness to reunite with those whom he brought to faith and concludes with a reference to the coming of the Lord that will fulfill the prophets' eschatological vision. Like Jeremiah, Paul speaks of God's powerful working in the lives of believers, to make love abound and to strengthen holy hearts. Luke 21:25–36 looks directly toward the king that Jeremiah speaks about—the Branch, now the Son of Man—and exhorts diligent vigilance in the space between the historical now and the eschatological future. The parable of the fig tree and Jesus' admonitions to pay attention to the signs of his coming remind readers that God is not absent or inactive in the interim but, to the contrary, powerfully at work in every present moment to bring about the redemptive end foreseen by the prophets.

L. DANIEL HAWK

Commentary 2: Connecting the Reading with the World

The Advent season opens with a promise to Jeremiah that God will fulfill the divine promise to establish David and his dynasty forever (2 Sam. 7:11–16). To people in exile, this promise gains specificity. It focuses on "a righteous Branch to spring up for David" who shall "execute justice and righteousness in the land" (v. 15). This righteous one brings safety to the people, saving them. This one will be called "The LORD is our righteousness" (v. 16; cf. Jer. 23:5–6).

Liturgical Context. This word of hope is appropriate for the First Sunday of Advent and reaches out to us, always. It looks forward, anticipating an action of God in caring for the people of God. The promised one will embody what God most desires: carrying out justice and righteousness. This one will save the people, as God through Israel's history had been the "God of salvation" (Ps. 68:20), leading to the affirmation: "Truly in the LORD our God is the salvation of Israel" (Jer. 3:23). Restoration of the exiled people to their homeland and the safety of the land and its people rests in the work of the righteous one.

The Christian church has seen this prophecy fulfilled in Jesus Christ. In Advent, the church anticipates the coming Christ, finding in him the reality of all God's promises (2 Cor. 1:20). Jesus Christ is the righteous one of David's line. He brings the strong hope of carrying out God's justice and righteousness in himself. He brings salvation through his life, death, and resurrection, establishing forgiveness, reconciliation, and peace with God forever. He protects and secures those who believe in him. He enables lives of safety marked by praise and thanks to Jesus, who is rightly called "The Lord is our righteousness." Liturgically, during Advent these words of promise find their reality in the coming Christ, who is "God with us" (Matt. 1:23). Jesus brings the blessings of God's continual presence with God's people. He enables new lives to be lived in relationships of love and trust with God and others.

Ecclesial Context. This Advent promise provides the church with its message and mission. The church proclaims there is a God of hope who has sent God's Son, the righteous one— Jesus Christ. The promise is that Jesus Christ does what is just and right. He shows us what living this way means in human life, giving us a model to follow. The church's mission is to continue this ministry and enact God's justice and righteousness in caring for the world and the needs of all people. Since Jesus himself is God's mission to the world, the church lives God's mission as it conveys Jesus Christ. As theologian Karl Barth put it, the church community is "the earthly-historical form of existence of Jesus Christ himself."[1] In and through the church, Christ's work is carried out.

To be the people of God means proclaiming there is salvation and safety in Christ. This is a message of power, hope, and peace for the world. The church declares that God's ancient promises to the prophet are now real in Christ. The God who has been Israel's salvation is also the God who saves us today. The church lives out its salvation by following the ways and will of Christ. We are led by the Holy Spirit to proclaim this good news in word and deed.

Social and Ethical Context. Advent is a time of hope that points us ultimately to God's coming reign or kingdom. Jesus Christ brings God's reign in himself. Early church theologians spoke of God's kingdom as *autobasileia*, a "self-kingdom"—a kingdom in Jesus Christ himself. God's righteousness and justice are found in Christ, as well as salvation and safety. This makes it possible for us to live in God's reign here and now. We can live in the freedom of serving God and receive the blessings of God's presence with us in Christ. This sustains us and launches us into participating in God's kingdom in Christ every day!

There is no greater impetus for the church and the Christian's involvement in the world than God's reign. This reign is with us now in Jesus Christ, the promised "righteous Branch,"

---

1. Karl Barth, *Church Dogmatics*, ed. G. W. Bromiley and T. F. Torrance, trans. G. W. Bromiley, 4 vols. (New York: Charles Scribner's Sons, 1956), IV/1:661.

who carries out justice and righteousness. This reign is the coming kingdom for which Jesus instructed his disciples to pray: "Your kingdom come" (Matt. 6:10). We work and serve Jesus Christ as people of his reign seeking the justice and righteousness that he embodies for the people of the earth. What is most worth doing for Christ's disciples is investing ourselves for the sake of others in this world because "the Lord is our righteousness." We do what is just and right on their behalf and because of God in Christ.

We can live out God's promise to Jeremiah, especially in Advent, when we *look for signs* of God's reign in Christ around us, and when we *plant signs* of God's reign in Christ with others.

If Jesus is our model of justice and righteousness, we will see Christ's reign when what is just and right prevails in our society. When right relationships are established between persons and institutions and among groups and persons, we recognize that the righteous one, Jesus Christ, is present. We see the reign of Christ happening.

By joining the struggle for justice, human rights, and peace, we can plant signs in our culture of God's reign in Christ. This is what Jesus himself desires and embodies. As Christ's disciples in the church, we join in seeking the righteousness Jesus showed and was in himself. Despite the fact that these struggles have to be made continually—and that nothing stays won in these arenas—the church continues its witness and work. We are pulled forward in faith by the promise of God's coming reign, and by the promise that God's reign is already present in the person of Jesus Christ, the "righteous Branch," who is God with us. This is what enables us to keep on through life. We obey Paul's word: "Brothers and sisters, do not be weary in doing what is right" (2 Thess. 3:13).

Personal Context. The message of Jeremiah was a word of hope and comfort for Israel and Judah. In Jesus Christ, this is a word of hope and challenge for the church. God's promise in Christ also touches our human hearts. The promise to Jeremiah means the future is now. In Jesus Christ, we live in the reign of God as we anticipate further the fullness of God's reign in the eternal life Christ gives us (John 10:28). We look to Jesus as the model for how to live— doing what is right and just in God's sight. He is "the righteous Branch." In him we will be saved. We receive God's forgiveness and reconciliation, knowing the joy of Christ's presence, and being led by the Holy Spirit, who unites us to Christ by faith. We are kept in safety, as Jeremiah was promised. As followers of Christ, we are sustained by God's love in Christ. We are enabled to live as Christ desires. We are given the deep personal assurance that nothing in all creation "will be able to separate us from the love of God in Christ Jesus our Lord" (Rom. 8:39).

DONALD K. McKIM

Psalm 25:1–10 *(1– 22)*

¹To you, O LORD, I lift up my soul.
²O my God, in you I trust;
   do not let me be put to shame;
   do not let my enemies exult over me.
³Do not let those who wait for you be put to shame;
   let them be ashamed who are wantonly treacherous.

⁴Make me to know your ways, O LORD;
   teach me your paths.
⁵Lead me in your truth, and teach me,
   for you are the God of my salvation;
   for you I wait all day long.

⁶Be mindful of your mercy, O LORD, and of your steadfast love,
   for they have been from of old.
⁷Do not remember the sins of my youth or my transgressions;
   according to your steadfast love remember me,
   for your goodness' sake, O LORD!

⁸Good and upright is the LORD;
   therefore he instructs sinners in the way.
⁹He leads the humble in what is right,
   and teaches the humble his way.
¹⁰All the paths of the LORD are steadfast love and faithfulness,
   for those who keep his covenant and his decrees.

Connecting the Psalm with Scripture and Worship

The season of Advent calls us to watch and wait, to prepare for God's coming again in judgment. The surrounding culture is not interested in this sort of Christmas preparation. The waiting is over by Halloween, as full-blown Christmas displays appear in stores, sales abound, and sidewalk Santas ring bells inducing generosity or guilt. Even those of us who observe the Advent discipline of waiting often "sweeten" the time. We count down the days with Advent calendars that help our children "wait" by opening something every day—a piece of chocolate, a tiny trinket, or a small picture window. Christian adults do not wait in penitential sackcloth. We don that Christmas sweater, tie, or pin, decorate trees, and attend parties. We await the birth of Jesus in all its Luke 2 joy, not the coming of the Son of Man in all its Luke 21 fear and foreboding.

Psalm 25:1–10 opens Advent with the desperate prayer of someone waiting on God to forgive and rescue. It begins with vivid contrasts. The psalmist prays: "To you, O LORD, I lift up my soul. O my God, in you I trust" (vv. 1–2a). Despite this upturned beginning, the psalmist then sinks low, overwhelmed by the weight of internal shame and external threat: "Do not let me be put to shame; do not let my enemies exult over me" (v. 2bc).

We do not know what sins lie behind this shame or the fear that enemies will celebrate the psalmist's ruin. Like us, this psalmist keeps shameful things hidden. At one point, the psalmist urges divine selective memory: God should *remember* the commitment to mercy, but *forget* the psalmist's long rap sheet (vv. 6–7)!

Psalm 25 contains the three most important biblical words for sin. The words "sin" and "sinners" used in verses 7, 8, and 18 mean "to miss the target." Behind the term "transgressions" (v. 7) is the word "to rebel." In verse 11, "guilt" carries the sense of being twisted out of shape, bent over, bowed down. As one scholar puts it: "Here, then, are three dramatic pictures of a life that is not headed in the right direction, off target, a life of rebelling; a life twisted out of shape."[1]

These three understandings of sin reflect Jeremiah's prophecy to the nation of Judah, which is facing its own crisis of internal shame and external threat. The enemy Babylon exults over Judah, toppling its king, destroying Jerusalem and the temple, and forcing God's people into exile. Judah's own sinfulness brought this calamity upon them. They have missed the mark, rebelled against God, and twisted God's commandments to suit their own desires. Punishment looms. They cannot save themselves.

Luke 21:25–36 joins in painting a grim picture of our circumstances; yet none of these texts leave us at a dead end. We are not without hope, because we are not without God.

The psalmist waits in trust (v. 2) as long as necessary (v. 5). His waiting is not passive. To "untwist" his life, the psalmist must relearn and humbly re-place his feet in God's ways (v. 4). No matter how off-target we become, God's paths remain open, cleared by truth (v. 5) and marked by steadfast love and faithfulness at every turn (v. 10).

Desolate Judah receives comfort. Babylon and its king appear in control, but God has not ceded ultimate power. In Jeremiah 33:14–16, God speaks, and a future opens. Into a landscape of destruction, God sends a green shoot of hope. A new ruler will come from David's lineage to lead with justice and righteousness. "Judah will be saved and Jerusalem will live in safety" (vv. 15–16).

Even Luke 21:25–36 offers hope. We stand up, raise our heads, because redemption is coming (v. 28). Creation greens again before the One coming to rule with justice and righteousness (vv. 30–31).

Psalms are often used for the Opening Sentences of a worship service, and Psalm 25:1–10 can be used in this way. A more robust contribution to the liturgy, however, would be as a prayer of confession and assurance of God's pardon. Composed by one overwhelmed by sin and shame, verses 1–7 could be adapted for a prayer of confession. Verses 8–10 shift abruptly from first-person to third-person speech. The waiting one becomes a witness. The psalmist becomes a liturgist. Imagine a congregation filled with the embattled people of Judah . . . or our own congregations filled with embattled survivors of other destructions: illness, grief, estrangement, addiction, violence, and sins undisclosed. Psalm 25:8–10 affirms that God creates a way forward marked by steadfast love and faithfulness. It becomes a responsive assurance of God's pardon to our confession of sin. It can also serve as an affirmation of faith elsewhere in the service:

> Good and upright is the Lord;
> > therefore God instructs sinners in the way.
> God leads the humble in what is right,
> > and teaches the humble God's way.
> *All the paths of the Lord*
> > *are steadfast love and faithfulness,*
> > *for those who keep God's covenant and decrees.*

Thankfully, we know that the gift of God's grace is not dependent on our ability to "keep the commandments and decrees." Psalm 25 and the book of Jeremiah emphasize our responsibility to walk in God's ways. Luke 21:34 lists behaviors to avoid, and 1 Thessalonians 3:13 prays that we will be found "blameless." Given this, the gracious words of Jeremiah 33 can fill out our assurance/affirmation as Advent begins:

> All the paths of the Lord
> > are steadfast love and faithfulness,
> > for those who keep God's covenant and
> > > decrees.
> The promise of God is fulfilled:
> > The Righteous Branch springs up
> > and we are saved.
> The One who has come
> > is coming again
> > in power and great glory!

KIMBERLY L. CLAYTON

---

1. James Limburg, *Psalms*, Westminster Bible Companion (Louisville, KY: Westminster John Knox Press, 2000), 80.

1 Thessalonians 3:9–13

⁹How can we thank God enough for you in return for all the joy that we feel before our God because of you? ¹⁰Night and day we pray most earnestly that we may see you face to face and restore whatever is lacking in your faith.

¹¹Now may our God and Father himself and our Lord Jesus direct our way to you. ¹²And may the Lord make you increase and abound in love for one another and for all, just as we abound in love for you. ¹³And may he so strengthen your hearts in holiness that you may be blameless before our God and Father at the coming of our Lord Jesus with all his saints.

Commentary 1: Connecting the Reading with Scripture

This brief lection invites us to read the texts for Advent 1 through the lens of joy: "How can we thank God enough for you in return for all the joy that we feel before our God because of you?" The reading was probably selected because of the reference in verse 13 to "the coming of our Lord Jesus with all his saints," but the readings from Jeremiah and Luke also frame their messianic expectation with joy. Jeremiah assures that the Righteous Branch will bring righteousness and justice to the land so that God's people will be saved and live in safety (Jer. 33:15–16). In Luke, Jesus exhorts those who see the fearful heavenly signs to "stand up and raise your heads [a posture of welcome rather than fear], because your redemption is drawing near" (Luke 21:28).

Although the church in Thessalonica was not the first that Paul founded, it is widely agreed that this is the earliest of Paul's letters. Indeed, this letter may have initiated the practice of reading letters (and the Gospels) in Christian worship. Paul concludes this letter: "I solemnly command you by the Lord that this letter be read to all" (4:27). Beverly Gaventa suggests that in so doing "the church entered into a permanent relationship with this text" and began the process of collection that led to the canonization of the New Testament.[1]

While we often think of Paul as a towering, solitary figure, seemingly always on the move planting churches, this letter makes it clear that

Paul is part of a ministry team that includes Silvanus and Timothy (1:1). They, together, are writing this letter back to a community that they love deeply. The capital of the region of Macedonia, Thessalonica was an important Roman city on the Via Egnatia, a road stretching from the Caspian to the Adriatic Sea. A cosmopolitan city, Thessalonica had a wide range of religious options, including a major shrine to Caesar Augustus.

Much of what we consider religious language today originated in a political context. For example, the Roman emperor was referred to as "Father," "Lord," and "Savior." The term for a monarch's arrival was *parousia*, the term Paul uses for the second "coming" of Christ. When Paul uses these terms to refer to Christ, he walks a fine line between cultural appropriation and sedition.

Acts 17 presents a very different picture of Paul's activity. First, it says that Paul was accompanied by Silas (or Silvanus), but makes no mention of Timothy. Second, it says that they went to the synagogue (the ordinary pattern, according to Acts), but there is little or no evidence of a Jewish community in Thessalonica. Finally, it implies that Paul and Silas were only in town briefly before trouble erupted, and they had to leave town. By contrast, the letter implies that the missionary team must have been there long enough to establish a strong community

---

1. Beverly Roberts Gaventa, *First and Second Thessalonians* (Louisville, KY: Westminster John Knox Press, 1998), 8.

("you became an example to all the believers in Macedonia and in Achaia," 1 Thess. 1:7). Further, by the time Paul and his colleagues write the letter, enough time has passed so that one of the questions is about the fate of those members of the community who have died before Christ's return (4:13). The letter gives us a much fuller picture of the relationship between Paul and the community and makes more sense of the depth of his prayers for them.

First Thessalonians may be divided into roughly two parts, and these verses conclude the first section with a summary statement (vv. 9–10) and a prayer (vv. 11–13), which serves as a bridge to the second half of the letter. Paul and his colleagues have been very worried about the Thessalonian community and whether their faith would stand in the face of rejection and persecution. Was the leadership strong enough? Were the practices of faith deeply embedded enough? Would the center hold? The affection that this ministry team has for the Thessalonians is also clear: "we were made orphans by being separated from you—in person, not in heart" (2:17). Finally, Timothy was dispatched to visit the community. He returned with the good news that the community was thriving. Hence, the theme of thanksgiving (introduced in 1:2 and recapitulated here). The phrase ("how can we thank God enough?") echoes Psalm 116:12 ("What shall I return to the Lord for all his bounty to me?").

The team is overjoyed but still longs to see the community "face to face." This longing leads into the prayer, which can be read as one sentence (RSV) or divided into its three component parts (NRSV). First of all, the team prays that God will direct their way back to the Thessalonians. God is the one who leads not only this team but the spread of the good news, and so they pray that their future will again connect them to people for whom they feel deep affection. Paul's work is relationship building, not just "church planting."

The second prayer goes to the heart of Christian identity and community: "May the Lord make you . . . abound in love for one another and for all." It has been said that if there is only one believer, what you have is not Christian faith. Just as Jesus created a community of followers, so the apostolic mission was the creation of communities of faith and practice wherever they went. Embracing Christ as Savior and Lord meant stepping away from traditional loyalties, both civic and religious. It could and did lead to social ostracism and persecution. In return, believers found a new community and a new family: people once separated by race and class became brothers and sisters to one another in Christ.

In this prayer, however, Paul and his colleagues remind us that the love that creates this community is not simply for the sake of the in-group. The prayer is that they (we) will abound in love "for all." This Christian community is to show love, compassion, care, and respect not only to one another but also to those who have rejected them. Christian life is not a closed loop or zero-sum game. The beloved community is one that "abounds" and overflows with love, a place where the door is always open and there is always room for more.

Finally, the ministry team prays that God will strengthen them in holiness (that is, in the holy life to which they have been called in Christ) and prepare them to meet Christ when he comes. Here the authors anticipate the rest of the letter, which reminds the readers of what a life pleasing to God looks like and offers words of comfort regarding those who have died without seeing Christ's return.

This prayer reminds us that we live in the in-between time. Christ has indeed come and brought us the gift of transformed life—abundant life now and the promise of life eternal—yet the transformation is not complete. Both we and the whole creation long to see God's promises fulfilled. We yearn for justice that rolls down like mighty waters. We hope that one day the wolf will lie down with the lamb and swords become plowshares. We long for the day when mourning and crying and pain will be no more. We already know what God's future looks like, and in beloved community with one another we experience the firstfruits. Because all that will be is not yet, we need to be strengthened so that we may walk in the light.

CYNTHIA M. CAMPBELL

Commentary 2: Connecting the Reading with the World

The epistle lesson for this First Sunday of Advent is fittingly from the oldest document in the New Testament, Paul's First Letter to the Thessalonians. In this letter, Paul picks up his pen, thinks of that struggling church dwelling in Thessalonica—the cosmopolitan Roman capital of Macedonia sitting strategically on the Egnatian Way—and memorializes for the first time the term *ekklēsia* as he writes to the faithful gathered there.

Paul exults in this Thessalonian church and is demonstrably joyful in its survival, even in the midst of hard times, distress, and persecution. His love for this dear congregation is abundant. Earlier in his letter to them, his pastor's heart is on display in the way he describes himself as a "wet nurse" (2:7) and a "father" (2:11–12); and in this text he is effusive in his praise: "How can we thank God enough for you in return for all the joy that we feel before our God because of you?" (3:9).

Here, in full view, is Paul's pastoral side. A planter of churches, he understands each one of them and their unique characteristics. Since the Thessalonian church is surely one of his favorites, his affirmations in this text are authentic and heartfelt.

In Acts 17:6, as the Reverend Rick Spalding, chaplain at Williams College, has written, "Paul and his cohorts are accused of being 'these people who have been turning the world upside down.' Paul would decline the honor of this marvelous phrase more readily than most of us would; he insisted that the intention of God was responsible for the vitality of faith in Christ wherever he found it. He would say that where preaching succeeds, God is already moving. We do not summon God in our sermons; God summons us."[2] God appears to be summoning that stalwart band of Thessalonian Christians, and this gives Paul joy.

Nonetheless, there is also a more sober note—a note of realism—woven in with the praise and affection. Speaking for himself and his partners in ministry, Silvanus and Timothy, Paul goes on to write, "Night and day we pray most earnestly that we may see you face to face *and restore whatever is lacking in your faith.*" Given Paul's apocalyptic understanding of reality, we are not surprised by this assessment. We do not learn specifically what is lacking, but we are reminded here that the Thessalonian church, just like your church and every other church dwelling in that creative tension between the "already" of the coming of Jesus Christ and the "not yet" of his return, is an ongoing work in progress.

Paul the pastor, like every other pastor across time who has shared with him the vocation of the gospel, has mixed emotions when he surveys even one of his most successful congregations. On the one hand, there is joy at the sheer contemplation of their being. The blood, sweat, and tears that went into the construction of the foundation of the gospel among them has not been in vain; to know that they are not floundering is good news for him, as it is for any pastor. On the other hand, he senses that there are some notes that are missing. So, however attached he is to them, he is willing to speak the pastoral truth in love regarding whatever is lacking in their faith.

Good pastors understand such truth-telling. At the funeral of a well-known and beloved parishioner, you get a special opportunity to tell the truth. Of course, you lift up the laudable things, the attributes, the noble aspects of that person's character. Because this is an occasion of grateful truth-telling, when perhaps your witness will be measured for its authenticity, maybe there is also occasion to lift up, with gratitude, the things that made him or her human. Paul here takes a risk, gently and in love, to tell the truth.

This sober note, though, is followed by an expansive benediction and a word of hope: "may the Lord make you increase and abound in love for one another and for all, just as we abound in love for you. And may he so strengthen your hearts in holiness that you may be blameless before our God and Father at the coming of our Lord Jesus with all his saints" (3:11–12).

He cannot stop being their good pastor;

---

2. From an unpublished paper on this text, by Rick Spalding, written for the annual meeting of the Moveable Feast cohort in January 1996.

and this drives him to the recognition of these things. He sees them as they are now, in the light of who they are meant to be when God has completed them. At the root of Paul's eschatological vision—however soon or delayed the redemptive completion of all things may be—is this claim: God holds the future, and God is pulling us, even now, toward that future. So it is that Paul yearns to lead that Thessalonian congregation toward restoring what yet is lacking in their faith.

At the beginning of Advent, when the world's grimness is somehow startled by new expectancy and hope as we begin another cycle of the Christian year, we are invited to take a fresh look at the ongoing work in progress that we in fact are. We are urged to consider who we are at our best—people who are forever "turning the world upside down" (Acts 17:6)—and to attend to what is yet lacking in our faith. Churches at their best are joyful, faithful, generous, courageous, and profound announcements, even embodiments, of what the realm of God looks like up close.

A number of years ago, a particularly beloved moderator of the General Assembly of the Presbyterian Church (USA)—the highest-ranking officer of that particular communion—went on a somewhat controversial visit to sister churches in a particular eastern European country. The Berlin Wall, the defining symbol of the cold war, had recently come down, and she and her entourage made plans to visit a particular parish in a remote mountainous area, and to worship with them. Weather conditions were icy and harsh. Diplomatic relations between this country and the United States were strained, and there was not a great deal of enthusiasm there for this visit.

The moderator's plane arrived much later than scheduled, getting through customs took longer, and then there was the weather. At best, her arrival in this mountain community would be far later than envisioned. This woman with her strong missional heart was not deterred, though; so the long drive up into higher altitudes and even more snow began. When the group arrived in the town, far later than scheduled, there was no certainty that anyone would still be at the church. Someone in town gave them directions, and they started off again. As they neared the area of the church, they noticed up ahead a long line of lights; and as they drew nearer, they beheld, one after another, the members of that church—each one of them bundled up against the cold and holding a candle. One light pointed them to another—hundreds of lights!—and they followed the light for the rest of the journey and to the front door of the church.

When the moderator encountered the host pastor, she asked him through an interpreter: "How long were you planning to wait out here in the dark and the cold?" He replied: "Until you came."

THEODORE J. WARDLAW

Luke 21:25–36

25"There will be signs in the sun, the moon, and the stars, and on the earth distress among nations confused by the roaring of the sea and the waves. 26People will faint from fear and foreboding of what is coming upon the world, for the powers of the heavens will be shaken. 27Then they will see 'the Son of Man coming in a cloud' with power and great glory. 28Now when these things begin to take place, stand up and raise your heads, because your redemption is drawing near."

29Then he told them a parable: "Look at the fig tree and all the trees; 30as soon as they sprout leaves you can see for yourselves and know that summer is already near. 31So also, when you see these things taking place, you know that the kingdom of God is near. 32Truly I tell you, this generation will not pass away until all things have taken place. 33Heaven and earth will pass away, but my words will not pass away.

34"Be on guard so that your hearts are not weighed down with dissipation and drunkenness and the worries of this life, and that day does not catch you unexpectedly, 35like a trap. For it will come upon all who live on the face of the whole earth. 36Be alert at all times, praying that you may have the strength to escape all these things that will take place, and to stand before the Son of Man."

Commentary 1: Connecting the Reading with Scripture

Our text belongs to a larger narrative unit concerned with calamity, redemption, and readiness (20:1–21:38). The whole is marked off by its location in the temple and its focus on Jesus as teacher—summarized well in verses 37–38: "Every day he was teaching in the temple. . . . And all the people would get up early in the morning to listen to him in the temple." Luke 20:4–21:4 emphasizes Jesus' status as the faithful interpreter of God's agenda, over against the Jerusalem leaders, generally portrayed as adversaries who use their positions to test him (20:1–44) and to tyrannize the helpless (20:45–21:4). Luke 21:5–36 portrays the coming calamity that marks the arrival of the new age.

Luke 21:25–36 has two parts. The first, verses 25–28, speaks of heavenly signs and earthly trauma in anticipation of the coming of the Son of Man. These verses signal the end of the longer discourse, in which Jesus responds to the request for a time line by which to track the coming disaster (v. 7). They show how Jesus moves from talking about the "sign" of the coming destruction of the temple (v. 7) to talking

about the "signs" of the coming of the end of this age (v. 25). The second, verses 29–36, concludes the entire section by showing how these calamitous signs ought to be understood in relation to God's program of redemption and by calling Jesus' followers to readiness and faithfulness. It is not too much to say that Luke 21:25–36 has two interrelated focal points: (1) God's people can trust God; (2) therefore God's people exercise faithfulness—even in the face of disaster.

The OT functions as a treasure trove from which Jesus, in Luke, has chosen images of the pending disaster. Isaiah 13 is especially significant, with its reference to the Lord's assembling an army in preparation for the Day of the Lord, a time of judgment, destruction, and rescue (see esp. Isa. 13:4, 6–11, 13; also Isa. 5:30; 8:22; 17:12; Ezek. 32:7–8; Joel 2:10, 30–31). This is important for two reasons. First, it urges that we understand the tragic events Jesus sketches as meaningful within God's plan to set things right. On the one hand, these events do not catch God by surprise, or suggest that God has forgotten God's people. On the other hand, they signal God's initiative to bring an end to arrogance, tyranny, and wickedness in all its guises. Second, whereas Isaiah anticipates the Day of the Lord, Jesus proclaims the coming of the Son of Man. In other words, Luke portrays the coming of the Son of Man as a theophany. Of course, throughout the Gospel of Luke, Jesus himself is identified as the Son of Man, but here the resonances with Daniel's vision ("I saw one like a human being coming with the clouds of heaven," Dan. 7:13) are especially strong. It is therefore worth reflecting on the consequence of the Son of Man's appearance in Daniel's vision: "To him was given dominion and glory and kingship, that all peoples, nations, and languages should serve him. His dominion is an everlasting dominion that shall not pass away, and his kingship is one that shall never be destroyed" (Dan. 7:14). Likewise, the Son of Man comes "with power and great glory" (Luke 21:27), and with him comes the final, decisive, universal establishment of God's reign.

Jesus anticipates three different responses to the calamitous events he has sketched. The nations react in bewilderment and "people will faint from fear" (vv. 25–26); these first two responses are inappropriate for God's people. In his address to them, Jesus counsels confidence (standing with raised heads), assured of God's intervention. For them, the Day of the Lord is not an occasion for dread, nor is it a day to be avoided. Rather, it is the realization of God's good news: "your redemption is drawing near."

What makes the difference is not a different set of events. They do not see different signs. They experience those events and read those signs quite differently. They grasp their significance as people whose frame of reference is guided by Israel's Scriptures, particularly as these have been interpreted for them by Jesus. Like fig-tree farmers who can set their calendars by observing their trees, those whose lives are shaped by Jesus' proclamation of God's reign grasp what time it is by what is happening around them. They see the same things as everyone else, but, formed in relation to Jesus' message, they see with different eyes.

Notice the repeated phrase: "When you see *these things taking place*, you know that the kingdom of God is near" (v. 31). "This generation will not pass away until *all things have taken place*" (v. 32). "Be alert at all times, praying that you may have the strength to escape *all these things that will take place*, and to stand before the Son of Man" (v. 36).

The first phrase is in the present tense, the second refers to a time yet to come, and the third uses the future tense. The future calls for present faithfulness. There is no one "season" for faithfulness; discernment, readiness, and prayer are always "in season." This is true even if the escalation of disturbing events, even harassment because of one's faithfulness to Jesus' message, tests the vigilant, expectant faith of Jesus' followers.

Jesus' pronouncement that "this generation will not pass away until all things have taken place" (v. 32) sometimes confuses interpreters. Which generation did Jesus have in mind? This confusion is misplaced, however, since the phrase "this generation" is less a marker of a set time and more a label for a particular kind of people. The phrase "this generation" is used of those who turned to violence and corruption in Noah's day (Gen. 7:1) and of the ungodly against whom the Lord guards the faithful (Ps. 12:7). In Luke's Gospel, "this generation" includes those who have rejected God's purpose for themselves (7:30–31), an evil generation that seeks signs and is set for condemnation (11:29–32), people who reject God's messengers (11:49–51), and those who reject the Son of Man (17:25). In other words, Jesus' followers can expect hostility and harassment from "this generation"—people who turn their backs on God's ways—until the very end. Those whose lives are determined, and sometimes rewarded, by this world will never be known for their hospitality to the new world, or to those whose lives are shaped by it.

Why would Jesus' followers need this firm reminder of the need for watchfulness? Perhaps they need to remember that God is faithful, that even cosmic calamity is no indication that God has forgotten God's people. The good news stands even when everything else falls. More pressing, perhaps, is the possibility that Jesus' followers share too much the inclinations and the practices of those who resist Jesus, that they too easily find their feet mired in the ways of "this generation": "weighed down with dissipation and drunkenness and the worries of this life" (v. 34). Faithful service in anticipation of the decisive revelation of God's peace and justice too easily gives way to a ho-hum attitude to everyday life. Jesus counters that the coming of the Son of Man and disclosure of God's

reign will be sudden, unexpected, at any time, and global. For those who trust God and whose trust of God is mirrored in their own faithfulness, the coming of the end is not a calamity to be feared but redemption to be welcomed.

JOEL B. GREEN

Commentary 2: Connecting the Reading with the World

Jesus speaks the prophetic word to us. He draws us into the future that he sees. He is inside human history, inside the history of his people, Israel, but he also brings Israel inside his history, the history of God and the time of God. If we lose sight of Israel's history inside Jesus' history and human history inside the time of God, then we will never grasp the message of Jesus for us today.

Too often interpreters of this passage have read it in one of two less fruitful ways. First, some have interpreted Jesus only as a figure in human history and Israel's history. They see Jesus as just another example of a unique seer who prematurely imagined the cataclysmic. This reading grows out of a historical habit of mind that narrowly interprets Jesus against the backdrop of human history and forgets to read human history against the backdrop of the life of Jesus. Jesus is in history, real history; but he will not be understood if we attempt to squeeze his life into any writing of history or into the time lines we construct. His life shows those historical constructs to be only our usual attempts to make sense of our time. Jesus has come to guide us in making sense of our time.

The other less fruitful way of interpreting this passage has been to obsess over the idea of interpreting signs, trying to pinpoint in his, or our, time exactly the connection between his words and world events. Jesus' words are meant to focus attention not on events, but on his life in our time, and our lives in his future. Jesus the prophet is neither simply an object (figure) in history nor the one who points us to objects (events) in history. These ways of interpreting this passage both represent shortsighted visions of the end times, that is, shortsighted

eschatologies that do not yet grasp the time of Jesus.

Jesus embodies God's own directing of our lives, not only in our space but also in our time. Jesus' stunning work intensifies what had been the case with the earlier prophets of Israel. The prophets always stood in a particular moment and invited the people of God to step into the depths of their faith by entering a future with God. They were asked to believe in a future that they could not see, because faith is never only for today. It is also always bright hope for tomorrow. Jesus describes the future; in so doing he is not trying to frighten us or to use fear as a tool for motivation. He describes the hour for the purpose of directing us toward the future.

God gives direction. In this passage, it has two implications. The first is that God is directing us in and through our time. It is always correct to place Jesus in his time, but it is never correct to limit him to his time. Jesus, like the other prophets of Israel, has entered that prophetic space, but now he claims it as his own space. Jesus expands that prophetic space to capture the entire cosmos, showing that God's direction is not thwarted by any events. Unlike a grand puppet master manipulating world events or even the events of our lives, God enters the everyday struggles of creatures and, from within the everyday, draws us toward our destiny in God. Jesus shows us the God of time moving in our time, walking with us in it and working with us through it.

Jesus is God's holy gift, a gift we need especially in times of uncertainty, especially when the world is shaking. In him we find a God who never keeps safe distance from chaos, holding the world at arm's length, but who will never be overcome by it. Jesus invites us to bring our lives into the divine life by following God's time. We must enter into God's time so that we are not overwhelmed by our times. The actions that Jesus wants from his disciples in uncertain and unstable times are precisely the opposite of what one would expect. Disciples stand up and raise their heads (21:28). Such actions are not examples of insanely blind faith or tragic denial of destructive forces; they suggest the recognition that our lives are in the hands of a God who has taken back from death and destruction the power to determine our future.

The second implication of the direction of God is to anchor our daily actions in the purpose of God. God's direction orients us in faith, not in fear toward our world. Even the cataclysmic events (as suggested in vv. 25–26), involving both the environment and nations, should not disorient us but turn us toward God, who has not and will not abandon this world. This orientation centers our efforts and does not evacuate them. Too often people have read this text in ways that resource political quietism and acquiescence to destructive forces, whether natural or social, economic or political. The words of Jesus outline the order of discipleship inside a politics of reading the signs of the times: see what

---

For Whom There Is No Room

Into this world, this demented inn, in which there is absolutely no room for Him at all, Christ has come uninvited. But because He cannot be at home in it, because He is out of place in it, and yet He must be in it, His place is with those others for whom there is no room. His place is with those who do not belong, who are rejected by power because they are regarded as weak, those who are discredited, who are denied the status of persons, tortured, exterminated. With those for whom there is no room, Christ is present in this world. He is mysteriously present in those for whom there seems to be nothing but the world at its worst. For them, there is no escape even in imagination. . . . It is in these that He hides Himself, for whom there is no room.

The time of the end? All right: when?

That is not the question.

To say it is the time of the end is to answer all the questions, for if it is the time of the end, and of great tribulation, then it is certainly and above all the time of the Great Joy. For the true eschatological banquet is not that of the birds on the bodies of the slain. It is the feast of the living, the wedding banquet of the Lamb. The true eschatological convocation is not the crowding of armies on the field of battle, but the summons of the Great Joy, the cry of deliverance: "Come out of her my people that you may not share in her sins and suffer her plagues!"

To leave the city of death and imprisonment is surely not bad news except to those who have so identified themselves with their captivity that they can conceive no other reality and no other condition. In such a case, there is nothing but tribulation: for while to stay in captivity is tragic, to break away from it is unthinkable—and so more tragic still.

What is needed then is the grace and courage to see that "The Great Tribulation" and "the Great Joy" are really inseparable, and that the "Tribulation" becomes "Joy" when it is seen as the Victory of Life over Death.

True, there is a sense in which there is no room for Joy in this tribulation. In the last analysis, the "joy" proposed by the time of the end is simply the satisfaction and the relief of getting it all over with. . . . That is the demonic temptation of "the end." For eschatology is not *finis* and punishment, the winding up of accounts and the closing of books: it is the final beginning, the definitive birth into a new creation. It is not the last gasp of exhausted possibilities but the first taste of all that is beyond conceiving as actual.

But can we believe it? ("He seemed to them to be jesting!")

Thomas Merton (1915–1968), "The Time of the End Is the Time of No Room," in *A Thomas Merton Reader*, ed. Thomas P. McDonnell, rev. ed. (New York: Doubleday, 1996), 365–67.

is happening and continue to do the work. His words are never heard rightly if they are understood to mean only to see what is happening.

We who follow Jesus must learn to read the signs—a complicated and dangerous business. Much mischief has taken place and continues to take place when people read signs poorly. Poor sign-reading has meant that Christians have often been guilty of reading the world in constant declension, so that every social, cultural, economic, or political occurrence comes to be interpreted through a lens of the world in decline and degradation. Too many Christians have seen justification in this passage for an impenetrable pessimism that dulls their senses to the beauty of God's creation and the joy of being alive even in difficult times.

Certainly, we can see in some events the operations of evil and human sin, which must never be taken lightly. However, for too long Christians have failed to frame this world within God's love and embrace, and have instead framed the world in horror and impending doom. This impoverished way of reading our times or any time loses sight of the purpose of prophetic reading: to look for Jesus' return and not to look for our escape from the world. Imagining that there are no signs is not an option for disciples of Jesus. In expectation we read of his soon return in order to sharpen our work and clarify our effort. We read signs in order to monitor our own actions. We read always in hope and toward hope.

It is precisely this prophetic dynamic that characterizes the life journey of disciples. We are swept up into his vision of the future, which teaches us how to live in the present. This is a Jesus-shaped present in which we follow his own life of expectation and trust, and his own faith and hope in God. Just as he waited on God, so too we enter his waiting bound up in his work. He is with us in the waiting and in the work, sharing in our challenges but offering us strength.

WILLIE JAMES JENNINGS

Second Sunday of Advent

Malachi 3:1–4
Luke 1:68–79

Philippians 1:3–11
Luke 3:1–6

Malachi 3:1–4

¹See, I am sending my messenger to prepare the way before me, and the Lord whom you seek will suddenly come to his temple. The messenger of the covenant in whom you delight—indeed, he is coming, says the LORD of hosts. ²But who can endure the day of his coming, and who can stand when he appears?

For he is like a refiner's fire and like fullers' soap; ³he will sit as a refiner and purifier of silver, and he will purify the descendants of Levi and refine them like gold and silver, until they present offerings to the LORD in righteousness. ⁴Then the offering of Judah and Jerusalem will be pleasing to the LORD as in the days of old and as in former years.

Commentary 1: Connecting the Reading with Scripture

Malachi is a little scroll that deals with a large crisis. Communities enduring a crisis or disaster are faced with terribly difficult decisions after surviving the initial shock: what to rebuild first? Of course immediate needs are the priority: shelter and food and, hopefully, relative safety. Then? Then the fights break out—the arguments, and the forming of factions. How do you rebuild a sense of actually living life and community?

It is clear that the community addressed by Malachi (lit. "my messenger") faced similar questions. Hebrews were returning to their devastated homeland from the eastern regions of the Persian Empire after the fall of Babylon (see Ezra 1–6). Returning to what? Nehemiah (c. 450 BCE), long after the time of Malachi, took his famous nighttime horseback ride to survey the *still devastated walls* of Jerusalem some 150 *years* after the destruction by Babylon in 587 BCE. Rebuilding was slow. Close to the time of Malachi, Haggai and Zechariah were also dealing with disputes in the community about what to rebuild, and how. It is hardly a surprise, then, that the book of Malachi is divided into a series of "disputations" or hard questions about the life of faith and the priorities of the rebuilding community early in the Persian Empire (ca. 539–533 BCE).

The previous verse, 2:17, ended with a demand for "the God of justice" to act! Too quickly some proclaimed: "What we need around here is pious reform and justice!"—believing, of course, that this meant *others* have to change. In Malachi 3:1–4 the message is clear: Be careful what you ask for! ("who can endure the day of his coming?"). The prophet warns that demands for justice may not end well for many folks who think that it is always "the other people's fault" that life is not back on track ("as in the days of old," v. 4)! The prophet announces that God does indeed intend to act; an important emissary ("my messenger") is coming! However, Malachi suggests that "purification" will extend even to religious leaders, the "descendants of Levi"! Were some of them perhaps among those clamoring for judgment and even restoration to positions of temple privilege, only to face warnings about the "refiner's fire and fullers' soap" themselves? Malachi warns the smugly self-righteous: not so fast with calls for judgment!

Asking for judgment can be treacherous. The book of Amos also mentions foolish people who asked for the Day of the Lord—a day of judgment. Amos's famous answer amounted to another version of "You do not know what you are asking!" The prophet exclaimed: "It is darkness, not light" (Amos 5:18b). Thus, in our passage, the messenger brings a portent of judgment (cf. the "messengers" who announce the destruction of Sodom and Gomorrah in Gen. 19).

It is true that many commentators have suggested that the messenger in Malachi 3 is to be understood as an "eschatological messenger,"[1] announcing judgments at the end of present times (cf. Isa. 1:25; 48:10; Jer. 9:7; Dan. 11:35; 12:10; Zech. 13:9), including apocalyptic themes of "washing" and "refining"—processes that use harsh soaps (lye? cf. Jer. 2:22) or intense heat (as in metal forges, cf. Jer. 6:29; 9:7; Ezek. 22:17–22). However, it is *also* true that readers have an interesting habit of postponing to some distant future any events that are particularly controversial, like destroying weapons (see Isa. 2//Mic. 4)! In this passage, purification will come "suddenly" (*pit'om*), and thus unexpectedly. Isaiah announced such a sudden turn of events and judgment from God ("And in an instant, suddenly . . . with whirlwind and tempest," Isa. 29:5c–6), and Jeremiah warned of sudden turns of events (Jer. 6:26, and the "sudden" fall of Babylon, 51:8), but these were hardly events that were safely cast into the future! To the contrary, the impact of "sudden" events is that they are *not* expected or planned for, which is surely part of the power of this passage. Judgment is not in our control! Maybe tomorrow!

One particular aim of the judgment in Malachi 3, however, appears to be the temple, and "divine judgement of social abuses" there,[2] such as the injustices enumerated in verse 5, which (in addition to religious infidelities and practices) features a powerful attack on the oppression of the "hired workers in their wages, the widow and the orphan, against those who thrust aside the alien." Unlike other, earlier prophets who critique the sacrifice so thoroughly that scholars wondered if they had any use for it at all (Amos 5:21–24; Mic. 6:6–8), Malachi appears to suggest that a time of purified worship will return, and even demands financial gifts to ensure the proper functioning of the revived and purified temple (Mal. 3:8–12). But equally clear is the theme that pure worship involves social justice!

Yet how often are piety and justice seen as opposing emphases in church?

It is important to keep in mind that the temple emerges after the exile as the central institution of Jewish life. For centuries, including right up to the time of Jesus under the Roman Empire, the temple was the main institution of identity, inclusive of political and economic power. Corruption, therefore, in the temple had to do with political and economic abuses as well as religious and cultic abuses, and deadly arguments about temple leadership were constant.

The purification noted in Malachi is presaged by the arrival of a messenger. Because this figure began to be merged with the eschatological expectations of Elijah the prophet heralding the coming of the Messiah, as in the New Testament (Matt. 11:10//Luke 7:27; Mark 1:2; Luke 1:76), Malachi 3:1–5 is often considered an Advent reading. Some early church fathers (Theodore of Mopsuestia, 350–428 CE) interpreted the figure as Jesus himself, but this was not widely shared, given the tradition connected with Elijah, already established in the New Testament. However, this image in Malachi may have influenced the more strident portrayals of Jesus in Revelation.

The late professor of Old Testament at Anabaptist Mennonite Biblical Seminary, Millard Lind, was fond of saying, "You can't have exodus without Sinai." What he meant was that liberation must also bring discipline, so that the liberation itself is not squandered away! In many of the celebrations of a positive future, the prophets warn about refining, discipline, cleansing, and judgment. Careful discernment is, therefore, necessary in the application of celebratory passages—especially those that seem to indulge in vengeful wishes of punishment of others (e.g., Ps. 137!). The prophets often warn: be careful what you wish for, since the judgment can be universal!

Practically, this surely is a call to careful consideration of how we ourselves are a part of the very circumstances that we object to—even the conditions from which we seek liberation. In what ways have we contributed to social and

---

1. A. Cody, "Malachi," in *The Jerome Bible Commentary*, ed. R. Brown, J. Fitzmyer, and R. Murphy (Englewood Cliffs, NJ: Prentice Hall, 1990), 349–61.

2. John Rogerson, "Malachi," in *The Oxford Bible Commentary*, ed. J. Barton and J. Muddiman (Oxford: Oxford University Press, 2001), 616.

economic conditions about which we so easily become upset—even angry? It is far too easy to blame others (and historically, this has often fallen on foreigners, migrants, and the weak).

The prophets often turn the mirror on ourselves. Who, indeed, can "endure the day"?

DANIEL L. SMITH-CHRISTOPHER

Commentary 2: Connecting the Reading with the World

Throughout Malachi, the prophet sets his oracles in the form of a disputation, a trial-like confrontation between God and the people. In the name of God, the prophet announces a charge, which is then challenged by the accused, prompting the prophet to return God's decisive rebuttal to the people's excuses. For the most part, Malachi levels his charges at the temple priests. The main accusations indicate a lack of integrity in worship, caused by insincerity and bad faith. To these main charges, Malachi adds broader secondary charges, namely, the social disorders that, in his view, follow on a corrupted cult: sorcery, adultery, perjury, defrauding the weak, and rejecting the migrant.

At one level, the protests of the accused priests over these charges simply serve to point out and deepen their guilt. They condemn themselves out of their own mouths. "You have spoken harsh words against me, says the LORD. Yet you say, 'How have we spoken against you?' You have said, 'It is vain to serve God'" (3:13–14). At another level, though, we hear an established bitterness, a people, disillusioned of their hopes, who despair of God's faithfulness: "'I have loved you,' says the LORD. But you say, 'How have you loved us?'" (1:2).

The scholarly consensus places these oracles in the period after Cyrus, the Persian emperor, allowed the return of Jewish exiles to Jerusalem (538 BCE). Understandably, many of those who took advantage of Cyrus's edict expected a new and blessed beginning. They would rebuild the temple, and God would triumph in glory, "The treasures of all nations shall come in, and I will fill this house with splendor" (Hag. 2:7 RSV). By Malachi's time, however, life in the Persian province of Yehud had undermined this enthusiasm through a wretched economy, high taxation, fiscal corruption, savage inequalities, and intermarriage with those who had lived in the land prior to the exiles' return.[3] The high hopes

and glorious visions of a renewed Zion had cooled into disappointment, then drifted into carelessness and, perhaps, a sullen, generalized resentment.

Malachi speaks to these conditions, bringing the words of God's judgment to bear on the religious decline under these dispiriting circumstances. For today's reader, though, this construction of Malachi's context raises a problem. Why rain down this furious series of denunciations on a culture already in despair? The contrast between this prophetic assault and Isaiah's promise of the servant who "will not break a bruised reed" (see Isa. 42:3) is painful. Is there, perhaps, a paradoxical blessing in Malachi's severity?

Among the condemnations, Malachi includes words of promise. In this passage, news of the coming messenger is one such declaration, following immediately upon another confrontation between God and his people: "You have wearied the LORD with your words. Yet you say, 'How have we wearied him?' By saying, 'All who do evil are good in the sight of the LORD . . .' Or by asking, 'Where is the God of justice?'" (2:17). Turning directly to the messenger who "will prepare the way" for God to make his presence known in the temple, the prophet answers the question—"Where is the God of justice?"—with a vision of God purifying his people. The prophet castigates the Levites and the people for offering an impure worship, a worship where the heart is not in the voice, nor the will in the action. Only a people purified by God himself, whose sacrifice aligns with the fullness of hearts and minds, can speak to God without "wearying" God.

When God comes then—ironically, the God "whom you seek" in such empty self-justifying questions—God comes, not to reward, and certainly not to justify God's self, but to purify. Here Malachi introduces something distinctive into

---

3. For a thorough discussion of the historical context, see Andrew E. Hill, *Malachi* (New Haven, CT: Yale University Press, 1998), 51–77.

his vision of the Day of the Lord. God's coming initiates neither ruinous destruction nor vindicating triumph but rather an interim period of refining, turning the corrupt and double-minded back to faithfulness and just dealing. That refining, moreover, will continue until God has restored the Levites—and those whose worship they present—to their integrity. Thus, the purified shall once again be fit to receive God's promise, "They shall be mine."

In Malachi, then, the word of judgment includes the promise of purification and, thereby, restoration to a covenantal relationship with God (3:1). Why, though, such fury of judgment in a situation arising, it seems, from disillusion and disappointment? This is where Malachi's words have a peculiarly sharp relevance for contemporary Western society. In God's judgment, the Levites and the people are asked to see themselves, not just as they have become, but as they are created and called to be. The blessing hidden in the intensity of condemnation lies in the seriousness with which God's judgment takes his people. God's call establishes a people who may and must live justly, who lift and protect the lowly, who speak a larger wisdom through their laws than self-interested prudence, who maintain faith in marital promise (2:14–17), and, above all, who approach the living God with confidence and joy (4:2). God's judgment insists on all of this, and refuses to let go the vision that the people have lost.

Among the most influential voices of our culture—politicians, journalists, entertainers, public intellectuals, especially natural scientists—some advocate, with vivid image and great passion, a morally and spiritually reductive account of our humanity. Beyond their destructiveness, humans are barely distinctive and have no more dignity than complex animals. The sense of moral freedom and responsibility is an illusion, and even our self-consciousness, a mere by-product, hides neurological processes ungoverned by any center. Viciousness and violence belong to us by nature, and altruism is always misdiagnosed self-concern. Religion is a cover story for oppression, neurosis, and an obdurate denial of reality, while tales of the trustworthy or of faithful love are only a pleasing opiate. As for politics, manipulative rhetoric barely covers the nakedness of power. A sense of cultural deflation, lost ideals, even cynicism, is quite widespread and has some spiritual analogy with Malachi's context.

Often churches promote their own versions of this loss of wonder over humanity. Human beings demand wonder: even our dealings in devilment stand out in their true horror only insofar as we keep catching glimpses of a divine calling, given in our making. The church, above all, cannot afford to fall for the popular disparagement of the species. Admittedly, the church version of this disillusion with humanity is generally a more upbeat one, but it equally misses the point.

Christians urge the love of God but forget God's desire. God yearns for a just and righteous and faithful humanity; if we ignore that, then we offer a cheap grace that sides with those who see so little in human beings. Listening, therefore, to such words of judgment as Malachi's reminds us of the blessing of God's desire, the intent of holiness. The church, therefore, must seek the strange blessing in the words of God's judgment, listening intently to this word that purifies and never flatters. When Christians accept God's calling, it is good news for the world, because the church, when it is willing to bear God's refining, represents the glory of humanity as it exists in God's desire. In the end, of course, what sustains the church, and all human beings touched by God's grace, lies beyond the words of judgment, in the faithfulness with which God shall complete the loving work of creation.

ALAN GREGORY

Luke 1:68–79

68"Blessed be the Lord God of Israel,
   for he has looked favorably on his people and redeemed them.
69He has raised up a mighty savior for us
   in the house of his servant David,
70as he spoke through the mouth of his holy prophets from of old,
   71that we would be saved from our enemies and from the hand of all who hate us.
72Thus he has shown the mercy promised to our ancestors,
   and has remembered his holy covenant,
73the oath that he swore to our ancestor Abraham,
   to grant us 74that we, being rescued from the hands of our enemies,
might serve him without fear, 75in holiness and righteousness
   before him all our days.
76And you, child, will be called the prophet of the Most High;
   for you will go before the Lord to prepare his ways,
77to give knowledge of salvation to his people
   by the forgiveness of their sins.
78By the tender mercy of our God,
   the dawn from on high will break upon us,
79to give light to those who sit in darkness and in the shadow of death,
   to guide our feet into the way of peace."

Connecting the Psalm with Scripture and Worship

In place of a psalm, the Second Sunday of Advent offers the canticle of Zechariah, one of three canticles in Luke's Gospel. Zechariah's canticle is the soaring poetic conclusion to a wonderful and detailed story concerning the birth of John, which Luke alone provides. Indeed, the first chapter of Luke uniquely braids together, in balanced strands, the foretelling of John the Baptist's birth followed by the foretelling of Jesus' birth, each announced by the angel Gabriel; the story of Elizabeth and Mary meeting in the joy of their unexpected pregnancies; and the birth of John the Baptist, which provides the final overlay of prophecy fulfilled.

John is a singularly striking figure who has the daunting task of turning "the hearts of parents to their children, and the disobedient to the wisdom of the righteous, to make ready a people prepared for the Lord" (Luke 1:17). In recognition of this weighty calling, two of the four Sundays

of Advent are devoted to his story. John is still at work, it seems, turning our hearts and making us ready to be "a people prepared for the Lord."

According to the witness of Luke–Acts, John was spectacularly successful. Crowds flocked to him in the wilderness, finding him so persuasive they wondered if he might be the Messiah (Luke 3:7, 15). John continued to draw people to his compelling message, garnering his own disciples (Luke 7:18ff.). The book of Acts mentions people who, years after Jesus' death and resurrection, still identified themselves with John, like Apollos (Acts 18:24–28) and a community of John's disciples living in Ephesus (Acts 19:1–7). Such a powerful messenger could not be ignored in Luke's time, so John is afforded a place of honor in the opening chapter of the Gospel. It ends there, however. Jesus is the Messiah and the focus of the good news being told.[1] With

---

1. Fred B. Craddock, *Luke*, Interpretation (Louisville, KY: John Knox Press, 1990), 31–32.

Jesus' birth in Luke 2, John recedes and never again stands on equal footing. John himself acknowledges as much in Luke 3:16: "I baptize you with water; but one who is more powerful than I is coming; I am not worthy to untie the thong of his sandals. He will baptize you with the Holy Spirit and fire."

Zechariah, the proud papa, acknowledges the divine differential in his canticle: He begins by praising of the God of Israel who "raised up a mighty Savior" (Luke 1:69) and lingers there for eight verses. Only after the Messiah is lifted up does Zechariah turn his attention to his own child for four verses. As "the prophet of the Most High," John will go before the Lord, preparing the way, giving knowledge of salvation by forgiveness of sins (Luke 1:76–79).

For the church, Zechariah's prophecy becomes the fulfillment of Malachi 3:1–4. Long ago, Malachi (a name that means "my messenger") prophesied that God would send a messenger "to prepare the way" for the Lord. Malachi addresses people who have returned from exile and rebuilt the temple, but whose worship life lies in ruins. From the priests to the people, there is corruption. Their sacrifices and offerings are unacceptable, and the people are wearing out God's ears with their questions and complaints. Into this state of apathy and corruption, someone is coming who will prepare the way for the Lord. Malachi's messenger does not sing the soft refrain of Isaiah 40:1, "Comfort, O comfort my people. . . . speak tenderly to Jerusalem." This messenger speaks not a word in these few verses, but is all action. The people and priests become harsh metaphors: the dirtiest stained cloth will be scrubbed until it is restored to its intended cleanliness and luster; the roughest metal dug from the earth will be placed in a blazing hot fire. The refiner will not be satisfied until we glint like 24-carat gold in the sunshine and sparkle like silver finer than sterling.

John not only speaks of cleansing and fire, but uses other painful metaphors as well. Although he appears in the wilderness, he has his eye on the temple and the empire itself. Just look at the names that crowd the way before him: an emperor, a governor, a Jewish ruler and his two brothers holding sway over their little fiefdoms, and a couple of high priests (Luke 3:1–2). Against these earthly and corrupt powers John, son of Zechariah, appears, preparing the Lord's way of light and peace (Luke 1:79).

On this Second Sunday of Advent, the narratives regarding Zechariah's prophecy and John's birth are lively contributions to the more formal account of Luke 3:1–6. Insights from that backstory can fill out a sermon on John's character and role.

The canticle can be a unison reading by the congregation between Malachi 3:1–4 and Luke 3:1–6. Alternatively, Zechariah's prophecy can also be sung. "Blest Be the God of Israel," text by Michael Perry, sung to MERLE'S TUNE is one option. This rather lilting tune is ironically at odds with the painful preparation Malachi and John portend.

For a different approach, read the canticle in unison after a sermon on John the Baptist. The congregation then has the chance to read backward into this prophecy with greater insight.

Select lines from Luke 1:68–69 or Luke 1:78–79 can be used for the Call to Worship/Opening Sentences. Who better to bring us to a prayer of confession of our sin than John the Baptist?

> John the Baptist came to prepare the ways of the Lord; and to give us the knowledge of salvation by the forgiveness of sins.

Luke 1:78–79 offers an evocative declaration of forgiveness:

> By the tender mercy of our God,
> the dawn from on high will break upon us,
> to give light to those who sit in darkness
> and in the shadow of death,
> to guide our feet into the way of peace.
> Let us walk in the ways of the Lord.

This canticle is beautiful in bits and pieces, but it is exquisite as part of the larger story of this singularly striking figure who needs two Sundays of Advent if we are to do him justice at all.

KIMBERLY L. CLAYTON

Philippians 1:3–11

³I thank my God every time I remember you, ⁴constantly praying with joy in every one of my prayers for all of you, ⁵because of your sharing in the gospel from the first day until now. ⁶I am confident of this, that the one who began a good work among you will bring it to completion by the day of Jesus Christ. ⁷It is right for me to think this way about all of you, because you hold me in your heart, for all of you share in God's grace with me, both in my imprisonment and in the defense and confirmation of the gospel. ⁸For God is my witness, how I long for all of you with the compassion of Christ Jesus. ⁹And this is my prayer, that your love may overflow more and more with knowledge and full insight ¹⁰to help you to determine what is best, so that in the day of Christ you may be pure and blameless, ¹¹having produced the harvest of righteousness that comes through Jesus Christ for the glory and praise of God.

Commentary 1: Connecting the Reading with Scripture

Perhaps one of the reasons that some Christians do not talk much about the coming Day of the Lord (or the second coming of Christ) is that we have fallen into the trap of thinking that it is all about doom and gloom. Because we reject the notion that faith in Christ is an insurance policy against eternal damnation, and do not believe that fear is an appropriate motivator for faithful living, we may avoid texts that seem to lift up the gloomy or fear-filled Day of the Lord. When we do that, however, we miss the joy that stands at the heart of Paul's proclamation of that day. For Paul, the second coming of Christ is a day in which all of God's promises will be fulfilled, God's people will be redeemed, and resurrection life will reconcile all to one another and to God (see Rom. 8:18–25). It is precisely the anticipation of that "day" that fuels the joy that pours out of his letter to the Philippians.

The readings for the Second Sunday of Advent are full of anticipation. Malachi asks, "Who can endure the day of [God's] coming?" He also says that God is the one whom the people *seek* and in whom they *delight*. The purpose of the refiner's fire is renewed and restored worship, surely a joyful thing. The Song of Zechariah celebrates the fulfillment of God's promises made to Abraham. Israel will be able to worship God without fear, and the dayspring (Luke 1:78 KJV; "dawn" NRSV) will guide the people into the ways of peace. In the Gospel reading, the ministry of John the Baptist is introduced with the words of Isaiah, which celebrates the promise that "all flesh shall see the salvation of God." In all of these readings, the Day of the Lord is anticipated with joy and longing.

The reading from Philippians follows immediately on the salutation and announces the themes that shape this letter: thanksgiving, joy, deep affection, partnership, and readiness for the "day" of Jesus Christ. Paul is in prison as he writes, but this in no way diminishes his sense of connection to the people of Philippi. The purpose of the letter is to reassure the Philippian community of his well-being, to thank them for their generosity, to encourage them in their faith and life together, and to warn them against false teaching. Paul is sending the letter with Epaphroditus and hopes to send Timothy later on. This letter is not abstract theology. Its purpose is not primarily instructive. This is a letter that shows what Christian friendship looks like and how deeply joyful it is.

Fred Craddock suggests that Philippians 1:3–11 can be divided into three sections reflecting Paul's relationship to the Philippian congregation over time.[1] In verses 3–6, Paul looks back in gratitude to God as he remembers this community, and his prayer is full of joy. In particular, Paul gives thanks for their "sharing in the gospel from the first day until now," which he (and his coworkers) have experienced with the Philippian community. *Koinōnia* can also be translated as "participation in" or "partnership" or "fellowship." This is a rich and important term for Paul that is far beyond what we think of as "fellowship activities" or even small-group ministries in the modern church.

Fundamentally, it means a shared relationship in Christ. Those who are baptized into Christ become a new community where boundaries of race, ethnicity, gender, and economic status are overcome (Gal. 3:28). In Christ, those separated by the world's categories become sisters and brothers, a new family in God. Baptism is the entry into this new relationship, and it is sustained by the *koinōnia* (or "sharing") in the body and blood of Christ in the Lord's Supper (see 1 Cor. 10:16). Paul goes on to describe what the new community looks like as he exhorts them to "have the same mind" with one another as they have in Christ. The partnership Paul celebrates is relationship grounded in and shaped by the person of Jesus Christ.

This partnership in the gospel is deeply theological, but also immediately practical. The Philippian community has not only shared spiritual fellowship and active ministry by building up their community. They have also been deeply generous to Paul and his colleagues by supporting their ministry in other cities. At the end of the letter, Paul expresses his deep gratitude for their financial support while he was starting the community in Thessalonica: "No church *shared* with me in the matter of giving and receiving, except you alone" (4:15). Spiritual transformation is evidenced by generosity. Paul concludes his remembrance of what God has begun among the Philippians by affirming that God will "bring it to completion by the day of Jesus Christ" (1:6).

Paul then turns to the present time in verses 7–8. The theme here is the affection Paul has for these friends in Christ. The Philippians are not only partners with him in God's grace. They are also in solidarity with him during his imprisonment. "I keep [or hold] you in my heart," Paul says. The Greek can be read either this way (as in the RSV) or as in the NRSV ("you [Philippians] hold me in your heart"). In context, the RSV seems to make more sense, because Paul is speaking of his affection. The other reading would imply that this affection is conditional on the affection or support of the Philippians for him. Clearly, Paul's care for those with whom he has shared Christian community is based on God's work among them. Indeed, he says that he longs for his friends with the "compassion" of Christ. The root of this word is the gut-wrenching feeling of "suffering with" that God in Christ has for humankind. Paul can hold the Philippians in his heart because he participates in the suffering of Christ as he longs to share in Christ's resurrected life (see 3:7–11).

Finally, Paul looks to the future in verses 9–11. Paul has told the Philippians that he remembers them in his prayers. Now he prays for them and for their future. What he wants for them is an intensification and deepening of mutual love, out of which, Paul says, will come wisdom, which will enable them to know how to live with one another and in the world. As God enables them to live ever more deeply into the "mind of Christ" and his self-emptying love, they will become the community that God intends. This is what will prepare them for "the day of Christ."

Paul is confident of this outcome, not because of the efforts that the Philippians have shown in the past or will continue to put forth in the future. Their readiness for "the day" does not hang in the balance, dependent on the amount of their faith. Paul's hope is grounded in what God has been doing with and among his friends. "For Paul, God is the power of good beginnings and good endings in all things, not the least in our relationships with one another," writes Dan Migliore. "The work that God has begun in us will be completed by God. It is the faithfulness of God, not our own or our friend's faithfulness, that is the source of the unwavering confidence that the goal of our life and that of our friends in Christ will be reached."[2]

CYNTHIA M. CAMPBELL

---

1. Fred B. Craddock, *Philippians* (Atlanta: John Knox Press, 1985), 15.
2. Daniel L. Migliore, *Philippians and Philemon* (Louisville, KY: Westminster John Knox Press, 2014), 32.

Commentary 2: Connecting the Reading with the World

The letter that Paul writes to the church in Philippi does not bear the formality, nor is it laced with what some might negatively identify as a mantle of authoritarianism, associated with more serious pieces of Pauline correspondence. Instead, this letter is intensely personal. In this portion of it, the salutation and introduction, there is an unusual warmth and informality—as if Paul is writing to a church that he obviously knows very well. Here he sets aside any sense of stiffness or attention to convention, and relaxes into a style of communication that signals he is clearly comfortable with these people to whom he is writing. This is a congregation with which, in a way that maybe happens just once in a pastor's life, he has fallen in love. "It is right for me to think in this way about all of you, because you hold me in your heart, for all of you share in God's grace with me, both in my imprisonment and in the defense and confirmation of the gospel. For God is my witness, how I long for all of you with the compassion of Christ Jesus" (1:7–8). This is not simply the sort of acknowledgment letter of a financial gift that, in any institution, is just spit out of a computer. It is a personal, handwritten letter that is laced with love.

It is not uncommon for pastors, perhaps on a continuing-education retreat with their feet kicked up at the end of the day, to go around the room sharing stories about that one special, favorite parish. As they each take their turn, that particular church is generally one that they are no longer serving—one that they look back to fondly, and remember the grace and generosity extended to them by laypeople who coaxed them patiently into the rhythms of ministry. Specific names are remembered, specific faces are conjured up, specific stories are told about

Renewing the Divine Image

Once again, a merely human king does not let [his] lands . . . pass to others to serve them, nor go over to other men; but he warns them by letters, and often sends to them by friends, or, if need be, he comes in person to put them to rebuke in the last resort by his presence, only that they may not serve others, and his own work be spent for naught. Shall not God much more spare his own creatures, that they may not be led astray from him and serve things of naught? Especially since such going astray proves the cause of their ruin and undoing, and since it was unfitting that they should perish which had once been partakers of God's image. What, then, was God to do? Or what was to be done save the renewing of that which was in God's image, so that by it men might once more be able to know him? But how could this have come to pass, save by the very image of God, our Lord Jesus Christ? For by men's means it is impossible, since they are but made after an image; nor by angels either, for not even they are [God's] images. Whence the Word of God came in his own person, that, as he was the image of the Father, he might be able to re-create afresh the man after the image. But, again, it could not else have taken place had not death and corruption been done away. Whence he took, in natural fitness, a mortal body, that while death might in it be once for all done away, men made after his image might once more be renewed. None other, then, was sufficient for this need, save the image of the Father.

For as, when the likeness painted on a panel has been effaced by stains from without, he whose likeness it is must needs come once more to enable the portrait to be renewed on the same wood, for, for the sake of his picture, even the mere wood on which it is painted is not thrown away, but the outline is renewed upon it; in the same way also the most holy Son of the Father, being the image of the Father, came to our region to renew man once made in his likeness, and find him, as one lost, by the remission of sins; as he says himself in the Gospels, "I came to find and to save the lost."

Saint Athanasius, Patriarch of Alexandria (d. 373), *On the Incarnation*, §§13–14, in Edward R. Hardy, ed., *Christology of the Later Fathers* (Philadelphia: Westminster Press, 1954), 67–68.

important mercies extended to a green, young pastor, and specific teaching moments are remembered and recited, often accompanied by tears or by frogs in the throat. "That was my Philippi," one or another of them may say.

Paul's Philippi—a church that is predominantly Gentile, marked by the leadership of women playing various significant roles, and noted for its repeated acts of generosity—is on his mind while he is in prison. He addresses his Philippi as colleagues in the gospel; and while there is the matter of his gratitude for money they have sent him, this letter is far more than a thank-you note. It is a deeply personal word of encouragement: "And this is my prayer, that your love may overflow more and more with knowledge and full insight to help you to determine what is best, so that in the day of Christ you may be pure and blameless, having produced the harvest of righteousness that comes through Jesus Christ for the glory and praise of God" (1:9–11).

There are moments when, in the midst of utter ordinariness, something breaks through; seen with the eyes of faith, that which is rudimentary is suddenly transformed into something holy. Sometimes people of faith are fortunate enough to see all of it, even themselves, with the eyesight of God; the only fitting response to it all is a great, unimaginable gratitude.

I was recently in Cuba with a group of seminary students. We went there to spend a week immersing ourselves in what is beautiful and inspiring and complicated and tragic and hopeful about that little nation—so near to our own shores and yet, in multiple ways, so far away. We encountered many churches and their people, and various mission agencies, and a variety of landscapes. Then, on our last day, a Sunday, with our hearts and heads full to overflowing, our last stop was a Catholic church near our hotel. We would be there for their 9:30 mass and would then have time to gather up our luggage and board a bus taking us to the Havana airport. When we entered the church, we quickly discovered that the service we had expected was an hour later, which meant that we were virtually alone there in that largely empty, soaring space. We decided to stay, to sit quietly and prayerfully, and to simply soak up its beauty.

About a half hour later, I witnessed the unfolding of a parable. Two or three elderly regulars in the life of that parish came in slowly—walking with canes—and settled quietly in the front rows of the church. Then a few more, and a few more, and finally they were seventeen people—sixteen women and one man, all of them sitting up front. In a little while, the place would be almost full, but these were the intrepid ones, the ones who came early.

They were there, along with a lay officer in that church, to join in a preparatory recital of the rosary. When the antiphonal liturgy between the lay leader and the people commenced, I was captured by its trance-like rhythm—almost like the sound of an energetically throbbing beehive—that for centuries has helped people enter the silence of their own hearts, where Christ's spirit dwells. In the midst of all those back-and-forth "Santa Marias" and "Gloria Patris," it dawned on me that this was a picture of "the church"—the people who stay, in this case the people who have stayed a long time, even as the clergy have come and gone. These were the people who came early, before the rest of the congregation gathered, to claim that empty space, once again, and to make it holy with their presence and their prayers.

It reminded me of what happened all over that country during the early days of the Castro revolution, after the new regime declared itself a secular, communist country. After that declaration, many of the wealthiest people took what they could and walked out the doors of their houses and fled the country, and many clergy did the same thing. The churches they left behind, which might otherwise have been seized and repurposed by the government, were saved if it could be demonstrated that religious activities were going on inside. So, across the denominations, the people in those churches went into their sacred spaces—certainly on Sunday but also daily—to pray, and to recite in their various ways the substance of their faith, and to hold meetings and Bible studies and certainly worship, so as to continually lay claim to those spaces in that difficult time, and to make them holy with their presence.

On that Sunday morning in Havana, I saw, in the ordinary act of devotion on the part of those faithful people, the embodiment, once again, of a kind of "Philippi"—indeed, the very spirit of Philippi—and I was filled with gratitude at the sight of it.

Before the letter to the Philippians is over, Paul is going to address some tough issues. The letter, though, begins with the assumption of relationship, which is strong enough to sustain difference of opinions. "I thank God every time I remember you, constantly praying with joy in every one of my prayers for all of you, because of your sharing in the gospel from the first day until now" (1:3–5).

THEODORE J. WARDLAW

Luke 3:1–6

[1]In the fifteenth year of the reign of Emperor Tiberius, when Pontius Pilate was governor of Judea, and Herod was ruler of Galilee, and his brother Philip ruler of the region of Ituraea and Trachonitis, and Lysanias ruler of Abilene, [2]during the high priesthood of Annas and Caiaphas, the word of God came to John son of Zechariah in the wilderness. [3]He went into all the region around the Jordan, proclaiming a baptism of repentance for the forgiveness of sins, [4]as it is written in the book of the words of the prophet Isaiah,

"The voice of one crying out in the wilderness:
'Prepare the way of the Lord,
   make his paths straight.
[5]Every valley shall be filled,
   and every mountain and hill shall be made low,
and the crooked shall be made straight,
   and the rough ways made smooth;
[6]and all flesh shall see the salvation of God.'"

Commentary 1: Connecting the Reading with Scripture

With its prominent chronological and geopolitical references, Luke 3:1–2 marks a new beginning for the Lukan narrative. Luke 1–2 tells the stories of the births and summarizes the childhoods of John and Jesus. Now Jesus is in the background, John in the foreground, as Luke unveils the character of John's prophetic ministry (3:1–20). Gabriel, the angel of the Lord, had given John's job description to Zechariah, John's father: "He will turn many of the people of Israel to the Lord their God. With the spirit and power of Elijah he will go before him, to turn the hearts of parents to their children, and the disobedient to the wisdom of the righteous, to make ready a people prepared for the Lord" (1:16–17). Celebrating John's birth, Zechariah's prophecy proclaimed that John "will go before the Lord to prepare his ways" (1:76). Now we discover, this is in fact what John does.

Luke has carefully structured John's appearance in verses 2b–3 by setting the stage in two quite different ways. The first, with its list of rulers, is sociopolitical (vv. 1–2a). The second, a citation of Isaiah 40:3–5, is redemptive-historical (vv. 4–6). Foreign rule and powerful rulers characterize the world into which John enters,

but it is precisely in this world that God intervenes to bring about the long-awaited restoration of God's people.

The onset of John's ministry in 3:1–2 reads like the beginning of several OT prophetic books—for example, Hosea 1:1: "The word of the Lord that came to Hosea son of Beeri, in the days of Kings Uzziah, Jotham, Ahaz, and Hezekiah of Judah, and in the days of King Jeroboam son of Joash of Israel" (see also Jer. 1:1–4; Ezek. 1:1–3; Joel 1:1; Jonah 1:1; Mic. 1:1; Zeph. 1:1; Hag. 1:1; Zech. 1:1). This suggests that Luke's first concern was not to provide modern readers with a precise dating for the beginning of John's ministry (the data Luke provides actually allows a window for dating the onset of John's ministry between 27 and 29 CE) but, instead, to portray John as a prophet who worked and spoke in the real world of human authorities.

On the one hand, Israel lives, sharply put, under foreign control. Even the references to the priestly dynasty of Annas and Caiaphas (Annas's son-in-law) further this image. After all, Mary's song had pronounced judgment on the rich and powerful, and the names of these two high priests are spoken in the same breath as the rich and powerful emperor of Rome and his appointed rulers. Indeed, in Luke's world, Rome controlled the appointment of high priests, who therefore exercised authority in civil affairs.

On the other hand, even though John enters an oppressive, top-heavy scene, his role as a prophet serves as a counterpoint to Roman authority. God's word does not find John in urban centers of power, but in the wilderness, a space where the power and privilege associated with emperors and their appointees have little currency and their pronouncements enjoy little cachet. God's word comes not to rulers, not even to ruling priests, but to John, a wilderness prophet.

The second introduction of John, in 3:4–6, does not compete with the first introduction of 3:1–2, but develops further what Luke has already begun to reveal. John's wilderness location stands in contrast to the elevated status and power of those who lord it over the civilized world from their urban hubs. With words borrowed from Isaiah 40:3–5, Luke reminds us that God's people too are wilderness dwellers; that is, they are not at home, but in exile. What is more, speaking directly to his audience, Luke declares that John's prophetic ministry sets in motion the end of exile by introducing the promised, hoped-for restoration. Drawing on Isaiah's vision of exile and return, Luke underscores his theological perspective that God's saving purpose—not human rulers or the way humans distribute power and privilege—shapes the history of the world in truly decisive ways.

Luke grounds John's appearance in Isaiah's vision with the phrase "as it was written in the book of the words of the prophet Isaiah" (3:4a). It is as if the Isaianic words come alive, as though they animate John and his prophetic ministry. John is the voice crying in the wilderness (vv. 3–4). John's repentance-baptism prepares "the way of the Lord" (vv. 3–4). John's proclamation of the forgiveness of sins (v. 3) makes good the messenger's promise of salvation (v. 6). Isaiah's announcement of good news (Isa. 40:9), realized in the coming of God in power (Isa. 40:6–11), comes to life in John's words regarding the coming, powerful one (Luke 3:15–17) and Luke's summary of John's mission as one of "proclaiming good news" (v. 18).

What kind of "baptism" does John practice? There are no clear precedents. In Jewish purification rites and in proselyte baptism (if proselyte baptism was a Jewish practice in the first century—a contested point), people bathed *themselves*; with John's baptism, they were washed *by John*. Ritual purification was directed toward specific impurities, whereas John's baptism was nonspecific and was for the forgiveness of sins. Ritual washings occurred again and again, whereas John's baptism seems to have been nonrepeatable. Without clear precedents for John's practice, we turn instead to the important and long-standing link between physical cleanliness and moral purity. In the opening chapter of Isaiah, for example, we read, "Wash yourselves; make yourselves clean; remove the evil of your doings from before my eyes; cease to do evil, learn to do good; seek justice, rescue the oppressed, defend the orphan, plead for the widow" (Isa. 1:16–17). Ezekiel writes, "I will sprinkle clean water on you, and you will be cleansed of all your pollution. I will cleanse you of all your idols" (Ezek. 36:25 CEB). As Ananias told Paul, "Get up, be baptized, and have your sins washed away, calling on his name" (Acts 22:16).

From this perspective, "baptism" would be an embodied act that marks a religious-ethical new start. This is fully consistent with the way Luke describes this central aspect of John's ministry: it is a "baptism of repentance," that is, a repentance-baptism. This realignment of hearts and lives in relation to God's agenda is the means by which God's people "prepare the way of the Lord" and "make his paths straight."

Isaiah's vision assumes an obstructed road, an uneven road, even a crooked one, when what is needed is a smooth, straight road. Roadwork is required; hence the call to make the road ready. The work of road repair is nothing less than repentance. In Isaiah 35, the "road" is for those who return from exile and a holy way on which only the "clean" shall walk. This road is for those who have embraced God's ways as their pattern of life. Isaiah's image in chapter 40, of "the way of the Lord," thus points both to God's restoration of God's people (the return from exile, portrayed like a second exodus) and to the way of life embraced by those people whom God restores. We therefore recognize that the repentance John proclaims is marked by baptism but it is not a one-time event. It refers to a continuing journey on an obstructed path requiring ongoing roadwork. God's people begin the conversionary journey with baptism, but baptism is not so much the arrival at one's destination as it is the beginning of a journey.

JOEL B. GREEN

Commentary 2: Connecting the Reading with the World

God speaks to those unimagined as recipients of the divine word. We tend to imagine those with power and wealth to be the ones who should be the first to receive the divine word. Surely, if God would speak directly to them, the world might be changed for the better. God is not averse to such direct speech. God spoke to the rulers and kings of Israel and other nations; but, even in Israel, God's preferred recipients of divine address were the prophets, who most often lived among the common people or at the edge of society. In this text, God again aims holy words in a remote direction—away from the centers of power and toward people outside of their influence. This word is bound for the wilderness.

This text illuminates a juxtaposition—power and powerlessness—that has always been crucial to understand. Emperor, governor, rulers, and high priests are on the one side, and a prophet in the wilderness on the other side. The emperor and the other rulers represent the world as it is with its structures of military, economic, political, social, and religious power fully intact and functioning. They collectively imagine that they already embody the will of God and that they have the word of God in hand. They need to hear no new word because they conceive that they are enacting such a word.

The prophet in the wilderness is under no such illusion. John knows that he lives in the vulnerability of reception, waiting to hear God's word and looking and listening to the land for his daily sustenance. It is a vulnerability he might have learned from his father Zechariah, whose voice was silenced until after John's birth and who only then received from God his voice again (1:62–64). The wilderness that John inhabits is not his undoing. It is the place that prepares him to hear the word that God will give, not one he will contrive. The word of God often comes to us in such places and times of vulnerable reception, when we are ready to hear what God will say, even if we do not think we are ready.

Prophets always need wilderness. The new will emerge out of the wilderness. John preaches an old word made new by the time. He is fulfilling a promise and making visible ancient prophetic word. This is the story of Israel's God, who now appears in redeeming light. God calls through John to a wayward people, inviting them to turn afresh to their loving Creator and to receive the gift fit for God's children, forgiveness of sins. God will once again draw life from the water. Their baptism will signal that the new has begun in them, not by their own efforts but only through the action of God. John shows us a renewing God whose faithfulness extends across space and time, overcoming every obstacle we might erect against grace. God renews Israel and in this moment reveals the divine love in its eternal power to be completely new each morning and ready for communion.

Who John is and what he is saying merge in this moment. He is John the Baptizer, and that identity means he is the one who announces that the time has come, a time that has captured him and all the rulers of this world, from the emperor to the high priests. While there is always the danger of confusing the messenger with the message, here John is not using the prophetic word to draw attention to himself. The energy moves in the opposite direction: John's life has been taken up into God's dramatic appearance in Israel. God has always worked in an economy of humility, where the divine life has been joined to human life, God's voice flowing in and with human voices. In this text, that economy is moving to its greatest strength as the one voice that cries from the wilderness is simultaneously the prophet's voice and the voice of God.

God's voice, woven into the voices of the prophets, is what love sounds like. God will be known and heard, seen and experienced. John announces what Israel longs for and the world needs: to see God. All that has obstructed the sight of God will be removed. Indeed, the world itself will make room for its Creator. Valleys filled, mountains and hills made low, crooked roads made straight and rough ones made smooth—all will be made to angle toward the divine life present in the world. There will be no need for an alternative route to God, no need for more maps to the Divine, because God has come to us, clarified the way, and sharpened the view. John announces a new question. No longer do we need to ask, "Where can God be found?" Now the only question is "Do you see the God who is coming to you?"

God comes to Israel, not simply to be seen, but to change the world. Divine visibility implies holy justice in the world. John announces the future that is coming. This is the salvation of God: Israel freed from oppression and a world made right under God's own rule. If God will be seen, so too will the clandestine operations of evil and injustice. They will no longer hide in the shadows and behind closed doors. Plans made and structures created that destroy the creation and damage the creature will no longer be able to hide through their political and social rhetoric or through those mechanisms that blind people to what is in front of their eyes. All flesh (3:6) means that all creatures—not only all peoples—will see and experience God's salvation.

This text refuses any privatization of salvation. It pushes against reading habits that would constrict gospel concern to the saving of souls and the healing of bodies. While life with God certainly means the redemption of body and soul, it expansively reaches out to the cosmos, to show the claim of God on a beloved creation. John heightens an expectation already present in Israel, that God will come and turn this world right side up. This expectation of Israel should never be spiritualized and used to escape John's urgent claim—that God is coming and will change this world. The time of salvation is upon us, and all who believe John's word have prepared themselves to see the change. The text invites us to enter the tension of this expectation. We live in its hope, yet are always edging toward frustration as we wait for a world filled with the sight, sound, and knowledge of God and shaped in the divine rule.

Jesus heard John. Jesus heard the voice from the wilderness speaking to him, and he too responded as John invited all of Israel to respond. We read this text poorly if we bypass this hearing as though it was inconsequential, as though Jesus would have come forward even without John. The text will not allow us such a poor reading of history. It was precisely this word of John that Jesus heard and took to heart. Jesus heard the urgency of John's message and realized that the time of God was indeed his time to act in obedience to God. John spoke a word from God about the overturning of this world and all its rulers, and Jesus, this child of Israel, heard that word. So too must we hear this word to be addressed to us.

WILLIE JAMES JENNINGS

Third Sunday of Advent

Zephaniah 3:14–20   Philippians 4:4–7
Isaiah 12:2–6   Luke 3:7–18

Zephaniah 3:14–20

¹⁴Sing aloud, O daughter Zion;
    shout, O Israel!
Rejoice and exult with all your heart,
    O daughter Jerusalem!
¹⁵The LORD has taken away the judgments against you,
    he has turned away your enemies.
The king of Israel, the LORD, is in your midst;
    you shall fear disaster no more.
¹⁶On that day it shall be said to Jerusalem:
Do not fear, O Zion;
    do not let your hands grow weak.
¹⁷The LORD, your God, is in your midst,
    a warrior who gives victory;
he will rejoice over you with gladness,
    he will renew you in his love;
he will exult over you with loud singing
    ¹⁸as on a day of festival.
I will remove disaster from you,
    so that you will not bear reproach for it.
¹⁹I will deal with all your oppressors
    at that time.
And I will save the lame
    and gather the outcast,
and I will change their shame into praise
    and renown in all the earth.
²⁰At that time I will bring you home,
    at the time when I gather you;
for I will make you renowned and praised
    among all the peoples of the earth,
when I restore your fortunes
    before your eyes, says the LORD.

Commentary 1: Connecting the Reading with Scripture

Jerusalem was occasionally referred to in a feminine form as daughter Zion, and in Lamentations "she" was filled with sadness (Lam. 2:10, 13); here she is invited to sing and rejoice! This is a rather startling ending to a book that begins (Zeph. 1:2–4) with a prophecy of doom and what may be called an "un-creation" (Zeph. 1 features a sweeping away of humans, then animals, then birds and fish, reversing the order in Gen. 1). The form of Hebrew poetry called a lament (a large number of psalms are such laments) also typically ends the otherwise sad poem on a note of hope and gladness—even thanking God for delivering the one who is praying for help.

The images of salvation are powerful here: God "takes away judgments," "you shall fear disaster no more" (v. 15); "The LORD, your God, is . . . a warrior who gives victory" (v. 17); "I will deal with your oppressors at that time" (v. 19). Oddly, in the final verse, translators often turn to a euphemism to suggest that God will "restore your fortunes before your eyes" (v. 20). The Hebrew is actually referring to returning captives, those who were taken, to restore *them* "before your eyes." Because of this reference to captivity, many have proposed that Zephaniah's older hopeful messages were added to in the days after the Babylonian exile.

Note how interesting the images are—images that are used to convey comfort in this passage: "disaster," "warrior," "oppressors," and so forth.

Such language strongly suggests a people having suffered a military trauma and its accompanying human losses, both casualties and those taken as prisoners of war. It is, of course, language that is all too familiar to twenty-first-century people as well. The problem is that sometimes encouragement that seeks to respond to abuse can itself become abusive, as if we want God to say: "I will defeat those who have defeated you."

Certainly this theme is familiar in the Old Testament, often associated with what a previous generation of scholars called Zion theology. This Zion theology is found in some psalms and in prophets that suggest a nationalistic hope for defeating the enemies of Jerusalem and clearly honoring the king who reigns there (Pss. 46, 48, and 76 are considered the main Zion theology

---

God Will Take Care of Us

It is true that a man cannot be serene unless he possesses something about which to be serene. Here we reach the high-water mark of prophetic religion, and it is of the essence of the religion of Jesus of Nazareth. Of course God cares for the grass of the field, which lives a day and is no more, or the sparrow that falls unnoticed by the wayside. He also holds the stars in their appointed places, leaves his mark in every living thing. And he cares for me! To be assured of this becomes the answer to the threat of violence—yea, to violence itself. To the degree to which a man knows *this*, he is unconquerable from within and without.

When I was a very small boy, Halley's comet visited our solar system. For a long time I did not see the giant in the sky because I was not permitted to remain up after sundown. My chums had seen it and had told me perfectly amazing things about it. Also I had heard of what were called "comet pills." The theory was that if the pills were taken according to directions, then when the tails of the comet struck the earth one would not be consumed. One night I was awakened by my mother, who told me to dress quickly and come with her out into the backyard to see the comet. I shall never forget it if I live forever. My mother stood with me, her hand resting on my shoulder, while I, in utter, speechless awe, beheld the great spectacle with its fan of flight spreading across the heavens. The silence was like that of absolute motion. Finally, after what seemed to me an interminable time interval, I found my speech. With bated breath I said, "What will happen to us if that comet falls out of the sky?"

My mother's silence was so long that I looked from the comet to her face, and there I beheld something in her countenance that I had seen only once before, when I came into her room and found her in prayer. When she spoke, she said, "Nothing will happen to us, Howard; God will take care of us."

O simplehearted mother of mine, in one glorious moment you put your heart on the ultimate affirmation of the human spirit! Many things have I seen since that night. Times without number I have learned that life is hard, as hard as crucible steel; but as the years have unfolded, the majestic power of my mother's glowing words has come back again and again, beating out its rhythmic chant in my own spirit. Here are the faith and the awareness that overcome fear and transform it into the power to strive, to achieve, and not to yield.

Howard Thurman (1899–1981), *Jesus and the Disinherited* (New York: Abingdon-Cokesbury Press, 1949), 56–57.

psalms, but Isa. 60–62 represents similar ideas). Here in Zephaniah, similarly, the writer understands a great day to involve the defeat of enemies, but there is more to this passage than mere vengefulness.

First of all, it is crucially important to hear the (typically angry) calls for revenge in the Bible as the *language not of the victorious and powerful but of the traumatized* (cf. Ps. 137, which clearly comes from the suffering of exiles). Therefore, the use of these kinds of passages in modern Christian faith and practice calls for caution. Secondly, it is crucial to point out that the message is not universally condemning of all "foreigners." There are more hopeful notes in Zephaniah. If punishment of "the nations" appears in Zephaniah 3:8, then are these the *same* nations that will be the recipients of a *positive change*, so that they will join Israel in praising God in 3:9? A number of commentators refer to a kind of universalism here in verse 9—a consideration that the nations have a place in God's future plans, even if chastised in the process. In any case, nations will also be impressed with God and God's people, according to verse 20.[1]

There is a critical role for a "pastoral reading" of biblical calls for revenge. If a friend or relative is heard spouting vindictive and angry calls for revenge, our normal response would probably involve two steps: first, reminding our friend or relative that this kind of language is never very helpful; second, we would quite rightly ask, "What's happened? Why are you so angry?" Surely this is the most important step in reading biblical anger—to listen to, and *thus identify*, suffering. When we read calls for revenge, or even celebrations of the defeat of others, a crucial response is to understand the suffering that has led to that point—and perhaps to better understand that the Bible comes from real people who suffered some very real tragedies. Our Scripture came at a price, and church folks who too easily forget this "humanity within the divinity" of the word will fail to appreciate its full message.

Finally, although it is a common motif in the

Hebrew Bible that liberation means defeat of enemies, there are equally important instances when it seems that what God is "destroying" is war itself, and this peaceful age is also because God is "in your midst": "Many nations shall join themselves to the Lord on that day, and shall be my people; and I will dwell in your midst. And you shall know that the Lord of hosts has sent me to you" (Zech. 2:11; cf. Zech. 9:9–10, Mic. 4:1–5). When the Hebrews were at their best, they wrote that former enemies will come to realize, to their shame, the nature of peace and justice, and thus they too will be included in God's intended future. After all, Jonah famously held out the possibility that even the Assyrians will come to realize their violent sins and repent, and Micah speaks of foreign nations bowing in shame (Mic. 7:16–17), not massacred in revenge. Wahl, for example, wrote that in the final verse of this passage in Zephaniah, the "protective presence of Yahweh contrasts with the threatening presence in vs. 5."[2]

It takes genuine strength to be actually concerned about transformation of enemies. Jesus was nearly lynched, according to Luke 4:25–30, for suggesting that God's liberating love (release to the captive, sight to the blind, and liberation for the oppressed) was actually going to include foreigners. When a Roman centurion, the very symbol of oppression in Jesus' homeland, confessed his unworthiness to Jesus, precisely because he was a Roman colonial soldier in the homeland of Jesus ("I also am a man set under authority," Luke 7:8), Jesus graciously complimented his confession of faith (Luke 7:9). It can certainly be argued that Jesus appealed to a Hebrew tradition of compassion and change, rather than the tradition of celebrating revenge. When nations come to realize their awful behavior, not only can they be spared, but they can be included in the mercies of God's future for humanity—even taking lessons from God's followers who can become, in the words of this passage, "renowned and praised among all the peoples of the earth" (v. 20).

The final verse confronts us with an interesting question: What is the kind of behavior

---

1. R. Mason, "Zephaniah," in *The Oxford Bible Commentary* (Oxford: Oxford University Press, 2001), 606.
2. Thomas P. Wahl, "Zephaniah," in *The Jerome Bible Commentary*, ed. R. E. Brown, J. A. Fitzmyer, Roland E. Murphy (Englewood Cliffs, NJ: Prentice Hall, 1990), 349–61.

that we can exhibit in the world—a behavior clearly based on our love for God—that would so deeply impress the nations of the world (even, perhaps *especially*, nations with whom we are angry!) that we are "renowned and praised" as a result? Surely it is not how effective we are at punishing enemies, but how effective we are at *impressing* enemies toward changed relationships. Such positive changes would indeed be "renowned and praised."

DANIEL L. SMITH-CHRISTOPHER

Commentary 2: Connecting the Reading with the World

Zephaniah concludes with this exultant announcement of homecoming. Jerusalem shall ring with song and despair shall vanish in delight. The final oracle ends the almost unrelieved storm of judgment and threat distinguishing the previous chapters. This good news, which begins in 3:9, comes as a startling change. Hitherto Zephaniah relentlessly condemns Judah's religious syncretism. Jerusalem has reduced the worship of God to a cult among cults, one of a variety of religious obligations. Zion bows before the Lord and tips her hat to Baal (1:4). Today, we might call this relegating God to one concern among others. We have religious interests, our "spirituality," and, alongside, much else that engages our passions but to which our faith is indifferent. God totally rejects such easygoing compromise, whereby we distribute our loyalties—God among them—according to taste, security, and public fashion. "'I will utterly sweep away everything from the face of the earth,' says the LORD" (1:2 RSV).

This book ends, however, not with ruin but with joy. Judah's enemies become the "peoples of the earth," who look gratefully to Jerusalem and "call on the name of the LORD" (3:9). The vision, however, lacks definition concerning restored Jerusalem. The images throw the emphasis upon the action of God, intimately present, rejoicing in the people, protecting and tending to them. The oracle, therefore, is strongly theocentric. Despite the exhortation, "Sing aloud, O daughter Zion" (3:14), it is God rather than the people whom the prophet sees singing over Jerusalem, celebrating as in the ecstasy of a festival (3:17). This Godward focus governs the underlying logic of judgment and restoration. On the one hand, God's judgment is unmitigated. It goes "all the way down" and

leaves no possibility of a human response to turn the condemnation. That judgment admits of no exception, though, it corresponds with the nature of God, with God's rightful claim to exclusive loyalty. However well or ill people behave, that they have God on a priority list along with other loves falsifies their faith, even if God is the top item.

On the other hand, though the prophet exhorts it (2:3), repentance plays no role in God's forgiveness and renewal. God has mercy, and the prophetic concentration remains entirely on God's action: "The LORD has taken away the judgments against you" (3:15). Only the joyful singing of the unexpectedly blessed is left for the people. God follows his unreserved judgment with an unqualified, unsolicited mercy. Moreover, Zephaniah leaves this blessing as God's final word. God's grace and God's judgment are not symmetrical. Mercy bursts as a surprise on scenes of devastation as God turns Jerusalem's "shame into praise and renown in all the earth" (3:19). Grace is the mysterious excess that outruns condemnation and covers all manner of ill.

With good reason, this passage is often read as future hope, the promise of a new world after the strife of history and the sway of sin is finally exhausted. The images of God's festival presence with God's people invite this, especially if one remembers the closing visions of Revelation, in which God and the Lamb indwell the "holy city, Jerusalem" (Rev. 21:10). Zephaniah's closing vision, therefore, belongs among the symbolic resources for imagining God's "new heaven and new earth."

If we leave interpretation with that, though, we miss something of the bite of this passage. Given the historical setting in the reign of

Josiah (640–609 BCE), Zephaniah's expectation belongs to history and looks for a glorious age within it. In other words, though our imaginations quite rightly complete these symbols in anticipation of heaven, they still give us hope set in the form of this world. God's blessing, therefore, takes burdened men and women, despised and spurned by their neighbors, and brings them joyfully into the common life (3:19). No longer will a constant shadow of fear and threat dampen all celebration. The penurious, the refugee, and all who dread what the next month may bring shall breathe freely as God rejoices over them. Our prayer and action must take their direction from this heavenly but also worldly hope.

Again, the passages of judgment help us draw out the shape of blessing in this final oracle, despite the lack of concrete detail. Zephaniah connects idolatry with oppression. His anger falls upon the officials and the royal court, and upon priests and prophets, "your proudly exultant ones" (3:11), who have submerged God's teaching in a parliament of idols. Riches and success, profitable trade, flourishing vineyards and luxurious houses suggest that all is well and better than well. The royal court apes the fashion of the great pagan empires (1:8) and so boasts in a foreign glory. The prophets give their support to these appearances of national flourishing, speaking out of their own inspirations, while the priests judge cases corruptly, serving their own interests (3:2–4).

Zephaniah denounces their arrogance, a self-confidence for which God is irrelevant, the prophetic word neither here nor there: "[They] say, 'The LORD will not do good, nor will he do ill'" (1:12 RSV). Judgment falls so heavily on Judah's ruling and privileged classes because their sponsorship of syncretism betrays the society whose care is their duty. They project a vision of their time and their nation wholly at odds with the reality of life before God. So God will strip Judah of its presence and influence (3:11).

Ideologies of national life are notoriously ambiguous; it is hard to keep our heads when we project our aspirations, fears, repressed rage, and narcissism upon our country and "way of life." We lose our frail grip on wisdom, as we curse strangers and foreigners, reserve our generosities for those like us, and refuse responsibility, piling condemnation on the media's latest flock of popular scapegoats. If Judah's official prophets packaged their own desires as God's word, we tend to substitute celebrity for moral example and reward politicians for channeling our least amiable urges. Societies need a collectively engaging vision of their common life; to the extent they lack one, they undermine the motivations for seeking the common good. Motivating symbols of national life are vital, but they are also ambiguous and subject to corruption, and such corruption falls under God's judgment. As many twentieth-century nations discovered, coming to know our national life justly can be bitterly painful, and following our best lights, in which God's grace beckons, demands courage. Thus, in Judah, when God topples the illusions of strength, God makes a path for the humble (3:12, 19).

God's final word, though, is mercy. Zion's people are to sing and shout with full hearts (3:14), because, though God has not taken back a word of the condemnation, God's grace exceeds the condemnation in the healing powers of renewal. By not confining interpretation of this passage to a future eschatology, we may recognize the presence in our lives, individual and corporate, of the grace that always exceeds, without denying, the truths we find so hard to hear. We discover the joy to sing of God's healing presence, renewing the world in wisdom, in goodness, and in the love that humbly seeks other than itself.

Judgment left us with nothing, but God's exceeding mercy gave us back God's self, which we now know is everything. In God's blessing, we have peace and a calling to make peace, forgiveness and a reason to reconcile, truth and the courage to speak it. If God's judgment goes down to the roots, as Zephaniah proclaims, then those who also know of God's mercy and of the persistence of grace, will always have much to sing about.

ALAN GREGORY

Isaiah 12:2–6

²Surely God is my salvation;
  I will trust, and will not be afraid,
for the LORD GOD is my strength and my might;
  he has become my salvation.

³With joy you will draw water from the wells of salvation. ⁴And you will say in
that day:
Give thanks to the LORD,
  call on his name;
make known his deeds among the nations;
  proclaim that his name is exalted.

⁵Sing praises to the LORD, for he has done gloriously;
  let this be known in all the earth.
⁶Shout aloud and sing for joy, O royal Zion,
  for great in your midst is the Holy One of Israel.

Connecting the Psalm with Scripture and Worship

To use a baseball analogy, Old Testament prophets are divided into the majors and the minors. Biblically speaking, the distinction is based solely on the respective lengths of their prophetic books. Still, some prophets do seem more "major league" than others. The difference is apparent in many a pastor's study. There are likely several commentaries on Isaiah and Jeremiah, unquestionably major prophets, while Habakkuk and Zephaniah merit no space on a shelf at all, tucked away in one commentary covering all twelve of the minor prophets. In any batting order, Isaiah is first up, the lead-off hitter; meanwhile, even among the minor prophets, Zephaniah bats ninth.

From the beginning of the church, Isaiah held a position of prominence. Isaiah is quoted in New Testament writings more than any other book of the Old Testament. Early church fathers (Eusebius, Theodoret, Jerome, and Augustine) read Isaiah's vision and understood it as prophecy foretelling Jesus Christ. They not only regarded Isaiah "as the first and greatest prophet, but as the first apostle and evangelist."[1] Today we seek to understand Isaiah in its own context within the history of Israel and avoid reading Jesus back into texts addressing a different time and circumstance. Still, the church's early affinity remains for seeing Isaiah as prophecy pointing to Jesus. Every Christmas Eve, Isaiah 9:2–7 is the Old Testament lesson. Among the candlelight and Christmas greenery, we hear "For a child has been born for us, a son given to us," and imagine Jesus, not an ancient Judean king like Hezekiah.

This Third Sunday of Advent, Isaiah 12:2–6 takes the place of a psalm, and it sounds very much as if it belongs in the book of Psalms. This canticle has much in common with the Old Testament reading, Zephaniah 3:14–20. Though written perhaps a century apart (Zephaniah after Isaiah), both prophets speak to Judah and Jerusalem in a time of great geopolitical turmoil. Threats from a northern alliance and from Assyria span the decades, bringing devastation. Both prophets pronounce God's judgment upon God's own beloved people. Nevertheless, amid the inescapable doom and gloom prophesied, both offer words of hope and restoration. Scattered promises

1. Christopher R. Seitz, *Isaiah 1–39*, Interpretation (Louisville, KY: John Knox Press, 1993), 1.

of God's ultimate faithfulness are lifelines in an overwhelming tide of terror. Zephaniah 3:14–20 and Isaiah 12:2–6 are concluding passages in which salvation and joy get the last word.

In the brief book of Zephaniah, hope does not outweigh doom; still, it concludes in rejoicing: God overturns harsh judgments and returns to the people's midst, gathering the vulnerable and outcast ones. God's gladness and love spill out; people of the earth take notice. Isaiah 12:2–6 concludes the first unit of the book of Isaiah. Chapters 1–12 pronounce judgment and punishment, with occasional glimpses of hope. Chapters 9 and 11 expand the hopeful vision, promising light, joy, a coming savior, and a world wholly at peace. After eleven chapters of prophecy, Israel is summoned to respond.

What a response it is! In both Zephaniah 3:14–20 and Isaiah 12:2–6, fear is replaced by trust and joy. Imperatives of praise pile up: Sing! Shout! Sing for joy!

Isaiah 12:2–6 is the sustained doxology of people who, despite their present condition of suffering and fear, know that death will not have the last word, because God controls the narrative. Isaiah 12:2 summons to mind Exodus 15:2, as Moses and the people sing their way through the sea on dry land. That definitive song of a people saved and set free by God echoes through the centuries, taken up now by those who will return from servitude and exile by the astounding power and mercy of God.

The Hebrew word for salvation, rarely used in the first thirty-nine chapters of Isaiah, appears three times in this brief passage. The prophet knows that God can and indeed will save the people from ultimate destruction. This repetitive use of "salvation" closes this unit of Isaiah, whose name means, "The Lord is Salvation."[2]

God forgives and saves. Isaiah 12:2–6 offers potent liturgy for the confession and pardon sequence:

CALL TO CONFESSION
Surely God is my salvation;
I will trust, and will not be afraid,
for the Lord God is my strength and my
    might;
God has become my salvation.

Following a prayer of confession, Isaiah 12:3–4, 6 embodies liturgical action. Stirring up the baptismal waters, the liturgist and people proclaim:

DECLARATION OF FORGIVENESS
With joy you will draw water from the wells
    of salvation.
Give thanks to the Lord; call on God's name;
make God's deeds known among the nations.
Proclaim that God's name is exalted!
God is in the midst of us.

Characterized by exuberant joy and reassurance, Zephaniah and Isaiah stand in contrast to the Gospel reading. John the Baptist preaches to a "brood of vipers," warning of the wrath to come. In good prophetic tradition, John pronounces judgment, preaches repentance, and calls people to God's righteousness. John's proclamation too leads toward God's salvation.

Isaiah 12:2–6 may also find use as a doxology following the sermon or as a joyful, hope-filled blessing and charge at the service's end. A sermon challenging us to repentance and right living in the spirit of John speaks to people in the wilderness. We are still seeking, waiting for God, beset by sin, surrounded by forces that threaten to overwhelm. Just as John preaches to people who have come to be baptized, we also come to the baptismal waters after the sermon or for the blessing and charge. There we remember that we are claimed, redeemed, and counted as the beloved of God, whose last word is always salvation.

In response to this good news, water is lifted and we join the ancient doxology:

With joy you will draw water from the wells
    of salvation.
Give thanks to the Lord!
Surely God is my salvation.
I will trust, and will not be afraid.
The Lord God is my strength.
Great in our midst is the Holy One of Israel.

What better conclusion could be offered by those being led into freedom, brought home along a miraculous path opened by the God who promises salvation?

KIMBERLY L. CLAYTON

2. Seitz, *Isaiah 1–39*, 112–13.

Philippians 4:4–7

⁴Rejoice in the Lord always; again I will say, Rejoice. ⁵Let your gentleness be known to everyone. The Lord is near. ⁶Do not worry about anything, but in everything by prayer and supplication with thanksgiving let your requests be made known to God. ⁷And the peace of God, which surpasses all understanding, will guard your hearts and your minds in Christ Jesus.

Commentary 1: Connecting the Reading with Scripture

This passage is a "fixture" in worship. It appears in the lectionary for Thanksgiving Day and can be used effectively at both weddings and funerals. It is exquisitely suited to Gaudete Sunday, the Third Sunday of Advent, when the church rejoices as Christ's birth draws ever nearer. The reading from Zephaniah exhorts daughter Jerusalem to rejoice at a vision of the city's (and nation's) restoration. Isaiah 12 is a resounding song rejoicing in God's salvation. While the Gospel reading centers on John the Baptist's ministry, the good news is that there are indeed lifestyle changes that can be made so as to be ready for God's Messiah. While the first three readings connect with the theme of rejoicing, the Gospel and Philippians are connected with the idea of how to live so as to be ready for the Day of the Lord.

Philippians is a very personal letter from Paul to a community that he knows well and is very close to his heart. The Philippians not only welcomed the good news into their lives; they have been loyal and generous supporters of Paul's ministry in other places. Paul is writing from prison to allay their anxieties about his safety and to encourage them to remain steadfast in faith. It is also clear that there are tensions in this community. False teachers (whom Paul calls "dogs" and "evil workers") are stirring up doubt and dissent (3:2). Paul's own imprisonment is evidence of tension with the larger society as well. Both abundance and tension are the context for this epistle of joy.

Paul's letters often follow a pattern of greeting, introduction, the body of the letter, concluding exhortations, and final greetings. Philippians

4:4–7 is the middle section of a three-part exhortation, and there is good reason to consider using the entire exhortation, as it provides context for the call to rejoice. First, in verses 2–3, Paul encourages two prominent leaders in the community to put aside differences and "be of the same mind in the Lord." This idea of having the mind of Christ figures prominently in chapter 2, where Paul uses a familiar hymn to remind the community that the self-emptying work of Christ should be the model for their life together. The naming of Euodia and Syntyche indicates the presence and importance of women in these early communities and reinforces the notion that leadership was understood as a partnership (or fellowship, *koinōnia*) in which many played key roles. Paul is perhaps not given enough credit for affirming patterns of shared ministry.

In the closing section of the exhortation, verses 8–9, Paul urges his friends to concentrate their attention and their lives on virtues that would have been familiar to Greek culture. Other philosophers taught that the good life was achieved by pursuing similar virtues, which not only built up the individual, but contributed to the flourishing of the whole community. Paul offers himself as an example and concludes that the result of the virtuous life will be God's peace.

The centerpiece of Paul's exhortation, our text builds on themes already explored in the letter. Paul opened this letter joyfully praying for his friends (v. 3). He himself rejoices, even in prison, because of their prayers for him (v. 19). Now he exhorts them to rejoice. Paul is thinking here of something much deeper than happiness or a sunny outlook or a "put on a happy face" form of denial. He *knows* that he is in prison; he knows that there are challenges for this community of believers both within and without. Nevertheless Paul has found in the gospel the source of deepest joy. Christ's self-emptying has become Paul's abundance. The joy that he has found in Christ seems like a paradox in view of his life circumstance, but Paul sees life now through a different lens: the grace of God poured out in Christ. Indeed, it is precisely this joy in the Lord that led Paul to write later: "I have learned the secret of being well-fed and of going hungry, of having plenty and of being in need" (4:12). The joy of knowing Christ sustains Paul in all circumstances, and he exhorts his friends to find that same joy.

"Let your gentleness be known to everyone." The Greek word *epieikēs* has a number of possible meanings, including "forbearance" (RSV) and "magnanimity" (NEB). Morna Hooker suggests that it "denotes generosity toward others that is a characteristic of Christ himself."[3] Christians are to welcome others; to be prepared to forgive one another; to bear with one another in the midst of the trials of life. Gentleness is the opposite of keeping score of wrongs done or seeking to get even. A similar theme is found in 1 Corinthians 13:5: "[love] does not insist on its own way." Christians are urged to get gentle or generous with each other and also with the world around them. This is not an ethic of "niceness," but rather a new way of life made possible by Christ's presence.

"The Lord is near." One could read this as a veiled threat ("be good to each other—the Lord is watching!"). However, it seems much more likely that Paul sees the immediacy of Christ's presence as what makes Christian life possible. Because God in Christ is with us, we are able to have "the mind of Christ" among us and live at peace with each other. There is also here a double meaning: God is near to all who call (see Ps. 145:8) and the Day of the Lord is drawing ever nearer.

Paul then exhorts his friends not to worry about anything. Jesus expressed the same sentiment: "Do not worry about your life, what you will eat, or about your body, what you will wear. For life is more than food, and the body more than clothing" (Luke 12:22–23). God knows our needs as well as or better than we do. Neither Jesus nor Paul romanticizes poverty, however. Their point is about worry or what we strive for (Luke 12:29). Strive for God's reign and realm, Jesus says, and then other things will sort themselves out.

The rest of verse 6 is a primer on prayer: "In everything by prayer and supplication with thanksgiving let your requests be made known to God." When we pray, we lift up our hearts to God full of our hopes and longings. We pray for ourselves and for others; we pray for healing, for safety, for justice, and for peace. But all of these requests are to be surrounded by thanksgiving. Prayer that is grounded in gratitude for what God has already done can make requests with confidence that God's grace is sufficient to all our needs.

When our lives with one another and with God begin with joy and are infused with gratitude, then Paul says, "the peace of God . . . will guard your hearts and your minds." Paul's final words echo the benediction in Numbers 6:24–26. Fred Craddock suggests that this is a military analogy. God's peace "will stand sentry watch" over our hearts and minds, perhaps in contrast to the soldiers that are guarding Paul. The day of Christ is near and God's peace is standing sentry; therefore the Philippians do not need to be anxious or distressed. "Because God's peace is on duty, they do not have to be anxiously scanning the horizon for new threats,"[4] Craddock writes. In that peace and confidence, all supplications can be made with thanksgiving and deep joy.

CYNTHIA M. CAMPBELL

---

3. Morna D. Hooker, "Philippians," in *The New Interpreter's Bible* (Nashville: Abingdon Press, 2005), 11:540.
4. Fred B. Craddock, *Philippians* (Atlanta: John Knox Press, 1985), 72.

Commentary 2: Connecting the Reading with the World

Maybe the first task for the preacher, on the Third Sunday of Advent—Gaudete Sunday, when worshipers light the pink candle on the Advent wreath for the relief of a lighter mood in the midst of an otherwise intentionally gloomy liturgical season—is to try to read this text without thinking of Henry Purcell's classical anthem "Rejoice in the Lord Alway." That iconic baroque piece is based on verses 4–7 of this epistle text, set to heartbreakingly beautiful music. Google it or pull the CD from your music shelf. Better yet, ask the choir to work it up as the main anthem of the day. It will help set the tone for preaching about joy—in the midst of suffering.

Paul writes this letter from prison, after all. In fact, as Fred Craddock once put it, "most of Paul's ministry was by mail."[5] In a jail cell, where he spent a lot of his time, he seeks to pastor that church as a veteran might write to foot soldiers still persevering on the field of battle. Even that gracious congregation in Philippi is not always the peaceable kingdom. The details of the dispute there are not known. Nonetheless, it is grave enough for Paul, knowing that this letter will be read in the context of worship, to call out Euodia and Syntyche as obvious contenders with one another (4:2, 3). How often do you do that on a Sunday morning? Whatever is going on in that church is no small matter. So, Paul, from prison—a place in which he may die this time—encourages joy.

He encourages joy, not happiness. You would do well to tease out the difference between these two values. You have the experience of stepping into a coffee shop after the Ash Wednesday service, and you have forgotten that the ashen cross marked on your forehead is still there in all of its countercultural starkness. Perhaps in an attempt to be helpful, a server, or a fellow patron wearing a smiley-face button on his or her lapel, remarks, "There is some dust on your forehead," and reaches for a Kleenex to wipe off the smudge. Maybe you have sometimes overcome the embarrassment of that moment to offer testimony: "No, I have been at an Ash Wednesday service." "What does

that mean?" comes the reply. "It means that God loves me even when all hell is breaking loose." Imagine, after silence, this response: "Can I put some on *my* forehead?" In a culture obsessed with acquiring or conjuring up happiness, there is still an often unspoken desire—hunger, even—for joy. Paul, in spite of the dankness and the darkness of that jail cell, is encouraging joy in the midst of suffering. "Rejoice in the Lord always; again I will say, Rejoice."

Why does Paul rejoice? He rejoices because, as he goes on to say, "The Lord is near." This is the heart of Advent's proclamation. Is it good news or bad news? The answer, of course, is Yes. It is arrogant to hear the news that the Lord is near, and not to imagine that news as a call to set about mending so much of what is broken in this world. It is timid to miss what that nearness also means: that the One who is coming, to live and to die just as we do, does this in order to stand with his people in their time, as well as at that moment toward which our world strains, when all time, through him, is fulfilled and redeemed.

Jon Maxwell Walton, one of America's most thoughtful preachers, stood up near the end of Advent a few years ago in his pulpit at First Presbyterian Church in New York City, and made this promise:

> In the next few days the world will probably become a little crazy, as people crowd into airline terminals and travel like Magi to distant places bearing gifts from afar. As children become so excited about the prospects of Christmas Eve that it will be all they can do to keep from wetting their pants . . . [and with] the carols on the CD player, the icicle lights strung outside on the house, and the trees on the lawn swaying in the night wind pleading for snow; all conspire to make of this darkest time of the year our brightest season of hope.
>
> And no matter how many times we have done it, it still will take us by surprise . . . to watch the shepherds and run with kings to a manger at the end of the world, where in the darkness of night,

5. Craddock, *Philippians*, 2.

in the farthest-away place in town, we see at last that the Lord is near.[6]

Paul ends this text with a benediction (vv. 8–9), even though his letter is still a good ways from being over. In worship, the benediction is predictably the last word in the liturgy. Paul's placement of a benediction here is a good reminder that benedictions come, more often than not, in the middle of things and not just at their end. Granted, the whole letter may be intended as a farewell address to that church so beloved by him, but Paul's words here, appropriately, are also reminders of how to be faithful in the middle of life. "Keep on doing the things that you have learned and received and heard and seen in me," he encourages the Philippian church, "and the God of peace will be with you" (v. 9).

The people who gather to worship on the Third Sunday of Advent may need to be reminded that they are, at the same time, those who need to *hear* a benediction for their ongoing equipping in the faith, as well as those whose own lives simply *are*, at their best, a series of benedictions—one benediction after another. The pastor on this occasion might endeavor to summon a measure of God's own eyesight, in order to behold his or her people in such a redemptive light. It is not uncommon for him or her, facing the people at the moment of benediction, to feel the frog in the throat and the sting of tears in the eyes when noticing their receptive faces and their faithful life stories. This is because of how much the pastor knows about so many of them. Even in the midst of the traumas and disappointments and tragedies of life, they are drawn—sometimes kicking and screaming, but still they are drawn—to church, where they will rejoice yet again in the Lord. Shell-shocked by what life deals out that is hard, or brimming with gratitude over some great new brush with goodness or mercy, they come. They keep on practicing the faithful things that they have learned and received and heard and seen. Wherever they are in the middle of life, they find another benediction—or, more to the point, they *become* another benediction, and another, and another—and just keep on being the church.

Paul suggests that this is what the church is made of, and why ultimately the church, even in the midst of suffering, finds reason to rejoice. On the Third Sunday of Advent, as he sits there in that prison cell, he takes pen in hand and celebrates it all with a great word of benediction.

THEODORE J. WARDLAW

---

6. From an unpublished paper written by the Rev. Jon M. Walton for The Moveable Feast lectionary cohort meeting in January 2001.

Luke 3:7–18

⁷John said to the crowds that came out to be baptized by him, "You brood of vipers! Who warned you to flee from the wrath to come? ⁸Bear fruits worthy of repentance. Do not begin to say to yourselves, 'We have Abraham as our ancestor'; for I tell you, God is able from these stones to raise up children to Abraham. ⁹Even now the ax is lying at the root of the trees; every tree therefore that does not bear good fruit is cut down and thrown into the fire."

¹⁰And the crowds asked him, "What then should we do?" ¹¹In reply he said to them, "Whoever has two coats must share with anyone who has none; and whoever has food must do likewise." ¹²Even tax collectors came to be baptized, and they asked him, "Teacher, what should we do?" ¹³He said to them, "Collect no more than the amount prescribed for you." ¹⁴Soldiers also asked him, "And we, what should we do?" He said to them, "Do not extort money from anyone by threats or false accusation, and be satisfied with your wages."

¹⁵As the people were filled with expectation, and all were questioning in their hearts concerning John, whether he might be the Messiah, ¹⁶John answered all of them by saying, "I baptize you with water; but one who is more powerful than I is coming; I am not worthy to untie the thong of his sandals. He will baptize you with the Holy Spirit and fire. ¹⁷His winnowing fork is in his hand, to clear his threshing floor and to gather the wheat into his granary; but the chaff he will burn with unquenchable fire."

¹⁸So, with many other exhortations, he proclaimed the good news to the people.

Commentary 1: Connecting the Reading with Scripture

Luke 3:1–20 forms a three-part presentation of John the Baptist's ministry. Part one sets the stage, portraying John as prophet (3:1–6). Part three has John imprisoned because of that prophetic ministry (3:19–20). Our text, 3:7–18, part two, presents a dialogue between John and the crowds about John's prophetic preaching and identity.

Elsewhere in Luke and Acts, the emphasis falls on John's role as baptizer, but it is here on the content of his message. Luke 7:29–30 portrays how people respond to John's baptism as the measure by which they embrace (or refuse) God's ways. In 20:3–7, Jesus questions some leaders in Jerusalem about the origin of John's baptism, and Acts repeatedly associates John with his baptism (Acts 1:5, 22; 10:37; 11:16–18; 13:24–25; 18:24–26; 19:1–7). Here, Luke presents John primarily as a preacher of repentance. Recalling that Luke paints John's baptism particularly as a "baptism of repentance," or a repentance-baptism (3:3), perhaps it is not surprising that Luke devotes so much space unfolding what repentance looks like.

Luke raises the stakes on the importance of repentance by the way he structures his presentation of John's ministry. On the one hand, John's prophetic preaching, in 3:7–9 and 3:15–17, emphasizes the *reason* why people need to repent: the coming judgment of God. In both texts, judgment is portrayed in fiery terms that trigger a crisis and the need to respond: Are we fruitful trees or fruitless? Are we like wheat or chaff?

On the other hand, John's interaction with his audience, in 3:10–14, explains what repentance *looks like*, that is, what it means to live as true children of Abraham. If Abraham's children will escape "the wrath to come," then the critical question is this: who are Abraham's children? For John, one's relationship to Abraham is not determined by a paternity test or by checking the genealogical records. Physical birth into the covenant community is not enough. Everything revolves around how one responds to God's gracious initiative in bringing salvation. In the Lukan narrative, "children of X" are those who share in X's character. God's children love their enemies, do good, and lend without expecting anything in return, and are thus like God, who is kind to the ungrateful and the wicked (6:35–36); a "son of peace" (my trans.) is someone who shares God's peace (10:6); and a "son of the devil" does not share the devil's DNA but, just like the devil, is deceptive and unscrupulous, and twists the Lord's ways (Acts 13:10). Accordingly, Abraham's children are known by family resemblance gauged in terms of their behavior. Those who have aligned themselves with God's agenda exhibit Abraham-like hearts and lives, just as Abraham-like practices cultivate ongoing repentance.

Luke is not content to present repentance (or conversion; Luke's terminology can be translated either way) as an abstraction. He has more to say than "turn around and go the other way." Nor does he allow room for conversion to be reduced to an interior decision. Rather, his account develops conversion in terms of Abraham-like performance. For John, this performance is consistently marked by its socioeconomic accent. The result is a focus on everyday life in which one's everyday network of relationships is touched by an ethical vision that makes conversion visible precisely in the everydayness of human existence.

"What then should we do?" The question posed by the crowds to John (3:10) is repeated by tax collectors (3:12) and soldiers (3:14). John identifies the character of Abraham-like life generally with sharing what one has with those who lack life's basic necessities, like clothing and food. Elsewhere in Luke's Gospel, care for the hungry and naked is attending simply and profoundly to Moses and the prophets (16:19–31). Reflecting on John's counsel, we should not imagine that he portrays care for the needy as the basis of one's membership among God's restored people. We could think this way only if we import into Luke's world a modern, Western portrait of humanity that allows us to

distinguish between a person's character and their behavior. For Luke's world, a repentant life, a life oriented toward "the way of the Lord," is a life that embodies "the way of the Lord"—in this case, care for those who have none.

From this general response to the crowds (3:10–11), Luke's account takes up the case of some tax collectors who came out to be baptized (3:12–13). This second scene builds on the first, providing a concrete example of John's message by centering on what would have been an offensive subset of those who came out to participate in John's ministry: tax collectors. The phrase "*even* tax collectors" anticipates the shock with which Luke's audience might greet the appearance of tax collectors among God's restored people. This is due to the disagreeable reputation shared by tax collectors in the Roman world, known as they were as meddlers, crooked, and deceitful. John does not take aim at the tax system itself, but instead concerns himself with the behavior of particular tax collectors: "Collect no more than the amount prescribed for you" (3:13). How much is too much? What percentage? We hear only that, for them, a repentant life does not exceed the amount set by those in authority over them. Apparently, it is possible to embody the faithfulness of Abraham *and* serve as a tax collector (see 19:1–10), though even here it is important to recognize that such faithfulness is not an abstraction but must be worked out in daily life.

In 3:14, soldiers play a similar role—a gathering of unexpected participants in John's mission, whose inquiry sets the stage for a further, concrete illustration of John's call to bear fruit appropriate to a conversionary life. As with the tax collecting system, so here John's response is not directed against the military complex as such. Instead, John calls for an end to the typical ways soldiers manipulated the public to their advantage. Again, routine interactions provide the setting for John to spell out the meaning of repentance.

In such ways, the behaviors John urges among his audience enact the covenant God has initiated. What Luke records would be exemplary of such conversionary behavior. If crowds and tax collectors and soldiers, what of jailors, fisher folk, synagogue leaders, and dealers in purple dye? Though John does not address this wider range of persons in their day-to-day circumstances, the prophet has begun to map the patterns of thinking, feeling, believing, and behaving that deserve the label "fruits worthy of repentance." These patterns reflect "the way of the Lord," who restores God's people, and they reach into the routine matters of life.

John's provocative preaching invites two different questions. The first centers on readiness for looming judgment: "What then should we do?" (3:10, 12, 14). The second centers on his identity: Is he the Messiah? (3:15). Apparently, the concept of messiah remained fluid enough that people could wonder if John fit the profile, just as John himself could later express doubt concerning Jesus' identity (7:18–20). This second

question allows John to clarify his role. He is the prophet who prepares the way for the coming one (see 1:17, 76; 3:4–6). The coming Messiah is superior to John and more powerful than John. Even John's baptism is preparatory, in this case of the outpouring of the Holy Spirit (see Acts 2). John's baptism points the way, calling people to align themselves with God's purpose by participating in a repentance-baptism. This prepares people for the work of the Messiah. John's mission thus participates in the good news by setting the stage for the coming of the Lord to bring God's reign of peace and justice.

JOEL B. GREEN

Commentary 2: Connecting the Reading with the World

John speaks a word that clears the ground, preparing the way of the one who will follow him. It is a word aimed at Israel for its renewal, not for its destruction; a word spoken in love, not in hatred: "Bear fruits worthy of repentance. Do not begin to say to yourselves, 'We have Abraham as our ancestor'; for I tell you, God is able from these stones to raise up children to Abraham" (Luke 3:8).

John's words are not anti-Jewish. They are for the people of God. We misunderstand the spirit of these words when we fail to hear in them God as an urgent lover pleading for commitment. Like the ancient prophets of Israel before him, John clarifies an alliance and demands a renewed allegiance. The way is being made plain, and Israel must repent through its deeds and its collective life. John's words upset the familial order, bringing a stunning disequilibrium. These words shake the foundations of family, lineage, kinship, and privilege, as John makes clear that only the fruits of repentance will designate Abraham's authentic children.

Such words are aimed at rededication, not at divorce or making distinctions among the elect people of God. They are Abraham's children and God's chosen by divine love and grace, not through legacy, ethnicity, or biology. John notes the power of God not only to create life but to create holy family as well. If stones may be turned into Abraham's children, then the power

of God is present to give new life. John brings us deep inside family business, with words harsh and strong, spoken between those who know each other deeply and may demand commitment just as deeply. The church has often handled these words poorly, imagining a freedom to scold Israel as if we are John. We are not. We may stand with Israel and overhear this demand to repent and realize that divine love and grace are not exclusive but inclusive of all who would hear and ask the crucial question, "What then should we do?"

This question already recognizes that grace has been received and mercy has been given. The question announces a people ready to hear and live a life that bears repentance's fruit. Such a moment of readiness can easily be abused and exploited by those who want only to control religious zeal and turn it toward destructive ends. "What then should we do?" It is a question that might suggest to some a dangerous docility, where people have opened themselves too much to the influence of a religious leader. Crowds are unpredictable, and for many they represent the worst site to offer theological instruction and articulate religious commitment. God, however, loves the crowd, because the crowd exposes the human creature in its purest form: needy, hungry, vulnerable, and helpless. God has drawn John into the dynamic that God desires: a crowd asking for direction. The question "What then should we do?" must be asked by the crowd and answered with a word from God.

John's answer to this crucial question brings us to the central difference between a response that sends people down a path toward destructive zeal and a response that draws people toward the divine life. John draws them toward a life that shows profound care and concern for their sisters and brothers. Clothes and food, the very things that speak of intimacy and life, must be shared. To show repentance involves, first, a sharing of the staples of life with anyone in need. The anonymity of the receiver speaks to the specific desire of God to care for those we see, regardless of their connection to us.

The work of repentance is reaching surprising people, even tax collectors and soldiers, each asking the question, "What should we do?" in the specific complexities of their work and lives. The tax collector and the soldier share an embeddedness in the ruling structure. Both are functionaries within governmental logics they did not create; yet both have heard the call to repentance, recognizing that their lives inside a system do not protect them from the wrath of God or the demand to live in covenant faithfulness. They do not ask, "What can we do, given the nature of our positions?" or "What is possible, given the constraints within which we operate?" Such questions would be reasonable but not born of repentance and the new age John announces. The life of repentance reverses the order of possibility. When it comes to our life and work, the life of repentance demands that we ask what *must* be done for the sake of God before we ask what *can* be done, given structural constraints.

John again draws them toward the divine life and away from oppression. From both the soldier and the tax collector, John demands economic justice. Both must shun extortion. Both must press against economic practices that advantage them and disadvantage others. John allows for governmental functionaries and for the ruling Roman system, but his words halt their advance at the expense of flourishing life. In fact, his words challenge that very system by making clear God's preference for those oppressed and in need. Both soldier and tax collector are answerable to God before they are answerable to the emperor. John instructs those imagined outside of godly instruction, and in so doing exhibits the expansive reach of God into all life and all creation.

Listeners knew the question that must be pondered after the initial question ("what should we do"). Is John the Messiah? This messianic expectation that John heightened now covers him. In response, his words, which turn that expectation in the right direction, away from him, rise to the level of a confession. One is coming who will baptize with the Holy Spirit and fire. John's own baptism will be engulfed in the baptism and fire that is coming. Luke turns toward a Pentecostal future and drives the attention of the people of God toward the One who himself is the baptizer. John points his listeners toward this One who will also be the end of history. From baptism with fire to an end in unquenchable fire, the One who is coming will separate wheat from chaff and determine the future of all things.

How can such a word be good news? John prophesies of God's coming to claim Israel. This judgment and the baptism, the word and the fire, are all inside the divine embrace. God is coming to Israel; *this is* the good news. Israel is not moving from divine absence to divine presence. John signals an intensification of presence; the faithful God of Israel will now make visible, touchable, and embraceable that very faithfulness. However, before God may be touched, John must be heard: Repent and believe the good news.

This text has always been read as precursor to the gospel message, but Luke does not reserve the term "gospel" for the words of Jesus. From the shaking of kinship and cultic foundations to the call to bring forth fruits of repentance— manifested in care and concern for others, especially within the economic realities of any society—John's words already bring the gospel message. Furthermore, John has prepared the way for the One in whom we pour expectations for our future, Jesus, the Messiah of Israel. The gospel that Jesus will announce will fulfill in word and deed this proclamation of John.

WILLIE JAMES JENNINGS

Fourth Sunday of Advent

Micah 5:2–5a
Luke 1:46b–55; Psalm 80:1–7

Hebrews 10:5–10
Luke 1:39–45 (46–55)

Micah 5:2–5a

²But you, O Bethlehem of Ephrathah,
    who are one of the little clans of Judah,
from you shall come forth for me
    one who is to rule in Israel,
whose origin is from of old,
    from ancient days.
³Therefore he shall give them up until the time
    when she who is in labor has brought forth;
then the rest of his kindred shall return
    to the people of Israel.
⁴And he shall stand and feed his flock in the strength of the LORD,
    in the majesty of the name of the LORD his God.
And they shall live secure, for now he shall be great
    to the ends of the earth;
⁵and he shall be the one of peace.

Commentary 1: Connecting the Reading with Scripture

Here the prophet Micah offers hope for a better future, for a people who have endured so much devastation (in the case of Micah, likely the invasion of Sennacherib in Judah in 702–701 BCE). It is also possible that verse 3, referring to a time when "the rest of his kindred shall return" was added when Micah was reread in the later time of the Babylonian exile (597–539 BCE). To read this passage as merely a vague promise of hope, however, is to miss some provocative details. Clearly Micah is offering a word about leadership. However, is Micah really so supportive of the present power structure in Jerusalem—the Davidic line? Why would Micah call for one who "is to rule in Israel, whose origin is from old, *from ancient days*"? In fact, it is God who is described as acting in ancient days and times of old (cf. Deut. 33:27; "God is my King of old," Ps. 74:12 KJV), not Israelite kings. Clearly Micah is looking back, perhaps to even before Judean kings. Or does Micah offer a far more *radical* word of hope than he has often been given credit for? Let's explore the possibilities.

To begin, to what location does verse 2 refer? The passage is almost universally amended to be a reference to Bethlehem. However, such a clear reference to the town eternally associated with David is somewhat surprising in a book that furiously criticizes the Jerusalem king and elite: Micah chapters 2 and 3 practically burn our fingers as we read the pages! Therefore, the reference to "one who is to rule," rather than meaning simply "king" (*melek*), may actually suggest that Micah is sending us back to the beginning, perhaps Bethlehem, in order to start all over—*with another king*. That would certainly be more consistent with Micah's fury directed at Hezekiah's line (and his administration) in Jerusalem!

To be fair, the fact that readers for centuries have assumed that this passage promises a birth to maintain the existing line of David makes some sense. After all, announcements of an impending birth are common in Isaiah, where there is little doubt that Isaiah wants to reassure Hezekiah that his line will carry on after the Assyrian invasion of 702–701 BCE. Certainly Isaiah often mentions Hezekiah in his reassurances, but Micah never does. Many of these "birth assurances" in Isaiah, like the passage here, are then taken by Christians to be references to Jesus at a much later time (Isa. 7:14, 9:6, etc.). Is Micah, in fact, merely offering reassurances to the same king in Jerusalem, as Isaiah did? Not so fast.

Micah calls for one who will "stand" and "feed his flock." Furthermore, the first part of verse 5 is often taken as the last phrase of this series of thoughts about future leadership. It can be read, "*He* will achieve peace" or "*He* will be one of peace." Other scholars read this as a reference to an era of peace, reading: "There *will be* peace." Some have even suggested that Micah might be proclaiming God to be the preferred king now! Certainly "strength" and "majesty" are often terms used to describe God, rather than a king, in Psalms (Pss. 93, 96).

Pannell, for one, supposes that it is the *premonarchic David*—the *shepherd* and not the warrior (one who will "feed his flock")—who is being recommended here, and that therefore this passage is consistent with Micah's antimilitary agenda (cf. 4:1–4).[1] However, as sympathetic as I am to Pannell's interesting suggestion, I think Micah implies a "starting over." Rather than an approving reference to the line of David in Jerusalem, Micah's hope is precisely the opposite: a summary *rejection of the line of David and a sentiment to go "back to the drawing board"* (e.g., back to Bethlehem) on Judean kingship! In Micah's day, the central Davidic authorities in Jerusalem responded to perceived Assyrian threats with force rather than diplomacy.[2] Micah and his people are exhausted and angry. Micah wants to go back to Bethlehem and find another line, one that will not resort to violence so easily. Micah's hope is rooted in change "at the top"!

What was to be done about unacceptable leadership among Israelites? Two solutions are often presented by the prophets: either a new king will come, or God will change the terms of the agreement and take the job (Zeph. 3:14–20).

---

1. Randall Pannell, "The Politics of the Messiah: A New Reading of Micah 4:14–5:5," *Perspectives in Religious Studies* 15 (1988): 131–43.
2. Daniel Smith-Christopher. *Micah: A Commentary*, Old Testament Library (Louisville, KY: Westminster John Knox Press, 2015), 170.

All Can Be Christian

I disagree very much with those who are unwilling that Holy Scripture, translated into the vulgar tongue, can be read by the uneducated, as if Christ taught such intricate doctrines that they could scarcely be understood by very few theologians, or as if the strength of the Christian religion consisted in men's ignorance of it. . . . To me he is truly a theologian who teaches not by skill with intricate syllogisms but by a disposition of mind, by the very expression and the eyes, by his very life that riches should be disdained, that the Christian should not put his trust in the supports of this world but must rely entirely on heaven, that a wrong should not be avenged, that a good should be wished for those wishing ill, that we should deserve well of those deserving ill, that all good men should be loved and cherished equally as members of the same body, that the evil should be tolerated if they cannot be corrected, that those who are stripped of their goods, those who are turned away from possessions, those who mourn are blessed and should not be deplored, and that death should even be desired by the devout, since it is nothing other than a passage to immortality. And if anyone under the inspiration of the spirit of Christ preaches this kind of doctrine, inculcates it, exhorts, incites, and encourages men to it, he indeed is truly a theologian, even if he should be a common laborer or weaver. And if anyone exemplifies this doctrine in his life itself, he is in fact a great doctor. . . . Only a very few can be learned, but all can be Christian, all can be devout, and—I shall boldly add—all can be theologians.

Desiderius Erasmus (d. 1536), "Paraclesis," in *Christian Humanism and the Reformation: Selected Writings* (New York: Harper & Row, 1965), 100–101, 102, 104.

The notion of God as shepherd (Pss. 23:1; 80:1) is particularly striking in light of Ezekiel 34, where God declares God's disgust with previous shepherds and then announces that God will "take back" (Ezek. 34:10) the sheep from the shepherds, and then, somewhat startlingly, declares, "I myself will be the shepherd of my sheep" (Ezek. 34:15–16). The New Testament picks up the theme of the "new Shepherd" (see John 10; Rev. 7:17). In other words, what Micah is dramatically suggesting—namely, *replacing* the shepherd—became an explicit tradition in later prophets. There is more.

Micah's call, as a prophet from a village devastated by war in 702–701 BCE, is also an appeal to a hoped-for ruler who *trusts in God rather than in military might*. Micah's ruler will be "one of peace." Why does this make sense? The prophet Isaiah (and here I am tempted to say "conveniently") survived the Assyrian onslaught in the walled bastions of Jerusalem and could afford comforting words to the Davidic king. Micah, on the other hand, a prophet from the devastated villages between the coast and Jerusalem, endured the horrific Assyrian destruction on Sennacherib's march to Jerusalem. Micah clearly was furious and, like so many others who have suffered, based his hope on *a change*, not on stability. The great Israeli human-rights activist Uri Avnery is fond of saying, "When you are on the top, you love stability. When you are on the bottom, you want change!"

If this is true, then the implications of reading this passage in Advent are far more revolutionary than we have typically supposed! For Christians, Jesus himself may be the *new* David, rather than the new *David*! It matters a great deal which word you emphasize! Powerful lessons are to be gained, not by blandly "comparing" Jesus to David (as a ruler or king, for example) but instead by *contrasting* Jesus to David! Micah was not looking back to shore up existing structures and powers. Micah was looking forward—and looking forward to a dramatic change. *Micah's ideal ruler is a person who brings about peace* (cf. Ps. 85:8; Isa. 9:6; 32:18; 52:7; 60:17). Furthermore, Jesus is likely seen not merely as a descendant from, but actually *as a corrective to*, the violent and flawed David in the spirit of Micah's call for change (Mark 10:43!). Micah is to be read at Advent because Jesus is understood to be the "one of peace," the one who was to come! Mary was right—this *is* a revolutionary change (Luke 1:52–54). We, like Micah, long for change from a stubborn pattern of human leadership that sets sister against sister, brother against brother. Who will feed the flocks in peace?

DANIEL L. SMITH-CHRISTOPHER

Commentary 2: Connecting the Reading with the World

It is hard not to read this passage through Christmas. "O Little Town of Bethlehem" has worn Micah's prophecy into a smooth familiarity. We read the words and hum the tune. However, unless we open our minds to more than these associations, the passage cannot speak freshly.

The substance of this oracle probably originates before the fall of Judah and the exile to Babylon. The prophet announces a worthy ruler, one who gains his right not from the shabby and ambiguous politics of the last Judean rulers but from "ancient days" (5:2). God shall secure God's people from the violence of nations, cherish them, and see that they live in abundance.

Rumor of God's greatness shall spread to the world's end and no enemy will dare challenge Israel's God.

The language here resonates with the ancient mythology of royal power. Egypt's pharaoh too set his staff on the foundation of an older world, and Mesopotamian kings also reigned from the earth's center, announcing their power to its circumference. The connection with the royal mythologies of the empires is clearer still in the strange statement "with a rod they strike the ruler of Israel upon the cheek" (5:1), which alludes to the ritual abasement of the king, perhaps part of the autumn harvest festival. A very similar humiliation was undergone by the Babylonian ruler, who, in a ritual of dedication to Marduk, received his royal dignity only after being first deprived of his kingly trappings and struck on the face. Each year, the festival reinserted the king into the cosmic order, the order that the gods mediate and that binds even them. The strength of the cosmos becomes the strength of the king. Thus rule is founded in the nature of things; sovereignty and empire belong among those inevitabilities that determine human lives.

That seems a far stretch from modern politics, until we recognize how we still mythologize human authority and human institutions, asserting their unimpeachable right among the inevitabilities. Freedom is an idea that gives us critical purchase upon the betrayals of politics. Yet we render freedom opaque when we bluntly identify it with particular nations and specific ways of life. This is the way to blindness, to binding a critical concept, a concept to inspire hope and energy, so that it now serves to elevate a particular human order into cosmic design.

Despite the outward resemblances, the way Micah (and many other voices in the Old Testament) uses royal and cosmological language differs fundamentally from these imperial myths and rituals. The God of Israel makes the difference here, simply because this God does not belong within the cosmos. Neither among its inevitabilities nor subordinate to them, Israel's God is Creator, the One who has life in God's self and owes the cosmos nothing. Since God is not among the cosmic powers, God's servants need not, and must not, abase themselves before them, nor rest their hope in them.

According to the cosmological vision of the empires surrounding Judah, the cosmos is the ultimate reality. The gods who inhabit its heavens are merely the supreme beneficiaries and mediators of its powers. The rituals of royalty enable earthly rule to mirror that of the gods. Divine and royal rule promise balance, rhythms of energy seeking equilibrium, assuring that there is "nothing new under the sun." The long history of prophetic protest shows how tempting Israel found this account of cosmos, divinity, and royal power. No room, however, exists in this cosmos for the unprecedented, for the God who makes something from nothing, justifies sinners, and raises the dead.

If the prophet uses this symbolism of cosmos and sovereignty, if he draws on this mythology, as did the royal courts of Israel and Judah, then it is as metaphor, as a broken myth, or even as irony. Micah, for instance, and those who collected his oracles, avoid the word "king," preferring always "ruler," to remind the reader that those who rule God's people gain their right solely from Israel's unique, incomparable God, who alone is king. The mention of Bethlehem—rather than Jerusalem, the center of Judean royal ideology and power—also signals God's transcendence, God's freedom over the order of earthly sovereignty.

The promised ruler shall come from David's birthplace, but God shall call him as a new beginning, a departure from the existing history of kings, a new start that goes to the very roots of Israel's ambiguous embrace of a monarchy "like the nations." The one who is to be ruler in "Israel" shall take his "origin . . . from of old, from ancient days" (5:2). Free over the creation, free to bless or to oppose, God shall inspire this promised ruler as a shepherd for God's people, unlike the "heads of Jacob and rulers of the house of Israel" (3:1). Those have failed to protect the people and robbed the hopes of families for the next generation (2:2). Their predations are monstrous, and leave nothing untouched. Like cannibals, they "eat the flesh of my people . . . like meat in a kettle" (3:2–3). The rich amass land for themselves, alienating the poor from their livelihood (2:1–3). God will now begin again, with one who rules for the good of all who struggle and work for life, who prefers peace to war, and who desires to secure their posterity in the land.

The God of Israel judges the integrity of human order, and the prophet measures that order against God's own faithfulness. Along with Judah's rulers, Micah also condemns both the priests, "who teach for hire" (3:11 KJV) and the prophets, who take bribes to judge the nation falsely, blessing this time in which the powerful revel in injustice (3:5, 9–11). Put in modern terms, Micah denounces the institutions of education and communication, the institutions responsible for teaching, interpreting, and guiding, for developing and sustaining the order of meaning. They betray their calling by defending society's savage inequalities, applauding them and the sacrifices they entail as inevitable and necessary. The prophet condemns both the social violence itself and the ideological practices that justify it.

Prophet and priest opinion formers, stewards of the symbolic, fashion the assumed social understanding of the way things are and have to be. Thus limits are set upon hope, upon what men and women may look for and trust in. Micah's announcement of the ruler who is to come from Bethlehem, "who [is] one of the little clans of Judah," rejects these limits in the name of the God who is not part of the cosmic order, who does not conform to the inevitabilities, and who judges the powers feared or imagined by men and women. The prophet speaks, therefore, of a new beginning, a ruler unlike those the people expect or to whom they resign themselves, one whose faithful leadership is inspired by God.

From this perspective, opened up by God's "majesty" over creation and over God's people (5:4), we can return to Jesus, and to Christmas, without the distracting tinsel or the sentimental nostalgia. Jesus' birth also happens in the world of empire and in the middle of a census, the bureaucratic mechanism of political control. Once before, a census had brought a curse upon Israel, when David attempted to count up the blessing of the God who will not be calculated like earthly powers (2 Sam. 24). Now, in David's birthplace, God slips through the census, through the powers of the world, to set up his rule against their pride, in the obscurity of Bethlehem and the weakness of the cross.

ALAN GREGORY

Luke 1:46b–55

46b"My soul magnifies the Lord,
    47and my spirit rejoices in God my Savior,
48for he has looked with favor on the lowliness of his servant.
    Surely, from now on all generations will call me blessed;
49for the Mighty One has done great things for me,
    and holy is his name.
50His mercy is for those who fear him
    from generation to generation.
51He has shown strength with his arm;
    he has scattered the proud in the thoughts of their hearts.
52He has brought down the powerful from their thrones,
    and lifted up the lowly;
53he has filled the hungry with good things,
    and sent the rich away empty.
54He has helped his servant Israel,
    in remembrance of his mercy,
55according to the promise he made to our ancestors,
    to Abraham and to his descendants forever."

Psalm 80:1–7

1Give ear, O Shepherd of Israel,
    you who lead Joseph like a flock!
You who are enthroned upon the cherubim, shine forth
    2before Ephraim and Benjamin and Manasseh.
Stir up your might,
    and come to save us!

3Restore us, O God;
    let your face shine, that we may be saved.

4O LORD God of hosts,
    how long will you be angry with your people's prayers?
5You have fed them with the bread of tears,
    and given them tears to drink in full measure.
6You make us the scorn of our neighbors;
    our enemies laugh among themselves.

7Restore us, O God of hosts;
    let your face shine, that we may be saved.

Connecting the Psalm with Scripture and Worship

By the Fourth Sunday of Advent, those who have zealously guarded the Advent season from becoming confused with Christmas soften, slipping in a carol to the congregation's delight and relief. This Sunday provides the ready excuse to do so. Micah 5:2–5a mentions Bethlehem, giving biblical warrant to sing that perennial favorite "O Little Town of Bethlehem." The hymn combines lilting tune with lovely images of stillness, dreamless sleep, and silent stars; of Christmas angels and meek souls receiving "the dear Christ" who enters in.

The Gospel reading (without vv. 46–55 in parentheses) paired with Micah seems sentimental enough: Bethlehem and shepherd king meet Elizabeth and Mary. The other texts are less cooperative. Psalm 80:1–7 is a lament psalm bordering on complaint; Luke 1:46b–55 is hardly a lullaby; and Hebrews 10:5–10 is chock-full of "sacrifices and offerings and burnt offerings and sin offerings"—hardly the gift list anyone has in mind this close to Christmas.

Two choices are provided for today's psalm: Psalm 80:1–7 and Luke 1:46b–55. If the Gospel reading includes Mary's song, Psalm 80:1–7 is the choice. This psalm contributes richly to both liturgy and preaching. Psalm 80:1–3 serves well as a call to worship; or, since this prayer is explicitly the "prayers of the people" (80:4), it may be used as that, guiding the prayers of intercession. Acknowledging God's sovereign, shepherding rule, we ask God to intercede—to be "stirred up" (v. 2b) against injustice, to heal those whose tears overflow (v. 5), to restore and reconcile. Its repeated refrain, "Restore us, O God; let your face shine, that we may be saved" (vv. 3, 7, 19), may be used as the people's response following each intercession.

The exact setting for Psalm 80:1–7 is uncertain, but it likely shares the context for Micah's prophecy: the reign of Hezekiah in the time of Assyria's threat. The lectionary omits Micah 5:1, but that verse sets the scene; the city of Jerusalem is under siege with the king publicly humiliated. Micah prophesies that God will send a ruler from a little out-of-the-way place, Bethlehem (Mic. 5:2). This ruler will restore and "feed his flock" with strength and majesty, universally recognized (Mic. 5:4–5a). That this one will come from David's hometown is not lost on the home crowd!

While Micah focuses on the coming ruler, Psalm 80:1–7 presents the voice of the imperiled people. It is the prayer uttered under siege. A series of imperatives calls God to urgent attention and action: Give ear! (v. 1). Stir up your might; come to save us! (v. 2). Restore us (vv. 3, 7). Their enemy worships a foreign god, so the people multiply their metaphors as though reminding God of God's own stature and power. God is shepherd: "O Shepherd of Israel" (v. 1a); king: "You who are enthroned upon the cherubim," (v. 1b); and commander of a great army: "LORD God of Hosts" (v. 4). God provided manna in the wilderness and water from a rock, but now God's people eat and drink only their own tears. They cry in repeated refrain: "Restore us, O God; let your face shine, that we may be saved" (vv. 3, 7, 19). Like the ancient blessing spoken by Aaron (Num. 6:24–25), God's shining countenance signals life and peace.

The other psalm choice is Luke 1:46b–55, Mary's testimony to the power of God. It can be used effectively as the call to worship or opening sentences (1:50–53). The entire passage read in unison or sung in hymn version becomes an affirmation of faith or response to the sermon. Here is a suggested prayer of confession and declaration of forgiveness:

> Holy God,
>> with strength you scatter the proud,
>> and bring down those who wield power unjustly.
>> you lift up the lowly ones, vulnerable and ignored.
> You fill those who are hungry for food and for justice.
> You empty those who take more than they need at the expense of others.
> Forgive us for our complicity in systems of greed, violence, and willful neglect.
> Forgive us for our complacency toward inequity and suffering.
> Remember your mercy, we humbly pray, and grant mercy in our generation.
> Help us to be your servants,

living according to your promises.
We pray in the name of the One who has
    come
    and is coming again, Jesus Christ. **Amen.**
We rejoice in God our Savior.
The Mighty One has done great things.
God's mercy endures from generation to
    generation.
Holy is God's name!

Just as Micah offers hopeful prophecy to besieged people, so Mary's song declares boldly what God will do to rescue desperate people. The lowliest receive God's attention and saving intervention. They are "lifted up"; the hungry are filled. At Mary's greeting, the child in Elizabeth's womb leapt for joy. Imagine a tiny John the Baptist in utero already celebrating the coming revolution when the mothers embrace belly to belly! Luke 1:51–53 forms the heart of this passage. A series of great reversals is announced: the proud, powerful, and rich are scattered, brought down, sent away empty; the lowly and hungry ones are lifted up, filled with good things. This theme of reversal, so prominent in Luke, is stated at the outset. The context only underscores the content of Mary's proclamation: it is uttered from a little Judean hill-country house, not from the temple in Jerusalem. It is announced by two women with no status, not by the learned official clergy. It anticipates a child who cannot yet live outside his mother's womb, so tiny and fragile is he; yet he will grow and—like his older cousin—become "strong in spirit" (Luke 1:80), the Savior of the world.

Micah also knows the God who orchestrates great reversals: From little Bethlehem, not Jerusalem, will come a great leader (5:2). People beleaguered "shall live secure" (5:4c). The present king, humiliated, will be succeeded by a ruler who will "stand and feed his flock" with strength and majesty recognized by the whole world (5:4).

Micah and Mary both speak of the future, but Mary does so using the past tense. In the Greek language, her verbs are in a past aorist tense unavailable in English. It is a "timeless tense," expressing what is true in the past, present, and future without differentiation. Mary is so sure that God will do these things she sings as though God has already accomplished it![1]

These reversals warrant a word of caution. The reversals declared by Mary (Luke 1:51–53) are framed within God's mercy (1:50 and 1:54). God's mercy and God's justice are never separated; therefore the mercy and the reversals interpret each other. Interpretations that promote vengeance or triumphalism are to be resisted, as though the lowly and hungry now hold sway over the formerly powerful and rich. Instead, God is replacing "an economy of scarcity and competition" with "an economy of generosity in which all have enough." The social transformation is dramatic and real, however; so it should not be sentimentalized or tamed either.[2]

The last verse of "O Little Town of Bethlehem" is hardly sentimental. It conveys the longing felt by Micah and Mary and the people praying Psalm 80. For those under threat *and* for those who wield power through systems and personal practices that widen the gap between the powerful and vulnerable, the coming of Jesus will be neither silent nor still. Indeed, "the hopes and fears of all the years" meet uncomfortably in him. If we dare to invite our Lord Immanuel to "come to us, abide with us," we can be grateful that he arrives with both justice and mercy.

KIMBERLY L. CLAYTON

1. Fred B. Craddock, *Luke*, Interpretation (Louisville, KY: John Knox Press, 1990), 30.
2. Sharon H. Ringe, *Luke*, Westminster Bible Companion (Louisville, KY: Westminster John Knox Press, 1995), 35.

Hebrews 10:5–10

⁵Consequently, when Christ came into the world, he said,

> "Sacrifices and offerings you have not desired,
> but a body you have prepared for me;
> ⁶in burnt offerings and sin offerings
> you have taken no pleasure.
> ⁷Then I said, 'See, God, I have come to do your will, O God'
> (in the scroll of the book it is written of me)."

⁸When he said above, "You have neither desired nor taken pleasure in sacrifices and offerings and burnt offerings and sin offerings" (these are offered according to the law), ⁹then he added, "See, I have come to do your will." He abolishes the first in order to establish the second. ¹⁰And it is by God's will that we have been sanctified through the offering of the body of Jesus Christ once for all.

Commentary 1: Connecting the Reading with Scripture

Hebrews 8 introduces a series of contrasts that will continue through chapter 10. It starts with a contrast between the old and new high priests (8:1–7; cf. 9:9–15) and then moves, citing Jeremiah 31:31–34, to a contrast between the old and new covenantal relationships. In chapter 9, the contrasts continue, now between the sacrifice of bulls and goats (9:12–13), which can purify the flesh (cf. 9:22, 23; 10:1) but not "the conscience" (9:14; cf. 9:9; 10:2, 22), and the efficacious sacrifice effected only by the blood of Christ (9:14). In 10:1–4 the author returns to this contrast, stating that "it is impossible for the blood of bulls and goats to take away [*apharein*] sins."

Verses 5–10 explain why this is the case: it was God's will that the sacrifice of Christ alone would make atonement. "When Christ came into the world" (v. 5) signals that the incarnation is not just a turn in the argument, but the source of his thought. The incarnate Christ speaks in the words of Psalm 40, declaring that God did not desire "sacrifice and offering" (v. 5), but instead "prepared a body for me" (see 11:3, where a variation of the same Greek word for "preparation," *katartizō*, describes the primordial creation). This announces that God willed the sacrifice of Christ's body even before

the establishment of the Sinai covenant and the ritual of sacrifice. Twice more in this passage, Christ speaks, both times declaring obedience to God's will (vv. 7, 9), which is that God's people are to be sanctified by the bodily sacrifice of Jesus Christ (10:10).

The interpretation of Psalm 40:6–8 (LXX 39:7–9) continues in verses 5–7. The author has focused on the psalm's thanksgiving section (vv. 1–12), rather than its lament (vv. 13–17), and especially on the psalmist's desire to do the will of God (v. 8). The author alters the psalm's claims through a modification of Psalm 40:6–8 (LXX, vv. 7–9), which he will further explicate in verses 8–9.

The use of the noun "offering" (*prosphora*, 10:5, 8, 10, 14, 18) and the verb "to offer" (*prospherō*, 10:1, 2, 8, 11, 12; see 8:3, 4; 9:7, 9, 14, 25, 28) recalls the thought of a perfected covenant, raised initially in 5:1–10 and distinctly expressed at 8:13. The contrast between continual animal offerings and the single offering of Christ (9:14, 25, 27, and 10:11–12) remains constant, but only here are we told that the new covenant in Christ is *the* will of God (10:7, 9, 10) and that, therefore, the prior practices of sacrifice were never intended to be permanent or capable of accomplishing full redemption, which has always, and only, been through the sacrifice of Christ.

The author first alters the original psalm by identifying the speaker as the incarnate Christ (10:5, 7, 8), so that the words "spoken to our ancestors in many and various ways by the prophets" (1:1) become words "spoken to us by a Son" (1:2). Next, the singular "burnt offering" and "sin offering" are made into plural nouns (v. 8), and the phrase "do not please you" (*ouk ēthelēsas*, 10:5, au. trans.) replaces the original verb "you have not required." According to our author, since animal offerings cannot address the entire human being's flesh *and* spirit, they are not pleasing to God. By adopting the LXX's paraphrase ("a body you have prepared for me") of the perplexing Hebrew phrase, "ears you have dug for me," the author connects the psalm to the self-sacrifice of Jesus and specifically to the ordained will of God (10:7, 9). Ultimately, he will identify the sacrifice as the offering (*prosphoras*) of Jesus Christ's body, once for all (10:10), thereby associating "body," "sacrifice," "offering," and singularity to the actions of God in Christ.

Next the author elides the last portion of Psalm 40:9 (LXX). Deleting its reference to the law and the verb "desire," as well as the phrase "my belly," implies that the initial covenant has been made secondary to the newer one and accentuates that the will of God requires Christ's total bodily commitment, both volitionally and operationally. Christ expresses this idea directly in 10:9: "behold, I have come *to do* [*poiēsai*] your will."

The author makes one more interpretive move in verse 7, playing on the Greek phrase "in the head [*kephalidi*] of the book, it is written about me."[1] Originally this referred "to the law, and in particular to the 'law of the king' as the word head often refers to a scroll," as Attridge suggests.[2] Our author expands the referent to claim that the essence of all Scripture bears direct witness to Jesus as obedient Christ (again in reference to 1:1–4).

These claims are reiterated with "when he said above" (v. 8) and the psalm verses are repeated in reverse order from verses 5–6. Once more the sacrifices and offerings are plurals, accentuating their insufficiency, and recalling 10:1–3. Their repetitions are juxtaposed to Christ's *once for all* (singular) offering of his body (v. 10), which *is* in accordance with God's will (v. 9). Therefore, even though the ritual sacrifices "are offered according to the law," they cannot be pleasing to God, because they cannot fully, finally cleanse. The author echoes this in 10:14 by reintroducing the quotation of Jeremiah 31:33–34 (see 8:10–12), as testimony spoken (*eirēkenai*) by the Holy Spirit (10:15–17) culminating with "where there is forgiveness . . . there is no longer any offering for sin" (10:18).

With verse 9 the author extends this claim, again through a proclamation of Christ ("then he added"; see 1:13; 4:3, 4; 13:5; and especially 10:15, where the verb *legein*, "to speak," is associated with the Holy Spirit bearing witness), "Behold, I have come to do your will" (v. 7 NKJV). This act resulted in the "doing away" (*anairei*) of the first covenant (based in cultic ritual) *and* the establishment of the second (based on the once-and-for-all obedient act of Christ). The verb *anairei*, translated as "abolishes" in the NRSV, is nowhere else used in this sense in the NT (though see Luke 22:2; Acts 2:23; 10:39 with regard to Jesus' own death). Whether the author intended it or not, an ironic reversal is created by this term, in that the death of Jesus actually results in the destruction not of Jesus, but of the cultic principles. The stress is on the last clause; the destruction occurs "in order that" the Christic reality may be "put into force" (*histēmi*, "establish"). This verb occurs in the immediate next sentence (10:11), which depicts the priests who "stand" day after day offering sacrifices and contrasts their labor with Christ, who, by virtue of a single perfecting sacrifice for sins (10:14), "sat down at the right hand of God" (10:12).

The pericope concludes noting that "our" sanctification (*hēgiasmenoi*) is accomplished by this death (cf. 1 Thess. 4:3). This, in accord with the will of God, is complete and definitive, shown by the use of "once for all" (*ephapax*, 7:27; 9:12), which recalls 9:12–14, "he entered *once for*

---

1. Author's translation. The NRSV translates this as "in the scroll of the book."
2. Harold Attridge, *The Epistle to the Hebrews: A Commentary on the Epistle to the Hebrews* (Minneapolis: Fortress Press, 1989), 274–75.

all into the Holy Place." As in 10:1–3, it is not with the blood of animals, but with Christ's own blood, that eternal redemption is obtained. The author has now returned to his initial premise (10:4), having argued that only in and through the obedient sacrifice of Jesus Christ is God's relationship to the world fully revealed, for in the offering of this body, "the heavenly and earthly realms of being intersect and become inextricably intertwined" (see 13:8, 21).[3]

STEVEN J. KRAFTCHICK

Commentary 2: Connecting the Reading with the World

The temptation looms large here, as it does in several places in Hebrews, to draw a sharp distinction between Christianity and Judaism. In this reading, the narrative could proceed: the Jews offered sacrifices, but God did not want those. Instead, God preferred the obedience of Jesus. Such sharp division between different religions skews the form and meaning of this passage, which was written by a Jewish believer in Jesus.

First, the words Hebrews places in the mouth of Christ are the words of Israel's Scriptures, namely, Psalm 40. If he envisions Jesus critiquing the sacrificial system, Jesus does so only by joining a long line of prophets who have done the same (see 1 Sam. 15:22; Ps. 50:8–15; 51:16–19; Isa. 1:11–13, 15–17; Jer. 7:21–22; Mic. 6:6–8; Hos. 6:6; Amos 5:21–24). The coming of Jesus has not changed the basic fact that God has always desired the obedience often made tangible by the sacrifice.

Second, if Jesus "abolishes the first in order to establish the second" (Heb. 10:9), he is not replacing sacrifice with something else, but fulfilling the previous sacrifices with the sacrificial offering of his own body. This is not Jewish sacrifice versus Christian obedience, but a scriptural (*Israel's* Scriptures, to be sure) affirmation of the obedient sacrifice of one Jew named Jesus.

God's displeasure over one sacrifice and acceptance of another, however, presents an additional quandary. If previous generations of faithful followers offered sacrifices commanded by God that somehow did not please God, congregants might wonder if they are similarly in danger of doing things that they *think* will please God but do not. In other words, this text from Hebrews forces the question, with what sacrifice is God most pleased?

The author of Hebrews, despite harsh words against the Levitical sacrifices, shows no opposition generally to presenting offerings to God.[4] At the close of the letter he encourages his congregation to offer up sacrifices of praise to God *continually* (13:15). In order to discern what God would have us do, Hebrews does not immediately solve all hard choices, but it does offer a helpful distinction. If our offerings ignore or seek to supplement the offering of Jesus, we are devaluing God's acceptance of us in Christ (a parallel exists in those in the early church who argued that rules need to be followed to gain salvation, *in addition to believing in Jesus*; see Galatians and Col. 2). On the other hand, when our offerings are caught up in his one-time full and final offering, we too can do God's will and please him (Heb. 13:21).

With this powerful affirmation, it is little surprise that this passage from Hebrews 10 echoes in the eucharistic liturgy of several denominations. As churches gather to remember and celebrate Jesus' gift of his body and blood for us, the *Lutheran Book of Worship* recalls him who was "obedient to your will even to giving his life."[5] Episcopalians proclaim that he "offered himself in obedience to your will a perfect sacrifice for the whole world."[6] In his

---

3. Ibid., 277.

4. Nicholas J. Moore offers an excellent treatment of ritual in Hebrews in his *Repetition in Hebrews: Plurality and Singularity in the Letter to the Hebrews, Its Ancient Context, and the Early Church*, Wissenschaftliche Untersuchungen zum Neuen Testament 2 (Tübingen: Mohr Siebeck, 2015), 388.

5. Holy Communion, Setting 1, in *Lutheran Book of Worship* (Minneapolis: Augsburg Publishing House, 1978), 69.

6. Rite II, Eucharistic Prayer A, in *The Book of Common Prayer* (New York: Oxford University Press, 1979), 362.

offering, we are made holy and therefore our offerings are made pleasing to God.

Hence this passage offers great personal spiritual encouragement. If a congregant wrestles with unworthiness before God, this passage, like many in Hebrews, clearly affirms the effectiveness and sufficiency of God's work in Christ. God's will, recorded long before in the psalm and enacted when the Son came, is that Christ makes humans whole and eternally holy. No matter how one might feel, it is good and right to hear the proclamation of one's true holiness in Christ. This is the power of God to rescue humanity, and that stirs gratefulness in those who have been sanctified by his offering.

Pondering the meaning of sanctification offers another opportunity to stir the minds and hearts of those who hear this text. Holiness has garnered a bad reputation, one in which the sanctified person avoids certain social activities in order to flaunt his or her superiority. The sanctification of which Hebrews speaks is much more earthy—the author will urge the audience to practice the mundane virtues of hospitality, fidelity, and gratitude (Heb. 13:1–5)—because it is first and foremost heavenly, proclaiming an intimate and eternal relationship with the God who reigns on high.

While this truth may mean a great deal for individuals, this passage affirms those individuals by affirming their place in the church. This passage is one of those places in the New Testament that contains the etiology of the Christian community. In offering his body, Christ created his body. By his one offering, the "we" of this little community—the author and the congregation—have been made holy, ready to serve God in the kingdom. Since this author has no doubt that Christ's offering affects *everything* (Heb. 1:2, 13; 2:8–9; 12:28), this sanctification extends way past this first-century congregation. We who confess Christ today have been sanctified as well; we too are his body through the offering of his body.

His sacrificial offering constitutes and orients the band of the sanctified by providing an example of willing obedience, even when the cost is immanently high. This is not to say that all sacrifice is laudable, or that God calls every believer to such intense sacrifice; but to be sanctified by this offering does set one apart wholly for God. The body finds encouragement that they are holy before God, and hears a challenge to live out that holiness in radical obedience.

The season when congregants hear this passage offers an interesting test for such obedience. As this text is read, listeners have Christmas in view. This is the last Sunday of Advent, the last week of preparation, and the celebration of Christmas finally arrives in a few days. As the author of Hebrews has set this text, Jesus utters it before "Christmas" as well. He speaks these words to God "as he is coming into the world." Temporal settings are often up for debate in Hebrews, but not so in this instance.

Commentators agree, because of the reference to the offering of Christ's body, that the incarnation is in view. That being the case, if the author imagines Jesus uttering these words as he comes into the world, that sets them not on Christmas Eve, but about nine months before. It is a good reminder that the anticipation for the coming of Jesus was not limited to a few weeks, but comprised, at least for Mary and her little band of confidants, the long spread of an entire pregnancy. The church year allows us to practice waiting for the coming of Christ over the four weeks of Advent, but this passage can serve as a reminder that sometimes the waiting for his arrival—not just in the flesh, but in pertinent ways in our lives—takes much more time than we would prefer.

Just like this band of believers in the first century, we eagerly await his second coming (Heb. 9:28); we study the words and lives of our forebears in the Scriptures of Israel and the church, who urged sacrificial obedience; and we practice it ourselves, knowing we are fully sanctified in Christ.

AMY PEELER

Luke 1:39–45 (46–55)

³⁹In those days Mary set out and went with haste to a Judean town in the hill country, ⁴⁰where she entered the house of Zechariah and greeted Elizabeth. ⁴¹When Elizabeth heard Mary's greeting, the child leaped in her womb. And Elizabeth was filled with the Holy Spirit ⁴²and exclaimed with a loud cry, "Blessed are you among women, and blessed is the fruit of your womb. ⁴³And why has this happened to me, that the mother of my Lord comes to me? ⁴⁴For as soon as I heard the sound of your greeting, the child in my womb leaped for joy. ⁴⁵And blessed is she who believed that there would be a fulfillment of what was spoken to her by the Lord."

⁴⁶And Mary said,

"My soul magnifies the Lord,
⁴⁷and my spirit rejoices in God my Savior,
⁴⁸for he has looked with favor on the lowliness of his servant.
Surely, from now on all generations will call me blessed;
⁴⁹for the Mighty One has done great things for me,
and holy is his name.
⁵⁰His mercy is for those who fear him
from generation to generation.
⁵¹He has shown strength with his arm;
he has scattered the proud in the thoughts of their hearts.
⁵²He has brought down the powerful from their thrones,
and lifted up the lowly;
⁵³he has filled the hungry with good things,
and sent the rich away empty.
⁵⁴He has helped his servant Israel,
in remembrance of his mercy,
⁵⁵according to the promise he made to our ancestors,
to Abraham and to his descendants forever."

Commentary 1: Connecting the Reading with Scripture

The first two and a half chapters of Luke weave together the remarkable stories of John and Jesus, whose mothers Elizabeth and Mary are identified in 1:36 as kinswomen. The conceptions of both children are heralded by angels— John's to his father Zechariah (1:8–23), Jesus' to his mother Mary (1:26–38)—and angels appear again to announce Jesus' birth to the shepherds (2:8–14). Divine promises concerning both children evoke songs of praise to God, Mary's here and Zechariah's in 1:67–79. Both births elicit amazement from neighbors and friends (1:57–66; 2:8–20). Both boys are duly circumcised on the eighth day, marking them as

part of God's covenant with Israel (1:59; 2:21), and both grow up prepared for their divinely appointed vocations (1:80; 2:22–52). God has sent John "to turn the hearts of parents to their children, and the disobedient to the wisdom of the righteous, to make ready a people prepared for the Lord" (1:17; cf. 1:76; 3:4), and Jesus to be "the Son of God" (1:35), "a Savior, who is the Messiah, the Lord" (2:11).

John arrives preaching repentance in 3:1 and raises expectations that he might be the long expected redeemer (3:15), only to point instead to Jesus, who John says is more powerful than he, John, is (3:16). Although Luke implies that

John is already in prison when Jesus is baptized, making for something of a long-distance baptism (3:20–21; cf. Mark 1:9; Matt. 3:15), it is clear that their lives and careers are linked by much more than their mothers' shared ancestry. John is the forerunner of God's redeemer. John and Jesus will not meet again in Luke's story after this scene, although John will appear several times more. At 7:18–35 his disciples approach Jesus, and Jesus interprets John's prophetic ministry as prelude to his own. At 9:7–9 Herod confuses Jesus with John "raised from the dead," as do the disciples in 9:18–20. At 16:16 Jesus divides salvation history into the time of "the law and the prophets," in effect until John, and the kingdom of God initiated in Jesus' ministry. At 20:1–8 Jesus affirms the divine origin of John's baptism. John thus functions as something like the hinge on the door that closes on the era of the prophets and opens to the time of Jesus. Luke alone of the evangelists makes a clear distinction among the times of salvation history: the time of Israel, the time of Jesus, and the time of the church, to say that God has planned since the beginning of time for the events that Luke narrates.

The passage has two parts, the meeting between Mary and Elizabeth (1:39–45) and Mary's song of praise (1:46–55). Mary goes to Elizabeth's house in response to the angel Gabriel's informing her that Elizabeth too is to have a child (1:36). There John pays in utero homage to Jesus: "The child leaped in her womb" (Luke 1:41; cf. v. 44). Both John and Elizabeth have prophetic powers, recognizing who has visited them and responding accordingly. Elizabeth identifies Mary's baby as "my Lord" (v. 43) and blesses her for believing that Gabriel's promise to her would be fulfilled (v. 45), which recalls Mary's faithful response to the angel at 1:38.

Although Luke does not say that Mary sings verses 46–55, the words are clearly poetic, and early on the church sang them.[1] The word "magnificat" that has come to identify the poem is the Latin word "magnifies." Much of Mary's song echoes Hannah's song in 1 Samuel 2:1–10, when she rejoices that she is to give birth to the prophet Samuel.[2] Hannah says, "My heart exults in the LORD; my strength is exalted in my God" (1 Sam. 2:1), and Mary says, "My soul magnifies the Lord, and my spirit rejoices in God my Savior" (Luke 1:46–47). Both women praise God's mighty power to reverse the fortunes of those who suffer: God lifts up the lowly and puts down the powerful. "The bows of the mighty are broken, but the feeble gird on strength. Those who were full have hired themselves out for bread, but those who were hungry are fat with spoil. The barren has borne seven, but she who has many children is forlorn. . . . He raises up the poor from the dust; he lifts the needy from the ash heap, to make them sit with princes and inherit a seat of honor" (1 Sam. 2:4–5, 8), says Hannah. "He has shown strength with his arm; he has scattered the proud in the thoughts of their hearts. He has brought down the powerful from their thrones, and lifted up the lowly; he has filled the hungry with good things, and sent the rich away empty" (Luke 1:51–53), says Mary. These women could be eighth-century prophets for the way they understand God to be emphatically on the side of the poor, the hungry, the weak, and the sad. Their praise of God for their unexpected and unlikely circumstances stands in sharp contrast to the circumstances of the world around them. Hannah prays in the context of Israel's shaky transition from a loose association of separate tribes to a monarchy, Mary in the context of Roman domination of Palestine.

Some manuscripts of Luke 1:46 and some early church fathers attribute Mary's song to Elizabeth instead of to Mary, even though the best manuscripts read Mary rather than Elizabeth. It is easy to understand why, since Elizabeth has more in common with Hannah than Mary does: both Hannah and Elizabeth are old and barren when they conceive their remarkable sons (Luke 1:7; 1 Sam. 1:6–7), while Mary is a virgin and therefore presumably young (Luke 1:26–38). There is a sense, though, in which the

---

1. Indeed four such songs appear in Luke's infancy narrative: Mary's Magnificat at 1:46–55, Zechariah's Benedictus at 1:67–79, the angels' Gloria in Excelsis at 2:13–14, and Simeon's Nunc Dimittis at 2:29–32. The traditional titles are the first words in each song in Latin. See Raymond E. Brown, *The Birth of the Messiah: A Commentary on the Infancy Narratives in the Gospels of Matthew and Luke*, updated ed., Anchor Yale Bible Reference Library (New Haven, CT: Yale University Press, 1999), 244–45.

2. Hannah's song is also echoed in David's song in 2 Sam. 22 (cf. Ps. 18), the two poems bracketing the whole of 1–2 Samuel. They praise God for reversing the fortunes of besieged people and raising up the Lord's anointed to rescue and restore them.

song belongs to both Mary and Elizabeth—and, beyond them, to all women and men who long for redemption, who chafe at the perdurance of poverty, warfare, injustice, racism, and oppression, who call on God to keep ancient promises and fulfill God's own purposes in creation.

The longing of Advent is rooted in the obscene contrast between the way things are in the world and the way God would have them be. The prayer "Come, Lord Jesus" (Rev. 22:20; cf. 1 Cor. 16:22) gives voice to that longing and directs the church's hope not simply to the birth of the Christ child but to the return of the risen Lord in glory (Luke 21:27).

The other lections for the day promise a king who will come from "Bethlehem of Ephrathah" who will rule the people in safety and peace (Mic. 5:2–5a), beg God for restoration of the people (Ps. 80:1–7), and quote Psalm 40:6–8 to say that Christ is given a body prepared by God in order to sacrifice it and thus to accomplish God's will (Heb. 10:5–10). The whole sweep of salvation history seems to be played out in these texts that point to God's promises of redemption and breathe confidence that God can be trusted to keep those promises.

E. ELIZABETH JOHNSON

Commentary 2: Connecting the Reading with the World

On the Fourth Sunday of Advent, the season of anticipation draws near to its close. Most of us have been busier than usual, and it might be worth asking: is it possible that in the chaos of holiday preoccupations we have put off the personal and relational preparation needed for fully embracing the incarnation for ourselves this year? If so, today's Gospel reading invites us to follow Mary, who, having heard the news of the coming child, now "went with haste" to deepen and to share the truth of it.

The annunciation story no sooner ends than Mary makes an active choice. She has consented to Gabriel's word and now wastes no time in *doing* something with it. His report of Elizabeth's miraculous pregnancy came with no instruction to go to her. The visitation was Mary's independent initiative. Given the length of the journey and no mention of traveling companions, it might well have been a risky one.

Why does she go? For confirmation that the promise is true? For companionship with the only person in the world who would understand? For the nurturing wisdom of the older woman? For the privilege of helping her through the last months of her pregnancy? For a mutual quickening of courage? For the sheer joy of it? Reasons such as these—confirmation of the promise, companionship with kindred hearts, the exchange of wisdom, support, and courage, and the flourishing of joy—are among the very reasons we join together in the church. How

can we not? The visitation is the first gathering of the community of Jesus. It invites us to recall how much we need each other, to draw fresh courage from each other, and to celebrate all that we share as bearers of the promise together.

If these two women are a prototype of church, they certainly embody how improbable and how subversive the church can be. They make quite a pair: a postmenopausal woman and a middle-school-age girl, both impossibly pregnant. Noticeably absent are their men. They both have men in their lives, but we are never told of a conversation with them. These two women confide only in each other, filled with power in a world that grants them little of it. In a few moments, Mary will sing of how God has "brought down the powerful . . . and lifted up the lowly." The setting anticipates the song. With their rather superfluous men nowhere in sight, two women—favored, empowered, exultant—lift their voices in praise of God's newness alive in them. So it will always be: the Spirit chooses whom it will to be voices and agents of the divine purpose, and the chosen will often be those who have little social status or economic power. In the church and beyond, *anyone* can be at the forefront of the Spirit's work, and it is the job of the rest of us to discern, to listen, and gratefully to follow their lead.

Meanwhile, like Mary toward Elizabeth, we go to each other; like Elizabeth toward Mary, we bless each other; and like the fetal John the Baptist (prophet leaping in utero!), we gladly respond to the Christ in each other.

Artistic representations of this delightful scene are innumerable. Mary is almost always the taller of the two, sometimes in part because Elizabeth is slightly stooped with age. In some depictions Elizabeth kneels, but most often she stands, her arms embracing Mary or holding her hand. In many cases Mary returns the embrace.

A contemporary sculpture at Ein Karem, the village traditionally designated the site of the visitation, yields fruitful reflection. Here the two women stand erect and very close to each other. Their faces are carved smooth and almost expressionless, except for their slight smiles. Mary's hands are on her hips; Elizabeth's arms hang straight down, open-palmed, while her torso tilts slightly backward, as a woman in later pregnancy will often do. The result is that the two women's bellies—Elizabeth's well rounded and Mary's barely convex—are very nearly touching. It is as if the two women are physically introducing their sons, who will be, like their mothers, wonderfully related and strikingly different.

This dynamic—of deep kinship embodied in indispensable difference—is always present in the community of Jesus. This is powerfully exemplified in the bond between Elizabeth and Mary. Both women bear in their bodies the children of promise, given wondrously by the Spirit; but they draw near to each other from different ends of more than one spectrum. Elizabeth, married to a priest, is established, secure, and known to be "righteous . . . living blamelessly according to all the commandments" (1:6). Mary, unwed and suspiciously pregnant, is socially the opposite. They also come from different ends of the spectrum of age and expectation. Elizabeth in her old age arrives from a circumstance too late for a child; Mary in her virginal youth comes from a circumstance too soon for a child. John is the miracle after the ending; Jesus is the miracle before the beginning. The slim space between the two women turns out to be a seam of history: the child brought forth by one of them will close an age; the other child will inaugurate a new one. In Advent perspective, we see that, like Elizabeth

and Mary, we stand in the between times, and that like them, as different as we may be from each other, we are "expecting" and rejoicing together.

Then comes Mary's song, and with it the question: can we sing with her? The church adores the Magnificat, as evidenced by so many musical settings of it. But the music is so sweet we miss the message. We pass over its ferocity, its chilling exultance in God's scattering the proud, dethroning the powerful, and banishing the rich into emptiness. What do we do with that?

Perhaps we can rejoice with Mary and with others like her. She is lowly, and God has favored her and done great things for her. Praise be that it is true. God *does* favor the lowly and has done and will do great things for them: the economically deprived, the socially excluded, the vulnerable, the threatened, the abused, the oppressed, the broken. Perhaps we are among them and have found ourselves by the favor of God to be wondrously included, enlivened, empowered, and lifted by the love of the faithful community. This is exactly the testimony of many, and we can be glad.

Yet Mary has more than this in mind. The lifting of the lowly comes in tandem with the falling of the powerful. The language of her declaration makes it clear that Mary's song celebrates social, economic, and political reversals. For this too we can render praise, but are there other applications to make? Since the mode of the text is prophetic vision and praise, a sermon should not reduce it to exhortation on seeking social justice. But how can we join in Mary's song without living into the Magnificat? This, for many of us, will include advocacy and action toward social and economic change in favor of the poor, the excluded, the vulnerable, the "lowly."

If we know ourselves to be proud, rich, and privileged, we would be wise above all to pray for dear life that the Mighty One will cast us down from our thrones, make us rightly poor, and lead us to our emptiness. Only from such a place do we begin to make our way toward joining Elizabeth and Mary: blessed, favored, and filled with newness.

PAUL SIMPSON DUKE

Christmas Eve/Nativity of the Lord, Proper I

Isaiah 9:2–7
Psalm 96

Titus 2:11–14
Luke 2:1–14 (15–20)

Isaiah 9:2–7

²The people who walked in darkness
    have seen a great light;
those who lived in a land of deep darkness—
    on them light has shined.
³You have multiplied the nation,
    you have increased its joy;
they rejoice before you
    as with joy at the harvest,
    as people exult when dividing plunder.
⁴For the yoke of their burden,
    and the bar across their shoulders,
    the rod of their oppressor,
    you have broken as on the day of Midian.
⁵For all the boots of the tramping warriors
    and all the garments rolled in blood
    shall be burned as fuel for the fire.
⁶For a child has been born for us,
    a son given to us;
authority rests upon his shoulders;
    and he is named
Wonderful Counselor, Mighty God,
    Everlasting Father, Prince of Peace.
⁷His authority shall grow continually,
    and there shall be endless peace
for the throne of David and his kingdom.
    He will establish and uphold it
with justice and with righteousness
    from this time onward and forevermore.
The zeal of the LORD of hosts will do this.

Commentary 1: Connecting the Reading with Scripture

The lectionary assigns these well-known words from Isaiah to Christmas Eve, reflecting the traditional and strong theological connection between Isaiah's joyous cry, "For a child has been born for us, a son given to us" (9:6), and the birth of Jesus. This long-standing link between Isaiah and Christmas constitutes both an opportunity and a warning for the preacher. The warning is that Isaiah should not be allowed to become merely background music for the Christmas story. Isaiah's words have their own context, their own history, and should be received as such. When the Isaiah passage is heard on its own ground—and this is the opportunity—it helps to interpret the Christmas story by shining light on the gritty political and social realities that are genuinely part of the Christmas narrative but that are sometimes sentimentalized and lost.

The original setting of this passage is the

geopolitics of the ancient world in the eighth century BCE. To understand Isaiah 9:2–7, we need to pull back the camera and view this passage in its larger literary context. In Isaiah 7, we meet King Ahaz of Judah, who was between a rock and a hard place. The rock, in this case, was Assyria, a major Mesopotamian military power intent on dominating the region. The hard place was an anti-Assyrian coalition forged between King Rezin of Syria (Aram) and King Pekah of Israel (Ephraim), leaders of two small and weaker nations who considered that their only defense against the Assyrian powerhouse was to combine forces in a military alliance. Rezin and Pekah wanted Ahaz to join in, but when Ahaz hesitated, the two kings decided that a regime change was in order and attacked

Judah, intending to depose Ahaz and to replace him with a compliant partner.

Ahaz now had two problems: the elephant of Assyria, who could roll over any moment and crush Judah, and the Syria-Israel coalition, which already had boots on the ground headed toward Jerusalem. What should Ahaz do? Snuggle up to Assyria, or roll the dice and join hands with Syria and Israel, thus rattling Assyria's cage?

In this anxious moment of political calculation, God sent the prophet Isaiah to intercept Ahaz as he walked out on one of the local Jerusalem roads (7:3ff.). God put a message in Isaiah's mouth for the king, essentially, "Do not be afraid, Ahaz. Sure, the soldiers of Rezin and Pekah are on their way to Jerusalem, but this is no threat. These two little 'smoldering stumps'

The Kingdom of Charity

When the King heard of the danger his son was in, he turned to Charity, his royal consort, and said, "Whom shall we send and who will go for us?" She replied, "Here am I. Send me." And the King said: "Victorious shall be your conquest; you shall set them free."

The whole heavenly court accompanied Charity, the Queen of Heaven, as she went out from the face of the Lord. When they made their way down into the camp, all who were inside were enlivened by the joy and strength of her presence. Turbulence subsided and upheaval came to rest. Light returned to these unhappy people and boldness came back to those who were cowed. Hope, who was on the point of running away, returned, and Fortitude, who was almost overcome, revived. Wisdom's whole army became firm once more.

Meanwhile the enemies who were besieging the city said: "What is happening? Why is there such rejoicing in the camp? Yesterday and the day before there was no such rejoicing. Woe upon us! Let us flee from Israel, for the Lord is fighting on their side."

As the enemies fled away, a torrent of divine grace gave joy to God's city, and the Most High made holy the place where he dwells. God is within, it cannot be shaken; God will help it at the dawning of the day. Nations are in tumult, kingdoms are shaken. He lifts his voice, the earth shrinks away. The Lord of Hosts is with us; the God of Jacob is our stronghold.

Queen Charity gathered up God's young son and carried him to Heaven and gave him back to God his Father. The Father came to meet him, full of mildness and gentleness. "Quickly," he said, "bring out the best garment and put it on him. Put a ring on his finger and shoes on his feet. Go and get the fatted calf and kill it. We must have a feast and rejoice, because my son, who was dead, has come back to life. He was lost and now is found."

There are four stages to be noted on the boy's return to freedom. Firstly, repentance, though not well grounded; secondly, flight, but rash and unthinking; thirdly, the battle terrible and frightening; and fourthly, victory in all its strength and wisdom. You will find that all who flee from the world pass through all these phases. At first they are weak and silly; then, with better times, they become precipitate and rash; when troubles come, they begin to be fearful and lose heart; and finally, when they arrive at the kingdom of Charity, they are far-seeing, experienced and made perfect.

Saint Bernard of Clairvaux (d. 1153), "The Story of the King's Son," in *Bernard of Clairvaux: The Parables and the Sentences*, trans. Michael Casey (Kalamazoo, MI: Cistercian Publications, 2000), 24–26.

are not in charge of Judah; I am. I have made promises to Jerusalem and to God's people, and I will keep them. Stand firm in your faith."

Then Isaiah added, "If you doubt God's promise, ask God for a sign. Make it as big as you need. As high as heaven or as deep as the underworld. Just ask." As if Ahaz did not already have enough problems, he now had one more: God. What if Ahaz asked for some really big sign, and God gave it? Then what? Ahaz would have to decide whether to trust God in the rough-and-tumble world of politics or to trust his own wits and finesse. Trusting God was perhaps all right for priests and prophets and little people, but kings had to stand on firmer realities; so Ahaz tried to wriggle free by answering Isaiah with fake piety: "Oh no, I would never put God to the test."

Isaiah responded sharply, "You tiresome idiot! OK, you will not ask for a sign, but God will give you one anyway!" What was this sign that was higher than heaven and deeper than the deepest pit? A baby. "Look," said the prophet, "a young woman is with child, shall bear a son, and shall name him Immanuel." In a world bristling with power and armies on the march with swords at the ready, the sign of God's promise of peace is that most fragile and vulnerable of human realities, a pregnant woman and her soon-to-be-born child.

Rolling forward to our passage, this promised child has now been born, and, as promised, the child is indeed Immanuel, "God with us." Historically, Isaiah 9:2–7, describing a newborn who would become the "prince of peace," may have begun as a royal coronation hymn or, more likely, as a poetic birth announcement for a new prince; but here in Isaiah these words have already begun their migration into something broader, a joyous proclamation of God's enduring intention to save God's people in distress.

The passage opens with a contrast between darkness and light (9:2). At one level, this darkness is the gloom of a nation in turmoil. King Ahaz turned his back on the God of life and the hope that only God can give drained out of society (God was "hiding his face" in 8:17). Panicked about security, food, and the economy, the people see only misery all around them (8:20–22). For wisdom, they desperately reach

out to false prophets—to necromancers or, perhaps for us, to pollsters, blathering pundits, and talk-show hosts (8:19)—but the darkness descends all around them.

At another level, though, this darkness is larger than one moment in history. Darkness represents the power of death and the disease, destruction, and decay threatening God's good creation. This power has shown up in the reign of Ahaz, but it keeps showing up—whenever military aggression is chosen over peace, whenever illness destroys hope, whenever fear overcomes faith, whenever death loudly boasts of another victim. The good news proclaimed by Isaiah is that God will not abandon God's people to the darkness; God is at work to overcome death and to bring wisdom, peace, justice, and righteousness, in ways as hidden and seemingly as weak as a newborn child. In the darkness, a light has shined.

Two images describe the newfound joy of the people (9:3). First, the people rejoice as they do at harvest time. Barren fields now burst forth with new life. Second, the people celebrate like victorious soldiers dividing plunder—a harsh, militaristic image, perhaps, but remember, the plundered enemy is death. Every child of God that death has claimed, every hope that death has dashed, is redeemed by the power of God.

Isaiah 9:4–5 is rhythmic, even dance-like (indeed, some commentators argue this is the liturgy for a performed victory ritual). One by one, the symbols of oppression—the rods, the boots of the enemy, the bloody uniforms—are brought forward and tossed on a fire, burning up the tools of evil. Finally, the promised child is pictured as a grown-up and majestic king. The language is Davidic, but it transcends any earthly king, even David. The child will be strong and authoritative, bringing wisdom, power, and endless peace. He will rule with justice and righteousness because "the LORD of hosts" is zealous to uphold him (9:7).

When Isaiah 9:2–7 is read on Christmas Eve, we join with the Gospel witnesses to proclaim that God's promise to send a child of hope, a promise fulfilled over and over again in history, has most definitively and gloriously been fulfilled in the child of Bethlehem. Isaiah's voice on Christmas Eve reminds us that God's salvation is not merely a spiritual victory to be serenaded with a lullaby. The Christ child took on the power of death, and this birth signals the time when the tools of war and injustice—the guns, the boots, the unjust laws, the oppressor's rod—will be consumed by the fire of God's great victory.

THOMAS G. LONG

Commentary 2: Connecting the Reading with the World

Some things cannot just be *said*; they must be *sung*. At times prose is insufficient; language must overflow into poetry. In seasons of sorrow or joy, in settings where we are mired in despair or swept up in hope, experience finds fullest voice not in sequences of words but in lines of melody. What seems too hard to endure or too good to be true can sometimes best make its way into understanding and acceptance through phrases that reverberate in cadence.

A celebration of Christmas shaped only (or primarily) in exposition and explanation is all but inconceivable. (Christmastide admonishment is more unthinkable still.) Of course we sing carols at Christmas! How can we keep from singing? Christmas sermons also need carol-like qualities, not simply as an accommodation to sensory and affective expectations of holiday churchgoers but because song and poetry are genres particularly appropriate for sharing incarnational theology. The joy and hope of "God with us"—enlightening, enlivening, liberating, and transposing our human condition—is Good News that needs to be danced in Christmas sermons rather than marched or plodded. This does not mean they should be composed in verse and sung as ballads or arias. This text from Isaiah 9 can be particularly helpful to preachers, not as a launching pad to conceptual sermon reflection but as an informing influence in the sermon's very "texture."

What kind of "caroling" best befits a Christmas sermon? The default lyrical elements in Christmas services are usually a mixture of jubilation ("Joy to the World") and tender awe ("Silent Night"). There is nothing wrong with those, but such sentiments, expected and well worn, can lose their edge. They can foster an environment of cocoon-like comfort and fond nostalgia. Such Christmas coziness is hardly consonant with the stark, confusing wonder of shepherds who go "in haste" to Bethlehem when their predictably ordinary world is interdicted by angels crying "Glory!" On Christmas Eve Isaiah's song can be taken hostage by seasonal sentimentality. How can that poetry of exultation be heard, instead, as a dumbfounded "too good to be true!" from shepherds spontaneously responding to a world-upending announcement from on high? How, to cite Marcus Borg's phrase, can those who hear it in church do so "again for the first time"?[1]

Probably the most recognized musical rendition of this passage is the chorus from Handel's *Messiah*, "For unto Us a Child Is Born." Some years ago, distinguished choral conductor Robert Shaw took a yearlong break from concert touring with his chorale. He immersed himself in a study of Handel's well-known oratorio. The reigning musical performance interpretation at the time was distinctively Victorian: tempos slow and dignified, instrumentation massive and ponderous, vocal production and tonal color in soloists and choir heavy (almost Wagnerian)—in short, sounding seriously religious!

Researching the original musical text in the context of its composer's art and its immediate cultural setting, Shaw determined that *Messiah* had become gummed up in layers of sentiment at odds with what he discerned as Handel's intent. Shaw shaped a concert production releasing the music from the weight of its Victorian accretions. Tempos moved like the wind; instrumentation was spare and sparkling; vocal production was nimble, light, and spritely. Emotional intensity was achieved through a sense of musical spontaneity that left listeners (and quite possibly singers) gasping for

---

1. Marcus Borg, *Meeting Jesus Again for the First Time: The Historical Jesus and the Heart of Contemporary Faith* (New York: HarperCollins, 1995).

breath. For the first few bars of "For unto Us a Child Is Born," the leaping, skipping, tumbling sounds of the altos, tenors, sopranos, and basses chasing each other sounded almost sacrilegious! Then listeners began to feel hearts leaping, bodies pulsing, tears falling. Expected holiday cheer was engulfed in fierce, explosive joy.

For the preacher on this occasion, the question is, how, with the help of Isaiah, can a sermon for Christmas Eve (or Day) foster an analogous experience of awe and joy—not the joy of happy times remembered but of unexpected liberation from apparently hopeless bondage? How can preachers approach Isaiah (and, the sermon, more broadly conceived) as Robert Shaw approaches George Frederick Handel? Here are some prompts for imaginative connections:

1. Listen to music, either prior to or in the process of sermon preparation: symphonies by Gustav Mahler or Carl Nielsen, folk songs by James Taylor or Joan Baez—any performing artist whose singing and playing is carried by a tension between despair and hope, in which surprise is always waiting to break in.

2. Peruse the texts of Christmas carols for theologically poetic articulations of liberation, understood not primarily as individual salvation but as communal liberation: familiar carols such as "Hark the Herald Angels Sing," "It Came upon the Midnight Clear," and "Of the Father's Love Begotten" (verse 3), and carols less well known, such as "From East to West from Shore to Shore," "And Every Stone Shall Cry," and "From Heaven Above to Earth I Come."

3. Revisit songs of liberation from the African American tradition, for the way they incorporate the eschatological energy of liberation: "Sometimes I Feel like a Motherless Child," "That Great Gettin' Up Morning," "Lift Every Voice and Sing," "I'm Going to Ride in the Chariot in the Morning, Lord."

4. Recall the liberation narratives and apocalyptic images in the biblical tradition—paying particular attention to how the dramatic sense of transformation is depicted and evoked. How might a sermon for Christmas take its place in the trajectory of that tradition?

5. Review recent historical events of protracted struggle against oppression that have undergone sudden, surprising reversals. How is the experience of liberation expressed by those who have been most immediately and deeply affected (as distinct from those who observe and report, regardless of how sympathetically)?

In all these exercises, the intent is not primarily to reference sources or incorporate information but to foster, in the process of sermon shaping, a sense of resonance with the poetry and musicality of God's "mighty acts" in "making a way when there was no way." The question underlying all of these: How can a sermon for Christmas not just "tell the story" or "reflect on the meaning" but really *sing* of incarnation and redemption?

In light of this invitation for a sermon to explore the relationship between theology and poetry, two issues merit an additional dimension of reflection. First, tucked into Isaiah's song of celebration is a twofold description of joys that are seen as analogous to the joy of liberation: "as with the joy at the harvest" and "as people exult when dividing plunder" (9:3). Both images express excitement at the gathering of "fruits" longed for and worked toward but ultimately "given." These joys come, however, from being in very different fields—farming fields and battlefields. Wars intended for liberation so often generate further cycles of strife, destruction, and oppression (notwithstanding the Isaiah poet's vision of "endless peace," in a kingdom established and upheld "with justice and righteousness"). This raises a question for poets of liberation (including Christmas preacher poets): what rhetorical centering is required, and what lyrical limits need to be in play, so that a hard-won peace is not misunderstood so as to grow into its very opposite? Especially in God's name!

Second, in Handel's *Messiah* the opening chorus powerfully reiterates the names by which the child of liberation "shall be called." For Christians, these names have come to be, in both song and statement, a signature way of sounding forth names they attribute to a different child named Jesus. In Christmas sermons, how might exegetical responsibility and interfaith sensitivity suggest that such poetry be employed—or alternatively rendered?

DAVID J. SCHLAFER

Psalm 96

¹O sing to the LORD a new song;
    sing to the LORD, all the earth.
²Sing to the LORD, bless his name;
    tell of his salvation from day to day.
³Declare his glory among the nations,
    his marvelous works among all the peoples.
⁴For great is the LORD, and greatly to be praised;
    he is to be revered above all gods.
⁵For all the gods of the peoples are idols,
    but the LORD made the heavens.
⁶Honor and majesty are before him;
    strength and beauty are in his sanctuary.

⁷Ascribe to the LORD, O families of the peoples,
    ascribe to the LORD glory and strength.
⁸Ascribe to the LORD the glory due his name;
    bring an offering, and come into his courts.
⁹Worship the LORD in holy splendor;
    tremble before him, all the earth.

¹⁰Say among the nations, "The LORD is king!
    The world is firmly established; it shall never be moved.
    He will judge the peoples with equity."
¹¹Let the heavens be glad, and let the earth rejoice;
    let the sea roar, and all that fills it;
    ¹²let the field exult, and everything in it.
Then shall all the trees of the forest sing for joy
    ¹³before the LORD; for he is coming,
    for he is coming to judge the earth.
He will judge the world with righteousness,
    and the peoples with his truth.

Connecting the Psalm with Scripture and Worship

Most of us are familiar with the concept of "thin places"—sites where the membrane between this world and the next is less opaque. On the shining night of Christmas Eve, we enter what you might call a "thin *time*." The waiting of Advent has brought us to this threshold of promise, awe, and joy. Psalm 96 ushers us in.

With opening and closing verses exhorting us to sing to God, this psalm describes God and suggests appropriate responses to the One who reigns over all. Because God creates everything, response is due from everything: "all the earth," "all the peoples," "all gods," "the nations," "the heavens," and the natural world (vv. 1, 3, 4, 9–12). It is a no-exceptions summons to praise.

All this leads to the doubled assertion that God "is coming" in judgment: God "will judge the world with righteousness, and the peoples with his truth" (v. 13). However, this is no threatening sort of judgment, no cause for dread. Although the earth has been urged to "tremble" (v. 9) before God, it is in awe, not in fear. In fact, God's omnipotence brings reassurance, because our "world is firmly established; it shall never be moved" (v. 10). Furthermore, not only will God graciously judge "with equity" (v. 10), but the very first attribute we were instructed to celebrate about this judge is that God offers "salvation" (v. 2).

Christians understand salvation as coming through Jesus Christ. That is why Christmas Eve is such a holy night: it is when we welcome God's Son as the zenith of God's "marvelous works among all the peoples" (v. 3).

Both Psalm 96 and Isaiah 9:2–7 speak of what God has done, is doing, and will do yet. Isaiah mentions grim realities—"darkness . . . oppressor . . . all the boots of the tramping warriors and all the garments rolled in blood" (Isa. 9:2–5)—that have already been defeated, and the psalm tells us how to respond now that we "have seen a great light" (Ps. 96:2).

The final two verses of the Isaiah passage most closely complement the jubilant passion expressed in the psalm: the wondrous "child . . . given to us" will wield "authority" (Isa. 9:6) on behalf of "peace . . . justice and . . . righteousness . . . forevermore" (v. 7). Isaiah ascribes this to "the zeal of the Lord of hosts" (v. 7), celebrating that it is God who acts and reigns on our behalf. This is the God to whom the psalmist invites us, saying, "bring an offering, and come into his courts" (Ps. 96:8).

Christmas Eve is a prime time to issue that invitation anew. We whose labors bring us to church every week may be tempted to disparage strangers who show up only on holidays. Instead, welcome these folks, rejoicing that the irresistible tug of the Savior's birth has led them to your door. By offering a banquet of ancient texts and beloved carols, you help them know that, no matter how long they are absent from the pews, they always have a place in God's house.

Heard every Christmas, today's Gospel lesson is among the New Testament's best-known passages. Compared to today's Old Testament texts, its style feels almost journalistic. Yes, the angels are impressive and the shepherds are impressed, but a preacher seeking to share the glorious exhilaration of Christmas Eve may find that Psalm 96 provides more to work with.

Holiday congregations deserve that. Defying the well-documented secularization of Christmas and modern culture, these texts together offer an awestruck, countercultural alternative. These texts together assert that Christmas Eve is a big deal! Not because Santa is on his way but because—as noted by the psalmist, and by Isaiah, and by Luke—*God* is coming.

The psalm's full-blown focus on God provides sure guidance for the preacher. This "thin time" is brought to us by God's choice to draw near. Congregants may be overwhelmed by the trappings of this season, but Psalm 96 turns our attention to God. The psalm enables the preacher to insist that, beyond those fortunate few in Bethlehem, all of creation is called to praise God.

Another homiletical angle suggested by Psalm 96 is the unprecedented nature of Immanuel. In the psalm, God can be described only via abstract attributes that attend upon the Divine: "honor and majesty . . . strength and beauty" (v. 6). What a difference Christmas Eve makes! God is now with us.

A third option is to preach about what kind of judgment Mary's child will bring. By knowing us, Immanuel will judge us graciously.

Liturgically, the psalm stands ready to serve. It is structured as two calls to worship (vv. 1–3 and vv. 7–12), each leading to reasons for worshiping God (vv. 4–6 and v. 13, respectively). Additionally, notice—or, better yet, *feel*—the poetic surging of three passages: "Sing to the Lord. . . . Sing to the Lord . . . . Sing to the Lord, bless his name; tell of his salvation from day to day" (vv. 1–2); "Ascribe to the Lord . . . ascribe to the Lord. . . . Ascribe to the Lord. . . . bring an offering, and come into his courts" (vv. 7–8); "Let the heavens . . . let the sea . . . let the field . . . Then shall all the trees of the forest sing for joy" (vv. 11–12). The triple repetition of each imperative builds an expression of praise with rhythm-like waves landing on a beach. Any of these segments could call your congregation to praise.

Also, heed the psalm's repeated instructions to "sing" (vv. 1–2). The psalmist asserts that even "trees of the forest sing for joy before the Lord" (vv. 12–13). Especially if you will not be worshiping as a congregation on Christmas Day, sing "Joy to the World." The hymn was written to paraphrase Psalm 98, but it also beautifully reflects the essence of Psalm 96.

In this thin time, the eternal call and response between heaven and earth unite in melody: angels and shepherds have done their part, star and magi are on their way, and God's Holy Spirit has created Earth's Holy Family. So sing to the Lord a new song!

LEIGH CAMPBELL-TAYLOR

Titus 2:11–14

[11]For the grace of God has appeared, bringing salvation to all, [12]training us to renounce impiety and worldly passions, and in the present age to live lives that are self-controlled, upright, and godly, [13]while we wait for the blessed hope and the manifestation of the glory of our great God and Savior, Jesus Christ. [14]He it is who gave himself for us that he might redeem us from all iniquity and purify for himself a people of his own who are zealous for good deeds.

Commentary 1: Connecting the Reading with Scripture

Titus 1:5–15 reveals a pastor concerned about the spiritual health of his congregation. Presented by a senior minister to his protégé, the letter begins with a charge to establish elders, who will assist with teaching, preaching, and community governance. The elders must display two fundamental traits: a stable character (1:6–8) and a firm grounding in the tenets of the faith (1:9). The pastor also insists that Titus teach and nurture the congregants so that they will display these same traits. If they accept this teaching, they will withstand the teachers who are "upsetting whole families by teaching for sordid gain what it is not right to teach" (1:11).

The pastor offers Titus a two-pronged strategy. First, instruct them to show reverence for order and civility, so as not to alarm their neighbors (2:1–10; 3:1–3). Second, teach carefully the elemental beliefs handed on from the earliest communities (2:11–15; 3:4–7). This advice is so critical that, prior to his final greetings, the pastor repeats it again (in reverse order, 3:8b).

Titus 2:11–14, one sentence in Greek, concentrates on the second prong. Having presented civic instructions, the pastor now expresses the religious tenets undergirding them. The focus is on the "grace" that is "training" us (vv. 11, 12), which is explicated through the sentence's remaining clauses. Similar instructions occur in 3:4–8a, so that "these verses, along with their counterparts in chapter 3, are the heart of the letter."[1]

The hortatory material concludes with a reminder to wear fidelity as an "ornament" that adorns the doctrine ("teaching," *didaskalian*) of God our Savior (2:10). The use of "ungodliness" (*asebeian*) and "worldly desires" (*kosmikas epithymias*) in verse 12 creates an aural and visual wordplay with "ornament," connecting verses 11–14 with the preceding moral exhortation. This is strengthened in verse 13, "great God and Savior" (*sōtēros*), which echoes the phrasing in verse 11, "the grace of God has appeared, bringing salvation [*sōtērios*] to all."

These verses are also connected by references to two epiphanies—one in the past (v. 11), and the other (v. 13) in the future. The first refers to the entry of Jesus Christ into human history (cf. 1 Tim. 3:16); the second to the return of Christ as cosmic judge. Together they frame the "present age/now time" as a time of anticipation, a typical Pauline idea (Rom. 12:2; 1 Cor. 2:16; 2 Cor. 4:4), but with atypical phrasing (cf. 1 Tim. 6:17; 2 Tim. 4:1).

Describing Jesus' life and death as an expression of God's "grace" focuses attention on God's actions toward, in, and for the world (cf. 2 Cor. 5:18–21). This is highlighted through the coupling of "to all" with "salvation" (v. 11), not to determine who is and who is not "saved" but to show the universal scope of God's graceful act. This sentiment foreshadows the liturgical language of 3:4: "God our Savior," whose "loving kindness" (*philanthrōpia*) has "appeared" (*epephanē*).

Connecting grace with "bringing salvation" (*sōtērios*) is conceptually obvious (cf. 3:4–5),

---

1. I. H. Marshall, *A Critical and Exegetical Commentary on the Pastoral Epistles*, International Critical Commentary (Edinburgh: T. & T. Clark, 1999), 262.

but the word itself occurs only here in the NT.[2] The *sōtēr* stem occurs seven times in Titus, all emphasizing salvation as present "deliverance" and proper behavior as a sign of right comprehension. A similar dynamic appears in Exodus 19:3–6, where the delivery of the law is a result of the deliverance from Egypt. The author alludes to this episode in Titus 2:14 ("a people of his own who are zealous for good deeds").

The "grace" of God is not only revelatory but also pedagogical (*paideuousa* ["training us," NRSV]). The use of *paideuō* is also rare in Paul (only 1 Cor. 11:32 and 2 Cor. 6:9) but occurs three times in the Pastorals (1 Tim. 1:20; 2 Tim. 2:25; and here), where it is connected to corrective teaching (influenced by Greco-Roman moral philosophy). "Grace," that is, the death of Jesus, provides the template for measuring and fitting one's behavior to God's redemptive act, while waiting for God's final revelation (cf. 2 Tim. 2:24–25).

In Galatians 3:23, Paul depicts Torah as a pedagogue until "faith would be revealed." Now that "faith" has appeared, grace is the trainer that transforms God's people. The rest of the sentence explains that spiritual training begins by renouncing (*arnēsamenoi*) "ungodliness" (*asebeian,* cf. *eusebeian* in 1:1) and earthly desires, that is, any activity that neglects the centrality of God. The verb "renounce," absent from Paul's major letters but frequent in the Pastorals (1 Tim. 5:8; 2 Tim. 2:12–13; 3:5; Titus 1:16; and here), creates a stark contrast to the rebellious teachers, who "profess to know God, but they deny [*arnountai*] him by their actions" (1:16; see 3:9–11).

The obverse of renouncing impiety is embracing virtue. By referencing three of the four fundamental Greek/Roman virtues— self-control (*sōphronōs*), uprightness (*dikaiōs*), and godliness (*eusebōs*)—the earlier allusion to Hellenistic moral exhortation is reinforced. The virtuous life may appear to be the self-disciplined life recommended by Plato and others; however, here it is the result of deliverance by God through Christ. The virtues become hallmarks of the Christian in the "present time."

Verse 13 underscores this, by instructing believers to "wait" (*prosdexomenoi*) expectantly for the object of "blessed hope," the eschatological manifestation of "glory" (1 Tim. 6:14). This is a deliberate echo of Job 2:9a (LXX), "while I wait for the hope of my deliverance."

Faithful waiting is almost a stock idea in the NT (Phil. 2:11; 1 Thess. 2:12; 1 Pet. 4:13; 5:1, 10), but "the great God and our savior Jesus Christ" is not. The phrasing is grammatically ambiguous, allowing for one or two objects of hope. The NRSV translates, "our great God and Savior, Jesus Christ" but also notes that "the great God and our Savior" is possible. Three factors suggest that the author intends one object, Jesus Christ: (1) the use of "the" (*tou*) and the possessive pronoun "our" (*hymōn*) link God and Christ, suggesting one rather than two persons; (2) the previous use of "epiphany" refers to Jesus, rather than God; (3) the author's blurring use of "savior" in referring to both God and Christ elsewhere (Titus 1:3, 4; 3:4, 6) suggests he is unconcerned with a subtle shift toward the divinization of Jesus.[3]

Verse 14 provides support for this, as the relative pronoun "who" introduces a fragment of a traditional confession (see 3:4–7 and Mark 10:45; Gal. 1:4) that refers to the death of Jesus: "who gave himself for us that he might redeem us." The term "redeem" (*lytrōsētai*) means "to set free," pointing again to salvation as deliverance, this time from iniquity (see Ps. 130:8). Redemption is not simply release but re-creation. God creates a "people of his own" (*laon periousion,* "a treasured people"), an allusion to Exodus 19:5 and Deuteronomy 7:6, a people "purified" (*katharizō,* see Heb. 9:14; Eph. 5:26) and desirous of "good deeds" (*kalōn ergon*), a favorite term for our author (cf. 1 Tim. 3:1; 5:10, 25; 6:18; Titus 2:7, 14; 3:8, 14). Here the readers are reminded of their true identity and the relationship of belief to lifestyle, an ethic counter to the rebellious teachers (1:13–16). The author can now move directly to the next section (3:1–8a), where the pattern of faithful obedience is repeated.

STEVEN J. KRAFTCHICK

---

2. Cf. the use of *sōtērion* in Luke 2:30; 3:6; Acts 28:28 (reference to Isa. 40:5); and Eph. 6:17 (reference to Isa. 59:17).
3. For a full discussion of the possible translations, see Marshall, *Pastoral Epistles,* 276–83. For an alternative translation, see J. N. D. Kelly, *A Commentary on the Pastoral Epistles* (Grand Rapids: Baker Book House, 1981), 246–47.

Commentary 2: Connecting the Reading with the World

Titus appears only twice in the Revised Common Lectionary. This section, 2:11–14, is the Proper I reading for Christmas Eve. This is the case for all three lectionary year cycles (A, B, and C). Christmas is a pregnant moment—play on words intended—in which past, present, and future fill to the brim this one beautiful day. Some preachers try to avoid the cliché of a three-point sermon, but as hard as I tried, this passage from Titus stubbornly persisted in a three-point direction. This passage encourages the congregation to pause in wonder and to observe the salvation of God in (1) the past baby, (2) the present teaching, and (3) the future glory, thus capturing every element of Christmas Day. The preacher could discuss all three or could focus on the one aspect most helpful for the congregation.

First, Titus 2 calls us to remember the first Christmas as it proclaims the good news in words reminiscent of Luke's angels, declaring the unveiling of grace that brings salvation for all. The liturgical setting of the Christmas service is so full, *literally*, with churches often bursting at the seams with families and guests, and *figuratively*, with the air charged with the arrival of the long-awaited celebration. Titus tells us that the celebration of remembrance has finally come. The little baby depicted in crèche or six-month-old wiggliness is the picture of God's saving grace.

Titus 2 offers several different avenues for the congregation to declare what God has done in song. The appearing of the grace of God (v. 11) and also the future appearing of the glory of God (v. 13) evoke images of dawning and light. Charles Wesley's hymn "Christ Whose Glory Fills the Skies" calls congregants to proclaim the dawning of salvation on the eve of the dawning of a glorious day:

> Christ, whose glory fills the skies;
> . . . .
> triumph o'er the shades of night.

It also recognizes the darkness of ungodliness of which the passage speaks, and it asks Christ to bring his light internally as he brings it to the whole world:

> Visit then this soul of mine;
> pierce the gloom of sin and grief.

Henry Ossawa Tanner's painting *The Annunciation* portrays, as the title indicates, not the birth of Christ but its announcement. Nevertheless, this might be a fitting image to discuss, because he conveys the presence of the angel only with blinding light. The glory of God as seen in Gabriel foreshadows the glory revealed in Christ at his first (and also second) coming.

For many congregants, however, the Christmas service simply must have familiar Christmas hymns, and John Mason Neale's translation of "Good Christian Friends, Rejoice" meets that need as it also reiterates the message of Titus 2. Along with words about the manger, Neale's hymn proclaims the salvation Christ has brought:

> Jesus Christ was born for this!
> He has opened heaven's door,
> and we are blest forevermore.

In its focus on the present, Titus also reminds us that we too have a role to play in the drama. In declaring the good news of Christmas and redemption, Titus declares that this rescue has transformed the believers into God's special people (v. 14). Titus then describes this people, the church, in several ways. First, the church is bound together as a class, a group of fellow learners. We are all learning together the right way to live, ways in which to grow, as we shed the immaturity of impiety, worldliness, and lawlessness to embrace instead living wisely, righteously, and in a godly fashion.

This particular passage may be short on the specifics of what that wise, righteous, godly life looks like, but the rest of the letter gives indications. The wise life would surely include those qualities of balance urged for church leaders (1:5–9), for different age groups in the church (2:2–8), and for all (3:1–2, 9–11, 14). The particular qualities are exemplary, but a dilemma arises with the realization that these exhortations are quite gendered and even urge submissiveness for slaves (2:9–10). Such texts may not be in this lectionary reading, but inquisitive parishioners will notice them, and the pastor can fully acknowledge the fallen reality in which these texts were written, even as both pastor and parishioner work to hear the calls to righteous living that shine in and through the first-century setting.

For contemporary readers of this text, this call "to do" rests in the reality of God's doing. Because God appeared, saved, taught, gave, rescued, and purified, God's people can slough off the former way of life and walk into the new. The hymn that most closely reflects Titus 2:11–14 is Isaac Watts's "So Let Our Lips and Lives Express," which specifically calls attention to the good works exhorted in the passage:

> So let our walks and virtues shine,
> To prove the doctrine all divine.

And again:

> Our flesh and sense must be denied;
> Passion and envy, lust and pride;
> While justice, temp'rance, truth and love,
> Our inward piety approve.

The temptation looms large here to let the call to holiness and the denial of "worldliness" recede into seclusion. Letting go of the ways of the world sometimes results in a retreat from the world in toto. The message from this passage must not forget its opening line. If God intends for salvation to come to all (v. 11), those good works must be lived out in such a way that those outside the walls of the church can hear the good news about the appearance of salvation and ultimately be folded into the patient instruction of God. The text will go on to say that members of this community were once outsiders caught in destructive behaviors (3:3), but God redeemed them. They too should be merciful, showing every consideration for all people (v. 2), just as God showed mercy to them. Therefore, this text is a rich one for reflecting on the kingdom of God and its inbreaking justice. The call to righteousness, then, must be both a personal call to holiness and a communal invitation to redemption.

The celebration of the nativity is not just memorial, however; it is also living out, here and now in the present, the future hope of the gospel. We, Titus says, "wait for the blessed hope" (2:13), the second appearing of the divine presence when our Savior returns as Messiah and God. The church, then, is on the cusp of something great, looking forward with expectation to his glorious return. In "Good Christian Friends, Rejoice," Neale too anticipates this great inclusion:

> Jesus Christ was born to save!
> Calls you one and calls you all
> to gain his everlasting hall.

Titus 2 strikes a fitting chord for a Christmas service. It proclaims the ineffable good news that salvation has come, but, as is fitting for a true *Christian* celebration of Christmas, it is not sentimental. It recognizes the cost of that salvation for God, that the Savior Jesus Christ gave himself to rescue us. It also acknowledges the life of discipleship demanded of those who enjoy this salvation, which is to grow in the zeal for good works. It tells the gathered congregation: we know where we have come from, what we need to work on, and where we are going. This is a text for celebration for this great day, because it looks back to what God has done and looks forward to what God will do in his Son and through his special people.

AMY PEELER

Luke 2:1–14 (15–20)

[1]In those days a decree went out from Emperor Augustus that all the world should be registered. [2]This was the first registration and was taken while Quirinius was governor of Syria. [3]All went to their own towns to be registered. [4]Joseph also went from the town of Nazareth in Galilee to Judea, to the city of David called Bethlehem, because he was descended from the house and family of David. [5]He went to be registered with Mary, to whom he was engaged and who was expecting a child. [6]While they were there, the time came for her to deliver her child. [7]And she gave birth to her firstborn son and wrapped him in bands of cloth, and laid him in a manger, because there was no place for them in the inn.

[8]In that region there were shepherds living in the fields, keeping watch over their flock by night. [9]Then an angel of the Lord stood before them, and the glory of the Lord shone around them, and they were terrified. [10]But the angel said to them, "Do not be afraid; for see—I am bringing you good news of great joy for all the people: [11]to you is born this day in the city of David a Savior, who is the Messiah, the Lord. [12]This will be a sign for you: you will find a child wrapped in bands of cloth and lying in a manger." [13]And suddenly there was with the angel a multitude of the heavenly host, praising God and saying,

[14]"Glory to God in the highest heaven,
  and on earth peace among those whom he favors!"

[15]When the angels had left them and gone into heaven, the shepherds said to one another, "Let us go now to Bethlehem and see this thing that has taken place, which the Lord has made known to us." [16]So they went with haste and found Mary and Joseph, and the child lying in the manger. [17]When they saw this, they made known what had been told them about this child; [18]and all who heard it were amazed at what the shepherds told them. [19]But Mary treasured all these words and pondered them in her heart. [20]The shepherds returned, glorifying and praising God for all they had heard and seen, as it had been told them.

Commentary 1: Connecting the Reading with Scripture

The lectionary appoints Luke 2:1–20 for both Christmas Eve and Christmas Day. This essay discusses 2:1–7, and the following one treats 2:8–20, since those are the two basic scenes in the first part of chapter 2.

Virgil's *Aeneid*, written in the late first century BCE, is a model of the ancient epic, telling the story of Aeneas and his journeys, leading to the divinely willed birth of the Roman people. Marianne Palmer Bonz argues that Luke's two-volume work of the Gospel and Acts is self-consciously modeled after the *Aeneid*.[1] The *Aeneid* is the epic performance of Rome's sacred history; Luke–Acts is an epic performance of God's sacred history. The *Aeneid* explores the theme of divine mission in the form of a journey, leading to the formation of a new people; Luke–Acts is a Christian version of this theme. The *Aeneid* includes stories of divine guidance and intervention, including instances of prophecy, visions, and oracles with divine messengers aiding or impeding the progress of the human agents; Luke–Acts also employs angels, theophanies, dreams, visions, and prophecies. The *Aeneid* employs ambiguous prophecies (prophecies that are open to misunderstanding or misinterpretation) and divinely imposed reversals are also a common

---

1. Marianne Palmer Bonz, *The Past as Legacy: Luke–Acts and Ancient Epic* (Philadelphia: Fortress Press, 2000).

feature; Luke–Acts frequently employs the motif of prophetic reversal, and its main character, Jesus, delivers ambiguous prophecies. Luke means to use the two volumes that are Luke and Acts, among other things, to set the empire of God in contrast with Rome's empire.

The first sentence of the Gospel reading for Christmas Eve sets Jesus' birth firmly within the context of Roman domination: "In those days a decree went out from Emperor Augustus that all the world should be registered" (Luke 2:1). Although a broad scholarly consensus agrees that Quirinius's census was conducted long after Herod's death and thus after Jesus' birth,[2] memory of the event allows Luke a mechanism to get Mary and Joseph to Bethlehem for Jesus to be born there.

Mary's name suggests her family is among those in first-century Palestine who long for God to free them from Rome. A remarkable number of first-century Jews name their daughters Mary—after the prophet Miriam, Aaron's sister, and in defiant memory of Mariamne, murdered by her husband, Herod the Great. "The name Mary is unambiguously political, brave, and resistive. Jesus was born into such a family."[3]

Although everybody in the early church knows that Jesus is from Nazareth in Galilee (the Gospels of Mark and John make no mention of Bethlehem and consistently name Nazareth as his hometown), both Luke and Matthew arrange in their stories to have him born in Bethlehem. Matthew says that is because his parents Mary and Joseph actually live in Bethlehem (Matt. 2:1) and move to Nazareth after fleeing Herod into Egypt and returning from exile (2:13–23). Luke says Mary and Joseph are originally from Nazareth and their baby is born in Bethlehem because the emperor attempts to move people around like pieces on a chess board, despite the fact that God is really in control. Both evangelists are more concerned with what the Bible says about God's shepherding of Israel than they are with journalistic reporting of Jesus' nativity. Both Gospel stories about Bethlehem—and they cannot be harmonized,

despite the efforts of popular Christian imagination—represent theological reflections on Scripture rather than historical reminiscences. Preachers do well not to force Matthew's and Luke's nativity stories into contrived conformity and instead to let Luke and Matthew tell their own stories.

Bethlehem is already an ancient city in the first century, the traditional site of the matriarch Rachel's tomb (Gen. 35:19), the home of a Levite the murder of whose concubine precipitates the move toward monarchy in Israel (Judg. 19), and the place Boaz and Ruth initiate the line that will result in the birth of King David. Their son Obed has a son named Jesse, whose son is David (Ruth 4:11–12; cf. Matt. 1:5–6). Much of the action surrounding David's ascension to the throne in 1 and 2 Samuel takes place in and around Bethlehem, and although it is Zion—Jerusalem—that comes to be thought of as the "city of David" in Scripture (2 Sam. 5:7, 9; 6:10; and so on), Luke twice uses that phrase to describe David's hometown of Bethlehem (Luke 2:4, 11). This is largely under the influence of Micah 5:2, "But you, O Bethlehem of Ephrathah, who are one of the little clans of Judah, from you shall come forth for me one who is to rule in Israel," the beginning of the Old Testament reading for the Fourth Sunday of Advent. Although Matthew has the chief priests and scribes quote the verse explicitly to Herod at 2:6, Luke simply assumes it and contrives to bring Mary and Joseph to Bethlehem before Jesus is born.

The competition in the tradition between Nazareth and Bethlehem finds voice in the Fourth Gospel. "Can anything good come out of Nazareth?" asks a skeptical Nathanael in John 1:46. "Surely the Messiah does not come from Galilee, does he?" asks an equally skeptical crowd when the chief priests and scribes attempt to arrest Jesus the first time. "Has not the scripture said that the Messiah is descended from David and comes from Bethlehem, the village where David lived?" (7:40–41; see Mic. 5:2). For the Fourth Evangelist, though, it does not matter where Jesus comes from geographically,

---

2. For an alternative view, see John H. Rhoads, "Josephus Misdated the Census of Quirinius," *Journal of the Evangelical Theological Society* 54, no. 1 (2011): 65–87.

3. Marianne Sawicki, *Crossing Galilee: Architectures of Contact in the Occupied Land of Jesus* (Harrisburg, PA: Trinity Press Int., 2000), 172.

because he really comes from God (7:28–29; cf. 1:1–18). For Luke, it is important that Jesus confirm the prophecy of Micah 5:2.

In Luke, Joseph goes to Bethlehem for the census because he is "from the house and family of David" (2:4). The emphasis on Joseph's lineage is curious in view of the fact that he is so emphatically not Jesus' biological father. Gabriel makes clear to Mary that it is the Holy Spirit, rather than a human man, who has caused her to conceive (1:35–37), and she is twice called Joseph's betrothed rather than his wife (1:27; 2:5). At 3:23, when the evangelist introduces Jesus' ministry, he says, "He was the son (as was thought) of Joseph." It is as though, for Luke, Jesus becomes a Davidide by adoption rather than by birth. Not surprisingly, in later Christian tradition Joseph becomes the patron saint of adoptive parents.

The other texts for Christmas Eve include the oracle in Isaiah 9 about a new king: "For a child has been born for us, a son given to us; authority rests upon his shoulders; and he is named Wonderful Counselor, Mighty God, Everlasting Father, Prince of Peace. His authority shall grow continually, and there shall be endless peace for the throne of David and his kingdom. He will establish and uphold it with justice and with righteousness from this time onward and forevermore" (Isa. 9:6–7). Psalm 96 is also about enthronement, calling all creation to praise God, who is king, and to sing the praise of God's glory and divine sovereignty. Titus 2:11–14 ties together the two impulses of Advent, our waiting for Jesus to be born and our anticipation of his return in glory: "For the grace of God has appeared, bringing salvation to all . . . while we wait for the blessed hope and the manifestation of the glory of our great God and Savior, Jesus Christ" (vv. 11, 13).

E. ELIZABETH JOHNSON

Commentary 2: Connecting the Reading with the World

No other occasion of worship seems more luminous than Christmas Eve. We gather in the night to a room lit with candles and lovely with familiar carols, all enveloped in an air of uncommon stillness—due partly to the fact that the stores have finally closed, and partly to the understanding that in the presence of the newborn holy child, a hush will fall over the room. Four weeks of expectation give way to wonder.

Not everyone will feel it this way. People in grief or other crisis may find the carols bittersweet. Memories and longings may disturb them, and the sight of apparently happy families may feel half-cruel. Whatever our emotional, relational, or spiritual differences, what most of us will hold in common is the feeling of *night*, and of the uniquely poignant fullness of this particular night.

The text will meet us there, but it does not begin there. Luke's nativity account begins with a stark declaration of the kind of world into which Jesus is born: empire, Caesar, governor, registration, taxation. The mention of Augustus, Quirinius, and a particular imperial mandate serves to remind us first that the Messiah's birth occurs within specific coordinates of historical time and space. The nativity story can feel gauzy and magical, but its opening verses warn us against reading it as a fairy tale. It happens in a prose world of known politicians, institutions, economies, and places locatable on an actual map.

This opening also reminds us that Mary gives birth within the oppressive, grinding machinery of empire, the same machinery that in the end will kill her son. The empire commands a census, the better to extract wealth from an occupied people. Joseph and Mary of Nazareth, like other peasants across the empire, are directed to a designated site so as to be more efficiently impoverished. The Word becomes flesh in a context of organized imperial oppression, as it still does. To the extent that we are captive to, threatened by, or benefiting from the current American Empire, the Christmas story has a powerful and subversive relevance for us.

What the Roman Empire does not know is that its very machinations are put to use by the sovereign purposes of God. Caesar's decree brings Joseph and Mary straight to Bethlehem, the little town of promise, and at just the right time. Even so, the conditions there are not welcoming. The teeming chaos that meets them offers no hospitality, "no room in the inn."

The Flemish painter Pieter Bruegel depicted the scene perfectly. *The Census in Bethlehem* (1566) is set in a sixteenth-century Flemish village. The town is filled with people, some of them working or playing in the snow, others walking with heavy burdens on their backs, and a crowd standing near a table outside an inn. One man behind the table holds out a big registration book, another writes in a ledger and takes the people's coins. Near the end of the line, a man carrying a saw is stepping forward. Behind him is a woman in blue, riding a donkey. We know who they are, but in the crowd they are mostly indistinguishable. Significantly, attached to the wall of the inn, above the table where people are paying taxes, is a plaque bearing the coat of arms of the Habsburg Empire, which ruled the Netherlands at that time in the person of Philip II of Spain, who was known for heavy taxation. Bruegel depicts the people's deprivation by placing broken wagons across the town and showing the small, local castle in ruins.

Perhaps we should do as Bruegel did and locate the story in our own time. The holy family is to be found among the systems of unfairness and indifference in which we live. Christ is born alongside the hard-pressed, the struggling, and the broken, some of whom are in church on Christmas Eve—and most of whom are not.

In such a place, "she gave birth to her firstborn son" (Luke 2:7). After the lengthy description of context, it is striking how briefly and simply the birth is narrated. Nothing is said of her pain or of who attended her or of the first cry of the baby; even his name is withheld. Apparently, all that matters is that Mary has brought to completion what she has consented to do, and that God's Son is now alive in the world.

How resourceful of her to put him in a feed box! Mentioned three times (2:7, 12, 16), and even a "sign" for the shepherds, the manger is clearly important. What shall we make of it?

That Christ is to be sought in lowly and unlikely places? That his sustaining gift is not just for humankind but for all of God's creation? Even that his birth prefigures his death? (Wrapping him in bands of cloth and laying him in a manger sounds oddly close to the actions of another Joseph, who "wrapped it [Jesus' body] in a linen cloth, and laid it in a rock-hewn tomb" [23:53]). The feed-box crib has much to say about lowliness, displacement, creation, sustenance, the sharing of our death, and more.

Some of the same themes are embodied in the shepherds: they too are in the natural world among animals, and they are lowly and displaced. Considered dishonest and "unclean," they are not just outside the city but outside the zone of social acceptability. To *them*, and only to them, the news is given. Perhaps they hold something in common with the people at the Christmas Eve service who feel estranged from the celebration. The shepherds bear an even closer resemblance to the socially abandoned people who are not in our candlelit sanctuaries. The news is especially for these.

The news comes in the night. The light shines in darkness. Naturally, the first response of the shepherds is terror, and the angel's first command is to get over it. Then the ravishing words: *See! Good news! Great joy! All people! To you! A Savior! Glory! Peace! Favor!* The sky erupts with it. For Mary, one angel was required, and so too for Zechariah—but for the shepherds, a sky full! From the beginning of time, the heavens were telling the glory of God, yet never with words (Ps. 19:1–3); now the words can be heard at last. What the heavens have always been singing is, "Glory to God, and on earth peace!"

Christmas Eve may not be much of a night for preaching. It is a time for the reading of Scripture, the telling of the old story, the lifting of song, the celebration of Holy Communion. It seems certainly not the time for admonition or instruction, except perhaps to remember the poor and to love one another as God has so loved us all. What Luke's narrative offers most of all is an invitation to receive the story again, to hear it and imagine it once more—and to do so noticing again the realities of empire, of systemic oppression, of personal dislocation and estrangement. All of these together constitute the place into which Christ is born. The nativity story itself does not change, but circumstances in our own empires, nations, communities, and families do, and we ourselves do. If we are to do as the shepherds did and "see this thing that has taken place" (Luke 2:15), we would do well to contemplate the present world as it actually is, and ourselves as we actually are, and to know that the holy child is born precisely there—and to hear the angels sing, precisely there, "Glory and Peace."

PAUL SIMPSON DUKE

Christmas Day/Nativity of the Lord, Proper II

Isaiah 62:6–12　　　　　　　　　　　Titus 3:4–7
Psalm 97　　　　　　　　　　　　　　Luke 2:(1–7) 8–20

Isaiah 62:6–12

[6]Upon your walls, O Jerusalem,
　　I have posted sentinels;
all day and all night
　　they shall never be silent.
You who remind the LORD,
　　take no rest,
[7]and give him no rest
　　until he establishes Jerusalem
　　and makes it renowned throughout the earth.
[8]The LORD has sworn by his right hand
　　and by his mighty arm:
I will not again give your grain
　　to be food for your enemies,
and foreigners shall not drink the wine
　　for which you have labored;
[9]but those who garner it shall eat it
　　and praise the LORD,
and those who gather it shall drink it
　　in my holy courts.

[10]Go through, go through the gates
　　prepare the way for the people;
build up, build up the highway,
　　clear it of stones,
　　lift up an ensign over the peoples.
[11]The LORD has proclaimed
　　to the end of the earth:
Say to daughter Zion,
　　"See, your salvation comes;
his reward is with him,
　　and his recompense before him."
[12]They shall be called, "The Holy People,
　　The Redeemed of the LORD";
and you shall be called, "Sought Out,
　　A City Not Forsaken."

Commentary 1: Connecting the Reading with Scripture

Isaiah's vision of a renewed Jerusalem after the Babylonian exile is assigned to be read on Christmas Day. Earlier in Isaiah, there is the announcement—"For a child has been born for us, a son given to us" (9:6)—pointing to a Davidic successor who is already born and who will in the future become a peaceful ruler (Isa. 9:1–7 [8:23–9:6 Heb.]; 11:1–5). At Christmas the joy over the newborn Christ child resonates with the hope for restoration of Jerusalem. Isaiah 62:6–12 unfolds the hope for a peaceful future brought through Christ by looking to a restored Jerusalem. For Christians, the Christmas hope for a secure, peaceful future is rooted in an array of images and ideas found in Isaiah's prophecy. Isaiah 62 presents at least seven major themes that together describe the hopeful restoration of Judah and provide encouragement for all exiles who follow.

1. Isaiah portrays the city of Jerusalem in feminine language, as "daughter Zion" (v. 11) and as a mother who provides resources for the inhabitants, her children. The city walls are her "crown of beauty" (vv. 3, 6), and her children will delight in the yield of the fields of grain and vineyards, which they formerly were forced to render as tribute to their oppressors (vv. 8–9). Zion-Jerusalem, presented in feminine terms, is a communal space mediating between Yahweh and her inhabitants. No longer enslaved, the rebuilt city becomes again the facilitator of communal life, passing on goods she has received from Yahweh.

2. Isaiah's picture of Jerusalem, rebuilt and fortified, is a sign of something larger than buildings and walls: the reestablishment of justice. When Isaiah was called to serve as a prophet, during the time of the ascendency of Assyria, he asked, "How long, O Lord," would his service last? God's answer was, "Until cities lie waste" (6:11). Now, Jerusalem is being restored, after a time of utter destruction (Heb. *shmamah*), a "laying waste" that both recalls and validates God's earlier pronouncement. The book of Isaiah tells of periods of both destruction and divine restoration. Destruction is announced against Israel and Judah (Isa. 6–8), and against Israel, Judah, and Egypt (Isa. 28–32; as well as against the nations in Isa. 13–23). However, there is no destruction without the promise of restoration. Reconstruction is consistently present in the book of Isaiah, in the themes of the restoration of the city (Isa. 62) and in the form of a return from exile (Isa. 35; 40–55).

3. The image of the watchmen on the city walls of Jerusalem is significant. The watchmen's task is to stand on the wall and to pray incessantly to God for the protection of the city (62:6). The watchmen symbolize the prophets (see Ezek. 3:17; 33:1–9; Jer. 6:17). To see the prophets as watchmen who intercede to God on behalf of the city is the result of a long development from their earlier self-identification as admonishers and deliverers of judgment (Isa. 6–8; 28–32) to the function of intercessors who pray for the citizens. The aim of the watchman is to hold God accountable and to transform Jerusalem into a city that is solidly and firmly established. In postexilic prophecy this image transcends this local Judean context; we see a universal understanding of a prophet as one who prays for the human community to be one of justice, peace, and righteousness.

4. Isaiah's prophecy shows the tension between what God is doing now and what is yet to come. On the one hand, Isaiah, like a watchman crying out in the night, prays fervently for the distressed city, pleading with God to come and restore Jerusalem. On the other hand, Isaiah calls God to accountability, reminding God of the promise ("sworn by his right hand and by his mighty arm") always to uphold Jerusalem, not in some unrealized future, but here and now. The text does not resolve the tension between the "already" and the "not yet," but instead invites the preacher to respect the tension between the hope for salvation and the deep anxiety about it not yet being fulfilled, and to discern whether the present moment is more one of rejoicing over what God is now doing or one of yearning for that which God will surely do.

5. Judah had been a colonized nation, under the rod of Babylon, but Isaiah challenges this exploitation by emphasizing Judah's autonomy. Isaiah 62 was most likely written at a time of Persian economic oppression, and the surprising exclusion of foreigners (v. 8), who will no longer eat the grain, should be understood in contrast to colonial rule, when foreigners seized the harvest. An emphasis on separation—the true Judeans from others—serves to condemn the exploitation Judah received in its recent past and to underscore Judah's new strength. The people now have the freedom to share their own goods with each other, rather than deliver those goods to the Persian oppressor (cf. Nehemiah's complaint about his predecessors, Neh. 5:15).

6. Isaiah 62:10 presents an image of a

pilgrimage toward the great and holy city. This motif of a pilgrimage to Jerusalem is repeated again and again in Hebrew Scripture and even sets the backdrop for the Christian story of Jesus moving to Jerusalem in the Synoptic Gospels. In Isaiah, the journey of the Judeans back to Jerusalem is the central metaphor for the end of the exile. Isaiah 40:1–11 points to this hopeful pilgrimage with the injunction to "clear the way for Yahweh through the desert" and with the majestic images of the valleys being lifted up, the mountains being made low, and the divine glory being revealed (Isa. 40:3–5). The pilgrimage to Jerusalem is a "homecoming" and a restoration for the people of Israel.

7. Finally, the prophet elevates the people of Judah by describing them, alone among the nations, as "The Holy People, The Redeemed of the LORD" (v. 12). The subsequent debate, reflected in much of Isaiah 56–66, about how exactly Judaism would understand itself after the exile in regard to the other nations, was intense. One inclusive voice envisions the foreigner included in the cult (Isa. 56:6–7), but the voice in this passage emphasizes Judah as a separate people over against "the foreigners." Again, because of the oppression of the colonizers, the former economic oppressors no longer deserve tribute.

How is Judah to be different? For the moment, this text refrains from pointing out ethical qualifications of the holy people. The role of the prophet now is simply to prepare the way for the people, to clear away the stones standing in the way of the community returning in strength and peace. The whole book of Isaiah demonstrates how the prophet's tasks are constructive for the community, as the prophet develops from one who announces judgment, to one who functions as a watchman, to one who becomes an ethical instructor.

How may the preacher unfold these images in Isaiah 62, the beauty of the restored Jerusalem, the glory of the pilgrimage of the people? Perhaps the preacher will describe an ethically pure and prophetic people, now safe in a walled city and finally freed from the oppressor. Perhaps the preacher will emphasize the subversive quality of this text, announcing God's promise to free all captives from their oppressors. Perhaps the preacher will emphasize Jerusalem's new role as a prophetic people, a role shared with the early Christian church, as a symbol of resistance against all forms of colonial power. In the New Testament, this was Rome (Rev. 21:1–5), but the oppressor appears in every age.

KLAUS-PETER ADAM

Commentary 2: Connecting the Reading with the World

This passage in Isaiah begins with a theme that is familiar to many of us on Christmas Day: exhaustion! The image of noisy clamor from sentinels on Jerusalem's walls (v. 6) may remind us of all the sounds and bustle of the last few weeks, as we angled for spots in parking lots, jostled with crowds in stores, and scurried to get a tree up and decorated. Along with the guards of Israel's glorious city, we too may feel that a silent night is far away—even as we herald its arrival. The text from Isaiah offers no rest for the weary, specifying that Jerusalem's watchers will *never* be silent. Never? Is it not finally time for some peace and quiet?

The prophet quickly specifies why the rest will not come. Those who are in relationship

with God cannot take a break. Isaiah's call to the sentinels is also a call to the church, and may seem surprisingly radical. Like the sentinels, we too are called to "remind the LORD" (v. 6). Why would God need our reminding? Does God not know everything there is to know? Perhaps the prophet's message portrays prayer—reminding God that we care—as far more than an optional or occasional activity. Prayer is a responsibility. Is there ever a time *not* to pray? Isaiah sees people in partnership with God through urgent petitions. We should not just expect God to take care of the work of the world, such as establishing Jerusalem, the city of peace (v. 7). People need to participate in partnership with God to establish God's realm here on earth.

However, the prophet quickly reminds us that God and humans are not on the same level. Underscoring God's superiority, Isaiah proclaims that the Lord has "sworn by his right hand and by his mighty arm" (v. 8). God means business and also speaks about the business world.

Our global economy distributes goods in a way that Isaiah abhors. "I will not again give your grain to be food for your enemies," God swears in an oath, "and foreigners shall not drink the wine for which you have labored." In Isaiah's time, hundreds of years before the birth of Jesus, the route from "farm to table" was very short, as most people ate food that they grew themselves. In stark contrast, today the average American plate (let alone a Christmas feast) has ingredients from five countries outside of the United States. Our food might be transported over thousands of miles before reaching our homes. This system of distribution increases food inequity across the globe, while transportation of food adds pollutants and greenhouse emissions to a rapidly heating atmosphere. Many farm hands and animal workers around the world scrape to feed their families and live in poverty, not eating or enjoying the fruits of their labor. Instead, they see their harvests shipped off to the world's wealthiest people. Can we blame these laborers in distant lands if they perceive voracious consumers, like us, as the enemy? Their grain is our food; we drink the wine for which they labored.

In contrast to this reality of inequality and greed, Isaiah proposes a vision based on equity (v. 9). Fairness generates gratitude. The harvesters will eat what they have produced, as they praise the Lord. Wine will flow in God's holy courts. Like the best of our Christmas celebrations, justice, joy, and worship intertwine through a prophetic vision of hope.

Perhaps like a holiday gathering, Isaiah 62:10 ushers in a feeling of welcome, with Jerusalem as the universal home. Isaiah invites people to gather in this sacred spot, repeatedly issuing the command, "Go through, go through the gates" (v. 10). Those who have visited the Holy Land know that Jerusalem is a walled city with seven gates. Made of large limestone bricks that are piled four stories high, Jerusalem's walls surround the old city and are flooded with spotlights at night. While these walls may appear ancient to us, they were built in the sixteenth century and are relatively modern by Jerusalem's standards. Even back to the time of Isaiah, walls surrounded Jerusalem, since walls were the distinguishing feature of a city in the ancient world. Throughout its history, entering Jerusalem meant going through gates.

The prophet realizes that first the people must arrive at the gates; a way should be prepared so that all may enter. Isaiah exhorts his listeners to build up a highway and clear it of stones (v. 10), which are ubiquitous in Israel. A banner should be raised over the peoples; those of any origin are welcome in Jerusalem, as the prophet again issues an encompassing invitation. This spirit of Isaiah's prophecy sets the tone for the king to come, born this day, who arrives on earth to show God's way to all the nations.

Verse 11 reiterates this theme of inclusion without limits: "The LORD has proclaimed to the end of the earth: Say to daughter Zion, 'See, your salvation comes.'" The one who is coming brings abundance, Isaiah promises. "His reward is with him, and his recompense before him." There is love in the generosity that the savior brings.

At Christmas, we generously share presents as a way of honoring someone else's presence in our life. One church I know has a "free store" for parents with few material resources to come and select toys that they can wrap and give to their children at Christmas. My guess is that this act gives at least as much joy to the parents as it does to the children. I am grateful that I am able to give presents to my family at Christmas, because this gesture is such a source of happiness. My favorite Christmas moments are when someone I love opens up that special gift that I have diligently found, purposefully purchased, painstakingly wrapped, and finally adorned with a red velvet bow. When they pull off the bow, they tear open the paper, and their eyes fly wide, I am elated. The present is the vehicle for showing love because of the joy of giving.

Unlike our Christmas purchases, God's gifts last forever. A glorious procession of all tribes and nations streams into Jerusalem; the watchers posted on its walls rejoice. With exaltation, they greet those passing through the gates as holy people, redeemed by God. Jerusalem is desired, "a city not forsaken." God gives the gift of relationship. How wonderful it is to belong!

The feeling of a happy homecoming—where everyone is welcome—gets to the heart of Christmas. Think of a return home in your life that was especially meaningful or memorable: perhaps your first return home from college, or when you introduced a new baby to the family, or the day you walked in the door after a tour of military service. Recall the moment you stepped across the threshold and those whom you love jumped up to embrace you, their eyes sparkling with tears of gratitude, just to see you again. These precious moments linger with us for a lifetime. These feelings reflect the joy that Isaiah describes: being welcomed, safe, cherished, and loved.

May Christmas be a time when we embrace each other with radical welcome. The hustle and bustle of this season must not overwhelm our celebration of the Redeemer's coming. As we honor the one born to us this day, may we be like the people of Jerusalem who celebrate, for God's glory has come to bring joy to the world!

JULIE FAITH PARKER

Psalm 97

¹The LORD is king! Let the earth rejoice;
   let the many coastlands be glad!
²Clouds and thick darkness are all around him;
   righteousness and justice are the foundation of his throne.
³Fire goes before him,
   and consumes his adversaries on every side.
⁴His lightnings light up the world;
   the earth sees and trembles.
⁵The mountains melt like wax before the LORD,
   before the Lord of all the earth.

⁶The heavens proclaim his righteousness;
   and all the peoples behold his glory.
⁷All worshipers of images are put to shame,
   those who make their boast in worthless idols;
   all gods bow down before him.
⁸Zion hears and is glad,
   and the towns of Judah rejoice,
   because of your judgments, O God.
⁹For you, O LORD, are most high over all the earth;
   you are exalted far above all gods.

¹⁰The LORD loves those who hate evil;
   he guards the lives of his faithful;
   he rescues them from the hand of the wicked.
¹¹Light dawns for the righteous,
   and joy for the upright in heart.
¹²Rejoice in the LORD, O you righteous,
   and give thanks to his holy name!

Connecting the Psalm with Scripture and Worship

Today's first reading, Isaiah 62:6–12, is not a text that makes us automatically exclaim, "Merry Christmas!" Yet the passage reveals a deep need of God's salvation and a trust in God's promised presence, and that is certainly a profound message for Christmas morning. Psalm 97 can help us preach that message from that text.

Psalm 97 is one of several psalms, including the psalm before it and the psalm after it, that emphasize God as the monarch of all creation. The psalm has three sections. Verses 1–5 describe God as a divine conqueror whose tremendous power obliterates adversaries (v. 3) and melts mountains (v. 5). This power is not brutal or arbitrary. Instead, God's very throne—a symbol of the ruler's reign—is built upon "righteousness and justice" (v. 2), a pair of concepts that also appear in each of the psalm's subsequent sections.

The second section, verses 6–9, explores an assortment of reactions to God's presence: the heavens announce it and the peoples behold it (v. 6); idolaters are shamed by it and idols bow down to it (v. 7); Zion—another way of naming Jerusalem—and Judah rejoice in it (v. 8). This section concludes with an elaborating restatement of the psalm's opening proclamation, this time declaring that God is the "exalted" ruler of all (v. 9).

The final section gives an expanded view of those who, as we were told in verse 8, rejoice in God: they are righteous and grateful to God (v. 12), and they hate evil (v. 10). Thus we encounter an acknowledgment that evil exists even in the lives of God's beloved. Furthermore, there is apparently something from which their lives must be "guarded" by God, and they must be "rescue[d] . . . from the hand of the wicked" (v. 10). Despite this reminder of reality, all three of the psalm's sections speak of gladness and rejoicing (vv. 1, 8, 11, 12).

In today's Isaiah text, we sense the need for and expectation of Psalm 97's divine king (Ps. 97:1): God's power should be acknowledged by all the earth (Isa. 62:7, 11); God has the "mighty arm" necessary to ensure that adversaries will no longer be able to take the people's food and drink (vv. 8–9); God has a profound impact on God's people, rendering them "holy" and "redeemed" (v. 12).

While Isaiah uses future-tense verbs and the vocabulary of anticipation, preparation, and approach (Isa. 62:6, 10, 11) to convey the persistent expectation of the arrival of this powerful God, Psalm 97 uses present-tense verbs to offer the reassuring perspective that God is already here and acknowledged by all (Ps. 97:9), and is already caring for the people (v. 10). While Isaiah looks to a future, when the rubble-ruined highway has been cleared, salvation has arrived, and Zion knows that it is "Not Forsaken" (Isa. 62:10, 11, 12), Psalm 97 can hearteningly report what that time is actually like: "Zion hears and is glad" (Ps. 97:8).

This emphasis in the psalm on gladness and rejoicing (vv. 1, 8, 11, 12) may help the preacher be in sync with the predominant emotions of Christmas morning. Meanwhile, the psalm's emphasis on righteousness and justice (vv. 2, 6, 8, 11, 12) provides a depth of hope to undergird our joy. Such well-grounded joyfulness is also evident in the epistle lesson, which shares Psalm 97's sense of God having already "appeared" and proclaims God's "goodness and loving kindness" (Titus 3:4).

When preaching on Christmas morning, this morning's Luke passage is difficult to resist. Putting the Gospel text into conversation with Psalm 97 enriches it with insights that extreme familiarity with the Christmas story may have dulled for us and for our congregants. Expanding beyond the psalm's image of the mighty, fearsome God obscured by "clouds and thick darkness" (Ps. 97:2) and "most high over all the earth" (v. 9), Luke's Christmas story introduces Jesus as a humble, vulnerable, accessible newborn (Luke 2:12, 16–17). Luke's presentation of this immanent God-with-us does not exclude the ongoing existence of the transcendent God-above-all, of whom the heavenly host exclaim, "Glory to God in the highest heaven" (v. 14). In fact, Luke's scene of angels and shepherds echoes the psalm's line, "The heavens proclaim his righteousness; and all the peoples behold his glory" (Ps. 97:6). A sermon on the heavenly God and the earthly God could be fitting Christmas fare.

The psalm's repeated language of gladness and rejoicing (vv. 1, 8, 11, 12) is reiterated in the angel's "good news of great joy for all the people" (Luke 2:10). Other vocabulary from Psalm 97 resonates with themes explored in Lukan prophecies that point to this Gospel passage: "Light dawns for the righteous" (Ps. 97:11) is echoed in Zechariah's prophecy that "the dawn from on high will break upon us, to give light to those who sit in darkness" (Luke 1:78–79); and the psalmist's emphasis on righteousness and justice (Ps. 97:2, 6, 8, 11, 12) is sung again in Mary's Magnificat (Luke 1:51–55). A sermon on fulfilled prophecy could also suit Christmas.

As liturgy for Christmas morning, the psalm's closing lines are an obvious choice:

> Light dawns for the righteous;
> *and joy for the upright in heart.*
> Rejoice in the Lord, O you righteous, and
> give thanks to God's holy name!
> *Let us worship God, the Light of the world!*

Or focus on the psalm's interest in God as Ruler:

> The Lord is king!
> *Let the earth rejoice!*
> The heavens proclaim God's righteousness;
> *and all the peoples behold God's glory.*
> *Let us worship God, the newborn King!*

As for hymns, traditional carols that are particularly well suited to these texts include "Come, Thou Long-Expected Jesus," "Break Forth, O Beauteous Heavenly Light," "What Child Is This," and "What Star Is This, with Beams So Bright." For something beyond the strictly seasonal repertoire, "I Love the Lord, Who Heard My Cry" or "Holy, Holy, Holy! Lord God Almighty" would be admirable choices. Merry Christmas!

LEIGH CAMPBELL-TAYLOR

Titus 3:4–7

⁴But when the goodness and loving kindness of God our Savior appeared, ⁵he saved us, not because of any works of righteousness that we had done, but according to his mercy, through the water of rebirth and renewal by the Holy Spirit. ⁶This Spirit he poured out on us richly through Jesus Christ our Savior, ⁷so that, having been justified by his grace, we might become heirs according to the hope of eternal life.

Commentary 1: Connecting the Reading with Scripture

The concerns and worries caused by disruptive and rebellious teachers (1:10–16) and addressed in 2:11–15, remain at the fore in chapter 3. The goal is not the direct rebuttal of the teachers, but the preparation of the audience to assess their claims. Our author realizes that some debates are futile, and sometimes the best way to settle them is to provide an audience with deeper learning. Social-conduct advice is provided when the author reminds the audience to focus on their civic behavior (3:1–2). This is followed by a personal example in verse 3, which contrasts the author's past life with his current existence as a member of God's "own people" (2:14), and serves to introduce the verses that follow.

It is difficult to comprehend how Paul could have characterized his pre-Christ life as "foolish, disobedient, led astray," which are terms that typically described Gentiles, and why he would need to describe his ministry in full detail (1:3) to Titus, his coworker (2 Cor. 2:13; 7:6, 13–14; 8:6, 16, 23; 12:18; Gal. 2:1, 3), suggesting that it is best to understand the author as a disciple of Paul, who invokes the names of Paul and Titus to authorize his letter and its instructions. Thus, as the term "we ourselves" suggests, this teaching is not a departure from the foundational preaching of Paul, but its recapitulation. In effect, the author is alluding to Paul's own stringent argument in Galatians, where he forswears any teaching that undermines the gospel of God's grace (1:6–10). This enables the author to categorize the rebellious teachers (Titus 1:16)

as interlopers who will destroy the fabric of the community, while authenticating his advice as that of the apostle whose ministries founded and upheld Gentile communities such as this one (cf. Rom. 1:11; Phil. 1:8–11).

This is substantiated by the author's modification of Paul's Hellenistic Jewish language with a more straightforwardly Roman religious tone, to express the advent of Christ both in terms of its Jewish roots and in regard to the gods and goddesses of Greco-Roman religion. The effect is to underscore the moral and spiritual transformation that occurs once one has comprehended God's actions and the actions and ideas that emerge from it.

One can see this in the phrase "God our savior" found in verse 4. The expression is similar to "the manifestation of the glory of our great God and Savior, Jesus Christ" (2:13). In both cases, the collocation of God with Savior, rarely used by Paul (Phil. 3:20), but typical of the Pastoral Epistles (1 Tim. 1:1; 2:3; 4:10; 2 Tim. 1:10; Titus 1:3; 2:10, 13; 3:4, 6) and General Epistles (2 Pet. 1:1, 11; 2:20; 3:2, 18; Jude 25), recalls Hebrew traditions of Yahweh as deliverer, while also resonating with the claims of the imperial cult that identify the emperor as Savior (*Sōtēr*).[1]

The dynamic of the instructions remains the same as at 2:11–14; the proper mode of behavior while awaiting the appearance of Christ requires renouncing "impiety and worldly passions" (2:12–13). However, the author's warrants have changed. In the previous section, the author used creedal tenets as the basis for

---

1. See Martin Dibelius, *The Pastoral Epistles* (Philadelphia: Fortress Press, 1972), 143–46.

the advice. Here the liturgical act of baptism is specifically invoked. In verses 4–7, the author "re-creates" for the mind's eye the act of baptism and the pronouncements that would have accompanied the physical act of immersion and one's future behavior (cf. Rom. 6:1–11).

It is to these statements and act that the author refers with the phrase "This saying is sure" (*pistos ho logos*) in verse 8a, which recurs throughout the Pastorals (1 Tim. 1:15; 3:1; 4:9; 2 Tim. 1:12; 2:11; Titus 3:8), but it is not found outside of them in the New Testament. The author employs it in different manners: sometimes with reference to materials just mentioned (1 Tim. 4:9), sometimes to those that will follow (1 Tim. 1:15; 3:1; 2 Tim. 2:11); but in every case, it underscores the trustworthiness of the claims being made. Most interesting is that the phrase is used to sanction different elements of Christian belief and actions: creedal statements (1 Tim. 1:15; 2 Tim. 2:11), qualifications for the office of the overseer (*episkopos*) (1 Tim. 3:1), and spiritual discipline (1 Tim. 4:7–9). Here the author uses it to remind the audience of the true change that took place in baptism.[2]

The author is using a traditional piece of worship liturgy. Unfortunately its poetic structure is obscured by the NRSV formatting of the verses. In Greek this is a series of couplets, bounded by the contrast of acts of "righteousness" (not from works of righteousness [*dikaiosynē*]), done by humans (v. 5), and the act of "justification by [God's] grace" (*dikaiōthentes tē ekeinou chariti*, v. 7). These depict salvation as an act of God's mercy (v. 4). Physically demonstrated in the act of baptism (through the water of rebirth), the Spirit, "poured . . . richly," renews the initiate both externally and internally, that is, in body and spirit.

Verses 4–7 expand upon the dichotomy between past and present existence, initially through the exposition of God's goodness (*chrēstotēs*) and "loving kindness" (*philanthrōpia*), then by a more direct reference to the rite of baptism and the renewal provided by the Holy Spirit (vv. 5–6). The baptismal materials not only inform; they evoke specific memory of the exact moment of spiritual rebirth

and the confession that accompanied it. Here the "renunciation" language of 2:12 and the creation of a people "zealous for good deeds" (2:14) are located as the results of being incorporated into Christ.

The term "goodness" appears elsewhere in the NT only in Pauline materials. Here the author is likely alluding to Romans 11:22: "Note then the kindness [*chrēstotēta*] and the severity of God: severity toward those who have fallen, but God's kindness [*chrēstotēs*] toward you, provided that you continue in his kindness; otherwise you also will be cut off." Our author offers a similar contrast between God's kindness as the source of salvation, which creates a life reflective of that kindness in the "hope of eternal life," and prior existence that was enslaved by human passions. The contrast is one not simply of historical record but of existential reality, the transformation of the self that is possible with the "appearance" (*epephanē*) of "our savior God" in history. Even this transformation should be understood as penultimate, since, as the author expresses it, if the Christ believers, "having been justified by his [God's] grace," continue in their faithful lives, they will become "heirs according to the hope of eternal life" (v. 7).

"Appearance" recurs throughout the Pastoral Epistles (*epiphainō*, cf. Titus 2:11, 13; *epiphaneias*, 1 Tim. 6:14; 2 Tim. 1:10; 4:8). As in 2:11, verse 4 reasserts that Jesus' actions were not incidental, but evidence of God's goodness and loving kindness (cf. 3:7; Rom. 5:1–11; Eph. 2:3–10). In this instance, the tradition is a reminder that the Savior Jesus opens the promise of inheritance of a birthright (cf. Gal. 4:7; Heb. 2:10–18). The terms "rebirth" (*palingenesias*) and "renewal" (*anakainōseōs*) (v. 5) recall the rite that incorporated them into Christ and into a communion of believers. A transformation occurred, enabling them to live in proper relationship with God, through God's mercy, goodness, and loving-kindness. Thus, at the deepest core of their existence, they must remember that they have been reconstituted, and so act according to the "hope of eternal life" (cf. 2:13; Gal. 5:13–26; Col. 3:1–4).

STEVEN J. KRAFTCHICK

---

2. See A. T. Hanson, *The Pastoral Epistles* (Grand Rapids: Eerdmans, 1982), 64.

Commentary 2: Connecting the Reading with the World

The Letter to Titus rates high in intensity. Its passion, even its vitriol, against the false teachings lurking in this community leads to language that is anything but mild (2:15–16; 3:9–11). This intensity—as in other letters of the New Testament, Galatians being the chief example—arises out of the deep concern to maintain the uncompromising graciousness of the gospel. Titus says that God "saved us, not because of any works of righteousness that we had done, but according to his mercy" (3:5). The false teachers in the community are quarreling about human righteousness (3:9–10), but no human righteousness, wherever it comes from, can compete with the mercy given by God. Titus 3:4–7 proclaims that great grace and so deserves careful attention as it celebrates the truth of the gospel, over against the pervasive and insidious teaching of human performance.

The echoes of Titus 2:11–14, the epistle reading for Christmas Eve, reverberate in Titus 3:4–7, the epistle reading for Christmas Day. Both speak of God and God's work, yet the emphases in Titus 3 are almost comprehensive. Students of the Bible are hard pressed to find a major theological category this passage does not cover: God, the Spirit, Jesus Christ, righteousness, regeneration, salvation, grace, hope, and eternal life, to name a few. Hence this passage offers the preacher an opportunity to proclaim the good news with incredible richness on Christmas Day.

This biblical text offers a powerful word of comfort for the church, especially in the sometimes stressful atmosphere of Christmas. In proclaiming so many amazing things that God has done for God's people—saved, washed, renewed, and justified them—Titus 3 makes it clear that none of these gifts was won by any works of righteousness that "we had done" (v. 5). This is the simple truth of the gospel, *sola gratia*; but on this day the gathered church may very much need to hear, even more than usual, the proclamation that God's mercy is not earned. The congregation may very well have in mind their need to be perfect—to host the perfect gathering, to bring the perfect gift, to wear the perfect clothes—on this day in which time slows and everything counts for so much because it comes only once a year. Christmas is, this text reminds, a celebration of *God's* good and loving appearing. That is what truly matters, no matter how amazing, or dismal, one is feeling on this Christmas morning; that grace comes richly (v. 6) through the Spirit and the Lord Jesus. This service, with the preaching of this text, can be a place of repose for the congregation. God's self-revelation makes grace abundant, no matter what any one person does or cannot do.

The church can be invited to respond with liturgy and song in affirmation of this amazing grace. The widely used hymn "Rock of Ages" sings of this unearned grace. It also appeals to the washing and salvation proclaimed here in Titus 3, and could provide a sung view of this salvation. The prayers of the service can also give the congregation an opportunity to listen and echo the profound truths of this passage. For example, the Catholic preface for the Mass at Dawn reflects the epiphany of Christmas, as well as the promised inheritance to be in God's kingdom, including the lines,

> though invisible in his own divine nature,
> he has appeared visibly in ours;
> so that he might . . . call straying humanity
>   back to the heavenly Kingdom.

The traditional collect for Christmas morning in the *Book of Common Prayer* offers these words for prayer that focus upon the regeneration and renewal proclaimed in the Titus passage:

> Almighty God. . . grant that we, being regenerate and made thy children by adoption and grace, may daily be renewed by thy Holy Spirit, through the same our Lord Jesus Christ.[3]

As congregants both hear and say the message of saving grace, they can be strengthened in their faith.

3. The Episcopal Church, *The Book Of Common Prayer* (New York: Seabury Press, 1979), 161.

In addition, Titus 3's reflection on the undeserved nature of salvation, the regeneration and renewal that come from God's mercy and not our works, lends itself to stirring examples from literature or film. Bishop Myriel's forgiveness and gifts to Jean Valjean in Victor Hugo's *Les Miserables* provide a classic expression of renewal prompted by undeserved grace. Valjean in turn shows mercy in his care of Fantine, the woman he rescues from a life of trafficking.

This story of grace—received and then given—points to another aspect of this passage. A focus upon grace does not indicate that Titus 3 advocates laziness with regard to moral behavior. In fact, the verses right before and after this eloquent—even poetic—reflection on God's grace call the congregation to behave in particular ways. Luther entitled his sermon on this text "God's Grace Received Must Be Bestowed."[4] The Letter to Titus states that the recipients were previously "in malice and envy, despicable, hating one another" (v. 3), but now that they have experienced God's grace, the author asks them to practice good works (v. 8), specifically to avoid controversies and dissensions (v. 9). This text calls the members of the church to be the radical agents of God's inbreaking kingdom through simple acts of civility, such as hospitality (1:8), self-control (1:8), sound speech (2:8), and the avoidance of factiousness (3:10). The message of God's grace in Christ cannot be compromised, but many things outside of that are not worth a battle. If congregants are on their way to a Christmas gathering, this is an imminently practical word: Be peacemakers, and in so doing you will be a lived demonstration of the Holy Spirit that has been poured out upon you.

After proclaiming God's grace and issuing a call to good works, the preacher might conclude with a focus upon God's action in the passage, lest the exhortation for good actions negate the message about grace. The passage consistently speaks of God taking the initiative. Motivated by mercy (3:5c), God saves through water, which brings about new birth, and the Holy Spirit, which makes the person new. This would be a perfect opportunity to remind the congregants of the transformation that was wrought in them through their baptism. God sends the Spirit to work through the tangible means of water to effect this great change. God does not do this in a small way but pours out this salvation abundantly (3:6).

Luther unites the message about grace and works in this way: "Take note, God pours out upon us in baptism super-abundant blessings for the purpose of excluding the works whereby men [*sic*] foolishly presume to merit heaven and gain happiness. Yes, dear friend, you must first possess heaven and salvation before you can do good works."[5] It is God's action both in the past and in the future that motivates those who hear their own story in this passage. Having been made righteous by his grace (3:7a), they look forward in hope to the inheritance of unending life (3:7b). Titus 3 offers, on Christmas morning, a chance to reset one's vision on God's unexpected appearing and its amazing grace.

AMY PEELER

4. Martin Luther, "Second Christmas Sermon: Titus 3:4–8," in *Sermons of Martin Luther*, ed. John Nicholas Lenker, trans. John Nicholas Lenker et al. (Grand Rapids: Baker, 1983), 6:142–65.

5. Ibid., 151.

Luke 2:(1–7) 8–20

¹In those days a decree went out from Emperor Augustus that all the world should be registered. ²This was the first registration and was taken while Quirinius was governor of Syria. ³All went to their own towns to be registered. ⁴Joseph also went from the town of Nazareth in Galilee to Judea, to the city of David called Bethlehem, because he was descended from the house and family of David. ⁵He went to be registered with Mary, to whom he was engaged and who was expecting a child. ⁶While they were there, the time came for her to deliver her child. ⁷And she gave birth to her firstborn son and wrapped him in bands of cloth, and laid him in a manger, because there was no place for them in the inn.

⁸In that region there were shepherds living in the fields, keeping watch over their flock by night. ⁹Then an angel of the Lord stood before them, and the glory of the Lord shone around them, and they were terrified. ¹⁰But the angel said to them, "Do not be afraid; for see—I am bringing you good news of great joy for all the people: ¹¹to you is born this day in the city of David a Savior, who is the Messiah, the Lord. ¹²This will be a sign for you: you will find a child wrapped in bands of cloth and lying in a manger." ¹³And suddenly there was with the angel a multitude of the heavenly host, praising God and saying,

¹⁴Glory to God in the highest heaven,
   and on earth peace among those whom he favors!"

¹⁵When the angels had left them and gone into heaven, the shepherds said to one another, "Let us go now to Bethlehem and see this thing that has taken place, which the Lord has made known to us." ¹⁶So they went with haste and found Mary and Joseph, and the child lying in the manger. ¹⁷When they saw this, they made known what had been told them about this child; ¹⁸and all who heard it were amazed at what the shepherds told them. ¹⁹But Mary treasured all these words and pondered them in her heart. ²⁰The shepherds returned, glorifying and praising God for all they had heard and seen, as it had been told them.

Commentary 1: Connecting the Reading with Scripture

The lectionary appoints Luke 2:1–20 for both Christmas Eve and Christmas Day. This essay discusses 2:8–20 and the previous one 2:1–7, since those are the two basic scenes in the first part of chapter 2. The passage itself is composed of two parts, verses 8–14 and verses 15–20. The first describes an angelic announcement to some shepherds in fields surrounding Bethlehem; the second describes the various responses to that announcement.

Angels are ubiquitous in the Old Testament, appearing over a hundred times as God's messengers to human beings or as courtiers who serve in God's presence. The first angel to appear to the shepherds in Luke 2 is identified as "an

angel of the Lord" and is accompanied by "the glory of the Lord" that shines all around the shepherds and terrifies them (v. 9). Angels are routinely seen as frightening, signaling not only their heavenly origins but also their capacity to speak and act on God's authority.

There is no small irony in the words "Do not be afraid" in verse 10, since fear is always the inevitable—and proper—response to seeing God (Gen. 15:1; 21:17; 22:12; 26:24). God's glory is overwhelming in its power; human beings cannot tolerate an unmitigated encounter with God's presence. Recall the ways Moses and Elijah hide their faces rather than gaze directly on the presence of God (Exod. 3:6; 1

Kgs. 19:13; cf. Gen. 16:13; 32:30; Judg. 13:22; Isa. 6:2). Sometimes there is a particular figure, "*the* angel of the LORD," who seems to be "almost another designation for God" (Gen. 16:7–13; Exod. 3:2; Num. 22:22).[1] That seems to be the case here, because, once the angel assures the shepherds that they have no need to fear because he brings them good news, he is joined by the "multitude of the heavenly host" (v. 13), all of God's court, as it were, celebrating the announcement of the Messiah's birth (see Deut. 4:19; 17:3; 1 Kgs. 22:19).

The angel's message is remarkable. "Do not be afraid; for see—I am bringing you good news of great joy for all the people: to you is born this day in the city of David a Savior, who is the Messiah, the Lord" (vv. 10–11). "Messiah," *Christos* in Greek, means "anointed." Although it is not always a royal designation—priests are anointed as well as kings (Exod. 28:41)—it is clearly intended here to refer to a king, since Bethlehem is identified as the city of David, the quintessential Israelite king. "Savior" and "Lord," though, are traditional epithets reserved for the Roman emperor, and Luke here applies them instead to the child Jesus. That Israel's God is so often referred to as "Lord," when *Adonai* replaces God's unspoken name *YHWH*, must

---

1. James M. Efird, "Angel of the Lord," in *HarperCollins Bible Dictionary*, ed. Paul J. Achtemeier (San Francisco: HarperSanFrancisco, 1996), 34.

How Do We Hear?

And so it is: the Christmas message, with its claim to be heard, demands a first decision from us. The Church does not really know herself unless she shows now that she is even more conscious of her human helplessness than "the children of this world," and humbles herself with all the world and before all the world to hear the message anew.

No one can say how it is done, not even the most devout and learned theologians of all times have been able to give the slightest hint of how one comes to hear the Christmas message. All we can say about hearing this message, hinges on the fact that it speaks for itself. We cannot reach it ourselves and we cannot even prepare for it, for such preparing would really be conforming with it. A bright Advent-tide must therefore borrow its light from a Christmas that, obviously, follows it. To know the Savior who is to come, we must first know the Savior who has come already. And help which can be obtained by some device of our own, is not the real, ultimate help. If the hearing of the Christmas message depended on the help we give ourselves, what else would we hear but something we can suggest to ourselves, and this would not alter our state of helplessness. This can mean one thing only; that in the night of Christ's Nativity the shepherds were told by the angel: "To you is born this day a savior." We cannot produce the angel, nor can we wait for him, as one waits for an inspiration or an experience. Inspirations and experiences are human possibilities. If we waited for them, we would look for something that we can tell ourselves. However, what we could tell ourselves, would not get us out of our helplessness. The angel is the *divine* possibility of human understanding, but one cannot ask if this possibility will occur one day, or hour. We must ask, however, if the angel is not already in our midst and is not speaking to us (in the manner in which angels do stand among men and talk to them) and if we are not being told before we have even begun to listen: "To you is born this day a Savior."

We cannot persuade ourselves or others that the angel stands in our midst and tells us that God has "prepared" us to listen. Perhaps we neither have had nor will have any spiritual experience or inspiration, and if we had, we might be rightly suspicious of it. But if God has prepared us to listen, then we do not need these things; for we are ordinary people, just as the shepherds were, and will listen with a sober mind. The Christmas story itself might pose the question for us: "Has not God Himself prepared us to listen and have we not already heard the message, while we are still asking if and how we can hear it?"

Karl Barth (1886–1968), "Hearing the Christmas Message: 1928," in *Christmas,* trans. Bernhard Citron (London: Oliver and Boyd, 1959), 26.

---

certainly have held resonance for first-century Christians; here, though, it is clearly taken from the emperor and given to a peasant infant. The good news (*euangelion*) in Greco-Roman society usually refers to Caesar's conquests and the much vaunted *Pax Romana* he imposes on his enemies. This Jesus looks nothing like Caesar, and all of these terms—anointed, savior, Lord, and good news—are redefined by the birth of this child.

The angel also announces a sign: "a child wrapped in bands of cloth and lying in a manger" (v. 12). Signs are portents, worldly events that point to heavenly or divinely ordered realities. This sign too proclaims a reversal of kingly expectations. The commonplace swaddling of an infant and the less common use of an animal trough for a baby bed suggest this child is anything but royal, despite his being Messiah, Savior, and Lord. He is indeed the king, but not one like Caesar, because he rules not with violence but with justice. Another recipient of a theophany hears the very same words. As Moses approaches the burning bush on Sinai, God says to him, "This shall be the sign for you that it is I who sent you: when you have brought the people out of Egypt, you shall worship God on this mountain" (Exod. 3:12).

Both signs point forward to acts of redemption yet to come: Moses and Israel will indeed worship God on Sinai, and the shepherds will see Christ the Lord. Several other momentous events in the Bible also share the divine promise that "this shall be the sign": Samuel's anointing of Saul (1 Sam. 10:1), Isaiah's promise to Hezekiah that God will defend the holy city against the Assyrians (2 Kgs. 19:29; Isa. 37:30), and Jeremiah's prophecy that God will punish the Judeans in Egypt for their faithlessness (Jer. 44:29). Jesus' birth in Bethlehem is the sign of what kind of king he will be: one whose power appears in weakness, whose life is marked by poverty and marginality, whose anointing by God destines him to be what Simeon calls "the falling and the rising of many in Israel, and . . . a sign that will be opposed" (2:34).

The angels' words of praise and benediction, what the church calls the Gloria in Excelsis, celebrate not only God's glory but also the peace the Messiah's birth portends for the world:

"Glory to God in the highest heaven, and on earth peace among those whom he favors!" (v. 14). The peace Jesus will bring is nothing like the *Pax Romana*; it is the *shalom* God intends for all creation, not a cessation of hostilities, but the fullness of life lived in God's presence, marked by justice and wholeness. God plans to reunite heaven and earth in the person of Jesus and the community he forms.

In the second half of this passage Luke reports a range of human responses to the angelic message. First, the shepherds act immediately: they go "with haste" (v. 16) to see what the Lord has told them. The great joy of the announcement and the promised peace from God are good news indeed. They find Mary, Joseph, and Jesus just as they have been told, and then they make known to others what they have seen and heard (v. 17). Everyone who learns their news is amazed by it, likely for the same reason the shepherds are (v. 18). Back in Bethlehem, "Mary treasure[s] all these words and ponder[s] them in her heart" (v. 19), presaging her other appearances in Luke's story,[2] particularly 2:51, where she keeps "all the words" (my trans.) about the child Jesus in the temple "in her heart." Finally, the shepherds return, "glorifying and praising God" (2:20). The shepherds join the heavenly chorus in praise of God. The various responses to the angelic announcement are likely designed to show readers how we are expected to respond—with obedience, proclamation, amazement, joy, and reflection.

The other lessons for Christmas Day—Isaiah 62:6–12; Psalm 97; Titus 3:4–7—all speak of theophanies, appearances of God to humans. Isaiah says, "The LORD has proclaimed to the end of the earth: Say to daughter Zion, 'See, your salvation comes; his reward is with him, and his recompense before him'" (62:11), which also points to the inevitable pairing of judgment and redemption that marks all of Luke–Acts. The psalmist says, "All the peoples behold [God's] glory" (Ps. 97:6), just as the angel tells the shepherds that the Messiah's birth is for "all people." The Letter to Titus says, "the goodness and loving kindness of God our Savior appeared" when Christ came (3:4).

E. ELIZABETH JOHNSON

---

2. Luke 2:22–52; 8:19–21; Acts 1:14.

Commentary 2: Connecting the Reading with the World

The appointed Gospel readings for Christmas Eve and Christmas Day are the same. Is this a good idea? Why preach the same text on two consecutive days? What determines the difference in how the same account is preached twice in a matter of hours?

The lectionary provides the first determining factor. Though the entirety of Luke 2:1–20 is given for both days, the Christmas Eve assignment sets verses 15–20 in parentheses, leaving the spotlight on Caesar's decree, the journey to Bethlehem, the birth, the manger, the announcement to shepherds, and the song of angels. Christmas Day sets verses 1–7 in parentheses, thus spotlighting the announcement to shepherds, the song of angels, the shepherds' visit to the manger, their testifying, Mary's pondering, and the shepherds' praise. Even with the overlap of verses 8–14, Christmas Eve accents the birth and Christmas Day accents responses to the birth.

The other justification for proclaiming the same story on Christmas Day as on Christmas Eve is that we have now entered a new kind of time. Telling or hearing a story in the broad light of morning is different from telling or hearing it in a candlelit night. The time gives the telling its particular tone—and this is all the more true of liturgical time. Christmas Eve is the apogee and fulfillment of expectation; the season of waiting comes to its happy conclusion. Christmas Day is the first day of a new season, twelve days of grateful responsiveness to the now-given promised child. For the secular culture, Christmas Day constitutes an ending; in the church, it is a beginning. We may be proclaiming a story that was told only hours ago, but we do so in new and perhaps more purposeful accents.

The Christmas Day nonbracketed portion of Luke 2:1–20 begins and ends with the shepherds. We should not lose sight of the fact that sheepherders were held in very low esteem in first-century Palestine. They were generally regarded as liars and thieves, were religiously "unclean," and were disallowed even from testifying in court. (Given their alleged noncredibility, the shepherds' eyewitness report of Jesus' birth is in striking parallel to the women's eyewitness report of his resurrection.) Anyone who feels like a distinctly unlikely candidate for divine encounter or for living a life of effective witness has a point of contact with these herders of sheep.

The extent of the story's focus on these men is remarkable. Notice the abundance of personal pronouns: the angel stood before *them*, the glory shone around *them*, the angel said to *them*: I bring *you* good news, to *you* is born, this will be a sign to *you*, *you* will find. The news has singled them out and honored them in the most exquisitely personal way. Heaven has chosen sheepherders, and makes them indispensable to the story. In fact, many more verses in Luke 2:1–20 refer to the shepherds than to Mary, Joseph, Jesus, or the angels. Strangely too, almost every Christmas carol we sing makes reference to them. The Christmas story is surely most of all about Jesus, but the shepherds are onstage far longer, as if his story cannot be told apart from theirs. Can the church ever speak of Jesus without telling of the outsiders to whom he is always joined?

They play their role perfectly. Having *heard*, they decide to go and *see*—a move so important that, instead of simply narrating it, the story tells how they encouraged each other to do it: "Let us go now to Bethlehem and see . . ." With this line, we have entered that part of the story that was in parentheses—optional—for Christmas Eve. The lectionary understands that the part of the story belonging especially to Christmas Day begins here: the act of *moving toward* the Christ child and *experiencing* the truth for ourselves.

We may wish to imagine that the shepherds brought gifts, as some of our carols and songs suggest; but that is for a different sort of visitor. The only business of the shepherds, for now at least, is to approach and to gaze at the child. This is the primary invitation of Christmas Day: to "see this thing that has taken place"—not to give, but to take in, to absorb, to imagine, to be grateful, to worship.

In the case of the shepherds, it leads to something else. Having finished seeing, they set about *telling*. "When they saw this, they made known what had been told them about this child, and all who heard it were amazed at what the shepherds told them" (vv. 17–18). Wonder opens outward into bearing witness. Given their low social status, we can imagine they are telling the news to marginalized people like themselves. The angel had told them that the good news of great joy is to be "for all the people," and already the shepherds are getting it started. We notice especially the change that has overtaken them. When we first met them, they were shaking with terror; now they are unabashed and eager to speak of all they have seen and heard,

The 1965 television Christmas special *A Charlie Brown Christmas* makes a nice, if subtle, reference to the change. Linus takes his place onstage to recite the Christmas story from Luke. As always, he is holding the security blanket that he is never, ever without. When he speaks the words, "Fear not," he lets his blanket slip from his hand and tells the rest of the story, using that hand to be more expressive as he speaks. True, when he is finished and ready to exit, he picks up the blanket again; but later we see him with his friends, now completely without it. News of God-with-us in the holy child is meant to take away our fear; but our newfound fearlessness is best discovered in sharing the news, and is mostly for the purpose of expressing it with greater abandon.

There is more to tell about the shepherds, but first we are shown Mary again, who unlike the shepherds did not go out and tell, but "treasured all these words [or things] and pondered them in her heart." Perhaps we can see in these words not only the unique role and remarkable depth of Mary, but also a necessary balance in the community of faith. The church must be publicly, visibly, and audibly expressive of our news; but we must also reflect, consider, imagine, meditate, and pray. We are communities of speech and silence, of action and reflection, of breadth and depth. We are active and we are contemplative. We are the shepherds who "made known what they had been told," and we are Mary, who "pondered these things in her heart." A church that does not engage in the practice of both has little future.

Neither are we complete without the final action of the shepherds, who, as they returned, were "glorifying and praising God." It is exactly what they had seen and heard when it all began. Out in the dark fields, the glory of the Lord shone around them, and the angels were praising God and singing, "Glory!" The shepherds are now exactly as doxological as the angels had been. They have, in fact, taken the place of the angels, bringing to others good news of great joy, and glorifying and praising God.

The Christmas Day Gospel describes responsiveness to the child. Angels proclaim to the unlikely and sing praise. Shepherds draw near and see and bear witness and glorify. Mary treasures and ponders. Our glad part in the unfinished, ongoing pageant of Christmas is to be all of them at once together.

PAUL SIMPSON DUKE

Christmas Day/Nativity of the Lord, Proper III

Isaiah 52:7–10
Psalm 98

Hebrews 1:1–4 (5–12)
John 1:1–14

Isaiah 52:7–10

7How beautiful upon the mountains
    are the feet of the messenger who announces peace,
who brings good news,
    who announces salvation,
    who says to Zion, "Your God reigns."
8Listen! Your sentinels lift up their voices,
    together they sing for joy;
for in plain sight they see
    the return of the LORD to Zion.
9Break forth together into singing,
    you ruins of Jerusalem;
for the LORD has comforted his people,
    he has redeemed Jerusalem.
10The LORD has bared his holy arm
    before the eyes of all the nations;
and all the ends of the earth shall see
    the salvation of our God.

Commentary 1: Connecting the Reading with Scripture

The triumphant mood of the liturgy on Christmas Day provides the setting for the announcement of Isaiah 52:7–10. Will the congregation prick up their ears to this ancient message delivered to the redeemed people of God after years in exile? Will the congregation join in a song of profound joy and thanksgiving to the God who has restored the ruins of Jerusalem rather than sing insipid tunes of anticipation of the soon-to-arrive Santa Claus? Will the preacher replace the radical vision of peace-through-strength in verse 7 with the radical hope of the Prince of Peace who eschews violence as Christmas Day is celebrated?

In rehearsing the promise of Israel's salvation, Isaiah 52:7–10 includes four scenes that bring to the foreground two related aspects that contemporary Christmas celebrations may fail to address: (1) salvation as a *collective* event, after more than a generation suffered exile, and (2) salvation as an event that is *intergenerational.*

Scene 1 is the victorious messenger's announcement from "the mountains" (v. 7). Isaiah describes the messenger's arrival on the mountain from the perspective of Jerusalem. The city's topography offers no natural defense on its northern border, which, as a consequence, is its strategically weakest point. The victorious messenger most likely drew near from the northern hills, today's Mount Scopus, northwest of the Mount of Olives.

Scene 2 contains the joyful shouting at the messenger's arrival (v. 8), when "in plain sight they see the return of the LORD to Zion" (v. 8). For Isaiah, God's good news always necessitates a joyful response.

Scene 3 is the prophet's invitation for a downcast people to "break forth into singing" (v. 9), because God has comforted the people and restored them to the holy city.

Finally, scene 4 promises that God's redemptive work is not limited to Jerusalem, but "all the ends of the earth shall see the salvation of our God" (v. 10). Surely, on Christmas Day the prophet's song is a carol for any congregation to sing.

Isaiah 52:7–10 in the Context of the Whole Book. The announcement of the messenger is part of the reflection on salvation throughout Isaiah 51–52. Isaiah 52:7–10 is one stanza of a poem, with each stanza opening with repeated imperatives. The poem portrays the new beginnings in a universal reflection of the (collective) history. Yahweh, the God of Judah, is the driving force behind every historical event. History is the stage upon which the drama of the divine will takes place. Deutero-Isaiah explicates this claim in light of his "monotheism." Consequently, the poem appeals first to Yahweh to come to the help of the people in Isaiah 51:9–11. Next, the poem speaks to the city of Zion, calling it to "rouse" and "awake" in 51:17–18 and 52:1–4. Finally, the poem directs its attention to the exiles as they leave Babylon to return to Jerusalem in 52:11–12. The God at work in Isaiah is immanent and active in bringing about restoration from exile and a new beginning for those still haunted by the past.

The theme of comfort (52:9) echoes in the beginning of the majestic overture in Isaiah 40:1–11: "Comfort, O comfort . . ." What does Isaiah mean by "comfort"? Comforting means to escape punishment. The comforter pauses, takes a breath, and rethinks the judgment, rather than executing it. In Isaiah, comforting means for God to interrupt the cycle of punishment in response to the people's transgression. For the convicted city of Jerusalem it means that they are spared any additional punishment, and that any pending verdict will be annulled. Seen through the lens of the city prophet of Jerusalem, the visible token of Yahweh's return to Zion (v. 8) is Jerusalem's restoration, an act that first presumes the forgiveness of guilt as proclaimed by Yahweh. In this regard, this text from Isaiah might challenge the Christmas Day preacher to reflect on how the coming of God entails the forgiveness of sin and the wiping away of guilt.

This text is full of difficult war metaphors. Yahweh's arm is a metaphor for power: God actively engages in history and fights on behalf of Israel. The victorious messenger's announcement of peace typically comes to the winners in battle (v. 7), and the metaphor (v. 10) of revealing a "holy arm" in the eyes of all nations is an image for Yahweh's military strength in Israel's favor. "Salvation," from the Hebrew verb *ys'*, "to come to help, save," designates coming to aid a covenant partner, usually by means of military power.

Isaiah 52:7–10 unfolds the proclamation of victory that is entirely grounded in divine help to which Judah could not contribute. How powerful it could be for preachers to take a text that celebrates the spoils of war made possible by God's military might, and on Christmas Day to help a congregation imagine the "beautiful feet" of messengers who bring a nonviolent word of salvation from God, who traffics not in violence but in the redemptive work of peace. What if preachers contrasted the violent, redemptive theology of Isaiah 52:7–10 with the Gospel portrayal of a Savior who eschews violence, even while being a victim of violence?

Eschatology in Isaiah. Deutero-Isaiah's postexilic proclamation intends to open itself toward the future. Spoken in today's context, the announcement of a victory may be heard equally as announcement of a victory yet to come. Isaiah 52:7–10 is rooted in the book of Isaiah's eschatological worldview. The designation "our God," points to the historical nation of Judah: Salvation takes place in a personal relationship between the Judean God Yahweh and God's people as a collective. It takes shape in Judah as a geographical space. Preachers are called to name for their congregation where and how they see signs of eschatological change happening in their midst and how they may point to the ongoing redemptive work of God.

In this text, Yahweh's involvement oscillates between the poles of small-scale Judean realities and a universal scale. Should preachers reflect on their own "political theology" on Christmas Day? Yes. Four options present themselves to preachers: First, they might strip the announcement of victory from any historical content and read it individualistically as announcement of success for one person. This is an option that neglects the grand scale of the announcement of God's saving work in Isaiah 52:7–10. Second, they might choose to read this text historically and biblically in light of Judah's history, and then to unpack its message in a reflection on overcoming a national or a collective defeat in light of the experience of a rise to power. This is an option that supposes salvation is the handiwork of the people of God, rather than an underserved and astounding gift from God. Third, preachers may read Isaiah 52:7–10 with an eye toward Christ's second coming. This is an option that needs to be navigated with care, lest Isaiah be wrenched from its historical and theological context. Finally, preachers may point to signs of restoration in the midst of broken places and broken people today. This option allows for preachers to be the "beautiful feet" of those who point to the ongoing redemptive work of God.

As preachers approach worship on Christmas Day, consider the power of first singing these less familiar words when walking to Bethlehem: "How beautiful upon the mountains are the feet of the messenger who announces peace, who brings good news, who announces salvation, who says to Zion, 'Your God reigns'" (v. 7).

KLAUS-PETER ADAM

Commentary 2: Connecting the Reading with the World

With an exuberant heart, Isaiah proclaims a message that gets to the heart of Christmas. His words provide an abundance of images for the preacher to consider. The image of the messenger's feet helps us immediately envision the news bearer as dusty, dirty, hot, sweaty, and exhausted after running a far distance to reach Jerusalem. Travel in the ancient world was physical and hard. Only royalty or high-ranking military officials would have access to a chariot. Riding a donkey would be luxury transportation for most people. (The Hebrew word for "to go" is the same as the word "to walk" [*halach*].) The prophet appreciates the arduous journey of the messenger who has endured hot, stony roads and all their inherent perils to arrive at the holy city and with breathless joy.

The sentinels understand the glory that the messenger's arrival portends and lift up their voices in singing (v. 8). They are delighted because their God has returned home to Zion, a mountain on which Jerusalem is built. This passage invites reflection on how singing expresses the depths of our souls in times of joyful reunion, perhaps at Christmas.

While filled with gladness, this passage comes after a painful period in Israel's history. In 587 BCE, the Babylonians conquered Judah and forced many of the people to leave their homes in the capital of Jerusalem. The Judeans (henceforth known as Jews) were forced to trek to Babylon (in modern-day Iraq), a walk of about nine hundred miles, where they remained in exile for fifty years. The prophet Ezekiel, writing during this time, has visions of God also in Babylon with the people (see Ezek. 1:1–3). God leaves Jerusalem with the people, abandoning God's own home in the temple. In this way, God is a refugee.

Another window into this text would be to invite listeners to see God in the face of refugees today, which is a staggering prospect. In 2017, the United Nations Refugee Agency reported that a stunning sixty-five million people were displaced around the globe. A refugee is someone who flees conflict or persecution in a recognized conflict and thereby is protected through international law from returning to their country. Refugees may have to endure harsh weather, precarious travel, dangerous living conditions, and merciless traffickers. Approximately twenty million people fit this definition of refugees now, over half of whom are children.[1] They leave their homes, often in ruins, to face an uncertain future.

A vision of a city in ruins can still be seen amid a modern-day pilgrimage to Jerusalem. Ruins abound. Low walls of limestone arranged in outlines of houses, stairs, or ritual baths silently whisper with muffled echoes from lives lived many centuries ago. Even in Isaiah's day, Jerusalem already had a long history. Predating King David, who reigned 1000–960 BCE and made Jerusalem the capital city of his kingdom, Jerusalem was a Jebusite stronghold belonging to the Canaanite people. No doubt ruins of

---

1. "Figures at a Glance," United Nations High Commissioner for Refugees, http://www.unhcr.org/en-us/figures-at-a-glance.html, accessed Jan. 28, 2017.

buildings littered Jerusalem in Isaiah's time too. This text speaks to those who find themselves separated from their home, a daunting proposition for many, refugee or not, especially at Christmas.

Preachers might explain why Isaiah addresses heaps of stones, an ostensibly odd action. The prophet's command, "Break forth together into singing, you ruins of Jerusalem," is like that of the prophet Habakkuk, who also called on stones to speak (Hab. 2:11). Later Jesus tells of stones that might cry out (Luke 19:40). Isaiah's words can prompt congregants to notice what they see in their neighborhoods and their homes, and how God gives them voice to sing even amid the rubble.

Preachers can speak from Isaiah's text to point out that the surroundings in our homes on Christmas Day speak volumes about our lives. Are there presents? Can we afford them? Is there someone to give them to? In many homes, heaps of perfectly wrapped presents look like piles of ruin after the wrapping has been torn off and thrown on the floor. Crumpled paper testifies to the exuberance of exchanging gifts. What we give to each other says a lot about us: our values, our economics, our culture, and our relationships. When relationships are broken, what kinds of gifts can reach across the divides of separation and division? Not only as individuals, but also in our communities and churches and among nations, we need to remember that the intangible gifts most valued are those that create an atmosphere of trust and appreciation, and even joy.

Preachers can reflect on the meaning of peace for people who need it most. Isaiah's image of the people of Jerusalem as comforted and singing together may feel as utopian to us as it did to those who first heard this euphoric prophecy. The ruins of Jerusalem today are not just the rubble of places but the ash heap of peace. The city is a military zone, with ubiquitous soldiers holding machine guns, a threat to those who would challenge Israeli rule. Palestinians maintain that they have had their homes destroyed and been driven from their ancestral lands, forced to live as refugees. Israelis counter that the land belongs to them as a refuge, promised since the time of Abraham, a homeland for Jews

who had none. Nowhere is this conflict more obvious than in Jerusalem. How sadly ironic that the "city of peace" is where peace feels nearly impossible today amid the ruins of distrust, denial, fear, and hatred. Is redemption from this political pit even possible?

At Christmas we speak of "peace on earth," while peace can feel so far away. Peace advocates and activists offer a solution that is as simple as it is hard: empower moderate voices. Why do the voices of calm and reason seem so hard to hear? When it seems that only shouting can be heard in social and political discourse, a preacher can suggest that it may be time to whisper. We need to aim for the goal of understanding. Why does the other person feel or think so differently? Listening to someone else and affirming any common ground can create a bridge of connection. When tempers flare and divisions emerge, both interpersonally and internationally, we do well to seek out the voices of calm and reason. Better, we can offer that voice.

When reading Isaiah, we may hear the voice of a baritone singing "comfort" from the aria in Handel's *Messiah,* "Comfort ye my people." The Lord is the comforter in Isaiah 52:9. Christmas can also be a comforting time when we are fortunate enough to be among people who love us and have all our bodily needs met. To live in comfort is a great blessing that we can all too easily take for granted. As preachers know, remembering our blessings puts many of our problems in perspective and can lead to a sense of comfort. However, the comfort of which Isaiah speaks is not having all our bodily needs met, but being met with the profound peace of God that brings comfort to our chaotic lives and calls us to bring comfort to others.

This passage ends with Isaiah's affirmation of God's power and strength (v. 10). It is easy to feel very small in the face of all the daunting forces that seek to hurt and destroy in this world. Yet no problem is too big—or too little—for God. The message of the church is that of Isaiah and the message of the tiny baby who incarnates God: may all the earth know the salvation of the Lord.

JULIE FAITH PARKER

Psalm 98

[1]O sing to the LORD a new song,
　　for he has done marvelous things.
His right hand and his holy arm
　　have gotten him victory.
[2]The LORD has made known his victory;
　　he has revealed his vindication in the sight of the nations.
[3]He has remembered his steadfast love and faithfulness
　　to the house of Israel.
All the ends of the earth have seen
　　the victory of our God.

[4]Make a joyful noise to the LORD, all the earth;
　　break forth into joyous song and sing praises.
[5]Sing praises to the LORD with the lyre,
　　with the lyre and the sound of melody.
[6]With trumpets and the sound of the horn
　　make a joyful noise before the King, the LORD.

[7]Let the sea roar, and all that fills it;
　　the world and those who live in it.
[8]Let the floods clap their hands;
　　let the hills sing together for joy
[9]at the presence of the LORD, for he is coming
　　to judge the earth.
He will judge the world with righteousness,
　　and the peoples with equity.

Connecting the Psalm with Scripture and Worship

The psalm for Christmas night is close kin to our psalm for Christmas Eve. Both open with "O sing to the LORD a new song" (Pss. 96:1; 98:1), both reference God's laudable works (96:3; 98:1), both emphasize that praise of God is due from all people as well as from all of creation (96:1, 7–9, 11–12; 98:4–8), and both conclude with anticipation of God's righteous judgment (96:13; 98:9).

The main difference is that Psalm 98 focuses exclusively on music as creation's proper response to God. Further, the psalmist has in mind all types of music from all types of sources. As six of the psalm's nine verses ring out with a total of fifteen references to audible praise—vocal (vv. 1, 4–5), instrumental (vv. 5–6), and jubilant sounds arising from nature (vv. 4, 7–8)—Psalm

98 comprehensively underscores the call to "repeat the sounding joy," as Isaac Watts wrote in "Joy to the World," his famous paraphrase of this psalm's closing six verses.

Psalm 98 begins with an imperative to sing and then identifies God's "marvelous" deeds as the reason for song (v. 1a). The psalmist immediately itemizes those divine deeds, emphasizing that these achievements belong purely to God. The thrust of God's accomplishment is salvation (NRSV, "victory"), mentioned in each of the psalm's opening three verses. Israel is specifically named as recipient of God's "steadfast love and faithfulness" (v. 3a), even as "all the ends of the earth" are witness to God's salvation (v. 3b).

Returning to imperatives, the psalmist exuberantly directs the people to offer their praise, repeating key phrases—"break forth into joyous song and *sing praises. Sing praises* to the LORD *with the lyre, with the lyre* and the sound of melody" (vv. 4b–5)—for an overlapping build that culminates in proclaiming God as "the King, the LORD" (v. 6). Next, the natural world is called upon to contribute its renderings of joyful adoration (vv. 7–8).

Just as the psalm's first verse provides rationale for singing a new song, the psalm's last verse also offers the reason for this worldwide harmony of praise: God "is coming to judge the earth . . . with righteousness, and the peoples with equity" (v. 9). The psalmist knows this promise is cause for celebration, and because we, as Christians, recognize this long-awaited righteous judge as the baby born in Bethlehem, we indeed celebrate.

Psalm 98 shares vocabulary and intent with today's Isaiah text. While the prophet cast a vision of a future in which the "ruins of Jerusalem" will sing (Isa. 52:9) and "all the ends of the earth shall see the salvation of our God" (Isa. 52:10), the psalmist celebrated an accomplished fact by declaring that God had already "remembered his steadfast love and faithfulness to the house of Israel. All the ends of the earth have seen the victory [salvation] of our God" (Ps. 98:3). For the prophet, it is a vision; for the psalmist, it is a done deal; for the Christian, it is Christmas.

Isaiah envisioned the approach of "the messenger who announces peace, who brings good news, who announces salvation, who says to Zion, 'Your God reigns'" (Isa. 52:7). Lookouts stationed atop Jerusalem's ruined walls would be the first to glimpse this messenger, and the prophet instructs us to listen that we may hear the joy of those sentinels (Isa. 52:8). By using Psalm 98 to add fuel to Isaiah's exhortation, the preacher can encourage the Christmas congregation to be today's singing sentinels.

Although Psalm 98 does not specify God as creator, it does make a point of involving all creation in God's praise. It therefore might be fruitful to link it to today's Gospel's assertion that "all things came into being through him" (John 1:3). Similarly, the psalm's anticipation of the coming of one who will judge us with equity could relate to the Gospel's statement: "And the Word became flesh and lived among us" (John 1:14).

For liturgy, especially because the psalm emphasizes God's activity and creation's response, it is prime material for antiphonal or responsive reading. Here's one arrangement that emphasizes the comprehensive nature of all that praises God:

> O sing to the Lord a new song, for God has done marvelous things!
> *All the ends of the earth have seen the victory of our God.*
> Make a joyful noise to the Lord, all the earth.
> *Let the sea roar and all that fills it; the world and those who live in it.*
> Let the hills sing together for joy at the presence of the Lord.
> *Let us worship God!*

To celebrate that which the psalm celebrates—the promise that God is coming to be the righteous judge of all (Ps. 98:9)—one might create an unexpected Christmas liturgy by finding ways to incorporate this call-and-response as repeated reassurance:

> God will judge the world with righteousness.
> *God will judge the peoples with equity.*

Since this is the ultimate day for singing Christmas carols ("Silent Night" would not be a good fit for this noisy psalm!), heed the psalmist's insistent call for joyful music. In addition to the Psalm 98–inspired "Joy to the World," consider "On Christmas Night All Christians Sing," "On This Day Earth Shall Ring," and "Go, Tell It on the Mountain." Additional options include "People, Look East," "Prepare the Way, O Zion," "Angels We Have Heard on High," "Hark! The Herald Angels Sing," and "Good Christian Friends, Rejoice." With such a wealth of widely known and loved music, you might sing all the liturgy, from gathering the congregation with "Prepare the Way, O Zion" or "People, Look East," to sending them forth with "Go, Tell It on the Mountain" or "On Christmas Night All Christians Sing."

Christmas is when we first meet, face to human face, our Savior, whose incarnation is the "revealing" of God's salvation (Ps. 98:2). It is also the ultimate example of the "marvelous things" God has done (v. 1). It is surely cause for making a joyful noise!

LEIGH CAMPBELL-TAYLOR

Hebrews 1:1–4 (5–12)

¹Long ago God spoke to our ancestors in many and various ways by the prophets, ²but in these last days he has spoken to us by a Son, whom he appointed heir of all things, through whom he also created the worlds. ³He is the reflection of God's glory and the exact imprint of God's very being, and he sustains all things by his powerful word. When he had made purification for sins, he sat down at the right hand of the Majesty on high, ⁴having become as much superior to angels as the name he has inherited is more excellent than theirs.
⁵For to which of the angels did God ever say,

"You are my Son;
  today I have begotten you"?

Or again,

"I will be his Father,
  and he will be my Son"?

⁶And again, when he brings the firstborn into the world, he says,

"Let all God's angels worship him."

⁷Of the angels he says,

"He makes his angels winds,
  and his servants flames of fire."

⁸But of the Son he says,

"Your throne, O God, is forever and ever,
  and the righteous scepter is the scepter of your kingdom.
⁹You have loved righteousness and hated wickedness;
therefore God, your God, has anointed you
  with the oil of gladness beyond your companions."

¹⁰And,

"In the beginning, Lord, you founded the earth,
  and the heavens are the work of your hands;
¹¹they will perish, but you remain;
  they will all wear out like clothing;
¹²like a cloak you will roll them up,
  and like clothing they will be changed.
But you are the same,
  and your years will never end."

Commentary 1: Connecting the Reading with Scripture

Just what are we to make of this decidedly odd letter, especially as we consider it on this holy day? It is plainly not from Paul; the language and theological thinking at times move in very different directions from his. It ends like an epistle, since in Hebrews 13 we are offered a closing benediction (vv. 20–21) and a final exhortation and greeting, including a reference to "our brother Timothy [who] has been set free." Exactly who this Timothy may be, and from what he has been set free, is not made clear.

More peculiar and unique is the beginning of Hebrews. No letter in the New Testament begins like this: "Long ago God spoke to our ancestors in many and various ways . . ." (Heb. 1:1). The author does not introduce himself or herself in any way, but focuses squarely on the real subject of the work: Jesus, the eternal and exalted Son of God. Here we listen to a theological preacher whose subject is the specific identity and superior nature of the one we call Christ.

Hear now one of the sermons of the Letter to the Hebrews, for this letter is a series of sermons. The subject of this first sermon is made clear in the four introductory verses. God has continually spoken to our ancestors in myriad and varied ways by the mouths and deeds of prophets. Though these prophets are not named, we know who they may be: Amos, Isaiah, Jeremiah, Micah, Hosea, and a host of others, including unnamed later prophets of the emerging gospel, all of whom have been the mouthpieces of the God who has spoken through them to our forebears.

Now "in these last days" carries the implication that the new activity of God in the Christ is somehow the fulfillment of God speaking. God has spoken to us now by means of a Son (some manuscripts say "*the* Son"). This new speech is unique, unprecedented, and complete. That is true because of the nature of the speaker; the fact that the speaker is the very Son of God makes this new speech of God genuinely new.

The sermon now moves from introduction to the first main point. He, the Son, is cocreator with God of all the worlds and at the same time is the heir of everything created. Not only that: he is the spitting image of God, reflecting precisely the glory of God. Said in another way, he is "the exact imprint of God's very being," God's full nature, and by his speech "he sustains all things by" the means of "his powerful word."

Christ's full nature, though, has not yet been revealed. After he had made "purification for sins" (the gift of his dying on the cross), he joined God ("the Majesty," v. 3) on high, sitting at God's right hand, a place of power and favor, indicating without doubt that he had become far superior to any angels, whose place was in the heavenly places, but not at the right hand of God. Also, his inherited name as he sat down with God became in every way far "more excellent than theirs."

This Son is thus exalted with God, but only after he has been humiliated on earth. That humiliation was the door to glory with the God who named him and chose him. The author focuses and illuminates the main point: Jesus is the unique spokesperson for God, because he is so like God in all things.

Now that the subject of the sermon has been announced, namely, the exalted Son of God, the author sets out to prove the case that God's new way of communicating with us in these last days through the Son of God is crucial for God's speaking henceforth. The author turns to a series of texts from the Psalms and other places in the Old Testament to prove the point. Psalms texts include Psalms 2:7 ("You are my son; today I have begotten you") and 104:4 ("He makes his angels winds; his servants flames of fire," from the Greek Old Testament), among other texts.

The Old Testament texts attempt to prove the main point: Jesus is far superior in every way to any who have preceded him. Did God ever say to any angel what God spoke in Psalm 110:1: "Sit at my right hand until I make your enemies your footstool"? The fact that the context of the Hebrew psalm may have been the coronation of a king does not for our author preclude its use now as proof of the Son's enduring uniqueness in these last days. We might rightly name such a use as eisegesis, a reading into a text of a predetermined idea, but for our first-century-CE author, such a reading is apparently quite traditional and appropriate. The Old Testament is thus made to prefigure and announce the Son as the unique gift of God.

The sermon does not end with the notion that the Son is superior to the angels. After a warning to pay careful attention to this sermon—it is given for our salvation—the author affirms that the earlier message through the angels was "valid" for us (2:2). Jewish belief was that the angels mediated the Torah from Sinai (see Heb. 12:18–21). Now we must hear the voice of the Son whose speaking was accompanied by "signs and wonders and various miracles, and by gifts of the Holy Spirit" (Heb. 2:4).

This initial sermon concludes with the claim that Christ is both savior and a most faithful and merciful high priest. The introduction of the language of "high priest" looks forward to further reflection on that theme in Hebrews 4–5, which itself is part of another sermon on faith (Heb. 3:1–4:13), concluding with a reiteration of Christ as high priest after the order of Melchizedek, that mysterious figure from Genesis 14:18–24 and Psalm 110:4.

Hebrews 1:1–14 makes a powerful accompaniment to the more familiar passage from John 1:1–14, the Gospel reading for the day. In both we hear of the Word of God, the preexistent Word, by and with whom the worlds were made and by whom the worlds may be "made whole," "saved" in the traditional language. In both texts we hear of the Son of God, exalted and humiliated, for us and for our salvation. In both texts we hear of the uniqueness of this Son, far surpassing all who have come before, full of grace and truth, both in speech and in action.

In short, the passage from the Letter to the Hebrews is a rich summary of a unique Christology that shaped and molded the church as it spread its gospel into the world. With the Gospel of John and the letters to the Colossians and the Ephesians, Christianity made enormous claims concerning the one it called the Christ, the Messiah of God. He is the humiliated and exalted one for us and for all, and his coming has made all things new.

To engage this text on Christmas Day is to remind our hearers that the babe in the manger will one day find his way to the cross and through the resurrection to sit at the right hand of God, thus fulfilling the plan of God to make the entire cosmos whole and complete again. More than reason enough for a grand celebration!

JOHN C. HOLBERT

Commentary 2: Connecting the Reading with the World

God who spoke Jesus into being. The poet who tells the first story of creation in Genesis begins this way: "In the beginning when God created the heavens and the earth, the earth was a formless void and darkness covered the face of the deep, while a wind from God swept over the face of the waters. Then God said, 'Let there be light'; and there was light" (Gen. 1:1–3).

God spoke and the world was created. The author of Hebrews begins by recalling God's speaking to his readers' ancestors through prophets. God spoke and the people were brought to righteousness and obedience. Now the writer reminds the reader that God has spoken again. God spoke and God's Son came into being and walked on the face of the earth.

On Christmas Day, and every day when we focus on gifts and giving and receiving, the author of Hebrews tells us that the greatest gift of all is that God spoke to the world in the person of God's Son. We are reminded that Jesus Christ, God incarnate, is the full reflection of the God of the universe and that, in and through Jesus Christ, all that God spoke into being in the creation is sustained by the Word made flesh.

In 2004, the United Church of Christ made news by producing a series of commercials promoting the denomination's openness and acceptance of all peoples through the use of the tagline "God is still speaking." Those who were critical of the phrase disputed not that God is still speaking but what the more liberal and open church was hearing. Some argued that while God is indeed still speaking, the church is hearing other voices and wrongly attributing those words to God. The controversy itself raises a serious question. While it may be true that God has spoken God's truest revelation in Jesus Christ, is it not possible that in our hearing we are distorting God's words and God's Word? The nature of a word spoken relies on the good work of the listener.

Cultures across the world are full of proverbs—spoken words that carry truth. The preacher would do well to remind the congregation of the power of these spoken words by recalling common proverbs, proverbs that carry importance when they are heard and the truth of them is taken to heart. A popular African proverb describes the difference between how Africans and Americans hear: When you see two Africans talking together, you see one person talking and the other person listening; when you see two Americans talking, you see one person talking and one person waiting to talk. Surely this proverb reflects the challenge of American culture, where the art of listening is in all-too-short supply. So much of what therapists do is to listen. The preacher could ponder what it says about a people when persons are so desperate to be heard that a whole profession of skilled listeners has emerged who are able to reflect with the speaker what is truly being said.

God spoke Jesus Christ, God's Son, into being. The important question for us is, while God is still speaking, are we simply waiting to talk, or are we actually listening?

The writer of the Letter to the Hebrews then goes on to help us understand why the word made flesh is worthy of our listening. Jesus Christ is seated at the right hand of God and is superior even to the angels. His character is clear. Not only has God spoken Jesus Christ into being. God also named him as God's Son and called the angels to worship him. Think about the times in Jesus' life when God spoke. At his baptism, God spoke, naming Jesus as God's Son in whom God is pleased. At the transfiguration, God spoke again and, after again naming Jesus as God's Son, told the disciples to listen to him!

For many churches, worship on Sunday is a given. For a number of churches, worship on Christmas Day is also a given; on the day when the church celebrates the birth of Jesus Christ, it is only right and good to gather to worship and praise God. For others, when Christmas does not fall on a Sunday, they are not in worship. When Christmas falls on a Sunday, some congregations choose not to worship, because the church has gathered the previous day and night for Christmas Eve services. One pastor reasoned that families and the church choir and staff members were so weary after Advent and Christmas Eve that the best "gift" the church could give was to offer a "Sunday off." It is difficult at best to take that rationale seriously, given the psalms that the writer of the Letter to the Hebrews quotes. One wonders how taking a break after a busy Christmas Eve schedule squares with God's introduction of the firstborn of all creation into the world

and God's words to "let all God's angels worship him." Perhaps the need to take a day off after a busy Advent and Christmas celebration is more an indictment of how even the church can fall victim to not listening to the Word spoken by God in Jesus Christ.

Many persons who gather for worship on Christmas Day may resonate with the desire to rest after the hectic Christmas season; that is not a bad thing in and of itself. The preacher could speak of God's own pattern of resting. After creation, God rested. After a particularly grueling period of healing and teaching, Jesus Christ went off by himself to pray and rest. We are called to rest as part of the rhythm of Sabbath keeping. Resting is faithful; but this day, when we celebrate the incarnation of God in Jesus Christ, is not a time for resting. This is a time for awe and worship and glory and praise.

The writer of Hebrews is telling us that God has already spoken the Son into being. This gracious act of God is worthy of our attention, worthy of our listening to God speaking. Surely in response to God's grace shown in Jesus Christ, the word from the church can be one that reminds and cajoles and nudges and calls the hearer to listen in a way that sets a pattern that is different from the never-ending lists of things that need to be done to make Christmas Day a day to remember. Remembrance has already been accomplished through the recollection of God speaking through creation and the prophets. The preacher might offer a grace-filled word to the hearer to remind all that, in God's speaking, grace has been fully revealed and the angels are forever rejoicing. In and through the incarnation God has dwelt among us, and all creation has been redeemed and transformed.

God has spoken God's Son, Jesus, into the world. Jesus is the fullest and greatest revelation of all who God is for us. He is seated with God at God's right hand—a place that demonstrates both God's favor and the place that Jesus holds in all of creation. Greater than even the angels, Jesus is worthy to be praised and worshiped. He will rule with God forever and ever. God is still speaking and creating even through us. So let all creation rejoice in the abiding love of the creator whose years will never end.

RODGER Y. NISHIOKA

John 1:1–14

¹In the beginning was the Word, and the Word was with God, and the Word was God. ²He was in the beginning with God. ³All things came into being through him, and without him not one thing came into being. What has come into being ⁴in him was life, and the life was the light of all people. ⁵The light shines in the darkness, and the darkness did not overcome it.

⁶There was a man sent from God, whose name was John. ⁷He came as a witness to testify to the light, so that all might believe through him. ⁸He himself was not the light, but he came to testify to the light. ⁹The true light, which enlightens everyone, was coming into the world.

¹⁰He was in the world, and the world came into being through him; yet the world did not know him. ¹¹He came to what was his own, and his own people did not accept him. ¹²But to all who received him, who believed in his name, he gave power to become children of God, ¹³who were born, not of blood or of the will of the flesh or of the will of man, but of God.

¹⁴And the Word became flesh and lived among us, and we have seen his glory, the glory as of a father's only son, full of grace and truth.

Commentary 1: Connecting the Reading with Scripture

John 1:1–18 is the theological prologue to the Fourth Gospel. It is a literary and theological whole. While preachers can follow the lectionary by focusing on various aspects today and on the Second Sunday after Christmas (John 1:(1–9) 10–18), the preacher should be alert for resonance between the lections on the two Sundays.

John 1:1–18 evokes a worldview within which to place the story of Jesus. This worldview, characteristic of Judaism influenced by Greek thought, interpreted much traditional Jewish theology as a two-story existence reminiscent of the middle-Platonism of Philo of Alexandria, a Jewish thinker who lived about the same time as Jesus. In this view, existence is a two-story universe with heaven above and the world below. God dwells in heaven, a sphere characterized by things such as life, love, light, truth, peace, joy, and abundance. The world is a decidedly negative place for John, as it is the dwelling place of the devil and is characterized by such things as death, hate, darkness, falsehood, violence, sadness, and scarcity. The contrast is not between a nonmaterial heaven and a material world but between two different qualities of life. The Gospel of John tells the story of Jesus in terms of this worldview.

Preachers can help the congregation grasp John's understanding of the relationship of God and Jesus. For John, Jesus is the word (*logos*) through whom God created all things (John 1:1–2). The Johannine Jesus is not yet God in the strictest Trinitarian sense, but is God's closest agent in creating the world and in revealing God's purposes. Two Jewish sources from the time of John provide background on this notion. The Wisdom of Solomon saw the figure of wisdom functioning similarly (e.g., Wis. 7:22b–8:1; cf. Sir. 24; Prov. 3:19–20; 8:22–31). Moreover, Philo comments on a grammatical construction similar to one that John uses: the *logos* ("word") does not refer to God but refers to an entity that God made and uses for God's purposes.[1] Jesus is such an agent for John. The preacher can help the congregation recognize how Jesus continues to be God's agent in making it possible to know God.

---

1. Philo, "On Dreams," 1.229–30, in *Philo,* trans. F. H. Coalson and G. H. Whitaker, Loeb Classical Library (Cambridge: Harvard University Press, 1968), 419.

Although God created "all things" through Jesus, the world did not know Jesus; that is, neither the world nor the Jewish people embraced Jesus as God's agent (John 1:10–11). As a remarkable demonstration of grace, God loved the world so much that God gave Jesus so that those who believe in Jesus will have eternal life (John 3:16). For the Fourth Gospel, the "gave" of John 3:16 refers not just to the cross but to the entire act of the Word becoming Jesus, descending from heaven, and returning (John 3:13). For John, however, "those who do not believe are condemned already" (John 3:18b).

Not only did God create "all things" through the Word, but God sent the Word into the world as flesh to live in the midst of the human family, so that we might behold the glory of Jesus (John 1:14). In the Fourth Gospel the incarnation is fundamental to the work of Jesus. As incarnate Word he offers those who are in the world the possibility of experiencing heaven on earth, that is, the qualities of heaven while still in the world. Indeed, to see the glory of Jesus in the Gospel of John is to see that these purposes of God are revealed through Jesus (John 1:14).

In a manner of speaking, the Word incarnate in Jesus turns on the light in the world, so that people can see the negative quality of life in the world, in contrast to the positive quality of life in heaven. By believing in Jesus, they can then expectantly await the time that he will return and take them with him to heaven (John 14:1–7). Without Jesus, inhabitants of the world assume that its negative qualities are the sum of the possibilities of existence. Those who believe in Jesus, by contrast, begin to experience many qualities of heaven—for example, love, light, peace, freedom, abundance—as they continue to live in the world. Indeed, the Johannine synagogue is a community in but not of the world,

---

Giving Ourselves to God's Will

Let us, then, cling to his blessing and note what leads to it. Let us unfold the tale of the ancient past. Why was our father Abraham blessed? Was it not because he acted in righteousness and truth, prompted by faith? Isaac, fully realizing what was going to happen, gladly let himself be led to sacrifice. In humility Jacob quit his homeland because of his brother. He went to Laban and became his slave, and to him there were given the twelve scepters of the tribes of Israel and if anyone will candidly look into each example, he will realize the magnificence of the gifts God gives.

So all of them received honor and greatness, not through themselves or their own deeds or the right things they did, but through his will. And we, therefore, who by his will have been called in Jesus Christ, are not justified of ourselves or by our wisdom or insight or religious devotion or the holy deeds we have done from the heart, but by that faith by which almighty God has justified all men from the very beginning. To him be glory forever and ever. Amen.

What, then, brothers, ought we to do? Should we grow slack in doing good and give up love? May the Lord never permit this to happen at any rate to us! Rather should we be energetic in doing "every good deed" with earnestness and eagerness. For the Creator and Master of the universe himself rejoices in his works. Thus by his almighty power he established the heavens and by his inscrutable wisdom he arranged them. He separated the land from the water surrounding it and fixed it upon the sure foundation of his own will. By his decree he brought into existence the living creatures which roam on it, and after creating the sea and the creatures which inhabit it, he fixed its boundaries by his power. Above all, with his holy and pure hands he formed man, his outstanding and greatest achievement, stamped with his own image.

We should observe that all the righteous have been adorned with good deeds, and the very Lord adorns himself with good deeds and rejoices. Since, then, we have this example, we should unhesitatingly give ourselves to his will, and put all our effort into acting uprightly.

1 Clement 31.1–4; 32.1, 3–4; 33.1–4, 7–8, in Cyril C. Richardson, ed. and trans., *Early Christian Fathers* (Philadelphia: Westminster Press, 1953), 58–59.

prefiguring the community of heaven in the midst of the world.

Jesus reveals, further, that the disciples are to love one another (e.g., John 13:31–35), that the disciples can expect conflict with agents of the world (e.g., John 15:18–16:4a), and that the Holy Spirit will continue the work of Jesus through the community (John 16:4b–15).

While there are no direct historical or literary connections among the readings for Proper III, they do present different perspectives on the similar theme of how we recognize God's work. The Gospel of John and Hebrews come from similar worldviews—Judaism interpreted broadly in middle-Platonic categories similar to Philo—and portray the work of Jesus in similar ways. In Hebrews 1:1–4 Jesus is the heir (Son) through whom God created all things (v. 2), the pioneer who came down from heaven to lead "many children to glory [heaven]" (Heb. 2:10).

Isaiah 52:7–10 uses the custom of a sentinel coming with an announcement of peace as a way of speaking about how we come to know God's work. "How beautiful upon the mountains are the feet of one who brings such news" to the exiles in Babylonia. Isaiah also suggests an appropriate response—the community lifting up voices to call attention to the news. While the prophet did not have Jesus in mind, the preacher could use this passage as a theological lens for interpreting the significance of exile for communities of faith that follow Jesus.

Psalm 98 is a royal psalm. While the psalmist did not have Jesus in mind as the royal figure, the preacher could use the royal personage to which the psalm points to prompt the church to recognize that, through Jesus, we experience the salvation, love, and faithfulness of which the psalm speaks.

Three of the most important questions in the Gospels and letters are, Who is Jesus? What does Jesus offer? and What does Jesus ask? The different authors of the Gospels and letters share the common conviction that God worked (and continues to work) through Jesus to help human and cosmic communities experience more fully God's purposes of love, justice, peace, and abundance, now and in the future. The authors refract this conviction through their different theological perspectives, with attention to issues at work in their particular historical, literary, and theological contexts. For John, as we have said, Jesus is the Word become flesh to reveal God. For Hebrews, Jesus is the heir, the pioneer, and perfecter who leads many children to glory.

Paul, Mark, Matthew, and Luke share a similar apocalyptic perspective on Jesus, but they interpret Jesus' role in the apocalypse and the timing of the apocalypse in different ways. Christmas is an ideal day on which to honor the differences and name the range of gifts they give rather than put them in a theological blender that muddles the dissonances and keeps us from pondering, creatively, what they might mean to our lives of faith. Indeed, preachers might use the different christological emphases in the Gospels and letters as inspiration for sermons in which they challenge us to think in multi-faceted ways about who Jesus is, and what he offers and asks.

RONALD J. ALLEN

Commentary 2: Connecting the Reading with the World

John's magisterial hymn to the incarnation, the first eighteen verses of chapter 1, is often named the prologue. Some selection of these familiar verses appears in all three cycles of the Revised Common Lectionary at Christmas time, often not only on Christmas Day but also on Christmas Eve and Sundays following Christmas Day. John 1:14 may indeed be a pivot verse for the Christian faith. It is so important that the lectionary offers similar verses from the prologue just two Sundays hence, something a preacher might keep in mind in preparing this Sunday's sermon.

The lectionary's practice reflects the fact that the church has long associated the doctrine of the incarnation with the birth of Jesus. Though most Christians hear the prologue as a Christmas text, it is not at all clear that John himself connected his theological affirmation of incarnation (v. 14) with Jesus' birth. John's intent is less to offer his readers a theological nativity story, but more to help them understand the relationship between Jesus and John the Baptist. By implication, understanding that relationship would shine light on the relationship between Jesus and his followers—both then and now. The prologue inserts the Baptist into the narrative twice, in verses 6–9 and again in verse 15. Subsequently, most of the balance of chapter 1 will offer the story of the encounter between John the Baptist and Jesus, an encounter that in John's telling includes no baptism. For John, the connection between the nativity and the prologue—though arguably theologically appropriate—is simply not as natural as we might think. For the Fourth Gospel, the doctrine of the incarnation is not merely about the birth of Jesus. Rather "becoming flesh and dwelling among us" is made manifest in Jesus' whole life and ministry, indeed his whole being. The incarnation shines through the cross, the resurrection, and the ascension as much as through the nativity.

Christmas preaching on the prologue to John's Gospel might provide an opportunity to explore what it means now, in our world, to make the daring affirmation that not only did God *once* come into the world in Jesus Christ, but that the living Christ *still* enters into our time and space, indeed into our very materiality—the mortal fleshliness we share with Jesus—now and always. Today's lectionary section of the prologue ends with John's affirmation of divine enfleshment in Jesus Christ, the one in whom God "lived among us" and through whom we glimpse the "glory," "grace," and "truth" of the Divine.

A sermon might explore the present and proximate meaning of incarnation for people in the pews. One of my seminary professors, J. Christian Becker, a noted New Testament scholar, often ridiculed what he called "the swoop-down theory" of the incarnation. Whenever he talked about the swoop-down theory, he became even more animated than he usually was. He pretended his hand was a bird flying along, high in the heavens. All of a sudden, it would swoop down to the earth for a visit, and then swoop back up to heaven. This idea, he would explain, suggested that God was up in heaven most of the time, but every once and again would swoop down, knock on our mortal door, and pay a visit—just for a while.

This was all wrong, Becker said. The truer understanding of the incarnation, he would tell us—and here he became rhapsodic—is that God is with us always, that God is forever proximate, always and everywhere as near to us as our own breath. The incarnation of Jesus Christ, he insisted, is the definitive expression of the great unfolding of the divine presence that *always was, always is, and always shall be* with us. The incarnation means that God is not "up there" or "back then." Rather, God is in the proximate; God is to be encountered in that which is close at hand; God is to be glimpsed in the ordinary. Theologian Belden Lane sums up this point nicely: "The one great practical truth of the incarnation is that the ordinary is no longer what it appears. Common things, common actions, common relationships are all granted new definition because the holy has once and for all become ordinary in Jesus Christ."[2] As the old chestnut of a rhyme has it, "Jesus shut within a book is hardly worth a passing look."

The preacher might consider quoting all or bits of Francis Thompson's "In No Strange Land," a poem written in the late nineteenth century, when he was a homeless opium addict in London. The second stanza, addressed obliquely to God, asks rhetorical questions that imply the incarnation:

> Does the fish soar to find the ocean,
> The eagle plunge to find the air—
> That we ask the stars in motion
> If they have rumor of thee there?

While sleeping in the rough on London streets near the River Thames, Thompson answers his incarnation question at the end of the poem:

> Yea, in the night, my Soul, my daughter,
> Cry—clinging to Heaven by the hems;

---

2. Belden Lane, "The Ordinary as Mask of the Holy," *Christian Century*, Oct. 3, 1984, 898.

And lo, Christ walking on the water,
Not of Gennesareth, but Thames![3]

Garrison Keillor posted an essay about the wonder of Christmas on the interactive internet magazine *Salon.* He wrote of "magic," in spite of all the regnant skepticism that lurks in our culture. The essay generated a lot of blog traffic. One young woman in New York responded by writing that she seldom went to church, but always did make a point to go at Christmas. She mentioned the magic about which Keillor wrote. She noted the kindness, the gentleness, the hospitality, the sweet generosity, and open welcome that so often rest in these special days. She said she adored it all, loved the carols and trees and candles, even the Christmas story itself. Finally, she lamented, almost bitterly, that it was all too soon gone. In no time, she said, Christmas was over and New York City was back to usual—no magic, not so kind, never gentle, and anything but sweetly generous. "Christmas just doesn't last," she sighed.[4]

The preacher might call the congregation to imagine ways to carry some of the "Christmas magic" into the days beyond Christmas Day into all the seasons of life. This is possible simply because—incarnationally speaking—Christmas actually *does* last. Incarnation is the declaration that just as God is in the spirit that often fills Christmas Day, God is also in the day after—indeed in every day to come. Incarnation suggests that *all* time and *every* place are saturated with the Divine. The preacher might call the congregation to look for incarnation in the world around them, and then to live their lives in the light of the incarnation, the daring and transforming truth that God is not "back then" or "up there," but that God is God-with-us, in every here and now. Liturgical tradition affirms that every Sunday of the year is a little Easter.

One might also declare that every Sunday is also a little Christmas.

MICHAEL L. LINDVALL

---

3. Francis Thompson, "The Kingdom of God—In No Strange Land," in *The New Oxford Book of Christian Verse* (Oxford: Oxford University Press, 1981), 256.

4. Garrison Keillor, "Away in an Awesome Manger," *Salon*, Dec. 5, 2007.

First Sunday after Christmas Day

1 Samuel 2:18–20, 26   Colossians 3:12–17
Psalm 148   Luke 2:41–52

1 Samuel 2:18–20, 26

¹⁸Samuel was ministering before the LORD, a boy wearing a linen ephod. ¹⁹His mother used to make for him a little robe and take it to him each year, when she went up with her husband to offer the yearly sacrifice. ²⁰Then Eli would bless Elkanah and his wife, and say, "May the LORD repay you with children by this woman for the gift that she made to the LORD"; and then they would return to their home. . . .
²⁶Now the boy Samuel continued to grow both in stature and in favor with the LORD and with the people.

Commentary 1: Connecting the Reading with Scripture

The life of Samuel is interwoven with the drama of king making. The rise and fall of Saul and the anointing of David come at Samuel's hands. Before we reach these larger events, we discover the root of Samuel's authority, this prophet whose words never fall to the ground (1 Sam. 3:19–20).

The strength of Samuel's example is foreshadowed by the pain his mother experiences before his birth. First Samuel opens with poignant words: "Hannah had no children" (1 Sam. 1:2). Hannah's childless status threatens to become the mark of her existence. Rather than slip into bitterness and despair, however, she persists in hope and faithfulness. God answers Hannah's prayer; she conceives and gives birth. Immediately Hannah dedicates Samuel to the Lord, giving back to the Holy One the gift she has received (1 Sam. 2:1–2).

As Samuel grows into a young boy, Hannah and Elkanah dedicate their annual sacrifice at Shiloh. Hannah gives Samuel a special robe. Her outward act of devotion is consistent with her heart's commitment.

This unity of purpose demonstrated by Hannah is an apt paradigm of the church's worship and communal life. Our congregations are marked by a tempo of dedication to community interwoven with an inner orientation of thanksgiving and trust in God. Conviction and action, theology and ethics go hand in hand. The particular God-given gifts we covet with passion are never reserved for us alone. In gratitude, all we receive is in turn to be offered to the church, our neighbors, and the Giver.

Hannah's life is a testimony to the bedrock of the Shema (Deut. 6:4–9): "You shall love the LORD your God with all your heart, and with all your soul, and with all your might. Keep these words that I am commanding you today in your heart. Recite them to your children . . ." Hannah's willingness to dedicate her son as an attendant at Shiloh ensures that the teachings of the law will fill Samuel's heart each day.

All the rich stories within 1 Samuel are interlaced with Samuel's lifelong fidelity. His equanimity, even when offstage, might be contrasted to the agitated decisions of Saul and David. Samuel is the relentless bearer of God's word, the heaven-sent guide, and the one who questions Israel's decision to anoint a king. Samuel stands as prophet, foreshadowing the judgment and restoration to come.

The influence of Samuel's story echoes far beyond the end of his life. Even though the announcement of his death (1 Sam. 25:1) appears as an afterthought as Saul and David are contesting for the throne, his life reverberates with determination. As a young boy, he opens himself to God's call (1 Sam. 3:10). He warns the people of Israel against choosing a sovereign, yet does not desert them when they insist (1 Sam. 8:4–22). He defies King Saul and anoints the youngest of Jesse's sons as king (1 Sam. 16:1–13).

Similarly, the fierce love of Samuel's mother becomes a symbol of perseverance throughout the Scriptures. Most notably, it serves as a model both in Mary's acceptance of her calling as mother of Jesus (Luke 1:26–38) and in her loyalty and love for Jesus, even after he challenges her to identify not only with him, but also with her new family—the community of his followers (John 19:25–27).

The faithful parenting of the mothers of both Samuel and Jesus might remind us that the creation stories in Genesis 1–3 make an intimate connection between humanity's creation in the image of God (1:26–27) and the charge to bear and raise children (Gen. 1:28). Such creative maternal modeling enriches our understanding of God's character. The witness of the Proverbs 31 woman and many other women of faith joins that of Samuel's mother and mother Mary, preparing us to more fully encounter God.

Isaiah uses maternal imagery for God quite explicitly: "Listen to me, O house of Jacob . . . who have been borne by me from your birth, carried from the womb; even to your old age I am he, even when you turn gray I will carry you. I have made, and I will bear; I will carry and will save" (Isa. 46:3–4) and "Can a woman forget her nursing child, or show no compassion for the child of her womb? Even these may forget, yet I will not forget you" (Isa. 49:15). This maternal imaging of God finds succinct expression in A Brief Statement of Faith, a Presbyterian confession: "Like a mother who will not forsake her nursing child . . . God is faithful still."

The maternal divine presence is depicted in one biblical narrative after another. Deuteronomy sings of God's motherly care for Israel in the wilderness (Deut. 32:10–14). Even when faced with quarreling and disobedience, our Mother God does not abandon Israel, but is unceasing in encouragement (Neh. 9:16–21). Sarah and Abraham receive the promise of a son, Isaac, and he becomes the confirmation of God's provision. Along the way Isaac also

witnesses the exile of family, Hagar and her son, and the nick-of-time intervention of the angel (Gen. 21–22). Maternal devotion reaches a crescendo in the faithfulness of Mary, revered in Orthodox Christianity as *theotokos* (God-bearer). Mary refuses to fear or doubt at the announcement of a promise almost too great for human hearts (Luke 1–2).

The preacher might reflect on the fact that Mary and Hannah share not only maternal devotion but similar life stories. Each sacrifices a beloved son to a life far different from what they first imagined. Both continue in gratitude and faithfulness, despite the disappointments they experience.

As we marvel at the stories of these godly women, we might discern opportunities to point to the inbreaking God at work in our lives and world. We, like them, may be called by God to embrace family life, with children first received and then offered to God and the world. A sermon rooted in the life and love of Hannah and Mary will point to the joy of giving back to God the best gifts we receive. Our self-giving reflects the Holy One's gift of the Son. As Hannah and Mary find the strength to lift their voices in trust, crying, "Here am I, the servant of the Lord; let it be with me according to your word" (Luke 1:38), so we, by the power of the Holy, may discover the goodness that lies beyond our desires to hold tightly to the best we have been given.

Selfless giving is a theme of the biblical witness that comes into sharp focus again in Matthew 12:46–50. Jesus is speaking to the crowds, sharing the great good news, when a friend announces that his mother and brothers are outside waiting for him. "But who is my mother, and who are my brothers?" Jesus asks. Then pointing to his followers, he proclaims, "These are my mother and brothers! For whoever does my Father's will is my brother and sister and mother." Here Jesus is not diminishing the maternal role of Mary, but praising her alongside all who, like her, faithfully embrace God's calling.

The preacher might reflect on the fact that Samuel dies beyond the spotlight, without a final word. Similarly, the path of Jesus leads to a new family as well as to the scandal and surprise of the cross and empty tomb. Like Samuel and Jesus, and like Hannah and Mary, we are invited to receive with gratitude our best gifts—family and community in every shape and color and

circumstance—and then offer them up to God. As we discover the grace to do so, we will discover our deepest identity as God's children.

GLEN BELL

Commentary 2: Connecting the Reading with the World

The biblical record is clear: Eli's sons were scoundrels. First Samuel 2:12–13 tells us, "They had no regard for the LORD or for the duties of the priests to the people." These weren't just preacher's kids being mischievous at church; it was far worse. They were stealing the offering, sleeping around, and threatening violence—all within the sacred space of the temple.

The idea that sin can be found at church should not surprise us. As the teacher in Ecclesiastes would say, *there is nothing new under the sun.* We know all too well that privilege, power, and position can be used for good, and can be used for narcissistic and self-serving ends. We see it in government when those elected seek more power rather than serve the common good. Even closer to home, we witness how easily sacred spaces can become havens for sin and corruption. These sons of Eli sat in the shadow of power—their father a respected priest—but instead of following his model of service and leadership, they chose a different, darker path.

From the text, we know that Eli was deeply troubled by his sons' actions. What disappointment he must have experienced. Perhaps he consoled himself by looking back and remembering the days of their births. There must have been great rejoicing for Eli on the days his sons were born. As he held them in the moments after their births, it is likely that he prayed that they would follow the same call that God had placed on his life, that they would be wise and kind and good.

Perhaps this is why the text in 1 Samuel contrasts the stories of Eli's sons with the story of young Samuel. As the chapter weaves back and forth between stories of the scandalous sons and the story of the boy who heard God, we begin to see something true and hopeful. We remember Mary, pregnant with Jesus, proclaiming that God "has brought down the powerful from

their thrones, and lifted up the lowly; [God] has filled the hungry with good things, and sent the rich away empty" (Luke 1:46–55).

As Mary reminds us, it is better to be hungry than to steal the offerings from the temple to fill your belly. It is better to be lowly than to be powerful. It is better to be poor than to be rich. In the end God will shake up everything in order to repair the world.

A preacher working with this passage might consider the Jewish concept of *tikkun olam*, which translates from the Hebrew as "mending the world." This is the idea that human beings join with God in the work of healing pain and stopping injustices in the world. In the passage for this day, God is repairing the world through a little boy who serves in the temple, a boy who was loved and prayed for before his birth, a boy who got a new robe from his mama each year when she brought her offerings to the temple. In this young boy and in the story of his praying mother, we find deep hope that all that has been lost can once again be saved. We pray that the preacher in Ecclesiastes is wrong—that there is something new under the sun, and its name is hope.

Parenting Hope. What do we do with hope once it has been born? The preacher might suggest that, in this season of Christmastide, our waiting is over: the new baby Jesus has been born in the world again, and this time he is ours to raise. He is inviting us to join him in making all things new. In between Christmas and Easter we will watch Jesus grow up. We will follow him to Egypt, where he will live as a refugee; we will go with him to the temple, where he will amaze all who hear him. In these formative times, we have some parenting work of our own to do. Like Hannah and Mary, we are invited to birth justice into the world, to nurture hope in its infancy, to watch it grow and show us all a new way of living.

When we feel helpless in the face of injustice, it is often because we think we do not have enough power to overthrow the powers that be. Perhaps our paradigm is wrong. Jesus did not enter the world as a military ruler, but as a baby so vulnerable he could have been easily killed by a king. Jesus said to give to Caesar what is Caesar's. He did not run for office or even vote in an election. He knew politics would never save us. Instead, he offered a more hopeful paradigm: that of parenting and nurturing justice into being. The prophet who proclaimed the new world that would come was not a sage or seer but Jesus' mother, pregnant with hope. She echoed the words of another mother before her, Hannah, who was barren but bore a son who reestablished justice in the temple at Jerusalem.

Learning How to Parent Justice. The world we live in is far from just and is often not fair. It is time to ask ourselves the question: what new models of transformation are needed to repair the world? Mary and Hannah give us one such model. We can parent justice into the world. Whether we are biological parents or not, this is work we can all do. For this parenting does not ask that our children be biological. Neither Mary nor Hannah was a biological parent. Mary became pregnant via virgin birth; Hannah, in her barrenness, had a pregnancy that was considered the work of miracles. Both women were asked to parent the hope that God was bringing into the world.

When we look around we can find miracles to adopt and nurture as our own. Hope springs up in unexpected places; children lead the way when our rulers are corrupt. When we listen and look and pray, we will find that we are bombarded with opportunities to repair the world. The small boy in the temple wearing a robe his mama made him learned to listen to God. The preacher of this text would do well to point out that we can too.

Eli's Helplessness and Hannah's Hope. When we and our parishioners hear this story, it is possible we will identify more with Eli than with Hannah. We may be overwhelmed with hopelessness, feeling as if the scoundrels who are not the sons we hoped to raise will soon take over the temple. Even within our own faith, we question how some can call themselves Christians when they seek political gain instead of love of neighbor. We worry that they may undo the work God has done in our midst.

Yes, injustice abounds, but God's justice always wins in the end. No system of governance has ever lived up to the justice that God expects. Our hope comes in knowing that it is within our power to do the work of justice and mercy here and now, even when our rulers are scoundrels.

If we step back and take a long look, we see it over and over again. When those in power do not serve God or care for the people, God will raise up someone. The prophets, the poets, the artists, the leaders, the people who will change the world are here in our midst. Our job as a community is to parent this justice into being as we live in the deep hope that together we can repair the world.

MELISSA BROWNING

Psalm 148

¹Praise the LORD!
Praise the LORD from the heavens;
>   praise him in the heights!
²Praise him, all his angels;
>   praise him, all his host!

³Praise him, sun and moon;
>   praise him, all you shining stars!
⁴Praise him, you highest heavens,
>   and you waters above the heavens!

⁵Let them praise the name of the LORD,
>   for he commanded and they were created.
⁶He established them forever and ever;
>   he fixed their bounds, which cannot be passed.

⁷Praise the LORD from the earth,
>   you sea monsters and all deeps,
⁸fire and hail, snow and frost,
>   stormy wind fulfilling his command!

⁹Mountains and all hills,
>   fruit trees and all cedars!
¹⁰Wild animals and all cattle,
>   creeping things and flying birds!

¹¹Kings of the earth and all peoples,
>   princes and all rulers of the earth!
¹²Young men and women alike,
>   old and young together!

¹³Let them praise the name of the LORD,
>   for his name alone is exalted;
>   his glory is above earth and heaven.
¹⁴He has raised up a horn for his people,
>   praise for all his faithful,
>   for the people of Israel who are close to him.
Praise the LORD!

Connecting the Psalm with Scripture and Worship

A Call for Universal Praise. Psalm 148 calls the world to praise Yahweh. The call includes all creation, from the highest heavens (vv. 1–6) to the deepest seas (v. 7) and everything in between (vv. 8–14). There are no exclusions and no excuses. Everything must praise Yahweh, because Yahweh created everything. Yahweh gave the word, and the world was established (vv. 5–6), so now the creation has something to say in response: "Hallelujah!" The psalm begins and ends with this very phrase, actually a command to the whole universe: "Praise Yah(weh)!" (vv. 1, 14).

As the psalm calls creation to praise, it reveals an ancient understanding of the structure of the cosmos. The psalm invokes the heavenly bodies (vv. 1–4) and catalogs them: the sun, moon, stars, and "the hosts of heaven." In the religions of the ancient Near East, these heavenly bodies—all in perpetual motion—were deities in their own right and worshiped as such. They propelled themselves, giving order to the world as they ran their courses across the sky. This psalm maintains that these heavenly bodies are in fact creations of one God. It was Yahweh who set them in place and governs their movement (v. 6).

As the psalm progresses, the forces of nature join the heavenly bodies in praise. The praise extends to the seas and their most mysterious and terrifying creatures (v. 7). Even though they epitomize the chaotic power of water, these creatures also praise their creator. All manner of meteorological phenomena then add their voices to the chorus. Lightning, hail, snow, frost, and wind express Yahweh's power (v. 8) as they buffet and nourish the earth and all its inhabitants (vv. 9–10). The psalm concludes by calling all humans to

We Must Knock at God's Door

Great are you, O Lord, and surpassingly worthy of praise. Great is your goodness, and your wisdom is incalculable. And humanity, which is but a part of your creation, wants to praise you; even though humanity bears everywhere its own mortality, and bears everywhere the evidence of its own sin and the evidence that you resist the proud. And even so humanity, which is but a part of your creation, longs to praise you. You inspire us to take delight in praising you, for you have made us for yourself, and our hearts are restless until they rest in you.

The house of my soul is too narrow for you to enter it: it needs you to widen it. It is in ruins: rebuild it. It contains things that will displease your eyes: I admit it, I know it. But who will cleanse it? Who else can I cry to, if not to you?—"cleanse me from my secret faults, O Lord, and keep your servant safe from the sins of others." I believe, and therefore I also speak, Lord: you know. Surely I have denounced my sins to you against myself, O my God, and surely you have forgiven my heart's lack of reverence? I am not contending in a court of law against you who are Truth; and I have no desire to deceive myself, lest my sin bear false witness against itself. So I do not contend with you in a court of law, because if you were to examine my sins closely—Lord, Lord, who shall endure that?

Even then you will rest in us, as now you are at work in us; and so that rest of yours will pervade us just as those works of yours pervade us now. But you, Lord, are always at work and always in repose: you do not see in time, act in time, rest in time; but yet you create our seeing in time, and time itself, and rest in time.

At one time, we had the impulse to do good, after our heart conceived by your Holy Spirit; in former times we were being impelled to do evil, while we abandoned you. But you, O God, the One, the Good, you never ceased to act well. There are works we have done that are good—by your gift—but they are not everlasting: after them, we hope to repose in your immeasurable hallowing. You are the Good, you need no good thing, you are always at rest, since you yourself are your own rest.

What human being can give another the power to understand this?
What angel can give it to another angel?
What angel can give it to a mortal?
We must ask it of you.
We must seek it from you.
We must knock at your door.
This, this, is how it will be received.
This is how it will be found.
This is how it will be opened.

Saint Augustine (354–430), *Confessions* 1.1, 1.6, 13.53, in *Confessions*, ed. and trans. Carolyn J.-B. Hammond, vol. 1: Books 1–8 and vol. 2: Books 9–13, Loeb Classical Library (Cambridge: Harvard University Press, 2014 and 2016), 26:3, 11; 27:425, 427.

praise God. As the psalm catalogued the skies, so too does it describe all types of people, starting with the most powerful, the kings, princes, and rulers (v. 11), and moving throughout the community, male and female, old and young together (vv. 12–13). Finally, the psalm names the people of Israel, who have been given unique insight into Yahweh's character as creator and savior (v. 14).

Liturgical Usages. This psalm is the quintessential call to worship. It should be certainly used in that way if it appears nowhere else on the First Sunday after Christmas. Its exuberance sets the perfect tone for the season. The Lord of creation (v. 5) and author of salvation (v. 14) has entered the world in a new and immediate way. This advent summons everything to worship.

The imagery of this psalm has sparked the musical imaginations of numerous composers. The best of these musical settings of Psalm 148 can be found in Gustav Holst's "Two Psalms for Chorus, String Orchestra, and Organ" (1920).[1] Holst sets a short paraphrase of the psalm by F. R. Gray and employs the hymn tune GEISTLICHE Kirchengesäng. Most will know this tune from the popular hymn "All Creatures of Our God and King" and/or the doxology, "Praise God from Whom All Blessings Flow." These hymns will echo in the congregation's ears as they encounter Holst's version of Psalm 148, set to a rolling triple meter along with a polyphonic vocal setting. The cascading tones convey the movement of the heavenly spheres and the churning of the sea. Holst has given us a masterpiece of sacred music and liturgical theology.

Another beautiful musical setting of the psalm is that of the late-Renaissance/early-Baroque composer Jan Pieterszoon Sweelinck (1562–1621). His setting ("Vous tous les habitans de cieux") requires an unaccompanied seven-part choir full of skilled musicians. With its stunning text painting and rhythmic intensity, this piece is well worth the effort, but only with the right personnel. Much more accessible for both choirs and audiences is John Rutter's setting "O Praise the Lord of Heaven." The text of Psalm 148 serves as the ninth part of his *Psalmfest* (1996), and it is a real crowd-pleaser.

Psalm 148 and the Lectionary Cycle. The season of Christmas focuses our attention on the central theme that God would save the world by entering it in an immediate and tangible way. In the Old Testament, Israel held that the name of God, Yahweh, was the clearest revelation of the divine character and activity. The psalmist highlights this name twice (vv. 5, 13) and calls all creation to recognize the divine name of Yahweh through the repeated command: Hallelujah, "praise Yah(weh)!" By using this psalm at Christmas, we answer the psalmist's call to praise, acknowledging the revelation of the divine character through the Word made flesh. In fact, Jesus' very name means "Yahweh is salvation." The name of Jesus demonstrates an essential continuity between the Old and New Testaments. Thus the entire canon of Scripture attests God's nature and God's specific mission in the world.

The psalm, the first lesson (1 Sam. 2:18–20, 26), and the Gospel lesson (Luke 2:41–52) all highlight the role of children in the service of God. Psalm 148 calls children specifically to join their voices in praise of God alongside the rest of creation (v. 12). The first lesson presents a picture of a child who does just that. Samuel, who would become one of Israel's greatest prophets, is dedicated to ministry at a young age. He grows up in God's service (1 Sam. 2:18, 26) and lives in the temple. In Luke's Gospel, the childhood of Jesus mirrors that of Samuel. Jesus is also at home in the temple (Luke 2:49). Like Samuel, Jesus grows in divine and human favor (1 Sam. 2:26; Luke 2:52).

God's ultimate self-revelation could have come through overwhelming displays of power. Yet the almighty creator of the universe comes as a vulnerable child. In the context of the Christmas season, Psalm 148 highlights both the majesty of God and the mystery that this God would enter creation in such a way. The psalm and other lections together witness to the surprisingly important role of children in the economy of salvation and how God's purposes are revealed as the Christ child matures.

JOEL MARCUS LEMON

---

1. While strings are ideal, piano or organ can suffice to accompany the voices.

Colossians 3:12–17

[12]As God's chosen ones, holy and beloved, clothe yourselves with compassion, kindness, humility, meekness, and patience. [13]Bear with one another and, if anyone has a complaint against another, forgive each other; just as the Lord has forgiven you, so you also must forgive. [14]Above all, clothe yourselves with love, which binds everything together in perfect harmony. [15]And let the peace of Christ rule in your hearts, to which indeed you were called in the one body. And be thankful. [16]Let the word of Christ dwell in you richly; teach and admonish one another in all wisdom; and with gratitude in your hearts sing psalms, hymns, and spiritual songs to God. [17]And whatever you do, in word or deed, do everything in the name of the Lord Jesus, giving thanks to God the Father through him.

Commentary 1: Connecting the Reading with Scripture

Scholarship on the book of Colossians focuses attention on whether or not it is an authentic letter of the apostle Paul. That discussion remains unsettled, as do the date and provenance of the letter. Was the letter even intended for Colossae, a town almost completely destroyed by a huge earthquake in 60–61 CE, and not much rebuilt until the second century?

Despite these and other historical problems, the letter is important for the preacher and teacher of the gospel. The purpose for the letter is stated most clearly in two places: 1:23 and 2:4–5. In the former, the author urges the reader "to continue in the faith, stable and steadfast, not shifting from the hope of the gospel that you heard" (ESV). The author apparently assumes that the teacher of this gospel was Epaphras (Col. 1:7–8), "our beloved fellow servant," who has brought news concerning the community to whom the letter is addressed. That news is, in the main, quite positive, since Epaphras has "made known to us your love in the Spirit" (1:8). However, he then goes on to say, "For I want you to know how much I am struggling for you, and for those in Laodicea, and for all who have not seen me face to face. I want their hearts to be encouraged and united in love" (2:1–2). The source of this unity and love is none other than the Christ who is "God's mystery . . . in whom are hidden all the treasures of wisdom and knowledge" (2:2–3). That leads to the summary of the purpose: "I say this in order that no one may delude you with beguiling speech. For though I am absent in body, yet I am with you in spirit, rejoicing to see your good order [my trans.; NRSV "morale"] and the firmness of your faith in Christ." My translation is more literal than many. It might imply morale, but could also mean merely a well-functioning community.

This particular view of Christ is one key to the letter. In the thought of Colossians' author, Jesus of Nazareth is the "cosmic Christ," who has in his resurrection and his place beside God in heaven become a vast figure, ruling over much more than the earthly church and its believers. He is master of the whole universe, a universe he loves with his God as its cocreator. In addition, he is the full image of God. Such an all-encompassing Christ is fully worthy to call his followers to a new way of life, rooted in him.

With that description of the cosmic Christ, the author launches into an extensive catalog of admonitions about false teachers (2:6–23). The content of this dangerous teaching may be summarized under three distinct categories: (1) rigorous ascetic practices, (2) the worship of angelic beings, and (3) the veneration of certain unnamed cosmic powers. The warning against ascetic practices arises from a perceived value and the necessity of severe self-denial. At Colossians 2:18, 23, a Greek word translated in NRSV as "self-abasement" suggests harsh treatment of the body to aid some sort of spiritual practice. This kind of "self-imposed piety" (2:23) is to be avoided. The author urges strongly that castigation of the flesh does not add to the depth of one's piety.

The warning against the worship of angels can be understood in two quite different ways, depending on the ambiguity of Greek grammar. If in 2:18 "worship of angels" means the actual worship by the readers of angelic beings (a subjective genitive), the caution is against worshiping the wrong object—not Christ but angels. If, however, the worship of angels means angels worshiping (an objective genitive) then the warning might be against those who "dwelling on visions" claim to join the angels in their own special worship after an exalted journey to the heavenly spheres. Whichever the author has in mind, such practices are to be avoided as impediments to the correct worship of God through the Christ.

The third category of dangerous false teaching and practice is not easy to define, but clearly has to do with "cosmic elements" or, as the NRSV translates, "the elemental spirits of the universe" (2:8, 20). Whatever these mysterious forces may be, they appear to be identical to the "principalities and powers" (NRSV "rulers and authorities") in Colossians 2:15. These powers are said to have control over the readers of the letter, and control over them can only be achieved, according to the false teaching, by devotion to the ascetic, ritual, and cultic practices that are rejected by the letter writer (2:20–23).

This leads us to the lection of the day. When believers devote themselves to the worship of the Christ as he is described in the magnificent hymn of Colossians 1:15–20, that Christ who is nothing less than "the firstborn of all creation," who is "the head of the body, the church," in whom "all the fullness of God was pleased to dwell," all false teachings are swept aside. All harsh ascetic practices, all so-called visionary journeys, all fear of unseen powers of the universe, become moot. The results of right worship and belief are described in Colossians 3:12–17. They may now readily clothe themselves with "compassion, kindness, humility, meekness, and patience." They may now "bear

with one another, and if any has a complaint against another," may "forgive each other, just as the Lord has forgiven you." "Above all, clothe yourselves with love, which binds everything together in perfect harmony." These signs of devotion to Christ are set in sharp contrast to the results of the false teachings that were outlined in Colossians 3:5: "fornication, impurity, passion, evil desire, and greed (which is idolatry)."

In short, the writer concludes, "let the peace of Christ rule in your hearts, to which indeed you were called in the one body. And be thankful" (3:15). The author calls us to be thankful for our freedom from the false teachings that lead to the terrible outpourings of rage, fury, greed, and evil desires; those "self-imposed pieties" that lead us away from love and peace that are the gifts of the Christ who has "reconciled to himself all things, whether on earth or in heaven, by making peace through the blood of his cross" (Col. 1:20).

For anyone deeply concerned about the environmental problems that we all face, this portrait of a cosmic Christ, a Christ who is "all in all," who has reconciled all things to himself, serves as the basic scaffolding for any genuinely Christian discussion of environmental issues. Such issues are then far more than "liberal vs. conservative" ones, but are centrally Christian ones, since Christ has acted as "the image of the invisible God" both "on earth and in heaven," acting as reconciler of all things, and bidding us to join him in the task of reconciliation.

The grand sweep of the portrait of the Christ in Colossians calls to mind the rich picture of the heavenly high priest of Hebrews, as well as the painting in John 1 of Jesus as the Word made flesh, living and loving among us. On this First Sunday after Christmas Day, we can begin to flesh out the multiple meanings of the birth of this one who is before all worlds, yet who comes to us first as the innocent babe of Bethlehem. A wondrous paradox from a wondrous God! More than enough to call forth our thanks and praise!

JOHN C. HOLBERT

Commentary 2: Connecting the Reading with the World

Wearing the practices of faith. The apostle gives to the new believers in the new church in Colossae a new image for living out their faith: Since you are now believers in Jesus Christ, and part of the body of Christ, put on the new clothes of Jesus Christ. Wear these things that demonstrate who you are now. Wear compassion and kindness and humility and meekness and patience. Above all, clothe yourselves with love.

One of the mantras of the consumer world in which we live is "You are what you wear." This mantra supports a global textile industry that is worth an estimated three thousand trillion dollars annually. It is this claim that causes persons to purchase clothes even when their walk-in closets are full to overflowing. Indeed, the very idea of a room dedicated to one's clothing and shoes is anathema to much of the world's population.

While the preacher might rail against this consumerism, the idea here of clothing one's self is not for ostentation or self-gratification but rather as a witness to one's dedication to Christ and the community of followers of Jesus of Nazareth. The idea here is very much in keeping with the mantra of "you are what you wear." Think of the countless T-shirts sold at conferences and concerts and sporting events. In wearing a shirt celebrating your favorite team or commemorating an event you experienced, you are making a claim about what is important to you. That is the concept here.

"Compassion, kindness, humility, meekness, and patience": this is not only a list of the traits of what it means to be followers of Jesus; it is a list of the spiritual practices of the people of God. People of God are compassionate and kind and humble and meek and patient and loving. They not only wear these characteristics like clothing; they embody them as part of their very being. Make no mistake; spiritual practices are named so for a reason. They take practice. We do not do them easily at first. We practice because there is a standard here that we are trying to maintain or to which we are trying to attain.

What does it take to "put on" or to wear the Christian practices of love and compassion and kindness? It takes hours and hours of practice. Through the gift of being chosen by God and sustained by God's Holy Spirit, we are to embody these practices, these traits, in response to the amazing grace shown to us in Jesus Christ.

In his book *Outliers*[1] author Malcolm Gladwell cites a study done in Berlin in the early 1990s. A team of psychologists studied a group of professional violinists and measured their practice habits over their years from childhood through adolescence and into adulthood. The question the psychologists asked each violinist was this: over the course of your career as a violinist, from the first moment you picked up a violin, how many hours have you practiced?

Gladwell reports that according to the study, all of the violinists began to play roughly around the age of five. But at eight, practice times began to diverge. By the time they reached twenty, the elite violinists, the best of the group, who had achieved a high status in the field and were playing with some of the most prestigious symphonies, orchestras, and ensembles across Europe and around the world, had practiced for more than ten thousand hours each. The less accomplished violinists, who were employed but not considered among the elite of their craft, averaged around four thousand hours of practice.

One especially fascinating finding in the study was the question about those who were thought to be "naturally gifted." The psychologists found no statistical difference in the hours of practice between those who were described as gifted and those who worked hard. Even for those who were thought to have a special gift, the hours of practice were similar. There were no shortcuts.

The apostle also calls on the people of Jesus Christ to bear with one another—an important invitation to remember that our practicing is not a solo endeavor. We are to do this with one another and support one another—at times calling each other to be accountable and to forgive and to be joined with one another as the one body of Jesus Christ. These words were not

---

1. Malcolm Gladwell, *Outliers* (New York: Little, Brown & Co., 2008), 38–39.

written to one individual. They were written to a community of people who together were doing their best to be Christ's new community. This is the best way that we practice who we are becoming: with one another.

To understand this even further, reflect on a spiritual practice not as an individual venture but as a communal one. The city of Philadelphia in Asia Minor was so named because it was known throughout the Roman Empire for the ways it embodied love. Think of it: A whole city known for its hospitality and love for others. Congregations are similar. Congregations have a culture that becomes known. Some will say one church is a "warm" one, or conversely, another church is a "cold" one. Some will say this congregation is generous and another congregation is known for welcoming the stranger. This text affords the preacher an opportunity to ponder with the congregation some questions: How are we known to others? What particular spiritual practices do we embody? What practice do we need to hone and refine?

The passage closes by lifting up love as the binder that draws everything together. The essence of Edwin Friedman's systems theory, explained in his crucial work *Generation to Generation,*[2] resonates here. Friedman describes the power of an individual in a smaller system or a small group of persons in a larger system to infect the whole. A toxic individual will spread that toxicity to others. Likewise, in a system a small group of leaders who treat one another with love and who embody the peace of Christ will infect the whole with the love and peace of Christ. American anthropologist Margaret Mead is often quoted as saying, "Never doubt that a small group of thoughtful, committed citizens can change the world. Indeed, it is the only thing that ever has." Mead's words ring true in light of Friedman's systems theory.

A word of hope from the preacher is the reminder that Jesus gathered a small group of men and women to walk with him during his public ministry, to witness to all he did. Then after his death and resurrection, this small group continued to tell others and to show others a new way of living. That way of life spread to other small groups, even to a fledgling gathering in Colossae in Asia Minor; together, these small groups changed the whole world. It is the same today.

This text invites preachers to reflect on what it means to wear love. Wear compassion. Wear kindness. Wear humility. Put these on as you do new garments after your baptism as a new creature in Jesus Christ. Live into them so they become more comfortable and part of your being. In this way, the apostle says to the believers, Christ will dwell in you, even as you abide with him.

RODGER Y. NISHIOKA

---

2. Edwin Friedman, *Generation to Generation* (New York: The Guilford Press, 1985).

Luke 2:41–52

⁴¹Now every year his parents went to Jerusalem for the festival of the Passover. ⁴²And when he was twelve years old, they went up as usual for the festival. ⁴³When the festival was ended and they started to return, the boy Jesus stayed behind in Jerusalem, but his parents did not know it. ⁴⁴Assuming that he was in the group of travelers, they went a day's journey. Then they started to look for him among their relatives and friends. ⁴⁵When they did not find him, they returned to Jerusalem to search for him. ⁴⁶After three days they found him in the temple, sitting among the teachers, listening to them and asking them questions. ⁴⁷And all who heard him were amazed at his understanding and his answers. ⁴⁸When his parents saw him they were astonished; and his mother said to him, "Child, why have you treated us like this? Look, your father and I have been searching for you in great anxiety." ⁴⁹He said to them, "Why were you searching for me? Did you not know that I must be in my Father's house?" ⁵⁰But they did not understand what he said to them. ⁵¹Then he went down with them and came to Nazareth, and was obedient to them. His mother treasured all these things in her heart.

⁵²And Jesus increased in wisdom and in years, and in divine and human favor.

Commentary 1: Connecting the Reading with Scripture

Many North Americans are interested in the personal lives of public figures. Since the text today provides the only biblical material focusing on Jesus between his infancy and his immersion, people often come to this vignette with biographical curiosity. However, many scholars today think the point of the story is more theological than historical.

The realm of God is the larger thematic context in which to interpret today's lection. Luke presupposes an apocalyptic worldview that sees history divided into two ages. The old age is characterized by the rule of Satan and the demons, idolatry, injustice, violence, fractiousness, sickness, scarcity, enmity with nature, and death. To rectify this situation, God will destroy the old creation and replace it with the realm of God, a new world characterized by the rule of God and the angels, true worship, justice, peace, community, health, abundance, harmony with nature, and eternal life. The realm includes the reunion of Jewish and Gentile peoples.

According to Luke, God has begun the transition from the old world to the realm of God through Jesus. The realm is manifest in part in the present and will appear in fullness at the second coming. The church continues the ministry of Jesus.

When telling the story of major figures, writers in antiquity sometimes described remarkable qualities that were a part of the birth and childhood of the figures. These stories helped establish the identity and the authority of the figure by showing that the deity shaped that person from the beginning (e.g., Jer. 1:5). Such stories sometimes foreshadowed themes that would emerge later in the figure's life. They often located the figure in relationship to significant places and peoples.

The stories of Jesus' conception, birth, and presentation function in all the preceding ways. Luke 2:41–52 joins Luke 1:26–56 and 2:1–40 in affirming that God's hand was on Jesus from the moment of conception to shape Jesus as prophet of the realm.

Luke 2:41–52 reveals that Jesus has impeccable Jewish credentials. Not only do his parents faithfully make a pilgrimage to the Passover festival in Jerusalem (2:41–42), but Jesus—exercising his own initiative at the age of twelve—stays behind to engage the teachers in the temple (2:46). When Jesus engages the teachers, he participates in the Jewish interpretive practice of the time, as he does continuously in the Gospel and as the church does in the Acts. Moreover, "all who heard [Jesus] were amazed at [Jesus'] understanding and his answers" (2:47).

By staying behind, Jesus interrupted the lives of his parents. They intended to return home, but they had to interrupt their trip to return to Jesus. When they found him with the teachers in the temple, they saw a clue to his identity and work. Jesus' invitation to the realm of God interrupted the lives of many others in the Gospel and Acts. For Luke, the ministry of Jesus is the model for the apostles and the church. How might we interrupt our lives, as Jesus did, by staying behind (so to speak) to be in the Parent's house, or to be about the Parent's business (the realm of God)?

By the time Luke wrote, the Romans had destroyed the temple. Nevertheless, the temple was still a central symbol of Judaism. Luke wants the reader to think that Jesus was familiar with the temple and its teachers. On the one hand, this shows that the ministry of Jesus and the church continues in the tradition of the temple and Judaism. On the other hand, this familiarity adds credence to Luke's criticism of temple leadership, especially to the claim that God destroyed the temple because of the unfaithfulness of Jewish leaders (Luke 13:31–35; 19:41–45).

The text notes Jesus would still grow "in wisdom and in years, and in divine and human favor" (2:52). Although Jesus was a child prodigy, he gained even more wisdom about the realm of God as he grew and matured. While "favor" is an adequate translation of *charis*, that word has multilayered meaning, as it is often elsewhere rendered "grace." Jesus continued to mature in the awareness of God's grace pouring out through the realm. A preacher might ask, "How do we position ourselves to grow in God's grace?"

As noted, Luke used this story to help the ancient congregation recognize that the ministry of Jesus pointed to the realm of God. The sermon might consider how the ministries of the church continue to point to the realm of God by being about the Parent's business.

The church focuses on children during the Christmas season. A sermon inspired by this text might consider how "Jesus is our childhood's pattern"[1] with respect to growing in wisdom and maturity.

Reading 1 Samuel 2:18–20, 26 in connection with Luke 2:52 illustrates a Lukan literary pattern with theological implications. Throughout the Gospel and Acts, Luke echoes the language of the Septuagint. Luke uses the literary technique of making the Gospel and the Acts sound like the Septuagint, to emphasize that the work of God in the Septuagint continues through Jesus and the church. Just as God guided the life of Samuel, so God guided the life of Jesus. In a way similar to Samuel being instrumental in the reorganization of Israel (from tribal confederacy to monarchy), Jesus was instrumental in the reconstitution from old age to the realm of God.

Psalm 148 invites all nature to praise God for raising up a "horn," a ruler for Israel. According to Psalm 72, the monarch is to lead the community in living in covenant with emphasis on justice. The psalm did not anticipate Jesus, but it fittingly invites praise to God for Jesus because, in Luke–Acts, Jesus announces the realm with characteristics of the just community of Psalm 72.

While Colossians 3:12–17 does not have the psalm in mind, it alerts listeners to qualities of relationship that should characterize life in the community moving toward the realm. These characteristics evoke the sense of covenant per Psalm 72.

Several noncanonical materials, some of which are called the "infancy gospels," tell stories about Jesus' birth and childhood, for example, *Infancy Gospel of Thomas, Infancy Gospel of James, The Book about the Origin of the Blessed Mary and the Childhood of the Savior*.[2]

1. Cecil F. Alexander, "Once in David's Royal City," *Chalice Hymnal* (St. Louis: Chalice Press, 1995), 165.
2. A collection of apocryphal materials, including some infancy gospels, can be found in Bart D. Ehrman and Zlatco Pleše, *The Apocryphal Gospels: Texts and Translations* (New York: Oxford University Press, 2011).

A preacher might tell some of these stories, compare and contrast them with Luke and Matthew, and pursue pertinent questions. Why does the Bible contain only the infancy narratives of Matthew and Luke? Why did people in the early church tell these stories? How does our awareness of them help us think about Christian faith?

The preacher could take the presence of the noncanonical gospels in the church for a sermon on broader considerations of canon and authority for the church. What does it mean to call the material in the Bible "canonical"? Is the canon open or closed? Why do the canonical materials have more authority than materials that the church did not include in the canon? The preacher might help the church consider why it is essential for us to continue to have conversation with and about the Bible.

RONALD J. ALLEN

Commentary 2: Connecting the Reading with the World

In this text, the story of the child Jesus' visit to the temple, the child Jesus is like us in two ways that are both jarring and important to our understanding of Jesus. First, the child Jesus finds himself, as do we all, in a tension between competing loyalties: his loyalty to his parents (v. 48) and his loyalty to his heavenly Father (v. 49). Second, the story affirms that Jesus' humanity means that he, like us, grew and developed. Jesus matured. He was like us in that he was not omniscient; rather, he *learned* things he once did not know. The last verse of the lection is clear: "And Jesus *increased* in wisdom and in years, and in divine and human favor."

Conventional American culture is often so radically family-centered as to be family-idolatrous. Parents live for and through their children, hovering over them, doing almost anything to further their educational advancement, their athletic prowess, and their general comfort. Parents will sometimes cheat and lie for their children. Anything in this world can become an idol, an object of adoration in place of God—even family. Speaking a public word putting family in its place, especially on the Sunday after Christmas, will perhaps be as uncomfortable as it is needful.

The preacher could emphasize our struggle with conflicting loyalties, pointing out how any number of things in our world can beg apotheosis, clamoring to be our little deities. Few stories of hard choices have captured the attention of more people than that of Eric Liddell, the phenomenal Scottish runner and devout Christian who refused to run on the Sabbath in the 1924 Olympics, forgoing an almost certain gold medal in the 100-yard dash. Liddell was a hero in his day (he won gold in the 440) and became a hero again when his story was retold in the 1981 blockbuster *Chariots of Fire.*

More recently, Duncan Hamilton's biography of Liddell, *For the Glory: Eric Liddell's Journey from Olympic Champion to Modern Martyr,*[3] unfolds the story of this man of remarkable integrity who time and again made costly choices out of loyalty to God and his understanding of God's claim on his life. Liddell was always clear about two things: that his athleticism was a gift from God to be used for glory of God, and that sport came in third, behind family and behind God's call to serve as a missionary in China during the tumultuous years before and during World War II. Liddell became a beacon of hope and exemplar of compassion and humility in China, first as a teacher and pastor, and later as a prisoner in the Japanese internment camp where he died in 1945.

Luke's candid acknowledgment that Jesus matured as a person can indeed catch us off guard. That Jesus "grew in wisdom" suggests both a Christology that confesses Jesus' full humanity and an anthropology that confesses that we, like him, are called to "grow in wisdom." New York City, where I live, is eternally under construction, even in the relatively staid neighborhood around the church I serve. Second Avenue is episodically

3. Duncan Hamilton, *For the Glory: Eric Liddell's Journey from Olympic Champion to Modern Martyr* (New York: Penguin, 2016).

torn up for the eschatological Second Avenue subway. Who knows exactly what has been going on under Madison Avenue? There are jackhammers and single-lane traffic week after week. The windy high-rise at Madison and 89th is surrounded by sidewalk scaffolding yet again. They are putting in a new Zabar's where Jackson Hole used to be. The entire city seems to be eternally under construction.

When we first moved to New York, I naively imagined that there would come a day when all the streets would be fixed, the jackhammers would fall silent, all the sidewalk scaffolding would come down, and everything that needed to be built or fixed or remodeled would be finished at last. I now understand that it is *never* going to be all done. In fact, part of New York's identity is that it is always under construction. Likewise, an integral part of Christian identity—our identity with Christ—is to be always under construction, never finished, forever "growing in wisdom." Martin Luther made the point this way: "This life . . . is not godliness but the process of becoming godly, not health but getting well, not being but becoming. . . . We are not yet what we shall be, but we are on the way. . . . This is not the goal but it is the right road . . . all does not gleam and sparkle, but everything is being cleansed."[4]

Some years ago, I heard about Sally, a working mom with a very sick baby. Her young son, John, had developed severe asthma. The young child spent many nights in pediatric intensive care. Often Sally and her husband, Bill, found themselves following the ambulance to the emergency room, praying that their son would be alive when they got there. As so often happens, this fell at a time when the family had inadequate health insurance, the couple having gone through job transition and the insurance company having declared John's illness a preexisting condition. Nights in intensive care cost thousands of dollars. New prescriptions and medical equipment meant selling family antiques, until soon there was nothing left to sell.

At around that time, an article appeared in the paper, reporting on the state's recent decision to go after individuals and families with outstanding hospital debts, referring to them as "deadbeats." With that, Sally had enough. She called the paper, telling what such hospital debt looked like from her family's perspective. The next week, another story appeared in the paper, reporting on John's struggles. As a result, things began to change. Various charitable organizations and churches took the family under their wing, offering assistance with John's bills. The hospital reduced those bills, and John's story was instrumental in the creation of a state fund to help cover catastrophic childhood illnesses.

John is now in his twenties, in good health, and about to graduate from college. He is creating for himself a life of purpose and service to others. Like his, our stories are forever being written. We are always under construction. The challenge ever before us is to be, like the child Jesus, growing in wisdom.

MICHAEL L. LINDVALL

---

4. Martin Luther, *Career of the Reformer II*, ed. George W. Forell, vol. 32, *Luther's Works* (Minneapolis: Fortress, 1958), 24.

Second Sunday after Christmas Day

Jeremiah 31:7–14
Psalm 147:12–20

Ephesians 1:3–14
John 1:(1–9) 10–18

Jeremiah 31:7–14

⁷ For thus says the LORD:
Sing aloud with gladness for Jacob,
    and raise shouts for the chief of the nations;
proclaim, give praise, and say,
    "Save, O LORD, your people,
    the remnant of Israel."
⁸See, I am going to bring them from the land of the north,
    and gather them from the farthest parts of the earth,
among them the blind and the lame,
    those with child and those in labor, together;
    a great company, they shall return here.
⁹With weeping they shall come,
    and with consolations I will lead them back,
I will let them walk by brooks of water,
    in a straight path in which they shall not stumble;
for I have become a father to Israel,
    and Ephraim is my firstborn.

¹⁰Hear the word of the LORD, O nations,
    and declare it in the coastlands far away;
say, "He who scattered Israel will gather him,
    and will keep him as a shepherd a flock."
¹¹For the LORD has ransomed Jacob,
    and has redeemed him from hands too strong for him.
¹²They shall come and sing aloud on the height of Zion,
    and they shall be radiant over the goodness of the LORD,
over the grain, the wine, and the oil,
    and over the young of the flock and the herd;
their life shall become like a watered garden,
    and they shall never languish again.
¹³Then shall the young women rejoice in the dance,
    and the young men and the old shall be merry.
I will turn their mourning into joy,
    I will comfort them, and give them gladness for sorrow.
¹⁴I will give the priests their fill of fatness,
    and my people shall be satisfied with my bounty,
    says the LORD.

Commentary 1: Connecting the Reading with Scripture

The temptation of a quick and cursory reading of Jeremiah 31:7–14 is to take refuge in the grand celebration. God will gather the people and lead them home; they will rejoice and be fulfilled. It is all too easy to hear the prediction as a freestanding promise from God of existential comfort and everlasting blessing.

The rich context of these verses points to the underlying spiritual rhythm of Jeremiah's prophecy. We are caught up in a drama far beyond ourselves, a drama of judgment and restoration, desolation and consolation, God's turning away *and* God's turning toward. This pattern of weeping and rejoicing is damaged by the limits of the lectionary, which only excerpts the full story. Adding Jeremiah 3:15–17 into the mix restores the rhythm in the Jeremiah moment (the joyous promises of God amid the wretched division of Israel) and the future (in Matt. 2:18, the weeping parents following the slaughter of the innocents in the context of the joy of Jesus' birth).

In our text, God's salvation is announced with gladness. The preacher might invite hearers of the sermon to join in the great song by asking questions like, Why the party? What are we celebrating?

As the Lord promises to bring the children of Israel "from the land of the north," we encounter a key image in Jeremiah. Beginning in the first chapter and recurring with regularity (1:14–16; 4:5–10; 5:14–17; 6:1–26), God declares judgment through the coming conquest of Judah by Babylon. Jerusalem will not be spared. The people in Jerusalem will go into exile. God has found both Israel and Judah wanting and has sent them away. God has seen and heard the unfaithfulness of the people and delivered them into judgment. Then and only then, as a faithful shepherd, God will gather the exiled sheep and bring them home.

This rich dynamic is the very fabric of Jeremiah 31. God's people suffer the sword and endure the wilderness, but in God's time will be restored with merrymaking (vv. 2–4). Their experience includes bitter weeping and the fulfilled hope that follows the lament (vv. 15–17). The Lord both disciplines Ephraim and has mercy on him (vv. 18–20). God announces destruction and rebuilding (v. 28). This cadence is highlighted in the proclamation of a second covenant, a new promise, resting on—yet different from—the first (vv. 31–34).

The proper understanding of this rhythm is recounted in Jeremiah 2:7–13. God claimed the people and led them into a bountiful land. There they turned away, going after other gods. The preacher might point out that we cannot grasp the tension of scattering and gathering until we recognize the story that lies beneath: God's initial rescue of the people of Israel from slavery in Egypt is followed by God's sending them to wander in the wilderness for forty years before guiding them into the promised land. Clearly, God is the only one who delivers and provides.

This prior relationship provides the impetus to look for repentance and return (3:11–14; 7:5–7). The eyes and ears of the people, however, prove to be closed to Jeremiah's warnings (6:10).

The framework of Jeremiah's prophecy models for us today the church's openness to divine action. God's ways with humanity are indelibly marked with judgment and mercy (12:14–15). This rhythm delineates the ways of the Holy One with humanity and God's relationship with Jeremiah himself. "Your words became to me a joy and the delight of my heart," Jeremiah testifies. "I did not sit in the company of merrymakers, nor did I rejoice; under the weight of your hand I sat alone, for you had filled me with indignation" (15:16–17). For the church and Jeremiah, to join the song is to accept the divine assessment of our faults and failings *and* receive the healing balm of mercy and restoration. The polarities of this pattern are presented in stark relief (16:9–15).

Only as we look and listen carefully can we avoid viewing Scripture as a kind of existential lollipop, designed simply for our succor and well-being. Only after honest reflection on the range of God's choices are we enabled to submit ourselves to divine direction. Such faithfulness readies us to be molded by the Holy One (18:1–11) and to respond with trust in God's intentions (18:6).

In our era of "truthiness" and suspicion, the

preacher might emphasize that the call of the prophet Jeremiah (26:1–3) is to speak the truth, no matter how unpopular or unacceptable. In a sound-bite world filled with self-centered yearnings, the church may desire quick promises of restoration and homecoming (29:11–14). Overhearing the prophet's words to Judah can alert the church to both warnings of judgment (34:2, 17) *and* promises of restoration (33:6–9).

Jeremiah is the prophet of God's long view, always looking through the present moment to a place and time over the horizon. His words echo the message that follows the Shema and the great commandment in Deuteronomy 6:1–9. God promises the bounty of the land, a good land filled with fine cities, houses, vineyards, and olive groves—and God is also the one we fear and serve, the one by whom we swear. This God of amazing grace is a jealous God, demanding loyalty and faithfulness. The push-and-tug of life with the Lord is unending. The question of Jeremiah is always this: How do we discover God's direction through judgment and redemption? What more is there to learn? How will we experience God anew, through and beyond this moment?

Two of the other lections today echo the trust in which God's promises are received. Psalm 147:12–20 affirms God's commitment to the people of Israel in this rhythm. Again, readers need to look just beyond the limits of the lectionary. Verses 10–11 declare that our rejoicing is rooted not in strength or victory, but in the hope in God, which finds expression by the church through the vicissitudes of life.

Ephesians 1:3–14 invites the church to live into hope, to see and hear far more than first imagined or immediately experienced. The mystery of God's will is not yet completely revealed, and we cherish the daily blessings of forgiveness and wisdom, trusting God's pledge for the future.

The clearest reverberation of the Spirit's voice is the Gospel reading in John 1:10–18. God's ways are revealed through every circumstance. In the gut-level joy/sorrow of our lives, symbolized and enacted by the pain and rejoicing of childbirth, the Divine breaks into our world. God's glory becomes tangible. The curtain is pulled back on the Holy. The richness of God's Word—bane and blessing, chiding and enlivening—becomes transforming grace.

Jeremiah 31:7–17 proclaims the moment-to-moment gift of God's empowering presence in every circumstance of life. The bedrock promise of God's salvation is discovered each day, through honor and dishonor, wealth and poverty, living and dying (2 Cor. 6:1–10). Salvation is never only a result or product, but always an experience and journey.

This perspective frees and impels us to receive the entire scriptural witness—law, prophets, writings, Gospels, epistles—as the church's ongoing encounter with the Lord through consolation and desolation. As the preacher might remind God's people, we are not allowed to hurry to the end, searching only for some positive, tidy resolution. Instead, we are found by God, the one who shakes the foundations, as we live out the divine promises in every moment.

GLEN BELL

Commentary 2: Connecting the Reading with the World

Preachers might invite listeners into the themes of this text by inviting them to reflect on their experiences of home. For some folks, home might mean the house in which they live. For others, it might conjure up memories of the place where they grew up. Home might be where we go for the holidays or where we return each night. In the best of circumstances, home gives us joy, not terror. The preacher might ask, though, what happens when home is associated not with comfort and safety, but with brokenness and violence? How might you hear this text if you are part of a people who has been scattered to the wind? What does home mean when home has been ravaged by war and bloodshed?

In recent years we have seen the numbers refugees and internally displaced people in our world rise at an alarming rate. According to the United Nations High Commissioner for Refugees (UNHCR), there are 65.3 million forcibly displaced people in our world and 21.3 million of those are refugees, meaning they are forced to leave their country. Of these, 10 million people are considered "stateless people," meaning they no longer have a home country and no country has yet received them. According to the UNHCR 2016 statistics, 33,972 people are forced to leave their home each day because of conflict and persecution.[1]

What does home mean to these 65.3 million people who no longer have a home? How might they read Jeremiah's words of hope that proclaim God's people are going home?

Refugees across East Africa tell vivid stories of flight and survival. In recent years, I've had the privilege of hearing some of these stories in the context of working with two organizations in particular: Amani ya Juu in Nairobi, Kenya, and Refuge and Hope in Kampala, Uganda.

Jacob and Esau, twins from Refuge and Hope, fled South Sudan as teenagers when war broke out in the middle of the night. They followed a convoy into Uganda, and from there they were on their own. Brilliant and resourceful, they managed to find people to help them. After spending too much time sleeping on the street in Uganda, they finally managed to find a

---

1. United Nations High Commissioner for Refugees, "Global Trends: Forced Displacement in 2015," http://www.unhcr.org/576408cd7.pdf.

Dispose Us to Be Thankful

Oh thou God of all the nations upon the earth! We thank thee, that thou art not respecter of persons, and that thou hast made of one blood all nations of men. We thank thee, that thou hast appeared, in the fullness of time, in behalf of the nation from which most of the worshipping people, now before thee, are descended. We thank thee, that the sun of righteousness has at last shed his morning beams upon them. Rend thy heavens, O Lord, and come down upon the earth; and grant that the mountains, which now obstruct the perfect day of thy goodness and mercy toward them, may flow down at thy presence. Send thy gospel, we beseech thee, among them. May the nations, which now sit in darkness, behold and rejoice in its light. May Ethiopia soon stretch out her hands unto thee, and lay hold of the gracious promise of thy everlasting covenant. Destroy, we beseech thee, all the false religions which now prevail among them; and grant, that they may soon cast their idols, to the moles and the bats of the wilderness. O, hasten that glorious time, when the knowledge of the gospel of Jesus Christ shall cover the earth, as the waters cover the sea; when the wolf shall dwell with the lamb, and, the leopard shall lie down with the kid, and the calf and the young lion and the fatling together, and a little child shall lead them; and when, instead of the thorn, shall come up the fir tree, and, instead of the brier, shall come up the myrtle tree; and it shall be to the Lord for a name and for an everlasting sign that shall not be cut off. We pray, O God, for all our friends and benefactors in Great Britain, as well as in the United States: reward them, we beseech thee, with blessings upon earth, and prepare them to enjoy the fruits of their kindness to us, in the everlasting kingdom in heaven; and dispose us, who are assembled in thy presence, to be always thankful for thy mercies, and to act as becomes a people who owe so much to thy goodness. We implore thy blessing, O God, upon the President, and all who are in authority in the United States. Direct them by thy wisdom, in all their deliberations, and O save thy people from the calamities of war. Give peace in our day, we beseech thee, O thou God of peace! And grant that this highly favored country may continue to afford a safe and peaceful retreat from the calamities of war and slavery, for ages yet to come. We implore all these blessings and mercies, only in the name of thy beloved Son, Jesus Christ, our Lord. And now, O Lord, we desire, with angels and archangels, and all the company of heaven, ever more to praise thee, saying, Holy, holy, holy, Lord God Almighty: the whole earth is full of thy glory. Amen.

Absalom Jones (1746–1818), "A Thanksgiving sermon, preached January 1, 1808, in St. Thomas's (or the African Episcopal) Church, Philadelphia, on account of the abolition of the African slave trade, on that day, by the Congress of the United States." (1808: NP)

Good Samaritan who paid for their high school education. They share that they are still waiting for someone who might sponsor them for university. Esau says he is proud to be from South Sudan and one day he hopes to return home to help his country, once there is peace. Jacob is not so optimistic. When he talks about home, he begins to cry and to say there was too much bloodshed. He says the only reason he would go home was if he were ready to die.

Jacob and Esau recently joined fifty other refugee youth at Refuge and Hope for a poetry night. They performed a spoken-word piece where they imagined child soldiers choosing peace over war and completely transforming a war-torn nation. Another youth at the gathering performed a poem in which he talked about what heaven would look like and how he was sure there would be no borders, because the borders that divide nations and turn people against people could belong only in hell.

In the passage from Jeremiah, the people are being gathered. The remnant of Israel is being called from the farthest parts of the earth to come back home. Today's passage begins by saying,

> Sing aloud with gladness for Jacob,
>   and raise shouts for the chief of the
>   nations;
> proclaim, give praise, and say,
>   "Save, O LORD, your people,
>   the remnant of Israel."
> See, I am going to bring them from the land
>   of the north,
>   and gather them from the farthest parts of
>   the earth,
> among them the blind and the lame,
>   those with child and those in labor,
>   together;
> a great company, they shall return here.

The biblical Jacob was a twin who wrestled with his brother Esau in his mama's belly. Once he grew up, Jacob deceived his brother in order to steal his birthright. We find his legacy here again in this passage. The nation that has been scattered is finally returning home.

When I asked Jacob and Esau, the twins from South Sudan, if they knew the meaning of their names, they said they grew up not knowing. As children living in a time of war, they lost

their father to the violence. Their mother never mentioned it. When they came to Uganda and joined the youth at Refuge and Hope, they were given a Bible and found their names in its pages. Now they lament that they never had a chance to ask their father or mother to tell them more about why they were named after these twins who became two nations.

The themes of longing for land and longing to return home are ever-present in Hebrew and Christian Scriptures. If there is anything we can say about our own legacy as people of faith, it is that we come from a long line of sojourners, refugees, and nomads. It is no wonder we find so many Scriptures that command us to practice hospitality to refugees and immigrants. Leviticus 19:33–34 says, "When an alien resides with you in your land, you shall not oppress the alien. The alien who resides with you shall be to you as the citizen among you; you shall love the alien as yourself, for you were aliens in the land of Egypt."

We have not yet learned how to choose the citizenship of the kin-dom of God over the kingdoms of this world. The borders that define nations too often define our interactions with one another. In a world where racism and ethnocentrism have become commonplace, how might we live as people who are called to serve a God whose love and grace transcend borders?

For refugees who have lived too long without a home, the idea of settling into a place that is their own can be an overwhelming joy. Jeremiah's words easily resonate with those who truly long for home. Preachers on this text would do well to reflect on the stories of refugees who share in the life of the community or congregation listening to the sermon.

When refugees are resettled in the United States, churches can help them in their transition. By volunteering with organizations such as Catholic Relief Services and World Relief, a church or individuals can adopt a refugee family and stock an apartment with furniture and basic supplies before they arrive. They can fill their fridge or cook a hot meal for them to eat when they arrive after long flights. They can help a refugee family navigate a new culture by helping them read their mail or learn how to shop in unfamiliar grocery stores.

As people who come from a long line of sojourners, we must always be people who help others find their way home. The story in Jeremiah reminds us that our ancestors knew the pain of the wilderness and exile. We come from wandering people whom God pulled together to create a great community. While we rejoice that we serve a God who has turned our weeping into dancing, we must also do God's work by welcoming others into this kin-dom celebration. Our work in this world is to share God's great joy, to be agents of transformation who proclaim the good news of the gospel—that all God's children are welcomed home.

MELISSA BROWNING

Psalm 147:12–20

¹²Praise the LORD, O Jerusalem!
  Praise your God, O Zion!
¹³For he strengthens the bars of your gates;
  he blesses your children within you.
¹⁴He grants peace within your borders;
  he fills you with the finest of wheat.
¹⁵He sends out his command to the earth;
  his word runs swiftly.
¹⁶He gives snow like wool;
  he scatters frost like ashes.
¹⁷He hurls down hail like crumbs—
  who can stand before his cold?
¹⁸He sends out his word, and melts them;
  he makes his wind blow, and the waters flow.
¹⁹He declares his word to Jacob,
  his statutes and ordinances to Israel.
²⁰He has not dealt thus with any other nation;
  they do not know his ordinances.
Praise the LORD!

Connecting the Psalm with Scripture and Worship

Psalm 147 belongs to the so-called Hallelujah Psalms, the five psalms that conclude the Psalter (Pss. 146–150). Each of these psalms begins and ends with the Hebrew phrase *hallelujah,* meaning "Praise Yahweh." Taken together, these psalms provide a climax to the Psalter, calling the entire world to praise and justifying this praise by describing the character and activity of God.

Psalm 147 argues that God is at work in the world, that God is active and visible in nature through the intervention of the divine command, the word of God (vv. 15, 18). God brings together clouds and causes rain to fall (v. 8). God also sends snow, frost, and hail (vv. 16–17). God causes grass to grow and gives food to all animals (vv. 8–9). God causes the temperature to change (vv. 17–18) and moves the wind and water (v. 18).

To be sure, the ideas presented in this psalm are very different from modern views of nature. Today science attributes such phenomena to atmospheric pressure systems, evaporation and condensation, photosynthesis, the force of gravity, and the like. To acknowledge these natural processes does not deny that God is at work in the world, but the modern preference for scientific knowledge over theological knowledge complicates such claims.

It is important to realize that the psalmist's claims were complicated in their ancient context as well. Numerous deities were understood to be governing the forces of nature. Indeed, many of these forces of nature were personified as gods themselves. Israel's neighbors, and many within Israel itself, worshiped these gods. So when the psalmist claims that God orders the ecosystem, it is an exclusive claim about God's power over and against other divine agents.

Moreover, the psalmist argues that God has uniquely revealed God's self to the community. At the beginning of the lection, the phrase "Praise your God, O Zion" (v. 12) calls the people to acknowledge their special relationship with their God. At the end of the reading, the psalm maintains that the community of Israel has unique access to God because God's word is revealed through God's statutes and ordinances (vv. 19–20). The God who is in control of the workings of nature extends that control though a series of laws to the community. Verses 18 and 19 make this connection clear through a shared grammatical structure: "he sends out his word [*dabar*] and melts [the snow and hail]" (v. 18), and "he declares his word [*dabar*] to Jacob, his statutes and ordinances to Israel" (v. 19). God's word orders the ecosystem and orders the human community that inhabits it.

The first lesson for this Sunday, from Jeremiah 31:7–14, begins like the psalm with a call to praise God (v. 7). For Jeremiah, the call to praise accompanies a plea for salvation: "Save, O LORD, your people" (v. 7). To be sure, both praise and plea acknowledge that God is in control. Otherwise, there would be no reason for speaking to God in these ways.

One difference in the rhetoric of Psalm 147 and Jeremiah 31 is this: While the psalmist heralds God's ordering work in the world, Jeremiah focuses on God's reordering work. God must reconstitute the community that has been devastated by exile. This community has a unique relationship with God that was predicated on God's giving the law to the people. Despite the strain of Israel's sin and its consequences (v. 10), the relationship cannot be broken. Indeed, Jeremiah describes God as Israel's father (v. 9), shepherd (v. 10), and redeemer (v. 11). All of these roles suggest that God is both powerful and active in supporting the community. Such claims are complicated by the agony of exile, but Jeremiah argues that God's word is still valid.

Jeremiah announces a time when the reordered people will come together and sing on Mount Zion. The multitude will come from all corners of the earth. It will include people who are in need of great care and who are thus the most vulnerable: "the blind and the lame, those with child and those in labor" (v. 8). God's reordered community excludes no one. As they travel to Mount Zion, God provides ample water for the journey ("I will let them walk by brooks of water," v. 9). And when they arrive, the fruits of the earth gladden these people (vv. 13–14), a bounty that includes abundant grain, wine, oil, and flocks (v. 12). Jeremiah does not include the song that the people will sing on Mount Zion, but one can imagine a song of praise like Psalm 147, one which describes an ecosystem under God's control and care. In fact, Jeremiah describes the people like a "watered garden," one that thrives because of God's constant attention (v. 12). Thus, the reordered people themselves reflect the ordered ecosystem that God causes them to inhabit.

In the context of the Christmas season, we can appreciate the various ways that the "word of God" appears in both Psalm 147 and Jeremiah 31. For the psalmist, God's word is the divine order that is apparent in God's control of nature (Ps. 147:15, 18). The psalmist also understands God's word as the law (Ps. 147:19–20). The law gives the community a mode of living that will promote God's order—right relationships among the people. In Jeremiah 31, the word of God appears through a prophecy of hope that allows for a new order to emerge for a disordered community: "Hear the word of the LORD, O nations, and declare it in the coastlands far away" (v. 10).

The advent of the word of God made flesh in Jesus Christ gives a further and fuller way of understanding God's word at work in the world. In this season, we offer praise to God because God continues to order and reorder the world through the person and work of Jesus Christ.

JOEL MARCUS LEMON

Ephesians 1:3–14

³Blessed be the God and Father of our Lord Jesus Christ, who has blessed us in Christ with every spiritual blessing in the heavenly places, ⁴just as he chose us in Christ before the foundation of the world to be holy and blameless before him in love. ⁵He destined us for adoption as his children through Jesus Christ, according to the good pleasure of his will, ⁶to the praise of his glorious grace that he freely bestowed on us in the Beloved. ⁷In him we have redemption through his blood, the forgiveness of our trespasses, according to the riches of his grace ⁸that he lavished on us. With all wisdom and insight ⁹he has made known to us the mystery of his will, according to his good pleasure that he set forth in Christ, ¹⁰as a plan for the fullness of time, to gather up all things in him, things in heaven and things on earth. ¹¹In Christ we have also obtained an inheritance, having been destined according to the purpose of him who accomplishes all things according to his counsel and will, ¹²so that we, who were the first to set our hope on Christ, might live for the praise of his glory. ¹³In him you also, when you had heard the word of truth, the gospel of your salvation, and had believed in him, were marked with the seal of the promised Holy Spirit; ¹⁴this is the pledge of our inheritance toward redemption as God's own people, to the praise of his glory.

Commentary 1: Connecting the Reading with Scripture

The author of Ephesians, whether Paul or a Pauline follower, argues that Christ is the head of a church that possesses cosmic status no less than its head. This theme is related to but different from that of the sibling letter Colossians, which focuses primarily on the cosmic status and role of Christ. The great hymn of Colossians 1:15–20 enumerates the portrait of the universal rule of Christ over all things in heaven and on earth. In Ephesians, by contrast, the church itself finds its very reason for existence and discovers its purpose for the believers in its midst. For the Ephesians author, Christ is head of the church, but because that is so, the church has also a cosmic status in the plan of God.

The Ephesians and Colossians letters clearly arise from the same world of thought, sharing several ideas: (1) Christ is head of the church, which is his body (Col. 1:18; 2:19; Eph. 1:22; 4:15–16; 5:23); (2) a believer's resurrection with Christ has already been experienced (Col. 2:12–13; 3:1; Eph. 2:4–7; (3) a divine "fullness" (*plērōma*) in Christ is possible (Col. 1:19; 2:9; Eph. 1:10, 23; 3:19; 4:13); (4) the plan of God is a great mystery (Col. 1:26–27; 2:2; 4:3; Eph.

1:9; 3:3, 4, 9; 5:32; 6:19); (5) all things will one day be "reconciled" (Col. 1:20, 21–22; Eph. 2:16). Both letters offer these crucial New Testament themes, many of which are illuminated further especially in the Gospel of John.

One gift Ephesians offers to the communities of emerging Christianity is its emphasis on the full participation of the Gentiles in the promises of God, a participation that is nothing less than a fundamental part of the divine plan "to gather up all things in him [Christ], things in heaven and things on earth" (Eph. 1:10). One is reminded of the account of the Jerusalem council in Acts 15, where the inclusion of the Gentiles is affirmed in the presence of Paul and Barnabas. This plan is the content of "the mystery of the gospel" (Eph. 6:19), called elsewhere in the letter "the mystery of God's will" (1:9) or "the mystery of Christ" (3:4). This "plan of the mystery" has been hidden for long ages (3:5), but has now been revealed in the power of the Spirit to the church's "holy apostles and prophets" (3:1–6).

The church is far more than the vessel of this great mystery; it itself is a crucial part of the revelation of God, because it is itself the "fullness" of Christ and hence shares in Christ's cosmic status. The church is the locus of a new humanity and of a cosmic peace (2:15–16). Indeed, "through the church the manifold wisdom of God might now be made known to the principalities and powers in the heavenly places" (3:10 ESV). In short, the church through Christ has become the center of God's power in the world to confront the forces of wickedness and evil that threaten to overwhelm the emerging communities of faith.

Reflecting on these purposes of the letter, we may see the argument of the long sentence of Ephesians 1:3–14 more clearly. Because the church is a central and crucial part of the plan of God, its continued existence means far more than the struggles of one or two individual congregations. Though we believers are by necessity vitally concerned with those in our churches with whom we worship and pray, Ephesians bids us raise our eyes far beyond our local community to witness the vast role that the Church—with a capital C—is called by God to play. God's Church moves well beyond boundaries of time and place: believers are chosen for salvation, for wholeness, "in the heavenly places . . . before the foundation of the world" (1:3–4). They are destined to be children of God and to receive the grace given by Christ (1:5–6), both destined and chosen (called) to live for the praise of God (1:12) and—because of those heavenly realities—"created in Christ Jesus for good works, which God prepared beforehand" (2:10). It is therefore the Church that serves as both earthly location for believers and heavenly home for those who have been called from the foundation of the world, explicitly for the performance of "good works."

Each congregation serves as a localized home for its members, and at the same time participates in the cosmic work of God through Christ. A recognition of this vast divine calling makes our good actions for Christ a part of God's larger goals for the cosmos, our smallest good actions a significant part of what God has determined for the universe, loved and redeemed in Christ Jesus. This is fully reminiscent of Matthew 25:31–46, where any action for the marginalized is an action directly for Jesus himself.

Surely the author of this letter is intent on convincing the earliest Christian communities that they are involved in something far greater than tiny gatherings for worship and prayer and the singing of hymns. As believers, they are destined to be in their chosen communities, and have been called and appointed before time itself to participate in the heavenly plan of God, which is to reconcile all things to God's self. Through their head, Christ, and beginning with the inclusion of the Gentiles into their communities along with the Jewish Christians, they have formed the backbone of the earliest churches. They have all been called precisely for the doing of good works, the works of justice and righteousness that God demanded from the beginning of the life of Israel and is still demanding from those who claim the name Christian. Ephesians 1:3–14 reiterates the heart of the gospel, that we have received "the forgiveness of our trespasses, according to the riches of [Jesus'] grace." This message leads inexorably to the reality that we have been "created in Christ Jesus for good works" (Eph. 2:10).

Because Christ has been raised and is seated "at [God's] right hand in the heavenly places," God has given Christ a throne and has designated him as "the head over all things for the church" (1:20–23; 4:10). This same Christ has granted power to the believers (1:19); thus God "has raised [them] up with [Christ] and seated us . . . in the heavenly places in Christ Jesus" (2:6 ESV). The baptized have already found salvation (2:4–6); their hope is already fulfilled (1:18–19). Nevertheless, the saved and fulfilled ones still have a "calling" (4:1) to exercise within their earthly histories. We are called and we are saved, but for those very reasons and because of those very realities, we have work to do, as Ephesians 4:2–6 makes plain.

On this second Sunday after the celebration of Christmas Day, the colossal role of the Church (and all churches) in the plan of God may be equally celebrated as God's gift to us, the heirs of Christ in the world. It may be especially significant to emphasize this letter's call for a larger vision of the Church on Sundays after the joy and excitement of Christmas is over, when church attendance tends to be quite low. Though the larger Christmas crowds have disappeared from many of our sanctuaries, Ephesians reminds us that the Church remains as the living embodiment of Christ in the world, and as such continues to have eternal significance in the plan of God.

JOHN C. HOLBERT

Commentary 2: Connecting the Reading with the World

By God's grace, we are members of a family in which we have always been chosen to be a part—even before we were birthed. The fact of each one's adoption into the family of God underscores the fact that adoption is not a lesser way of entering a family than biological connection. Adoption might be understood, in fact, as making manifest familiar relationships that have always been real.

Sarah Lynn was adopted by a loving family as an infant. As a child, one of her favorite activities was to sit with her parents and older brother at night and read a book together. One evening, her mother was reading to her from a book that had become one of Sarah Lynn's favorites. It was a children's picture book about a little girl being adopted and finding her new family. As her mother was reading, Sarah Lynn interrupted and, as if understanding for the first time, said to her Mom, "I am adopted too." Her Mom said, "Yes, you are adopted too, Sarah Lynn." Then Sarah Lynn looked at her and said, "Only you are not my new family. You are the family I was supposed to be with from before I was born."

Sarah Lynn has it right, as the text from Ephesians affirms. As members of the family of God, adopted as God's children through Jesus Christ, we are not part of a new family. Much of American culture places great emphasis on the biological family. This is a very Western and fairly recent perspective, even in our brief national history. The preacher would do well to provoke the congregation to reexamine their own biases about biological children versus adopted children. Many have a sense that being adopted, while lovely, is still less than ideal and even less than what God intends. It is a surprise then when we encounter families who either have biological children or are able to have biological children but choose instead to adopt. We view adoption at best as a magnanimous gesture to heal some of the brokenness in the world and at worst as a burden or even curse. If anything, these words from Ephesians tell us that adoption is not a curse or a burden but, rather, God's plan for all God's children.

In reflecting on cultural attitudes about adoption and families, the preacher might note that a challenge for many nuclear families today is an increasing sense of isolation. While there are still pockets of extended families that live in proximity to one another, this is more unusual than the norm. Peter Wenz argues that one invention that has significantly changed how we live as families and communities is the air conditioner.[1] No longer are families sitting on front porches in the late afternoon and early evening watching each other's children and talking with one another. We spend our time now indoors, more isolated from one another than ever, thus emphasizing the biological family rather than the communal one.

All of us need relationships beyond our biological family. The preacher would do well to remind the listener that the writer of the Letter to the Ephesians is speaking in the plural. This adoption is not for an individual but for a community—a whole family that is defined not by biology but by God's claim upon us all.

The preacher can recall the proverb that "it takes a village to raise a child." In many families and cultures, children are truly raised by the whole family and whole community—the village. If one's biological parents are in a difficult place or time, many think nothing of helping to raise nieces or nephews or friends' children. For years, anthropologists and sociologists diminished such adoptive relationships by calling them fictive kinships. The term "fictive" meant

---

1. Peter Wenz, "Synergistic Environmental Virtues: Consumerism and Human Flourishing," in *Environmental Virtue Ethics*, ed. Ronald Sandler and Philip Cafaro(Oxford: Rowman & Littlefield, 2005), 197–213, 204.

that the kinship was fictional or imaginative and neither true nor real. Fictive relationships were considered less than real because they were neither consanguineal (the result of shared blood ties) nor affinal (the result of marriage ties). One can readily see how damaging and biased this way of thinking would be for families.

Being destined by God for adoption as God's children is neither fictive nor imaginary. Rather, being brought into God's family through Jesus Christ is an extraordinary demonstration of God's love and grace for us all, and at the same time normative and a sign of God's covenantal love.

The preacher could raise up the congregation as the best example of God's intended family. Many educators and pastors make the claim that the congregation is one of the last remaining intergenerational spaces in American culture. If that is true, then in what ways is the congregation taking advantage of its role as an intergenerational village for grandparents whose children and grandchildren live far away, for grandchildren who see their grandparents only once or twice a year for a few days at a time, and for the young mother and young father who need help raising a new baby? Possibilities abound for the congregation to live out the adoption that we all share by the grace of God in Jesus Christ.

One young man, upon his graduation from high school, asked for a moment of personal privilege to speak to the congregation. His father had died suddenly when he was five years old; he and his mother had been cared for through their grieving and in the years that followed. Before leaving for college, he stood up before the whole church and read from a list in a shaky voice, thanking persons by name for teaching him to drive and helping him learn how to knot a tie for his prom; for taking him golfing and coming to see him in the school play. He told them that they helped raise him and showed him that he was part of this church family. If the preacher were to go beyond making more general references to the congregation as an "intergenerational family" and instead—like this young man—also named persons and the particular role each one played in the family, the concept of being the "body of Jesus Christ" for one another would become an actuality.

What follows, then, as children of God, is that we are part of an inheritance that God bestows upon us all as the body of Christ. In the legal sense, inheritance refers to the transfer of actual property or goods received after a family member's death. For the Jewish people, one's inheritance extended beyond physical goods to name and status. In the theological sense, inheritance is more like this: we are heirs together with Christ, recipients of God's amazing gift of grace, not at some moment in the future, but in the here and now. Salvation is not some far-off gift but one we receive today. Being welcomed into the kingdom of God—into a joyful existence with God—is not just for the afterlife; it happens here and now. When we baptize, we proclaim that the baptized one has been "marked as Christ's own forever." This is as clear a statement of inheritance as there can ever be. We are adopted into God's family as children of God. As the children of God, we share in the inheritance of the God who, in Jesus Christ, has marked us as God's own today, for eternity.

RODGER Y. NISHIOKA

John 1:(1–9) 10–18

¹In the beginning was the Word, and the Word was with God, and the Word was God. ²He was in the beginning with God. ³All things came into being through him, and without him not one thing came into being. What has come into being ⁴in him was life, and the life was the light of all people. ⁵The light shines in the darkness, and the darkness did not overcome it.

⁶There was a man sent from God, whose name was John. ⁷He came as a witness to testify to the light, so that all might believe through him. ⁸He himself was not the light, but he came to testify to the light. ⁹The true light, which enlightens everyone, was coming into the world.

¹⁰He was in the world, and the world came into being through him; yet the world did not know him. ¹¹He came to what was his own, and his own people did not accept him. ¹²But to all who received him, who believed in his name, he gave power to become children of God, ¹³who were born, not of blood or of the will of the flesh or of the will of man, but of God.

¹⁴And the Word became flesh and lived among us, and we have seen his glory, the glory as of a father's only son, full of grace and truth. ¹⁵(John testified to him and cried out, "This was he of whom I said, 'He who comes after me ranks ahead of me because he was before me.'") ¹⁶From his fullness we have all received, grace upon grace. ¹⁷The law indeed was given through Moses; grace and truth came through Jesus Christ. ¹⁸No one has ever seen God. It is God the only Son, who is close to the Father's heart, who has made him known.

Commentary 1: Connecting the Reading with Scripture

The Gospel of John plays such a large role in Christian theology that its prologue appears twice in the lectionary in the span of two weeks. The first time, on Christmas Day, the emphasis is on the event of the incarnation itself. The reading occurs also on the Second Sunday after Christmas Day, to focus more on the redemptive effects of the incarnation. The preacher who focuses on the Gospel today should consult the comments on Christmas Day Proper III for the worldview of the Gospel of John and the function of John 1:1–18, commonly known as the prologue.

The prologue reveals the identity of Jesus, establishes the authority of Jesus, and introduces the work of Jesus as revealing God and the possibility that Jesus' followers can experience heaven on earth. These themes would be an appropriate follow-up to Christmas Day, especially if the Second Sunday after Christmas is the first Sunday in the new calendar year. To whom—and for what—do we listen in the new year?

The immediate and larger literary contexts evoke an unfortunate theme in John: a negative relationship between the leaders of traditional synagogues that did not believe in Jesus (whom John often calls "the Jews") and the congregation to whom John wrote (the Johannine synagogue) (e.g., John 1:19; 5:16; 9:22–23). Following J. Louis Martyn, many scholars think that traditional synagogues had banned John's group because those leaders saw the excommunicants as insufficiently Jewish (e.g., John 9:22, 34; cf. John 12:42; 16:2).[1] John writes, in part, to assure the Johannine synagogue that they are truly Jewish and the authentic heirs of Judaism, to the exclusion of Jewish people who did not believe in Jesus (e.g., John 8:44).

From this perspective, scholars note that

1. J. Louis Martyn, *History and Theology in the Fourth Gospel.* New Testament Library (Louisville, KY: Westminster John Knox Press, o.p. 1967, rev. 1979, rev. 2003).

John's picture of "the Jews" is less a recollection of historical information from the time of the historical Jesus and more a retelling of the story to discredit leaders of traditional synagogues in John's own time, and to reinforce the authority of leaders in the Johannine synagogue.

Against this backdrop, speaking of "the beginning" and the "word," John 1:1 implies that Genesis 1 gives an incomplete picture of the act of creation: Christ is the true agent, the Word, through whom God made the world. The real children of God are not the people Israel, but those who believe in Jesus (John 1:12–13). John 1:14 uses the same word for "lived" ("dwelled," "pitched a tent") that occurs in the Greek text of Exodus 33:9; 40:34; and Ezekiel 37:27. This indicates that Jesus replaces the mode of divine presence invoked in Exodus and Ezekiel. Preachers could emphasize that Jesus the Word travels with the church through wilderness and exile in a way similar to God traveling with Israel.

For John, the law (Torah) and Moses are insufficient religious expressions, since they do not fully reveal grace or truth (John 1:17; cf. John 1:45; 6:31–33; 9:28, 35). In contradiction to Exodus 24:9–10, John claims that no one except Jesus has seen God (John 1:18).

While John's larger purposes include assuring the Johannine synagogue of its Jewish legitimacy, John's strategy unnecessarily discredits Jewish tradition through caricature and misrepresentation. These theological moves contributed to the swell of anti-Semitism that climaxed in the Holocaust.

A preacher could move from this text to a reflection on the relationship of Christianity and Judaism today. After a sketch of John's view of the relationship, the sermon could critique it as historically and theologically inadequate, posing the idea that Jews and Christians today can live in mutual respect and solidarity.

A preacher might name and condemn caricature, misrepresentation, and polarization evident in religious circles and in wider public life. Such behavior is not consistent with a gospel that calls for people to love one another (e.g., John 13:34–35)

The prologue is a kind of first-century elevator speech, a speech summarizing a big issue that a person gives in the two minutes an elevator takes going from the ground floor to the top floor. The speech sets out the bare bones of an idea as directly as possible. In the spirit of an expanded elevator speech, the sermon could explain the notion of the Word becoming flesh so that people in the elevator have the possibility of knowing God, living in God, and experiencing heaven in the midst of the world.

The commentary on Christmas Day Proper III considers the major themes of the prologue in relationship to the Gospel of John as a whole. For today, the text invites us to focus on references to John the Baptist (John 1:6–9, 15; 19–42; 10:41–42). Scholars think there was rivalry between John's disciples and Jesus' disciples over which leader was more important. While the four Gospels agree that John was insightful, they indicate that Jesus was categorically different. A preacher might ponder where we encounter figures and forces similar to John today—insightful but incomplete.

Additionally, the Fourth Gospel uses John the Baptist to indicate the proper role for those who recognize revelation in Jesus: they *point* to Jesus. How can the congregation point to Jesus as they "testify to the light"?

While the four lections are not connected by direct literary allusion, the readings share the theme of God acting in redemptive ways. Jeremiah 31:7–14 is excerpted from an oracle of salvation, spoken during the exile, to assure the community that God would end the exile and gather the exiles in their homeland. Psalm 147:10–20 is a hymn of praise for God's care that gives peace (Ps. 147:10–14a), that provides through nature (vv. 14b–18), and that teaches through statutes and ordinances (vv. 19–20). Ephesians 1:3–14 is a Jewish prayer blessing God for redemption through Christ and pointing to God's intention "to gather up all things in [Christ]" (Eph. 1:10).

While sermons deal optimally with one text, the preacher could use these passages as different perspectives on God's saving work through the Word-made-flesh. While Jeremiah and the psalm were not originally spoken in reference to Christ, the preacher can help the congregation see that God's work in Jesus continues God's desire to end exile and bring about homecoming

(Jeremiah) and to provide things necessary for life (the psalm). Ephesians points to cosmic redemption as God's goal, while positively connecting redemption to God's work in Judaism.

The motif of the preexistence of Christ connects this passage to a larger canonical discussion. This notion receives its fullest statement in John 1 (John 3:13, 31; 5:36–38; 6:46, 62; 7:28–29; 8:23, 58; 17:5, 24), but also comes to expression elsewhere in the NT (1 Cor. 8:6; 2 Cor. 8:9; Phil. 2:5–11; Col. 1:15–20; Heb. 1:1–4; 1 Tim. 3:16; Rev. 3:14). Biblical writers use the notion of preexistence in several ways: to establish the authority of Christ, to point to the continuity of God's purposes from the very beginning of history, and to underscore the reliability of the claim that God redeems through Christ.

A preacher could take several approaches to a sermon around what a congregation might believe about the preexistence of Christ. The preacher could clarify the concept of preexistence for the modern listener. A preacher might argue that preexistence is a foreign category for the early-twenty-first-century postmodern mind-set, and ask what categories today would be at home in a way similar to the notion of preexistence in John's day. In a Trinitarian congregation, the preacher might explore the role of the preexistence of Christ in Trinitarianism, while a pastor in a non-Trinitarian congregation could consider what sense that congregation might make of preexistence.

RONALD J. ALLEN

Commentary 2: Connecting the Reading with the World

Should a preacher begin the Gospel reading at verse 10 or read all eighteen verses of the prologue? The lectionary offers both options, and the decision will affect the direction of a sermon preached on this richest of texts. Verse 10 begins with the pronoun "he," perhaps ambiguous to some hearers without the preceding nine verses, which make it clear that the "he" is "the Word," though the Gospel writer has not yet identified the Word with Jesus Christ. It is only in the first nine verses that the Gospel writer connects the Word with the creative activity of God, and only in these nine verses that John uses the image of light and darkness.

One might reflect on the powerful implications of John's use of the concept of "logos," signaling as it does order and meaning, and his image of light overcoming darkness, a rich metaphor for hope. Our postmodern world is often profoundly skeptical about any overarching order or meaning to the universe. It is often equally incredulous of claims that "light" really is overcoming—and finally shall overcome—the forces of "darkness."

In a cultural context often weighed down with cynicism, John's familiar and fundamental affirmations of "logos" and "light" cut radically against the grain. The Greek *logos*, usually translated as "word," suggests much more than the fragment of speech denoted in English. *Logos* implies order and purpose, reason and rationality, as in its English derivatives "logic," "logical," and "-ology." In a world that despairs of any order and purpose, an affirmation that there is indeed a *logos* governing creation and the arc of history is radically countercultural and good news indeed!

For John—for all Christians—hope is the trust that the light does indeed overcome the darkness. For people of faith, this hope is rooted not so much in us, but in the resurrection of Jesus Christ, God's definitive declaration of the ultimate victory of life over death, light over darkness. Our early-twenty-first-century world is curiously pessimistic about the future. We find ourselves chided by the stunning human toll of twentieth-century totalitarianisms, present environmental concerns, political chaos and dysfunction in Washington, and media that successfully stream into our living rooms global horrors that once stood at a distance from us. In the wake of such realities, many people in our time are distrustful of all institutions, the church included, and the ability of leaders to chart a future of promise.

I say "curiously pessimistic" because there is credible, documentable reason for optimism.

One might refer to Steven Pinker's magisterial study *The Better Angels of Our Nature: Why Violence Has Declined*.[2] The book is a thoroughly documented 700-page argument that, while the current human condition may seem bad, it used to be much, much worse. One could quote Martin Luther King Jr.'s hope-filled line from a 1965 sermon delivered at Temple Israel synagogue in Hollywood: "The moral arc of history is long, but it bends toward justice." Christian hope is more than a human disposition toward optimism—whether merely a positive attitude or Pinker's documented historical positivity—because our hope is grounded in what God has done, is doing, and shall do in history.

The lection includes two references to John the Baptist. These are more than narrative asides. John the Evangelist is eager to have the reader understand John the Baptist's secondary role in the narrative of salvation. He wants to make it clear to his readers that John is only the one who points toward the One. Just so, in a sermon the preacher might declare that, in a parallel way, our role as followers of Jesus is to be secondary. Like John, we are called to point away from ourselves to the one who is at the center, the *logos*. A sermon likening our call to pointing away from ourselves to John's vocation to do the same would be perfectly faithful to the text. Indeed, ministers too often can be lured into mistaking themselves for the One, rather than merely one whose call is to point toward the One.

When I was a younger minister, a preacher friend called to ask if I would preach in his church. I was simultaneously flattered and humbled when he told me he was including me in a series of "great preachers" he was inviting into his pulpit. Come sermon time, I climbed the steps into the pulpit and noticed a little cardboard sign taped to the upper edge of pulpit, where only the preacher could see it. The Scotch tape keeping the sign in place was yellow and brittle. The little sign itself was carefully lettered in Indian ink; water had obviously been spilled on it more than once. It said: "'He was not the light, but came to bear witness to the light.' John 1:8."

John and Jesus are often portrayed together in religious art. They appear most frequently at two points in their lives: on that day when John baptized Jesus, and years earlier as infants in their cousin-mothers' arms. Whatever their age, when the two of them occupy the same canvas, they usually appear in symbolic postures that speak more than words about who each of them is. Jesus, whether a grown man or an infant, is always at the center of the painting. He often has his index finger slightly raised in a gesture of blessing. John, whether a wild-eyed adult in a loincloth or a child in Elizabeth's arms, is always to the side of the painting. With his hand, he is almost always pointing, pointing to Jesus, pointing with a long, bony prophet finger or with a chubby, little baby finger.

In his book *The Road to Character*, *New York Times* columnist David Brooks talks about what the calls the "Big Me" culture of our day. He notes that there is a survey called the Narcissism Test that asks respondents to identify with statements like "I like to be the center of attention because I am so extraordinary," or "Somebody should write a biography about me." Brooks points out that the median narcissism score has gone up 30 percent in the last twenty years.[3]

We live in a world with magazines with names like *People* and *Us*, even one named *Me*. Ours is a world of Facebook "likes" and selfie-sticks, a world of entitlement, rights, and quests for personal power. Even more daunting is the fact that even religion, even church, even ministry, can become all about *me*. Faith is something to make *me* happier. Ministry fulfills *me*. Prayer gives *me* direction. Worship gives *me* peace. John's gracious movement away from the center, his pointing away from self to the one who is the center, is the very liberating movement we are called to make ourselves: to step out of the spotlight, to point toward the *logos*, and confess with the Baptist: "It is not about me. It is not about you. It is not about my career. It is not about my psychological needs. It is not even about my spiritual needs. It is about the One to whom we point."

MICHAEL L. LINDVALL

2. Steven Pinker, *The Better Angels of Our Nature: Why Violence Has Declined* (New York: Viking Penguin Books, 2016).
3. David Brooks, *The Road to Character* (New York: Random House, 2015), 6, 7.

Epiphany of the Lord

Isaiah 60:1–6
Psalm 72:1–7, 10–14

Ephesians 3:1–12
Matthew 2:1–12

Isaiah 60:1–6

¹Arise, shine; for your light has come,
   and the glory of the LORD has risen upon you.
²For darkness shall cover the earth,
   and thick darkness the peoples;
but the LORD will arise upon you,
   and his glory will appear over you.
³Nations shall come to your light,
   and kings to the brightness of your dawn.

⁴Lift up your eyes and look around;
   they all gather together, they come to you;
your sons shall come from far away,
   and your daughters shall be carried on their nurses' arms.
⁵Then you shall see and be radiant;
   your heart shall thrill and rejoice,
because the abundance of the sea shall be brought to you,
   the wealth of the nations shall come to you.
⁶A multitude of camels shall cover you,
   the young camels of Midian and Ephah;
   all those from Sheba shall come.
They shall bring gold and frankincense,
   and shall proclaim the praise of the LORD.

Commentary 1: Connecting the Reading with Scripture

The custom in many churches during Holy Week is to have an evening worship service—sometimes on Maundy Thursday, sometimes on Good Friday—where the lights are gradually dimmed, and the service ends in complete darkness. The point, of course, is that the events of the passion—Jesus' betrayal, trial, and crucifixion—mark a time when the powers of darkness prevailed, leaving people of faith desperately yearning for the breaking forth of Easter light. That same movement—from darkness to light—is at work in Isaiah 60:1–6.

Until recently it was the fashion of critical scholarship on Isaiah to speak of two, or even three, Isaiahs, and to think of Isaiah as a kind of small library containing two or three separate literary works. Lately, however, the scholarly

pendulum has swung back some toward an emphasis on the unity of Isaiah. Yes, material in the book of Isaiah comes from different historical moments, and there are several authorial and editorial hands at work, but all these hands are like quilters working together to make a single quilt.

A significant pattern in the quilt of Isaiah involves the contrast between darkness and light. One of the sins of an unjust society is to confuse the two, to "call evil good and good evil, [to] put darkness for light and light for darkness" (Isa. 5:20). When society is broken and unfaithful, people will look up to heaven and look down to the earth "but will see only distress and darkness" (8:22). When God acts to redeem, the experience is like a powerful light suddenly shattering the darkness. "The people who walked in darkness have seen a great light" (9:2). In the Servant Songs of Isaiah, God's Servant is given as "a light to the nations" and called to "open the eyes that are blind, to bring out the prisoners from the dungeon, from the prison those who sit in darkness" (42:6–7).

The material that comes just before our passage makes it clear that the people are in a season of darkness:

> Therefore justice is far from us,
> and righteousness does not reach us;
> we wait for light, and lo! there is darkness;
> and for brightness, but we walk in gloom.
> We grope like the blind along a wall,
> groping like those who have no eyes;
> we stumble at noon as in the twilight,
> among the vigorous as though we were
> dead.
>
> Isa. 59:9–10

When is this time of darkness? What historical moment is referred to here? Perhaps this is a reference to the Babylonian exile or, more likely, the time of Jerusalem's rebuilding, after the exile has ended and the exiles have returned home to Jerusalem. Then there was a chance to remake society around the ways of God, but it was not to be. God had ended their time of exile and delivered them from oppression, but they came home to live not as the grateful, but as the corrupt. "The way of peace they do not know, and there is no justice in their paths. Their roads they have made crooked; no one who walks in them knows peace" (59:8).

Isaiah is referring to some specific time, but he is also referring to *every* time. Whenever people in any society expect wisdom from their leaders, but get only raw ambition and deceit; whenever people hope for justice from the law courts, but receive only indifference and partiality; whenever people cry out for food, but get only empty plates and hunger; whenever people yearn for truth, but receive only lies and empty promises: then we have come to one of those times when, as Isaiah aptly describes, "we wait for light, and lo! there is darkness" (59:9).

When darkness falls upon the land, what is God doing? God, says Isaiah, is "displeased" when there is no justice and "appalled" whenever human beings do nothing to battle the

darkness (59:15–16); so God takes matters into God's own hands. "His own arm brought him victory, and his righteousness upheld him" (59:16). Even when the people do not keep the covenant with God, God vows to keep the covenant with them.

The images Isaiah uses to describe God's actions in the face of injustice are both terrifying and full of hope. We have all seen news videos of floodwaters spilling over riverbanks and sweeping houses and cars into the raging torrent; we have watched on the Weather Channel as hurricane winds rip away roofs of buildings and pluck large trees out of the ground like twigs. So it is with God. Whenever the structures of injustice stand proud and tall, God comes "like a pent-up stream that the wind of the LORD drives on" (59:19b). This is terrifying, and yet also hopeful, because all this divine fury is an act of salvation. God "will come to Zion as Redeemer" (59:20).

Now we come to our passage. It is as though we have been awake all night during the storm, during the darkness. We have heard the scream of the winds, howling through the trees; we have listened fearfully to the churning of the floodwaters surging by during the long night. Now, as morning dawns, we look anxiously out the window to see what the storm has done. Suddenly the strong and clear voice of Isaiah announces good news:

> Arise, shine; for your light has come,
> and the glory of the LORD has risen upon
> you.
> For darkness shall cover the earth,
> and thick darkness the peoples;
> but the LORD will arise upon you,
> and his glory will appear over you.
>
> Isa. 60:1–2

What Isaiah sees is almost too wonderful for us to imagine. The light that shines in this new day is not simply the morning light but the light of God's glory. In that light, we can see that the divine storm that raged all through the dark night did not bring destruction; it brought redemption. The winds roared terrifyingly, but what they blew down were all the flimsy structures of injustice, and the surging floods washed away all evil, falsehood, and deceit. What is left standing, now glowing with beauty in the light, is the city of God, the beloved community, Mount Zion.

Isaiah describes what he sees and what he wants us to see, and the images dazzle. The city is now so full of light that all the surrounding people stream to it. Even kings are beckoned by "the brightness of your dawn" (60:3; see also Isa. 49:22–23). Broken community is restored, and shattered families are healed. "Look around you," Isaiah says, "and you will see your children coming home" (60:4; see also Isa. 49:18). What is more, that swollen river we feared all through the stormy night now appears to be "an abundance of the sea" (60:5), bringing blessing and prosperity for all. The nations of the earth make a grand procession to the city, praising the God of Israel and bringing the very best gifts they have, gifts so fine they are fitting to be placed on the altar in the house of God—camels, gold, frankincense, rams, and more (60:5–7).

Isaiah asks us to "lift up your eyes and look" (60:4), and when we do, we will see this new community of God shining in surprising places. Isaiah's words are read at Epiphany because of the church's faith that the wise men who journeyed from the east following a star—Gentiles who brought their very best gifts—found the glory of God and the hope of salvation shining powerfully in the face of a baby in a manger in Bethlehem.

THOMAS G. LONG

The Light Not Dimmed by Sharing

The sun never leaves its orbit, never divides. It gives light to all the world, to everyone who wants to be warmed by it. This sun is not defiled by any uncleanness. Its light is one. So is the Word, my Son, one with me and I with him. His most gracious blood is a sun, wholly God and wholly human.

The sun, this light, has in it the color of your humanity, the one united with the other. So the light of my Godhead became lightsome with the color of your humanity. That color became lightsome, fully divinized by the resurrection. The person of the Incarnate Word was penetrated and kneaded from one dough with the light of my Godhead, the divine nature, and with the heat and fire of the Holy Spirit. By this means, you have come to receive the light.

Just as the sun cannot be divided, so neither can my wholeness as God and as human be divided. Even if the host is divided, I would be there, wholly God and wholly human. Nor is the sacrament itself diminished by being divided any more than fire. If you had a burning lamp, and all the world came to you for light, the light of your lamp would not be diminished by the sharing. Yet each person who shared it would have the whole light. True, each one's light would be more or less intense, depending on what sort of material each one brought to receive the fire.

Imagine that many people brought candles. Each candle, the smallest as well as the largest, would have the whole light. Yet the person who carried a one-ounce candle would have less than the person whose candle weighed a pound. This is how it is with those who receive the sacrament. Each one of you brings your own candle, that is, the holy desire with which you receive the sacrament. Your candle is unlit and is lighted when you receive the sacrament. It is I who have given you the candle with which you can receive the light and nourish it within you. Your candle is love, because it is for love that I created you. Without love, you cannot have life.

Your being was given to you for love. In Holy Baptism, which you received by the power of the blood of this Word, you were made ready to share this light. There is no other way you could come to share it. Indeed, you would be like a candle that has no wick and therefore can neither burn nor receive the light. So if you would bear this light, you must receive the wick that is faith. To this grace that you received in baptism, you must join your own soul's love. For I created your soul with a capacity for loving—so much that you cannot live without love. Indeed, love is your food.

Saint Catherine of Siena (1347–1380), *Dialogue* 110, in Suzanne Noffke, trans., *Catherine of Siena, The Dialogue* (New York: Paulist Press, 1980), 206–9.

Commentary 2: Connecting the Reading with the World

The season of Epiphany is a several-week light celebration. The opening line of this first reading for the first day of the season sets the tone immediately: "Arise, shine, for your light has come." Before picking up and running with the image, however, preachers may want to remember that today's hearers carry connotations as to how light "comes" that are a world away from that of the prophet. For us, light can be turned on with the flick of a switch. It is easily accessible—(seemingly) self-initiated—and the illuminated area goes instantly from dark to bright.

Metaphorical associations with "light" often come with analogous connotations. If someone deemed as in "the darkness of ignorance" comes at last "to see the light," that might well come in an "aha moment." Yet enlightenment seldom comes all of a sudden or on cue. Even so-called Damascus-road experiences of spiritual transformation are usually transition points in an extended process of development, a process—as for the apostle Paul—still far from complete.

When God's light comes, as announced by Isaiah, it is not like the night-to-day illumination of high-powered klieg lights. The coming of light experienced by the subdued and chastened faith community to which Isaiah speaks is like the imperceptible dawning of the morning sun, like the slowly building brightness of a kindled fire. As in other poetic oracles (see the text for Christmas Eve, Isa. 9:2–7), the reiteration in cadence of complementary images of darkness and light underscores the felt sense of God's light arising slowly, imperceptibly, rather than in a burst of clarity coming all at once.

Neither such dazzling brilliance, nor the attention-snatching, sense-saturating glare of blinking neon lights is the kind of light Christians anticipate, behold, and celebrate in this season. Rather, Epiphany tracks a light trajectory commencing in gentle dawning awareness, such as Isaiah proclaims, coming gradually over time toward ever greater, richer brightness. That is what a sermon on the feast of the Epiphany will try to prepare for and engender. The brightness of the star of Bethlehem did not require the

magi to put on sunglasses. It was an attention-catching glimmer providing direction for a journey. The glory to which it eventually led its followers was nothing like the aura surrounding the stars of stage, screen, and athletic field.

Physical-chemist-turned-philosopher Michael Polanyi[1] employs a helpful image for envisioning the light of Epiphany. What we can see and understand clearly, he says, is like the circle of focal illumination emitting from a high-powered spotlight. Outside the center circle of brightest light is a penumbra—a "gray area"—partially illuminated in varying degrees. No matter how large or bright the circle of light at the center, the penumbra never goes away. Indeed, as the light source gets wider and brighter, the penumbra gets larger. The illumination of divine revelation is like that. Attention to such an ever-expanding focus is a central thrust in preaching during the succeeding weeks of Epiphany—illumination dawning upon illumination. It might be helpful for preachers to draw attention, with respect to biblical texts and contemporary contexts, to what areas of *partial* illumination may be in shared peripheral vision, on the horizon, in the penumbra of brighter, more focused light.

The prophet's call is for the people of God, in response to the arising and shining glory of God, to "arise and shine"—to become progressively brighter. The appeal is not so much an imperative as an invitation. The more we become aware of ourselves as shined upon, the more we are able to reflect, and the more we are able to shine.

What images and instances of progressive illumination—glory, arriving not as a fixed flash, but as light upon further light—can today's preachers draw? Preachers can surely draw from other places in Scripture (e.g., the prophetic renewal of the ideal of covenant), from the unfolding trajectory of church history (e.g., insights of medieval scholars leading to Reformation illumination), from emerging patterns and structures in society and culture (e.g., the slowly dawning awareness of gender

---

1. See Michael Polanyi, *The Tacit Dimension* (New York: Barnes & Noble, 1966) and *The Study of Man* (Chicago: University of Chicago Press, 1959).

equality and different sexual identities), from distinctive growth dynamics in communal and congregational life, as well as from the preacher's own expanding personal epiphanies (intellectual, psychological, spiritual). To hold up for attention a variety of images that bear witness to sources of gently but relentlessly growing light can itself foster illumination.

Isaiah's promise to listeners who are "nobodies" is that "nations shall come to [their] light," and that displaced sons and daughters will "gather together" and "come to you." Part of the increasing benefit for faith communities that shine with God's growing and reflected glory is that, as they become more enlightened, they become more fully constituted as communities of vocational identity. Imagine the light dancing in the eyes of fathers and mothers as sons and daughters who have been given up for lost or dead begin, from all directions, in widening streams, to make their way home! God's people begin to be seen as enlightening by those in other nations who have previously treated them with disregard and contempt. In this recognition, God's people are enabled to embrace former enemies in a more radically inclusive community. Resources in abundance flow in their direction as former foes, seeing their glory, find them worth investing in. As they "see and [are] radiant," their hearts "shall thrill and rejoice." The poet is replicating in image, phrase, and cadence the progression of light building in ever-growing intensity. The poet's language not only reports what is happening; it contributes to the growing of the light in the celebrating of it.

Preachers will do well to name similar dynamics-in-process in their own communities. Where has a dawning awareness of revelation been attended by the convening of a critical mass of community members? Where has the faith community's influence—previously unrecognized, ignored, discounted, or even ridiculed—begun to attract more favorable attention, gain greater respect? Into what places might a recognition of growing light lead to the faith community "arising and shining" in ways that would evoke a similar arising and shining from forces that they have previously experienced as "dark"?

Isaiah's imagery of increasing resources made available to those who have suffered economic devastation is couched in terms clearly antiquated and, frankly, materialistic: the abundance of the sea, the wealth of nations, camels (lots of camels!), gold, and frankincense. It would be easy to employ the influx of economic resources as a "glory index"—a measure of spiritual brightness—as registered in bigger bank balances, eye-catching programs, more flashy facilities. Any combination of those could, perhaps, be an indirect indication of the energy being released in divine illumination.

It is well to remember, however, that, at the end of the day, according to the prophet, the most important thing that the nations bring to God's people is not camels and such. Rather, both the reconstituting of displaced sons and daughters, and the convening of nations are for one purpose: to proclaim the praise of the Lord. The ingathering of glory, as an end in itself or as an elevation of human beings in whom it is reflected, is nothing more than an insignificant glare. To retain its radiance, glory must ultimately be returned to its Source.

DAVID J. SCHLAFER

Psalm 72:1–7, 10–14

¹Give the king your justice, O God,
and your righteousness to a king's son.
²May he judge your people with righteousness,
and your poor with justice.
³May the mountains yield prosperity for the people,
and the hills, in righteousness.
⁴May he defend the cause of the poor of the people,
give deliverance to the needy,
and crush the oppressor.

⁵May he live while the sun endures,
and as long as the moon, throughout all generations.
⁶May he be like rain that falls on the mown grass,
like showers that water the earth.
⁷In his days may righteousness flourish
and peace abound, until the moon is no more.
. . . .
¹⁰May the kings of Tarshish and of the isles
render him tribute,
may the kings of Sheba and Seba
bring gifts.
¹¹May all kings fall down before him,
all nations give him service.

¹²For he delivers the needy when they call,
the poor and those who have no helper.
¹³He has pity on the weak and the needy,
and saves the lives of the needy.
¹⁴From oppression and violence he redeems their life;
and precious is their blood in his sight.

Connecting the Psalm with Scripture and Worship

Psalm 72 portrays Israel's ideal king. The form of the psalm is a prayer for this king, one whom God empowers to bring about justice. The psalm opens with a request: "Give the king your justice, O God, and your righteousness to a king's son." The community prays that the king's rule will be an extension of God's order, that the monarch's power will realize divine justice on earth. "The king's son" is a royal epithet that expresses the idea that the king has come to power through birth rather than through violence. The king then is no usurper, but an heir to a long and stable dynasty. This stability is another indication of the right relationships that the king enjoys with his family, his community, and his God.

After the opening plea, verses 2–11 present a series of petitions that give a full picture of what Israel hopes for in its leaders. They are looking for a king to be the instrument of divine justice both at home and abroad. Justice is the chief desire of those suffering oppression, the poor and needy. Since the king has the most power within the community, his primary task is to protect those without power. This royal imperative to support the weak appears over and over again in this psalm, underscoring this as the essential task of the king (vv. 1, 2, 4, 12–14).

The king also exerts power throughout the world (v. 8). The king receives tribute from far-off lands (v. 10), with rival kings doing acts of obeisance before him (vv. 9, 11). His preeminence on the world stage is a witness to God's power. For in the ancient world, the patron deity of a king received glory whenever the king exercised domination over his foes.

The psalm also depicts the salutary effects that the king will have on the earth itself. Under just rule, the land is productive. The agricultural economy hums right along. Indeed, the psalm likens the king's just administration to the blessing of rain that enlivens the fields and yields abundance (v. 6).

The psalm refers to the king in the third person throughout. It does not give the king's name. The superscription suggests the prayer should be related to Solomon, but this superscription is most likely a later interpolation. That the king is nameless in this text is highly significant. Leaving open the precise identity of the king allows for readers to apply the psalm's criteria for righteous leadership in multiple different contexts. The psalm thus becomes an instrument by which to measure whether a leader is just and effective.

Based on what is written about Israel's kings in 1–2 Samuel, 1–2 Kings, and the entire corpus of prophetic literature, the psalm's picture of righteous kingship was never realized. In fact, only a handful of kings can even begin to approach the standards of justice and righteousness that the psalm presents. This vision of kingship remained an ideal.

The final verses of Psalm 72 reveal a fundamental shift in perspective. After describing the ideal king in great detail, the psalm abruptly moves to a blessing on Yahweh, "the God of Israel, who *alone* does wondrous things" (v. 18). The psalm thus moves from an extended benediction upon the king to a benediction upon Yahweh alone. Faced with the failure of the monarchy throughout Israel's history, these final verses were appended to the psalm to refocus the attention of the reader toward Yahweh

as king. Yahweh alone, and not any human, is capable of bringing about righteousness and justice within the world.

The first lesson from Isaiah 60 was also written during a time in which there was no king. The failure of the monarchies of Israel and Judah is a painful memory. Those kings were not effective in bringing about God's justice on earth, but Isaiah 60 employs language derived from the royal ideology of the Persian period in which it was written. In this context, the Persian king, the leader of the world's greatest empire, was associated with the sun, whose beneficent rays enlightened the entire world. Isaiah 60 describes this radiant king: "Arise, shine: for your light has come" (v. 1).

However, the light is neither the Persian emperor nor a Judean king. Instead, Yahweh is king. This divine king illuminates the world and blesses it, filling it with abundance. Yahweh as divine king receives tribute from every nation. Dignitaries from foreign lands bring gold and frankincense and camels (v. 6). This procession of tribute testifies to the fact that Yahweh as king exercises total control of the world.

Of course, on the Epiphany of our Lord, Isaiah 60 and Psalm 72 help point us to the kingship of Jesus. Both texts draw from the royal ideologies that were dominant in their culture. The texts also reframe those notions of what kingship means. Isaiah 60 and Psalm 72 suggest that God alone is king, over and against any human who might claim authority as the divine representative on earth.

In Jesus Christ, we see the king who finally enacts God's justice, whose power extends throughout the entire world. Jesus illuminates the darkness. He draws the nations together. He causes the world to rejoice. He delivers the poor and needy. He redeems those who are oppressed. Jesus is the Messiah, the ideal king.

On Epiphany, our attention turns to kings. Traditionally, the wise men are portrayed as kings, though Matthew does not actually make that claim. Jesus is the true king and the focus of our attention. Portions of Psalm 72 can serve as a call to worship to establish at the outset of the service that the one king, Jesus, outshines all other rulers who vie for our attention and loyalty. Since this king comes as child, it would be particularly meaningful to have a child read or sing this psalm, especially the verses that list the characteristics of righteous kingship (vv. 12–14). This would highlight how Jesus overturns all expectations about power, from his coming as child king to his suffering in adulthood and death at the hands of the state.

JOEL MARCUS LEMON

Ephesians 3:1–12

¹This is the reason that I Paul am a prisoner for Christ Jesus for the sake of you Gentiles— ²for surely you have already heard of the commission of God's grace that was given me for you, ³and how the mystery was made known to me by revelation, as I wrote above in a few words, ⁴a reading of which will enable you to perceive my understanding of the mystery of Christ. ⁵In former generations this mystery was not made known to humankind, as it has now been revealed to his holy apostles and prophets by the Spirit: ⁶that is, the Gentiles have become fellow heirs, members of the same body, and sharers in the promise in Christ Jesus through the gospel.

⁷Of this gospel I have become a servant according to the gift of God's grace that was given me by the working of his power. ⁸Although I am the very least of all the saints, this grace was given to me to bring to the Gentiles the news of the boundless riches of Christ, ⁹and to make everyone see what is the plan of the mystery hidden for ages in God who created all things; ¹⁰so that through the church the wisdom of God in its rich variety might now be made known to the rulers and authorities in the heavenly places. ¹¹This was in accordance with the eternal purpose that he has carried out in Christ Jesus our Lord, ¹²in whom we have access to God in boldness and confidence through faith in him.

Commentary 1: Connecting the Reading with Scripture

Ephesians 3:1–12 is a celebration of the inclusion of Gentiles within the people of God. It proclaims that bringing non-Jews into the people of God is the culmination of an eternal divine plan. Yet it is a surprise. There was significant antipathy between Jews and non-Jews throughout the Greco-Roman period. Anti-Semitism was well known in the ancient world, and the derisive Jewish views of non-Jews (Gentiles) are clear here in Ephesians (4:17–19; cf. Rom. 1:18–31). In the earliest days after Pentecost, all church members were Torah-observant Jews. The controversy that erupted over allowing Gentiles to be full members without becoming Torah observant raged for decades, in some places for centuries. By the time Ephesians is written, most church members are Gentiles, but the ethnic distinction between Jews and Gentiles remains clear. While being Jewish brought members and leaders authority in the earliest days (see, e.g., 2 Cor. 11:21–23), the church Ephesians addresses is wondering whether it needs to maintain the connection to its origin in a Jewish church. Ephesians insists that it must.

This letter describes the membership of Gentiles in the church and their receiving of salvation as being brought into what were blessings originally given only to Jews. This is correct both chronologically and theologically. Our whole passage is a description of Paul's apostleship. That apostleship is defined by its mission: bringing Gentiles into the blessings of God. The text makes the salvation of Gentiles a signature feature of the eschatological age. This element of God's plan for the cosmos was not known in previous times, but now, in the eschatological time, it has been revealed to Paul, the apostles, and the church's prophets (3:3–5).

The author of Ephesians, whether Paul or a disciple of Paul, sounds amazed that God's plan to give salvation includes Gentiles. The content of the mystery that has been hidden from all previous times is that God will bring together Jews and Gentiles into a single community of the saved in Christ (3:6). This astounding intention of God has now come to pass. God's eternal plan is to heal the rift between ethnic groups that have been at odds for centuries.

Ephesians goes back and forth in the way it thinks about Gentiles before they have faith. In places they are immoral outsiders who constantly pollute the world with their sin (4:17–19). They are alienated from God's promises to and blessings on Israel (2:11–13). In other places, though, Ephesians recognizes something of a common humanity, as all peoples are named and so claimed by God (3:14–15). Most significantly, Ephesians recognizes that all people need the gospel because all are sinners. Chapter 2 begins by saying that Gentiles were dead because of their sin and were children of disobedience, living as the powers of the world told them. Then Ephesians says "we all" were children of disobedience (2:3). Here Jews and Gentiles have the same need for the gospel.

Jews and Gentiles had been separated by real and important things, but all those are overcome by their common identity as fellow heirs of God's salvation, as members of the same body, and as fellow participants in the promises given through Christ (3:6). They have a common identity and a common heritage. It is not just any heritage; it is the heritage of the historical people of God, Israel. Ephesians emphasizes this to stress the importance of the church maintaining its connections to the God of Israel and so to the blessings of that God. God is not a God who remained unknown until the coming of Christ. The God that the multiethnic church knows in Christ is the God known in the saving acts of Israel's past. Ephesians says the plan of God's multifaceted wisdom was always to bring all people together as a single people in Christ (3:10–11). This unification manifests the vastness of God's wisdom. God's ultimate plan for the world includes healing the divisions among opposing ethnic groups.

Now, in the eschatological age inaugurated by Christ, all are one in being given the invitation to share in the promises of God. Together all are given the boldness to enter God's presence because of Christ's work for them and their life together in Christ. In Christ they can be confident of their acceptance by God and of the salvation God has in store for God's people.

The unity of the church is a central theme of Ephesians. Earlier in the letter we hear that Jews and Gentiles have been reconciled through the cross, so that they are together a single people. They have been given peace, and through the same Spirit they together can approach God (2:14–18). Now together they are God's building, even God's temple, because together they are the place God's presence dwells (2:19–22). In 4:1–6, the unity theme comes to expression in the well-known list of things that all believers share. It culminates with, "one God and Father of all, who is above all and through all and in all."

The distinctive emphasis of 3:1–12 is that it interprets this oneness as an eschatological reality. As the new age breaks into the world in the church, God's plan for making peace by making all one in Christ has become a reality. Of course, it is not fully realized in the church. If it were, Ephesians would not have been needed. Still, our text proclaims this oneness as the ultimate plan of God for our salvation, a plan that will not be thwarted.

The inclusion of Gentiles is also an important aspect of the Gospel reading for today. Although Matthew addresses a Torah-observant church, Gentiles are participants in God's plan from the beginning of the narrative. God calls them with the star, and they are the first to worship Christ. Their gifts to the child acknowledge that he is the one who brings the possibility of being a part of God's covenant people to all peoples. From the beginning of the gospel story, God's plan is to draw all peoples into the people of God. Our Ephesians passage shows how hard it was for the early church to think of God's grace in this expansive way. At the same time, it celebrates the breadth of the salvation brought by Christ.

The Isaiah reading also points to a mission beyond Israel. The postexilic Isaiah looks to the day when all nations will see the light of the knowledge of God and come to Jerusalem. This prophet would certainly be surprised at the interpretation the church gives to the nations coming to Israel. Still, he sees God act to honor the promises to Israel, even as Gentiles are blessed through those promises. Understanding the election of Israel to include bringing a blessing on all people goes all the way back to the call of Abram. There all families of the earth will be blessed through him (Gen. 12:3).

Ephesians sees the present eschatological gift

of the church as the culmination of all the promises of God's blessing of the whole world through the blessings of Israel. The salvation believers receive includes not only the reconciliation of individuals to God, but also a reconciliation of opposed ethnic groups. The breach of relationship that separated Jews and Gentiles, the wall between them, has been taken away. As much as differences continue (and Ephesians sees them as continuing realities), there is the more basic oneness founded in shared dependence on the grace of God received through the work of Christ. In Christ believers are saved from alienation from God and alienation from one another regardless of their differences.

JERRY L. SUMNEY

Commentary 2: Connecting the Reading with the World

We read Ephesians 3:1–12 on the Epiphany of our Lord, which begins a new liturgical season. In this season of Epiphany, we celebrate God's light in the world, manifest through Jesus Christ, and extended to all persons. In his letter to Ephesus, Paul reaches explicitly toward the Gentiles, preaching that they too are included in God's plan: "The Gentiles have become fellow heirs, members of the same body, and sharers in the promise in Christ Jesus through the gospel" (Eph. 3:6). Paul describes himself as a servant dedicated to and empowered by God's grace "to bring to the Gentiles the news of the boundless riches of Christ" (3:8). What a powerful message with which to begin the new calendar year: that the light of Christ is not for ourselves, but for the world of which we are a part. Thus the church begins the season of Epiphany and the new calendar year with a call for outreach and inclusion, to carry forth the good news of Christ to all the world.[1]

In this strikingly personal pericope, Paul offers more than a call to go forth and make disciples. With reference to his own journey and precarious circumstance, he reminds us that the mission of the church begins with perceiving the presence and power of God in the world. Paul reminds us of the revelation made known to him, this unveiling of the mystery of Christ through whom God's divine purposes are also revealed. Paul describes this revelation as an experience of grace. God makes Godself known even to Paul, the "very least of all the saints" (3:8).

To put this in contemporary language, we might say that Paul reminds us that our doing begins with our being. Our outreach to others is made possible by God's outreach to us. We are participants in a story and empowered to share that story with others. The sharing, the outreach, grows out of our awareness of relationship with God. We know ourselves to be part of the body of Christ, and we see others as members of the same body. Outreach and identity are intertwined. This text, then, offers an occasion for thinking with the congregation about the movement between spiritual growth and social ministries. Are these two expressions of church life informing one another, strengthening one another? Is there integration between worship and outreach?

That Paul writes these words from prison should also be underscored. The joy with which Paul communicates the power and grace of God must be bound together with the suffering this public witness cost him. The pericope begins, "I Paul am a prisoner for Christ Jesus for the sake of you Gentiles" (3:1). Biblical scholars note the meaning of this sentence for authorship of the letter. One might also consider its importance as a declaration of identity that runs deeper than authorship. Paul identifies himself as a "prisoner for Christ Jesus for the sake of you Gentiles," connecting himself in the most powerful and personal terms to both Christ and those considered "other." The fiber of this connection is love, the love of God made known through Christ and extended to all the world.[2]

---

1. Gail R. O'Day, *Epiphany: Interpreting the Lessons of the Church Year* (Minneapolis: Augsburg Fortress, 1994), 4–8.
2. John Paul Heil, *Ephesians: Empowerment to Walk in Love for the Unity of All in Christ* (Atlanta: Society of Biblical Literature, 2007), 133–48.

Rembrandt's 1627 painting *St. Paul in Prison* depicts this prisoner for Christ among materials and in clothing of seventeenth-century Europe. Rembrandt places an open manuscript on his lap and surrounds him with papers. Paul seems lost in thought, pen in hand, while light streams in to cover him. Isolated, Paul continues to preach through writing. Alone, Paul feels the loving presence of God. Meditating on this painting in connection with the passage from Ephesians, we might ask what it means to be a "prisoner for Christ Jesus for the sake of" others. What forms of outreach does the revealed grace of God empower us to risk? How do we remain attentive to the loving presence of God when we feel isolated and exhausted? How can we encourage spiritual formation for outreach that so thoroughly connects our sense of service to others with service to Christ?

There is also a difference between the way Paul writes about taking the gospel to the Gentiles and the experience that many contemporary Christians have in the work of outreach. Paul describes a unilateral movement, taking the gospel to the Gentiles, and there are likely Christians who continue to understand mission this way. However, the language of mission and outreach is also shifting to describe an experience of finding the light of Christ in the world rather than taking it there. Christians involved in outreach regularly describe learning from and growing through these experiences, indicating a dynamic movement between church and the world, rather than a unilateral movement from church to world.

Indeed, a persistent theme in contemporary writings on mission and in personal accounts of mission is that mission is not a one-way street. Rather, influence, agency, and love flow in multiple directions. We are not carrying God's love and light into the world so much as discovering that it is already there. Whether working in a soup kitchen down the street, participating in a short-term mission trip abroad, or living for years in partnership with people perceived to be "other," frequently we find ourselves on the receiving end of insights about divine love, presence, and grace.

For example, in her reflections on decades of refugee ministry, Sister Marilyn Lacey writes about "viewing those who are 'other' as revelation rather than threat" and as agents of grace rather than recipients of our lessons about grace. Sister Marilyn continues, "Grace—those leading strings of love connecting us all—permeates all of creation. Nothing is left outside this holiness. God is always flowing toward us."[3] Paul's experience of invitation to the Gentiles and the call to outreach that the contemporary church draws from this text must be supplemented with this awareness of the ways in which God's love and grace flow toward us through the lives of those we consider "other."

In religiously diverse settings, this passage raises some questions with which we must wrestle. It is one thing to affirm that God's love extends to all people. It is another thing to affirm Paul's claim to exclusive revelation of God's mystery: "In former generations this mystery was not made known to humankind, as it has now been revealed to his holy apostles and prophets by the Spirit" (3:5). Knowing the history of violence that accompanies the history of Christian mission, it is crucial for us to wrestle with Paul's claims to exclusive revelation through Christ. To put it positively, knowing the rich insights to be gained through interfaith and interreligious dialogue, it is appropriate to broaden our understanding of God's revelation. As we move out into the world with the light of Christ, what do others help us to see and understand? Where do we see God at work in the world in unexpected places? How does God reveal Godself to us in surprising encounters? How does our knowledge of God's grace help us to move into diverse and different places with a posture of openness, curiosity, and humility?

ELLEN OTT MARSHALL

---

3. Marilyn Lacey, RSM, *This Flowing toward Me: A Story of God Arriving in Strangers* (Notre Dame, IN: Ave Maria Press, 2009), 181, 196.

Matthew 2:1–12

[1]In the time of King Herod, after Jesus was born in Bethlehem of Judea, wise men from the East came to Jerusalem, [2]asking, "Where is the child who has been born king of the Jews? For we observed his star at its rising, and have come to pay him homage." [3]When King Herod heard this, he was frightened, and all Jerusalem with him; [4]and calling together all the chief priests and scribes of the people, he inquired of them where the Messiah was to be born. [5]They told him, "In Bethlehem of Judea; for so it has been written by the prophet:

[6]'And you, Bethlehem, in the land of Judah,
   are by no means least among the rulers of Judah;
for from you shall come a ruler
   who is to shepherd my people Israel.'"

[7]Then Herod secretly called for the wise men and learned from them the exact time when the star had appeared. [8]Then he sent them to Bethlehem, saying, "Go and search diligently for the child; and when you have found him, bring me word so that I may also go and pay him homage." [9]When they had heard the king, they set out; and there, ahead of them, went the star that they had seen at its rising, until it stopped over the place where the child was. [10]When they saw that the star had stopped, they were overwhelmed with joy. [11]On entering the house, they saw the child with Mary his mother; and they knelt down and paid him homage. Then, opening their treasure chests, they offered him gifts of gold, frankincense, and myrrh. [12]And having been warned in a dream not to return to Herod, they left for their own country by another road.

Commentary 1: Connecting the Reading with Scripture

The season of Epiphany is a season of revelation, a time to recognize the arrival of God's plan in Jesus, and a time to look forward to God's ongoing action through the Christ event. So what difference does God's revelation make?

The story in Matthew 2:1–12 is about birth and the changes great births bring to the social order. In some ancient societies, births brought the potential for political revolution. At the least, the privileged class was not always pleased with certain births. Some considered change positive news; others interpreted the same events as the beginning of potential chaos.

In a more contemporary world, the outcome of political elections can create anxiety for many. Ancient births created their own kind of political anxiety. According to our Gospel text, this was the case with Jesus' birth. News of his birth drew the attention of King Herod, as well as visitors from afar. The visitors arrived "from the East"; Herod was supported by the West (Rome). This is a story in which East and West clashed over the birth of a little Jewish boy. The tension between the agent of God and the agent of Rome (i.e., Herod) eventually led Jesus' family to flee to Egypt (Matt. 2:13–16). Celebrations of Jesus' birth may have caused others to respond with terror, fright, and anger. Some in Jerusalem were "deeply disturbed" (Gk. *tarassō*) by the news (2:3). (This Greek verb, *tarassō*, also describes the disciples' reaction when they thought Jesus was a ghost [Matt. 14:26].) Herod's desire to kill Jesus is not explained explicitly (v. 13); the text simply records that he was "frightened" (NRSV) or "troubled" (CEB) or "disturbed" (NIV) (v. 3). Loss of political power probably lay at the root of his concern (cf. 2:6). In light of Herod's willingness to massacre infants, fleeing Jerusalem was a wise move for the family of Jesus.

The arrival of the magi drives this Gospel lesson. It is their epiphany that shapes the opening of chapter 2. The *magoi* (Gk.), translated as "wise persons" or "astrologers" or even "magicians" (as in the NRSV's translation of the same Greek word in Acts 13:6, 8), were persons capable of interpreting stars and dreams. They follow a star in order to locate Jesus' birth. Seemingly unaware of the jealousy of regional rulers, the magi seek Herod's advice and he, through his religious agents, sends them to Bethlehem (vv. 3–8). The star confirms the scribes' interpretation of Scripture. Matthew contrasts the magi with Herod, who desires to locate Jesus for no good; the magi, on the other hand, wish to pay homage and offer gifts (v. 11). Due to a timely dream, they choose not to assist Herod in return (vv. 12, 16).

Summoned westward by a star, the magi return home, guided by a dream of warning. Dreams play a minimal role in the Gospel tradition, but they are central to the opening chapters of Matthew's Gospel. They do even more than move along the plot; they also encourage people to avoid death threats on Jesus' life. In an earlier scene, an angel appears to Joseph in a dream, to encourage him to take Mary as his wife (1:20); the angel also informs Joseph of the significance of Jesus. Another dream forewarns the wise men to avoid Herod (2:12). In similar fashion, an angel tells Joseph, in a dream, to take the family to Egypt to escape Herod's wrath (v. 13). The angel comes again to inform Joseph to return to Israel after Herod's death (vv. 19, 22). The political refugees are able to return to the land of their birth.

The Gospel of Matthew links key elements of this story to Israel's story. Jesus' birth would occur in Bethlehem, as predicted by the prophet Micah (2:6). Micah's words address a people in exile longing to be returned to their place and space in the world. The prophet anticipates a time following exile when a leader "who is to rule in Israel" will rise up (Mic. 5:2) and rule over other nations (Mic. 5:5–6). While connecting Jesus to Bethlehem, the first canonical Gospel also recalls 2 Samuel, the selection of David as one "who shall be shepherd of my people Israel" after Saul's death (2 Sam. 5:2).

The antagonism between King Saul and David may be the subtext behind Matthew's reporting of Herod's fear of the rise of Jesus. The magi initially ask King Herod the provocative question, "Where is the child who has been born king of the Jews?" (v. 2). Furthermore, it is not until Herod's death that Joseph and family return to the region (2:19). Eventually, in this Gospel Jesus will die with the mocking charge of "king" posted over his head: "This is Jesus, the King of the Jews" (27:37). The label "king" was not one of Jesus' own self-identifying markers (cf. Matt. 21:5; 25:31–34; 27:11–14). Rather, it is how the Gospels portray Jesus' mission as one in line with Davidic lineage.

In addition, Matthew's Jewish audience would have heard in the Herod/Jesus saga echoes of the Pharaoh/Moses tradition. Moses' birth was also surrounded by political intrigue. Pharaoh desired to kill all male babies among the Hebrews (Exod. 1:22), as a way to manage the growing population of the Israelites. Jochebed hid Moses from this public travesty but was unable to raise him without deceit (see Exod. 2:1–10). Just as God sent Moses to lead the people of Israel out of Egypt, so God sent Jesus—according to the angel who appeared to Joseph—to be a savior (see Matt. 1:21). One major difference between the two accounts is that Egypt functions as a city of refuge in Matthew's account, rather than a city of bondage, as it was in Exodus.

As a form of communication, dreams have a complicated history in Jewish tradition. Certain dreams may provide insight into the divine will. Many would agree with Ben Sira's mixed message that "dreams are unreal" since "the mind has fantasies," while still recognizing that God may use them to communicate God's will (Sir. 34:5–6). Jeremiah frequently complained about his opponents utilizing the medium of dreams, even juxtaposing the prophetic uses of this form over against a direct word from the Lord (Jer. 23:28; cf. Jer. 29:8–9). While direct communication from God was preferred, divine use of dreams was occasionally practiced for favorable purposes (Num. 12:6–8). The problem was the message not the medium (cf. Deut. 13:2–6; Zech. 10:2). Discernment was key! Positive instances of dreams guiding Jewish heroes—like Jacob, Joseph, and Daniel—abound in the tradition.

The season of Epiphany is about revelation, a time shortly after the excitement of the arrival of God's Son, Jesus. So what difference does God's revelation make during this season, a season full of promise and chaos, full of joy and sorrow?

If Advent is about waiting for the promised visit, Epiphany is about the grand expectations that will come after the visitor has arrived. Sometimes we have to be open to new resources for revelation, like dreams and stars or advice from children and words of hope from unexpected places. As Langston Hughes's poem "I Dream a World" beautifully expresses, so may this be our dream: "I dream a world where all will know sweet freedom's way."[1]

EMERSON B. POWERY

Commentary 2: Connecting the Reading with the World

The appearance of the magi constitutes one of the most peculiar stories in the Gospels. Unnamed, unnumbered, and guided by stars, the travelers enter and exit the narrative surrounded in mystery. Interpreters often describe them as exotic figures. The magi's theological significance nevertheless demands that we refuse to view them as the cartoonish figures they appear to be in typical nativity scenes. Their inclusion in Matthew causes us to see the arrival of "God with us" (1:23) as a seismic event on the world stage. Their unique insights and the dangerous game they play with Herod characterize the serious and far-reaching political implications of the Messiah's birth.

There is no simple way to describe the longstanding association that the story of the magi has shared with January 6, the day after the twelfth night of Christmas. Their arrival marks the culmination of Christmastide for many. Whether through the gift giving and foods that mark Día de Los Reyes in Mexico or through the public processions that enliven Trzech Króli in Poland, the "three kings" are front and center as the Christmas season concludes in various cultures that have been influenced by Western church traditions. Without denying the importance of these celebrations, when preachers and teachers work with Matthew 2:1–12 on or near Epiphany, they have an opportunity to let this text direct our vision forward, so we can see the new realities that the Messiah continues to bring into being. The arrival of the magi need not be seen, as it is in most Christmas pageants, as the final scene that occurs around the manger. Gifts of gold, frankincense, and myrrh do not declare the official end of Christmas; they point the way forward into the impact that Jesus Christ will have upon human societies and the things that vie for our loyalties.

The Portentous Magi. This passage provides a bridge that carries us from Christmas's introspective rhetoric to an encounter with the world-altering ramifications of the Messiah's arrival. If Epiphany's onset focuses our attention on the question of how this child born into a relatively unremarkable family will become known to the world as God's Messiah, Matthew's strange story of foreign visitors arriving in Bethlehem offers a basic yet mysterious answer: the world will take notice and come to him. Matthew insists that the Messiah's arrival fulfills God's promises to Israel. The magi's trek implies that even the nations of the world will now arrive at a new understanding of God's intentions through the Messiah. A new political order is taking shape.

The magi's prominent place in Matthew's narrative underscores the importance of what they symbolize. The first people to recognize the arrival of "the king of the Jews" are outsiders. Originating "from the East," evoking the customs of probably Babylon or Arabia, they represent the wider Gentile world to whom Jesus' followers will be sent when the Gospel ends (28:18–20). Guided by signs in the night sky, their astrological wisdom makes them appear suspicious—and maybe dangerous—because of the Old Testament's prohibitions of divination

1. *The Collected Poems of Langston Hughes*, ed. Arnold Rampersad (New York: Vintage, 1995), 311.

and augury (e.g., Deut. 18:9–14). No one else in this Gospel resembles the magi; their amazing cameo suggests that God finds ways to attract others—or that others discover ways of finding God.

The magi also set the stage for forthcoming developments in the Gospel. Aware of Jesus' royal identity even at the beginning of his life, the outsiders possess the insight that religious insiders will tragically lack when they deride him on the cross as the counterfeit "king of Israel" (27:42; cf. 21:5; 27:37). The strangers' curiosity and insight make the Jerusalem-based leaders look bad by comparison. Accordingly, Matthew contains many passages that caution readers against assuming that it is easy to tell who the true insiders are (e.g., 5:3–12; 20:1–16; 25:1–13, 31–46).

The arrival of the magi also signals that "the kingdom of heaven has come near," even before John and Jesus begin to announce such things (3:2; 4:17). The precious gifts of the magi recall Isaiah 60:1–6 and Psalm 72:10–11, texts that are also assigned for Epiphany. Insofar as the magi and their offerings recall scriptural images, they intimate that God's promised future has begun to materialize with Jesus' birth. The glory of the Lord (Isa. 60:2) revealed in Christ has a magnetic quality. It will attract, potentially, all people. The nativity of the Messiah means fruition is at hand.

The Magi's Discernment. When the shadowy visitors from the East display keen vision while Herod the Great and "all Jerusalem" fall into distress, one might presume that Matthew celebrates Gentiles as faithfully responsive and discredits Judaism as ignorantly apostate. That interpretation is too hasty. It neglects key dimensions of the magi's quest to find Jesus. These men's techniques, their attempts to read the natural world for evidence of God's intentions, bring them remarkably close to Jesus. Ultimately the travelers need to learn additional things from Jewish sacred writings to pinpoint their destination. The priests and scribes impart knowledge and direct the magi to Micah 5:1–3, 3 and 2 Samuel 5:2. Scripture clarifies. At the same time, the Jewish elites, because they had not perceived what the magi discerned on their

own from the heavens, can hardly be said to hold a monopoly on God's revelation themselves. Matthew describes the world's discovery of the Messiah's birth taking place through dialogue; natural revelation and special revelation work cooperatively in this passage to uncover theological truth.

The passage therefore opens doors to discuss interfaith dialogue and what it means to proclaim Christian faith graciously in religiously diverse modern societies. The magi's religious hunches come from purportedly unorthodox means; yet they uncover truth. Like the Athenians whom Paul addresses in Acts 17:22–29, the magi are capable of discerning theological realities according to their own intuitions, observations, and canons. The outsiders have something to teach the presumed insiders. The passage might urge congregations to listen more carefully to their neighbors.

At the same time, however, the New Testament has limits in its ability to model constructive multifaith dialogue. Matthew depicts the magi as submitting to Jesus instead of conversing about theology with his parents. When the easterners pay homage to him as a king, they acknowledge the Messiah's superiority, especially when this passage receives scrutiny in connection to Isaiah 60:1–6. There is nevertheless no warrant here for Christian triumphalism. The magi bear witness to Jesus' majesty; the narrative does not humiliate them for doing so. Matthew simply does not devote attention to learning from the magi's particular theological insights or wondering how this experience may have changed them once they returned to "their own country." Their role in Matthew is to assert that Jesus deserves adoration as the one who announces and institutes the kingdom of heaven.

The magi succeed in paying homage to Jesus the king, which is something no one else in Matthew 2 appears willing to do. When the magi show up in Jerusalem, they make it plain that a new king will arise, news that agitates and soon will unhinge Herod. Without the magi, Matthew's Christmas story might be solely about an inconspicuous birth. With these visitors and the startling news they bring to Jerusalem, Matthew colors the whole narrative with a revolutionary hue. The world cannot remain the same once the Messiah enters. King Herod sees that truth. He responds not with wisdom, wonder, praise, or gifts. Rather than bend his knee to God's anointed, Herod chooses terror, as tyrants still do. That must not be our choice, as those who recognize it is not only our world the Messiah changes, but also our very lives.

MATTHEW L. SKINNER

Baptism of the Lord

Isaiah 43:1–7
Psalm 29

Acts 8:14–17
Luke 3:15–17, 21–22

Isaiah 43:1–7

¹But now thus says the LORD,
    he who created you, O Jacob,
    he who formed you, O Israel:
Do not fear, for I have redeemed you;
    I have called you by name, you are mine.
²When you pass through the waters, I will be with you;
    and through the rivers, they shall not overwhelm you;
when you walk through fire you shall not be burned,
    and the flame shall not consume you.
³For I am the LORD your God,
    the Holy One of Israel, your Savior.
I give Egypt as your ransom,
    Ethiopia and Seba in exchange for you.
⁴Because you are precious in my sight,
    and honored, and I love you,
I give people in return for you,
    nations in exchange for your life.
⁵Do not fear, for I am with you;
    I will bring your offspring from the east,
    and from the west I will gather you;
⁶I will say to the north, "Give them up,"
    and to the south, "Do not withhold;
bring my sons from far away
    and my daughters from the end of the earth—
⁷everyone who is called by my name,
    whom I created for my glory,
    whom I formed and made."

Commentary 1: Connecting the Reading with Scripture

Our text begins with a dramatic pivot: "But now" (43:1). Right at the beginning of our passage Isaiah is announcing that things used to be one way, *but now* things have changed. In this case, what used to be was Judah's captivity in Babylon, and what has changed is that God has ended their captivity, brought the exiles home, and restored the community.

Isaiah interprets this shift from what was to what is, from the "then" to the "but now," from the before to the after, in theological terms. What happened before was that God's people were "deaf" and "blind" to the ways of God (42:18), and in response, God turned away from the people. God, says Isaiah, "gave up Jacob to the spoiler . . . [and] poured upon him the heat of his anger and the fury of war" (42:24–25). In other words, the Babylonian exile is described by Isaiah as a punishment, or at least a consequence, of the people's faithless disregard for the law of God, and the result was that the people were plunged into hopelessness. Isaiah dramatically depicts the exiles as "people robbed and plundered . . . trapped in holes and hidden in prisons." The people had no hope because they were locked in the prison of exile with no one to spring their cells. They had no savior; there was "no one," says Isaiah, "to say, 'Restore!'" (42:22).

"But now," proclaims Isaiah, there is someone to say, "Restore!" Now there is a savior, and that one is God the creator, the God of Abraham, Isaac, and Jacob:

> But now thus says the LORD,
>   he who created you, O Jacob,
>   he who formed you, O Israel:
> Do not fear, for I have redeemed you.
>   Isa. 42:1

The people of God were in exile because of their own doing, and there was no one to save them. *But now*, the God who created them has risen up as their redeemer and restorer.

The "but now" that begins our text signals not only a change in circumstances but also a shift in tone. The verses leading up to our text (Isa. 42:14–25) are words of judgment and warning, but with the "but now" the mood changes to comfort and reassurance. Twice in our text appears the command from the Lord, "Do not fear" (43:1, 5), and, indeed, the charge not to fear is a refrain throughout this section of Isaiah (see also 40:9; 41:10, 13, 14; 44:2; 51:7; 54:4).

This is not the first time in Scripture that we have heard "Do not fear," and it will not be the last. In the New Testament, these words will be spoken many times, for example, by the angels in the Christmas story, by Jesus to his disciples, and by the risen Christ at Easter. Here, however, Isaiah is not looking ahead to the story of Jesus, but instead looking back to Genesis and the story of Israel's formation. Specifically, Isaiah is echoing four occasions in Genesis when God says, "Do not be afraid": to Abram (Gen. 15:1), to Hagar (Gen. 21:17), to Isaac (Gen. 26:24), and to Jacob (Gen. 46:3). Each of these Genesis passages has three key elements: God *self-identifies*, God gives the *command* not to be afraid, and God makes a *promise* to make a great nation around the person being addressed. For example, in Genesis 26:24–25, God says to

Isaac, "I am the God of your father Abraham" (self-identification); "Do not be afraid" (command); and, "I am with you and will bless you and make your offspring numerous" (promise).

Some biblical scholars see our passage in Isaiah as modeled closely on this Genesis formula,[1] as follows:

God's Self-indentification:	"Now says the LORD, he who created you" (43:1a)
Command:	"Do not fear, for I have redeemed you" (43:1b)
Promise:	"When you pass through the waters, I will be with you" (43:2)
God's Self-indentification:	"I am the LORD your God, the Holy One of Israel" (43:3–4)
Command:	"Do not fear, for I am with you" (43:5a)
Promise:	"I will bring your offspring from the east, and from the west I will gather you" (43:5b–7)

Again, Isaiah's point in this connection to Genesis is theological. In Genesis, God not only created the heavens and the earth from the void and nothingness; God also created Israel, the children of Abraham, from nothingness, from "no people" to "my people." The Israelites acted as if they were not God's people and found themselves captives, exiles, and strangers, locked in a prison of their own making. *But now* God comes as redeemer to re-create the people of God, to break open the prison cells, to bring their sons and daughters home, and to make of them a nation of blessing and glory once again.

It is important to note that this action of restoration is initiated by God and not by the people. Redemption occurs not because Israel has suddenly come to its senses. It springs rather from the character of God. God is creator, and God will create again. The salvation of the people comes not because they love God, but because God loves them: "You are precious in

---

1. See, e.g., Edgar W. Conrad, "The 'Fear Not' Oracles in Second Isaiah," *Vetus Testamentum* 34, no. 2 (1984): 143–47.

my sight, and honored, and I love you" (43:4). The people are ensnared; they cannot come to God. It is God who comes, who advents, to them. When Dietrich Bonhoeffer was imprisoned, he once compared life in a prison cell to the season of Advent, because "the door is shut and can be opened only *from the outside*."[2]

In the background of this theological affirmation of redemption are, of course, actual events in history. In the sixth century BCE, the Persians, first under Cyrus and then others, conquered many nations, including Babylon, Egypt, Ethiopia, and Seba. As a result, in 539 BCE, the Jews in exile in Babylon were allowed to return to their homeland. For Isaiah, this history was evidence of the saving power of God on behalf of Israel, who "gave people in return for you" (v. 4) and "gave Egypt as your ransom, Ethiopia and Seba in exchange for you" (v. 3).

The lectionary places this passage on the Sunday observing the baptism of the Lord. Some have assumed that the connection between Isaiah 43 and baptism is made because the Isaiah text alludes to the exodus, and baptism is often understood as a type of new exodus. However, the link between Isaiah 43 and the exodus story may not be as strong as it first seems. Old Testament scholar Christopher Seitz, commenting on Isaiah 43, argues that the images that seem to refer to the exodus likely do not. For example, "pass through the waters" is, in Isaiah, an image of judgment (see Isa. 8:5–8), and the phrase "Egypt as your ransom" refers to the Persian conquest of Egypt, rather than to the rescue of the Hebrew children through the parting of the Red Sea. According to Seitz, the connection of Isaiah 43 to the exodus is, at best, "secondary and allusive."[3]

So rather than trying to nail down some tight exodus-baptism analogy, it is perhaps better for the preacher to look for poetic and theological connections between Isaiah and baptism—Jesus' baptism and ours. In both our passage and in baptism, people pass through the waters under the protection of God, are called by name, and are formed and re-formed into God's people.

THOMAS G. LONG

Commentary 2: Connecting the Reading with the World

When, at the church's observance of the baptism of the Lord, preachers hear Isaiah's words "Do not fear, for I have redeemed you," two connections quickly occur.

A similar "I have your back!" assurance comes to Jesus at his baptism via a voice from heaven. The declaration is a centering energy source for his ministry—a designation of identity, a touchstone for vocation. A promise, previously made to God's people, is personalized for Jesus—a promise liberating and empowering.

If that is so, then those who in baptism are "marked as Christ's own forever"—and those presenting or supporting them—may hear such assurance, claim such a promise, and anticipate analogous empowerment as they are enfolded into the faith community or as they welcome the newly baptized.

In both cases, what is offered *to* those thus freed from fear can be offered *by* them. Just as fear can be contagious, so can comfort and security, conveyed in word and embodied in deed—especially when we deeply trust someone who has *our* back. Drawing on everyday examples of fear-assuaging support we share with each other, preachers can echo Isaiah's words.

But "do not fear" is "easier said than done." Regardless of assurances from strong, supportive sources, none of us lives free from fear. Fears come in all sorts of shapes and sizes, and abstract assurances are cold comfort. It is noteworthy that Isaiah, our predecessor preacher, moves immediately to make the claim credible by making it concrete. He speaks of passing *through* the waters and walking *through* fire—not around or away from, but through what are legitimate occasions of genuine fear.

What are particular fears our listeners may be

2. Dietrich Bonhoeffer, *Letters and Papers from Prison* (New York: Touchstone, 1997), 135.
3. Christopher R. Seitz, "The Book of Isaiah 40–66," in Leander Keck et al., *The New Interpreter's Bible* (Nashville: Abingdon Press, 2001), 6:375.

undergoing? Answers will be diverse and complex. The fears of children can differ from the fears of adolescents, mature adults, and those in old age. Our sense of security can be upended by concerns related to health, economics, threat of physical or emotional abuse, social unrest, political conflict, vocational challenge, interpersonal relationships. Fears can come as sudden shocks, grave doubts, stark terrors, nagging worries, gnawing dreads. Some fears persist as incapacitating chronic anxieties. The "presenting problem" of a fear can be a mask for (and a distraction from) an underlying issue. Fears can be rational and realistic—essential to the health of those they seem to threaten; fears can be grounded in misinformation, misrepresentation, and projection.

"Fear" is an umbrella term overarching a spectrum of dis-eases that cannot be addressed by a "one size fits all" assurance. We nurture coping mechanisms to deal with fears by skill development, intellectual resources, collaboration with colleagues, the support of friends and family. These questions arise in and through such a spectrum: Can the preacher connect? Has he or she "been there" to "know what it feels like"? *What* should our listeners "not fear," and *how*?

The exploitation of individual and communal fears is one of the most commonly employed (and dependably successful) strategies of authoritarian leaders. Fear can be channeled as resentment, spawning hostility and violence among those who, even for generations, have lived peaceably together. What Isaiah does *not* say is that there is nothing to be afraid of.

In the divine reassurance proclaimed by Isaiah's prophetic poetry, there is, in its rhythmic repetition, recognition that one of the elements often most effective in addressing fear is the quiet, continuing, measured assurance that personal support for dealing with various fears is readily available and will be there, no matter what. At some level, regardless of age or circumstances, none of us ever outgrows the need of frightened infants to be rocked to sleep. Assurances that cannot be appropriated all at once can have, over time, a cumulative effect. It may be helpful for preachers to recall and reference instances of how someone they regarded

as strong, even intimidating, by persistent presence, over time, calmed and transformed their fears.

There are, however, at least two elements in Isaiah's efforts to quiet fears that might well raise the eyebrows of those who are not directly affected or addressed. There is, about this promise of fears relieved, one element that is pragmatically unrealistic and one that is morally suspect.

"When you pass through the rivers, they shall not overwhelm you; when you pass through the fire, you shall not be burned" (v. 2bc). With due regard for metaphorical license, this promise does seem a bit of a stretch. Experience strongly suggests that some fears are not so easily assuaged; or, if they *can be*, they *should not be*. In passing through fire or water, there is no assurance that drowning or burning will not occur *this* time.

"I give people in return for you, nations in exchange for your life" (v. 4b). While those locked in fear may well find the prospect of preferential, even exclusive treatment attractive, a declaration such as this sounds suspiciously like a promise to throw one's enemies or aliens "under the bus"—to alleviate the fears of the "precious," "honored" chosen by giving the "other" something for which they should "be afraid, be very afraid."

In a political and social climate, both national and international, beset by surges of nationalism, nativism, and identity politics, there is a particular problem in knowing how best to engage this biblical text. Unrealistic promises made to certain aggrieved segments of society, coupled with raised expectations that other groups will be put in their (decidedly and deservedly lower) place is a potentially toxic combination—one that plays on and stokes fears, rather than fostering reflective conversations regarding how social apprehensions can be responsibly and creatively de-escalated. Invoking divine sanction as "payback" for perceived injustice is a rhetorical strategy often tried with tragic consequences across the course of history. How can preachers, engaging this text, avoid fearmongering in their fear addressing?

Perhaps the most fruitful underlying strategy for addressing various dimensions of fear is the act of *naming*—naming the fears themselves[4] and, more important, naming those who are undergoing them. Naming others—individuals, families, communities—is a fundamental act of establishing relationship and connection. Such naming, and claiming as "beloved," is an affirmation of distinctiveness that need not lead to preference over or the active exclusion of "others." The pursuit of identity politics is fraught with moral and pragmatic problems. At its heart, identity politics addresses a deep human need, however—the need for distinctive identity, the honoring of individuality, a recognition of and connection with those we know by name. The fire and water of our fears can be negotiated if we are accompanied by someone who knows and names us. As Isaiah sees it, the God who creates, forms, and redeems, honors, and loves them, not only knows the names of all the chosen; God bestows the divine name upon them, each and all, as a badge of bonding identity, as a means for facing fear.

On this day, it is worth noting that he who went through fire and water for us began his ministry in a baptism of blessing—being named as cherished by the One from whom he came. The Gospel writer employs Isaiah's words to describe, not the inoculation of Jesus from all possible fears, but the ongoing available antidote to them. For those "named as Christ's own forever" in baptism on this day, in the presence of a faith family all bearing God's name, this can be a tangible act of being identified and strengthened for going "through" fear.

DAVID J. SCHLAFER

---

4. Naming of fear has a prominent place in trauma theory. For a brief overview, see *Trauma Theory Abbreviated*, by Sandra L. Bloom, MD, at iheartenglish.pbworks/Trauma+Explanation+14+pages.pdf.

Psalm 29

¹Ascribe to the LORD, O heavenly beings,
  ascribe to the LORD glory and strength.
²Ascribe to the LORD the glory of his name;
  worship the LORD in holy splendor.

³The voice of the LORD is over the waters;
  the God of glory thunders,
  the LORD, over mighty waters.
⁴The voice of the LORD is powerful;
  the voice of the LORD is full of majesty.

⁵The voice of the LORD breaks the cedars;
  the LORD breaks the cedars of Lebanon.
⁶He makes Lebanon skip like a calf,
  and Sirion like a young wild ox.

⁷The voice of the LORD flashes forth flames of fire.
⁸The voice of the LORD shakes the wilderness;
  the LORD shakes the wilderness of Kadesh.

⁹The voice of the LORD causes the oaks to whirl,
  and strips the forest bare;
  and in his temple all say, "Glory!"

¹⁰The LORD sits enthroned over the flood;
  the LORD sits enthroned as king forever.
¹¹May the LORD give strength to his people!
  May the LORD bless his people with peace!

Connecting the Psalm with Scripture and Worship

Immediately identified as a hymn of praise, Psalm 29 proclaims God's glory through its illustration of God as the power behind the storm. The psalmist begins with a four-part call to worship repeating the opening phrase ("ascribe to the LORD") three times before moving to a slight variation the fourth time ("worship the LORD"). This call to worship is directed to the heavenly beings who are urged to attribute strength, glory, and holiness to God (vv. 1–2). The psalmist then expresses the content of this worship into which the heavenly beings are being called: God's strength depicted through images of lightning, thunder, and chaotic waters

(vv. 3–10). This hymn of praise presents a glorious demonstration of God's power that concludes with a prayer for peace and strength for God's people (v. 11).

Psalm 29 echoes the sovereignty of God made clear in the prophet Isaiah's declaration of God's promised restoration and protection (Isa. 43:1–7). Echoing God's promise to Israel of safe passage through the waters and protection from the fire, the psalmist acknowledges God as the one who dominates the waters that represent chaos. Through a sevenfold proclamation of power described as a mighty thunderstorm (vv. 3–7), God's control of the storms through the "voice of the LORD" reassures hearers of God's powerful rule. God is the Sovereign One enthroned over the unruly waters, and the source of strength and peace for God's people.[1]

For those preaching the texts for Baptism of the Lord, Psalm 29 offers two distinct approaches: a summons to glorify God, and a focus on God's sovereignty in the midst of chaos. In Isaiah and Luke, God's power and glory are depicted through natural elements, water and fire, with God being the one who protects (Isaiah), and Jesus being the one who baptizes by fire and the Holy Spirit. Similarly, the organizing image of Psalm 29 is glory. The opening call to worship uses the term "glory" (vv. 1–2), and the term is present at the beginning and the end of the proclamation of the voice of the Lord (vv. 3, 9). The psalmist uses this term both to describe the attributes of God (v. 3) and to display the manifestation of divine power (v. 9). First, the psalmist speaks of the strength, power, holy splendor, and majesty of God (vv. 1–2), and brings these attributes together by naming God as the "God of glory" (v. 3). Then the term "glory" is used as a way of verbally responding to God's divine royalty in the world (v. 9). The psalmist makes this very clear by reporting at the proclamation's conclusion that everyone in the temple, both the heavenly palace and the earthly sanctuary, is saying, "Glory!" in recognition of what that proclamation means.[2]

Using the language of ancient mythology, Psalm 29 also draws a focus on God's sovereignty in the midst of chaos. At first glance, the waters, thunders, cedars breaking, flashes of lightning, and shaking in the earth all appear to be chaotic natural occurrences; certainly people all around the world can identify with these phenomena. However, the psalmist positions these environmental happenings under "the voice of the LORD," and poetically displays them in cycles that lead to a proclamation of the fullness of God's glory. The first cycle bursts with thunder (v. 3) and ends in the calmer tone of majesty (v. 4). The second cycle depicts the angry, breaking

storm (v. 5) and moves to flashes of lightning (v. 7). The third cycle presents a powerful sound that can be imagined as loud thunder—so strong that it shakes the wilderness (v. 8) and causes a whirlwind of force (v. 9), all culminating in a shout of praise. While the scene presented is chaotic, it unfolds at the voice of the Lord, reminding us that God is in control of that which seems to be uncontrollable and that God's sovereignty is proclaimed through nature. While in our preaching we may not typically use the same type of language, we can express and understand God to be the celebrated one who keeps us from being overwhelmed, the one who is enthroned over the metaphoric floods of our lives.

The opening call for the heavenly host to glorify the Lord is a liturgical way for the congregation to equate its own praise with what is right and required in the heavenly palace-temple. Worship planners might follow the psalmist's lead in using Psalm 29 as a responsive opening to the worship service, with one voice leading and the congregation responding as a proclamation of God's glory, using verse 2 as the central call to praise through the response sequence.

> Leader: Verse 1
> People: *Verse 2*
>
> Leader: Verses 3–4
> People: *Verse 2*
>
> Leader: Verses 5–8
> People: *Verse 2*
>
> Leader: Verses 9–10
> People: *Verse 2*
>
> Leader: Verse 11
> People: *Verse 2*

An opening of this type can then be followed by a lively hymn of praise. This call-and-response style may be presented through a dramatic reading with multiple leaders and the congregation offering the consistent response from verse 2.

The psalm can also be presented as either the opening hymn of praise or a bridge between the first reading and the Gospel lesson. For example, the hymn "Sing Glory to the Name of

---

1. Tremper Longman III, *Psalms* (Downers Grove, IL: InterVarsity Press, 2014), 157.
2. James Luther Mays, *Psalms*, Interpretation (Louisville, KY: John Knox Press, 1994), 136.

God" by David Gambrell presents a full expression of the psalm, balancing speech with song in the worship service. The musical expression of this psalm allows the congregation to embody the robust nature of the language and to move through the bursts and lulls of the psalm's cycles.

In summary, Psalm 29 is a doxology in praise of God as sovereign of the universe. The psalmist calls us not only to worship God, but to worship God in the fullness of God's power.

KHALIA J. WILLIAMS

Acts 8:14–17

¹⁴Now when the apostles at Jerusalem heard that Samaria had accepted the word of God, they sent Peter and John to them. ¹⁵The two went down and prayed for them that they might receive the Holy Spirit ¹⁶(for as yet the Spirit had not come upon any of them; they had only been baptized in the name of the Lord Jesus). ¹⁷Then Peter and John laid their hands on them, and they received the Holy Spirit.

Commentary 1: Connecting the Reading with Scripture

Luke packs a lot into Acts 8:14–17. These verses touch a number of theological themes that are important to Luke. The first thing to note is that the spread of the gospel to Samaria opens a new stage in the church's mission. In Acts 1:8, the risen Christ tells the apostles that they will be his witnesses in "Jerusalem, in all Judea and Samaria, and to the ends of the earth." The gospel has already been preached in Jerusalem and Judea; now it moves outside the bounds of those whom the original disciples would have recognized as the people of God. The movement to Samaria seems like both the logical choice and an unexpected move.

This development makes sense because Samaritans are related to Jews. Samaritans are the descendants of the Israelites of the northern kingdom who married non-Israelites after the exile of 722 BCE. The centuries-old ethnic conflict between Samaritans and Jews was so bad that when the Maccabees reigned in Jerusalem (first century BCE) they razed the Samaritans' temple. Still, they and the Jews—and now believers in Christ—believe in the same God. Their antipathy toward each other grew in part from their differing religious claims, somewhat different Bibles, and each claiming that the legitimate place for God's temple was in their territory. Jews saw the Samaritans as, at best, apostates. Some interpreters suggest that in this section of Acts the Samaritans and the Ethiopian eunuch of the next story (Acts 8:26–40) are both seen as outcasts in Israel. In any case, this mission to them represents the next step in the growth of the church that will soon include Gentiles, and so the whole world.

This mission also seems to be the result of persecution in Jerusalem. Philip, the one who brings the gospel to Samaria, is one of the church leaders who leaves Jerusalem in the wake of Stephen's martyrdom (8:4–5). His mission to Samaria is successful. A number of people have been baptized, but something is wrong. The earliest church expected the coming of the Spirit to accompany baptism. Acts makes this coming of the Spirit a hallmark of the church's existence, a sign that it is the community of the eschatological age. Peter's sermon in Acts 2 named the coming of the Spirit as a distinctive mark of God's new acts of salvation. He promised those in Jerusalem that whoever was baptized would receive forgiveness of sins and the Spirit. In Samaria, however, many had been baptized, but no one had received the Spirit.

Acts has the Spirit act in unusual ways in the two most important moves the church makes to expand its membership beyond observant Jews. This episode in Samaria is the first; the second is the Cornelius story, in which the first Gentile becomes a member of the church (Acts 10:1–33). In the Samaria incident, the Spirit is given only after the apostles arrive. In the Cornelius narrative, the Spirit comes early, before baptism, and essentially forces Peter to admit Cornelius into the church. Each of these episodes assumes that readers will see these episodes as anomalies to the usual connection between baptism and the Spirit. When we are told that the Spirit had not fallen on anyone in Samaria, we are supposed to know that means something needs to be done to set things right.

The solution is introduced before readers

know about the problem. This brief notice about the Spirit begins by saying that when the apostles in Jerusalem hear about the Samaritan mission, they send Peter and John. The purpose of their visit is to bring the Spirit to the new mission. This visit signals the apostolic and divine approval of this step outside of observant Judaism. Only apostles are commissioned to bestow the Spirit (see vv. 18–19, where Simon sees that the Spirit comes through the apostles), and doing so here signals the unity of the church. While Philip seems to have acted independently, the apostles see his sharing of the gospel with this new and surprising population as part of God's will.

Philip baptized the Samaritans "in the name of the Lord Jesus." The phrase "in the name of" appears nowhere in the LXX and seldom anywhere else. Acts uses it to distinguish the church's baptism from all others, including John the Baptist's. John's baptism was about repentance and forgiveness (Luke 3:3), but for Luke, baptism "in the name of Lord Jesus" is more. This formula signals that baptism brings the recipient into relationship with Jesus. Through the establishment of this relationship with Jesus, Luke associates the church's baptism with forgiveness of sins, reception of the Spirit, and entrance into the church. Baptism was perhaps the church's earliest rite, the one through which a person was brought into the community and came to share in the blessings of salvation.

Ritual baths of various sorts were a part of Judaism and other ancient religions. Such baths were often seen as cleansing in the sense that they prepared one to enter the presence of a god. John's baptism was for sin rather than ritual cleansing. In addition to forgiveness, the church's baptism is seen as an act that brings one into the eschatological sphere of existence, as the tradition Paul cites in Galatians 3:27–28 shows. Through it one receives the Spirit, that new presence of God that strengthens the believer to live a life governed by the values of the coming kingdom.

While the usual pattern in Acts and in the rest of the New Testament is that the Spirit comes to believers at baptism, we have seen it delayed in the case of the Samaritans. It is also delayed in Luke's telling of Jesus' baptism. Matthew and Mark say the Spirit and voice from God came as Jesus was coming up out of the water, but Luke has these things happen while Jesus was praying. While this reflects Luke's tendency to portray Jesus at prayer and perhaps allows Luke to distance the Spirit from John's baptism, it also makes his baptism and the coming of the Spirit be what equips Jesus to begin his ministry. As the Spirit empowers Jesus to do God's will in his ministry, so it empowers believers in Christ to do God's will.

The reality of this reassuring and empowering gift of the Spirit brings us to the end of the lectionary reading but not the end of the paragraph in Acts. The rest of the story has Simon attempt to buy the power to give others the Spirit. This part of the story is a stern warning against greed and against any thought that the Spirit is owned by believers, so that they can make demands or selfishly profit from it.

In this week's Old Testament text, the Isaiah of the exile assures the people in Babylon that God loves them and that God will do whatever it takes to claim them as God's own. Isaiah promises that God is with them in the difficulties they face in Babylon. It is not the mention of water that connects this text to baptism, but rather God's promise to save. It is now through baptism that believers in Christ are identified with Christ and so made God's people, made those who will be brought into God's presence and blessings. Acts 8 widens the circle of those who are included among God's people, and thereby receive God's blessings, by including Samaritans. This step in Acts' story of the march toward including all humankind in the salvation that comes in the "name of the Lord Jesus" is affirmed by the coming of the Spirit, the coming of God's intimate presence to live in God's people.

JERRY L. SUMNEY

Commentary 2: Connecting the Reading with the World

We read Acts 8:14–17 in a collection of baptism-related texts on the First Sunday after Epiphany, the Baptism of the Lord. Through the lectionary readings for this day, we trace the movement of the Holy Spirit, who anoints the prophet in Isaiah 61:1, descends on Jesus at his baptism in Luke 3:22, and spreads with the gospel to Samaria in Acts 8:17. On Epiphany, we reflect on the light of Christ extended throughout the world. On this First Sunday after Epiphany, we are reminded that the "spread of the Gospel was accompanied by the spread of the Holy Spirit."[1]

Acts 8:14–17 is particularly generative for reflection on a theology of baptism because it distinguishes between baptism in the Lord and reception of the Holy Spirit. In Acts 8:12, we read that the people of Samaria "believed Philip, who was proclaiming the good news about the kingdom of God and the name of Jesus Christ, [and] they were baptized, both men and women." However, when Peter and John come from Jerusalem, we learn that the Samaritans "had only been baptized in the name of the Lord Jesus." When Peter and John prayed for them and laid hands on them, then "they received the Holy Spirit" (Acts 8:14–17). Some hearers of the word find this distinction unsettling. There is only one baptism, right? Preachers might connect with this unsettling feature in the text to explore debates over baptism, historically and in our diverse Christian family. Is there a difference between baptism by water and baptism in the Holy Spirit? Who can baptize in the name of the Holy Spirit? This text offers a great teaching moment, an opportunity for the preacher to connect their baptismal language and practice to these lines of text and some of the debates they engender.

For example, one effect of this passage is that it prompts us, as readers, to reflect on the importance of prayer and physical touch as part of the baptism ritual. It is not enough to pronounce baptism while the congregation looks on; we invite the community of faith to participate in baptism through prayer and the laying on of hands. The preacher might draw attention to the movement of bodies during baptism. Who holds the baby and when? Who places hands on the adult receiving baptism? Think about the proximity of bodies as people gather around the baptismal waters. What do these movements and touch suggest or reinforce about the meaning of baptism for the congregation as a whole? As the Holy Spirit descends on the Samaritans, we are encouraged to think afresh about the "meaning of becoming God's child." We are invited to remember our baptism, to "ponder the significance of the prophetic proclamation, 'The Spirit of the Lord is upon me' (Isa. 61:1)."[2]

This event occurs at a time of persecution of the church at the hands of Saul. We read that "all except the apostles were scattered throughout the countryside of Judea and Samaria" (Acts 8:1). Despite a history of tension between Jews and Samaritans, Philip—one who was scattered to Samaria—proclaimed the Messiah and was believed (Acts 8:4–8). The text indicates that Philip's teaching and healing brought "great joy in that city" (Acts 8:8). His ministry there enables the Samaritans to transcend both generations of division and fear of persecution. John and Peter then add their confirmation to Philip's, and through their prayers and laying on of hands, the Holy Spirit descends upon the "outsiders," bringing all into unity in Christ.[3] Particularly striking is the way in which the descent of the Holy Spirit is mediated through the ministrations of Philip, John, and Peter.

This is not abstract preaching about unity in Christ. John and Peter pray over the Samaritans and lay their hands on them. God confirms this outreach to the "other." In addition to providing space for reflection on baptism and the presence of the Holy Spirit, therefore, this passage also encourages us to reflect more generally on the power of ritual in community formation. In

---

1. Gail R. O'Day, *Epiphany: Interpreting the Lessons of the Church Year* (Minneapolis: Augsburg Fortress, 1994), 13.

2. Fred Craddock, John H. Hayes, Carl R. Holladay, and Gene M. Tucker, *Preaching the New Common Lectionary: Year C: Advent, Christmas, Epiphany* (Nashville: Abingdon Press, 1985), 119.

3. Alexandre Vieira, "Holy Spirit, Church, and the Outsiders: A Brief Study of the Relation between Baptism and Holy Spirit in Acts 8:14–17," *Missio Apostolica* 22, no. 1 (May 2014): 109–17.

contexts of division, do we enact religious practices that make us attentive to the movement of the Spirit? How do we actually live out our convictions about unity in Christ?

Studies on engaged Buddhist and Christian prayer practices for peace note an encouraging correspondence between forms of compassion meditation and an openness to engaging the other in the work of peace building. Forms of meditation strengthen our capacity to remain open and receptive to one who is different and historically perceived as enemy. We also find evidence that religious rituals emphasizing connectedness and relationality play an important role in the willingness of divided communities to participate in processes of restorative justice. These contemporary examples of religious peace building through prayer and ritual that affirm relationship offer another lens through which to read Acts 8:17, in which John and Peter pray for and lay hands on the Samaritans. Their actions facilitate the coming of the Holy Spirit, who confirms the loving presence of God within and among these divided communities.

In addition to these ecclesial connections and sociopolitical connections, the preacher might also prompt congregants to make personal connections to the text. How do parishioners experience the movement of the Holy Spirit in relationship to the liturgical rhythms of worship? Do the two descriptions of being baptized in the Lord and receiving the Holy Spirit provide some space to think together about the head and the heart or about liturgical tradition and spontaneous religious expression? Does intellectual clarity converge with a

sense of being filled with the Spirit, or do these dimensions of growth occur in less synchronous ways? What role does communal prayer or physical touch play in the life of faith? How do our study circles also attend to the movements of the Spirit? How do we reflect together on those moments that stir the soul?

Recalling the context of persecution and vision surrounding this baptism narrative, we are also prompted to reflect on the fears that obstruct our openness to the other. This story is filled with courageous people who take tremendous risks for their faith. How does our faith call and equip us to risk relationship or change? How do we support one another in those risky moments? In short, how do we continue to remember our baptism?

As we reflect on the baptism of the Lord on this First Sunday after Epiphany, we might also consider the prayer that is part of the Episcopal liturgy for Holy Baptism. Taking the liberty to change the pronouns, we might pray, "Sustain [us], O Lord, in your Holy Spirit. Give [us] an inquiring and discerning heart, the courage to will and persevere, a spirit to know and to love you, and the gift of joy and wonder in all your works. Amen." Baptism into the household of God is baptism into a different way of living in the world. One lives differently in the world because of the ongoing presence of the Holy Spirit in one's life. Acts 8:14–17 reminds us that the act of baptism must be accompanied by ongoing and fervent prayer, enhanced by the power and touch of community.

ELLEN OTT MARSHALL

Luke 3:15–17, 21–22

[15]As the people were filled with expectation, and all were questioning in their hearts concerning John, whether he might be the Messiah, [16]John answered all of them by saying, "I baptize you with water; but one who is more powerful than I is coming; I am not worthy to untie the thong of his sandals. He will baptize you with the Holy Spirit and fire. [17]His winnowing fork is in his hand, to clear his threshing floor and to gather the wheat into his granary; but the chaff he will burn with unquenchable fire." . . .

[21]Now when all the people were baptized, and when Jesus also had been baptized and was praying, the heaven was opened, [22]and the Holy Spirit descended upon him in bodily form like a dove. And a voice came from heaven, "You are my Son, the Beloved; with you I am well pleased."

Commentary 1: Connecting the Reading with Scripture

"As the people were filled with expectation" (3:15) is a phrase that nicely defines the season of Epiphany. During the season of Epiphany, celebrants wish to see the evidence of God's revelation in Jesus. The events surrounding Jesus' baptism feature the significance of this humble act: Jesus' willingness to be baptized by another.

Immediately preceding our lectionary passage, John the Baptist's message embodies the symbolic, mystical nature of the baptism he inaugurates, as he emphasizes the need to act morally with specific examples like sharing clothes and food (3:11), collecting fair taxes (3:13), and accepting fair wages (3:14). Despite his wilderness appearance, as a preacher of justice John the Baptist was attentive to the common needs of people. So was his greatest disciple.

Compared to other Gospels, Luke's sequencing of John's imprisonment (3:20) and Jesus' baptism (3:21–22) is odd. Basically, Luke downplays John's role in this ritual act, by (1) not mentioning John's direct contact with Jesus and (2) interspersing the literary side note that Herod imprisoned John, which occurred later. Similar to the Fourth Gospel, in which the baptism of Jesus was not recorded explicitly at all, Luke's account diminishes John's role in relationship to Jesus. In this sequence, the baptism is not so much about John's role as it is about Jesus' identity, especially through the Spirit's

empowerment and God's acknowledgment of Jesus as God's Son (3:21–22). It is an epiphany of its own.

As the piously portrayed Jesus is praying (3:21), heaven opens, as a sign of divine approval. This apocalyptic sign was typical of divine disclosure throughout biblical literature (see below). This coverage of the scene portrays the Spirit's descent "in bodily form like a dove." Ultimately, a heavenly voice speaks and announces the news that Jesus is God's Son. Apparently, the only audience in tune with this proclamation is Jesus. Luke offers no crowd reaction to the announcement. Finally, the narrative link between the baptism of Jesus and the genealogy that follows is significant. The baptism confirms what the genealogy concludes ("son of Adam, son of God," 3:38): that Jesus has been announced as God's Son. Earthly confirmation endorses divine acknowledgment of Jesus' identity.

Much more than the other Gospels, Luke portrays Jesus as a practitioner of prayer, one who regularly sought deserted places to pray (5:16). This emphasis on the piety of Jesus cannot be divorced from a clear depiction of Jesus' dependence on God's Spirit, which marked Jesus at his baptism. The prayer life of Jesus accompanies many of the most significant events in his mission. At the baptism scene, he is in prayer as the heavens open, the Spirit lands, and God announces him to be

God's Son (3:21). Jesus' prayer also accompanies other extraordinary moments in his life, like his bodily transfiguration on a mountain (9:28–29) and his prayer at another mountain (the Mount of Olives) that "this cup may pass" (22:40–46). Prayer also immediately precedes other special episodes: the appointment of the twelve disciples (6:12); his question to the disciples about his identity, when Peter confesses him as "God's Messiah" (9:18); his teaching the disciples how to pray (11:1).

Prayer is also a feature of Jesus' teaching. He tells a parable to emphasize the importance of praying continuously (18:1) and another parable about the need for unpretentious prayers (18:10–11). Along with this last parable, he warns of scribes who "say long prayers" (20:47). In Luke's Gospel, prayer is a central feature in Jesus' life. So his first narrative prayer unsurprisingly is at his baptism.

As mentioned above, Luke's narrative downplays John's role in the baptism of Jesus. This is striking when compared to the earliest Gospel, Mark: "In those days Jesus came from Nazareth of Galilee and was baptized by John in the Jordan" (Mark 1:9). For Luke, the baptism does not occur as an isolated event; Jesus is simply included among others in the crowd (3:21). No baptizer is named. By implication, readers may assume John the Baptist performed the act. What distinguishes Jesus' baptism, for Luke, is not the specific action itself but Jesus' humble prayer and the apocalyptic sequence that follows (vv. 21–22). Announcing the true identity of Jesus, God's voice (v. 22) replaces John's voice (vv. 16–17).

The opening of the heavens usually signifies divine revelation, action, or interference in earthly activities. In Jewish tradition, it is associated with blessings (Mal. 3:10). In Noah's day, the disaster of the flood poured out when "the windows of the heavens were opened" (Gen. 7:11). When heaven opens for Ezekiel, he sees visions (Ezek. 1:1), a tradition that continues with John the Revelator, who also experiences visions, when gazing into an open heaven (Rev. 4:1; 19:11). Nearing death, Stephen looks through an open heaven to visualize

the "Human One" standing next to God (Acts 7:56 CEB). Similarly, in Acts, Peter sees heaven opened and receives a vision that points to the inclusion of the Gentiles (Acts 10:11). In addition, Jesus tells Nathanael that he will see heaven opened and the activities of angels assisting the work of the "Son of Man." For most of these scenes, access to the heavens provides insights into divine revelation and thoughts.

The passage in Luke does not imply that Jesus' prayer opened heaven; rather, an open heaven signifies God's initiation. In Mark's parallel, Jesus sees heaven open (1:10), an action only implied in Luke. For Luke, the downplaying of Jesus' baptism by water elevates the revelatory moments exemplified in an open heaven. More than an act of baptism as a symbolic act of joining the community, an act that others should emulate, Luke's baptism narrative more likely emphasizes the disclosure of Jesus' identity from God. The open space implies an accessible opportunity between that which separates the heavenly from the earthly, in order for God to reveal an eschatological plan for the people of Israel. This baptism is God's identity marker, not John's.

John lived the prophetic life, protesting things gone awry in society. Any desire to separate religion from the political was unknown in first-century Jewish life. John's protests integrated the political and the spiritual in ways that move some contemporary Christians to march against injustices in our own day. For some of us, publicly and communally questioning political power when it fails to serve the "least of these" is indeed a spiritual act of commitment. The lectionary's unfortunate omission of verses 18–20 seeks to avoid the mention of John's political enemies, especially Herod, who imprisoned him (3:20). This tension is central to John's life and to Jesus' mission as well. These wilderness prophets spoke truth to power and suffered for it.

Finally, there is no separation between prayer and protest in this story. Prayer fuels the protest and mission of Jesus. Martin Luther King Jr.'s nonviolent resistance movement drew on the words of Jesus for support to "pray for them which despitefully use you, and persecute you"[1]

---

1. Martin Luther King Jr., *Why We Can't Wait* (New York: Harper and Row, 1964), 76.

(see Luke 6:28). To bless those who may wish you harm requires more than a theological commitment; it requires a spiritual act of courage grounded in deep-seated prayer. In the Gospel of Luke, protest against ruling powers drives the content of one's prayer: "Your kingdom come. Give us each day our daily bread. And forgive us our sins, for we ourselves forgive everyone indebted to us" (Luke 11:2–4).

EMERSON B. POWERY

Commentary 2: Connecting the Reading with the World

Preaching about the baptism of Jesus should not quickly transition into reflections on the value and meaning of Christian baptism. First and foremost, this passage urges readers to consider who Jesus is, as well as his role in the salvation that God provides.

The distinction between identity and role is important, because too often texts like this one tie us in knots with questions about what baptism must have meant to Jesus and why he had to be baptized, taking congregations down doctrinal rabbit holes like the one John the Baptist starts to dig in Matthew 3:14. Before long, sermons and Bible studies based on the Synoptic accounts of Jesus' baptism turn into lessons about the nature and significance of a Christian sacrament. That is unfortunate, not because our baptisms do not deserve attention, but because the main focus in Luke 3 and parallel passages falls on Jesus' identity and purpose. Only after pursuing those important dimensions of Lukan Christology can we wonder further about what it means for us to undergo baptism in Jesus' name.

Jesus' Identity and His Submission to God. Luke actually draws very little attention to Jesus' baptism itself. After all, this is the Gospel that famously implies John may have little to do with Jesus' baptism, since Luke reports

---

Grace That Is Complete and Sufficient for All

Whoever hears "spirit" cannot impress on his mind a circumscribed nature, or one subject to changes and alterations, or one at all similar to creation. Rather, he must advance to the highest heights in his thoughts and conceive of a necessary, intellectual substance that is infinite in power, unlimited in greatness, immeasurable by time or ages, and generous with the good that it has. Everything that needs holiness turns to him. All that live virtuously desire him, as they are watered by his inspiration and assisted toward their proper and natural end. He perfects others, but himself lacks nothing. He lives, but not because he has been resorted to life; rather, he is the source of life. He does not grow in strength gradually, but is complete all at once. He is established in himself and present everywhere. He is the source of holiness, an intellectual light for every rational power's discovery of truth, supplying charity, so to say, through himself. He is inaccessible in nature, but approachable in goodness. He fills all things with power, but only those who are worthy to participate in him. He is not participated in all at once but shares his energy in "proportion to faith." He is simple in substance, but manifold in powers. He is present as a whole to each and wholly present everywhere. He is portioned out impassibly and participated in as a whole. He is like a sunbeam whose grace is present to the one who enjoys him as if he were present to such a one alone, and still he illuminates land and sea and is mixed with the air. Just so, indeed, the Spirit is present to each one who is fit to receive him, as if he were present to him alone, and still he sends out grace that is complete and sufficient for all. The things that participate in him enjoy him to the extent that their nature allows, not to the extent that his power allows.

Saint Basil the Great (ca. 329–79), *On the Holy Spirit* 9.22, trans. Stephen Hildebrand (Yonkers, NY: St. Vladimir's Seminary Press, 2011), 53.

John's arrest in 3:20, prior to mentioning Jesus' baptism. The passage's emphasis falls on what occurs subsequently: the opening of heaven, the Holy Spirit's arrival, and a declaration from God. Those pivotal events happen separately from the baptism, apparently at a later time and perhaps in a different location, when Jesus prays. Prayer, according to Luke–Acts, creates a context in which people receive divine guidance or find themselves cooperating with God's work (e.g., Luke 6:12–16; 9:28–29; 22:41–42; Acts 1:24–26; 10:9–16; 13:3). As Jesus prays, presumably alone (see Luke 5:16; 6:12), God addresses him, confirming his identity as God's beloved Son. In the aftermath of his baptism, Jesus discovers who he is. Actually he rediscovers this knowledge, along with Luke's readers (Luke 1:35; 2:49). The divine words confirm truth that has already been declared.

Jesus therefore does not commence his ministry until first he is told again who he is, to whom he belongs. His ministry thus exists as a prolonged expression of his identity as God's chosen and sent agent. We might say similar things about Jesus' followers, including ourselves. The church perpetuates Jesus' ministry not because Christians' primary task is to imitate our Lord or do whatever we think he would do in our circumstances; rather, believers promote and embody the reign of God because first we know who we are: witnesses of Christ, the Son of God, and beneficiaries of the salvation he brings (cf. Acts 1:8; 5:32).

Luke also describes Jesus' identity in connection to Jesus' willingness to submit himself to God and God's intentions. By participating in "baptism of repentance for the forgiveness of sins" (Luke 3:3), Jesus commits himself to participating in the fulfillment of Isaiah's vision that John's ministry anticipates (Luke 3:4–6; Isa. 40:3–5 LXX). John knows what everyone in Luke 1–2 also knows: God's salvation and a new restoration of Israel are at hand (cf. Luke 2:38; 24:21). God is making good on old pledges that anticipate the reconfiguration of the whole human landscape. In his baptism, then, Jesus commits himself to what God has in store—for him and for the soon-to-be-expanding community of God's people. Jesus aligns himself with the new realities God envisions. In our

meditations on Jesus' baptism, Jesus' followers discover opportunities to align ourselves in the same way.

Jesus and the Holy Spirit. God's new realities reveal themselves in the narrative that follows this passage, first in the multifaceted salvation Jesus provides throughout his public ministry, and later in the creation of Spirit-filled communities in Acts. The Holy Spirit comes to Jesus here, early in the Gospel, so that the Spirit may eventually come to all of Jesus' followers, when the book of Acts tells its story.

The words John speaks in Luke 3:15–17 are therefore quite important for understanding the comprehensive Lukan portrait of salvation and, as a result, the church's identity and mission. When John announces that the Messiah "will baptize you with the Holy Spirit and fire," he anticipates what occurs on Pentecost (Acts 2) and elsewhere in the Gospel's sequel (e.g., Acts 8:17; 10:44). The connections between Luke and Acts encourage us to read Luke's baptism scene as more than literary foreshadowing or unfulfilled eschatological longings. Luke–Acts understands the giving of the Holy Spirit as the full and complete expression of the salvation Jesus provides. Jesus' identity as "Lord and Messiah," according to the apostle Peter's Pentecost sermon, becomes undoubtedly and finally *publicly* confirmed through the conclusion of a series of connected events: his death, his resurrection, his ascension to God's right hand, and his outpouring of the Holy Spirit (Acts 2:32–36; cf. 1:5; 11:16).

John's announcement in Luke 3:16–17 thus highlights more than Jesus' authority; it points forward to the power Jesus will share and the communities he will create. In that regard, the passage directs the contemporary church's vision forward when it is read during the time after the Epiphany. Epiphany provides occasions for considering how Jesus' work continues now in the lives of his followers. According to the larger story Luke–Acts tells, Jesus remains especially manifest through the Spirit that propels, redirects, and surprises believers. What Epiphany celebrations promise when the Holy Spirit comes upon Jesus and God addresses him as "Son" in a hidden and apparently private moment, the texts of Pentecost will confirm with great and unavoidable fanfare.

Jesus' Baptism, Our Baptism. The purpose of the Synoptic Gospels' accounts of Jesus' baptism is not to provide archetypes. In other words, they are not primarily about showing us how a ritual is done. Nor do the Gospels imagine the event as Jesus' vague expression of solidarity with human frailty and brokenness. Rather, we should see Jesus' baptism as his declaration of a revolutionary commitment to God's plan and to the well-being of God's people. It signals his willingness to be a part—the crucial part—of the new order God has pledged to enact and God begins to enact in Jesus' public ministry. Through his baptism and prayerful reception of the Holy Spirit, Jesus receives confirmation of his identity as the one who will eventually bestow the Holy Spirit upon others. After we recognize first that this is who Jesus is in Luke–Acts, only then may we choose to reflect more deeply on Christian baptism, especially the significance of being baptized in Jesus' name (e.g., Acts 2:38; 10:48; 19:5).

A Lukan perspective on baptism in Jesus' name involves believers' finding a new identity in Christ, an identity that allows them to share in the new realities God has brought into being, marked by forgiven sins and the reality of sharing together with God's own self through the Holy Spirt. This identity empowers the church to be part of Isaiah's vision of God's future, when God arrives and "all flesh shall see the salvation of God" (Luke 3:4–6). This future, characterized by human flourishing and divine compassion, starts to come into being when Jesus presents himself as willing to play his costly part in the prophetic ministry and cosmic drama God sets before him. Jesus' baptism involves his recognition that God means business. The baptisms of us who share in the salvation that comes through Jesus declare similar things about what God is determined to accomplish in, for, and around us.

MATTHEW L. SKINNER

Second Sunday after the Epiphany

Isaiah 62:1–5
Psalm 36:5–10

1 Corinthians 12:1–11
John 2:1–11

Isaiah 62:1–5

¹For Zion's sake I will not keep silent,
  and for Jerusalem's sake I will not rest,
until her vindication shines out like the dawn,
  and her salvation like a burning torch.
²The nations shall see your vindication,
  and all the kings your glory;
and you shall be called by a new name
  that the mouth of the LORD will give.
³You shall be a crown of beauty in the hand of the LORD,
  and a royal diadem in the hand of your God.
⁴You shall no more be termed Forsaken,
  and your land shall no more be termed Desolate;
but you shall be called My Delight Is in Her,
  and your land Married;
for the LORD delights in you,
  and your land shall be married.
⁵For as a young man marries a young woman,
  so shall your builder marry you,
and as the bridegroom rejoices over the bride,
  so shall your God rejoice over you.

Commentary 1: Connecting the Reading with Scripture

Biblical prophetic writings such as this may be compared to a symphonic musical piece: as a symphony contains many motifs and chords, in various keys, voices, and pitches, so prophetic texts have a multitude of themes, layers, and nuances. These have developed over time as faithful authors have joined their voices to the score to create the symphony of the text.

Jerusalem, the Beautiful Bride, in Isaiah. The book of Isaiah presents one of the most elaborate symphonies in the prophetic corpus. Isaiah proceeds from a somber voice announcing judgment against Judah in Isaiah 2–12 (esp. chaps. 6–8), to the announcement against the nations (chaps. 13–23), to the joyful interlude of chapters 33–35, and to a historical narrative about King Hezekiah (chaps. 36–39). It then

moves to a triumphant second part (chaps. 40–55) in which a mixed reprisal of themes is included. To continue the symphony analogy, chapters 56–66 take up voices and motifs of many earlier parts.

Isaiah 62 serves as a joyful coda full of promise for the future, like the end of a majestic symphony. The piece has been performed and reedited time after time. One may think of it as part of a musical telling of the story of Judah between the sixth and fourth centuries BCE (Second Temple Period). The themes of vindication on one side and divine marriage on the other side designate the extremes of Judah's collective experience. The dialectic between vindication from former punishment and Zion-Jerusalem's marriage with a divine bridegroom (Isa. 52, 54) reveals its own theological

177

tension. The prevailing theme, though, of Isaiah 62:1–5 is that of an identity restored by God. By God's grace, the former exiles are to jettison their former exilic names, "Forsaken" and "Desolate" (v. 4), in order to embrace a restored identity that will frame their future, the new community named "My Delight."

Restoration. Isaiah 62:1–5 unfolds its overarching theme of restoration with two recurring motifs. The first concerns establishing justice that materializes in the city's external restoration. Justice is accomplished by way of Zion's vindication (62:1–2), as rehearsed throughout the book.

Isaiah develops justice as obligation toward the God of Jerusalem, the owner of Jerusalem, a well-kept vineyard (Isa. 5:1–7). Instead of yielding an abundant crop of justice *(tsedaqah)* from a fecund vineyard, the vineyard/city yields a foul and smelly harvest, with "cries of injustice," *ts'aqah* (Isa. 5:7).

The tone of Isaiah 62:1–2, in which the author presents his future plans for Zion's vindication, is promissory; the divine promise of peace is put in place by Zion's industrious God. It is a promise yet to be realized, but it is nonetheless sure.

Adorned Bride. The second theme of the passage is developed through the metaphor of marriage. The popular personification of Zion as God's bride, for instance, in the hymn "Zion's Daughter, O Rejoice! Shout Aloud, Jerusalem!" has its roots in Isaiah 62:1–5. The metaphor is cast as a prophetic message of Isaiah as "city prophet." Zion-Jerusalem in Isaiah is an epitome for Judah as a whole. When Zion-Jerusalem is humiliated, it signifies Judah's suffering during the Babylonian exile. When Zion-Jerusalem is the place where Judah rejoices, Zion-Jerusalem stands as the seat of glory.

Isaiah 62:1–5 describes the image of the beautifully adorned bride, already alluded to in Isaiah 61:10–11. Zion's husband, who will not forget her, will continue to speak on her behalf. Jerusalem, the capital, is a mediator through which Yahweh blesses Jerusalem's inhabitants. Isaiah proclaims the divine care of Yahweh against the backdrop of Judah's brutal subjection under the empires of Assyria, Babylonia, and Persia.

The frame of reference in Isaiah 6–8 points to how religious leaders in Jerusalem damage Israel's relationship with Yahweh. They do not hear or listen. As a consequence of the rejection of the stubborn King Ahaz (Isa. 7:10–17), Isaiah is led to highlight the teaching of Isaiah 8:16–18 so that future generations, in hindsight, may more fully understand what Isaiah means by his warnings. The prophet announces that Judah has been, by and large, swallowed by the Assyrian Empire at the time of Hezekiah. The allusions to Judah's former humiliation are plain. Isaiah 62 refers to the change of Jerusalem-Zion's position by pointing to her honor. This honor is symbolized through the images of the royal diadem, an image for the city's restoration (v. 3) and through the metaphor of the "hand of your God" (v. 3b). Formerly, the city had from that same hand received the "cup of staggering" (51:22). God is bringing restoration of the identity of Jerusalem-Zion despite the hardships of exilic and postexilic life.

Rhetorical Strategies. How can we flesh out the marriage metaphor of Isaiah 62:1–5? Throughout antiquity the marriage metaphor communicates a relationship between nonequals, an alliance between uneven partners. Bride and groom are in an asymmetric relationship; the bride receives her honor through the bridegroom's kin. Biblical covenant theology assumes an inherently hierarchic setting analogous to a close kinship relationship that a marriage forges between a woman and husband. Marriage is a covenantal agreement and, as a consequence, a key passage, Jeremiah 31:31–34, interprets Yahweh as "husbanding" Israel.

In a patriarchal society the two partners are not of equal status and have different responsibilities. The groom is the bride's owner and her representative in all matters legal; at the same time, he is also responsible for all aspects of her well-being. Yahweh, the God of Israel, enters into a relationship with Jerusalem. Their interaction is as personal as a covenant with a spouse. God's history with God's people is told as a variant of the narrative of the ever-dutiful, ever-loving, ever-forgiving, and ever-patient lover.

Put for a modern audience: Isaiah's point is not to reinforce the pattern of patriarchal obedience. Instead, Isaiah points to the amazing perspective of a caring God through all times and spaces. He casts this thought into a metaphor valid for his own days. God is provider who is in charge of life-giving food, and God's people need to be fed. The patriarchal groom-and-bride metaphor, despite the dissonances it creates for contemporary hearers, is meant to portray God in a way that reassures the Israelites they will be provided for and protected. God is not portrayed as a domineering husband, but as a compassionate spouse who attends to the needs of God's beloved.

In addition to providing preaching insights into a caring God, Isaiah 62:1–5 invites reflection on modern gender concepts. Could the image of the female queen Zion-Jerusalem inspire the preacher to draw her in a female imaging of humanity, as provider to her inhabitants, rather than in the typically patriarchal, male imaging of God and God's relationship with God's people? Isaiah 62:1–5 also offers a gender-neutral image of God to be considered along with the marriage metaphor, the builder/creator: your builder marries you. Seen through this lens, the actual quality of the relation between the two partners becomes more relevant; God is not acting with patriarchal authority but God is suffering along with Jerusalem. God instead exercises compassion and grieves over God's lover's defeat. Even in the midst of defeat, God redeems and restores the identity of God's "forsaken" and "desolate" people.

How can the preacher perform this symphony from Isaiah 62:1–5? Listen for the music of restoration. Attend to the promise of a new identity. Rejoice in the promise of a God who rejoices over God's people when they are broken and forlorn. It is a symphony waiting to be performed in the season of Epiphany, as God reveals a future in which joy is music to the ears.

KLAUS-PETER ADAM

Commentary 2: Connecting the Reading with the World

Isaiah 62:1–5 is a poem celebrating a love triangle between the prophet Isaiah, the city of Jerusalem, and God. Preachers might compare this text to popular movies in which the lovers' relationship seems unlikely at first. Here in Isaiah 62, the unexpected pairing does not come from the predestined couple's improbable first encounter (think of *Notting Hill*) or their lukewarm friendship turned passionate (as in *Harry Met Sally*) or a courtship shrouded in mystery that finally ends in a union (*Sleepless in Seattle*). The love relationship that Isaiah describes is startling because it is not between two people at all.

Just as study in film technique helps viewers to appreciate the scenes that flash on the screen, recognizing elements of Hebrew poetry enhances readers' understanding of this passage. Congregants appreciate learning about the nuances in the text. For example, Isaiah 62:1–5 offers a clear example of parallelism, a literary device in which one line of a poem is echoed in the next. The second line nuances the previous line, somewhat like an emoji in a text message. In this passage, the parallelism is synonymous, meaning that the lines agree with each other in meaning. Appropriately, the synonymous couplets of Isaiah 62:1–5 resound in poetic harmony, as the prophet sings a love song for Jerusalem.

Once the reader of the Bible understands parallelism, the poetry is much clearer. Many people in the pew do not realize that Zion is the name of the mountain on which Jerusalem sits. In the biblical books of poetry, references to Zion refer to Jerusalem, as in verse 1. The NRSV tells of Jerusalem's "vindication" (vv. 1, 2), but the Hebrew word here (*tsidqah*) would be better translated as "her righteousness." The prophet explains his attraction to Jerusalem—she is righteous and radiant, shining like the dawn or a burning torch.

The preacher might point out that Isaiah is boastful in verse 2, heaping praises on Jerusalem. This invites reflection on the difference between boasting and pride. What are the hallmarks of each? When does pride (in our children or our accomplishments, for example) become obnoxious? Here, Jerusalem is adored and the prophet proclaims her luminary status.

The desire for fame is extraordinary in modern North American culture. Through YouTube, Instagram, Facebook, Twitter, SnapChat, and other social-media venues, anyone with an internet connection has the access to become a celebrity. Here the preacher might offer some caution. Whom do we adore, and why? Media spew forth details about renowned glamorous people whose main claim to stardom is being famous. In contrast, Isaiah does not obsess over Jerusalem's fame. Rather, the prophet moves the relationship between God and the city forward with a focus on a name.

Preachers might explore questions about the ramifications of our names. Shakespeare's famous question about names, voiced by Juliet, has almost become a cliché: "What's in a name? That which we call a rose by any other word would smell as sweet" (*Romeo and Juliet*, act 2, scene 2). Is this well-known dictum true? If we called deep red roses "ripped-up blood bulbs," would you be eager to give a bouquet of them to your true love? Isaiah recognizes that a name is deeply significant and promises Jerusalem that God will give her a new name, without revealing (at first) what this name will be. The names the prophet gives Jerusalem show that she is cherished (v. 4). How do congregants name what is precious to them? How does the church do the same?

The importance given to Jerusalem's name shows how much names matter. Cities are gendered as feminine in the Bible and, like many

---

Living in Christ and the Neighbor

Therefore, if we recognize the great and precious things which are given us, as Paul says, our hearts will be filled by the Holy Spirit with the love which makes us free, joyful, almighty workers and conquerors over all tribulations, servants of our neighbors, and yet lords of all. For those who do not recognize the gifts bestowed upon them through Christ, however, Christ has been born in vain; they go their way with their works and shall never come to taste or feel those things. Just as our neighbor is in need and lacks that in which we abound, so we were in need before God and lacked his mercy. Hence, as our heavenly Father has in Christ freely come to our aid, we also ought freely to help our neighbor through our body and its works, and each one should become as it were a Christ to the other that we may be Christs to one another and Christ may be the same in all, that is, that we may be truly Christians.

Who then can comprehend the riches and the glory of the Christian life? It can do all things and has all things and lacks nothing. It is lord over sin, death, and hell, and yet at the same time it serves, ministers to, and benefits all men. But alas in our day this life is unknown throughout the world; it is neither preached about nor sought after; we are altogether ignorant of our own name and do not know why we are Christians or bear the name of Christians. Surely we are named after Christ, not because he is absent from us, but because he dwells in us, that is, because we believe in him and are Christs one to another and do to our neighbors as Christ does to us. . . .

We conclude, therefore, that a Christian lives not in himself, but in Christ and in his neighbor. Otherwise he is not a Christian. He lives in Christ through faith, in his neighbor through love. By faith he is caught up beyond himself into God. By love he descends beneath himself into his neighbor. Yet he always remains in God and in his love, as Christ says in John 1, "Truly, truly, I say to you, you will see heaven opened, and the angels of God ascending and descending upon the Son of man."

Enough now of freedom. As you see, it is a spiritual and true freedom and makes our hearts free from all sins, laws and commands, as Paul says, I Tim. 1, "The law is not laid down for the just." It is more excellent than all other liberty, which is external, as heaven is more excellent than earth. May Christ give us this liberty both to understand and to preserve. Amen.

Martin Luther (1483–1546), *The Freedom of a Christian*, trans. W. A. Lambert, rev. Harold J. Grimm, in *Luther's Works* (Philadelphia: Fortress Press, 1957), 31:367–71.

women who marry, Jerusalem is faced with the prospect of a name change. Most married women in the United States today take their husband's last name, but in recent decades changing one's name has become more of a choice. Approximately 20 percent of women who marry retain the names that they have had throughout their lives. Another 10 percent of women choose another option, such as hyphenating their last name or keeping their birth name only in their careers.[2] Reasons for changing or retaining one's name are as individual as the people making these decisions. Preachers can invite members to think deeply about what they call the people in their lives and what our names say about our origin and our relationships.

In Isaiah 62:4, God offers Jerusalem names that show she is loved. Who would want to be called "Forsaken" when you can have the name "My Delight Is in Her"? She who was called "Desolate" is now "Married." In Hebrew, these four words have rhyming last syllables (*Azubah, Hephzibah, Shemamah,* and *Beulah,* respectively), enhancing the poetic quality of this verse. Form mimics meaning, as carefully chosen phrases resound with God's exquisite love for Jerusalem.

The language of love saturates this passage, which ends, not surprisingly, like a romantic comedy culminating in the promise of marriage. Marriage is the ready happy resolution in love relationships that our culture promotes; the preacher might invite speculation on this assumption. In this text from Isaiah, the glorious final scene (v. 5) shows the bridegroom rejoicing over the bride, strengthening this culture ideal. Isaiah's focus is on the man of this couple, metaphorically God, who is clearly full of delight. Yet the poetic prophet does not describe the bride in these moments. The concern for mutuality in a true love connection is ours, not Isaiah's.

Mutual love might seem like a modern concern, and in some ways this focus is anachronistic when drawn from the biblical text. Preachers can remind congregants that mutuality is the hallmark of a healthy relationship. How many people in a relationship work to please their partner, who does not care about pleasing them? Giving members of our churches tools of awareness that can lead to interpersonal appreciation and understanding can save congregants from dangerous relationships. Often the church avoids discussion of domestic strife or even abuse. This passage gives the chance to point out that relationships are a blessing when filled with reciprocated care and concern from all parties involved.

Isaiah calls readers to imagine a wedding scene of delight, not distress. Preachers know that weddings are full of drama, and often tension. People come together for an event that is often laden with pressure. Under this weight, family histories can all too frequently devolve into histrionics. How easy it is to lose sight of the rejoicing amid all the wedding details and planning. Christians know that we should keep love at the center of all of our lives, but so easily the demands of our lives distort our view, and we lose sight of what matters most. This text helps the preacher keep a focus on the joy of the celebration of God's love.

During the season of Epiphany, when Christmas is over and weeks of winter still stretch ahead, Isaiah 62:1–5 invites us to a metaphorical wedding. Often this time of year is relatively uneventful in congregational life. The liturgical calendar offers a lull between the exuberance of Christmastide and the somber repentance of Lent. Instead of seeing this as a dull period in need of excitement, ministers can offer an invitation not to a wedding but to the joy behind everyday love. There is joy in quiet and even relaxation. God's love comes to us in all moments, not just those filled with fanfare.

At its core, this passage invites the preacher to think about God's love and to be bold in raising questions about what makes our love genuine.

JULIE FAITH PARKER

2. Claire Cain Miller and Derek Willis, "Maiden Names, on the Rise Again," *New York Times,* June 27, 2015, https://www.nytimes.com/2015/06/28/upshot/maiden-names-on-the-rise-again.html.

Psalm 36:5–10

⁵Your steadfast love, O LORD, extends to the heavens,
   your faithfulness to the clouds.
⁶Your righteousness is like the mighty mountains,
   your judgments are like the great deep;
   you save humans and animals alike, O LORD.

⁷How precious is your steadfast love, O God!
   All people may take refuge in the shadow of your wings.
⁸They feast on the abundance of your house,
   and you give them drink from the river of your delights.
⁹For with you is the fountain of life;
   in your light we see light.

¹⁰O continue your steadfast love to those who know you,
   and your salvation to the upright of heart!

Connecting the Psalm with Scripture and Worship

"For with you is the fountain of life; in your light we see light" (v. 9). These magnificent words found in Psalm 36 depict the central message of this entire psalm: humanity's dependence on God. Placed between a description of the wicked (vv. 1–4), and a petition (vv. 11–12), verses 5–10 ground the psalmist's prayer for help. These verses fully praise God's love, which encompasses the world and reaches the heavens. The psalmist offers praise to God for accepting humanity, and all creation, into God's presence to be nurtured by divine love.

Knowing that people who had forgotten their faith in God surrounded the community, the psalmist uses metaphors of greatness, presenting attributes that are cosmic in dimension. Heavens and clouds mark the upper limit of the world; mountains and the great deep are terms of immensity.[1] These cosmic dimensions are connected to the attributes of love and faithfulness (v. 5), and righteousness and judgment (v. 6). Israel had come to know these attributes of God in its history with God. Israel's encounter with God (Isa. 62:5)

is illustrated through images of marriage and delight. God's love vindicates Israel, and God rejoices over them. This same imagery is present within Psalm 36. When taken in the context of the entire psalm, verses 5–10 illustrate this salvific love that is extended to all living things, human and animal alike.

The psalmist's faith and trust offer one key focus for preaching on the Second Sunday after the Epiphany: the entire world is founded upon love, faithfulness, righteousness, and justice.[2] Humanity and all creation are dependent upon God's providential care. Even the host of the wedding at Cana (John 2:1–11) unwittingly depended upon divine intervention to provide hospitality for his guests. The psalmist emphasizes this dependence on God's saving help through images of shelter (v. 7b), food and drink (v. 8), and God as the very source of life (v. 9). Everything that sustains life comes from God; therefore, every living thing is dependent upon God. This provision described by the psalmist is not just limited to Israel; rather, it is for all creation, and we have an open invitation

---

1. James Luther Mays, *Psalms*, Interpretation (Louisville, KY: John Knox Press, 1994), 156.
2. C. Hassell Bullock, *Psalms, Volume 1: Psalms 1–72* (Grand Rapids: Baker Books, 2015), 273.

to embrace God's love and protection as God's children.

The psalm text reflects the compassion and love found in Isaiah's message to Israel. God loves God's people and allows for a much deeper experience of God. We are offered the blessed privilege of encountering the very nature of God as sustainer, redeemer, nurturer, and savior. This personal encounter is seen through the psalmist's complete trust in God's immeasurable and unfailing love. God is compassionate and cares for all of God's creation. Through vindication and preservation (Isa. 62:1–5), God protects us and shows us the way through God's divine light. Upon this promise of love and spiritual nourishment, the psalmist rejoices with trust in God's eternal love.

Psalm 36:5–10 may be used in worship as a prayer of response to the sermon. Utilized as a sermon response, the psalm reminds the congregation of God's great love, and invites a moment of focused praise for God's faithfulness through prayer. This can provide a change in the way in which the congregation offers praise to God, departing from hymns of praise or using the psalm as an opening to worship. Instead, this petition becomes a centering opportunity, allowing time for people to reflect on the preached word and then respond with praise, recognizing that God provides all things, even the word that is preached. The response can be led by two voices with the congregation offering a response of praise.

Voice 1: God of Light and Love . . . Verse 5
People: *For your steadfast love, O God,*
we give thanks.

Voice 2: Verse 6
People: *For your steadfast love, O God,*
we give thanks.

Voice 1: Verses 7–8
People: *For your steadfast love, O God,*
we give thanks.

Voice 2: Verse 9–10
People: *For your steadfast love, O God,*
we give thanks.

The responsive nature of this psalm allows for a personal prayer of thanksgiving to become a communal statement, acknowledging that we all receive the gift of God's divine and steadfast love. This love is not only personal; it is for all who are gathered and thus connects us one to another through God's love.

These verses may also be adapted for use as a benediction, offering words of blessing and a reminder to walk confidently in the love of God, as we seek to be human expressions of God's love in the world. The preacher might speak the blessing, and the congregation may respond with thanks and praise.

Leader: Find joy and comfort
in these words
as we depart from this place.
God's steadfast love extends
to the heavens,
and God's faithfulness to the clouds.
God's righteousness is
like the mighty mountains,
God's judgments are
like the great deep;
God saves humans and animals alike.
May you experience the precious
steadfast love of God,
and take refuge in the shadow
of God's wings.
May you feast on the abundance
of your house,
and drink from the rivers
of your delights.
God is your fountain of life,
and in God's light may you see light.
Give praise to God,
and go and in peace.
People: *We praise you, God,*
for your steadfast love,
and for your salvation
to the upright of heart.

Psalm 36:5–10 calls us to reflect on God's love in all of its grandeur and pause in thanksgiving for our personal proximity to God. All of creation—human and animals alike—is dependent on God; and God's righteous and saving love sustains us all. "For with you is the fountain of life; in your light we see light" (v. 9).

KHALIA J. WILLIAMS

1 Corinthians 12:1–11

[1]Now concerning spiritual gifts, brothers and sisters, I do not want you to be uninformed. [2]You know that when you were pagans, you were enticed and led astray to idols that could not speak. [3]Therefore I want you to understand that no one speaking by the Spirit of God ever says "Let Jesus be cursed!" and no one can say "Jesus is Lord" except by the Holy Spirit.

[4]Now there are varieties of gifts, but the same Spirit; [5]and there are varieties of services, but the same Lord; [6]and there are varieties of activities, but it is the same God who activates all of them in everyone. [7]To each is given the manifestation of the Spirit for the common good. [8]To one is given through the Spirit the utterance of wisdom, and to another the utterance of knowledge according to the same Spirit, [9]to another faith by the same Spirit, to another gifts of healing by the one Spirit, [10]to another the working of miracles, to another prophecy, to another the discernment of spirits, to another various kinds of tongues, to another the interpretation of tongues. [11]All these are activated by one and the same Spirit, who allots to each one individually just as the Spirit chooses.

Commentary 1: Connecting the Reading with Scripture

The task before the church in Corinth was to create a new form of community centered on the Christian faith received in baptism. Paul's letter offers concrete advice, principles for discernment, models to follow, and a picture of Christian life playing out in the extended space between baptism and eschaton.

Members of the church in Corinth were distinguishing themselves from one another based on a number of characteristics and behaviors, in order to claim superior status. Paul names one source of division and pride in chapter 1: members of the church are dividing into factions based on their teachers. Various Corinthians said, "'I belong to Paul," or "I belong to Apollos," or "I belong to Cephas," or "I belong to Christ" (1 Cor. 1:12). Other points of contention among the Corinthians include lawsuits (6:1–8), marriage (7:1–16), and eating food that has been offered to idols (8:1–13). While Paul takes the time to offer detailed advice on each individual issue, his primary response to their quarrels is given right up front and echoes throughout the letter: "I appeal to you, brothers and sisters, by the name of our Lord Jesus Christ, that all of you be in agreement and that there be no divisions among you, but that you be united in the same mind and the same purpose" (1:10).

On its own, this sentence sounds like a parent urging contentious children to get along: "For the love of Jesus, stop fighting!" However, for Paul there is great theological depth to unity in Christ.

The baptismal formula in Galatians 3:28 declares that distinctions of social status do not hold sway within the community of those who follow Christ. "There is no longer Jew or Greek, there is no longer slave or free, there is no longer male and female; for all of you are one in Christ Jesus." The Corinthians have busily created other divisions and hierarchies within their own community, including among the spiritual gifts of individuals. The Corinthians gave ecstatic speech, or speaking in tongues, pride of place as a mark of spiritual superiority.[1] Paul addresses this directly by reminding the members of the church that many of them had ecstatic spiritual experiences in the cults they had participated in before coming to know Jesus (12:2). Speaking in tongues—on its own—is unreliable evidence of spiritual maturity.

1. Luke T. Johnson, *The Writings of the New Testament: An Interpretation* (Philadelphia: Fortress Press, 1986), 287.

Paul then offers a principle of discernment of true spiritual gifts, writing, "Therefore I want you to understand that no one speaking by the Spirit of God ever says 'Let Jesus be cursed!' and no one can say 'Jesus is Lord' except by the Holy Spirit."

Paul is making plain the primary criterion for discerning any claims to spiritual knowledge or wisdom: Jesus Christ. Any theological or spiritual utterance in the church that disregards or contradicts the life, ministry, death, and resurrection of Jesus Christ is not empowered by the Holy Spirit. Conversely, we can be confident that lived faith in Jesus is Spirit-led. When Paul writes, "No one can say 'Jesus is Lord' except by the Holy Spirit," he is not indicating a mere verbal declaration of faith in Jesus. Rather, he is referring to an affirmation of faith that involves a person's entire life in commitment and trust.

While Paul begins chapter 12 discussing *pneumatika,* or things concerning the spirit, he divides them into *charismata* ("gifts"), *diakonia* ("services"), and *energēmata* ("activities") (12:4–6). His discussion of gifts is emblematic of the whole. Paul reminds the Corinthians that the varied spiritual gifts in the church are not the innate possessions of individuals. They are precisely gifts, which means they do not have their origin in the individuals who display them but have, rather, been bestowed on these individuals by another. The word itself (like the word "gift" in English) implies a relationship between giver and receiver.

Similarly, service (*diakonia*) implies a relationship between one who serves and one who receives service. The word for activities in 12:6 (*energēmata*) highlights that the activities of the Corinthians are the outworking of the divine activity of the Spirit. This is also a relational term, for it implies that the work of one results from the energy of another. Gifts, service, and activities are dynamic and relational terms.

The poles of the relationship are clearly delineated by Paul: God and the community. The varieties of spiritual gifts are given by the same Spirit, Lord, and God (12:6), and each "manifestation of the Spirit" is given "for the common good" (12:7).

The origin of the different gifts is the same, and so is their destination. It makes no sense for a particular Christian to boast of possessing a certain spiritual gift, for that gift was given *by* another and intended *for* the whole community.

In this way, the spiritual gifts are similar to the wine at the wedding in Cana (John 2:1–11). The hosts of the celebration do not have, from their own stores, enough wine to serve the guests. Jesus transforms water into wine, bestowing a great blessing on the host family. Jesus clearly intends that the hosts to whom he has given wine will, in turn, give wine to the rest of the gathered community. How odd it would seem if the hosts shut the party down in order to save the fine wine for themselves! It would be stranger still, and profoundly ungrateful, if they were to take this gift as indication of their superiority over their neighbors.

This chapter of Paul's letter is a stern but loving scolding of the Corinthians. He reminds them that of their own accord they have been "led astray to dumb idols" (12:2), but he does not doubt their faith or their gifts. Instead, he offers guidance on how to discern true spiritual gifts and use them well. Paul's comments reject self-aggrandizement and urge unity in Christ. For the Corinthians, living into their baptism—which dismisses using differences as a means to stratify people—necessitates understanding that difference does not have to be hierarchical or divisive.

Later in the letter, Paul chastises those Corinthians who have been denying the resurrection of the dead (15:12–28). In their confidence that they have received the truth and the Spirit, these members of the church have forgotten that the fulfillment of God's new creation has yet to come.[2] The structure of the letter—with mention of conversion and baptism (1:12–17) at the beginning and a chapter on eschatology near the end (chap. 15)—echoes and underlines his comments on spiritual gifts. The Corinthians have forgotten that they do not possess the spiritual gifts. Rather, they are blessed to be the go-betweens—the people who receive a boon in order to pass it along to the whole community. In similar fashion, they have forgotten that they

---

2. Johnson, *Writings,* 276.

are living in-between—after the inauguration of the new creation, but before its consummation. Their task of passing on the spiritual gifts to the whole community fits within their larger vocation, which is to live the faith they have received until it is perfected in the resurrection.

In the season of Epiphany, Paul's words encourage reflection on the relational nature of spiritual gifts, as they flow between God and the community. He portrays a kind of holy regifting. We receive gifts in order to give them to others. What are we regifting? What changes if we remember that we are go-betweens, living in-between?

SHANNON CRAIGO-SNELL

Commentary 2: Connecting the Reading with the World

God bless whoever it was God had tapped to lead the nascent gathering of Christians in Corinth following Paul's founding of the congregation. Little could they have known that the contentious members of this congregation were simply prefiguring the subsequent two thousand years of Christian existence. Reading this letter and positing the letter that prompted it, I imagine an ecclesial family feud. Picture various sides conferring among themselves about the top ten issues that have split the congregation and have diminished church unity since the first century. Which of the many disputes deserved Paul's attention? Jealousy over which teacher to follow? Taking each other to court? Quarrelling over matters of sexual morality? Exploiting the most vulnerable in Jesus' name? Succumbing to the worship of idols? Showing contempt for each other at the table?

As Paul tackles each new issue using the words "Now concerning," he inches closer to the No. 1 issue, which will take him three chapters to address. "Now concerning spiritual things," Paul begins in general, but everyone in the community knows that the spiritual thing in question, the spiritual thing creating a dangerous hierarchy among worshipers, is speaking in tongues during the service of worship. Reading between the lines, Richard Hays suggests that those who spoke in tongues, or who were prone to prophetic utterances, "considered themselves authorities on such matters" and were treating these manifestations of the Spirit as signs of their own sophistication and power."[3] Paul knows that this behavior can threaten the community with schism. How does Paul address this particular division in the community he founded only a few years earlier? How does his argument tutor our own when dealing with Christians who think more highly of themselves than they ought?

Some preachers may want to follow Paul's lead as he shows his own humanity in what could be read as a slight rant. Asserting his teaching office and pastoral authority with a gentle turn of the screw, he addresses those who are acting as though they have a direct line to the Spirit. "I do not want you to be uninformed"—a kind way of saying both that they *are* uninformed and that he is *better* informed. This is what spiritual mentors must do sometimes. He next reminds them that he knew them "when": when they were Gentile nonbelievers, vulnerable to every spiritual huckster that blew into town. The words invite them to step down from their self-declared spiritual heights. Finally, he lifts up the truth that the Spirit alone leads believers to say, "Jesus is Lord." Any tongues that deviate from that confession are as good as cursing Christ.

How is a minister to deal with the spiritually haughty in the congregation? As eager as we have been in the last few decades to downplay the authority of the pastoral office, in most traditions, the minister/pastor/priest has been set apart by the community to be its teacher. This is not to say that the minister is closer to God or is privy to insider spiritual information. It simply means that the minister has taken pains to be informed through the study of scriptural and confessional resources and practices that have

---

3. Richard Hays, *First Corinthians*, Interpretation (Louisville, KY: John Knox Press, 1997), 208.

served as vehicles of the Spirit in times past. For the health of the body, sometimes we have to risk the exercise of the authority we were given by God and the church when we knelt to be ordained. At the very least, by exercising that authority in the next few chapters, Paul has the Corinthians' undivided attention!

Other preachers might want to take Paul's theological lead as he renames the subject at hand. What makes the church the church is not "spiritual things" attributed to individuals, but diverse spiritual gifts given by the one God for the good of all. Therefore if the church is to live into the unity given by the Spirit, its members must understand three things: (1) their contributions to the life and health of the community are not their own doing (not spiritual things that they have achieved as an individual) but are a gift (a charisma) given to them for the sake of the whole; (2) the services and activities they have been given, in order to give away, are diverse by God's design; (3) it is the same Spirit/Lord/God who is the source of each gift.

Paul is making a pivot that the twenty-first-century church, set in a society that lauds the individual and struggles with diversity, misses at its own peril. Christian ethicist Paul Lehmann articulates best what is at stake theologically: "This is the *communio sanctorum,* the fellowship of Christians, in the world. It does not mean that there are no diversities in the fellowship. But it does mean that diversities, whether in society or in the church, cannot be preferentially used to disrupt and destroy the fellowship."[4]

Diversities in the church, if they are of the Spirit, are designed to express the reality and maturity of the fellowship. Foreshadowing the first paragraph of his famous chapter 13, Paul names the Spirit's diverse gifts to the Corinthian church. He cites speech characterized by wisdom and by knowledge; faith, the sort that moves mountains; healing and the working of miracles; prophecy and the discernment of spirits. Finally, he includes speaking in tongues and interpretation of tongues. No gift is privileged over another; each gift is necessary but not sufficient.

When we speak of diversity in the church today, we are more likely to think of theological diversity, diversity in the ways we worship, diversity in racial-ethnic identity or in socioeconomic class, diversity in the music we play and sing to the glory of God. Were we to write Paul for advice, our top ten issues would be different from those that occupied the first eleven chapters of Paul's letter, seeking his mediation as we quarrel with each other over competing interpretations of Scripture, styles of worship and music, social-justice commitments, and ideological agendas.

Finally, preachers in the season of Epiphany could easily spend the whole sermon on what has not changed over the past two thousand years. The No. 1 issue that has literally caused the church to divide is mistaking the manifestation of Christ's presence in the world as cause for one group of believers to consider themselves better than, more holy than, more saved than the rest.

If the church in this season is to live into the unity given by the manifestation of God's Spirit, we would do well to follow Paul's lead: gently remind the spiritually superior that faith is not their own doing but a gift of God that cannot be preferentially used to disrupt and destroy the fellowship; name and give thanks to God for the diversity of gifts given to express the reality and maturity of the fellowship; live together as though our humanity as Christ's church rises or falls by our relationship to the same Spirit, same Lord, same God. Finally, because this is the season of Epiphany, invite the congregation to discern where the Spirit is leading the church, as together we seek to bear witness to the light presently piercing the darkness of our deepest divisions, even the divisions in Christ's body of believers.

CYNTHIA A. JARVIS

---

4. Paul Lehmann, *Ethics in a Christian Context* (New York: Harper & Row, 1963), 66–67.

John 2:1–11

¹On the third day there was a wedding in Cana of Galilee, and the mother of Jesus was there. ²Jesus and his disciples had also been invited to the wedding. ³When the wine gave out, the mother of Jesus said to him, "They have no wine." ⁴And Jesus said to her, "Woman, what concern is that to you and to me? My hour has not yet come." ⁵His mother said to the servants, "Do whatever he tells you." ⁶Now standing there were six stone water jars for the Jewish rites of purification, each holding twenty or thirty gallons. ⁷Jesus said to them, "Fill the jars with water." And they filled them up to the brim. ⁸He said to them, "Now draw some out, and take it to the chief steward." So they took it. ⁹When the steward tasted the water that had become wine, and did not know where it came from (though the servants who had drawn the water knew), the steward called the bridegroom ¹⁰and said to him, "Everyone serves the good wine first, and then the inferior wine after the guests have become drunk. But you have kept the good wine until now." ¹¹Jesus did this, the first of his signs, in Cana of Galilee, and revealed his glory; and his disciples believed in him.

Commentary 1: Connecting the Reading with Scripture

The season of Epiphany is a season of revelation, a time to recognize the arrival of God's plan in Jesus and a time to look forward to God's ongoing action through the Christ event. So what difference does God's revelation make?

Contemporary wedding ceremonies draw people together as witnesses to a union between two loving people. That union is the central event of the celebration. Much effort goes into the preparation of such events, both for the ceremony itself and the festivities following the ceremony. We do not always know all of the backstories connected to the complicated preparation: family squabbles, rearranged wedding invitation lists, financial stress, and more. Love is complicated. In antiquity, marriage was a social arrangement between families, with much less fanfare over the actual wedding ceremony. Nevertheless these families too enjoyed a good party. John 2 provides one backstory that played itself out at a wedding gathering in Cana, when a potential crisis ensued.

Mary's relation to the wedding party is unclear. As a mother and possibly a close family friend, she wants the events of the celebration to go well. That much is clear. The Fourth Gospel, surprisingly, omits her specific name, referring to her only as "the mother of Jesus." That designation, of course, is crucial to her role in this narrative. In the opening scene, Mary plays the leading role. When the crisis happens, she pushes her son into action. Jesus expresses reluctance (2:4), but his next step indicates that he is an obedient son, one who will spend more time with his family (2:12) before beginning his public mission.

What a crisis for the servants responsible for monitoring the drinking supplies! Imagine what will happen to them when the head of the household discovers this predicament. It is possible that these servants (*diakonoi*) were hired for this occasion and were not necessarily household slaves (*douloi*). Sometimes, however, a *diakonos* was a synonym for a *doulos*. In either case, Jesus' later words ring true in first-century culture: "The slave does not have a permanent place in the household" (John 8:35). These servants could be dismissed (or worse) for lesser offenses. They are desperate to heed Mary's advice, if only to save their own jobs. The chief steward (*architriklinos*) was oftentimes an enslaved individual responsible for managing a feast. So Jesus—and his mother—served the servants, by helping them out of a potentially life-threatening jam.

The chief steward's reaction is priceless. He credits the bridegroom with an intentional act of withholding the best wine until people are less aware of what they are drinking. With no reaction from the bridegroom, the steward's declaration stands, uncorrected. This slave knows his place. A bit of humor or narrative irony is seen, insofar as the bridegroom is given credit for this unusual cultural decision (2:10). The reader knows that the steward compliments the wrong "bridegroom" (cf. 3:29). Jesus' "sign" is less public than we might hope; his mother, who instigates the miracle, knows about it (2:5), as do the servants (2:9) and the disciples (2:11). The other guests who are present seem completely unaware.

From John's perspective, this story is not ultimately about a wedding, miraculously produced wine, or obedience to a mother's command. As with most of the stories in the Gospel tradition, this one elevates Jesus' status. One objective of John's Gospel is to provide evidence for its opening claim: "The Word became flesh and lived among us, and we have seen his glory" (1:14). Jesus' action is not simply to save the wedding party, but functions as a "sign" (*sēmeion*) that points to something beyond the miracle itself. These signs show Jesus to be God's agent acting on God's behalf (3:2), what the narrator calls Jesus' "glory," a key Johannine concept from the beginning of the Gospel (e.g., 1:14) to the end ("The glory that you have given me I have given them, so that they may be one, as we are one," 17:22). That edification leads to "belief" in Jesus, which is another key Johannine idea. Both "glory" and "belief" are central to John's theological renarration of the story of Jesus. Neither concept is prevalent in the Synoptic Gospel tradition. It all begins with a crisis at a common wedding and a mother's wish.

A few wedding narratives in the First Testament highlight the nature of the weeklong feasts surrounding weddings (e.g., Gen. 29:21–28; Judg. 14:10–12). Within the New Testament, the focus falls elsewhere. Jesus tells a wedding parable to symbolize God's mission (Matt. 22:1–14). In Matthew 22, a king throws a wedding reception for his son but has few friends willing to come. Worse, some of the king's slaves are killed for making the request. When the king finally gets a full wedding hall, he condemns a man to death for wearing inappropriate wedding attire. Perhaps other guests refuse the initial invitation because they know this king's antics well. The king of the parable represents a disturbing image of God, if that were Jesus' point. His own emphasis, however, seems to fall elsewhere: "many are called, but few are chosen" (Matt. 22:14). Traditional scholarship assumes appropriate clothing refers to purity concerns.

Also, the wedding reception motif is apocalyptically imagined in the great end-time marriage of the Lamb (Rev. 19:1–9). In this eschatological marriage, the bride "has made herself ready" with "fine linen, bright and pure," a reference to "the righteous deeds of the saints" (Rev. 19:7–8). At this banquet, similar to Jesus' parable in Matthew 22, the guests must be prepared. One distinction from the parable, in which the guest list seems vast, is that only some will be "invited to the marriage supper of the Lamb" (Rev. 19:9).

The John 2 wedding reception is distinctive in the New Testament. It is not that anyone *deserves* better wine because they act more purely or perform a righteous deed. Rather, Mary insists that her son, "the Lamb of God who takes away the sin of the world" (1:29), perform this act, and he does so. This activity becomes, in turn, the first sign that reveals Jesus' glory.

The new/old wine motif has symbolic significance for the new mission Jesus has initiated. In the Synoptic tradition, the emphasis falls on the "new wine" and the splintering wine jars (Mark 2:22 and par.). In John, the stone jars contain the new wine without problem. Whatever the old and new represent, there is less disjunction between the two in John's Gospel. Jesus even has a better relationship with his family in this Gospel (cf. Mark 3:19b–21 CEB). In John, the focus shifts to the miracle worker, the one who produces new wine. Jesus performs the first of his signs and apparently by doing so brings about belief and reveals his glory.

The season of Epiphany is about revelation, a time shortly after the excitement of the arrival of God's Son, Jesus. So what difference does God's revelation make during this season, a season full of promise and chaos, full of joy and sorrow?

If Advent is about waiting for the promised

visit, Epiphany is about the grand expectations that come after the visitor has arrived.
Sometimes we have to adjust our expectations.
Because sometimes Jesus simply turns water into
wine at a neighbor's wedding feast, and only a
few hear about the sign. With appropriate eyes
to see, sometimes this story implies turning
scarcity into plenty for all. With such signs God
reveals the glory of Jesus. Perhaps God is saving
the best for last! During this season of Epiphany, we hope so!

EMERSON B. POWERY

Commentary 2: Connecting the Reading with the World

Few texts are better suited for Epiphany meditations than this one. The first "sign" Jesus performs
in John connects to Epiphany's basic concern: to
consider how and why God's Messiah becomes
manifest to the broader world. Vital theological
questions animate this period of the church year:
How can Christ and the gospel be made known?
What does it mean to encounter God through
Christ? What kind of God does Christ reveal?
The story of the wedding at Cana does not give
comprehensive answers to those questions, but it
does feed our imaginations by serving up entic-
ing metaphors that evoke themes of urgency,
grace, abundance, delight, and wonder.

Urgency. As nearly all biblical authors attest,
given the desperate state of the world, God's
intervention is urgently needed. John's Gospel
acknowledges this; it presents Jesus as ready to
deliver now, ready to initiate eternal life now
(3:15; 6:54; 17:3). This Gospel has little interest
in depicting gradual discoveries. Disciples draw
accurate conclusions early (1:40–49). Jesus'
glory bursts into the open, bright enough for
his followers to see, at the wedding, which is
the first extensively narrated episode in John's
account of Jesus' public ministry.

For some reason, in Cana the time has
come for Jesus to demonstrate and share his
glory, his unique relationship with the Father
(1:14; 8:54; 11:40; 17:22). His mother seems
to sense that the timing is right, for although
Jesus initially dismisses her concern about the
wine, still she persists, telling the servants to be
ready for whatever is coming next. Perhaps she
knows how urgently the world needs to experience the glory Jesus has to share. Maybe she
yearns for our shadow-filled societies to experience life-giving light (1:5–9), and therefore she
expects—or prods—Jesus to act.

Grace. According to John, the coming of the
Word means the arrival of "grace upon grace"
(1:16). This Gospel includes no calls to "repent,"
no warnings about a Christ who waves a "winnowing fork" (cf. Matt. 3:12; Luke 3:17). When
John's Jesus speaks about judgment and condemnation, his focus is on judging the devil, "the
ruler of this world"; those who receive eternal life,
however, avoid judgment (3:17–19; 5:24; 9:39;
12:31, 47; 16:11). It is fitting then that the first
of Jesus' seven signs is not a warning but a gift.
By providing wine for a wedding, Jesus tacitly
endorses things that make human life meaningful and pleasant: relationships, sexuality, community, hospitality, meals, family, and celebration.
By enabling the festivities to continue, Jesus
locates himself in places where life flourishes and
human relationships thrive. The Messiah will be
seen there in Epiphany, just as the signs that Jesus
performs elsewhere in John indicate that he will
be found also in fractured communities, vulnerability, grief, and death.

Abundance. Those who study leadership
sometimes strike contrasts between mind-sets
of abundance and mind-sets of scarcity. Interest
in these categories has seeped into theological
circles and attracted attention to the wedding at Cana and certain miracles (e.g., Mark
6:30–44; Luke 5:1–11) as indications that the
church should not be fooled by appearances,
but should instead trust in a God who abundantly provides. When churches idolize abundance, however, they risk allowing prosperity
theologies to infiltrate them as through a Tro-
jan horse. God's grace flows abundantly indeed
in Cana, but that must not keep us from seeing the Messiah also in places of want, where
real need and undeniable despair exists (Matt.
25:31–40).

At the same time, when Jesus produces the equivalent of six hundred to nine hundred bottles of fine wine, we can linger for a while over extravagance. There will be no shortages or rationings when the messianic banquet opens its doors (Isa. 25:6–9; Amos 9:13–14). John's Jesus expresses little interest in remaining hidden or counseling moderation; he promises a life lived abundantly (10:10). Christians, therefore, should refuse to rely on dour methods of assessing our ministry's proper limits. We cannot do everything, but limited time, energy, and resources should not make us stingy in our dispositions toward God and neighbors.

Delight. In this story, the chief steward is undoubtedly desperate; he needs wine. Imagine his delight when he samples the new stuff that the servants have brought and discovers its quality. Imagine the servants' relief or amusement when they see that Jesus has done more than save the wedding with a merely passable beverage. This wine bursts with flavor—it has a joyful body, with hints of amazement and a finish of enduring fulfillment.

The practical benefits of Jesus' first sign are simple and hardly world-changing in and of themselves: a party continues, while a bridegroom and chief steward avoid the shame that could have resulted from their poor planning. Not every act of God has to turn the world upside down or otherwise carry cosmic significance. Something about Jesus Christ's manifestation, according to John, is simply about sowing delight. The Messiah's work strikes a chord deep in human experience and emotion. Jesus' signs are less about cognitive instruction than they are about existential knowing; through the signs Jesus provides an embodied encounter with divine love. According to the chief steward, this encounter exceeds "good enough." The vintage Jesus serves tastes fabulous.

Preachers might consider the fact that tastes conjure strong memories and emotions. Like smells, they share close neurological connections with memory in the human brain. Tastes can bring us back to meaningful moments in the past—home-cooked meals, first dates, holidays—and make our stomachs growl for more, as when someone suffering from thirst receives a first sip of what they need. Jesus provides superior wine, not because he is trying to impress a gathering of elite guests, but because he wants everyone to hunger for more and not to be satisfied with inferior substitutes. Likewise the psalmist says about God, "You give them drink from the river of your delights" (Ps. 36:8).

Wonder. Part of this passage's beauty and theological richness resides in the ambiguity. Would not the chief steward and bridegroom be incredibly confused by the sudden appearance of all this great wine in jars reserved for purification rituals? Were the disciples present for everything that the narrative describes? These questions seem as immaterial as they are unanswerable, given how the passage proceeds. John describes a manifestation of Jesus' glory that is immediate, dramatic, exciting, and fully revelatory; yet it is also limited in scope. Only some people—evidently the disciples, the servants, and the mother of Jesus—have access to all the details of Jesus' sign; yet the brimming jars of wine benefit a multitude of wedding guests. The insiders, at least the disciples, respond with belief; the wider community responds with wonder, and probably no small amount of joy.

That is a familiar biblical dynamic, the notion of a confined revelation with wide-ranging consequences. It can inform Christian communities' self-understanding and ministry. Sometimes Christ becomes glimpsed through the consequences of the gifts he bestows. Even though not everyone witnesses Christ's glory from an unobstructed perspective, still that glory—that intimate relationship Jesus enjoys with the Father and shares with others—radiates outward to bless human existence.

Modern societies tend to regard the church as a house of doctrine. The wondrous and semiprivate sign in John 2:1–11 might provoke Christians to change or supplement that reputation. What if Christian churches, in response to the divine glory they see and share alongside Christ (John 1:14; 17:20–23), aimed to nourish wonder in the wider world? Jesus remains manifest when his followers follow his lead, promoting abundant wholeness through their public proclamation, advocacy, service, charity, artistic expression, and imagination.

MATTHEW L. SKINNER

Third Sunday after the Epiphany

Nehemiah 8:1–3, 5–6, 8–10 1 Corinthians 12:12–31a
Psalm 19 Luke 4:14–21

Nehemiah 8:1–3, 5–6, 8–10

¹All the people gathered together into the square before the Water Gate. They told the scribe Ezra to bring the book of the law of Moses, which the LORD had given to Israel. ²Accordingly, the priest Ezra brought the law before the assembly, both men and women and all who could hear with understanding. This was on the first day of the seventh month. ³He read from it facing the square before the Water Gate from early morning until midday, in the presence of the men and the women and those who could understand; and the ears of all the people were attentive to the book of the law. . . . ⁵And Ezra opened the book in the sight of all the people, for he was standing above all the people; and when he opened it, all the people stood up. ⁶Then Ezra blessed the LORD, the great God, and all the people answered, "Amen, Amen," lifting up their hands. Then they bowed their heads and worshiped the LORD with their faces to the ground. . . . ⁸So they read from the book, from the law of God, with interpretation. They gave the sense, so that the people understood the reading.

⁹And Nehemiah, who was the governor, and Ezra the priest and scribe, and the Levites who taught the people said to all the people, "This day is holy to the LORD your God; do not mourn or weep." For all the people wept when they heard the words of the law. ¹⁰Then he said to them, "Go your way, eat the fat and drink sweet wine and send portions of them to those for whom nothing is prepared, for this day is holy to our LORD; and do not be grieved, for the joy of the LORD is your strength."

Commentary 1: Connecting the Reading with Scripture

Public service and faithfulness in God's name is trying, but it comes with great opportunity. As the governor of Jerusalem, Nehemiah faces misunderstanding, deceit, and opposition. He perseveres at every step, and through his determination, God reveals a blessing.

The story begins before Nehemiah's appointment and return to Judah. Nehemiah is a minor figure in the court of Artaxerxes, king of Persia, just another participant in the Jewish Diaspora following defeat and exile. The book of Nehemiah opens with a discouraging gut check, as he hears a firsthand report from those recently returned from their homeland: "The survivors there . . . are in great trouble and shame; the wall of Jerusalem is broken down, and its gates have been destroyed by fire" (Neh. 1:3). The emotional foundation for this saga is discovered

in Nehemiah's reaction: "When I first heard these words I sat down and wept, and mourned for days, fasting and praying before the God of heaven" (1:4).

Above all, Nehemiah is a conservator, determined to renew the best of Jewish law and tradition, no matter the obstacles. The glass may be much less than half full, but the situation is rich with possibility. With the support of the God who keeps covenant and welcomes all who repent, Nehemiah vows a return by the people of Israel to the tradition of Moses. He risks everything on the promises of God in Deuteronomy 30:1–5.

The stage is set for the crescendo within today's biblical text through a series of twists and turns. Nehemiah, pleading for the chance to restore the graves of his ancestors, is named governor by the king. Upon his arrival he immediately faces the opposition of Sanballat and Tobiah, regional officials in Judah, but he focuses on his mission. After an inspection of the badly broken wall around the city, he rallies the Jewish community: "Come, let us rebuild the wall of Jerusalem, so that we may no longer suffer disgrace" (2:17).

Things get worse before they improve. The local officials ridicule his efforts and question his loyalty to the king; they poor-mouth any success and criticize the quality of the workmanship. Nehemiah faces challenges both internal and external, from the threat of armed intervention by his enemies to the failing strength of the workers—and their complaints about the cost. At every turn, Nehemiah's posture is confident, even adamant. "Do not be afraid," he announces. "Remember the Lord, who is great and awesome, and fight for your kin" (4:14).

Through this threat of violence, the Jews are called to an even deeper level of commitment, arming themselves and working constantly without pause. Nehemiah notes that he and his closest colleagues never have the opportunity to lay down their weapons or enjoy a good night's sleep (4:23).

Finally the wall and gates are complete, and Nehemiah invites the Jewish community to come home from exile. Known as the First Return, Nehemiah gathers thousands of Jews, both those who had remained in and around Jerusalem and those coming from the east.

Nehemiah calls a grand assembly. The people mark a holy day with the reading and interpretation of the law of Moses. Hour after hour, "the ears of all the people were attentive to the book of the law" (8:4). This celebration and dedication is the apex of the story of Nehemiah. The restoration of the wall is identified not in and for itself, but as an offering and sacrifice to the Lord. The testimony of the struggle echoes the witness of Nehemiah. "The joy of the Lord is your strength" (8:10). Through the striving, a deep spiritual heritage is rediscovered.

This assembly presages the next in which Ezra recites the salvation history of the Israelites (Neh. 9), reminding God's people that their corporate and personal identity is rooted in the covenant of their Creator and Lord. With the rebuilding of the wall and religious renewal comes a new opportunity for all to "stand up and bless the Lord your God from everlasting to everlasting" (9:5).

Each element in the remainder of the story—the feast of booths, the public confession of sin, the renewal of the covenant, and the further reforms—springs from the recognition that God's initiative and our responses are joined in joyful purpose.

In this era of unbridled individualism, Nehemiah proclaims the power of life's context. We discover our purpose only as we love God and our neighbors in the here and now. Each of today's lectionary readings echoes this theme and rests on the bedrock of the Great Commandment to love God and neighbor wholeheartedly (Matt. 22:37–40).

Nehemiah's work culminates, not with the laying of the final stone or brick but, instead, with the wonder found in ritual and liturgy, centered on the law of Moses. Psalm 19 reminds us that the law is not only sure and solid. The law renews and empowers us from the inside out: "The law of the Lord is perfect, reviving the soul; the decrees of the Lord are sure, making wise the simple; the precepts of the Lord are right, rejoicing the heart; the commandment of the Lord is clear, enlightening the eyes; the fear of the Lord is pure, enduring forever; the ordinances of the Lord are true and righteous altogether" (Ps. 19:7–9). We discover our very identity as we respond to the Holy One's guidance and direction.

Similarly, after Christ's baptism, filled with the power of the Holy Spirit, Jesus proclaims the meaning of his life and ministry. He does so, not with original phrasing or novel ideas, but through the impetus and commands of Scripture. He is designated, he announces, to fulfill God's promises: to proclaim the great good news and deliver the devastated and bound.

"The Spirit of the Lord is upon me," Jesus says, "because God has anointed me to bring good news to the poor. God has sent me to proclaim release to the captives and recovery of sight to the blind, to let the oppressed go free, to proclaim the year of the Lord's favor" (Luke 4:18–19).

First Corinthians 12 points to the practical

reality of Nehemiah's quest. A great work cannot be accomplished by self-defined individuals without a common vision. God's people reject the limiting labels either as the remnant who remained around Jerusalem or as leaders who were faithful in far-off exile. Instead, only as one community united in faithfulness can their God-given mission be achieved. "Indeed, the body does not consist of one member but of many. . . . If all were a single member, where would the body be? As it is, there are many members, yet one body. The eye cannot say to the hand, 'I have no need of you,' nor again the head to the feet, 'I have no need of you.' . . . But God has so arranged the body . . . [that]

the members may have the same care for one another" (1 Cor. 12:14, 19–21, 24–25).

Today the church lives in an internet age of novelty and self-revelation. We often discount history and dismiss the wisdom of others—and even Another. In determined contrast, Nehemiah unearths the delight of a renewed tradition. He invites us to come together in God's name, to listen attentively to the Lord, and to offer our best work with faithfulness and determination. As we follow Christ and find ourselves empowered by the Spirit, we will discover that the joy of the Lord is our strength.

GLEN BELL

Commentary 2: Connecting the Reading with the World

The God who turns weeping into joy shows up when we least expect it. In times of worry and grief, we can easily forget that "the joy of the LORD is [our] strength" (Neh. 8:10). Sometimes, when life and faith become overwhelming, when we live in communities that are fractured and divided, we need a commandment to put aside our grief and sing for joy, because in this celebration we can learn how to become the community that God has called us to be.

In this passage in Nehemiah we meet the people as they are coming together to hear the word of God read aloud. The text tells us that the people have called this meeting, and as we encounter them in the story, we know from previous chapters that this is a fractured community, where neighbors have been at odds with one another and where injustice has become commonplace. The people want something different. So the community gathers around the text to search for healing and reconciliation.[1]

In this time period, the Scripture was not yet gathered into one book, so Ezra and his assistants would have been reading from scrolls. As he read, the text reminded the people of their journey out of Egypt and through the wilderness and the long struggle to find the promised

land. It reminded them of God's law and their covenant. As they read the Scripture together, the stories they heard caused them to weep and grieve. The promised land of the past was no longer theirs. In the sacred words that were being read, they saw their own faithlessness to God, and they were filled with regret.[2]

The people's custom during this ritual reading of Scripture was to weep and cry, but on this day, Ezra, Nehemiah, and the Levites instructed the people, saying, "This day is holy to the LORD your God; do not mourn or weep." Instead, they were told to make the day holy through their eating, drinking, and rejoicing.

The commandment we find here might strike us as odd. This is a fractured community with deep and abiding problems. Yet rather than be overwhelmed with the problems, the people are told to build community by throwing a party. There is no need to stay for a town-hall meeting and lament the issues that divide them. They need to celebrate!

Often when the church encounters what we call broken or impoverished communities, or broken or impoverished people, we have the same response. We mourn an individual's situation or lament the crime and brokenness of a place without recognizing any assets. We

1. Johanna W. H. Van Wijk-Bos, *Ezra, Nehemiah, and Esther,* Westminster Bible Companion (Louisville, KY: Westminster John Knox Press, 1998), 75.
2. Ibid.

label failing schools and crime-ridden blocks, we identify "at-risk" youth and abandoned housing. We talk about unemployment, and the percentage of people in poverty, and how there are no jobs. We are rather good at making a depressing list of issues, and when we're done, we decide the problem is too overwhelming to actually fix, so we just give away bags of food or open a clothes closet.

There is a different way of living in community. The asset-based community development approach asks us to love our neighbors by celebrating the gifts and talents that they bring to their community. Rather than starting with a list of problems, we start by mapping the assets. We look for libraries and reading groups, gatekeepers and do-gooders, talents and stories and teachers. We gather the community together, not to tell them statistics about how terrible their neighborhood is, but to spark a catalyst of change by asking them to celebrate the things they love about their home.

In this spirit of appreciation, the assets that are already present are able to grow and bloom. The people who were hopeless suddenly see things differently, when they realize that they do not have to wait on outside help, but they can work together to transform their community now. When we learn to celebrate the gifts that God has given, "the joy of the Lord" can be our strength to create change.

Our world is full of scenarios where joy and celebration can be experienced in the midst of grief and worry. The Epiphany is one such story. When we celebrate the arrival of the magi, we cannot help but remember the violence of King Herod and that Jesus and his parents were refugees in a foreign land. We often hear the story of Jesus fleeing with his family to Egypt, but in our Christmas-friendly versions of these stories, we might not fully appreciate the deep danger and profound fear that Jesus' parents must have experienced. They have been chosen to bring God incarnate into the world, to raise him and care for him, yet while he is still an infant, they are forced to flee in order to save his life.

In my work with refugees through the years, I've met many people who remind me of the baby Jesus, who was marked and targeted by a king. The story is too familiar—friends who fled because they or their parents ended up on the wrong side of a dictator; friends who fled because a bomb or a police force destroyed their house; friends who were singled out because they spoke out against injustice or simply because of their race/ethnicity. In the midst of hiding, the magi still come, reminding the refugees that they are seen and known and loved by God.

If we truly listen, the word of God always comes to us sharper than a sword, piercing our heart with its compelling message to do justice and love mercy. We cannot live up to all that is required. The kin-dom of God is difficult to build, even if we spend our whole lives trying. For people who were likely illiterate and did not have mass-produced copies of Scripture on their bookshelves at home, hearing the word of God read aloud was a sacred and rare opportunity. When they heard the word of God, they were in the habit of weeping with their face pointed to the ground. I wonder how it must have felt to be given permission to stop crying and rejoice.

For refugees and displaced peoples, for communities who are labeled as "bad neighborhoods," working to create a safe and welcoming community to call home can be an inexpressible joy. As we work with people and communities who are fractured and broken, we literally and actually live out Matthew 25, where we hear Jesus, here speaking as the king, say, "I was a stranger and you welcomed me," or "I was hungry and you gave me something to eat." We like to think that we would give up time or a bedroom or resources if we were asked to care for an infant Jesus fleeing for his life.

When Jesus is from Syria or Somalia, or the resource-poor neighborhood across town, the question becomes more difficult. When our poor neighbors need more than a bag of food, we find it hard to commit. Like the magi and like the people in the Nehemiah text, we are called to create community through our celebrations. When we throw parties for refugees or work to identify the assets of our neighbors, we are celebrating God's joy through building community. The work will not be easy, but the "joy of the Lord is our strength."

MELISSA BROWNING

Psalm 19

¹The heavens are telling the glory of God;
    and the firmament proclaims his handiwork.
²Day to day pours forth speech,
    and night to night declares knowledge.
³There is no speech, nor are there words;
    their voice is not heard;
⁴yet their voice goes out through all the earth,
    and their words to the end of the world.

In the heavens he has set a tent for the sun,
⁵which comes out like a bridegroom from his wedding canopy,
    and like a strong man runs its course with joy.
⁶Its rising is from the end of the heavens,
    and its circuit to the end of them;
    and nothing is hid from its heat.

⁷The law of the LORD is perfect,
    reviving the soul;
the decrees of the LORD are sure,
    making wise the simple;
⁸the precepts of the LORD are right,
    rejoicing the heart;
the commandment of the LORD is clear,
    enlightening the eyes;
⁹the fear of the LORD is pure,
    enduring forever;
the ordinances of the LORD are true
    and righteous altogether.
¹⁰More to be desired are they than gold,
    even much fine gold;
sweeter also than honey,
    and drippings of the honeycomb.

¹¹Moreover by them is your servant warned;
    in keeping them there is great reward.
¹²But who can detect their errors?
    Clear me from hidden faults.
¹³Keep back your servant also from the insolent;
    do not let them have dominion over me.
Then I shall be blameless,
    and innocent of great transgression.

¹⁴Let the words of my mouth and the meditation of my heart
    be acceptable to you,
    O LORD, my rock and my redeemer.

Connecting the Psalm with Scripture and Worship

Psalm 19 is a poetic hymn of praise that depicts creation coming into being through the proclamation of God's voice (vv. 1–6), the Torah's proclamation of God's word (vv. 7–11), and the psalmist's reflection and prayer (vv. 12–14). The first part of the psalm attests to the world's witness of God through creation's glory, and is based on the notion that every creature acknowledges the Creator.[1] In Psalm 19, the heavens do exactly what humans do: proclaim God's glory by simply being the product of God's creative works. The psalmist is careful to avoid a pantheistic point of view in this hymn of praise and intentionally keeps creation separate from the creator by illustrating the silent praise of creation as a result of God's work. This praise offered by creation leads the psalmist to uplift the magnificence of God's law and thus illustrates God's connectedness to humanity through God's law. The creator of the awe-inspiring universe is the same God who gives us a transformative law.

The psalmist understands the law of God (Torah) to be just as glorious as the creation described in verses 1–6. It is not a law that condemns or restricts; rather, the psalmist describes the law as life giving and desirable. Adjectives of perfection, purity, clarity, luxury, and sweetness (vv. 7–10) all appeal to the human senses and desire. The psalmist is suggesting the law of the Lord is more than one can ask for, and should be sought after, just as one seeks expensive jewels and sweet-tasting honey. This is the law the psalmist praises. Just as Ezra in Nehemiah 8 encourages the people to hear the word of the Lord with joy and not grief, the psalmist celebrates God's law with great joy and admiration.

However, the psalmist does not simply praise God's law for its ability to appeal to humanity; instead, the psalmist praises God's law for its ability to transform the one who keeps the law. God's law has the power to transform human life, and the transformation is sweet and pure. The transformational nature of God's law further emphasizes the psalmist's understanding that humanity must follow God's law (or instruction) in order to be transformed. Therefore, God did not give the law simply for the sake of its establishment, but to be intimately involved with humanity, offering a guide for transformational living.

Paired with the companion lectionary texts, Psalm 19 provides one particular approach for preaching on the Third Sunday after the Epiphany: God's glory is revealed in both creation and divine revelation. From a declaration of God's glory through creation to a praise of God's law, the psalmist recognizes the power of God on both cosmic and human levels. God's glory is so far beyond our human reach that we must look to creation's silent praise to witness it. At the same time, God makes God's self visible through the very law that we have been given— through God's own instructions for human living. No matter where we look, we can see God's glory, as it is on full display all around us. This points to the psalmist's closing petition (vv. 13–14), a posture every preacher should take in preaching and living: sin does not rule us, but God's instruction guides—even the words of our mouths and the meditations of our hearts.

Psalm 19 carries a vibrant, energetic tone in its poetic language. Often used as two separate texts in liturgy and hymns, it is filled with images of celebration and rejoicing, as well as a centering on the wholeness of God's law. The tone and rhythm of the psalm make it fitting to be used both as an opening for worship and as a prayer for illumination before hearing God's word. Verses 1–5 may be adapted for use as a responsive call to worship:

Voice 1: The heavens tell the glory of God;
and the firmament proclaims
his handiwork.

People: *Day to day pours out speech,*
and night to night
declares knowledge.

Voice 1: There is no speech,
nor are there words;
their voice is not heard;

People: *yet their voice goes out*
through all the earth,
and their words to the end
of the world.

---

1. James Luther Mays, *Psalms*, Interpretation (Louisville, KY: John Knox Press, 1994), 97.

Voice 1: As our voices join with nature,
come—let us worship God!

This litany (or one similar) begins the service with immediate congregational participation and can be paired with visuals representing various facets of nature, if the space and worship components allow (e.g., on screens, in the order of service, posted throughout the sanctuary). This visual presentation reminds the congregation to appreciate God's glory in the creation we engage every day. The second half of Psalm 19 might also be used as a prayer for illumination before the reading of Scripture or preaching.

Praying verses 7–14 centers the congregation on the wholeness of God's word and reminds us of God's grace gifted to us through God's word.

In summary, Psalm 19's declaration of God's glory through creation and the law reminds us that God's glory is everywhere. Just as creation declares God's glory through its silent beauty and majestic nature, so are Christians to proclaim God's glory by living according to God's law through the meditations of our hearts and the words of our mouths. In this there is sweet transformation.

KHALIA J. WILLIAMS

1 Corinthians 12:12–31a

¹²For just as the body is one and has many members, and all the members of the body, though many, are one body, so it is with Christ. ¹³For in the one Spirit we were all baptized into one body—Jews or Greeks, slaves or free—and we were all made to drink of one Spirit.

¹⁴Indeed, the body does not consist of one member but of many. ¹⁵If the foot would say, "Because I am not a hand, I do not belong to the body," that would not make it any less a part of the body. ¹⁶And if the ear would say, "Because I am not an eye, I do not belong to the body," that would not make it any less a part of the body. ¹⁷If the whole body were an eye, where would the hearing be? If the whole body were hearing, where would the sense of smell be? ¹⁸But as it is, God arranged the members in the body, each one of them, as he chose. ¹⁹If all were a single member, where would the body be? ²⁰As it is, there are many members, yet one body. ²¹The eye cannot say to the hand, "I have no need of you," nor again the head to the feet, "I have no need of you." ²²On the contrary, the members of the body that seem to be weaker are indispensable, ²³and those members of the body that we think less honorable we clothe with greater honor, and our less respectable members are treated with greater respect; ²⁴whereas our more respectable members do not need this. But God has so arranged the body, giving the greater honor to the inferior member, ²⁵that there may be no dissension within the body, but the members may have the same care for one another. ²⁶If one member suffers, all suffer together with it; if one member is honored, all rejoice together with it.

²⁷Now you are the body of Christ and individually members of it. ²⁸And God has appointed in the church first apostles, second prophets, third teachers; then deeds of power, then gifts of healing, forms of assistance, forms of leadership, various kinds of tongues. ²⁹Are all apostles? Are all prophets? Are all teachers? Do all work miracles? ³⁰Do all possess gifts of healing? Do all speak in tongues? Do all interpret? ³¹But strive for the greater gifts.

[handwritten annotation: discernment – the quality of being able to grasp and comprehend what is obscure; an act of perceiving]

Commentary 1: Connecting the Reading with Scripture

In this passage, Paul continues his instructions on the subject of spiritual gifts. Earlier in the letter, Paul gave two principles of discernment regarding them: (1) that which comes from the Spirit will be manifest in committed faith in Jesus Christ (1 Cor. 12:3), and (2) spiritual gifts are to be used for the common good, rather than to elevate the status of a particular individual (1 Cor. 12:7). Here Paul weaves these together. Because the community is the body of Christ, caring for the common good is what faith in Jesus looks like.

The apostle begins by reiterating part of the baptismal formula from Galatians 3:28.

Baptism is the starting point of the new identity the Corinthians are struggling to embody. A vital element of the ordering of Christian communities is the rejection of social stratification. The power of identity categories to divide people, and in particular to elevate some and denigrate others, is undone by baptism. Paul offers a different way for the community to understand their relationships with one another.

The metaphor of the body was familiar in Paul's context as a way to understand members of a community having different functions that all work together, as it appeared in the works of Aristotle, Plato, Plutarch, and Seneca. Paul alters the metaphor in two important ways.

First, Paul pushes the body beyond a metaphor for corporate identity by naming it clearly the body *of Christ*. While the body metaphor on its own says something about how individuals within the body should treat others (as serving necessarily different functions for the common good), Paul's claim that the church is the body of Christ is also instructive about how the group as a whole should treat others outside the body. Jesus, a poor Jewish man living under Roman occupation, fully identified with the marginalized of his society, including those who were oppressed and those who had made seriously objectionable moral choices. He spent his days teaching, serving, and healing others, as well as rejecting injustice and subverting social structures of domination. By naming the collective body of the church the body *of Christ*, Paul enjoins the church to imitate Jesus in all of these ways. The church—not just individuals within it—should identify with the marginalized, serve others, reject injustice, and subvert domination.

Paul's metaphor is, at times, taken almost literally. The church is seen as the ongoing incarnation. One familiar saying states, "Christ has no body now but yours. No hands, no feet on earth but yours. Yours are the eyes through which he looks compassion on this world. Yours are the feet with which he walks to do good. Yours are the hands through which he blesses all the world."[1] Here Paul's image is used as an ethical exhortation to do good and bless all the world. Unfortunately, for some Christians, a near-literal reading of Paul's words leads not to challenge but to comfort. In this case, the logic runs backwards: if the church is the body of Christ, then what the church is doing is right and good, and the traditions of the church are beyond question. Such interpretations of Paul's declaration that the church is the body of Christ run counter to the message of 1 Corinthians.

The second way Paul alters the common metaphor of the body appears in verses 22–25.

This includes some rather confusing language, to the effect that we honor our private bits with clothing, while we do not need to clothe our less embarrassing parts. This is not Paul's shining moment as a philosopher, as this argument alone would not be persuasive. However, verses 24 and 25 state, "But God has so arranged the body, giving the greater honor to the inferior member, that there may be no dissension within the body, but the members may have the same care for one another." This is not an argument or even an illustration about clothing, but rather a theological claim about God. As such, it is consistent with the rest of 1 Corinthians and with the entirety of the gospel. God honors the least among us, not to create another hierarchy in reverse, but so that "the members may have the same care for one another."

When God became incarnate in the particular body that is Jesus Christ, God honored the marginalized. Any expectation that God loves those of high status best is upended in the incarnation and utterly rejected in the life and ministry of Jesus Christ. At the beginning of his ministry, Jesus reads the words of Isaiah in the synagogue, saying,

> The Spirit of the Lord is upon me,
>   because he has anointed me
>   to bring good news to the poor.
> He has sent me to proclaim release to the
>   captives
>   and recovery of sight to the blind,
>   to let the oppressed go free,
> to proclaim the year of the Lord's favor.
>   Luke 4:18–19

Paul's words are an articulation of the preferential option for the poor, which is a premise of liberation theologies and widely accepted in Roman Catholic theology.[2] God loves everyone. Given our human tendency toward social hierarchies, we are continually tempted to see worldly success or status as a sign of God's favor. God, like a parent caring first for the child who has been injured, leans toward the oppressed. This does not negate God's love for everyone.

---

1. The authorship of this saying is contested. It is often misattributed to Teresa of Avila.

2. ". . . a theme that is central in liberation theology and has now been widely accepted in the universal church: the preferential option for the poor" (Gustavo Gutiérrez, *A Theology of Liberation*, 15th anniversary ed., trans. and ed. Sister Caridad Inda and John Eagleson [Maryknoll, NY: Orbis Books, 1988], xxv).

Rather, it teaches Christians to care for one another with similar compassion and respect.

The latter half of chapter 12 gives an extended metaphor to reinforce the messages of the first half. In baptism, Christians are inducted into a new humanity that requires new forms of community. Such new forms should be marked by an appreciation for difference, without a hierarchy of social status. The good of the whole is prioritized, and the collective whole should itself be about the business of caring for others as Jesus did.

At the end of the chapter, Paul does offer a list of spiritual gifts that are ranked. Yet the organizational principle is that those gifts that build up the whole are at the top of the list, and speaking in tongues—which had been used as an individual claim to status in the church at Corinth—is put at the bottom. As the affirmation of God's preferential option for the poor lifts up that which had been lowered, this list lowers that which had been lifted up. All spiritual gifts, if they are true gifts of the Holy Spirit, will serve the whole community, which is, in turn, to serve the world.

In Epiphany, we celebrate recognition. The wise men not only found the infant Jesus; they also recognized his holiness and worshiped him (Matt. 2:10–11). In Corinth, some individuals sought to be recognized as particularly spiritual

---

A God Who Creates Diversity

We should thank God, then, if both effects are always together in the Christian church and are always reacting upon each other. The immediate testimony of the Lord's efficacy in the soul must continually animate the effects of the Word; the holy authority of the Word must provide a firm rule for all that happens in the hearts of Christians, so that all may be held together in the unity of faith and each may submit to the consensus of the community. So may we all remain in the truth that makes us free. . . .

How should each individual relate to these two effects that our spiritual life rests upon? In answering this question, we must consider above all the word of the apostle, "The body is one and has many members," each one of a distinctive kind. Within the Christian congregation, God appointed one person to one task, another to another, and no one can do everything. In the Christian church, both effects must be united: the clear, intelligible, and easily communicable efficacy of the Word, and the more mysterious but immediate truth of the Redeemer that stirs the depths of the soul. An equal measure of the two effects, however, has not been ordained for everyone. God is a God of order in the church only because he is a God who creates diversity; it is only in diversity that order occurs and is rightly maintained.

Each, then, must cling to the particular task to which he is called. We should value those who cling to God's Word with lively zeal and sincere faithfulness, relying on the Redeemer's teaching and example that they draw from the Word. . . . And we want to regard those who lay special claim to such experiences of the Redeemer's spiritual presence in the same way. . . .

If each of us goes his own way, however, and merely accepts with gratitude the task to which God called and appointed him, then we are not yet doing justice to brotherly love. . . . But love requires that each remain open to the special gift of another. Fellowship exists—the many and various members are one body—only insofar as all devote themselves to such a mutual influence and each respects and uses as a manifestation and gift of the Spirit the good that arises from the distinctive life of another. . . . Each of us should make his own inner experiences and every blessing we receive from the Lord into a common blessing by returning and communicating to others what has happened to us and how it happened. We are pupils of one Teacher, disciples of one Master, all called by him in the same way for this end: to edify, strengthen, and establish one another in faith and love for the Lord by means of everything he gives to each of us from his fullness and according to his grace and mercy.

Friedrich Schleiermacher (1768–1834), "The Effects of Scripture and of the Redeemer," in Dawn de Vries, trans., *Servant of the Word: Selected Sermons of Friedrich Schleiermacher* (Philadelphia: Fortress Press, 1987), 115–16.

because of their gifts. Paul changes the lens, so that these same individuals can recognize (a) themselves as members of a body, (b) their interdependence with other members of the church, and (c) the value of the gifts of their fellow Christians. Furthermore, the church as a whole should be recognizable as the body *of Christ*. Do we recognizably embody God's love and intentions—good news to the poor and release to the captive? Do we recognize one another's gifts? Do we recognize our own?

SHANNON CRAIGO-SNELL

Commentary 2: Connecting the Reading with the World

The one has many, and the many are one. Paul is not simply offering advice about how we ought to relate to one another in the church; he is making a statement about the new humanity we have been given in Christ, the new humanity into which we have been reborn through the waters of baptism, the new humanity that is the church. Dietrich Bonhoeffer's words in *Life Together* make explicit what is implicit in these verses:

> What determines our brotherhood [our relatedness] is what that man is [what being human is] by reason of Christ. Our community with one another consists solely in what Christ has done in both of us. This is true not merely at the beginning, as though in the course of time something else were to be added to our community; it remains so for all the future and to all eternity. I have community with others and I shall continue to have it only through Jesus Christ.[3]

That must be why, when we think Paul is going to say, "So it is with the church," he says, "So it is with Christ." The genesis of the one having many and the many being one is Christ, in whom all things are held together (Col. 1:17b).

Then, for the next twelve verses, Paul addresses the behavior among Corinthian Christians that looks to all the world like the behavior of those who gather in the agora of Corinth. Clearly there are some in the community who have been made to feel as though they do not belong; there are others who think they alone embody Christian existence; and there are a few who out-and-out say to the most vulnerable, "I have no need of you." Likely the only discernible difference in their relationships with one another now, compared with their lives before Christ, is that the stronger members use their moral superiority or their purer spiritual relationship with Christ as justification for their treatment of the weaker members. So it still goes in the church two thousand years later.

"As it is," Paul counters, as the reality of our new humanity is, God has arranged the body as God chose. That is to say, our behavior notwithstanding, God sees us whole through Christ's redeeming love; God sees us from the perspective of eternity—from beginning to end (fulfillment, completion)—through the body of him in whom we have already been knit together. His is a body that, in time, bore our infirmities and weaknesses, a body that was despised and rejected, a body that assumed the very abuse we visit on one another in his name. God has chosen him to redeem all these things and, in this way, has chosen to reveal in him the indispensability of the weak, the honor of the dishonored, the respectability of the disrespected. As it is, as we are held together in him, the suffering of one causes all to suffer; when one is honored, all rejoice. This is not our own doing, even when we actually manage to behave as God's redeemed! Like the gifts mentioned at the beginning of this chapter, our interrelatedness in our diversity, our identity in our interrelatedness, is in Christ.

Only in this way can Paul declare, "Now you are the body of Christ and individually members of it," a sentence that could just as well be the last in the previous paragraph instead of the first in the next paragraph, as the NRSV reckons such things. If Christ's body is made manifest

---

3. Dietrich Bonhoeffer, *Life Together* (New York: Harper & Row, 1954), 25.

through the witness of a community marked by interdependent relationships and diversity, surely the relational dysfunction within denominations and congregations over the past few decades—over precisely those issues that necessitate our being interdependent and diverse—has split the church and resulted in the growth of "nones" and "dones" according to the latest research polls. Millennials, in particular, have simply gone looking outside the church for Christ's body in the world.

Thinking the problem was relevance and style, the church began going after every new technique or theory that promised to bring the next generation back: bands, songs displayed on screens, lattes in the narthex, preachers in jeans, services in Starbucks or the local bar, virtual worship on social media, marketing campaigns. Seminaries began training church leaders to be "missional," believing that the church's decline was a result of the church's failure to be in mission or even to *have* a mission beyond its own institutional survival. Emergent congregations responded by offering a postmodern, make-it-up-as-you-go, come-as-you-are community that eschews metanarratives, systematic theology, and evangelical fervor. Yet none of these responses dealt with the relational dysfunction that Paul identified as being the heart of the matter for those who are the body of Christ and individual members of it.

That is why I imagine Paul would simply nod in recognition if he were to read Rachel Held Evans's account of her departure from church life, and the journey that eventually returned her to it. Having grown up in the bosom of evangelical faith, she discovered cracks in the certainty her upbringing had instilled in her. She felt disquieted by the treatment LGBTQ persons received in the churches she knew. She found little help in relating her faith creatively and affirmatively to science; her questions about Scripture and Christian belief went unanswered; few would join her in openly expressing doubt.

Seen through the lens of Paul's letter, Evans left because her faith community was acting just like the Corinthians.

> What finally brought me back, after years of running away, wasn't lattes or skinny jeans; it was the sacraments. Baptism, confession, Communion, preaching the Word, anointing the sick—you know, those strange rituals and traditions Christians have been practicing for the past 2,000 years. The sacraments are what make the church relevant, no matter the culture or the era. They don't need to be repackaged or rebranded; they just need to be practiced, offered and explained *in the context of a loving, authentic and inclusive community.*[4]

The italics are mine and might as well be Paul's. What brought Evans back? The church doing what the church has done from the beginning and doing these things in the context of a loving, authentic, inclusive community. Evans is not the only millennial trying to tell the church what Paul told the Corinthians long ago. God has so arranged the body that, in the words of my own denomination's *Book of Order*, "The organization rests upon the fellowship and is not designed to work without trust and love."[5]

Paul concludes this part of his attempt to address the spiritual hierarchy at Corinth by returning to the things that need doing in the church and the people set apart to do them: apostles, prophets, teachers, miracle workers, healers, and speakers in tongues. One is not more important than the other; all need the others to be who they are and to do what they do. Each must strive together for the greater gifts of the one Spirit, gifts that thus far have coincided with the particular tasks they have been given to do. All these gifts are useless without the greatest gift the church has been given in Jesus Christ: the gift of love.

CYNTHIA A. JARVIS

---

4. Rachel Held Evans, *Washington Post*, April 30, 2015, http://wpo.st/1MbH2.
5. *The Constitution of the Presbyterian Church (U.S.A.),* Part II, *Book of Order* (Louisville, KY: Office of the General Assembly, 2016), G.-1.0102.

Luke 4:14–21

¹⁴Then Jesus, filled with the power of the Spirit, returned to Galilee, and a report about him spread through all the surrounding country. ¹⁵He began to teach in their synagogues and was praised by everyone.

¹⁶When he came to Nazareth, where he had been brought up, he went to the synagogue on the sabbath day, as was his custom. He stood up to read, ¹⁷and the scroll of the prophet Isaiah was given to him. He unrolled the scroll and found the place where it was written:

¹⁸"The Spirit of the Lord is upon me,
    because he has anointed me
        to bring good news to the poor.
He has sent me to proclaim release to the captives
    and recovery of sight to the blind,
        to let the oppressed go free,
¹⁹to proclaim the year of the Lord's favor."

²⁰And he rolled up the scroll, gave it back to the attendant, and sat down. The eyes of all in the synagogue were fixed on him. ²¹Then he began to say to them, "Today this scripture has been fulfilled in your hearing."

Commentary 1: Connecting the Reading with Scripture

This well-known text presents interpreters and preachers with some challenges. While the scene is often regarded as paradigmatic for Jesus' ministry, what actions does the Isaiah citation (4:18–19) describe? How do scene and citation connect with the rest of Luke's Gospel? How are we to understand the claim of fulfillment in 4:21 when—two thousand years later and counting—the poor, blind, and oppressed still inhabit the earth? Clichés will not suffice. How does the people's apparently favorable response to Jesus in verse 22 connect to verses 28–30, if at all, when within six verses they try to kill Jesus (important for next week's reading)?

The scene, the beginning of Jesus' public activity, builds on previous scenes that have established Jesus' identity as God's agent: Son of God (1:32, 35; 3:22; 4:3, 9), descendant of David (1:32), Savior (2:11), Messiah (2:11, 26), Lord (2:11). These scenes have also established the Spirit as the source of and power for Jesus' activity (1:35; 3:21–22; 4:1). His baptism (3:21–22) and temptation by the devil (4:1–13)

have announced and demonstrated his faithfulness to God as God's Son or agent. However, there has been little clarification of *how* Jesus will express his identity as God's agent. What sort of Son or Messiah or Savior will Jesus be? What will he do?

This scene starts to address these questions. First, it summarizes Jesus' teaching activity in synagogues in Galilee empowered by the Spirit (4:14–15) in continuity with the Spirit's previous roles in empowering Jesus' activity (4:1) and relocating him in Galilee (2:39)—a report about Jesus that elicits universal praise. The only activity mentioned is his teaching (4:31; 5:3, 17; 6:6, etc.).

An elaboration follows that places the scene geographically in the synagogue of Jesus' hometown of Nazareth (1:26; 2:4, 39, 51) and culturally on the Sabbath. Then comes the enigmatic citation from Isaiah 61 (4:18–19). Most of the passage that Jesus reads comes from Isaiah 61:1–2, with a couple of omissions and an addition from Isaiah 58. A somewhat literal translation reads:

The Spirit of the Lord is upon me
    for it has anointed me
To announce good news to the poor, he
    has sent me,
    [Omits—to bind up the
    brokenhearted]
To proclaim to the captives release,
To bring sight again to the blind,
To set the oppressed in release [added
    from Isa. 58:6],
To proclaim the year of the Lord's favor.
    (Omits—and a day of recompense/
    vengeance/judgment)

The Isaiah citation defines four features of Jesus' identity. (1) Lines 1–3 end with "me," defining Jesus as the sent-one anointed or commissioned by the Spirit. (2) The infinitives at the beginning of lines 3 to 7 name five tasks that comprise Jesus' mission. (3) The term "release" is repeated in lines 4 and 6 at the end of the line for emphasis, with line 6 added from Isaiah 58:6 to highlight this action. (4) The reference in Isaiah 61:2 to a "day of recompense or judgment" has been omitted, thereby emphasizing the merciful, transforming work of God's favor.

The central question concerns what Jesus is anointed to *do*. Unconvincing are readings that restrict the passage's significance to religious meanings and spiritualize its language as descriptions or metaphors of human sinfulness (poor in spirit, bound by sin, blind to God's favor, etc.) from which Jesus is to save. More convincing options emerge from recalling the context of Isaiah 61 and connecting its language to the rest of Luke's Gospel.

Isaiah 61 addresses exiles who returned from Babylon to the land after 539 BCE. Their expectations of a new creation, expressed in Isaiah 40–55, did not materialize. The promised salvation of a flourishing community did not occur, amid conflicts over negotiating Persian rule. Isaiah 61 restates a vision of an expected material, somatic, economic, and political transformation marked by prosperity, physical wholeness, and release from Persian rule.

Luke's use of the citation's language maintains the focus on material transformation. Interpreters have often sought to blunt the economic force of "the poor" by claiming it refers to people of diminished or marginalized status.

While they are included, the crucial observation is that some 70–90 percent of inhabitants in Rome's world can be classified as "poor" to varying degrees, struggling either permanently or sporadically with food insecurity and subsistence existence. There is little reason to avoid this economic reading, even as it embraces those of diminished or marginalized status. Throughout, Luke's Gospel emphasizes God's transforming favor for the material poor (6:20; 7:22; 14:13, 21; 16:20–22; 18:22; 19:8; 21:3). All of these instances denote economic poverty and, often, material/somatic transformation.

This use shapes the material interpretation of the remaining terms. Jesus' announcing of good news and divine favor enacts the presence of God's reign or empire in subsequent acts of healing the blind, lame, lepers, deaf, dead, and poor (7:22; cf. Isa. 35:5–6). These acts enact God's work of healing the damage inflicted on the poor by Rome's imperial rule through limited resources, poor nutrition, low immunity, and abundant stressors (cf. the good news of God's reign over Babylonian power in Isa. 52:7–10). The "blind" consistently denotes the literal blind (6:39; 7:21–22; 14:13, 21; 18:35). The terms "captives" and "oppressed" (from the Isaiah passage) appear only here and so can entertain a broad range of referents, including release from Roman rule, as well as from the power of the empire-controlling devil (4:5) in exorcisms.

The twice-repeated term "release" occurs in relation to sin (1:77; 3:3; 24:47). Is this only personal sin, or also structural and institutional sin? The latter possibility gains support from the observation that the term appears in jubilee or "release" traditions in Leviticus 25, referring more than ten times to the release of slaves, of people from debts, and of land from productivity (also Deut. 15:2). The cognate verb in the Gospel covers a similar range of releases that Jesus accomplishes: release from or forgiveness of sins (5:20–24; 7:47–49; 17:3–4); release from sickness (4:39; 5:20–24); release from or forgiveness of debts (11:4); release from everyday life in calling disciples (5:11).

The Isaiah passage thus offers a vision of God's transformative work of healing and release that Jesus as God's Son and agent is to perform. The work, while underway, remains incomplete, as a glance at the world, ancient and modern, makes clear. That suggests its ultimate completion will be eschatological. As Paul, the Gospels, and Revelation assert, the final release from all that is contrary to the divine will in Rome's world—and ours—awaits Jesus' return and the establishment of God's favor in a renewed world (Luke 21:25–28). In the long meantime, the Isaiah vision provides an agenda of hope and transforming actions for Jesus' followers to perform.

It takes a village—or a body of varying members and ministries, as Paul says in the reading from 1 Corinthians 12—to continue this work.

Animated by the Spirit, the church, the body of Christ, has a huge mission, as well as the personnel, resources, skills, and energy to work hard to change the world. Everyone has a contribution to make to this mission.

Jesus' announcement, then, that the Scripture has been fulfilled today in their hearing (4:21) cannot mean the accomplishment of the citation's claims. At most, the claim refers to Jesus' role as God's agent anointed to enact the divine will, a task that Jesus' followers are to continue.

WARREN CARTER

Commentary 2: Connecting the Reading with the World

In this text Jesus uses a prophetic passage from Isaiah in order to commence and proclaim the character of his messianic mission. The account comes early in Luke, while in Matthew (13:53–58) and Mark (6:1–6) it occurs late in Jesus' Galilean ministry. This difference may be due to Luke's emphasis not so much on chronology as on the themes and purposes of Jesus' mission of compassion and liberation. This passage, very much an inaugural address, serves as the introduction to the opening scene of the messianic drama. Following the account of the three temptations in the desert, Luke quickly shifts to the period of Jesus' ministry, lifting the curtain on the narrative of the momentous things that are about to happen in Galilee and beyond.

Luke strongly links the beginning of Jesus' ministry to his Jewish roots. From the start, harkening back to the Spirit's role in incarnation itself and Simeon's later blessing of him as an infant, Jesus is repeatedly directed and empowered by the Spirit. Luke frequently alludes to the power of the Spirit in the ongoing work of Jesus, and links Jesus with his Jewish roots in the genealogy that closes the previous chapter. Luke reports (2:41–52) that Jesus' family customarily journeyed to Jerusalem to observe the Passover. The work of the Spirit and the ongoing power of the tradition figure large in Luke's Gospel. Jesus chooses Galilee as the location for his announcement, and he teaches and worships

in the synagogue "as was his custom." Thus Luke positions Jesus firmly within the Jewish tradition. This is significant, since prophets most often speak from within their traditions, and by the time Luke writes his Gospel (a Gentile writing to a non-Jewish audience), a distinction between Christianity and Judaism already existed. Positive reports spread throughout the countryside and Jesus is praised "by everyone."

Luke is setting the stage for a highly dramatic moment. Following the tradition of synagogue worship, in which adult worshipers would be invited to read from the Scriptures and offer comment, the already-popular Jesus takes his place in his hometown synagogue, unrolls the scroll, finds his intended text, and reads from Isaiah 61:1–2, a passage from the Servant Songs of the great prophet. He begins to read: "The Spirit of the Lord is upon me, because he has anointed me." This anointing refers to his commission by the Spirit "today," to serve as Christ and Messiah.

The prophetic text is the vehicle for announcing the character of his mission: "to bring good news to the poor . . . to proclaim release to the captives and recovery of sight to the blind, to let the oppressed go free, to proclaim the year of the Lord's favor" (vv. 18–19).

To Jewish ears, this sounds like a clear reference to the year of jubilee, the fiftieth-year celebration at the end of seven cycles of seven years, when debts were to be forgiven, slaves were to be freed, the land was to be given rest, and a new era was to begin (Lev. 25:8–13). Thus, the need for economic justice and spiritual renewal are a powerful theme.

Jesus neatly rolls up the scroll as all eyes are upon the one sitting before them. He looks up to the gathered worshipers, and the drama is heightened when he says, "Today this scripture has been fulfilled in your hearing."

Note that the first word spoken by the public Jesus in Luke's Gospel, other than the reading of Isaiah, is "today"—not yesterday, not tomorrow, not someday. "Today this scripture has been fulfilled in your hearing." A stress on immediacy pervades Luke's Gospel. The time of divine action is always now. This today continues throughout Jesus' ministry. Now is always the time to release the captives, to give sight to the blind, to free the oppressed, to proclaim the year of the Lord's favor.

This text is pivotal in the seasons of the church. After Advent and Christmas, after the Epiphany and Baptism of the Lord, it is time to proclaim and interpret the Galilean ministry of the grown-up Jesus, Jesus who has, Epiphany-style, appeared on the public scene. The Gospel reading for this Sunday is a strong statement of the mission of the Messiah to those marginalized by the kingdoms and systems of the world.

The immediacy of this account is a good place to start in forming the sermon's message, given Jesus' first public word, "today." Too often, the prophetic word is followed by those who will answer, "Tomorrow"—or simply, "Wait." History is full of examples of how people of faith have been tragically slow to embrace the cries of the prophets or the opportunities to "do justice, love kindness, and walk humbly with God" (Mic. 6:8).

When Martin Luther King Jr. gave his clarion call for racial justice, some wanted to be supportive of his cause but feared acting too soon. Their message was, in essence, that it was a good idea but the time was not right. They told him to wait. Then, in his "Letter from Birmingham Jail," he replied, "This 'Wait' has

almost always meant 'Never.' We must come to see, with one of our distinguished jurists, that 'justice too long delayed is justice denied.'"[1] This text gives the preacher a rich opportunity to address contemporary examples of social and economic injustice, racism, and the plight of refugees, among others. Like King, we affirm that the time for justice is always today.

It should be noted that this dramatic Gospel reading lifts the curtain on who Jesus is and what he has come to accomplish. The Isaiah text is fulfilled in Jesus' arrival on the scene, while it will continue to be fulfilled and enfleshed in the unfolding of his ongoing ministry, crucifixion, and resurrection. Like all good preaching, this pivotal announcement stresses the fullness and breadth of the gospel. In a time when many stress the "spiritual" over the "religious," the danger is a contentless, individualistic Christianity, a faith characterized by feelings rather than substance and corporate advocacy.

This public inaugural appearance of Jesus is the proclamation of the content of what he has come to do: to announce good news to the poor and release to the captives, to give sight to the blind, to free the oppressed, and to proclaim the year of the Lord's favor. This is not a contentless mission or a feel-good form of spirituality. Jesus' mission is focused and specific, and it is rooted in the deep identity of his people and his tradition, made all the clearer by his quoting the strong prophetic source. He is describing his mission as something to fulfill the tradition, not to replace it. His inaugural message is also a clarion call to those who would follow to join in his work of healing, liberation, and grace.

As congregations today get about the work of crafting their mission and vision statements, as they shape the ways they will, together as the church, strive to make real in the world the mission of Jesus, they would do well to take this text as a guide and a model, for what Jesus describes here is nothing less than a statement of his own mission and vision as the long-awaited Messiah. As we move to our strategies, we should continually strive to achieve Jesus' mission "today."

BLAIR R. MONIE

---

1. Martin Luther King Jr., *Why We Can't Wait* (New York: Harper and Row, 1964), 83.

Fourth Sunday after the Epiphany

Jeremiah 1:4–10
Psalm 71:1–6

1 Corinthians 13:1–13
Luke 4:21–30

Jeremiah 1:4–10

⁴Now the word of the LORD came to me saying,

⁵"Before I formed you in the womb I knew you,
and before you were born I consecrated you;
I appointed you a prophet to the nations."

⁶Then I said, "Ah, Lord GOD! Truly I do not know how to speak, for I am only a boy." ⁷But the LORD said to me,

"Do not say, 'I am only a boy';
for you shall go to all to whom I send you,
and you shall speak whatever I command you.
⁸Do not be afraid of them,
for I am with you to deliver you,
says the LORD."

⁹Then the LORD put out his hand and touched my mouth; and the LORD said to me,

"Now I have put my words in your mouth.
¹⁰See, today I appoint you over nations and over kingdoms,
to pluck up and to pull down,
to destroy and to overthrow,
to build and to plant."

Commentary 1: Connecting the Reading with Scripture

The call of Jeremiah comprises four sections that convey the dialogic character of the prophet's relationship with the Lord: Jeremiah's appointment as a prophet (1:4–5); a response in the form of a protest (v. 6); a message of assurance (vv. 7–8); and a confirmation of the calling by divine action (vv. 9–10). The sequence echoes other call accounts (e.g., Judg. 6:11–12; Isa. 6:1–8; Ezek. 1:1–3:27) and presents the calling as entirely an act of divine initiative.[1] While other call accounts take place within the context of a vision, Jeremiah introduces his calling with a simple formula that is employed throughout the book to introduce prophetic speech (1:11, 13; 2:1ff.): "Now the word of the LORD came to me." The visionary component is given a nod by a pair of brief vision reports (vv. 11–13) that connect the account to an announcement of invasion and an exhortation (vv. 14–19) but are not part of the unit.

The passage links Jeremiah to Moses in a number of ways. First, the sequence of commission-protest-assurance-sign pattern follows the call of Moses (Exod. 3:1–4:17). Second, the language of the assurance and sign ("you shall speak whatever I command you" and "the LORD put out his hand and touched my mouth") pick up the language of Deuteronomy 18:18, which is situated in a passage that enjoins obedience to a prophet like Moses, whom the Lord will raise up in the land (Deut. 18:15–22). Finally,

---

1. N. Habel, "The Form and Significance of the Call Narratives," *Zeitschrift für die alttestamentliche Wissenschaft* 77 (1965): 297–323.

Jeremiah's objection that he does not know how to speak recalls Moses' protest that he is "slow of speech and slow of tongue" (Exod. 4:10). These allusions, along with the fact that the Lord specifically commissions Jeremiah as a prophet (in contrast to Isaiah and Ezekiel, who are not so designated in their call narratives), suggest that readers are to view Jeremiah as a prophet like Moses in the manner elaborated by Deuteronomy.

Although the commission comes when Jeremiah is yet unborn, it is not announced until Jeremiah is a young man. This creates a measure of uncertainty about the relationship between the commissioning and the announcement. The book's superscription places the beginning of Jeremiah's prophetic ministry in the thirteenth year of Josiah, that is, 627 BCE (1:2).

One view takes the note as a reference to the announcement, so that Jeremiah undertakes his ministry during his early teens, in coordination with Josiah's reform. Another view takes the reference to the thirteenth year as the time of Jeremiah's birth (and thus his commissioning just prior), which would place the beginning of his ministry during the reign of Jehoiakim, perhaps inaugurated at the age of eighteen by his temple sermon in 609 BCE (Jer. 26:1).

An intricate structure, centering on a series of parallel couplets, elaborates the interaction between the Lord, the prophet, and the message. The declaration that the Lord knew and consecrated Jeremiah before his birth underscores the scope of his prophetic ministry (1:5). Knowing in this context speaks of a deep relational bond (12:3; 31:34), while consecration

---

Go Preach the Gospel!

Between four and five years after my sanctification, on a certain time, an impressive silence fell upon me, and I stood as if some one was about to speak to me, yet I had no such thought in my heart.—But to my utter surprise there seemed to sound a voice which I thought I distinctly heard, and most certainly understand, which said to me, "Go preach the Gospel!" I immediately replied aloud, "No one will believe me." Again I listened, and again the same voice seemed to say—"Preach the Gospel; I will put words in your mouth, and will turn your enemies to become your friends."

At first I supposed that Satan had spoken to me, for I had read that he could transform himself into an angel of light for the purpose of deception. Immediately I went into a secret place, and called upon the Lord to know if he had called me to preach, and whether I was deceived or not; when there appeared to my view the form and figure of a pulpit, with a Bible lying thereon, the back of which was presented to me as plainly as if it had been a literal fact.

In consequence of this, my mind became so exercised, that during the night following, I took a text and preached in my sleep. I thought there stood before me a great multitude, while I expounded to them the things of religion. So violent were my exertions and so loud were my exclamations that I awoke from the sound of my own voice, which also awoke the family of the house where I resided. Two days after I went to see the preacher in charge of the African Society, who was the Rev. Richard Allen, the same before named in these pages, to tell him that I felt it my duty to preach the gospel. But as I drew near the street in which the house was, which was in the city of Philadelphia, my courage began to fail me; so terrible did the cross appear, it seemed that I should not be able to bear it. Previous to my setting out to go to see him, so agitated was my mind, that my appetite for my daily food failed me entirely. Several times on my way there, I turned back again; but as often I felt my strength again renewed, and I soon found that the nearer I approached to the house of the minister, the less was my fear. Accordingly, as soon as I came to the door, my fears subsided, the cross was removed, all things appeared pleasant—I was tranquil.

I now told him, that the Lord had revealed it to me, that I must preach the gospel.

Jarena Lee, *Religious Experience and Journal of Mrs. Jarena Lee* (Philadelphia: NP, 1849), 10–11.

marks the prophet as belonging to the Lord. Consecration, while commonly associated with priests, is unusual with reference to a prophet and so marks Jeremiah as a unique servant who, like a priest, carries out his ministry within the sphere of God's holiness.

Knowing and consecration together form the foundation upon which Jeremiah's ministry to the nations rests. Jeremiah, however, responds to the enormity of the task with a declaration of "not knowing" (how to speak) because he is only a boy (v. 6). The Lord in turn responds by negating the prophet's words ("Do not say, 'I am only a boy,'" v. 7a), before moving to a couplet that admonishes the prophet to complete obedience (v. 7b) and to another that assures him that the Lord will deliver him out of fearful situations (v. 8). As a whole, then, the interplay conveys a sense of back and forth as the Lord sets an enormous task before the prophet, hears his misgivings, asks for complete obedience nonetheless, and concludes with words of comfort and assurance.

That Jeremiah does indeed receive the Lord's word is emphasized by repetition, first as a report that the Lord touched his mouth, and then as direct speech that confirms what the Lord has done (v. 9; cf. Isa. 6:7). The Lord then expands on and particularizes the mandate of verse 5 to encompass nations and kingdoms (v. 10). Three pairs of infinitives signal that the prophet's impact will correspond to the vast range of his recipients. Just as Jeremiah will speak to the nations of the world, so the word that he speaks will bring cataclysmic changes. The infinitival forms indicate that the prophet's words will not just admonish and predict. They will bring into being what they declare; the utterance of the word of the Lord will set in motion the reality that the word proclaims. Together, the three pairs signal the content and proportionality of the word Jeremiah will speak; two pairs announce destruction while a third announces rebuilding.

References to plucking up, pulling down, planting, and building occur throughout the book to underscore both destruction and promise for Israel and the nations at large. The Lord uses the same language to summarize the overturning of powers (45:4) and to envision a future restoration

and return to the land (24:5–7; 31:27–28). Most notably, the language appears as Jeremiah watches a potter shaping clay, to express how the Lord deals with any nation that responds or rejects what the Lord has spoken to it (18:5–10).

The various aspects of the passage thus introduce fundamental themes that will thread through the book. The revelation that Jeremiah was appointed a prophet while in the womb, along with his protest to the revelation, establishes the framework for understanding Jeremiah's compulsion to prophesy and his protests against the Lord (15:10–21; 20:7–18); the prophetic word is etched in his DNA. His designation as a prophet and association with Moses alert the reader to see in him the marks of the authentic prophet, in contrast to the false voices that contest the word he speaks (14:13–18; 23:9–40; 28:1–17). The scope of his ministry to the nations signals the reader to see in the prophecies, sermons, and narratives to follow a larger theological vision that extends beyond the particularities of Judah's situation to encompass the Lord's working among the kingdoms of the world.

Psalm 71:1–6 reads as if it could be Jeremiah's response to the Lord's calling and the prophetic ministry that ensues. The psalmist's acclamation that "Upon you I have leaned from my birth; it was you who took me from my mother's womb" expresses the human response of trust and praise that befits the Lord's declaration that "before I formed you in the womb I knew you." The interaction between the texts invites readers to consider that the knowing and caring conveyed by the Lord's words to Jeremiah may extend beyond the particulars of the prophet's life to reveal a God who sees, knows, and plans for us even before we are born. First Corinthians 13:1–13 casts this interaction in loving terms and, in conversation with Jeremiah 1, directs us to the passage's conclusion, which speaks of us, like Jeremiah, as children who know only in part. Luke 4:21–30 presents a contrasting reality, when set against the hard reality of prophetic ministry in the world. Jesus' rejection by the people of Nazareth reminds those who speak God's words that they may expect to receive anger and rejection at the hands of those to whom they speak.

L. DANIEL HAWK

Commentary 2: Connecting the Reading with the World

The call of Jeremiah is a dramatic beginning to the ministry of a major prophet. God's words to the young man assured him he was known by God, even before his birth, and that God had set him apart, appointing him as a prophet—unilaterally!

Jeremiah resisted this call, arguing he did not know how to speak, since "I am only a boy" (v. 6). God turns this objection aside and promises Jeremiah a mission—"to speak whatever I command you" (v. 7). He is not to be afraid, for "I am with you to deliver you" (v. 8). Then God touches his mouth, indicating God will put words in his mouth. Jeremiah is appointed "over nations and over kingdoms." His work is "to pluck up and to pull down, to destroy and to overthrow, to build and to plant" (vv. 9–10). Here are four stages: appointment, objection, promise, and sign. These elements remind us of the calls of other important figures: Moses (Exod. 3:1–4:17), Isaiah (Isa. 6:1–13), and Ezekiel (Ezek. 1–3).

Liturgical Context. This story of Jeremiah's call is a reading for the season of Epiphany. This period marks a celebration of God's revelation in Jesus Christ to the whole world. The arrival of the magi to worship a newborn king (Matt. 2:1–12) begins this season. Jesus has come, not for a few but for the many—in fact, for all persons!

Epiphany is a significant context for noting the call of Jeremiah. He was called to be a spokesperson (prophet) for God, with God guiding him on what to say. As the book unfolds, Jeremiah's vocation (calling) was in his "calling all members of the community back to their vocation as followers of Israel's God."[2] This was Jeremiah's mission—to all the people.

In the Epiphany season, when we marvel that Jesus Christ has come for all the world, like Jeremiah, we recognize our calling to proclaim this message to all. As Jesus said: "Go into all the world and proclaim the good news to the whole creation" (Mark 16:15). The message of Christ is *for all*, and our calling during Epiphany—and in all seasons—is to proclaim this message *to all*.

A second significance to reflecting on Jeremiah's call during Epiphany is to realize that though his call shares similarities with other greats—Moses, Isaiah, and Ezekiel—God does not call just the "big names" to proclaim God's word. God's call is for all persons to serve God, no matter what their condition, situation, or status. Jeremiah himself was "only a boy," but the call of God came to him. We realize this when we recall that even the "greats" in the Bible were ordinary persons whom God used in extraordinary ways. The same is true for the disciples of Jesus; they were used by God, but not because of anything within themselves that earned them this privilege. They responded to Jesus' call. The Epiphany season says Christ came for all persons; and Christ came to use all persons to serve—in whatever ways. Despite objections, God promises to be with us. We can hear God's call to us in Jesus Christ—no matter who we are or what we are. God calls and connects with us and others, as Epiphany reminds us.

Ecclesial Context. The call of Jeremiah led to the work of Jeremiah. God was calling him to a life of experiences that would test his faith. Through it all, God was with him—as promised. In the broad strokes of his life, "vocation, for Jeremiah, involves being known by God, being equipped to proclaim God's will in the public square, being prepared to call others to account, and being fortified to face inevitable resistance."

The church is called by God to serve God through its life and mission. Its identity and its work are given by the God who calls disciples of Jesus Christ into the body of Christ to do God's work in this world. Like Jeremiah, the church is known by God; it is called into one body by the work of the Holy Spirit (Eph. 4:4). The church is equipped to proclaim God's will in the world by God's Spirit, who is with us. As the Confession of 1967 puts it: "wherever the church exists, its members are both gathered in

---

2. Carolyn J. Sharp, "Jeremiah," in *Theological Bible Commentary*, ed. Gail R. O'Day and David L. Petersen (Louisville, KY: Westminster John Knox Press, 2009), 226. The quote in "Ecclesial Context" comes from the same page.

corporate life and dispersed in society for the sake of mission in the world."[3] This is not always easygoing for the church—it was not for Jeremiah, either—but the church is equipped with the presence of God in Jesus Christ and with the power of the Holy Spirit to proclaim the Gospel, to seek reconciliation, and "to work with others for justice, freedom, and peace."[4]

The church's message and mission are concerned with the mission given to the prophet: to be "over nations and over kingdoms, to pluck up and to pull down, to destroy and to overthrow, to build and to plant" (v. 10). Jeremiah is sometimes said to be involved in "theopolitics"—bringing God's word to political situations. The church's mission moves in the same direction. Nations and kingdoms are the public contexts where the church's mission is carried out. Words of God's judgment must be spoken as sinful structures and practices must be dug up and pulled down and demolished. Words of God's grace come as well: "to build and to plant." Resistance emerges, but God's word and will are carried out. This can happen because "I am with you to deliver you, says the LORD" (v. 8).

Personal Context. The call of Jeremiah features a direct communication of God with the prophet. All Jeremiah was to do in his ministry was built on the conviction that God spoke to him, called and commissioned him, and appointed him to the ministries that lay ahead. He did not choose to be enlisted by God. Jeremiah knew what Jesus' disciples later experienced: "You did not choose me but I chose you" (John 15:16).

Throughout the Bible and in our own lives, the experience of Jeremiah is born out: God chooses us. God chooses us to serve God, to come to faith in Christ, to be drawn into the church, and to be witnesses and disciples of Jesus Christ in this world. The initiative in our salvation and in our callings and ministries is God's. The promises we receive from God are grounded in God's call, God's taking us as we are, and God's calling us into who God wants us to be as God's people engaged in mission and ministry.

God takes the initiative in calling us and continuing to be with us. We need not be afraid, for God is with us to rescue and deliver. This is the courage that comes from the conviction that God's purposes can guide our lives and that what God has begun in us will be brought to completion. This conviction strengthens our faith as we are upheld by God's Spirit and led in the ways to which God has called us. This is the trust—and the hope—we have, emphasized in the words of Jesus: "I am with you always" (Matt. 28:20).

DONALD K. McKIM

---

3. Presbyterian Church (U.S.A.), *Book of Confessions* (Louisville, KY: Office of the General Assembly, 2016), 9.35.
4. A Brief Statement of Faith, in *Book of Confessions*, 10.3.

Psalm 71:1–6

¹In you, O LORD, I take refuge;
  let me never be put to shame.
²In your righteousness deliver me and rescue me;
  incline your ear to me and save me.
³Be to me a rock of refuge,
  a strong fortress, to save me,
  for you are my rock and my fortress.

⁴Rescue me, O my God, from the hand of the wicked,
  from the grasp of the unjust and cruel.
⁵For you, O Lord, are my hope,
  my trust, O LORD, from my youth.
⁶Upon you I have leaned from my birth;
  it was you who took me from my mother's womb.
My praise is continually of you.

Connecting the Psalm with Scripture and Worship

Psalm 71 is a psalm of lament. It is often regarded as the lament of an elderly person who in the midst of a difficult time looks back on her or his life to find consolation in the fact that God has been present in the past and surely will be again. Like most psalms of lament, the structure includes an expression of distress, a plea for God's help, and an overarching expression of confidence in God. Psalm 71 is unique among laments in that the movement from distress to trust in God occurs three times.[1] The psalm verses appointed for this day express the first of these three movements, thus emphasizing the profound faith that the psalmist has in God. This sense of trust is further developed in the series of imperatives in verse 2, leading at least one scholar to suggest that the elderly speaker has "compose[d] a tribute to the value of a lasting friendship with God."[2]

Viewed as a response to the call narrative from Jeremiah, Psalm 71 highlights two particular angles of interpretation. The first is a reflection on the life stage of the two speakers; Jeremiah is referred to as a boy, while the psalmist seems to

have a lifetime of experience. The second examines lament as a response to the challenging prophetic vocation that is thrust on Jeremiah.

The psalm's evocative imagery of birth and "my mother's womb" (v. 6) draws our attention to the challenges that human beings face at every stage of life. While the psalmist speaks of her or his own birth, we might also pause to think about God's presence to the mothers who give birth to the figures in today's lectionary readings: the mother who gave birth to the psalmist; the mother of Jeremiah, who was known by God in his mother's womb; and Mary the mother of Jesus, whose presentation in the temple has recently been celebrated. Just whose wombs are we talking about in these readings? Motherhood is an understated and yet driving force behind these texts, and God's presence, not only to the children, but to the mothers who carried them, is pivotal.

The lectionary readings together offer a range of experiences from different stages of life. In Psalm 71, the expression "from my youth" suggests a wealth of years between that time and

---

1. J. Clinton McCann, "Psalms," in *New Interpreter's Bible* (Nashville: Abingdon Press, 1996), 4:958.
2. Konrad Schaefer, *Psalms,* Berit Olam: Studies in Hebrew Narrative and Poetry (Collegeville, MN: Liturgical Press, 2001), 133.

the present. The speaker's years of life with God have produced a kind of intimacy with God such that God is a "refuge" (vv. 1, 3) and support (v. 6). Although age does not mean that the speaker is free from the hands of those who are "wicked," "unjust and cruel" (v. 4), there is a hard-won wisdom to the psalm; the speaker knows that God was present in past struggles and will be present again.

In Jeremiah, we see a different stage of life. "Only a boy," the prophet does not yet understand what it means to have been known by God in the womb. Neither does he yet understand what it will mean to be a "prophet to the nations" (Jer. 1:5). He is a polite and modest boy, confessing his ignorance regarding public speaking, even adding the "truly" (v. 6) before trying to excuse himself. He does not confess fear, but perhaps it is evident, since God reassures preemptively, saying, "Do not be afraid of them" (v. 8). Finally, in the Gospel reading, we see Jesus as a young man, at the beginning of his career; in this moment, unlike the young and as yet innocent Jeremiah, Jesus comes to know what it means to be a prophet. Did he experience fear in the violence and rage of his community? How might the word of God to Jeremiah, or the words of the psalmist to God, inform a reading of the Gospel passage?

Considered as a response, today's psalm of lament can be heard as an appropriate reply to Jeremiah's call narrative. The call to be a prophet implies both intimacy with God and a resulting confrontational relationship with the world. The one who is appointed to "pluck up and to pull down, to destroy and to overthrow, to build and to plant" (Jer. 1:10) is likely to need a "rock of refuge" behind which to hide, or a rescuer ready to "incline [an] ear" (Ps. 71:2). Thus the psalmist could be heard as the voice of wisdom speaking through the ages to the young prophets Jeremiah and Jesus, and perhaps also to the prophets in the liturgical assembly. Can we picture an elderly Jeremiah speaking to God the words of the psalmist, as he reflects back on a life in which cruelty, injustice, and wickedness have been all too present, but in which God's presence also has been as continuous as the praise that is offered in the final verse? Can we picture Jesus, in the rocky beginnings of his ministry, finding consolation and refuge in the words of this elderly ancestor in faith? What response does the psalmist offer to the prophets in our own time and place?

This psalm of lament echoes the womb imagery from Jeremiah and offers a nuanced perspective on the challenges of a life with God in the midst of wickedness, cruelty, and injustice. The liturgical season suggests a framework of prophetic living and public witness.

RHODORA E. BEATON

1 Corinthians 13:1–13

¹If I speak in the tongues of mortals and of angels, but do not have love, I am a noisy gong or a clanging cymbal. ²And if I have prophetic powers, and understand all mysteries and all knowledge, and if I have all faith, so as to remove mountains, but do not have love, I am nothing. ³If I give away all my possessions, and if I hand over my body so that I may boast, but do not have love, I gain nothing.

⁴Love is patient; love is kind; love is not envious or boastful or arrogant ⁵or rude. It does not insist on its own way; it is not irritable or resentful; ⁶it does not rejoice in wrongdoing, but rejoices in the truth. ⁷It bears all things, believes all things, hopes all things, endures all things.

⁸Love never ends. But as for prophecies, they will come to an end; as for tongues, they will cease; as for knowledge, it will come to an end. ⁹For we know only in part, and we prophesy only in part; ¹⁰but when the complete comes, the partial will come to an end. ¹¹When I was a child, I spoke like a child, I thought like a child, I reasoned like a child; when I became an adult, I put an end to childish ways. ¹²For now we see in a mirror, dimly, but then we will see face to face. Now I know only in part; then I will know fully, even as I have been fully known. ¹³And now faith, hope, and love abide, these three; and the greatest of these is love.

Commentary 1: Connecting the Reading with Scripture

In this passage Paul picks up again his instructions on discernment and use of spiritual gifts. He has already explained in chapter 12 that authentic spiritual gifts are rooted in a lived commitment to Jesus Christ and function for the common good. Since others cannot understand ecstatic speech without someone to interpret it, the benefit of speaking in tongues accrues only to the speaker (14:4). Paul therefore puts ecstatic speech at the bottom of the list of spiritual gifts to be desired (12:28).

At the beginning of his statements on spiritual gifts, Paul writes, "You know that when you were pagans, you were enticed and led astray to idols that could not speak" (12:2). It appears that some of those speaking in tongues in the church at Corinth had similar experiences in religious cults before their conversion. Paul reminds them that ecstatic speech alone does not denote spiritual maturity. Paul's assertion that without love, one who speaks in tongues is "a noisy gong or clanging cymbal" (13:1) is another reminder of the possibility of ecstatic speech that is not fitting for Christian worship,

as gongs and cymbals were likely to be found in some of the various Greek and Roman temples in Corinth.

Paul is not condemning all ecstatic speech, only offering markers for discerning its appropriate use in worship. In addition to those offered in chapter 12 (attendant on trust in Jesus and offered for the common good), Paul now offers love as the final criterion. Not just glossolalia but all spiritual gifts are utterly negated without the presence of love.

There are four different words for love in the Greek of Paul's day. One, *eros*, refers to the love inspired by attraction, to passion and desire. This word is not used in the New Testament, nor was it used in the Septuagint (the Greek translation of the Hebrew Bible that Paul's readers would have known). Another, *storgē*, refers to the kind of natural affection, almost instinctual, that one has for a child, spouse, or pet. This term appears a couple of times in a negative form in the New Testament when its lack is noted. For example, in Romans 1, Paul describes the condition of fallen humanity as a distortion of its natural state. He writes, "claiming to be wise, they became fools," and worshiped images of mortal creatures rather than the fullness of immortal God (Rom. 1:22–23). In this fallen state, the natural affection of *storgē* is gone, and the people are "heartless" (Rom. 1:31).

A third Greek word, the verb *phileō*, refers to affinity, fondness, or friendship. It can be companionable and mutual, and it involves the lover's own enjoyment or pleasure. In the Synoptic Gospels, *phileō* often has negative connotations. For example, in Matthew, the hypocrites "love [*phileō*] to stand and pray in the synagogues and at the street corners, that they may be seen by others" (Matt. 6:5). It is used positively in the Gospel of John to describe the love of the Father for the Son (5:20), the love between Jesus and Lazarus (11:3, 36), and Jesus' love for his disciple (20:2).

The word for love John associates most closely with God is a fourth term, *agapē*. This kind of love longs for the well-being of the beloved. It is love directed or willed by the nature of the lover, which means it can remain strong even when the beloved turns away. This is the term used in John 3:16, "For God so loved [*agapē*] the world that he gave his only Son," and in 1 John 4:8, "God is love [*agapē*]."

It would be foolish to imagine firm lines of separation between these nuanced types of love. Surely love can be both erotic and agapeic, and the best friendships include the desire for the flourishing of the beloved. At the same time, the early Christians honored *agapē* as rooted in and reflective of God's love. While the term *agapē* was not used commonly in other literature of the period, it appears more than three hundred times in the New Testament. This giving and forgiving love always desires goodness for the beloved; this is the kind of love God gives to us, and therefore the kind of love we ought to have for one another. Paul's words in verses 4–7 offer the definitive portrait of *agapē*: "Love is patient; love is kind; love is not envious or boastful or arrogant or rude. It does not insist on its own way; it is not irritable or resentful; it does not rejoice in wrongdoing, but rejoices in the truth. It bears all things, believes all things, hopes all things, endures all things."

These verses reinforce all that Paul has said

previously. Spiritual gifts that are not offered in agapeic love—that is, given for the well-being of the beloved—are nothing. These verses also point forward to what Paul will do in the rest of 1 Corinthians. The Christians at Corinth are attempting to live out their baptism. For much of this epistle, Paul reminds them of the new identity they have gained in Christ and advises them on how to shape a new community in light of this identity. In 13:8, however, Paul starts looking forward. While Christian identity begins in baptism, it comes to fruition in the eschaton. Christians must live in the strange space between the two, when the coming kingdom has been inaugurated but not yet fulfilled. While Christians should be confident in the power of the Spirit given to us, we must also be humble and discerning, aware that our prophecies are partial, our knowledge incomplete, and our vision dim. Whatever spiritual gifts we may boast of, or even generously offer to the common good, are fleeting. What remains is love.

Throughout this letter, Paul balances between validating the true faith of the Corinthians and urging them to be more nuanced in their theology and more humble in their actions. He tells them they are right, but there is more to learn; they are spiritual people, but not the spiritual royalty they imagine themselves to be (4:18). Earlier in this epistle, Paul chides the Corinthians for imagining they are spiritually mature and in full possession of the richness of the Spirit. He reminds them that when he was with them, he spoke to them "as infants in Christ. I fed you with milk, not solid food, for you were not ready for solid food. Even now you are still not ready" (3:1–2).

In chapter 13, as Paul casts his vision forward to the eschaton, he invokes the imagery of childhood again: "When I was a child, I spoke like a child, I thought like a child, I reasoned like a child; when I became an adult, I put an end to childish ways." The spiritual gifts, in which the Corinthians have taken so much pride, are, finally, childish things. They too will be put away. While this might be a blow to a personal sense of status, it is ultimately cause for rejoicing. Paul is not interested in nostalgia for childhood, but in the full promise of maturity. In this awkward stage of adolescence, we glimpse something of that promise when we recognize love for what it truly is: eternal.

"Love never ends" (13:8). In so far as agape is present in our worship and our lives, we are dipping our toes in the new creation. Everything else will fall away—and therefore should be held lightly—but "faith, hope, and love abide . . . and the greatest of these is love" (13:13).

SHANNON CRAIGO-SNELL

Commentary 2: Connecting the Reading with the World

Sir John Templeton spent the first part of his life making money—lots of money—and the last part of his life giving it away. In 1973 he established the Templeton Prize for progress in religion (whatever that means) and awarded the prize first to Mother Teresa. Then in 1987 he formed the Templeton Foundation to promote research on what Sir John called the "Big Questions," questions dealing with the intersection of science, faith, God, and the purpose of humanity.

Templeton came of age during the Scopes trial, which was held near his home in Winchester, Tennessee. A Presbyterian by upbringing, he did not believe in the literal interpretation of Scripture and so was determined to do what he could to find common ground between science and religion. If science could study religious experience, perhaps such study might foster understanding of what he called "spiritual realities." Foremost among these realities for Sir John was love: unlimited love. In the summer prior to 9/11, Case Western Reserve received over $8 million from the foundation to underwrite research on unlimited love. What would Paul have said to this?

Paul's chapter on love is wedged in the middle of a longer discourse written in response to a particular division within the community. Chapters 12 through 14 concern the presumed hierarchy of spiritual gifts within the community, gifts that lent status to some and second-class citizenship to others, thereby causing divisions. Topping the list of better gifts, according to the beginning of chapter 13, was speaking in tongues, followed by prophetic knowledge of God and ostentatious stewardship.

To be given the gift of speaking in tongues is to be set apart to say the unsayable in the community, to express the ineffable through the aid of God's Spirit. Paul says the same of human knowledge about God, whether written by the theologian, proclaimed by the prophet, or acted out by the healer. Even though a person can have the outward appearance of knowing God theologically, receiving God's word prophetically, working God's works miraculously, and saying the unsayable, if that one is puffed up with knowledge or self-important about her or his faith, then there can be no witness to the One who in love emptied himself.

Paul first calls into question two aspects of discipleship that are unassailable in most Christian communities: sacrificial giving and social action. "If I give away all that I have and if I deliver my body to be burned, I gain nothing." These actions come as close as any can to the more excellent way Paul is commending, but even in an act of sacrifice on behalf of the neighbor, the love that really is love can be missing. If you go to Haiti to plant trees and, all the while, do not get out of yourself, divest yourself of yourself, remove yourself from the center of your concern, so that there is room to be with and for the other, then you might as well have stayed home. How many good deeds are ruined by the inner self-congratulation that places the doer in the moral spotlight? Likely the one who is the object of a loveless loving act sees right through to the pretense!

What then is this love without which our speech and knowledge and actions are in vain? According to the Institute for Research on Unlimited Love, "When the happiness, security and well-being of another feels as real to us as our own, or perhaps more so, we love that person. Unlimited love extends to . . . all humanity based on our shared dignity and interdependence with one another and with nature."[1]

1. See http://unlimitedloveinstitute.org/about.php.

With this definition in hand, the institute set out to trace, scientifically, how persons come to delight unselfishly in the well-being of the other. The assumption is that if a researcher can identify and even measure what makes a person love unconditionally, then it may be possible to reproduce the conditions—in the family, community of faith, nation, and world—that will make unconditional lovers out of otherwise selfish human beings. Ironically much of the funded research has to do with the benefits that accrue to a person who loves unconditionally—health, for instance, and long life or the salutary effects of prayer on healing—thereby compromising the unconditional aspect of the affective affirmation of the well-being of another!

Paul knows you just cannot say what love is without saying Jesus! He knows only Christ can make unconditional lovers out of otherwise selfish human beings. He knows this because Christ has done this for him. Hence he offers no definition but, instead, turns the Corinthians to the one who alone is love. Substitute Christ for every mention made of love in this chapter, and you begin to see through a mirror darkly the love for which you were made. "What is here called love," writes Dietrich Bonhoeffer in his *Ethics,* "is not this general principle but the utterly unique event of the laying down of the life of Jesus Christ for us. . . . The New Testament answers the question 'What is love?' quite unambiguously by pointing solely and entirely to Jesus Christ."[2]

However, when Paul considers the love revealed in Christ, he looks not to the teachings of Jesus or to the deeds of Jesus during his lifetime. He looks to the cross, where love is "shorthand for a narrative: death and resurrection," says theologian Robert Jenson, ". . . because, seen from faith's viewpoint, death and resurrection is what love concretely means. . . . The usual

promises we make each other stop short because we except the condition of death, because we reserve self-preservation; but to promise *myself* is to try to give up this reservation. Therefore to love is to accept death: it is to give up my cautious claims to hang onto myself."[3]

At the heart of the division in the Corinthian community was this cautious claim to hang on to the self: the wise self, the moral self, the righteous self, the "I am right and everyone else is wrong" self. Therefore, with the exception of Paul's first two positive words ("love is patient and kind"), we are given a negative litany that nails the various ways in which we hang on to ourselves: by our jealousy, boastfulness, arrogance, our rude behavior; by insisting on our own way, being irritable and resentful, rejoicing in the wrong rather than in the truth. We are full of ourselves such that we come to believe love of the other must be at the expense of ourselves. Indeed it must!

So, given the presupposition of the Institute for Research on Unlimited Love—that if we can know what makes a person love unconditionally, we can reproduce the conditions that will make unconditional lovers out of otherwise selfish human beings—Paul would say death is the only condition. Our jealous, boastful, arrogant, and rude selves must die, as Saul died on the road to Damascus. Our selves full of ourselves must be emptied, even as Christ emptied himself and took the form of a servant.

This is not a condition we can reproduce. Rather, if we love at all, we love because—when we were jealous and boastful, arrogant and rude, irritable and resentful and insisting upon our own way—the patient and kind God first loved us, is *still* loving our sorry selves, to the end that, with Sir John and all the saints, we may one day see Love face to face!

CYNTHIA A. JARVIS

---

2. Dietrich Bonhoeffer, *Ethics* (New York: Simon & Schuster, 1995), 54.
3. Robert Jenson, *Story and Promise* (Ramsey, NJ: Sigler Press, 1989), 55.

Luke 4:21–30

²¹Then he began to say to them, "Today this scripture has been fulfilled in your hearing." ²²All spoke well of him and were amazed at the gracious words that came from his mouth. They said, "Is not this Joseph's son?" ²³He said to them, "Doubtless you will quote to me this proverb, 'Doctor, cure yourself!' And you will say, 'Do here also in your hometown the things that we have heard you did at Capernaum.'" ²⁴And he said, "Truly I tell you, no prophet is accepted in the prophet's hometown. ²⁵But the truth is, there were many widows in Israel in the time of Elijah, when the heaven was shut up three years and six months, and there was a severe famine over all the land; ²⁶yet Elijah was sent to none of them except to a widow at Zarephath in Sidon. ²⁷There were also many lepers in Israel in the time of the prophet Elisha, and none of them was cleansed except Naaman the Syrian." ²⁸When they heard this, all in the synagogue were filled with rage. ²⁹They got up, drove him out of the town, and led him to the brow of the hill on which their town was built, so that they might hurl him off the cliff. ³⁰But he passed through the midst of them and went on his way.

Commentary 1: Connecting the Reading with Scripture

This scene continues last week's account of the beginning of Jesus' ministry in the Nazareth synagogue (4:14–21). Two aspects present challenges to interpreters and preachers.

The first concerns troubling triumphalist or supersessionist readings. The scene's violent ending tempts interpreters to read/preach against the synagogue (and Jews), stereotyping them as violent and unwilling to share God's favor with outsiders, while constructing Jesus (and Christians) as superior, generous hearted, and oppressed. Such a reading reinscribes an inaccurate and objectionable them-and-us, outsiders-and-insiders, binary. It is unloving, as the lectionary reading from 1 Corinthian 13 cautions us is always a possibility. The inclusion of Gentiles in God's favor is not a Christian discovery. Across the canon, the Hebrew Scriptures root it in God's creation of the world, in Abraham's call to bless "all the families of the earth" (Gen. 12:3), in Israel's task to be a light to the nations (Isa. 49:5–7), in Jeremiah's call to speak to the nations (Jer. 1:4–10, the Hebrew Bible lection), and in the prophetic ministries of Elijah and Elisha (Luke 4:25–27).

The second challenge concerns the difficult connections and translations across verses 22–24 and 28. Jesus finishes his citation of Isaiah 61 by declaring its accomplishment "today . . . in your hearing" (4:21). Given that no transformation of the world, ancient or modern, has occurred, the accomplishment refers at most to Jesus' anointing as God's agent to enact the divine favor identified in the citation. How do the hometown folks respond in verse 22?

One reading—the NRSV translation, for example—presents the response as positive and appreciative. They "spoke well of him and were amazed at his gracious words" (4:22). Joseph's boy (2:16; 3:23) is now God's anointed!

Problematic, though, is the subsequent shift in tone in verses 23–24. Suddenly Jesus seems to understand they are challenging him. The proverb "Doctor, cure yourself" expresses a demand that he perform beneficent actions for them, just as he has apparently done for others (though not described by the narrative). Then Jesus declares their rejection of him (4:24). The sequence is wobbly. Why does Jesus assume a challenge and a rejection if verse 22 is a positive response?

The most common explanation is that Jesus

hears in the positive affirmation of verse 22 an expectation that he will perform acts of God's favor for them—which he, strangely and without reason, declines to do. Some interpreters explain his refusal as rejecting their narrow understanding of his mission that claims divine favor only for themselves. This suggestion seeks to explain the strong change in tone through the next few verses and the remarkable change in the people's attitude to Jesus in verse 28, when they want to kill him.

A different reading of these verses understands the people's response of verse 22 negatively. The translation "spoke well of him" could be translated differently: "they witnessed against him" and "marveled" in opposition to him. How could a hometown boy—Joseph's son—claim to be God's anointed agent? They do not believe his identity claim. They do not accept that the words have been "accomplished" among them when they have not experienced any good news, release, or favor. Jesus will need to demonstrate some healings and "releases" before they believe.

On this reading, Jesus responds in verses 23–24 to their hostility. He anticipates their challenge that he demonstrate acts of favor in Nazareth just as he did in Capernaum (evoking 4:14–15). Jesus refuses to perform such acts, because they have not discerned his identity. He is not primarily "son of Joseph" but Son of God (1:32, 35; 3:22; 4:3, 9). They know the former but not the latter. Their "hearing" has rejected his claimed identity and not discerned Jesus' divine sanction (4:21). Second, using an authoritative introductory phrase ("Truly I say to you"), he names their response of rejection as typical of how hometowns react to prophets (Neh. 9:26), thereby asserting his own prophetic identity.

Neither interpretation is without its problems. Both options require interpreters to fill in gaps in the text to create a coherent narrative. Both options run the risk, though, sooner or later (4:28) of antisynagogal readings, as interpreters attribute negative motivations to the hometown audience. Decisions made about these verses influence the interpretation of the following verses' examples of Elijah and Elisha. Does Jesus provoke the violent reaction that follows in 4:28, or does he expose what has already happened in 4:22?

However we solve these issues, verses 25–27 provide two (rather awkward) examples of the extent of God's favor and of Jesus' mission as agent of God's favor and release. These scenes evoke 1 Kings 17:8–24 (Elijah) and 2 Kings 5:1–19 (Elisha). Both examples have parallel constructions. (1) They name situations of poverty and desperation: a three-and-a-half-year famine throughout "all the land" (4:25) and many diseased lepers (4:27). (2) They identify prophets as agents of divine transformation. Using the (divine) passive construction, verse 26 denotes God sending Elijah to the hungry widow. Verse 27 also uses a divine passive ("was cleansed") to signify divine healing through Elisha. (3) They locate the recipients among the poor and outsiders. Verse 26 identifies an unnamed, food-insecure, poor widow in Zarephath in Sidon, a Gentile. Verse 27 identifies the named male (Naaman) as a Syrian/Gentile and as a leper. Luke omits the descriptors of Naaman in 2 Kings 5 ("a great man . . . in high favor . . . a great warrior"), along with his conversion to Israel's God. Luke also reworks the Elijah scene, in which 1 Kings emphasizes reliance on God for food and healing of her son (omitted here), not the widow's Gentile identity.

The verses emphasize the beneficiaries' Gentile identity by naming location (Zarephath in Sidon, 4:26), using a personal name (Naaman), and employing the ethnic marker, "Syrian." They also employ parallel and repeated constructions that contrast Israel: "there were many widows/lepers in Israel" (4:25, 27) and "none of them . . . except" (4:26–27). The "except" phrase indicates no favor for Israelite widows and lepers. The Gospel has signaled Gentiles as recipients of divine favor previously in Simeon's praise to God for salvation that is "a light of revelation to the Gentiles and for glory to your people Israel" (2:32), John's declaration that "all flesh shall see the salvation of God" (3:6), and in tracing Jesus' genealogy to Adam (3:38). The favor of God that Isaiah declares, with which Jesus is aligned as God's agent and Son, extends to the poor and oppressed of every nation. Jeremiah in the Hebrew Bible lection is similarly sent to the nations (Jer. 1:4, 10)

What then are we to make of the hometown folks' rage (4:28–29)? Do they angrily resent sharing God's favor with foreigners, as is commonly preached? A better connection is at hand. They have heard Jesus refuse to manifest God's favor in their town. They have heard him cite two examples of prophets who shared God's favor with Gentiles but not with Israel, suggesting—staggeringly—that God's favor had been withheld from Israel. These factors suggest that the hometown folks express not anger at having to share God's favor but anger that Jesus seems to exclude Nazareth from it. The townsfolk rightly protest their exclusion from God's loving actions. They reject a prophet whom they understand—on the basis of his words in this scene—to announce a withholding of divine favor, love, grace, mercy. They appropriately demand God's agent, whether individual or community, to manifest God's favor, which extends to and embraces everybody, Jew and Gentile, male and female, rich and poor.

WARREN CARTER

Commentary 2: Connecting the Reading with the World

Today's Gospel reading picks up where last Sunday's left off (just after Jesus reads from Isaiah), repeating Luke 4:21, "Then he began to say to them, 'Today this scripture has been fulfilled in your hearing.'" Having read the prophet's summary of the mission of God's anointed servant, Jesus announces that this centuries-old Scripture concerns not only long-ago times; it also names the present reality of God's liberating work. What they hear in the synagogue today is Isaiah's message coming to pass. Something momentous is beginning before their eyes.

With these first public words of Jesus, the curtain goes up on Luke's narrative of Jesus' Galilean ministry. This statement is so pivotal that it is repeated from last week's lection. Now, however, we hear the response of the people: "All spoke well of him and were amazed at the gracious words that came from his mouth. They said, 'Is not this Joseph's son?'"

What is this amazement about? N. T. Wright suggests that the people were not amazed that Jesus was such a good speaker; rather, they are amazed at "his gracious words"—that is, his message of grace.[1] However, their amazement seems to quickly turn into doubt. Jesus was a familiar neighbor, merely "Joseph's son."

Quite likely they expected and wanted something else, for Jesus' listeners' expectations of the Messiah were rooted in the hope that the occupying foreign power of the Roman Empire would be soundly defeated. The Messiah was to be no mere messenger of grace, but a political and military leader who would take on the power of Rome. After all, there were passages in the Psalms and the Prophets that prayed that God would punish the foreign powers (e.g., Hag. 2:22: "I am about to destroy the strength of the kingdoms of the nations, and overthrow the chariots and their riders").

The passage Jesus chooses to read in the synagogue suggests only a mission of grace and, moreover, healing *for everyone*. Perhaps the all-inclusive character of the grace Jesus proclaims explains the people's anger. Unfortunately, the church has always included those who are upset with the preacher for not condemning their favorite enemies.

The rest of the verse seems to support the possibility that the people's amazement was not a positive thing: "They said, 'Is not this Joseph's son?'" One way to discredit the messenger when you do not like the message is to find petty faults. Familiarity, after all, can breed either pride or contempt—alternatives the preacher might explore.

Another way to discredit someone is to apply some well-worn platitudes. Now Jesus gets the jump on his critics by suggesting some. "He said to them, 'Doubtless you will quote to me this proverb, "Doctor, cure yourself!"'" (v. 23).

The next issue of the critics seems to be that, although they have heard stories of miracles and healings in other parts of Galilee, Jesus has not done any such things in Nazareth, his

---

1. N. T. Wright, *Luke for Everyone* (Louisville, KY: Westminster John Knox Press, 2004), 48.

own hometown. So they might be thinking, as Jesus suggests, "Do here also in your hometown the things that we have heard you did at Capernaum." His response is that "no prophet is accepted in the prophet's hometown" (v. 24).

The plot now thickens. Jesus points to two of the great Hebrew prophets. In the time of Elijah, "there were many widows in Israel" in a time of famine, yet Elijah was not sent to any of them (v. 25). Instead, he went to a widow of Zarephath in Sidon. The problem here is that Sidon is just the sort of foreign power that insiders like to despise (Jesus seems to say unexpected things often, such as making a Samaritan the hero of a parable in Luke 10). Next, he refers to Elisha, Elijah's successor, who seemed to ignore all the lepers in Israel, only to cleanse Naaman the Syrian. Naaman was not only a foreigner, but the commander of an enemy army. Jesus' God was healing all the wrong people. This is what made the people of the synagogue so angry—and what can make church congregants angry. N. T. Wright adds the comment, "That's like someone in Britain or France during the Second World War speaking of God's healing and restoration for Adolf Hitler. It's not what people wanted to hear."[2]

The people were "filled with rage" because Jesus proclaimed a grace that was wider and more generous than they were. Grace is more difficult to really embrace than we often assume. We are happy when the "right" people are forgiven, accepted, or healed, but we're not so sure that we want those things extended to people outside our favored circles, or that we want to extend that grace ourselves.

The irony is that Jesus was preaching for the very sort of people who became enraged with him. He was not preaching to people of power and authority; in all probability, he was preaching to the common folks of Nazareth. They were people who had suffered under the powers of empire. Many were poor. When Jesus, in reading from Isaiah, had communicated a gospel of grace for the poor, the captives, the blind, and the oppressed, he was talking about them! This announcement, after all, was good news for those oppressed by the Roman occupiers—but

we too have ways of rejecting the good news of the kingdom.

The preacher should be sure to help listeners avoid the assumption that the people of Nazareth are unlike us, for this is certainly not true, given so many contemporary church divisions and schisms, and the polarization that exists in society. This is a passage full of the themes of "us" versus "them." Jesus, you did it for them, so why not us? You speak of a grace extended to them when we believe they do not deserve it. On it goes.

At the heart of all this is the theme of privilege. As many social commentators have observed, privilege is a powerful reality in society, but generally only those who do not have it realize its power. The idea of privilege—that some people benefit from unearned and largely unacknowledged advantages—has a long history. In the 1930s, W. E. B. DuBois wrote about the "psychological wage" that enabled poor whites to feel superior to poor blacks, even as poor whites suffered their own forms of injustice. During the civil rights era, activists talked about "white-skin privilege," and the 1970s would bring heightened awareness of male privilege.

The people of Nazareth who gathered on the Sabbath that day in the synagogue may not have been wealthy or powerful, but many thought of themselves as God's people in terms of privilege in the negative sense of favoritism. That led them to resent a grace that was extended to others and, ironically, kept them from joyously receiving grace themselves, when it was so publicly announced.

This text offers an opportunity to explore ways we may have something in common with the Nazareth crowd who listened to Jesus that day. We do a disservice to such passages when we caricature biblical people as not like us. The similarity may be stronger than we imagine. In whatever context we find ourselves, from a makeshift chapel in a borderlands refugee center to a suburban megachurch, how we respond to messages of liberation and justice will reveal much about how we receive the Word.

BLAIR R. MONIE

---

2. Ibid.

Fifth Sunday after the Epiphany

Isaiah 6:1–8 (9–13)
Psalm 138

1 Corinthians 15:1–11
Luke 5:1–11

Isaiah 6:1–8 (9–13)

¹In the year that King Uzziah died, I saw the Lord sitting on a throne, high and lofty; and the hem of his robe filled the temple. ²Seraphs were in attendance above him; each had six wings: with two they covered their faces, and with two they covered their feet, and with two they flew. ³And one called to another and said:

"Holy, holy, holy is the LORD of hosts;
the whole earth is full of his glory."

⁴The pivots on the thresholds shook at the voices of those who called, and the house filled with smoke. ⁵And I said: "Woe is me! I am lost, for I am a man of unclean lips, and I live among a people of unclean lips; yet my eyes have seen the King, the LORD of hosts!"

⁶Then one of the seraphs flew to me, holding a live coal that had been taken from the altar with a pair of tongs. ⁷The seraph touched my mouth with it and said: "Now that this has touched your lips, your guilt has departed and your sin is blotted out." ⁸Then I heard the voice of the Lord saying, "Whom shall I send, and who will go for us?" And I said, "Here am I; send me!" ⁹And he said, "Go and say to this people:

'Keep listening, but do not comprehend;
keep looking, but do not understand.'
¹⁰Make the mind of this people dull,
    and stop their ears,
    and shut their eyes,
so that they may not look with their eyes,
    and listen with their ears,
and comprehend with their minds,
    and turn and be healed."

¹¹Then I said, "How long, O Lord?" And he said:

"Until cities lie waste
    without inhabitant,
and houses without people,
    and the land is utterly desolate;
¹²until the LORD sends everyone far away,
    and vast is the emptiness in the midst of the land.
¹³Even if a tenth part remain in it,
    it will be burned again,
like a terebinth or an oak
    whose stump remains standing
    when it is felled."

The holy seed is its stump.

Commentary 1: Connecting the Reading with Scripture

From the outset, the most important thing to say about Isaiah 6 is that the entire chapter is a unit; so the interpretation and proclamation of this chapter should *not* end at verse 8, which is what the lectionary suggests with its unfortunate placement of verses 9–13 in parentheses, indicating that those verses are optional. One might argue that ending at verse 8 concludes the lectionary's (apocopated) reading on a high point with the prophet's "Here am I; send me!", but that would be a wrong and premature conclusion. The high point in verse 8 is actually anything but, since the story of Isaiah's calling and particularly the hard facts of his prophetic commission come *only later*, in verses 9–13.

It would be perilous to sign on to a task before one knows what one has signed on for! Of course that is exactly what Isaiah does—and what so many sermons that end with verse 8 do. When the hard facts of prophetic calling do come, Isaiah, no less than other prophets, wants out (see v. 11a). So, while ending at "Here am I; send me!" may make for a nice sermon(ette), like far too many sermon(ette)s, it would be shortsighted, creating a false impression of Isaiah and of this chapter. The entirety of the chapter demonstrates that Isaiah's statement in verse 8 is overly hasty and ill advised. Perhaps it was occasioned by the flush of Isaiah's newfound forgiveness (v. 7). Whatever the case, it was a rush to judgment in two ways. First, it was a rush to Isaiah's judgment that he really wanted this task, was truly eager for this job. Second, it was also a rush to God's judgment, since that is the substance of Isaiah's prophetic calling: the unremitting, unrelenting, almost complete eradication of God's people—even if 10 percent remains, it will all be burned again (v. 13a).

The altogether sobering sentiment in verses 9–13 is no doubt what led the lectionary to want to spare us their despair, but this is an unfortunate censorship, demonstrated not only by the chapter's formal coherence, but also by the use of Isaiah 6 in the New Testament. Verses 9–10 are among the most frequently cited Old Testament texts in the New Testament, where they often serve as Jesus' explanation for why he teaches in parables—namely, so that no one will

understand (Matt. 13:14–15; Mark 4:12; Luke 8:10; cf. John 12:40; also Acts 28:26; Rom. 11:8).

Isaiah 6 begins with a chronological notice—the year of King Uzziah's death—that seems somewhat out of place (6:1; cf. 1:1; 2:1; 7:1), but may be included for historical and compositional reasons. If the chapter reflects Isaiah's initial call to ministry, it dates that call to about 738 BCE. Some scholars believe that chapter 6 could not be Isaiah's inaugural call, because comparable calls found in other prophetic books tend to appear at the very start of the book (e.g., Jer. 1:4–10; Ezek. 1:1–3:9). Why then should Isaiah's inaugural call come only in chapter 6? The placement issue should not be overthought. The chronological indicator may only signal that the call report was composed (or presented) sometime after the actual experience of it (see J. J. M. Roberts, *First Isaiah: A Commentary* [Minneapolis: Fortress Press, 2015], 91–92). Further, not every reference to prophetic commissioning is found in initial position (e.g., Amos 7:12–15). Regardless of book placement, these call reports often function to legitimize a prophet's words and ministry, and such a function is also at play in Isaiah 6.

Perhaps then the placement of Isaiah's call in chapter 6 has to do with now irrecoverable details about the final composition of the book. What cannot be denied, regardless, are the formal similarities between Isaiah 6 and other call reports that are presented as the prophet's initial calling (esp. Jer. 1; Ezek. 1–3), such that Isaiah 6 too should be considered an account of his inaugural call. In this light, verse 1's chronological indicator is less important in terms of history or composition as *theology*: at an uncertain political moment, when the great King Uzziah died (v. 1), Isaiah had a vision of the true "King, the LORD of hosts" (v. 5). Here, no less than elsewhere, the prophetic task is one that is profoundly and politically fraught.

Isaiah's vision may have taken place in the Jerusalem temple itself, but what he ultimately catches sight of is the heavenly throne room. While God is not directly described, the text makes clear that God is massive (just the edges of the divine robe fill the temple, v. 1b) and served by fantastic beings: six-winged seraphim that proclaim the holiness and glory of God (vv. 2–3) to such an extent that the very building shakes (v. 4). Isaiah is rightly overcome—even terrified—by what he sees, which is an altogether proper response in the face of the holy God (cf. Exod. 3:5–6). Indeed, Isaiah is not only overcome; he fears that he is undone, that he is finished; that is how holy God is and how unclean, how unholy, all else, including Isaiah himself, is in comparison (v. 5).

As if in direct response to Isaiah's concern and his specific words about his unclean lips, one of the seraphs cleanses him with a coal taken from the altar. Etymologically, a seraph is a fiery creature (Heb. *srp*), but even this blazing servant must retrieve the coal with tongs (v. 6). What is left unsaid explicitly, but implied nevertheless, is that Isaiah's cleansing was unbelievably painful. It was also completely effective (v. 7), with the flow of verses perhaps suggesting that it is only now, with forgiveness of his guilt and sin, that Isaiah is finally ready (and able) to hear God's own voice.

What Isaiah hears is God asking whom to send—but the conversation seems midstream, as if Isaiah has suddenly burst into the middle of a complex deliberation (v. 8a). First Kings 22:19–23 reflects a comparable but fuller account. That story shows that God's question could well be intended for the heavenly entourage, but no matter. Isaiah, perhaps emboldened

by his cleansed lips, blurts out his willingness to go (v. 8b).

Here is where the lectionary leaves off, where the chapter gets uncomfortable, but where it also becomes truly profound: the prophetic commission is to *failure*, at least by contemporary measures. Isaiah's task is not to win more repentances but to *prevent* all repentance (vv. 9–10). It is no wonder that he immediately regrets his offer to serve. Isaiah's "How long, O Lord" (v. 11a) is no polite inquiry about the duration of the mission but a lament, akin to similar statements in the Psalms, that begs for immediate cessation (Pss. 6:3; 74:10; 80:4; 82:2; 90:13; 94:3).

There can be no release from Isaiah's dread task; the work is too important. Isaiah's success will not be measured by fruit but by fidelity to God's word of judgment. The prophetic mission will not be complete until the land is devastated, until everyone and everything rests . . . in peace (vv. 11–12). Even the little that survives will be burned a second time, ensuring that the divine winnowing is comprehensive (v. 13a).

All that will be left, in the end, is a stump, but that stump will be the holy seed (v. 13b). It is the tiniest of things, the slenderest of hopes. Perhaps the recovery of that seed is what the judgment is all about. Those who know Scripture know that the tiniest of things can sometimes turn out to be the greatest (Matt. 13:31–32).

BRENT A. STRAWN

Commentary 2: Connecting the Reading with the World

In most Protestant traditions, as well as in the Roman Catholic Church, the Sundays following the feast of the Epiphany properly belong to Ordinary Time, rather than to an Epiphany season. Even so, many congregations treat these Sundays as a special season unto itself, with preaching and worship attending to such themes such as light, vision, theophany, revelation, and the church's mission to the whole world. Without the cultural and consumer pressures that congregants often feel during Advent and Christmas, the Sundays after Epiphany can

provide a welcome opportunity to consider in a more focused way the implications of divine incarnation and the invitation for human response. Many of the lectionary readings for these Sundays shine with Epiphany light; this text from Isaiah certainly does.

Considered liturgically, this reading not only reflects multiple Epiphany themes; it illuminates the meaning and character of our ongoing congregational worship. Like the congregants who listen to a sermon on this text, Isaiah has entered the place of worship. Was he expecting anything unusual to happen this time? Are we? The order of our own public worship typically mirrors the experience Isaiah had in the temple—praise, confession, forgiveness, response—but the connections between his experience and ours seem to end there. The room fills with smoke. The structures shake. Angels wing their way around the throne, calling out to each other, shouting, "Holy!" The border between heaven and earth dissolves. Isaiah is undone.

Every week we go to church, sing our hymns, lift our prayers, read our Bibles, offer our sermons. We move through the elements of worship—toward what end? We can manufacture neither the grandeur nor the intimacy that Isaiah encountered in the temple, yet his vision invites us to consider the invisible reality toward which all our hymns, prayers, and sermons point: the dazzling, devastating presence of a holy God.

Isaiah's experience of God's presence was shockingly direct. Our own personal and congregational experiences may feel less so, but the seraphs tell the truth: "the whole earth is full of [God's] glory." The Hebrew word for glory has at its root the concept of heaviness. It is as if God's character—beauty, truth, and goodness beyond our comprehension—is so substantial that it cannot be confined to a heavenly realm; the weight of it breaks through the veil. In fact, the declaration of the seraphs blurs the margin between heaven and earth: *all* of it is loaded with glory.

English poet Elizabeth Barrett Browning famously wrote, "Earth's crammed with heaven / and every common bush afire with God; / But only he who sees takes off his shoes, / The rest sit round it and pluck blackberries."[1] Priest and poet Gerard Manley Hopkins likewise proclaimed, "The world is charged with the grandeur of God."[2] While Victorian poets such as these two often articulated deeply spiritual understandings of the natural world, poets throughout the ages, like the prophet, have given voice to the breakthrough of God's glory in the world.

Contemporary poets, whether religious or not, could be put in fruitful conversation with Isaiah's vision of God's holiness. Mary Oliver and Wendell Berry offer particularly accessible avenues for exploring how the whole earth is full of God's glory. Indigenous poets Joy Harjo and emerging poet Lyla June Johnston help us to move beyond comfortable understandings of the sacred. "To pray you open your whole self / To sky, to earth, to sun," Joy Harjo writes.[3]

Like the poets, Isaiah challenges us to expand and clarify our own perception of the truth we proclaim. The fact that he caught his vision in the place of worship is instructive. If we are going to look for and find God's glory in the common bush, public worship is where we come to sharpen our eyesight. We come not to replicate or approximate Isaiah's reality-shattering experience (not that we could do so, even if we tried), but to renew our imagination, our expectation, and our perception. Perhaps our own experience of God is limited less by the border between heaven and earth than it is by the firm boundaries around our own imagination. Isaiah gives us a glimpse of the terrain beyond those boundaries.

Shaken by what he witnesses, Isaiah makes the only response he can: confession. True awareness of God's holiness draws us toward true awareness of our human horror: we have failed to live in harmony with that holiness. Perhaps all human failure has its origin in our inadequate awareness of the glory of God shimmering in every atom of the cosmos. If this is so, might it be true that attentiveness to manifestations of God's glory could lead us toward right relationship with God's sovereignty and God's good purposes in the world? Perhaps, but not without an acknowledgment of the truth: in humanity, God's gorgeous glory is distorted. It is also damaged in the natural world, to be sure, but only inasmuch as we humans have done the defiling. Seeing the glory, Isaiah cannot help but also see the distortion. As a prophet, he will

1. Elizabeth Barrett Browning, "86. From 'Aurora Leigh,'" in *The Oxford Book of English Mystical Verse*, ed. D. H. S. Nicholson and A. H. E. Lee (Oxford: Clarendon Press, 1917), http://bartleby.com/236/86.html.

2. Gerard Manley Hopkins, "God's Grandeur," in *Gerard Manley Hopkins: Poems and Prose*, ed. W. H. Gardner (London: Penguin Classics, 1985), 27.

3. Joy Harjo, "Eagle Poem," http://ohio.edu/people/hartleyg/poems/JH%20Poems.doc, accessed Jan. 5, 2017.

pronounce judgment against nations, but his first judgment is against himself.

Our modern sensibilities may shrink from the language of shame and self-judgment, but Isaiah's response actually invites us toward true liberation. Read in light of the vast array of social conflicts and ethical failures in the contemporary Western world, his frank assessment of culpability shows us our necessary starting point. In simple, straightforward language, he confesses sin on both the individual and systemic levels: "Woe is me! I am lost." Isaiah reminds us that transformation of systemic evil begins with admitting our own part in the mess. On a personal level too, our best hope of change starts here. The disruption and subversion of entrenched patterns of sin always depend on telling the truth, including our individual part in it.

As soon as Isaiah speaks his sin, it is destroyed. From a psychological perspective, we know how this works: when we name our shame, we take away some of its power to hurt us (or others). Theologically, Isaiah's story points to something more profound: God does not seek our guilt, but its obliteration. As old as Isaiah's story is, this core truth always seems fresh, a beautiful repudiation of our twisted understandings of God's nature. Our many stories about Catholic/Jewish/Baptist guilt demonstrate our deep, painful suspicion that God desires our shame and our punishment. Isaiah's experience in the temple dares us to see past such fears, to behold the radical reality that God's intention has never been our shame.

Now a voice calls out, and God's desire becomes plain: "Whom shall I send, and who will go?" The divine longing is for someone to speak God's word to the world. Has God been calling all along? Is Isaiah able to hear only after he has been freed from his own self-judgment? He is not called by name; he volunteers. Set free from sin and guilt, Isaiah shows us what freedom is for: for listening, for hearing the divine voice of longing for the world, and for responding. In freedom, we go into the world to seek and to serve God's glory, which is all around.

STACEY SIMPSON DUKE

Psalm 138

¹I give you thanks, O LORD, with my whole heart;
    before the gods I sing your praise;
²I bow down toward your holy temple
    and give thanks to your name for your steadfast love and your faithfulness;
    for you have exalted your name and your word
    above everything.
³On the day I called, you answered me,
    you increased my strength of soul.

⁴All the kings of the earth shall praise you, O LORD,
    for they have heard the words of your mouth.
⁵They shall sing of the ways of the LORD,
    for great is the glory of the LORD.
⁶For though the LORD is high, he regards the lowly;
    but the haughty he perceives from far away.

⁷Though I walk in the midst of trouble,
    you preserve me against the wrath of my enemies;
you stretch out your hand,
    and your right hand delivers me.
⁸The LORD will fulfill his purpose for me;
    your steadfast love, O LORD, endures forever.
    Do not forsake the work of your hands.

Connecting the Psalm with Scripture and Worship

Psalm 138 is generally regarded as a postexilic psalm of thanksgiving. While it is written in the voice of an individual, references to the heavenly court and earthly temple suggest communal worship. The psalm is distinct as a psalm of thanksgiving in that although the psalmist begins by giving thanks for God's faithfulness, love, and deliverance, she or he also concludes this section of the psalm with a prayer for God's ongoing presence and assistance; the idea of "trouble" (v. 7) persists, even in the midst of thanksgiving.[1] The imagery of the psalm, especially "all the kings of the earth shall praise you" (v. 4), points to a cosmopolitan worldview that is especially appropriate to the Epiphany season.

In the lectionary context, Psalm 138 is paired with the call narrative from the book of Isaiah. This is the second Sunday in a row that

has featured a call narrative. In contrast to the psalm of lament that is the response to Jeremiah's call, here we find a psalm of thanksgiving that attends both to the transcendence of God and to the experience of God's presence mediated through place and symbol. The prophetic readings and psalm responses can be seen to correspond to the Epiphany Gospels focusing on the early days of Jesus' public ministry. Thus, in the season of Epiphany, one theological emphasis might be on the call to witness the glory of God revealed to the nations through the incarnation.

The psalm highlights God's power and transcendence through reference to the "holy temple" (v. 2), which has been described at greater length in the first reading; Isaiah's vision provides context for the psalm. When the psalmist bows

---

1. J. Clinton McCann, "Psalms," in *New Interpreter's Bible* (Nashville: Abingdon Press, 1996), 4:1232.

down toward God's holy temple, the modern worshiper, hearing these readings in the liturgical context, can picture the heavenly court above the temple, filled with the praise of the seraphs, who with their six pairs of wings (Isa. 6:2) and voices that can shake the pivots on the thresholds (v. 4) are capable of inspiring human awe in their own right. What human would not, as the psalmist does, bow down (Ps. 138:2) toward the God whose voice is at the center of this image of the heavenly court? What human, the text from Isaiah seems to suggest, would not be moved to say, "Send me!" upon hearing God ask, "Whom shall I send, and who will go for us?" (Isa. 6:8). The psalm and prophetic reading together suggest the possibility of human participation in the heavenly liturgy: "before the gods I sing your praise" (Ps. 138:1).

This sense could be heightened through emphasis on the liturgical singing of the Sanctus and the connection that the psalm makes between Isaiah's vision and temple worship. Isaiah sees "the Lord sitting on a throne" and describes the temple seemingly at God's feet; "the hem of [God's] robe filled the temple" (Isa. 6:1). God's garment provides the point of connection between the earthly temple and the heavenly court. One can almost imagine reaching out to touch the hem of this garment, which is located in heaven and yet trails onto the earth in the "holy temple" (Ps. 138:2) toward which the psalmist turns. This sense of proximity is heightened by the psalmist's references to the hands (v. 7) of God, which are stretched out for deliverance in the midst of danger. The closing reference to the speaker as "the work of [God's] hands" (v. 8) emphasizes the sense of God's commitment to the individual from creation, through danger, to the fulfillment of God's purpose.

Christ Alone Is Lord of Salvation

Christ is now a king and reigneth, and hath received power of all that he prayed for to do it himself, and that whensoever the elect call for aught in his name he sendeth help even of the power which he hath received, yea, ere they ask, he sendeth his Spirit into their hearts to move them to ask: so that it is his gift that we desire aught in his name. And in all that we do or think well he preventeth us with his grace: yea, he sendeth to call us, and draweth us with such power that our hearts cannot but consent and come and the angels stand by and behold the testament of the elect, how we shall be received into their fellowship, and see all the grace that Christ shall pour out upon us. And they rejoice and praise God for his infinite mercy, and are glad and long for us, and of very love are ready against all help. . . .

Now if an angel should appear unto thee, what wouldest thou say unto him? If thou prayedst him to help, he would answer: I do. Christ hath sent me to help thee, and believe that the angels be ever about thee to help. If thou desiredst him to pray for thee, to obtain this or that, he would say: Christ hath prayed, and his prayer is heard for whatsoever thou askest in his name, and would shew thee all that God would do to thee and what he would also have thee to do: and if thou believest so, then wert thou safe. If thou desiredst him to save thee with his merits, he would answer that he had no merits, but that Christ only is Lord of all merits, nor salvation, but that Christ is Lord of salvation. Wilt thou therefore be saved by merit? Would the angel say, then pray to God in Christ's name, and thou shalt be saved by the merits of him. . . .

And if thou speak to Paul of his merits, he can none otherwise answer thee than he answered his Corinthians: That he died for no man's sins, and that no man was baptized in his name, to trust in his merits. He would say, I builded all men upon Christ's merits, preaching that all that repented and believed in his name should be saved and taken from under the wrath, vengeance and damnation of the law and put under mercy and grace. . . . If thou desire therefore to enjoy part of my merit, go and read in my gospel, and thou shalt find the fruit of my labour, the knowledge of Christ, the health of the soul and everlasting life.

William Tyndale (ca. 1494–1536), "An Exposition upon the First Epistle of St. John," in David Daniell, ed., *William Tyndale: Selected Writings* (New York: Routledge, 2003), 65–66.

In some ways, the psalm of thanksgiving seems an odd response to the desolate vision of empty cities and desolate lands (Isa. 6:11) with which the passage from Isaiah ends. In contrast to "this people," whose mind will be dulled, ears will be stopped, eyes will be shut (v. 10), Isaiah both sees and hears God. The clarity of Isaiah's heavenly vision will not be available to those to whom Isaiah is sent. The first reading ends on a note of desolation, with an apparent reference to the exile (v. 12) and only a small symbol of hope in the stump of the burned tree. The psalm's dual emphasis on thanksgiving as well as "trouble" and "the wrath of [one's] enemies" (Ps. 138:7) make it an especially appropriate response both to Isaiah's experience of exuberance in the presence of God and concern ("how long, O Lord," Isa. 6:11) in light of God's message of judgment.

In addition to this mirrored response, the psalm can also be seen to pick up on a worldview that reflects the experience of the exile. Isaiah's prediction of a time when "the LORD sends everyone far away" (Isa. 6:12) may be reflected in the experience of the psalmist, who is not in as close proximity to God as Isaiah experiences himself to be.[2]

In contrast to Isaiah, the psalmist does not even seem to be in the earthly temple, although she or he bows down "toward" it (v. 2). The speaker, however, does have a sense of the broader world, perhaps indicating an exilic or postexilic worldview. The cosmopolitan reference to the "kings of the earth" who shall sing and praise God (vv. 4–6) suggests consideration of a worldview beyond that of Israel and the Jerusalem temple. These foreign kings will respond (like Isaiah) to "the words of [God's] mouth" (v. 4). In terms of the liturgical season, these "kings" might point to the three magi, who come to represent worldwide recognition of the God of Israel. In relation to the Gospel, the disciples, like the psalmist, found both "trouble" and the presence of God when "they left everything and followed him" (Luke 5:11).

This psalm highlights the significance of communal worship, while acknowledging that a life of thanksgiving does not provide a solution to every problem. The epiphany context draws out the wider implications of God's presence among the nations of the world.

RHODORA E. BEATON

---

2. Konrad Schaefer, *Psalms*, Berit Olam: Studies in Hebrew Narrative and Poetry (Collegeville, MN: Liturgical Press, 2001), 323–25.

1 Corinthians 15:1–11

¹Now I would remind you, brothers and sisters, of the good news that I proclaimed to you, which you in turn received, in which also you stand, ²through which also you are being saved, if you hold firmly to the message that I proclaimed to you—unless you have come to believe in vain.

³For I handed on to you as of first importance what I in turn had received: that Christ died for our sins in accordance with the scriptures, ⁴and that he was buried, and that he was raised on the third day in accordance with the scriptures, ⁵and that he appeared to Cephas, then to the twelve. ⁶Then he appeared to more than five hundred brothers and sisters at one time, most of whom are still alive, though some have died. ⁷Then he appeared to James, then to all the apostles. ⁸Last of all, as to one untimely born, he appeared also to me. ⁹For I am the least of the apostles, unfit to be called an apostle, because I persecuted the church of God. ¹⁰But by the grace of God I am what I am, and his grace toward me has not been in vain. On the contrary, I worked harder than any of them—though it was not I, but the grace of God that is with me. ¹¹Whether then it was I or they, so we proclaim and so you have come to believe.

Creed

Commentary 1: Connecting the Reading with Scripture

At first it appears that 1 Corinthians 15 is tacked on to the letter, as if Paul is addressing a question or problem within the community, as he does in chapters 5–14. On closer examination one realizes that his treatment of the resurrection provides the theological foundation for what goes before. Not only is the gospel the power of God (1:17; 2:4) for salvation; it is the ground for Christian living in the present time (3:16; 6:13–14, 19–20) and future hope (1:8; 15:20–23). Without the resurrection the gospel loses its meaning and power.

In 15:1–11 Paul provides the necessary prologue to his discussion of the resurrection by establishing the credibility of his message and the genuineness of his apostleship. Both of these were instruments through which the Corinthians came to faith. "In Christ Jesus I became your father through the gospel" (4:15). Yet even as the Corinthians and outsiders question Paul's apostleship (1:12; 4:3), he points out that the validity of their own faith is at stake (15:2, 14). This comes through clearly in the *exordium* or introduction in 15:1–2:

The gospel that I proclaimed to you,
which you in turn *received,*
in which you also *stand,*
through which you *are being saved*
If you hold firmly to the message that I
proclaimed to you—
unless you have come to believe in vain.

The conditional clause at the end (if you hold firmly . . .) exhorts persistence in faith, but points to the possibility that faith may be purposeless or "in vain." Faith's value, meaning, and purpose are tied to the question of the resurrection, which he deals with in verses 12–19.

In verses 3–11 Paul lays out his case by reminding them of the basic tradition he passed on to them and on which their faith is based. He places himself within the chain of testimony to the risen Christ and reminds them of the basis of his apostleship. The tradition he cites is foundational for his later comments on the resurrection.

"Christ died for our sins in accordance with the scriptures" (v. 3). The forgiveness of sins connects not only to the cross (1:17–18,

23, 30; 2:2) and resurrection (15:17–18), but also to the apocalyptic expectation of final judgment (1:8; 3:13; 15:23–28). The prospect of facing God without a provision for forgiveness of sins was apparently unacceptable to the Corinthians. While Christ's death for sins may echo the Suffering Servant tradition in Isaiah 52:13–53:12 (scholars are divided on this), the reference to the Scriptures points to the earliest belief that Jesus' death had been foretold and hence was according to God's plan.

"He was buried" (v. 4). It is notable that this brief phrase was preserved in the tradition. It succinctly summarizes the fact of Jesus' death as a prelude to the resurrection and points to the first evidence of Jesus' resurrection, the empty tomb. It accompanies the affirmation that Christ was raised from the dead. Paul will return to this point later in verses 12–19 to counter the argument of the "some" (v. 12).

"He was raised on the third day in accordance with the scriptures" (v. 4). As the passive form of the verb indicates, Jesus did not raise himself but was raised by another. Paul consistently credits God as the one who raised Jesus, albeit in the power of the Spirit (1 Cor. 6:14; 15:15; 2 Cor. 4:14; Rom. 8:11; 10:9). As with Christ's death (v. 3), this was according to God's plan as laid out in the narrative of Scripture.

The third day should not be restricted to a single Old Testament passage, although some see an allusion to Psalm 16:9–11 (LXX) or Hosea 6:2. For Paul, the larger scriptural narrative provides the frame of reference for understanding the resurrection and Christ's work as a whole. Furthermore, the phrase "in accordance with the scriptures" is a subtle reminder that the Christ event is God's project and fulfills God's purposes as laid out in Scripture.

"He appeared to Cephas, then to the twelve" (v. 5). Testimony of credible witnesses was considered to be the most trustworthy evidence in the Jewish legal system. In verses 5–8 Paul gives a list of appearances of the risen Christ. These are intended to give evidence to the fact of Jesus' bodily resurrection. When he mentions that most of the five hundred are still alive (v. 6), he implies that they are available to bear witness to their experience.

While scholars have debated the nature of the appearances, whether they are subjective, internal visions or more objective, external ones, Wright correctly notes: "Experience of the Spirit and seeing the risen Jesus are never, in early Christian writings, assimilated to one another."[1] Interpreting the experiences as spiritual visions rather than sightings of the bodily resurrected Christ would seem to undercut the uniqueness of the witnesses' testimony. Anyone can have a spiritual vision, but not everyone has seen the bodily resurrected Christ. Experience and Scripture are the two bedrock evidences for the gospel.

"Last of all, as to one untimely born, he appeared also to me" (v. 8). Here Paul offers the most definitive defense of his apostleship, citing one of the most significant criteria for being an apostle, seeing the risen Christ. Placing himself last in the list of witnesses and recognizing that he had not accompanied Jesus during his earthly ministry, Paul describes himself as an "untimely born" apostle (the Greek term *ektrōma* may signify miscarriage or abortion). In spite of his previous behavior as persecutor of the church and the unlikely late appearance of the risen Christ to Paul, his apostleship is just as real and valid as that of other apostles.

Paul responded to God's grace of his birth (calling) as an apostle by working "harder than any of them [other apostles]," although it was grace that energized his efforts ("the grace of God that is with me," v. 10).

Paul rounds out his argument (v. 11) by pointing out that whether it was one of the other apostles (of which there are many) or he (who has been derided by some in Corinth, 4:3, 18; 9:1–3), the Corinthians came to faith through their proclamation. Their response to the gospel determines their standing before God, but they have received it from a trustworthy, apostolic source.

The lectionary readings in Isaiah 6:1–8 and

---

1. N. T. Wright, *The Resurrection of the Son of God* (Minneapolis: Fortress Press, 2003), 325.

Luke 5:1–11 are both call narratives. Paul's dramatic encounter with the risen Christ on the road to Damascus and Isaiah's vision of the Lord on the throne resonate strongly with one another. Isaiah the prophet answered the Lord's call, "Whom shall I send, and who will go for us?"; Paul became apostle to the Gentiles. Luke 5 gives the account of another apostolic call, as Jesus tells Simon Peter, "From now on you will be catching people" (Luke 5:10). In both Isaiah and Luke, personal encounter with God leads to missional engagement and is not an end in itself.

While the Bible is full of stories of people's experience of God that lead to faith and incorporation into a covenant community, Romans 10 offers a clear parallel to the thinking behind the process that moves from proclamation to faith to salvation. Paul mentions "the word of faith that we proclaim" (v. 8). The hearers are to confess with their lips Jesus' lordship and believe in their heart "that God raised him [Jesus] from the dead" (v. 9), resulting in salvation. He also includes the necessity of one being called and sent to proclaim the gospel (vv. 14–17).

MARK ABBOTT

Commentary 2: Connecting the Reading with the World

Here begins Paul's long explanation of the resurrection, both the past resurrection of Jesus and the future resurrection for which all humanity hopes. Paul is setting up a larger argument that is going to make claims on every part of us, body and soul. To offer resurrection hope, Paul first reminds us of the story of Jesus, and then he connects that story to his own life, inviting us to connect the story to our lives too. The most important connection in this text is that between Jesus and us. This is no disembodied, purely spiritual connection. Paul wants us to connect the flesh of Jesus Christ to our own flesh. The text takes the story of the risen Jesus and invites us to remember that it is our story, and so to live within that story.

The text meets us in the coldest darkness of the liturgical year and, for those of us who live in wintry climates, of the natural year as well. The dead of winter may be weighing on us in so many different senses. Ruthless cold and lack of light are at their most depressing. Work and school cycles are in their depths of drudgery, and vacations seem far away. The joys of Christmas and Epiphany are behind us, though the credit-card bills and tax bills may still loom large before us. For many, this is a brutal time, a time when it is all too easy to forget where we fit in the story of Jesus. We may feel as though this time of year, though we have only recently celebrated seeing God face to face, is a time when we are furthest from such a vision.

In this context, in the dead of literal and spiritual winters, Paul offers us hope, and he makes it clear that said hope rests firmly on Jesus and all that Jesus has already done. When we find ourselves inadequate, beaten down, and broken, it is a relief to remember that our hope is outside of us. Hope rests, not on our own persons, but on the person of Jesus, who has defeated all that would oppress us, including death itself, and so offers us new life for body and soul. The heart of this passage is the connection Paul makes between Jesus and us. He asks his readers to remember the basics of the Jesus story, and he focuses those basics on the resurrection. He connects that Jesus story to his own life. Though he is "last" and "least" of the apostles, the resurrected Christ is for him and for us. This grace comes to us in even in the darkest of times, and only this grace can carry us through. Only this grace is the basis for action.

Here the church finds the power of God, even in the darkest winters of our hearts and of our life together. The people of God are the people who tell the story of Jesus. When we are trudging through the sometimes bleak day to day, we need to repeat that story again and again. Here, Paul distills the story down to the risen flesh of Christ. We are the people who repeat the gospel story, "that Christ died for our sins in accordance with the scriptures, and that he was buried, and that he was raised on the third day in accordance with the scriptures, and that he appeared" (vv. 3–5). The story bears repetition. It is infinitely rich. Even those who have heard it hundreds of times need constant reminders of who Jesus is and what he has done.

Repetition of "in accordance with the scriptures" reminds us that we are the people who become who we are as we read and hear God's verbal revelation to us. That revelation is a blessed given. We do not have to create it. We do not have to strive for it. It just is, and we are asked to remember it, and we turn to it anew as we ask God to re-create us. The story of the risen Jesus is a story of grace. Though we may have trouble feeling that Christ is present in the darkness, the *givenness* of Jesus' story and the *givenness* of the Scriptures are nonetheless here and true. They are given for us, and they make us who we are. We do not have to produce ourselves as the people of God. We are the ones who are being produced by the story and by the flesh of Jesus who is risen from the dead.

After the repetition of "in accordance with the scriptures," we meet another repetition in Paul's accounting of those to whom the risen Jesus "appeared." Paul wants to remind us that the risen flesh of Jesus was made apparent, in the flesh, to other believers. Jesus "appeared to Cephas, then to the twelve. Then he appeared" (vv. 5–6) to many believers, then "to James, then to all the apostles" (v. 7). Last he appeared to Paul, who now recounts the Jesus story to us. Those resurrection appearances are to famous leaders, to be sure, but they are also to ordinary, unnamed believers. Paul notes their number ("more than five hundred," v. 6). The anonymity, the multitude, and the diversity of those believers asks us, by extension, to identify ourselves with them. When he reminds his audience that most of these believers were still alive, Paul invites that audience to connect themselves to those who saw the risen Jesus.

The text suggests that any of us might, at any moment, encounter one of these to whom Jesus appeared. It creates a chain of witnesses leading from those first-century sisters and brothers who encountered Jesus between his resurrection and ascension, to Paul and those with whom Paul shared the story of Jesus, through to us today. The resurrected Jesus of Nazareth showed himself in the flesh, to a chain of witnesses, and we are included in that chain. We are the next link in the chain of those created by the resurrection of Jesus, but we are not to be the last link in that chain. Though we do not see Jesus in the flesh, we are connected to this line of witnesses, to the fleshly eyes that saw him so, and we are called upon to join in this chain of witnesses to the resurrection and to offer the resurrection story to others who stand in need of its hope.

The text offers us hope for being such witnesses and hope for getting through our work, even when—maybe especially when—the days are short and the nights are long. The text asks us, like Paul and with Paul, to get to work, and at the same time it releases us from the strain of trying to produce that work by our own power and strength. Paul suggests that he has "worked harder" than any of us, but he is not asking us to grit our teeth and try to work like him. Instead, he is releasing us to work, as he did, only by "the grace of God." In the darkest winters of the heart, we need good work to do, but those winters are often when we are least able to produce such work. The text opens up the possibility of release. The work has already been produced. Christ has already been raised. Christ's solid flesh is the grace we need to put one foot in front of the other and so to press on, to press forward, to do what needs to be done.

BETH FELKER JONES

Luke 5:1–11

¹Once while Jesus was standing beside the lake of Gennesaret, and the crowd was pressing in on him to hear the word of God, ²he saw two boats there at the shore of the lake; the fishermen had gone out of them and were washing their nets. ³He got into one of the boats, the one belonging to Simon, and asked him to put out a little way from the shore. Then he sat down and taught the crowds from the boat. ⁴When he had finished speaking, he said to Simon, "Put out into the deep water and let down your nets for a catch." ⁵Simon answered, "Master, we have worked all night long but have caught nothing. Yet if you say so, I will let down the nets." ⁶When they had done this, they caught so many fish that their nets were beginning to break. ⁷So they signaled their partners in the other boat to come and help them. And they came and filled both boats, so that they began to sink. ⁸But when Simon Peter saw it, he fell down at Jesus' knees, saying, "Go away from me, Lord, for I am a sinful man!" ⁹For he and all who were with him were amazed at the catch of fish that they had taken; ¹⁰and so also were James and John, sons of Zebedee, who were partners with Simon. Then Jesus said to Simon, "Do not be afraid; from now on you will be catching people." ¹¹When they had brought their boats to shore, they left everything and followed him.

Commentary 1: Connecting the Reading with Scripture

This scene connects in several ways to Luke 4. There, Jesus declares his commitment to proclaim "the good news of the kingdom/empire of God" (4:43–44). Now he does so. The term "the kingdom/empire of God" connects back to the Isaiah vision of good news, release, and favor that Jesus read in the Nazareth synagogue in 4:18–19 in describing his anointing as God's agent. How does he enact this vision, and what does the kingdom/empire of God look like when Jesus manifests it? Luke 5:1–11 provides examples to further the healings and exorcisms of 4:31–44.

Jesus' first demonstration of the presence of God's kingdom/empire in 5:1–3 continues the emphasis on proclaiming good news in 4:43–44. Despite the statement in 4:44 that he did so in Judea, this scene is set in Galilee. From the sea of Gennesaret/Galilee, Jesus speaks "the word of God" to a crowd from a boat. As with 4:15, no content is stipulated, though the context of 4:18–19 and the reference to the kingdom/empire of God indicate the teaching's likely focus.

Verse 2 prepares for the subsequent encounter with Peter by depicting a fishing business comprising two fishing boats and fishermen washing their nets. This latter detail signifies that their futile nighttime fishing has ended. It provides the context for Jesus' surprising instruction to Peter in verse 4 to return to "the deep water" and to the group to "let down your nets" (the imperative is plural). Verse 3 introduces Simon/Peter as the owner-operator of the boat in which Jesus sits to teach the crowd, thereby preparing for the encounter between Peter and Jesus. It also foregrounds Peter as the first male disciple to be called (6:14), giving him a prominence that will continue through the Gospel as spokesperson for the disciples and close, though not always reliable, companion of Jesus.

Verses 4–10 are structured as a protracted call story. The Hebrew Bible lection features Isaiah's call narrative with typical elements: an epiphany or revelation of the Divine (Isa. 6:1–4), Isaiah's reaction of unworthiness (6:5), reassurance (6:7), commission (6:8–13), and obedience. The epistle reading follows the same form in referencing Paul's call: a divine epiphany in the form of resurrection appearances (1 Cor. 15:3–8), a response of unworthiness (15:8–9), reassurance (15:9–10), commission and obedience (15:9a, 11). In this passage, in a very different context, these first disciples experience an epiphany or revelation of the Divine (Luke 5:4–7), react with objections (5:5a) and unworthiness (5:8b), hear reassurance (5:10b), are commissioned (5:10b), and obey (5:11).

Verses 4–7 describe the revelation or epiphany to Peter of Jesus' identity as agent of God's reign. Jesus commands them to put out into the deep of the lake and let down their nets to catch fish. Since Jesus is the agent of God's purposes and of God's reign/empire of good news and favor (3:22; 4:3, 18–19, 43–44), these commands express God's rule over people and creation (the sea and fish). True to the form of a call story, Peter initially resists or, less strongly, wonders how the predicted catch of fish is possible when the night's efforts produced nothing (5:5a; similarly Mary wonders in 1:29, 34). Perhaps recalling Jesus' healing or release of his mother-in-law from a fever (4:38–39), Peter obeys, calling Jesus "Master" in recognizing his authority. Jesus' commands are efficacious, expressing his identity as a trustworthy, authoritative prophet. When obeyed, the commands yield a net-breaking, boat-sinking extravagant yield of fish (5:6–7).

Interpreters often see this abundant catch as anticipating the large numbers of disciples that Peter will subsequently "catch" when Jesus commissions him to catch people (5:10). However, at this point in the scene the abundance of the catch has a much different epiphanic function, namely, to manifest Jesus' identity as agent of God's reign.

Across the canon, God supplies food in situations of need. Moses (Exod. 16), Elijah (1 Kgs. 17:8–16), and Elisha (2 Kgs. 4:1–7, 42–44) provide ready examples. More significant are scenes that present abundant and extravagant food as a feature of the world created when God's rule is fully established. Isaiah 25:6–10a envisions God's rule as a feast "for all peoples, a feast of rich food, a feast of . . . well-aged wines strained clear." God removes "from all nations" death and tears and establishes God's awaited salvation. In Revelation's vision of God's re-created world, the tree of life produces "twelve kinds of fruit, producing its fruit each month; and the leaves of the tree are for the healing of the nations" (Rev. 22:2). In 2 Baruch, written around the time of Luke's Gospel, the new earth "will also yield fruits ten thousandfold. On one vine will be a thousand branches, and one branch will produce a thousand clusters, and one cluster will produce a thousand grapes" (2 Bar. 29:5). This renewed fertile earth "shoots out speedily" its products so that reapers and farmers never grow weary and no one goes hungry (2 Bar. 74). Subsequently in Luke, Jesus multiplies five loaves and two fish to feed more than five thousand people with a surplus of twelve baskets of broken pieces (Luke 9:10–17). Abundant food signifies the establishment of God's reign/empire.

The abundant catch of fish reveals God's rule/empire at work through Jesus' words of command. It is an epiphany, and Peter responds as do others in call narratives when they encounter God's reign and presence. Moses "hid his face, for he was afraid to look at God" (Exod. 3:5–6). Isaiah encountering God in the temple cries, "Woe is me! I am lost, for I am a man of unclean lips" (Isa. 6:5). Peter falls down before Jesus (as others do in the Gospel who seek or experience God's power manifested through him, 8:41; 17:16). Peter begs Jesus to leave him, and names himself "a sinful man" (5:8). The latter is not a moral confession of a sinful life; it expresses awe in the presence of a manifestation of Jesus' identity as agent of God's rule/empire. This response of awe is repeated in verses 9–10. Peter's amazement is shared by "all who were with him" (employees) and his business partners, James and John, who also become followers (6:14). A miraculous display of power produces insight into and commitment to God's working (also 5:25–26; 7:16).

Three features, typical of commissioning stories, close the scene. The first is reassurance (5:10b). The reassuring "fear not" is commonly spoken to people who encounter divine workings: Zechariah (1:13), Mary (1:30), shepherds (2:9–10), the girl's parents (8:50). The second is Jesus' commissioning of Peter to "catch people" (5:10c). The image evokes hunting and war, but here the purpose is not death but the good news of release in the service of God.

The third feature is obedient response (5:11). The language is now plural; at least Peter, James, and John follow Jesus, perhaps others also. "Following" can denote both physical movement and commitment to Jesus (5:27–28). In naming their leaving everything, the text suggests they abandon or divest possessions and family (also 18:18–24). Other scenes, though, present different practices with possessions: hospitality (4:38–39); celebration, despite leaving everything (5:27–29); redistribution to benefit those in need without repayment (6:34); maintaining possessions (7:10); supporting Jesus' mission (8:1–3; 9:1–6); giving alms and restoration (19:1–10).

This scene has used typical features of call/commission stories to depict the call of three male disciples. Luke's Gospel indicates that women disciples also followed Jesus *throughout his ministry* (8:1–3; 23:49). Though no woman is accorded a call/commission scene, we must make explicit the presence and contribution of women disciples, especially when the Gospel narratives render them invisible.

WARREN CARTER

Commentary 2: Connecting the Reading with the World

In today's Gospel passage Luke describes the calling of the first disciples. While the parallel accounts in Mark 1:16–20 and Matthew 4:8–22 are sparse and to the point, Luke's account is extended and includes details not found elsewhere. Luke begins the story with "once," leaving the reader unclear as to the chronology of the story in relation to the accounts that precede it. We can assume, however, that this act of calling comes early in Jesus' ministry, for the forming of a community of followers and learners is a core aspect of his ministry.

The setting is "the lake of Gennesaret," Luke's name for the Sea of Galilee. Similar to the Gospel readings for the previous two Sundays, Luke portrays Jesus as highly popular, gaining the attention of the crowds, who are "pressing in on him to hear the word of God." Fortunately, two fishing boats are nearby. Jesus gets into Simon's boat and asks him to put out "a little way from the shore." Simon's boat then serves as Jesus' pulpit. How fitting, then, that some pulpits have been designed in the shape of a ship's prow, and some architectural elements of churches borrow from nautical terminology, such as the "nave," which comes from the same root as "navy."

Jesus, seated in rabbinical style, teaches the crowd from the boat. We are not given the content of his message, probably because Luke's purpose is to focus on the drama that follows (we have previously seen Luke's interest in the dramatic, pivotal elements of Jesus' ministry).

After concluding his time of teaching, Jesus turns from the crowds to Simon and tells the experienced fisherman to "put out into the deep water." Simon, who has been fishing without results all night long and probably wants to go home, may well doubt that a rabbi has superior knowledge of fishing. However, Simon responds, ". . . if you say so." For Luke, this is evidence of the power of Jesus' persuasive, if disconcerting, presence.

The result is a great haul of fish—so great that they need help from another boat, and still all the fish nearly sink both boats. Simon, overwhelmed by an event far beyond his understanding, responds, "Go away from me, Lord, for I am a sinful man!" Simon is probably overwhelmed by the recognition that he is an ordinary, fallible person, while this Jesus is someone unique and extraordinary. Again, Luke wants the reader to know that the presence of Jesus is powerful—powerful enough to draw ordinary people to himself.

Jesus tells Simon, who is now joined by brothers James and John, "Do not be afraid," followed by the famous command, "from now on you will be catching people." Immediately, the fishermen "left everything and followed him"—another illustration of the compelling power of Jesus. Leaving it all behind is a recurring theme for Luke, as in the account of the rich young man (18:18–23) and in Jesus' saying that "any of you who does not give up everything he has cannot be my disciple" (14:33 JUB).

Preachers will recognize a number of meaningful connections.

1. Many listeners to a sermon on this text will connect with the theme of *call*: the question of what we are to do with our lives. As a seminary teacher, I am struck by the call stories of students, who often have left other careers or educational directions to respond to a sense that God is calling them to service, the forms of which are not always clear at the time. Note that in this case Jesus calls fishermen who have no prior educational background. They are common people, doing necessary jobs. John Calvin used this passage as an opportunity to make a case for theological preparation, suggesting that although Jesus called unlearned fishermen, he later called Paul, "who had been carefully educated from his childhood," to teach those previously called.[1] Calvin seems to see Paul as the "theology professor" who is called to educate the previously called disciples.

2. Other listeners will connect with the experience of the fishermen, who have been fishing all night, with nothing to show for it. Studies of American workers consistently show that the majority (around 70 percent) of workers are dissatisfied with the amount of stress they experience in the workplace. Economic uncertainty, job insecurity, and inadequate wages are prime sources of stress among workers and families; these fishermen were not exempt from such daily stresses. There are many who know the frustration of working hard and "not catching a thing."

3. Luke goes to great pains to describe the huge catch of fish the fishermen hauled in as a result of Jesus' words. As emphasized in the Gospel reflections two weeks ago, God's grace and blessings are often more than we expect, so much so that the blessings can surprise and even discomfit people!

4. Simon's response is to feel unworthy: "Go away from me, Lord, for I am a sinful man!" While this may be seen as the normative response to the powerful presence of Jesus, it may also speak to many people's response to the church as full of "religious" people with whom they would not fit in. Either the church is a hospital for imperfect sinners, or it is "the champagne toast of the spiritually proud." Many people experience it as the latter, but this text supports the former. Luke often stresses Jesus' ministry to the outsider and the sinner: "Those who are well have no need of a physician, but those who are sick" (5:31). Simon's reply to Jesus exhibits a paradox that Martin Luther would have recognized: those who see their need of grace are in the best position to find it.

5. Simon's sense of inadequacy is met by Jesus' message not to be afraid, followed by the gift of purpose: "from now on you will be catching people." This is, once again, similar to John 21, in which Jesus gives Simon Peter a threefold mission: "Feed my sheep . . . tend my lambs . . . feed my sheep." The interpreter of this passage would do well to link its two themes, "Do not be afraid" and "catching people." Obedience is described here as first casting off both goods and fear, after which the mission is given. Given Jesus' prior announcement of his mission, "to bring good news to the poor, . . . to proclaim release to the captives and recovery of sight to the blind, to let the oppressed go free, to proclaim the year of the Lord's favor" (4:18–19), being "fishers of people" is suggestive of gathering together and including such people.

6. Finally, the response of the fishermen is a willingness to "leave everything and follow." Is such radical obedience literally required of us today? Perhaps not. However we interpret it, only a strong sense of call and a robust sense of purpose can accept the necessary losses that commitment may cost. As Dietrich Bonhoeffer said, "Only he who believes is obedient, and only he who is obedient believes. . . . The first step of obedience makes Peter leave his nets, and later get out of the ship; it calls upon the young man to leave his riches. Only this new existence, created through obedience, can make faith possible."[2]

BLAIR R. MONIE

---

1. John Calvin, *Commentary on Luke* (Titus Books, Kindle ed.), Kindle locations 2651–57.
2. Dietrich Bonhoeffer, *The Cost of Discipleship* (New York: Touchstone, 1959), 63–64.

Sixth Sunday after the Epiphany

Jeremiah 17:5–10
Psalm 1

1 Corinthians 15:12–20
Luke 6:17–26

Jeremiah 17:5–10

⁵Thus says the LORD:
Cursed are those who trust in mere mortals
    and make mere flesh their strength,
    whose hearts turn away from the LORD.
⁶They shall be like a shrub in the desert,
    and shall not see when relief comes.
They shall live in the parched places of the wilderness,
    in an uninhabited salt land.

⁷Blessed are those who trust in the LORD,
    whose trust is the LORD.
⁸They shall be like a tree planted by water,
    sending out its roots by the stream.
It shall not fear when heat comes,
    and its leaves shall stay green;
in the year of drought it is not anxious,
    and it does not cease to bear fruit.

⁹ The heart is devious above all else;
    it is perverse—
    who can understand it?
¹⁰I the LORD test the mind
    and search the heart,
to give to all according to their ways,
    according to the fruit of their doings.

Commentary 1: Connecting the Reading with Scripture

This short collection of wisdom sayings is presented as a prophetic utterance ("Thus says the LORD"). It begins with two similes that contrast the cursed state of those who turn away from the Lord with the blessed state of those who trust in the Lord (vv. 5–8) and concludes with two declarations concerning the human heart (vv. 9–10). Another reference to the heart—the seat of intentions, motives, and decision making—occurs at the beginning of the passage (v. 5), thus prompting the reader to view the unit as a revelatory pronouncement on human personality and dispositions. The first two instances comprise a frame that strikes a decidedly negative tone, equating a wayward heart with trust in human strength (v. 5) and pronouncing the heart itself as devious and perverse (v. 9). In light of these associations, the declaration that the Lord tests the human heart and recompenses for its fruit concludes the passage on an ominous note.

The similes of the shrub (vv. 5–6) and the tree (vv. 7–8) make the point that one's condition results from what one chooses to trust. Those who put their trust in human beings and human power turn away from the Lord. Their cursed condition is compared to a solitary shrub, a spindly, fragile plant amid a landscape

239

of utter desolation and unrelenting thirst, isolation, and lifelessness. The contrasting blessedness of those who trust in the Lord takes the extreme in the opposite direction. This person is like a tree planted in a place where water is always available, enabling it to extend the roots that provide stability and nourishment, and so to produce luxuriant foliage and continuous fruit.

Two sayings (vv. 9–10) then move toward general pronouncements about the human heart, in the form of a declaration, a question, and a response. The declaration that the heart is deceitful in the Hebrew text puns on the name "Jacob" and so suggests the patriarch as an example. The question is rhetorical: "Who can understand it?" The Hebrew verb here translated "understand" encompasses the entire

sphere of knowing and so communicates both the scope and impossibility of the question. The Lord nevertheless responds with something of an answer (v. 10). The unusual first-person pronouncement, followed in the Hebrew text by participial verbal forms, not only identifies the Lord as one who inspects and examines, but also signifies that the Lord does so constantly. The mention of both the heart and its fruit indicates that the Lord's examining and recompensing process takes into account both the inner disposition and the outward act, both intention and deed.

The passages that precede and follow this unit suggest that Judah's disposition and deeds can be viewed as a particular example of the wisdom pronouncements that comprise the unit. The larger unit (17:1–18) opens with a

---

All Shall Be Well

Then our Lord took my mind back to the longing I had for him before. And I saw that nothing had held me back save sin; and I beheld the same thing in us all. And I thought that if it were not for sin, we should all have been clean and in our Lord's liking, as when he made us. And so it was that, in my folly, before this time I would often wonder why in God's great foresight and wisdom sin had not been forestalled in its beginning; for then, thought I, all should be well. These thoughts were hard to forsake and I turned them over endlessly with no proper reason or discretion until they made me mourn and sorry. But Jesus, who in this vision had informed me of all that I needed, answered with these words saying: "Sin is necessary, but all shall be well. All shall be well; and all manner of thing shall be well."

In this naked word "sin" our Lord brought to mind in general everything that is not good, and the shameful despising, the utter humiliation that he bore for us in this life, and his dying and the many pains that all his creatures also suffer, both in spirit and in body—for we all share in his humiliation, that way we follow our master Jesus until we are fully purged; that is to say, until we be fully rid of our mortal flesh and of all our inward affections which are not true and good. Such was my beholding, along with all the pains that ever were or ever shall be; yet compared to all these, I understood that the passion of Christ was the most pain by far. But all this was shown in a touch and then it swiftly passed over into comfort; our Lord never meant to terrify a soul with such an ugly sight.

But all this while, I never once saw sin. For I believe it has neither manner of substance nor part of being, and it would not even be known save for the pain it causes. Yet this pain is indeed something, as I see it for it purges and makes us know ourself as we ask for mercy, while the passion of our Lord comforts us against all this, all according to his blessed will. And our good Lord, with all the tender love he has for all those that shall be saved, comforts readily and sweetly, for thus is his meaning: "It is true that sin is the cause of all this pain, but all shall be well, and all shall be well, and all manner of thing shall be well." This was said so tenderly, without blame of any kind toward me or to anybody else. Therefore it would be a great unkindness to wonder or complain of sin to God, since he puts no blame on me.

Julian of Norwich (b. 1343), *Revelation of Love*, trans. John Skinner, chap. 27 (New York: Image/Doubleday, 1997), 47–48.

judgment oracle (vv. 1–4) that particularizes the heart condition that verses 5–10 generalize: "the sin of Judah is written with an iron pen . . . it is engraved on the tablet of their hearts" (17:1). The oracle indicts Judah for particular instances of turning aside, in the form of idolatrous worship and sacrifice, of trusting in human power in the form of "your wealth and all your treasures," and promises the Lord's recompense: "I will give for spoil as the price for your sin" (v. 3). The reference to the fire of the Lord's anger, furthermore, introduces an image that the second simile picks up: the tree by the water does not fear when the heat comes (v. 8). Judah in Jeremiah's time, in short, is presented as Exhibit A of the wayward crookedness that verses 5–10 ascribe to all humanity.

The proverb that follows the passage (v. 11) picks up the theme of wealth, retribution, and loss with a third simile concerning a partridge and hatchlings, thus redirecting the focus back to the historical particularity of the judgment oracle (vv. 1–4). A brief hymn then interjects a note of hope by acclaiming the sovereign Lord as the hope of Israel, before returning to a final elaboration of the shame and destiny of those who turn aside from and forsake the Lord (vv. 12–13; v. 5).

The hymn's concluding phrase, "they have forsaken the fountain of living water, the LORD," names the Lord as the source of the water that nourishes the blessed one of verses 7–8. This in turn elicits a response from the prophet, who evokes hope with a plea that the Lord heal and save him (v. 14). The rest of his prayer reiterates the motifs of verses 5–10 via personal testimony. Unlike devious Judah, Jeremiah declares that he has not run away. He recognizes that the Lord knows what comes out of his lips. He calls for recompense by asking the Lord to shelter him but destroy his enemies (vv. 15–18).

When set within the first main section of Jeremiah (1:1–25:38), a network of associations more tightly casts Judah as a particular manifestation of the universal wisdom revealed in verses 5–10. Judah's persistent turning away to worship other deities "under every green tree" (2:20, 27; 3:6, 13) stands in ironic counterpoint to the luxuriant tree associated with the trusting and blessed. Images of water and dryness signify the consequences of Judah's decision to trust in human power, most poignantly in Jeremiah's declaration that the people have forsaken the Lord, "the fountain of living water," and have dug cisterns that are cracked and cannot hold water (2:13).

The widespread and deep-seated deviousness of the human heart resonates in Jeremiah's pronouncement that "from the least to the greatest of them, everyone is greedy for unjust gain" (6:13) and therefore will bear "the fruit of their schemes" and their rejection of the Lord (6:19). The Lord refines and tests the people, whose tongue is deceitful, and recompenses them accordingly (9:7–9). The devastating outworking of retribution, in the destruction of Jerusalem and the exile of the nation, gives historical particularity to the picture of desolation that marks the accursed person who turns aside from the Lord (25:18).

As noted above, verses 5–10 transpose wisdom motifs into a prophetic idiom. The idea that one's situation in life is determined by one's choice to walk in one of two ways occupies a prominent place in wisdom thinking. The similes that illustrate the two ways in this passage have counterparts in Psalm 1. The psalm introduces the Psalter as a book of instruction for right living and orients right living to observation of the law. It focuses on conduct and its consequences, as opposed to trusting. In this case, foliage, water, trees, and fruit symbolize the benefits that come from following the law, whereas dryness, symbolized by chaff, signifies the emptiness of not following (as opposed to the dire fate of the accursed).

The other two lections draw out different aspects of the passage. First Corinthians 15:12–20 responds to the intransigent perversity of the human heart with the good news that Christ has been raised from the dead, freeing those who believe from the perverse waywardness of the heart and the curse and deathliness that humans bear as a result. In Luke 6:17–26 Jesus takes up the motifs of recompense and the contrasting states of blessedness and woe. In true prophetic fashion, he announces a reversal of affairs and status for those who enjoy the benefits of life and those who are deprived of those benefits.

L. DANIEL HAWK

Commentary 2: Connecting the Reading with the World

In the midst of Jeremiah's social and political situations, we find this short section which may be called Wisdom poetry. A stark contrast is set between those who trust themselves and whose hearts are turned away from God (v. 5) and those who "trust in the LORD" (v. 7). The result of a devious heart, set against God, is disaster (v. 6), while those whose trust is in God are like trees that bear fruit (v. 8). These blessings and woes remind us of portions of Old Testament wisdom sayings in which "two ways" are contrasted (Ps. 1) and the way of wisdom is to follow God and not one's own desires (e.g., Proverbs and Ecclesiastes).

Social and Ethical Context. The contrast between two potentials for trust—in "mere mortals" and "mere flesh," and trust in the Lord—is at the core of the human heart. From these two disparate ways of committing one's self emerge actions that on a large scale define social contexts and ethical actions of humans within cultures. That is, orienting ways of action spring from the commitments of the human heart: to ways of self-trust and self-reliance ("mortals"/"flesh") or to ways of God. Actions arise from interior desires that turn either to human strength or to the strength of God. As one Old Testament scholar put it: "The prophets hammer home the folly of dependence on human physical strength . . . 'flesh' then means transitoriness and moral corruption."[1]

As this passage indicates, God is concerned with the inner life and also with outward actions that express the inner heart: "I the LORD test the mind and search the heart, to give to all according to their ways, according to the fruit of their doings" (v. 10). Thus, the result of expressions of the heart, "fruit" of one kind or another, is what we can expect to see from this analysis of the question, whom do you trust—the "flesh" or God?

Examples of the social and ethical expressions of trusting in "mere mortals" and the "flesh" abound. In Jeremiah's time, a temptation was to trust in foreign powers to preserve the nation.

Militaristic might was a manifestation of trust in humans to fulfill desires for safety and peace. Entrusting one's self or a nation to the visible powers apparent in military muscle in an army that can be seen was an appealing alternative to trusting in the Lord, who cannot be seen and whose power is not so visibly apparent.

This same temptation to trust "the flesh" is with us today. Arms buildups, standing armies, aggressive military threats and actions—all these are powerful seducements toward trust. Nations rely on their military prowess, but these cannot ultimately bring the safety and security needed over time. A stronger military power can always emerge. Military "solutions" may appear viable for a time, but can be changed by other forces that impact them and lead into an intensifying spiral of further military escalations and brinkmanship.

Jeremiah was told that those who trust in mortals and make "the flesh" their strength will be like "a shrub in the desert, and shall not see when relief comes." They "live in the parched places of the wilderness, in an uninhabited salt land" (v. 6). In other words, there is no source of life and renewal that can move them beyond the limits of their situations. Like desert shrubs, no new life is possible. There is no water of renewal that can relieve their parchedness. When might feeds upon might, and the answer to weapons is more weapons—there is no breaking the cycle, no means of relief. The folly of trusting human power and force is exposed. No good fruit results from a devious and perverse heart that trusts in presumed human strength.

By contrast, trust in the Lord leads to blessedness (v. 7). A tree planted in the soil of trust is planted "by the water." It sends out its "roots by the stream" so "it shall not fear when heat comes, and its leaves shall stay green." When drought comes, "it is not anxious, and it does not cease to bear fruit" (v. 8). Trusting in the Lord means a renewing source of nourishment is always available. Even in the midst of the drought—when all else seems hopeless and a tree in itself may appear helpless—its roots

---

1. Christoph Barth, *God with Us: A Theological Introduction to the Old Testament*, ed. Geoffrey W. Bromiley (Grand Rapids: Eerdmans, 1991), 21.

receive needed nurture from the stream that gives life to the tree. The "invisible" resources sustain, even when, to all outward appearances, disaster seems imminent. The "leaves shall stay green"; the actions of the human heart that trusts in God will continue vitally, in ways pleasing to God, because the heart trusts in the living Lord. Social and ethical actions—even when the just and right seem endangered by surrounding evils—continue because they are nourished by the life-giving God who ensures that this trusting heart "does not cease to bear fruit" (v. 8).

Personal Context. Jesus made it plain that "you will know them by their fruits" (Matt. 7:20; cf. 7:16). Our outward actions express our inner heart. In Jeremiah's Wisdom poetry, the great difference between trust in mortals (including ourselves) and trust in God is shown in all humanity, according to the biblical witness. Humans are sinners, turned against God's will and purposes, loving self rather than loving God and neighbors. This is the biblical portrait from the opening chapters of Genesis through the testimony of the prophets, of Jesus, and of the New Testament writers (e.g., Rom. 2:5; Eph. 4:18). As Jeremiah put it: "The heart is devious above all else; it is perverse" (v. 9). The heart is the seat of sin, which leads to trusting in the wrong things: "mere mortals" and "mere flesh" (v. 5).

The counter to this is "those who trust in the Lord," whose hearts are directed to God instead of self. Through the biblical witness, God's work with God's people is giving them a "new heart," as promised to the prophet Ezekiel: "A new heart I will give you, and a new spirit I will put within you" (Ezek. 36:26; cf. 18:31). This work of God is focused in establishing new orientations, new loves, new loyalties, and new affections—now directed to God through Jesus Christ. By the work of God's Holy Spirit, Jesus Christ is known and confessed as the savior from sin (Gal. 2:16). One is "born from above" (John 3:3), reconciled to God (Rom. 5:10), and "alive to God in Christ Jesus" (Rom. 6:11) with a "new life of the Spirit" (Rom. 7:6). This is, in short, a "new creation" (2 Cor. 5:17).

Only God's power can overcome a "devious" and "perverse" heart (v. 9). God does this by the radical transformation of a human being. Self-love and trust in "mortals" and "the flesh" is replaced by "trust in the Lord" (v. 7). Trust is faith. Trust is enacted faith, a faith directed toward its object, God in Christ. Faith is the trust that responds to Jesus' command: "Follow me" (Mark 1:17). Faith is the trust to love others. Faith is the trust to continue living as God desires and as Jesus showed us, even "when heat comes" and "in the year of drought" (v. 8). Faith enables us to "trust in the Lord with all your heart" (Prov. 3:5).

DONALD K. McKIM

Psalm 1

[1]Happy are those
   who do not follow the advice of the wicked,
or take the path that sinners tread,
   or sit in the seat of scoffers;
[2]but their delight is in the law of the LORD,
   and on his law they meditate day and night.
[3]They are like trees
   planted by streams of water,
which yield their fruit in its season,
   and their leaves do not wither.
In all that they do, they prosper.

[4]The wicked are not so,
   but are like chaff that the wind drives away.
[5]Therefore the wicked will not stand in the judgment,
   nor sinners in the congregation of the righteous;
[6]for the LORD watches over the way of the righteous,
   but the way of the wicked will perish.

Connecting the Psalm with Scripture and Worship

The first psalm in the Psalter can be seen as a kind of prologue that both sets the tone for all that is to follow and makes a connection to the Wisdom literature with which the Psalms are grouped in the canon. Thus the entire Psalter begins with the word "happy" or "blessed."[1] The psalm presents human happiness and flourishing as choices in keeping with God's intentions, and issues of happiness or blessing do indeed follow in the remaining 149 psalms. At times, the psalmist praises God and gives thanks for the happiness that life has brought. At other times, as in the laments, the psalmist questions God regarding the loss of happiness amid the difficulties of life.

While Psalm 1 presents the matter of happiness as a straightforward choice for God and against the "wicked," the remaining psalms demonstrate that the path to happiness is not as clear-cut as one might hope; injustice, cruelty, and abandonment can stand in the way. As the first reading from Jeremiah suggests, sometimes even the human heart can become a source of unhappiness: "the heart is devious above all else; it is perverse—who can understand it?" (v. 9). This complex reality, presented throughout the Psalter, leads to questions about how happiness can be understood, perhaps pointing to the idea that it should continuously be sought, even in the midst of difficulty. The Gospel reading for today picks up on this question, as Jesus preaches in the Beatitudes an inverted understanding of happiness and blessing.

Psalm 1 is classified as a Wisdom or Torah psalm. It makes reference to the "law" of the Lord, which may be a direct reference to the Torah, or may, as many scholars suggest, be understood as the divine law more broadly.[2] As with much of the Wisdom literature, Psalm 1 offers a worldview that suggests happiness and prosperity are to be found through prayer, meditation, and the law of the Lord. Such a life

---

1. J. Clinton McCann, "Psalms," in *New Interpreter's Bible* (Nashville: Abingdon Press, 1996), 4:960.
2. Konrad Schaefer, *Psalms,* Berit Olam: Studies in Hebrew Narrative and Poetry (Collegeville, MN: Liturgical Press, 2001), 3–8.

will lead to stability and protection. Those who "delight in the law of the Lord" (v. 2) will leave a strong legacy for their families and loved ones. Like a tree that produces fruit for many seasons, their names will endure. In contrast, those who are wicked will lack stability and be blown away like the chaff, or waste (v. 4) from the threshing floor; they will be forgotten by history, since the deeds of the wicked have no power in the face of the "law of the Lord" (v. 2). The "two paths" motif is common in the Wisdom literature, as is the idea that those who follow the way of God will be sustained by God. It may be important to remember that the book of Job, also classified as Wisdom literature, calls this worldview into question.

As a response to the first reading from the book of Jeremiah, Psalm 1 can be seen as an inverted echo of the prophetic vision. Speaking the word of the Lord, Jeremiah first offers a desolate vision of a shrub withered and parched in the desert. The vision represents those who are cursed, who "trust in mere mortals" and in their own strength (Jer. 17:5). In contrast to this parched shrub is the image of a tree, representing those who trust in the Lord, which is echoed in Psalm 1. God's action is implied here, as those who trust in themselves are left parched in the desert of their self-sufficiency, while those who trust in the Lord are brought to the nourishment that they need. The text from Jeremiah suggests the possibility of change in the Hebrew word that might better be translated as "*trans*planted."[3]

Given this imagery, the context of the liturgical season is important. Since Epiphany is traditionally associated with baptism, the water images in these two readings have particular significance. In the Christian context, those who "trust in the Lord" (Jer. 17:7) or whose "delight is in the law of the Lord" (Ps. 1:2) may be seen

as strong trees growing up around the font of baptism. In the Lenten season, the desert imagery might signify testing or strengthening, but here dry husks and salt land are presented in negative terms associated with idolatry. The text from Jeremiah suggests that "trust" in the Lord is foundational. The psalm elucidates the fruits of this trust in study and meditation. In both cases, the choice should be clear to the one who is wise. The repeated image of the trees planted by water is an enduring one.

While the psalm and the first reading seem to pair well together, the Gospel text presents a more complicated worldview, perhaps pointing us toward that other "tree," the cross. Here those who are described as blessed, those who trust in God, do not seem to flourish according to the standards of the world. Instead, Jesus promises "your reward is great in heaven" (Luke 6:23). Here we find a different sort of eschatology, one in which trust and worldly flourishing are not neatly aligned, but one in which poverty, hunger, persecution, and sorrow are acknowledged. This acknowledgment can point us back to the Psalter as a whole, which adds depth to the seemingly simple choices presented in Psalm 1. Subsequent psalms of lament almost revel in the suffering that the speaker has endured, building the sorrow only to come back to the expression of trust. In the Beatitudes, Jesus offers a similar message, encouraging his listeners to trust in God's presence with them, both in the difficulties of life and in the promise of the future.

This psalm introduces the theme of happiness or blessing in life, echoing the powerful image from Jeremiah of trees planted by water. Liturgically this can be linked to Christian baptisms, which have historically been associated with Epiphany.

RHODORA E. BEATON

---

3. Patrick D. Miller, "Jeremiah," in *New Interpreter's Bible* (Nashville: Abingdon Press, 1996), 6:708.

1 Corinthians 15:12–20

¹²Now if Christ is proclaimed as raised from the dead, how can some of you say there is no resurrection of the dead? ¹³If there is no resurrection of the dead, then Christ has not been raised; ¹⁴and if Christ has not been raised, then our proclamation has been in vain and your faith has been in vain. ¹⁵We are even found to be misrepresenting God, because we testified of God that he raised Christ—whom he did not raise if it is true that the dead are not raised. ¹⁶For if the dead are not raised, then Christ has not been raised. ¹⁷If Christ has not been raised, your faith is futile and you are still in your sins. ¹⁸Then those also who have died in Christ have perished. ¹⁹If for this life only we have hoped in Christ, we are of all people most to be pitied.

²⁰But in fact Christ has been raised from the dead, the first fruits of those who have died.

Commentary 1: Connecting the Reading with Scripture

After Paul's prologue to the theme of the resurrection in 15:1–11, in which he establishes the credibility of his message and the genuineness of his apostleship, he takes on the core issue that puts Christian faith at risk. He addresses a small but influential group, "some of you," who believe there is no resurrection of the dead.

Scholars differ as to the specific beliefs this group may have held regarding the dead and what may happen afterwards, since Paul does not specify it. Certainly the Corinthians had filtered the Christian narrative through their pagan beliefs, but these were not uniform.

The four most common options for what the "some" believed are these: (1) Denial of any life after death. This option seems unlikely, since in 15:17–19, 32–34 he seems to argue against this. There seems to be an implicit belief in some existence after death. (2) Belief that the resurrection had in some sense already happened. Second Timothy 2:18 refers to some who believe the resurrection has already happened. Such proto-gnostic ideas certainly deny any bodily character of the resurrection. (3) Denial of the bodily character of the resurrection. From a pagan point of view, resurrection would probably be understood as the resuscitation of a corpse. This would help explain Paul's lengthy explanation of the nature of the resurrected body (15:35–54).

Belief in the immortality of the soul would also fit this category. (4) Due to the mixed sociological makeup (and possible variety of philosophical backgrounds) of the Corinthian community, Paul may have been facing a variety of different understandings.

Option 3 seems to be the most likely. There is general agreement that Paul's apocalyptic eschatology in general and his view of the resurrection in particular basically follow the contours of Pharisaic Judaism, modified by his Christology. He responds to paganism and to the Corinthians' confused understanding from this foundation.

Paul proceeds to point out the absurd and costly conclusion to their line of logic. If the premise that the dead are not raised is true, then it follows (15:13–19):

- "Christ has not been raised." Paul's (and all the apostles') proclamation has been "in vain" (*kenos*: worthless, foolish), and as a consequence,
- "Your faith has been in vain." Paul (and all the apostles) have misrepresented God because they proclaimed that God raised Christ; the Corinthian believer's faith is useless or worthless.
- "You are still in your sins." Those who

died as believers in Christ have perished and have no hope of life after death. Putting trust in Christ only for the present life makes believers pitiful people.

The Corinthians did respond to Paul's proclamation of the gospel and put their faith in Christ. If the premise of the "some" is true, then the bad joke is on the Corinthians, because they have allowed themselves to be taken for fools. For those who think they are "wise" (3:18), this would be particularly painful.

Verse 19 gives a clue to the connection Paul sees between the Christian's future hope and present life. Paul does not see value in trusting in Christ without the hope of resurrection. This implies not only that present Christian existence is sustained by the resurrection hope, but that the vision of new life with God becomes the ground for present living. Just as the future vision shapes our present living, so what we do in our bodily existence now matters for our future (1 Cor. 6:12–20). The gift of the Spirit is the power and presence connecting the present and the future (1 Cor. 3:16; 6:11, 17, 19; 12:13).

Paul ends his rebuttal of the absurd denial of the resurrection with a positive statement of his thesis: *"But in fact Christ has been raised from the dead, the first fruits of those who have died"* (v. 20). This is a prelude to a prolonged discussion of the implications of this truth (vv. 21ff.).

Christ raised as the firstfruits not only gives hope of the future harvest but refers to the order of things. In Jewish apocalyptic eschatology, the resurrection of the dead would occur on the Day of the Lord, the day of judgment, but the gospel proclaims that God raised Christ first as a guarantee of the future resurrection. This was totally new in Judaism, the raising of the Messiah in anticipation of raising those who belong to him.

With this affirmation in verse 20, Paul turns the vanity or worthlessness of his proclamation and of their faith into acts of supreme worth. Christ's resurrection assures the basis of the forgiveness of their sins (resurrection as a vindication of the crucified Christ) and their future hope of life with God after death. By implication Paul also confirms the legitimacy of his

calling (15:7–11; 1:1) and the value of his suffering as an apostle (4:10–15; 9:1–18).

The lectionary reading in Jeremiah 17:5–10 contrasts the one who trusts in "mere mortals" (v. 5) with those who trust in the Lord (v. 7). The object of one's faith and trust matters. The mortals in Jeremiah sound like those who trust in human wisdom in 1 Corinthians (1:17, 26–29; 2:1). The faith elicited by the gospel is placed in the God who raised Jesus from the dead. Faith in mere mortals produces barren shrubs with no recourse in a dry desert with poisoned salty land, whereas trust in the Lord leads to resources in the midst of the desert, so that the plant produces fruit even in drought. Faith in Christ is not worthless or empty, because the object of that trust is the God who raised Christ from the dead.

In Jesus' Sermon on the Plain in Luke 6:17–26, people come to Jesus "to hear him and to be healed of their diseases," and to be cured of unclean spirits (v. 18). For those who trust and become his disciples, Jesus proclaims the blessings of God's kingdom. Jesus' ministry proclaims and manifests God's kingdom. His deeds and teachings serve as signs to elicit trust in future blessings, on the one hand, and as a call to a life true to God's character as revealed in Jesus, on the other. The anticipated inbreaking of God's kingdom with Jesus' coming inspires lives that point to the future consummation. God's kingdom comes with Jesus, but is not consummated. In a similar way, Christ's resurrection manifests transformed humanity, but the resurrection of those in Christ is still in the future.

Paul rightly identifies God's raising Christ from the dead (and implicitly his life and death) as a nonnegotiable foundation for faith and life. Simply put, our new life in Christ is grounded in the resurrection. As his discussion of the first and second Adam (vv. 21–22) indicates, resurrection is tied to God as creator and to God's plan to renew both creation (Rom. 8:19–23) and humanity (2 Cor. 5:17). Sin and death threaten to frustrate God's creative purpose. Death is an enemy to be destroyed, not a condition to be cured. God's redeeming grace manifested in the incarnation enables redemption, new creation, and the fulfillment of God's creative purpose. Christ's resurrection as a first-fruit gives us the horizon of our destiny. This new horizon provides the navigation coordinate for our present existence. The gift of the Spirit brings the future into the present as both reality and future promise. God's presence and power in the Spirit enable us to stay on course, to be the new humanity in Christ.

MARK ABBOTT

Commentary 2: Connecting the Reading with the World

The passage connects the first Easter Sunday to every Sunday that comes after. It connects the past resurrection of Jesus Christ to God's future purposes for all of humanity, and it connects Jesus' resurrection to the general resurrection. Paul insists that the connection between Jesus and us is so intimate, so deep, and so real that his resurrection guarantees our future hope. Jesus' body is linked to our bodies in such a way that the end of Jesus' body is the end of our bodies too, and this end is not an ending but a *telos*: a purposeful life in which human beings glorify God with our bodies (1 Cor. 6:20). Because of Jesus, "the dead" have hope. Because of Jesus, the dead will be raised. Because of Jesus, the dead have a future, and it is an embodied future. Resurrection, by its very nature, makes claims on our bodies. Paul's "the dead" here means all of us, both our loved ones who have died and we who, though still living, are mortal and bound to die.

Contemporary North American culture might be read as a culture obsessed with the limits of mortality. Vampire stories and zombie apocalypses seem to dominate the cultural imagination, and sci-fi quests for everlasting life continue to capture our attention. We have longer life spans than any group of people in human history, but we try desperately to insulate ourselves from death. Still, we remain mortal, and we are fascinated with the limits of human life. Death is the universal human horror that we try to defeat, but despite our medical advances and safety precautions, that horror remains ever before us. The text speaks into that horror. It offers God's promise that *the enemy we cannot defeat has nonetheless been defeated by God in Jesus Christ*. We will die, but Jesus has been raised from the dead, and his resurrection is the pattern for and the guarantee of our resurrection.

The church's ministry to the dying has always been central to our work as the people of God, and this text reminds us that the ministry to the dying is really a ministry to every human being. We are more aware of our calling to this ministry when death is imminent—when, for instance, a member of our congregation goes into hospice care or gets in a serious accident. The text asks us to be more aware, all the time, of the fact that we—and all those to whom we minister—are dying. Interpretation of the text might recall the church to the ministry of comfort to and hope for the dying. The source of our comfort and hope is not medical, humanist, or technological; it is christological.

Christological hope is, by the text's definition, resurrection hope. The resurrection of Jesus involves his whole person, body and soul, and Paul's promised resurrection for all of us who are "the dead" is for divine redemption and transformation of us as whole persons, body and soul in union. This is surprising, for there are other kinds of possible hope. In the ancient context, gnostic hope was a menacing alternative to resurrection hope. Gnosticism presumed a hierarchical dualism, which set body against soul and the material world against the spiritual world, and so Gnosticism hoped for release from the body or the destruction of the body. Gnosticism hoped for escape from this world and this flesh. Resurrection hope is for the redemption of this world and this flesh.

Interpretation of this text might consider ways in which new forms of Gnosticism are prevalent in contemporary Western culture. Our new Gnosticisms have been stripped of the metaphysical and religious baggage of the ancient forms, but they retain and perhaps even heighten the hierarchical dualism that despises bodies and material creation. Even while we discipline our bodies at the gym, we assume that the true person is spiritual and not physical. We talk about the real self as an interior, not a physical, reality. We rebel against embodiment or strain against the limits of physicality and material finitude. We long to escape our bodies and the problems in this world, instead of hoping and working toward God's redemption of our bodies and this world. When we treat our bodies as prisons or problems, instead of treating them as good gifts from God that are being redeemed, we embrace a hope that is *not* the hope of this text. Not all hope is resurrection hope; Paul rejects those other possibilities as false hopes.

Because the resurrected Jesus is the "first fruits of those who have died" (v. 20), we are invited to make connections between Jesus and us. We expect the hope we have seen embodied in the resurrection of Jesus to reveal something about the shape of our hope, the shape of hope for "the dead." Interpretation of this text then will be helped by considering it alongside those texts that recount Jesus' resurrection appearances and imagining how those appearances might shape our hope. In Jesus' resurrection, we see him appear as the *same* man he was before his death, and we also see him *transformed*. He is the same, since he is resurrected in the same body. The tomb is empty. The marks of his crucifixion are visible in his flesh. He eats fish. He is the same in that he carries on the work and relationships that were his before he died. However, he is also transformed, so that sometimes people recognize him and sometimes they do not. He passes through locked doors. He is transformed, as his flesh is now victorious over death.

Paul's identification of this sameness and transformation as the pattern for our hope invites us to consider ways that God is redeeming us and will finally redeem us. We have seen that redemption in Jesus' flesh, and we can expect our redemption to leave us in some ways the same and in some ways transformed. Redemption does not erase us or destroy us. We, the people being redeemed by God, are the same people we were when God began to work in our lives. We are the same, body and soul, and God loves and cares for us, body and soul, even as we are being made new.

There is comfort here for those who have been told they are worthless, for those who have believed they are beyond redemption. God does not want to destroy us. God wants to redeem us. At the same time, we need transformation. There is comfort here for "the dead," for all of us who groan against our mortality, for that very mortality is being transformed and overcome. There is comfort here for all of us who long for change, who battle some habit or pain that seems intransigent. No hurt is intractable before the God of resurrection, who has worked, is working, and will work dramatic transformation in human lives.

The text invites reflection on God's work in our lives. It invites reflection on those aspects of our lives that have stayed the same and those that God has transformed, and it invites reflection on that which still needs to be transformed. It invites hope and trust in the God who is able to work transformation. It invites us to understand the intimate and redemptive connection between Jesus and us. It invites us to see that what has been done in the flesh of the resurrection can be done and is being done in our own flesh.

BETH FELKER JONES

Luke 6:17–26

¹⁷He came down with them and stood on a level place, with a great crowd of his disciples and a great multitude of people from all Judea, Jerusalem, and the coast of Tyre and Sidon. ¹⁸They had come to hear him and to be healed of their diseases; and those who were troubled with unclean spirits were cured. ¹⁹And all in the crowd were trying to touch him, for power came out from him and healed all of them.

²⁰Then he looked up at his disciples and said:

"Blessed are you who are poor,
    for yours is the kingdom of God.
²¹"Blessed are you who are hungry now,
    for you will be filled.
"Blessed are you who weep now,
    for you will laugh.

²²"Blessed are you when people hate you, and when they exclude you, revile you, and defame you on account of the Son of Man. ²³Rejoice in that day and leap for joy, for surely your reward is great in heaven; for that is what their ancestors did to the prophets.

²⁴"But woe to you who are rich,
    for you have received your consolation.
²⁵"Woe to you who are full now,
    for you will be hungry.
"Woe to you who are laughing now,
    for you will mourn and weep.

²⁶"Woe to you when all speak well of you, for that is what their ancestors did to the false prophets."

Commentary 1: Connecting the Reading with Scripture

In this passage, Jesus begins his Sermon on the Plain, so called because of its location on a flat spot or plain and because of a good bit of shared content with Matthew's Sermon on the Mount. These blessings differ from Matthew's—both in number (Matthew has nine, Luke has six) and in content (e.g., "poor" in Luke vs. "poor in spirit" in Matthew). Luke also includes "woes" that Matthew does not have. This is consistent with the sharpness of Luke's Gospel, more urgent in judgment than Matthew's version. What sound like statements of wisdom in Matthew resonate as cautionary statements in Luke. This is heard in the parallel oppositions of blessings and woes, which recall the same kinds of distinctions made by the Hebrew prophets. The lectionary emphasizes this as it places Jeremiah's cautionary words alongside those of Luke's Jesus. The truthfulness of the prophetic claims is weighed not only by verification in history, but also by self-application, moral clarity, and the way in which it creates a community of obedience out of a collection of individual hearers.

The rhetorical appeal is to *ethos*, to the character of the one making the claim and the righteousness of the world the blessing imagines (where the hungry of this world are fed and the satisfied of this world are found wanting, and so reality is set right). Woe to you if the paradoxical truth of this blessing does not change your way of life! So this is a statement not only about the way things are, but also about how disciples are to live.

Sociohistorical Context. Regarding socioeconomic class, Luke–Acts features well-to-do supporters of Jesus' and Paul's ministries (Luke 8:1–3; Acts 16:14; 17:4) right alongside the needs of the poor among the Jerusalem converts, to whom the early believers distributed goods according to their needs (Acts 2:42–47). Jesus' family was poor in Luke 1 (Mary's Magnificat) and Luke 2 (the sacrifice of the turtledove indicates humble estate). The first Lukan beatitude is the first time the class of Jesus' followers is mentioned.

Immediate Context. In Luke 6:13–16, Jesus ascends a hill to pray, then selects the twelve who will form his inner circle. These are differentiated from the throngs of disciples by the term "apostle." Thus, when the narrator has Jesus come down with the twelve into a great throng of "disciples," the reader is not confused. This connects to Matthew, who also sees concentric circles of followers, in that case "disciples" and "crowds."

Jesus descends the hill with his newly named apostles to this great throng who have come from the regions of Jerusalem, Judea, Tyre, and Sidon. In fact, this crowd is the lion's share of the population of those regions. Luke takes this expansive description of Jesus' followers from Mark 3:7–9 and economizes. This throng has come "to hear him and to be healed of their diseases." For his part, Jesus responds in the opposite order: he heals first, then teaches. This is suggestive for the preacher. We may not know the order of our needs, but Jesus does.

Power "came out of Jesus" (6:19), so crowds clambered to touch him. Other references to this sort of power include the hemorrhaging woman in Mark, who sneaks up to touch Jesus' garment with the same expectation of healing (5:24–34), a scene that Luke picks up in 8:45–46, and in Acts, when Peter's shadow (5:15) and Paul's handkerchiefs (19:12) heal people.

Rarely do the Gospels report a comprehensive healing, but here Jesus "healed all of them."

It seems unclear whether this refers to all who came forward or all who were able to touch him, but the sense of an expansive ministry and a significant healing event is unequivocal. Modern Western culture tends to individualize healing; so a connection here to shared experience is worth noting. Jesus' healing is communal event.

The narrator hints at this complex connection by having Jesus include a second-person-plural pronoun with each declaration to this great crowd: *yours* is the kingdom of God, *you* will be filled, *you* will laugh (rather than *theirs*, as in Matt. 5). The woes, similarly, are spoken to *you* who are rich, *you* who feast now, *you* who laugh now, and *you* who are well regarded. This shows Luke's direct style again. The crowd includes both the blessed and the cursed, the poor and the rich. What that says about the composition of the audience for this Gospel is unclear, except that it is also complex and plural.

The Blessings and Woes. Having blessed the crowds by healing the diseased and those who have been cursed (by evil spirits), Jesus now clarifies who is blessed and who is woeful. Each of these declarations surprises normal expectations, turning them on their heads.

In making this shift, there is a change in how Jesus is depicted. The crowd sees him as a miracle worker, from whom they seek personal benefit as well as teaching. When he begins teaching, however, Luke presents Jesus as more in line with the prophets, naming urgent truth and calling people to embrace what is not expected, for the sake of God's promised kingdom. For while those who are healed of disease or possession are the first to appear blessed, Jesus challenges appearances by associating blessing and warning with a call to discipleship. Who is blessed and who is woeful are to be determined by how one waits on God and whether one serves the Son of Man. He takes his message to a level more profound than the immediate meeting of a presenting need.

These blessings and woes pick up strong OT forms (see e.g., Deut. 28, Ps. 1, and Hab. 2:6–20). Structurally, they follow a pattern:

A—A current state (poverty/wealth) masks reality.

B—A reversal to come—from hungry to well fed/from filled now to hungry later.

B—A reversal to come—from weeping to laughing/from laughing now to weeping later.

A—The deception of human approval: the persecuted should rejoice and the popular should weep.

This structure shows this flow of meaning, taking what appears true to a deeper, paradoxical plane where the blessing of God follows a new logic. For blessing in the kingdom of God is independent of, or prior to, a material manifestation. The poor are blessed even in their poverty, the hungry fed, the sad joyful, and those who sacrifice for the truth of this kingdom and the one who tells it have a reward stronger than the hands who oppress them. Even in their suffering, they can sing the truths of Psalm 1 (the lectionary psalm appointed alongside this passage): "Happy are those who do not follow the advice of the wicked, or take the path that sinners tread, or sit in the seat of scoffers; but their delight is in the law of the LORD, and on his law they meditate day and night" (Ps. 1:1–2). Woeful are those who put their trust, instead, in mere appearances. We find the same in the Old Testament reading (Jer. 17:5–10) that accompanies our Gospel text. Those who "trust in mere mortals and make mere flesh their strength" have in so doing placed themselves under God's curse. In the same way, "those who trust in the LORD, whose trust is the LORD" are blessed.

WES AVRAM

Commentary 2: Connecting the Reading with the World

Two thousand years later, the so-called Sermon on the Plain still messes with our heads. Just as, I assume, it messed with the heads of the apostles, disciples, the curious onlookers, and a small but significant group who were either infirm or "troubled with unclean spirits." Everything is topsy-turvy here. The things that common sense and common custom maintain as desirable are suddenly said to be undesirable. In the words of Jesus, the hungry, the poor, those who hurt, those who mourn are those to be celebrated.

This is the gospel of the reviled, the persecuted, and the alien. Radical stuff.

Not surprisingly, this passage appears regularly in sermons of churches and congregations that daily, in a very real way, face those very issues. In the African American church, these words are spoken in whispers from the pulpit, sung with thunder in hymns and gospel songs. Few populations over the past two hundred years have been more persecuted, reviled, and hated than African Americans. The events of the twenty-first century have done little to dispel that assessment.

Yet, in any black church this Sunday you'll find laughter ringing through the sanctuary—no matter how big or small—before, during, and after the service. You will find joyful congregations, extraordinary hats (better known as crowns in the black church community), towering sermons, and mighty songs of praise and hope sung in glorious harmonies. In the poorest neighborhoods, in the smallest storefront churches, my family and I have experienced this phenomenon firsthand, almost without exception. We have always, always been made to feel welcome, like long-lost children returning home for the first time in years.

Why is that?

Perhaps a clue can be found in the Sermon on the Plain, with humble folk from Tyre and sun-darkened fishermen from Sidon, with widows and waifs from Jerusalem, with crippled and diseased beggars from all of Judea. Jesus spoke *to* them, *for* them, *of* them.

A fascinating dichotomy is going on in Luke 6:17–26. Three things jump out at even the casual reader. First, the blessings are carefully, systematically paired with woes. "Blessed are you who are poor . . ." is paired with "But woe to you who are rich . . ." "Blessed are you who are hungry now . . ." is paired with "Woe to you who are full now . . ."

This pattern continues throughout the chapter. There is a definite balance here. As the old spiritual says, "Trouble don't last always." The strict parallel sequencing allows Jesus to be very clear. Those who are hungry will be *filled*. Those who weep will *laugh again*. Those who were hated, excluded, reviled, defamed—why, they will be *blessed!* When faced with such a bold, in-your-face construction, it is hard to escape the conclusion that Jesus believes these words to be very, very important.

Second, the blessings are in the present tense, and the woes are in the future tense. Those who are listening to the Sermon on the Plain are poor people for the most part, living under Roman occupation. This teacher says that it is better to be poor, hungry, weeping, and hated now? Even his disciples must have struggled with this one. Jesus is promising that good times are ahead—but only if we faithfully endure.

This is, of course, a tough sell—not just to folks living two thousand years ago, but to people living today. These words are difficult for Christians who have rarely, if ever, known want or pain or exclusion; but for those who have—black and white, alien and native born, male and female—when Jesus says, "Blessed are you who are hungry *now,*" few words resound as powerfully through the centuries.

Perhaps this means that one way to resolve this disconnect is for us, the rich Christians, to minister to the people Jesus is blessing. We are called to feed the poor, comfort the afflicted, house the homeless. It is one thing to give to the mission offerings of your church. It is quite another to volunteer at a homeless shelter, serve at a soup kitchen, mentor a disadvantaged third-grader. Giving money is good, giving of your time and presence is even better. We are to be God's instruments in transforming their woes into blessings.

Third, the blessings and woes in the Sermon on the Plain are in the second person (you), while in the Sermon on the Mount the listeners are addressed in the third person. Jesus does not make arbitrary rhetorical decisions. If he says, "Blessed are *you* who weep now," and "Woe to *you* who are laughing now," then there is a point to be made, an insight to be understood, a message to be shared. Each listener, each reader is

being addressed, each in his or her own individual circumstance, each in his or her own moment in time.

If that is the case, then who is doing these things now? If you are a middle-class, comfortable, safe American, are you the one who is weeping now, or are you the one who is laughing now? If you are a penniless refugee living in a massive camp, are you weeping now or are you laughing now? For whom is this message?

Luke 6:17–26 can certainly be read as one of those passages that comfort the afflicted and afflict the comfortable. It is altogether valid to read it as a challenge to *you* (and me). So many of us have been given much, at a time when the need is so great around the world. The poor and hungry who gathered around Jesus during the Sermon on the Plain are still with us. If that is the case, Jesus is not particularly subtle here. Taking care of the least of these is a mandate, not a suggestion.

On that dusty plain in northern Galilee so long ago, Jesus spoke to the poor, the hungry, those who mourned and cried out in pain and who wept. He told them to take heart, rejoice, and know that if they had been excluded, hated, reviled, and defamed as they earnestly sought to follow the Son of Man, their reward would be great. Looking at these words in one way, it was—and is—a message to the oppressed, not the oppressor.

At the same time, Jesus was and is speaking to the rich Christian today, reaching across time and gender and race and geography and beyond.

Visit one of those small, predominantly African American congregations away from the wealthy parts of town sometime. Virtually all of them will have food pantries and soup kitchens, offer ESL classes, support prison ministries, and take donations for the poor. There you will find groups of people earnestly trying to live out the words of the Sermon on the Plain. They weep, they laugh, they sing and cry and sing again.

The words of Jesus are both instructional and preparatory. This is a bold new way of looking at life, at faith. The opening section of the Sermon on the Plain is a sea change, an extraordinarily well-reasoned, well-argued theological discourse that upends the old, well-established ways of thinking about what it means to be a

Christian in the twenty-first century. It also troubled the disciples two thousand years ago, disciples who stood in awe and wonder and listened with the "great multitude of people from all Judea, Jerusalem and the coast of Tyre and Sidon" to a message that was *already* changing the world.

ROBERT F. DARDEN

Seventh Sunday after the Epiphany

Genesis 45:3–11, 15
Psalm 37:1–11, 39–40

1 Corinthians 15:35–38, 42–50
Luke 6:27–38

2-24-19

Genesis 45:3–11, 15

³Joseph said to his brothers, "I am Joseph. Is my father still alive?" But his brothers could not answer him, so dismayed were they at his presence.

⁴Then Joseph said to his brothers, "Come closer to me." And they came closer. He said, "I am your brother, Joseph, whom you sold into Egypt. ⁵And now do not be distressed, or angry with yourselves, because you sold me here; for God sent me before you to preserve life. ⁶For the famine has been in the land these two years; and there are five more years in which there will be neither plowing nor harvest. ⁷God sent me before you to preserve for you a remnant on earth, and to keep alive for you many survivors. ⁸So it was not you who sent me here, but God; he has made me a father to Pharaoh, and lord of all his house and ruler over all the land of Egypt. ⁹Hurry and go up to my father and say to him, 'Thus says your son Joseph, God has made me lord of all Egypt; come down to me, do not delay. ¹⁰You shall settle in the land of Goshen, and you shall be near me, you and your children and your children's children, as well as your flocks, your herds, and all that you have. ¹¹I will provide for you there—since there are five more years of famine to come—so that you and your household, and all that you have, will not come to poverty.'" . . . ¹⁵And he kissed all his brothers and wept upon them; and after that his brothers talked with him.

Commentary 1: Connecting the Reading with Scripture

In several ways, the reading from Genesis 45 is the climax of the extended narrative centered on Joseph (Gen. 37–50). Since this is the first appearance of Genesis in Year C, the preacher will need to provide some background for this lesson. In brief, Joseph is in Egypt because his brothers turned on him and sold him into slavery (chap. 37). Their act, while heinous, is not entirely incomprehensible, given what appears to be a certain haughtiness on Joseph's part, not to mention his favored status (37:3, 33–35) and his (in)famous dreams that invariably signified his superiority vis-à-vis his brothers and his parents (37:6–7, 9). Joseph, it would seem, had a lot to learn.

In Egypt, or so it seems, Joseph learns a lot! Here Joseph experiences great success, working himself up from a slave to head of Potiphar's house (39:1–6), only to experience another crushing turn of events, ending up in prison after he refuses the advances of Potiphar's wife and she lies about the incident (39:7–20). Even in prison Joseph's abilities are recognized, and he again secures a supervisory position under the jailer (39:21–23). What Joseph is learning, it would seem, is a good deal of patience, virtue, and prudence—but not on his own!

God is everywhere and always involved. This is explicitly noted at key junctures in Genesis where we learn that the Lord "was with" Joseph (39:2a, 3a, 21a, 23a); these statements typically precede comments about Joseph's success (39:2b, 3b, 21b, 23b). Indeed, two verses make the connection crystal clear: it is God who is responsible for Joseph's success (39:21, 23). Even outsiders like Potiphar and Pharaoh are somehow aware of God's presence with Joseph (39:3; 41:38). Joseph knows it too. After he proves successful as a dream interpreter (chap. 40) and has the chance to get out of prison by interpreting the dreams of Pharaoh himself (41:1–36), Joseph gives all the credit to the Lord: "It's not me. God will give Pharaoh a favorable response" (41:16 CEB). So for a third time Joseph finds himself as head supervisor, second only to Pharaoh (41:37–57).

Here the story comes full circle, back to the family struggles with which it began. When the famine that Joseph predicted hits, it also hits Jacob and sons back in Israel. The brothers who sold Joseph to Egypt must go there to buy food (42:1–5) and just happen to run into Joseph. He recognizes them, though they cannot say the same (42:6–8). They bow to him, exactly as the dreams predicted so long ago (37:7, 9; 42:9a). Now Joseph's mettle will be tested as never before. He has been wise and virtuous with others, but what about with his family? Family can bring out the worst in us.

It is not surprising, then, to hear Joseph speaking "harshly" to his brothers (42:7) and then unleashing "an incredible three-chapter assault" on them.[1] Joseph, it seems, is taking his sweet time exacting some sweet revenge.

Or is he? What Joseph puts the brothers through could be seen as a step back from the wisdom and virtue he has manifested since being sold into slavery. However, more generous interpretations are possible. First, perhaps Joseph is testing his brothers to see if they too have changed. Have they also gained virtue and wisdom over the years? Second, perhaps even the great Joseph must work through the complex feelings he has after his brothers' profound betrayal of him. His virtue may not have gone out of the window, but must nevertheless be shifted into low gear to surmount a mountain of filial treachery. Joseph has seen serious tests of his character, but the narrative arc of Genesis suggests that this moment will be the most difficult of all.

This is what makes Genesis 45:1–15 so profound. Here both Joseph and his brothers pass the final test. Moved by Judah's appeal to save Benjamin (44:18–34), Joseph cannot maintain the charade any longer. He bursts into tears, reveals himself to his brothers, and immediately asks about the health of his father (45:1–3a).

The brothers are not only stupefied; they are "terrified" (CEB), or perhaps simply "confused" (45:3b; "dismayed" NRSV). Joseph again reveals himself as "your brother, Joseph," which he immediately defines with the contentious detail: "whom you sold into Egypt" (45:4). Joseph then comforts them (45:5a) by making a stunning theological claim: it was not the *brothers* who *sold* Joseph *out of spite*, it was *God* who *sent* him *to save lives* (45:5b)—a point he repeats twice more because of its importance and because the brothers surely cannot believe their ears (45:6–8). Repetition is also useful for difficult topics, and this one is almost incomprehensible: how could all that happened to Joseph be *God's will*? And *why*?

These questions are profound and should not be answered too quickly, especially with a simple-minded appeal to Romans 8:28, which is no less complicated! What we know for certain is that Joseph is the one making this claim. It is not the narrator's third-person perspective—like the notices of God being with Joseph—but is Joseph's own, first-person testimony. The two claims are not incommensurate, but one should not miss the difference: Joseph lacks the privileged knowledge of God's ways that the narrator manifests. Or does he? At this climactic moment, Joseph's testimony aligns with the narrator's, just as it did in 41:16. This then may be Joseph's most virtuous moment, and it comes at the tensest of times. Perhaps this is another reason why he repeats his theological assertion three times: not only to reassure and convince *his brothers*, but to reassure and convince *himself*. Family can bring out the worst in us, but also the best—though the best rarely comes easily.

That last point means that Genesis 45 should not be used as a simple illustration for the Gospel lesson from Luke 6. Nor should Luke 6 be used as a simple explanation of Genesis 45. Forgiveness, especially of those closest to us, whose betrayal is always the most painful, is never easy, especially once the tables have turned and we are the ones with power and opportunity to exact revenge. That is exactly what we are when our forgiveness is sought, even if we exercise that power only by withholding our forgiveness. Joseph, of course, is wise, and Joseph forgives.

---

1. John C. Holbert, "Genesis 45:3–11, 15," in *The Lectionary Commentary: The Old Testament and Acts*, ed. Roger E. Van Harn (Grand Rapids: Eerdmans, 2001), 74.

Evidently it was not easy, for him or for his brothers, who continued to worry and who needed Joseph's reassurance, even after Jacob's death (50:15–21).

Reconciliation will not happen in the space of a verse, or a day, or even many years. The one tasked with forgiveness will need virtue and prudence—often hard won—and a good dose of divine assistance . . . like Joseph. Those in need of forgiveness may also have to prove their worth,

their virtue, their good intentions . . . like Joseph's brothers. Nevertheless, reconciliation *can* happen. Even within families. Genesis demonstrates that family dynamics can move from the worst, fratricide (Gen. 4:1–16), to forgiveness (Gen. 45:1–15; 50:15–21). One small—but altogether crucial—way that one forgives and loves one's enemies (who are sometimes family members!) is by not retaliating against them.[2]

BRENT A. STRAWN

Commentary 2: Connecting the Reading with the World

The dense, rich story of Joseph makes but a single appearance in Year C of the lectionary (even then, it is included only if there are at least seven Sundays between Epiphany and Lent) with this climactic scene: the big reveal of Joseph to his brothers. Untethered here from its fuller context within Joseph's story (Gen. 37–50) and the wider story of the patriarchs, it gives us the part we like the most, Joseph's shocking revelation of his identity to the brothers who betrayed him. As with all plot twists, however, the impact of the payoff depends on the development of the setup. Listeners will appreciate the impact of this pivotal moment best if the preacher offers at least some of the backstory.

This text functions as a lens through which to view the whole narrative of deception, betrayal, heartbreak, reversal, and reconciliation. That narrative can be seen not only as the story of a single life, but also as the story of a single family, as the story of an entire family line, and as the story of Israel. Some also see within it a prefiguring of the story to come, of Jesus. Given the multiplicity of narratives for which this single episode provides a lens, this text could be considered as a kind of kaleidoscope. It invites repeated looks, offers many angles of vision, reveals different patterns and possibilities from the very same pieces. Like a kaleidoscope, it is also made up of little mirrors. How many ways will we see our own reflections in it?

"I am Joseph. Is my father still alive?" (v. 3). Both the pathos and the hope of the whole story are packed into these words. At the heart of both the pain and the redemption in this text lie core issues that concern every human in every time: identity and relationship.

"I am Joseph": here is the dramatic disclosure, the climactic catharsis after the emotional tension of Joseph's plotting and manipulation. His brothers had hated him for what he could not help being, the favored son of their father. During the long years since their betrayal, he has survived by becoming someone else. He "passes" as an Egyptian, and no one but God knows his true identity. We know something about this, do we not? We all make choices about how much we reveal of our true selves, and how much we adapt to the expectations of others. In many cases, we trade authenticity for acceptance, safety, or success.

For those whose true identity involves racial, religious, or sexual-minority status, or some intersection of these identities, the choice between authenticity and assimilation can entail real trauma and risk. While Joseph, now in a position of power and safety, had arrived at the right moment to reveal his true self, we also see throughout his story how acts of self-protective concealment can be necessary for survival.[3] Moreover, in all times, regardless of the identity

---

2. See further Matthew R. Schlimm, *From Fratricide to Forgiveness: The Language and Ethics of Anger in Genesis* (Winona Lake, IN: Eisenbrauns, 2011); and David L. Petersen, "Genesis and Family Values," *Journal of Biblical Literature* 125 (2005): 5–23.

3. I am indebted to Rabbi Jane Rachel Litman for the concept of Joseph "passing." She writes particularly poignantly about how Jews throughout history have had to make choices about passing or not ("Joseph Comes Out," http://www.beliefnet.com/faiths/2001/01/joseph-comes-out.aspx, accessed Jan. 1, 2017).

laid on Joseph—slave, prisoner, vizier—Joseph continued to embrace and use the gifts God had given him (dreams and interpretation), and God blessed what he did (Gen. 39:23) Sometimes we can be true to ourselves, even when we cannot be our full selves.

Joseph's self-disclosure comes with a tender question: "Is my father still alive?" All these years, father and son have been dead to each other. For Jacob, the grief was certain, as he believed Joseph had "without doubt" been torn to pieces (Gen. 37:33). For Joseph, the grief of separation was compounded by uncertainty; he did not even know if his father was still alive. Their story presents us with one of the most sustained treatments of grief in Scripture. In it, we see the various faces of prolonged pain, and how loss can shape a family. We are shown the father's sorrow, his refusal to be comforted (37:35), and his fear of losing his youngest son (42:4). The sons, burdened with the horrifying knowledge of their guilt, now live with the fear of causing their father more suffering (44:34), as well as the suspicion that they will pay the penalty for that crime (42:21). Over and over again, we are told of Joseph's weeping (42:24; 43:30; 45:1–2, 14–15; 46:29; 50:1, 17).

Joseph's trickery of his brothers (reminiscent of his father Jacob's own trickery of his brother Esau) sets him up to take revenge for their treachery; yet his first words, rather than being vindictive, are laced with anguish and hope. He once declared that God had made him forget all his hardship and all his father's house (41:51), but now we see his deep yearning for reunion. Even after everything that has happened, he still aches for family connection, not only with his father, but with his brothers. "Come closer to me," he beckons (45:4).

For anyone who has struggled with the deep grief that comes from family betrayal, alienation, or loss, the complexity of Joseph's emotions may strike a chord. His path is not straightforward; neither are his emotions. Is there any emotional pain more common or more complicated than family pain? We think of family as the people who are supposed to love us, keep us safe, and accept us, just as we are. Joseph's brothers hated him instead of loving him, and caused him harm instead of keeping him safe.

The dysfunction in Joseph's family runs back generations, as we see in the many stories of dishonesty, manipulation, sibling rivalry, and other bad behavior. From a family-systems perspective, it is unsurprising that such a legacy ends up playing out in the sibling jealousy and family violence we see from Joseph's brothers. What *is* surprising is how Joseph disrupts the old family pattern. In the episodes leading up to this text, he has toyed with his brothers, and cruelly so, but now he makes a choice that changes everything: he forgives them. Even within a family system loaded with manipulation, jealousy, and fear, a single person within the system has the power to transform relationships, and even the system itself, through an unexpected act of reconciliation.

"Do not be distressed, or angry with yourselves," Joseph tells his brothers (45:5). How do we release each other—and ourselves—from anger and regret? For Joseph, the answer lies in how he chooses to see things. He has reframed the horrific actions of his brothers, understanding now that, though his brothers intended him harm, God used what they did to him for good (v. 8; see also Gen. 50:20). His theological understanding transforms his suffering, so that, instead of passing on that suffering through retaliation, he can forgive. If God can use even family violence for good, how much more might God use acts of healing and peace?

Redemption in this story was initiated by God but interpreted by Joseph. That interpretation spurred him to act in partnership with God, whose redemptive purposes included not only Joseph and his family, but the people of Egypt and beyond. Redemption ripples far beyond us when we receive it, trust God is in it, and then cooperate with it.

Looking through the kaleidoscope of this story, we might see ourselves reflected in any number of ways. If we look again, we might also see God at work, taking our pieces and turning them toward something good. What will we do with what we have seen?

STACEY SIMPSON DUKE

Psalm 37:1–11, 39–40

¹Do not fret because of the wicked;
    do not be envious of wrongdoers,
²for they will soon fade like the grass,
    and wither like the green herb.

³Trust in the LORD, and do good;
    so you will live in the land, and enjoy security.
⁴Take delight in the LORD,
    and he will give you the desires of your heart.

⁵Commit your way to the LORD;
    trust in him, and he will act.
⁶He will make your vindication shine like the light,
    and the justice of your cause like the noonday.

⁷Be still before the LORD, and wait patiently for him;
    do not fret over those who prosper in their way,
    over those who carry out evil devices.

⁸Refrain from anger, and forsake wrath.
    Do not fret—it leads only to evil.
⁹For the wicked shall be cut off,
    but those who wait for the LORD shall inherit the land.

¹⁰Yet a little while, and the wicked will be no more;
    though you look diligently for their place, they will not be there.
¹¹But the meek shall inherit the land,
    and delight themselves in abundant prosperity.
. . . .
³⁹The salvation of the righteous is from the LORD;
    he is their refuge in the time of trouble.
⁴⁰The LORD helps them and rescues them;
    he rescues them from the wicked, and saves them,
    because they take refuge in him.

Connecting the Psalm with Scripture and Worship

Patience, patience, patience. That's the drumbeat of this psalm: "Do not fret" (v. 1). "Soon" (v. 2). "Be still and wait patiently, do not fret" (v. 7). "Refrain" (v. 8). "Yet a little while" (v. 10). What is experienced in the present differs from what is to come. Those who have the upper hand now will be brought low. The prosperity of the wicked will be reversed (v. 38).

The evildoers will wither away. Just wait. Just be patient.

Confidence is the colleague of patience, and so this psalm affirms and assures that God will act to make things right, granting fulfillment to the seeker, extending care to the righteous, and lifting the lowly. God "will give you the desires of your heart" (v. 4). God "will make your vindication

259

shine like the light, and the justice of your cause like the noonday" (v. 6). Just wait. Just be patient.

While urging patient confidence in the future that God is preparing, the psalm also recommends behaviors for the present time: faithfulness, righteousness, and devotion. The present is not simply a time for passive waiting but, rather, a time to actively pursue the things that further God's purposes and that build a meaningful life: "Trust in the LORD, and do good" (v. 3). "Take delight in the LORD" (v. 4). "Commit your way to the LORD" (v. 5). It is a diligent and hopeful posture, tending faithfully to the present while confidently anticipating the future and the fullness that will then be revealed.

The biblical story of Joseph is a grand and sweeping narrative, full of conflict and drama. Joseph is his father's favorite child. Jacob, we are told, "loved Joseph more than any other of his children, because he was the son of his old age; and he had made him a long robe with sleeves" (Gen. 37:3). Not surprisingly, the favor granted Joseph does not sit well with his brothers. In fact, "they hated him" (37:4). In addition to the fancy coat, Joseph also has a gift for interpreting dreams and the brashness to share what he has seen. Two of his dreams suggest to Joseph that in the future his entire family will bow down before him (37:5–11). When they hear these predictions, Joseph's brothers become all the more infuriated with him. An opportunity soon presents itself for them to act on their rage. They throw Joseph into a pit and then sell him to traders who take him to Egypt. Good riddance, they think.

Today's first reading, Genesis 45:3–11, moves us forward several chapters and many years. Using his gifts and abilities, Joseph has prospered in Egypt, rising to a position of prominence and authority exceeded only by Pharaoh. A regional famine forces the sons of Jacob to seek food from Egypt. They must appear before Joseph, bowing before him to make their request (42:6–9). He recognizes them, though they do not know him. After a few cycles of dramatic repetition, Joseph at last reveals his identity to them. It is a shocking moment, rendering the brothers speechless. Their silence of recognition is perhaps filled with regret for what they did or dread for what Joseph might do.

Joseph breaks the silence with words of assurance: "Do not be distressed, or angry with yourselves, because you sold me here; for God sent me before you to preserve life" (45:5). Joseph has come to understand that his brothers' actions long ago actually served a greater purpose, making it possible for him to be in Egypt in a position to provide food for the hungry Israelites. The fullness of time reveals that their hatred and their schemes had been redirected to fit into God's saving work. So Joseph affirms to them, "It was not you who sent me here, but God" (45:8). God simply refused to let Joseph's story end in a pit.

Joseph is the one who tends faithfully and diligently to the present, while waiting for God's future to be fully disclosed. Not fretting on the wrongdoing that brought him to Egypt, Joseph does what he can in the situation where he finds himself, using the gifts God has given him. The path to God's future is filled with complications, twists, and turns, but in time God does act to restore, nourish, and save. Joseph further embodies the psalm's admonitions, refraining from evil and forsaking wrath when retribution is within reach (Ps. 37:8). Instead, Joseph glimpses God's providential work and yields to God's reconciling intents. Joseph's maturity of spirit is neatly summarized in his final speech to his brothers a few chapters hence: "Even though you intended to do harm to me, God intended it for good, in order to preserve a numerous people" (50:20). Ours is a trustworthy God, and a God worth waiting for. Just be patient.

The day's Gospel lesson from Luke also continues some of the thematic elements of Psalm 37. Jesus' ethical teachings are directed toward the present time with an eye to God's future. Generosity, forgiveness, and righteousness are the behaviors to cultivate and pursue diligently. The wrongdoers persist, and the enemies remain; but, Jesus says, love them anyway. Love them in the present, motivated by the promise of what is to come. "Your reward will be great, and you will be children of the Most High" (Luke 6:35). Persistent faithfulness and surprising forgiveness here and now anticipate the day when God's entire family will be fully restored.

JOHN W. WURSTER

1 Corinthians 15:35–38, 42–50

³⁵But someone will ask, "How are the dead raised? With what kind of body do they come?" ³⁶Fool! What you sow does not come to life unless it dies. ³⁷And as for what you sow, you do not sow the body that is to be, but a bare seed, perhaps of wheat or of some other grain. ³⁸But God gives it a body as he has chosen, and to each kind of seed its own body. . . .

⁴²So it is with the resurrection of the dead. What is sown is perishable, what is raised is imperishable. ⁴³It is sown in dishonor, it is raised in glory. It is sown in weakness, it is raised in power. ⁴⁴It is sown a physical body, it is raised a spiritual body. If there is a physical body, there is also a spiritual body. ⁴⁵Thus it is written, "The first man, Adam, became a living being"; the last Adam became a life-giving spirit. ⁴⁶But it is not the spiritual that is first, but the physical, and then the spiritual. ⁴⁷The first man was from the earth, a man of dust; the second man is from heaven. ⁴⁸As was the man of dust, so are those who are of the dust; and as is the man of heaven, so are those who are of heaven. ⁴⁹Just as we have borne the image of the man of dust, we will also bear the image of the man of heaven.

⁵⁰What I am saying, brothers and sisters, is this: flesh and blood cannot inherit the kingdom of God, nor does the perishable inherit the imperishable.

Commentary 1: Connecting the Reading with Scripture

In 1 Corinthians 15:1–34, Paul responds to some at Corinth who claim there is no resurrection of the dead (vv. 12, 16, 29, 32). Paul argues that Christ's resurrection from the dead, a fundamental element of the gospel received by the Corinthians, guarantees believers' resurrection as well.

At 15:35, he poses two related questions that shift the discussion to a different facet of the same subject. Paul writes, "But someone will ask, 'How are the dead raised? With what kind of body do they come?'" These questions concern not whether there is a resurrection of the dead, but by what means they are raised and with what kind of body. He will answer these questions in reverse order, dealing with the second in 15:35–50 and the first in 15:51–58.

Here Paul employs a method of teaching known as diatribe, an approach commonly used by Hellenistic philosophers. A teacher poses a question supposedly raised by an imaginary interlocutor among his audience and then responds to it. Often this takes the form of a rhetorical question followed by its immediate answer, then a defense of that answer. By this method, a teacher anticipates and parries possible objections to his argument. Paul uses this approach elsewhere in his letters, especially in Romans, where it structures much of his argument (e.g., 3:1–9; 3:27–4:1; 6:1–7:25).

As with questions about the resurrection dealt with earlier in 1 Corinthians 15, scholars disagree as to the precise reason(s) why Paul addresses these potential concerns. Paul probably anticipated objections to his claim that the *body* was resurrected, because many Hellenistic thinkers thought of the body as something from which to escape. After all, so the thinking went, the body was corruptible and subject to death; only the soul was immortal. The idea of linking a body with immortality therefore was unthinkable.

Paul's response, in short, is that bodily resurrection entails bodily transformation. A corpse is not simply brought back to life; the body is raised in a different form. His argument employs two basic strategies. In verses 36–38, he argues with an analogy from nature. In verses 42–50, he draws an analogy between Adam and Christ, rooted in an interpretation of Genesis 2:7.

In verses 36–38, Paul appeals to the transformation that takes place when seeds sown in the ground grow into plants. The seed is not the same as the full-grown plant, but the plant does develop from the seed. Similarly, Paul asserts continuity between the earthly body and the resurrected body, while at same time illustrating the transformation necessary in moving from one to the other.

Paul's argument in verses 42–50 describes the nature of the untransformed and transformed body. The first part of this subsection is relatively clear. Paul contrasts the earthly and resurrected bodies (vv. 42–43). The earthly body is perishable, dishonorable, and weak. The resurrection body is imperishable, glorified, and powerful. Paul's point is that the preresurrected human body requires transformation in order to become fit for eternal life.

Beginning with verse 44, however, interpretive problems arise. Paul speaks of the preresurrected body and the resurrected body, using phrases that are difficult to translate. The NRSV's "physical body" and "spiritual body" can be misleading, since they suggest a dualism between the physical and spiritual that is foreign to Paul. Paul never speaks of the soul's being resurrected, as if resurrection leaves the body behind. Rather, Paul's overall point is that a continuity exists between a preresurrection *body* and a resurrected *body*. To get from one state to another requires transformation, but human existence never ceases to be bodily. Humans do not *have* bodies; they exist as bodies.

So how do we best make sense of Paul's words?[1] Paul provides clues in verses 45–49 when he compares the first Adam and the last Adam, Jesus Christ. According to Genesis 2:7, which Paul quotes in part, Adam was a "living being" made from the stuff of earth (1 Cor. 15:47). He was thus subject to decay and death because of sin. So he existed as a bodily being ill-suited for eternal life with God. The same holds true for all of Adam's descendants (v. 48). The last Adam, now raised from the dead as a transformed body, does not just receive life as did the first Adam, but also gives life (v. 45). Believers raised with

this last Adam will like him be transformed into a body whose life is suited for the age to come (v. 49). Anthony C. Thiselton helpfully translates these phrases as "a body for the human realm" and "a body for the realm of the Spirit."[2]

Paul's argument about *bodily* resurrection carries significance beyond its implications for understanding Christian resurrection alone. If to be human is to be embodied, then it would be a mistake to regard the body and what we do with it as unimportant. Paul combats such mistaken thinking in 1 Corinthians 5. Apparently one of the Corinthian Christians had been having sexual intercourse with his stepmother (5:1). Paul's concern lies foremost with the health of the Christian community, and he urges them to take strong action against this person (5:4–5). Why would a person do such a thing (regarded as revolting, even among nonbelievers, v. 1), and why would the Corinthian believers have not already taken action against him?

Although answers to these questions involve multiple factors, one element was likely a disregard for the significance of what one did with his or her body. After all, if the body is something humans inhabit for the time being but discard at death, why should what someone does with it matter? Paul will have none of that thinking or the practices it produces. Human life, preresurrection and postresurrection, is embodied life. Christ died to redeem us as whole human beings. What we do with our bodies, therefore, is of utmost significance.

Paul's teaching in this section of 1 Corinthians 15 warrants comparison with three other passages in his letters. In Philippians 3:20–21, Paul speaks of Christian resurrection in terms similar to those in 1 Corinthians 15. Believers wait for the Lord Jesus Christ, who "will transform the body of our humiliation that it may be conformed to the body of his glory." In 1 Thessalonians 4:13–18, Paul addresses questions regarding the resurrection that have arisen because some among the Thessalonians have died.

Most important, however, are Paul's parallels between Adam and Christ in 1 Corinthians

---

1. Here I follow Joel B. Green, *Body, Soul, and Human Life: The Nature of Humanity in the Bible* (Grand Rapids: Baker Academic, 2008), 173–75.

2. Anthony C. Thiselton, *The First Epistle to the Corinthians*, New International Greek Testament Commentary (Grand Rapids: Eerdmans, 2000), 1279. I owe this reference to Green, *Body, Soul, and Human Life*, 175.

15:45–49 and Romans 5:12–21. The Romans text demonstrates that Adam and Christ constitute the points of origin for Paul's entire worldview. Adam introduced sin and death into human experience. As a result, all humanity fell under the rule of sin as an enslaving power. Jesus Christ endured human death, yet was raised to new life by God. As a result, all humanity can be freed from sin's enslaving power by becoming joined with Christ (cf. Rom. 6:1–10). By appealing to Adam and Christ in 1 Corinthians 15:45–49, Paul likewise taps into the entire biblical narrative from its inception (see the quotation Gen. 2:7 in 15:45) to its consummation with Jesus' return and the transformation of those in Christ, whether dead or still living.

JAMES C. MILLER

Commentary 2: Connecting the Reading with the World

As Christian faithful, we cling—bind ourselves—to the resurrection hope that is the primary message of our faith. When considered against the backdrop of the central message of the resurrection, the Corinthians' detailed questions to Paul regarding the resurrection of the dead seem a petty squabble about minor details. However, the struggle is real. It is not just the Corinthians who are struggling with the scope of resurrection hope; so often we too find this hope unbelievable. At least we have trouble discerning how to move through the world as if this hope were a sure anchor of faith. Paul himself laboriously goes through the motions of explaining the significance and reality of the resurrection. Yet many of us today still cannot overcome the limitations of an imagination shaped by a culture filled with dualisms that split reality between the known physical world and an unknown spiritual world.

These questions are perennial. Living in this world while cleaving to resurrection hope is a constant and unnerving paradox for Christians. Superficial understandings of resurrection hope tend to establish a dualism between earthly and heavenly justice, fostering the disturbing sentiment among the faithful that they need not be concerned with the stuff of life in this world.

In contrast to this, Paul insists the ultimate promise of resurrection is the backdrop against which the faithful must live every single moment. It is the proleptic essence that ought to shape life in community, as the first fourteen chapters of the epistle instruct. The familiar 1 Corinthians 13 on the primacy of love must be understood against the backdrop of resurrection hope. Also, 1 Corinthians 12 on the building up of the community as different parts of the body must be understood against the backdrop of resurrection hope. The edification of the community and its members, Paul's goal throughout the epistle, must be understood against the backdrop of resurrection hope.

Central to this understanding of resurrection in Corinthians is its essentially communal nature. The resurrection can be understood only in the context of a community that prays and worships together, suffers together, and experiences loss and rebirth together. In the community Paul envisions, there is no room for an individualistic sense of salvation. This Pauline view of the Christian community flies in the context of so much of our being church today, when our sense of community so often is impacted by the individualistic tendencies of US consumer culture. The worshiping community experiences these texts on resurrection hope in the context of the ritualized remembering of Christ's death and resurrection on a weekly basis. Encountering this particular text then becomes an affirmation of the community's task of being witnesses to life in Christ, the new Adam, in ways that transcend our everyday deaths.

In this key, all attempts by the powers and principalities to deal death to humans and the natural environment must be resisted, much as the resurrection is both an act of resistance and victory over all forms of death. Death ought to be resisted as the last word, as imposed fatalism, as determining our total existence. For Paul, human existence is the story between birth in the first Adam and death in the new one (vv. 45–48). Therefore, life in this world ought to be a continual struggle against the forces of sin and all that deals death, especially unjust death. This requires a sharp eye ready to read the signs of the times. Throughout Corinthians, Paul admonishes the community to be watchful against those things that threaten their integrity as followers of Christ, that is, that threaten their steadfast witness to salvation in Christ. This is far from an otherworldly reading of resurrection hope. On the contrary, it is the historical witness to life in Christ as resistance to death.

As I write this, hundreds of protesters have joined the Standing Rock Sioux Tribe in North Dakota, who are resisting an oil pipeline slated to be built under their territory, threatening their water source and the integrity of their sacred lands. In addition to fossil fuels dealing death to our ecosystem, and therefore dealing death for the human family, especially to vulnerable communities in low-lying coastal regions, this particular case confronts us with a corporate project that also threatens death to the spiritual integrity of the Sioux Nation. The studies that declared that these were not sacred burial grounds for the tribe (and therefore available for digging the pipeline) were done without proper tribal input. More importantly, there are grave concerns that the pipeline threatens the safety of their primary water source.[3]

In the Christian tradition, water is both a symbol of God's life-giving gift of grace, poured out for us in baptism, and a necessity for all life in creation. Therefore, poisoned water and lack of access to safe water are death-dealing sins. They threaten the integrity of the community. What does it mean to witness to resurrection hope in this situation? Many Christian churches have pledged their solidarity and support with the Standing Rock water protectors and their allies through their direct participation, as well as their financial support.[4] In addition, faith communities have pledged to advocate with elected officials to protect the integrity and dignity of protesters. All the tribes and protesters gathered in North Dakota experienced the

preliminary victory of the denial of the final easement for the construction of the pipeline as a life-giving, life-affirming moment, brimming with hope, even while grounded in the reality of potential battles ahead.

This protest is but one example of the struggles into which the resurrection hope may lead us. When faced with a choice between death and life, the perishable and the imperishable, the physical and the spiritual, to use Paul's language, how will we choose to read the signs of the times? First, this passage from Corinthians applies directly to prior demands from Paul to do everything for the edification and integrity of the community. The faithful today are challenged to call out death by its many names: global warming and other environmental disasters; massive inequality; exclusion and marginalization of diverse groups; lack of food, health care, child care, education, and other elements that improve the lives of communities by improving the lives of women; human trafficking; political polarization. These all threaten the integrity of the human family and must be considered with a careful eye, attentive to the question of what kind of response the resurrection hope requires of us at the moment.

Second, the passage places the faithful as constantly interwoven in these binaries. We are constantly touched and impacted by extremes of both death and life. Paul does not demand that we run away from one to seek shelter exclusively on the other, because he knows this is not possible within history. Therefore, approaches to challenges to the human family that range from escapist, on the one hand, to fatalist, on the other, are not faithful. Disengagement from the world is not a faithful option. Our faith is lived in the existential tug between death and resurrection in concrete ways in the world. This passage provides a vision for discernment in this world, grounded on resurrection hope.

MARÍA TERESA DÁVILA

3. Leah Donella, "The Standing Rock Resistance Is Unprecedented (It's Also Centuries Old)," Nov. 22, 2016, http://www.npr.org/sections/codeswitch/2016/11/22/502068751/the-standing-rock-resistance-is-unprecedented-it-s-also-centuries-old.

4. For example, David Paulsen, "Episcopalians Rally behind Native American Protests of ND Pipeline," Aug. 26, 2016, http://episcopaldigitalnetwork.com/ens/2016/08/25/episcopalians-rally-behind-native-american-protests-of-nd-pipeline/; "UMC Bishops Support Standing Rock Sioux Nation," Oct. 25, 2016, http://www.cedarcross.net/2016/11/02/umc-bishops-support-standing-rock-sioux-nation/; and "ELCA Presiding Bishop Issues Statement on Standing Rock," Nov. 14, 2016, https://www.elca.org/News-and-Events/7865.

Luke 6:27–38

27"But I say to you that listen, Love your enemies, do good to those who hate you, 28bless those who curse you, pray for those who abuse you. 29If anyone strikes you on the cheek, offer the other also; and from anyone who takes away your coat do not withhold even your shirt. 30Give to everyone who begs from you; and if anyone takes away your goods, do not ask for them again. 31Do to others as you would have them do to you.

32"If you love those who love you, what credit is that to you? For even sinners love those who love them. 33If you do good to those who do good to you, what credit is that to you? For even sinners do the same. 34If you lend to those from whom you hope to receive, what credit is that to you? Even sinners lend to sinners, to receive as much again. 35But love your enemies, do good, and lend, expecting nothing in return. Your reward will be great, and you will be children of the Most High; for he is kind to the ungrateful and the wicked. 36Be merciful, just as your Father is merciful.

37"Do not judge, and you will not be judged; do not condemn, and you will not be condemned. Forgive, and you will be forgiven; 38give, and it will be given to you. A good measure, pressed down, shaken together, running over, will be put into your lap; for the measure you give will be the measure you get back."

Commentary 1: Connecting the Reading with Scripture

The Moral Exhortation (Luke 6:27–31). If the woes and curses of verses 17–26 surprise us, so do these exhortations: love enemies, do good to those who do you ill, bless your cursers, and pray for your abusers. Jesus goes through a list of the least-likely-to-be-loved.

In the immediate context, Jesus follows the blessings and woes of previous verses with a strong adversative: "*But* I say to you." Why? The woes that immediately precede it are directed to well-fed, highly regarded, socially powerful, personally secure people. It would make sense to make a contrast here with an exhortation to give up money, ease, and prestige. The call is not to give things up, but to love, to regard others with mercy, and to sacrifice one's comfort on their behalf. This is a call to be like those who are "blessed" in the kingdom, who do not hate when hated, do not resent when oppressed, do not seek revenge when persecuted.

Compared with Matthew's Jesus in the Sermon on the Mount, Luke's Jesus universalizes. He refers to "sinners," rather than "Gentiles and sinners," as the group that can "love those who love them." Note how Jesus defines the audience (v. 27): "You the listening/hearing ones."

The next three exhortations concern material possessions: add to a thief's demand by offering more, give to whoever begs from you, and do not demand stolen property back. In the trail of these unconventional commands comes Jesus' Golden Rule: "Just as you wish that people would act toward you, act precisely that way toward them" (v. 31, my wording).

A famous parallel from the renowned Jewish scholar Hillel has a defiant student approach Shammai, saying, "I will convert if you can teach me the whole law while I stand on one foot." Shammai declines. Hillel says, "That which is despicable to you, do not do to a fellow. That is the whole Torah, and the rest is commentary. Go and learn it" (*Shabbat* 31:7).[1] Again, unlike Matthew, where Jesus makes a similar claim (Matt. 7:12), Luke's Golden Rule does not stand on Torah authority, even if it assumes it.

---

1. Isadore Epstein, ed., *Shabbath*, vol. 1, *Babylonian Talmud: Seder Mo'ed* (n.p.: Socino Press, 1938), 31a, 140.

Is it a general precept amid specific ones, or a "this is the simplest way to meet what otherwise feels impossible" kind of guide? Is there is a third alternative, that because verse 31 is both preceded and followed by specific, albeit difficult, exhortations, those exhortations may be commentary on verse 31, rather than verse 31 being a summary of them? Do you want to know how to treat others as you would like to be treated? Treat them with unmerited favor, just as you appreciate favor when given to you. This renders verse 36 as its parallel, with the giving of mercy a summary of counterintuitive love, reflective of the Father's.

The Moral Reference Group (Luke 6:32–36).
Jesus juxtaposes two comparison points relative to which this kind of love can be seen. The first is "sinners," whose ethics thrive in a world defined by exchange: loving those who love them, doing good to those who treat them well, and lending to those who pay back. The second is God, who "is kind to the ungrateful" and so merciful (6:36). Jesus hopes to transfer his crowds from a "keeping up with the sinners" approach to a "keeping up with God" way of living. By imitating God, one shows why one is a child of the Most High (v. 35).

Making God's unmerited mercy the reference point connects with Luke's further treatment of the Golden Rule in chapter 10, where the story of the man who fell among the thieves joins an account of Martha and Mary serving Jesus. If the story of a man receiving mercy can be taken to explain the Golden Rule, one might in parallel fashion decide that Mary, who sits at the feet of Jesus to receive his love, is more devout than the one who is busy with service but not ready to love mercy. There may be a rhythm of giving and receiving in the work of mercy.

The reference point for what it means to love shifts here. To underscore this, consider how Luke views "sinners" throughout the Gospel. There are fourteen unique references to "sinners" in the Gospel (see 7:37, 39; 13:2; 15:1, 2, 7, 10; 18:13; 19:7). Almost every one of these features someone who was transformed, from being judged by others to being a subject of God's mercy. Could Jesus' use of "sinners" also be a juxtaposition of the old self to the new self, from

a former definition to a new definition, a social ethic to a religious ethic? There are parallels to Paul's understandings here (Gal. 2:20).

Verse 36 ("Be merciful, just as your Father is merciful") presents an interesting question of connection. If it is indeed a parallel to verse 31, then the verses that are before, in between, and after these parallel truisms may illustrate how to live out this core ethic. Opting for this approach opens interesting pathways for preaching. It positively triangulates the Golden Rule with discipleship. If how one would like to be treated is a reference point for how one is to treat others, and if the Father's character, as one full of mercy, is the reference point for extending mercy, and if these two reference points are similar in meaning, then grace-filled favor to the unfavorable (i.e., mercy) is the reference point for how we are to understand both human and divine being. Waiting on God, loving enemies, absorbing injustice for the sake of goodness, and resisting the intrigues of human power become lively examples of how to live within the triangle of self, other, and God. The triangle also grounds Christian ethics.

More Exhortations (Luke 6:37–38).
The final verses of this section continue to exemplify this transformed ethic, raising to new heights the prophets' calls to love. The balanced logic of the blessings and woes become a kind of karmic-sounding cadence, with the passive voice summoning God as actor:

- Do not judge, and you will not be judged;
- Forgive, and you will be forgiven;
- Give, and it will be given to you.

Here the exegetical question circles around the agent in the predicate, where all three verbs are future passive. Is this a Wisdom saying, insinuating that the world works in such a way that we will get back what we gave? Is this, rather, an eschatological saying, suggesting that God will not judge those who have refrained from judging, will forgive those who have forgiven, and will give back to those who have given? The reference may move in both directions, allowing us to conclude that acts of love for others will cultivate love in return—here and beyond.

The third of these pairings includes a colorful extension: "A good measure, pressed down, shaken together, running over, will be put into your lap" (v. 38b). The imagery may come from the vineyard, where vintners filled their vats as full as possible. Pressing down and shaking compact the grapes to minimal size, but still the contents exceed the limit and run over the brim. Others claim dry measures are envisioned—hence the shaking. The image remains one of abundance, both shared with others and personal. We hear resonance of Ephesians 3:20, where "God can do exceedingly abundantly more than we can ask or imagine." Such is the spiritual reward of a mercy-based ethic.

WES AVRAM

Commentary 2: Connecting the Reading with the World

Jesus continues the Sermon on the Plain, speaking to a host of people who have gathered on a broad "level place" to hear more about a revolutionary new message that turns their understanding of faith and love upside down. It is more than a sermon. It's a revelation. It tells about a supremely loving and merciful God. It is at one and the same time a call and a promise.

The Fellowship of the Crucified

How then does love conquer? By asking not how the enemy treats her but only how Jesus treated her. The love for our enemies takes us along the way of the cross and into fellowship with the Crucified. The more we are driven along this road, the more certain is the victory of love over the enemy's hatred. For then it is not the disciple's own love, but the love of Jesus Christ alone, who for the sake of his enemies went to the cross and prayed for them as he hung there. In the face of the cross the disciples realized that they too were his enemies, and that he had overcome them by his love. It is this that opens the disciple's eyes, and enables him to see his enemy as a brother. He knows that he owes his very life to One, who though he was his enemy, treated him as a brother and accepted him, who made him his neighbor, and drew him into fellowship with himself. The disciple can now perceive that even his enemy is the object of God's love, and that he stands like himself beneath the cross of Christ. God asked us nothing about our virtues or our vices, for in his sight even our virtue was ungodliness. God's love sought out his enemies who needed it, and whom he deemed worthy of it. God loves his enemies—that is the glory of his love, as every follower of Jesus knows; through Jesus he has become a partaker in this love. . . .

This commandment, that we should love our enemies and forgo revenge, will grow even more urgent in the holy struggle which lies before us and in which we partly have already been engaged for years. In it love and hate engage in mortal combat. It is the urgent duty of every Christian soul to prepare itself for it. . . . And how is the battle to be fought? Soon the time will come when we shall pray, not as isolated individuals, but as a corporate body, a congregation, a Church: we shall pray in multitudes (albeit in relatively small multitudes) and among the thousands and thousands of apostates we shall loudly praise and confess the Lord who was crucified and is risen and shall come again. And what prayer, what confession, what hymn of praise will it be? It will be the prayer of earnest love for these very sons of perdition who stand around and gaze at us with eyes aflame with hatred, and who have perhaps already raised their hands to kill us. It will be prayer for the peace of these erring, devastated and bewildering souls, a prayer for the same love and peace which we ourselves enjoy, a prayer which will penetrate to the depths of their souls and rend their hearts more grievously than anything they can do to us.

Dietrich Bonhoeffer (1906–1945), *The Cost of Discipleship* (New York: Simon & Schuster, 1995), 150–51.

Jesus addresses it "to you that listen"—so we had best pay attention! If we do, it holds the possibility, for anyone with ears to hear, of a radically transformed life.

This life is not easy; it asks a lot. It requires us to abandon the cycle of violence and retribution, rejecting at last the self-defeating logic of "an eye for an eye, a tooth for a tooth." It calls us to expand the circle of our concern beyond the narrow boundaries of group or tribe. In directing us to give even the shirt off our back, it demands a radical dependence on the God who has promised to provide for us. Most of all, it asks us to sacrifice our long-cherished sense of aggrievement toward our enemies, rendering them in the process not enemies at all, but fellow sinners forgiven by God.

Stern though the call might be, greater still is the promise. We are blessed, and we become children of God. By implication, the call holds an even more startling hope: by lending, by loving, by giving, by forgiving, by showing mercy: by doing all of these things, we enter into the very life of God.

In verse 27, the words "But I say to you that listen" introduce a parallel set of sayings that radically change what has gone before, but *only* if we are willing to listen with open ears and an open heart. Jesus does not waste time or mince words. He goes right to the heart of the matter in that same verse: "Love your enemies." That includes those who hate, curse, strike, and steal from you. No exceptions.

How is this mandate to love your enemies to be accomplished? Jesus answers the unspoken question in verse 31: "Do to others as you would have them do to you." "Others" is the operative word here, because it includes both your loved ones *and* your enemies. It does not read, as some have apparently interpreted it, "Do to those you love or those you have need of as you would have them do to you." The *why* is provided in verse 36: "Be merciful, just as your Father is merciful."

This has been called the Golden Rule, and it is at the heart of what Jesus teaches here. Christians have struggled with these words for centuries, asking questions like, "How can I love my neighbors if they're actively doing hurtful things to the people I love?" Obviously, we need some

discernment, since we cannot allow an innocent to be harmed or oppressed. Neither can we make the call that someone is unlovable, knowing, as we do, that God loves them—because that's who God is.

That is the crux of the matter, which Jesus addresses in verse 37: "Do not judge, and you will not be judged." Christians tend to be wildly judgmental of other people doing things that Christians are already doing themselves. It is that kind of spiteful judgment that makes Christians look like hypocrites. How many times have you been cut off on the highway by someone who has a bumper sticker with a Christian symbol?

Perhaps the problem lies in the fact that a lot of people have trouble loving themselves and thus judge themselves harshly, which makes them more likely to judge *others* harshly as well. It is difficult to forgive and love your enemies when you do not forgive and love yourself. Feelings of low self-esteem (and sometimes self-loathing) create an easy pathway to the judgment of others. Jesus knew that, of course; that may be why he said, "Be merciful, just as your Father is merciful." We have to believe that *we* are worthy of that mercy. Jesus believes that God thinks so. Why can we not? Jesus says (in v. 35) that the Most High is "kind to the ungrateful and the wicked." So why are we not?

The Sermon on the Plain is full of these seeming dichotomies. The crucifixion and resurrection may only be the greatest (to conquer death, Jesus had to die), but other such dichotomies are equally unsettling for the modern mind: "Give, and it will be given to you." "If anyone strikes you on the check, offer the other also." These are counterintuitive commands.

That is why this is the perfect passage for the Seventh Sunday after the Epiphany. Jesus' words force us to deliberate on the *ongoing* revelation of Christ. This continued outpouring of wisdom tosses previous beliefs and tenets into disarray. Like so many of the words of Jesus, they operate on multiple levels. Jesus dares listeners in verses 27–31 to compare ourselves not with the heroes and prophets of the Old Testament, but with the sinners and beggars of *our* day. Verses 32–38 then take it a step further. We are told to love the unlovable, no questions asked—even if we ourselves are the hardest persons to love and forgive.

Of course, sometimes our eagerness to believe that God will forgive us is not matched by a similar expectation on our neighbor's behalf. We often want judgment for everyone else, but mercy for ourselves.

If these passages are true, the institution that should be at the forefront of the forgiveness movement is the Christian church. It was created to be the model for what the world to come will look like. However, instead of forgiving and nurturing, the church often is the first to condemn. Sometimes the church assumes the lead—for example, the work of Nobel Peace Prize–winner Archbishop Desmond Tutu, the chair of South Africa's amazingly successful Truth and Reconciliation Commission—but that sort of forgiveness is rare.

The ideal of forgiveness has long provided a rich subject for storytellers, including filmmakers. Some of the best films in recent decades have been built around this theme: *Tender Mercies, A Trip to Bountiful, Babette's Feast, Smoke Signals, Ordinary People, Dead Man Walking,* *Places in the Heart,* and so many others. It could be argued that forgiveness is the most crucial theme of C. S. Lewis's *Chronicles of Narnia,* from *The Lion, the Witch and the Wardrobe* to *The Last Battle.* It is a powerful, reoccurring theme in film and literature, because forgiveness *is* so hard for ordinary people to do.

There is an elegant chemistry in these verses from the Sermon on the Plain. Jesus distills his message and boils it down to its essence: love others and love yourself, because God loves you. If you love the least of these in your life, everything else will work out. This passage is about what God wants from us, God's will, God's plan for our lives.

If we understand this, then verse 38, which speaks of the "good measure" that will overflow into your lap, becomes clearer. The more love we give away, the more love will come back to us, in greater and greater measure, until it cannot be contained.

ROBERT F. DARDEN

Eighth Sunday after the Epiphany

Isaiah 55:10–13
Psalm 92:1–4, 12–15

1 Corinthians 15:51–58
Luke 6:39–49

Isaiah 55:10–13

¹⁰For as the rain and the snow come down from heaven,
 and do not return there until they have watered the earth,
making it bring forth and sprout,
 giving seed to the sower and bread to the eater,
¹¹so shall my word be that goes out from my mouth;
 it shall not return to me empty,
but it shall accomplish that which I purpose,
 and succeed in the thing for which I sent it.

¹²For you shall go out in joy,
 and be led back in peace;
the mountains and the hills before you
 shall burst into song,
 and all the trees of the field shall clap their hands.
¹³Instead of the thorn shall come up the cypress;
 instead of the brier shall come up the myrtle;
and it shall be to the LORD for a memorial,
 for an everlasting sign that shall not be cut off.

Commentary 1: Connecting the Reading with Scripture

Isaiah 55 is the last chapter of what biblical scholars have long called Second Isaiah. Most agree that this section (chaps. 40–55) stems from an anonymous prophet active during the Babylonian exile, which has now been combined with chapters 1–39 (First Isaiah) and chapters 56–66 (Third Isaiah) to form the complex masterpiece that is the final form of the canonical book of Isaiah. If Second Isaiah is placed in the exilic period, First Isaiah is associated with the preexilic, eighth-century prophet who lends his name to the whole book (1:1; 2:1); Third Isaiah is usually located in the postexilic period, after the exiles returned to the land. The fine details of the process(es) that produced the book as it now stands are unclear and will probably remain that way.

Whatever the case, to this point in Year C, not including Christmas Day and Epiphany, the lectionary has included one text from Third Isaiah (62:1–5, Second Sunday after Epiphany), two texts from First Isaiah (12:2–6, Second Sunday

of Advent, and 6:1–8 [9–13], Fifth Sunday after Epiphany), and one text from Second Isaiah (43:1–7, Baptism of the Lord). Isaiah 55:10–13 (Eighth Sunday after Epiphany) is the second text in Year C from Second Isaiah. Given that it follows these other texts from Isaiah, some discussion of the larger literary context will be important, though it will best be done with reference to the text itself, not with heavy-handed hypothetical compositional theories.

The transition from Isaiah 39 to Isaiah 40 has always appeared abrupt. Indeed, Isaiah 36–39 is largely a prose account of Jerusalem during the time of Hezekiah, much of which is also found elsewhere (see 2 Kgs. 18–20; cf. 2 Chr. 32). Isaiah 40 thus comes as something of a surprise with its return to poetry, its call to comfort God's people, and its reference to Jerusalem's double payment for her sins (40:1–2). This and the later references to Cyrus of Persia by name (44:28 and 45:1; cf. 41:2, 25; 45:13;

46:11; 48:14–15) are among several indicators that chapters 40–55 are considerably later than the eighth-century prophet Isaiah ben Amoz. The time in question appears to be the Babylonian exile, at some point after Cyrus had come to prominence but before he took Babylon (539 BCE), at which point he issued his famous edict allowing the exiles to return to Judah (538 BCE). This time frame is suggested because the return home is only promised and imaginatively envisioned (e.g., Isa. 43:16–21; 51:9–11), not discussed as already experienced.

The time then is a fraught one. God's people are in exile, the temple in Jerusalem lies in ruins, much is uncertain. Comfort is desperately needed, but several voices in the Old Testament, prophetic and otherwise, considered the exile as deserved judgment; the people were reaping what they had sown. How shocking, then, to hear this Isaianic voice of comfort declaring that Jerusalem's debt has been paid in full—indeed twice over (40:2)! Second Isaiah has long been seen not only as an expression of hope to the exiles, but also as something of an argument convincing them to return home once they can (see 48:20; 52:11–12).

However, things are not quite as straightforward as that.[1] While we cannot assume that every exile was familiar with, say, the account of Judah's fall in 2 Kings or the threatening oracles of the prophets, the people are in Babylon, not Israel. Even without extended theological explanation, such a situation could be read, then as now, as proof of divine displeasure, that God was unwilling and/or unable to help the exiles in their plight (both concerns are placed on the exiles' lips in 40:27). One cannot simply speak "comfort" into a situation where significant and palpable damage has been experienced, with the effects enduring for years. To do so is the very definition of "trite." The damage in this case cuts both ways: Israel has suffered exile at God's hand, and God has suffered frustration over Israel's recalcitrance and disobedience. It is not just the time that is fraught, therefore. It is the God-Israel relationship itself.

Isaiah 40–55 addresses this via a complex interlacing of poems that do not tell a story or make an argument so much as present a presence: *God's* presence. The prophets often speak for God in the first person, but this is especially dense and pronounced in Second Isaiah.[2] That is because this is precisely what Israel needs to hear: God's voice. They need to hear it straight and honest. This is why the poems in Second Isaiah contain some of the greatest promises in all of Scripture but also candidly admit of the Lord's displeasure and anger (e.g., 41:28–29; 42:17; 42:25; 43:22–24, 27; 48:8; 50:1–2; 54:7–8). How could it be otherwise? The exiles' life in Babylon is definitive proof of the latter. That fact cannot be ignored, therefore, but must be acknowledged, even while is taken up with—even superseded by—unmatched expressions of grace and forgiveness.

There is, then, a kind of poetic conflict taking place. Will the promised comfort of 40:1 be realized? How? The conflict comes to a final resolution at the end of the poetic sequence in chapters 54–55. Chapter 54 decides once for all in favor of God's comforting and forgiving of Israel. While God's displeasure and wrath are acknowledged even here, both are delimited by the briefest of temporal markers: just "a moment" (54:7a, 8a). God's mercy and love, however, are large and everlasting (54:7b, 8b). The Lord even promises never to be angry with Israel again—just as God promised never again to flood the earth (54:9)!

After the zenith of chapter 54, one might wonder what else chapter 55 could say. More of the same, it seems, if not still more! Chapter 55 is addressed to "all" (55:1a) who thirst and hunger, promising provisions that are free, delicious, and satisfying (vv. 1–2). The poem then promises an everlasting covenant like that made to David, resulting in recognition and praise among the nations (vv. 3–5). Next, the poem enjoins the listener to seek this good God (v. 6)—and why not? God is the one who shows mercy and pardons abundantly—even beyond all human capacities to understand (vv. 7–9; cf.

---

1. In what follows I am heavily dependent on the excellent study of Katie M. Heffelfinger, *I Am Large, I Contain Multitudes: Lyric Cohesion and Conflict in Second Isaiah* (Leiden: Brill, 2011).

2. As much as 60 percent of the verses are presented as God's voice, according to Heffelfinger. The next largest percentage (25 percent) belongs to the prophet's voice.

the responsorial Ps. 92). Finally, verses 10–13 indicate the utter reliability of God's word; it is as trustworthy as the natural cycle of water on the earth and the fertility it brings (v. 10). That cycle is entirely dependable, regular, virtually automatic. So is God's word; it will not return unfulfilled but will succeed precisely according to divine intent (v. 11; note, however, that the imperative of v. 6 would be unnecessary if God's word were altogether irresistible).

Verses 12–13 indicate what this divine intent is: the people will "go out in joy" and "be led back in peace"—both verbs having exodus or, better, new exodus connotations (cf., e.g., 40:3–5; 41:17–20; 42:14–16; 49:8–12)—and creation itself will rejoice over this new exodus. It will testify to the Lord's "stature" (CEB) or serve as a kind of "memorial" (NRSV) to God's reputation—an everlasting sign that cannot be denied. The return from exile that Scripture recounts, that Second Isaiah promised, is precisely such a sign to this very day.

BRENT A. STRAWN

Commentary 2: Connecting the Reading with the World

Only occasionally are there enough weeks between Epiphany and Lent to get this far in the lectionary, and on the years when this is the last Sunday before Lent, many churches will opt to celebrate this Sunday as Transfiguration Sunday. The congregation choosing instead to observe the Eighth Sunday after Epiphany will be rewarded with a text that sparkles with its own luminous and transfiguring possibilities. Having celebrated at Christmas the Word made flesh, and having contemplated at Epiphany how the manifestation of this Word invites our gifts and alters our paths, we have spent the weeks following the Epiphany with the expansive truth of the incarnation and its transformative claim on our lives.

The lectionary texts during the time after the Epiphany make it increasingly clear that the truth of the incarnation wants to press further into our lives; it confronts us with choices about how—or if—we will allow the Word to take on flesh in our own lives. Throughout the season, the Scriptures burst with images of abundance, and we see with growing clarity that such abundance, given freely, also asks something of us. Like water turned to wine, blessing is meant to be shared. Here was the divine intention from the beginning, as God told Abraham, "I will bless you . . . so that you will be a blessing" (Gen. 12:2).

The blessing comes to life in Jesus of Nazareth, who embodies the fulfillment of the Scriptures. He makes possible the hauling up of a great catch from empty waters; the fishermen respond not by hoarding their bounty but by dropping their attempts to contain it, and by following him (Luke 5:1–11). Now we see just how far the incarnation of God's blessing is meant to go—to the very center of our lives, where, giving us everything, it also asks everything. We cannot help but wonder what we will need to leave behind in order to follow.

We are almost ready for Lent now. First, before that season of emptying, we arrive at a moment of fullness. Either next Sunday, or the Sunday after that (depending on whether there are eight or nine Sundays after the Epiphany), a desert awaits us, but today a prophet shows us luscious truth on a global scale: a new creation unfolds ahead of us. Perhaps we, as Isaiah himself did, will witness the glory of God in this vision and, by that light, see our own truth so clearly that we cannot help but respond with confession (Isa. 6:1–8).

The four gorgeous verses of today's Old Testament reading are only the final portion of the final chapter of Second Isaiah (chaps. 40–55); the larger portion of this chapter (vv. 1–9) will appear on the Third Sunday in Lent. This chapter thus straddles two seasons, moving us from vision to call, from fulfillment to promise. The movement may look backward to us—we read the end of the chapter before we will come back and read its beginning—but journeys of hope always begin with the end in mind. The preacher who prepares today's sermon with a view toward the coming Sundays can consider building on the bridge the lectionary has provided. In three or four weeks we will hear the prophet calling, "Ho, everyone who thirsts, come to the waters!" (Isa. 55:1). Today he sings to us of the Source that will slake all thirst.

Written for a people in exile, Second Isaiah as a whole, and this passage in particular, connects in a profound way with the church's situation in post-Christendom. Whereas the church once seemed to hold a central place in American culture, our decline over the last several decades—in numbers, influence, reputation, and respect—is steep and well documented. While Christians in America are not in literal exile, we have lost our place.

It is not just the church. In our rapidly changing digital era, traditional patterns of communication, community, and meaning making are disrupted; old forms pass away while the multiplying and emerging new forms shake everything. Institutions of commerce, entertainment, economy, education, and politics—all, to varying degrees, grapple with a loss of place, destabilization of identity, and anxiety about how successfully to adapt. Individuals too feel the personal effects of so much change; isolation, alienation, and free-floating anxiety increase, even as many of the institutions, shared rituals, and social patterns that once helped us deal with such feelings are shifting or disintegrating.

In the face of disruption, destabilization, disorientation, and fragmentation on every level—global, societal, ecclesial, individual—the prophet speaks. Just as Second Isaiah began in chapter 40 with God announcing, "Comfort, O comfort" (Isa. 40:1), Isaiah now reassures with a promise that at once both transcends all time and impinges directly on our present time. The whole of Second Isaiah is framed by texts that celebrate the word of the Lord as standing forever (40:6–8; 55:8–11), calling us to remember that whatever new things emerge, whatever old things pass away, one thing is always sure and true and eternal: the word of God. Even as everything else changes, withers, fades, or dies, we can rely on this. God is bigger than our institutions. God is bigger than anything else we have staked our hope on.

Isaiah directs our gaze now to the natural world, which offers us a moment to pause and consider how disconnected we may have become from the good earth. It is time to look up from our screens and really *see* what God has created. See how the rain and the snow come down, how they do not return to heaven until they have accomplished their life-giving purpose, which is to water the earth, to make it "bring forth and sprout" (v. 10). See how the earth itself does not create this life; the water from above does. Notice too how the pattern moves forward—the water comes down, giving life to the earth, and what does the earth then do with the gift? It gives "seed to the sower and bread to the eater"! (v. 10). Here, in the very design of nature itself, we see the generative character of God's giving; what we receive from God grows and cannot be contained. Just as rain and snow reliably water the ground, transforming the earth, and creating the conditions for life, so too the word of God.

It goes out from God to accomplish God's purpose, which is to transform us, and indeed the whole world, creating in us the conditions for life. When this life blooms within us, we, like the earth, yield fruit; we participate in God's purpose by passing the gift forward. The success of this work depends not on our efforts but on our yielding. Can we let go of our frantic attempts to contain and control what we have been given?

The word goes out and does not return empty; it continues its forward movement, unfolding into the future. Like many exiles, we may long for restoration, for what was lost to be returned to us, for what was destroyed to be rebuilt. Sooner or later all exiles learn the truth: there is never any going back. So we move forward now. We leave behind what needs to be left, we follow Jesus, we trust God, we share the blessing. We look forward with Isaiah, and we see. The new creation spins into view, the mountains bursting into song, the trees clapping their hands, the earth blooming with lush new growth where thorns once pricked; and there is also this: you and me, exiles transformed, going out in joy, led back in peace.

STACEY SIMPSON DUKE

Psalm 92:1–4, 12–15

¹It is good to give thanks to the LORD,
    to sing praises to your name, O Most High;
²to declare your steadfast love in the morning,
    and your faithfulness by night,
³to the music of the lute and the harp,
    to the melody of the lyre.
⁴For you, O LORD, have made me glad by your work;
    at the works of your hands I sing for joy.
. . . .
¹²The righteous flourish like the palm tree,
    and grow like a cedar in Lebanon.
¹³They are planted in the house of the LORD;
    they flourish in the courts of our God.
¹⁴In old age they still produce fruit;
    they are always green and full of sap,
¹⁵showing that the LORD is upright;
    he is my rock, and there is no unrighteousness in him.

Connecting the Psalm with Scripture and Worship

These verses from Psalm 92 affirm God's goodness and the blessings of a life devoted to praise and righteousness. Music is the language of worship; so it is fitting that the psalmist's praise involves lute, harp, and lyre (v. 3), as well as voices raised in song (vv. 1, 4). Joining heart and soul, music represents a whole-body response to God's steadfast love. The musical references in this psalm resonate with the first reading from Isaiah 55, in which mountains and hills burst into song and trees clap their hands at the promised restoration of Israel (Isa. 55:12). So great and joyful is the coming triumph of God that the natural world is moved to join in resounding praise. Let heaven and nature sing! The music continues in today's epistle reading as Paul links God's transformative work of resurrection with the sounding of the trumpet (1 Cor. 15:52). Throughout the Bible, God's saving work has its own musical accompaniment.

The very first psalm in the Bible introduces a tree deeply planted by streams of water as an image of those who seek to live righteously (Ps. 1:3). In contrast to the insubstantial chaff, which represents the wicked, the tree of the righteous has full leaves, and its fruit is abundant. The tree image is repeated in Psalm 92: the righteous flourish like a palm and grow like a cedar (Ps. 92:12). They are rooted and strong, nourished by their devotion and refreshed by God's faithfulness. These are the trees that bear fruit abundantly, even "in old age" (v. 14). Grounded and healthy, the righteous bear witness to God's goodness all of their days. Their commitments produce a harvest of love, justice, and mercy, the bounty of a life lived for God.

Planting, growing, and bearing fruit are prominent motifs in the day's readings from Isaiah and Luke. Like snow and rain, God's word falls to the earth with a purpose, watering the ground and making new life possible (Isa. 55:10). The word of God is filled with vitality and potential, eventually providing seeds to the sower, eventually providing bread to the eater, eventually providing sustenance for the journey, eventually providing shelter from stormy blasts, eventually providing companionship through the valley of the shadow of the death. What might God's nourishing word bring forth in our lives? What are the areas in need of refreshment? Where is the parched ground desperate for water?

The passage from Isaiah concludes with an image of fruitfulness. The barrenness of the desert, represented by the thorn and the brier, is transformed to a place of abundance and lushness, a place where trees like the cypress and the myrtle grow, a place where righteousness can flourish, a place that signifies God's life-giving word (Isa. 55:13).

In his Sermon on the Plain, Jesus uses the relationship between a tree and its fruit to teach a lesson about the products of a faithful life: "No good tree bears bad fruit, nor again does a bad tree bear good fruit; for each tree is known by its own fruit" (Luke 6:43–44). Deeds of righteousness, acts of mercy, and works of love evidence a life that is deeply rooted in God's word. Thorns and brambles do not produce figs and grapes. Rather, delicious fruit is borne by healthy plants, carefully tended and well nourished. There is a sequential logic to a successful harvest: good soil promotes deep rootedness that results in abundant fruit. The quality of the soil is foundational.

As he develops the lesson on the importance of a solid base, Jesus concludes his sermon with a transition from agriculture to construction, noting that a sturdy house, one that is able to withstand floods and circumstance, is one with the foundation laid on rock. The one who builds a house in this way, Jesus says, the one who begins constructing by digging deeply, is "what someone is like who comes to me, hears my words, and acts on them" (Luke 6:47–48). A strong base makes for a strong house. It is first a matter of taking the time and making the effort to locate the solid rock. The song of praise that is Psalm 92 concludes with the affirmation that God "is my rock" (Ps. 92:15). That is the place to build; that is the foundation to seek.

In the epistle reading, Paul makes his famously emphatic statement of God's triumph over all things, "Thanks be to God, who gives us the victory through our Lord Jesus Christ" (1 Cor. 15:57). Then he immediately follows with an admonition to be "steadfast and immovable, always excelling in the work of the Lord" (1 Cor. 15:58). In response to what God has done, the text encourages us to seek a solid foundation and on that rock build a life that shows forth God's goodness.

These texts all encourage the preacher to lift up formative practices that nourish a deep-rooted, well-founded faith. Developing and maintaining a base on which a significant faith can grow or on which a significant faith can be built requires regular and committed attention to core activities like worship, study, and service. There is a cumulative effect to these practices. Over time, they yield a bountiful harvest; over time, they construct a house that cannot be shaken.

JOHN W. WURSTER

1 Corinthians 15:51–58

⁵¹Listen, I will tell you a mystery! We will not all die, but we will all be changed, ⁵²in a moment, in the twinkling of an eye, at the last trumpet. For the trumpet will sound, and the dead will be raised imperishable, and we will be changed. ⁵³For this perishable body must put on imperishability, and this mortal body must put on immortality. ⁵⁴When this perishable body puts on imperishability, and this mortal body puts on immortality, then the saying that is written will be fulfilled:

"Death has been swallowed up in victory."
⁵⁵"Where, O death, is your victory?
   Where, O death, is your sting?"

⁵⁶The sting of death is sin, and the power of sin is the law. ⁵⁷But thanks be to God, who gives us the victory through our Lord Jesus Christ.
⁵⁸Therefore, my beloved, be steadfast, immovable, always excelling in the work of the Lord, because you know that in the Lord your labor is not in vain.

Commentary 1: Connecting the Reading with Scripture

In 1 Corinthians 15:50–58 Paul completes his discussion of the resurrection of Jesus Christ and of Jesus' followers begun at 15:1. More specifically, these verses round off Paul's answers to two related questions posed in verse 35. Paul asked, "How are the dead raised?" and "With what kind of body do they come?" Paul answered the second question in verses 36–49. Now in verses 50–58 (esp. vv. 50–54), he answers the first. As an answer to one of two related questions, Paul's line of thought in these verses bears strong similarities to the discussion just concluded at verse 49.

Paul prefaces his questions of verse 35 with the words, "But someone will ask . . ." By doing so, he employs the method of teaching known in the Hellenistic world as diatribe, which involves asking a question as if it had been posed by an interlocutor among the audience, then answering it.[1]

At verse 50, Paul abruptly breaks off his argument in order to draw it to a close. The NRSV's translation of the opening clause, "What I am saying, brothers and sisters, is this," properly conveys the sense that Paul will summarize what he has said so far.

The terse statement that follows almost carries a confessional tone. The two clauses stand in synonymous parallelism, in which the second line restates the first in different words. This is a common stylistic feature in biblical literature, especially in the poetry found in the Hebrew Bible. We can display the parallelism as follows:

Flesh and blood cannot inherit the kingdom of God,
nor does the perishable inherit the imperishable.

The contrast is not between present and future so much as the present *body* and the future transformed *body*. This is Paul's point: the human body *must* undergo transformation.

Paul now returns to the issue raised by his first question in verse 35: How then will the resurrection take place? He offers no detailed explanation. He merely asserts that the dead in Christ and the living in Christ will receive transformed bodies in a moment when Christ returns. Paul labels this information a "mystery," meaning something about God's purposes that was once hidden but has now been made

1. For more on the diatribe, see Commentary 1: Connecting the Reading with Scripture, on 1 Cor. 15:35–38, 42–50, Seventh Sunday after the Epiphany, in this volume.

known by revelation (cf. Rom. 11:25; 1 Cor. 2:7). Once again, Paul highlights continuity as well as discontinuity between the mortal bodies and the imperishable ones. According to verses 53–54, the perishable will "put on" the imperishable as one puts on clothing. This common Pauline metaphor (2 Cor. 5:2–5; cf. Eph. 4:24; Col. 3:12) suggests the perishable body will not be done away with, but will somehow be encompassed in the new.[2]

Paul sees this bodily transformation from perishable to imperishable as the final defeat of sin and death (15:54b–56). Paul goes to the OT prophets to support his claim:

> "Death has been swallowed up in victory."
> "Where, O death, is your victory?
> Where, O death, is your sting?"

The first line comes from Isaiah 25:7, while the last two are from Hosea 13:14. The book of Revelation quotes from the following verse of this passage in Isaiah ("he will wipe every tear from their eyes," Rev. 21:4/Isa. 25:8). As in 1 Corinthians, John the Revelator speaks of this moment as one when "death will be no more." The two NT texts witness to a common early Christian belief that resurrection and accompanying victory over death stand as the final purpose in God's salvation of those in Christ. So Paul concludes triumphantly, "Thanks be to God, who gives us the victory through our Lord Jesus Christ" (v. 57). These words from Isaiah, picked up both in 1 Corinthians and in Revelation, speak to the truth of the Old Testament reading for this Sunday. Isaiah writes that God's word spoken by Isaiah "shall not return to me empty, but it shall accomplish that which I purpose, and succeed in the thing for which I sent it" (Isa. 55:11). Both Paul and John the Revelator attest to that truth.

Paul draws his conclusion in verse 58: "Therefore, my beloved, be steadfast, immovable, always excelling in the work of the Lord, because you know that in the Lord your labor is not in vain." This exhortation serves multiple functions. First, it draws to a close Paul's arguments in chapter 15 about the resurrection. Note how the language of verse 58 echoes that of 15:1–2. Paul proclaimed the gospel in which the Corinthians "stand" and through which they are being saved; unless they have come to believe "in vain." His language thus creates an *inclusio* around this section of the letter, marking it off as a unified whole.

Secondly, within the practices of ancient rhetoric, verse 58 functions as the *epilogos* of Paul's argument in the letter as a whole. As such, this exhortation both recapitulates Paul's key points from the beginning of the letter and appeals to the emotions of his audience in an attempt to seal his case before the Corinthians. What then has Paul been arguing for since chapter 1? Margaret Mitchell has demonstrated that the rhetorical burden of 1 Corinthians consists of Paul's appeal for unity.[3] First Corinthians 1:10 serves as the prosthesis or thesis for the argument of the entire letter: "I appeal to you . . . that all of you be in agreement and that there be no divisions among you, but that you be united in the same mind and the same purpose."

The letter body that follows consists of Paul's response to one problem after another that has arisen among the Corinthians. Paul sees all these issues through the single lens of threats to the community's unity in Christ. By means of this closing appeal in 15:58, Paul looks back on these varied problems and exhorts the Corinthians not to become distracted from the "work of the Lord." Within 1 Corinthians that work centers on maintaining the unity as God's people caught up in God's saving work in Christ (1:4–9). Such work will never prove futile, for the formation of a people to be God's own has been at the heart of God's purposes since the call of Abraham (Gen. 12:2–3). Thus this single verse plays an oversize role within the entire letter.

Finally, this verse marks the end of the body of the letter with an upbeat note of triumph and hope. Paul's long series of responses to problems among the Corinthians has now ended. Beginning in chapter 16, Paul will launch into new

---

2. Richard B. Hays, *1 Corinthians*, Interpretation (Louisville, KY: Westminster John Knox Press, 1997), 274–75.
3. Margaret Mitchell, *Paul and the Rhetoric of Reconciliation* (Louisville, KY: Westminster/John Knox Press, 1993).

subject matter—travel plans and final greetings—typical of ancient letter closings.

This final exhortation, placed at the end of a lengthy discussion, demonstrates that God's resurrection of the dead, whether of Jesus in the past or of those in Christ at Jesus' return in the future, carries moral implications for the present. Paul repeatedly claims that, apart from the resurrection, all Christian labor is in vain

(15:12–19, 29–32). By affirming the truth of the resurrection proclaimed in the good news they received and through which they are being saved (15:1–2), the Corinthians have the confidence to walk faithfully and courageously in that truth. Such a life will entail firm resolve to maintain their unity through love for one another (see the final exhortation in 16:13).

JAMES C. MILLER

Commentary 2: Connecting the Reading with the World

This passage presents us with words that definitively witness to our hope and trust in the resurrection:

> "Death has been swallowed up in victory."
> "Where, O death, is your victory?
>   Where, O death, is your sting?"
>
> The sting of death is sin, and the power
> of sin is the law. But thanks be to God,
> who gives us the victory through our
> Lord Jesus Christ. (1 Cor. 15:54b–57)

Paul's poetic mockery of death echoes the mockery of Jesus by the soldiers at the foot of the cross during the crucifixion. Paul's mockery triumphantly transcends the soldiers' mockery, as in the resurrection nothing remains of death but a mockery of its previous hold on humanity. The faithful through the ages have held on to Paul's words when facing death in its many forms, personal and communal. The change that Paul foretells to the community in Corinth (1 Cor. 15:51b–52) is inevitable, as the end of all history is inevitable. Whether we are talking about the consummation of all things, when God creates the new heaven and new earth, or we simply mean the "last things" that all members of the human family will face at the end of life, we must heed Paul's admonition that the time is close when the faithful must put on imperishability and witness to the promises of the resurrection and God's power over death.

In the context of 1 Corinthians, victory over death does not stand apart from history. Clearly Paul's statement immediately after this

declaration of victory attests to the paradox of life in history: *The sting of death is sin*. As a community, Christians move from Sunday to Sunday, and in our daily devotional life, through examination of conscience, prayer of contrition, and acceptance of the forgiveness that is Christ's holy reconciliation. Whether or not we look for an imminent end of the world, each of us is called to the journey of acknowledging the spiritual death of sin and moving into forgiveness and new life. Along that path, the resurrection serves as our victorious Yes! to urgent calls for life and reconciliation in today's world. Our hope of new life in Christ, despite the grand failures of this world and the constant reminders of our sinfulness, both personal and corporate, is not just a gift of our faith, but a requirement of the same. Paul insists that indeed this is not a futile hope, for "you know that in the Lord your labor is not in vain" (1 Cor. 15:58).

Paul's acknowledgment that sin infects even the best of our intentions stands at the head of a long stream of Christian tradition. That stream flows broad and deep through the teachings of Augustine; in more recent years we see it running through the work of Reinhold Niebuhr, Jean Bethke Elshtain, and others. This stream of "Christian realism" attends to the paradox of sin and salvation in history, and how the two present themselves even in society's most noble projects. To appreciate Paul's resurrection hope properly, we have to see it against the backdrop of sin and its consequences, especially at the social and corporate level.[4]

---

4. E.g., Reinhold Niebuhr, *Moral Man and Immoral Society: A Study of Ethics and Politics* (1932; repr. Louisville, KY: Westminster John Knox Press, 2001).

Communities of faith in particular must understand fully how this paradox shapes their projects. Resurrection hope without an awareness of the ongoing power of sin sets the table for a false and destructive triumphalism. Ignorant of the ironic possibility that our good intentions will not save us from our worst inclinations, we harm the very ones we seek to help. When our grandest plans or our finest projects result in the exclusion of particular groups, or the perpetuation of systemic evils, a false sense of victory over sin may indeed blind us to these flaws, or worse, see the victim of our own sin as the enemy or disrupter of the peace we have built.

In *Dear White Christians*, ethicist Jennifer Harvey witnesses to what it means to hold on to Paul's paradox of being attentive to how sin infects our projects, while clinging on to the power of the imperishable, and the hope that in the Lord our labor will not be in vain.[5] This is hard work. The liturgical practice of confession, contrition, and reconciliation prepares the community for the hard work of examining our collective projects within the context of this paradox. Harvey's attention to why prior efforts at racial reconciliation by mainline and evangelical Christian churches have failed is not aimed at castigating our failures, but at striving for true justice that includes the resurrection hope of historically excluded and oppressed groups in the United States. In other words, the project of living into resurrection hope and witnessing to Christ's victory over death—within history— requires vigilance against the sin of exclusion and a false trust in our own ability to safeguard against it.

Hope in the resurrection means a hope for a life with dignity for all, one that must be constructed patiently and intentionally. Like Paul in Corinthians, Harvey notes the many ways communities interrupt the project of edification and justice, sometimes unintentionally, but often quite so, such as cutting short denomination-wide conversations on racial justice and calling them a failure, establishing special programs and spending resources without input from the very groups one seeks to enter into covenant with, systematically ignoring the goals or rationale of black Christian leaders, beginning processes of "racial reconciliation" that fail to examine the ways in which white Christians have historically contributed to racial injustice. The hope of racial justice, working toward the oneness of the human family, is essential to the identity of Christian churches and our project for wholeness in Christ's reconciling all to Christ's own self.

Paul's letter to Corinthians has much to offer regarding how hard it is to work toward the edification of the community—often fractured by sin—within history. Aware as Paul was of the deep hold sin exercises over our communities, we should pay attention to the fact that the discourse on resurrection hope and putting on of imperishability comes close to the *end* of the letter. In 1 Corinthians Paul's rhetoric slyly reveals his theology: resurrection gets the last word. In his wisdom Paul knows that only when we hold onto the promise of victory over death and all that deals death in this world are we able to face our sins and our brokenness with ever-renewing hope for wholeness. Resurrection hope is what makes realistic view of human history and behavior possible.

Likewise, groups that have been at the receiving end of exclusion, oppression, and violence hear in the closing chapters of 1 Corinthians the promise of a wholeness and justice that is beyond the scope of human understanding, but that appears within history in Christ's victory over death. It is this hope that freed Cesar Chavez, Dietrich Bonhoeffer, Martin Luther King Jr., and others to proclaim victory over the deaths dealt wrongly and unjustly to so many, knowing full well the consequences that such claims have on their persons. Against the backdrop of their quest and so many others' quest for wholeness within Christian communities and beyond, Paul's mockery of death becomes a brazen invitation to life truly lived in resurrection hope.

MARÍA TERESA DÁVILA

---

5. Jennifer Harvey, *Dear White Christians: For Those Still Longing for Racial Reconciliation* (Grand Rapids: Eerdmans, 2014).

Luke 6:39–49

³⁹He also told them a parable: "Can a blind person guide a blind person? Will not both fall into a pit? ⁴⁰A disciple is not above the teacher, but everyone who is fully qualified will be like the teacher. ⁴¹Why do you see the speck in your neighbor's eye, but do not notice the log in your own eye? ⁴²Or how can you say to your neighbor, 'Friend, let me take out the speck in your eye,' when you yourself do not see the log in your own eye? You hypocrite, first take the log out of your own eye, and then you will see clearly to take the speck out of your neighbor's eye.

⁴³"No good tree bears bad fruit, nor again does a bad tree bear good fruit; ⁴⁴for each tree is known by its own fruit. Figs are not gathered from thorns, nor are grapes picked from a bramble bush. ⁴⁵The good person out of the good treasure of the heart produces good, and the evil person out of evil treasure produces evil; for it is out of the abundance of the heart that the mouth speaks.

⁴⁶"Why do you call me 'Lord, Lord,' and do not do what I tell you? ⁴⁷I will show you what someone is like who comes to me, hears my words, and acts on them. ⁴⁸That one is like a man building a house, who dug deeply and laid the foundation on rock; when a flood arose, the river burst against that house but could not shake it, because it had been well built. ⁴⁹But the one who hears and does not act is like a man who built a house on the ground without a foundation. When the river burst against it, immediately it fell, and great was the ruin of that house."

Commentary 1: Connecting the Reading with Scripture

This passage sounds a bit like a grab bag of wisdom sayings, one after the other, as if Luke put together a string of Jesus' sayings that bear a family resemblance but not much more. One recalls the book of Proverbs in hearing these truisms: the blind cannot lead the blind, good trees bear good fruit, sweet fruit will not come from a bramble bush, houses built on strong foundations will better withstand the weather. However, as one explores possible connections, an overriding theme comes through. It resonates with the intimacy between Christian ethics and divine character described in the previous section, with our linking of verse 31 with verse 36 in an ethic of love defined by God's mercy. The theme moving through this section is the necessary unity of character and action in Christian discipleship.

Paragraph 1: Seek Humility. Jesus' first parable in this chapter paints an odd picture: someone who is unable to see the path ahead is being directed by another who sees no more,

saying, "I'll show you the way!" For Jesus, this introduces the question of who is qualified to lead, just as it raises the question of the nature of leadership itself. The claim that comes next is not clean and resolute. We might expect a call to proper subordination, "Therefore, students ought to follow their teachers!" or something like that. Instead, just as Luke's Jesus asserts the necessity and authority of the "sighted" teacher, he also makes space for the student to become "qualified" (NRSV), "fully trained" (NIV), or "perfect" (KJV), and thus equal to the teacher—though never superior. The logic is hidden, especially when the next sentence turns to critique by the unqualified-to-judge crowd. The order goes like this:

1. The blind need a sighted guide.
2. The parable applies to teacher and students, but not really, because students can become equally sighted with their teachers, though never clearer sighted.

3. Personal failings (our log-in-the-eye) may leave us self-deceived, and therefore insufficiently self-aware to either understand or critique others (whose vision, if still cloudy, may yet be clearer than our own).

The first and third parts of the paragraph promote proper humility. The second gives hope that, if we interpret the metaphor of blindness as it relates to insight, unlike the one who will not see, the student who may have cloudy vision at first can yet become better sighted—in fact, fully qualified. That possibility bridges the irremediable state of metaphorical blindness in the parable and a very remediable case of log-in-eye. So the moral of the three seems that anyone aspiring to become a fully trained/qualified disciple, ready even to be a teacher, begins by removing the logs from her or his own eye. In short: tend to yourself in humility. Learning begins with that step.

To delve into the full connectivity of this teaching, one might look at how Luke speaks of a "teacher" throughout the Gospel. The Greek term for "teacher" appears seventeen times in the Gospel—most often in the vocative by people inquiring of Jesus, but also of John.

2:46   Teachers in the temple converse with the boy Jesus.

3:12   John the Baptist is addressed as teacher.

7:40   Simon the Pharisee addresses Jesus.

8:49   Jairus's servants say, "Do not trouble the teacher," after his daughter has died.

9:38   A desperate man summons Jesus to help his son.

10:25   A lawyer asks Jesus how to be saved.

11:45   A lawyer cries foul.

12:13   A brother calls on Jesus to settle an inheritance squabble.

18:18   A rich ruler asks Jesus how to get eternal life.

19:39   Pharisees on Palm Sunday plead with Jesus to get his disciples to stop shouting.

20:21, 28, 39   Jewish leaders test Jesus.

21:7   A temple audience asks about things to come.

22:11   Jesus is self-referential as Last Supper arrangements are made.

Disciples join Jesus as guide and teacher when their inward devotion is strong, with their outward actions consistent and expressive of that inward faith. Here again is the ethic of the Golden Rule. The question is character: consistency between the personal and the social leads to a strong tree that bears sweet fruit. The key is not mere consistency, but integrity congruent with the character of God.

In the history of interpretation, one sees connections with the Eastern Orthodox understanding of *divination*, when through the work of divine grace in Christ's atonement a believer can approach equivalent nature with God. The split between word and act, faith and life, is narrowed.

Paragraph 2: The Heart Will Win Out. The second parable in this section completes this movement, turning our eyes toward fruit trees. Matthew's Jesus uses this image to help his followers sort true teachers and prophets from false teachers and prophets, and to understand the integrity of faithful discipleship: "By their fruits you will know them" (Matt. 7:15–20 NKJV). Luke's Jesus does not draw that application directly. Rather, he makes a general statement about humanity that derives behavior from the inner person.

Whether one concludes that Luke or Matthew is closer to their shared source, Q, may depend on whether one thinks that Luke has restated the source to universalize Jesus' Jewish ethic or Matthew has restated it to render Jesus' words most helpful in sorting true from false teachers. In either case, the canonized material allows both purposes.

Related to our musings on the first paragraph, however, another problem arises: fruit (like soil in Mark 4/Matt. 13) cannot change itself. If a tree can give only fruit that it is destined to give by its variety, how can a disciple be perfected as implied in verse 42? Is our goodness or badness a given? Is this a theologian's predestination or a sociologist's determinism? Is Jesus simply making a point that does not need to be verified by theological or scientific accuracy, but simply asks for intuitive application? That point would be that the quality of discipleship is measured by integrity between what's inside and what's outside. This seems more consistent with the movement of the text.

Paragraph 3: Find a True Foundation. At first look, the section concludes with another apparent contradiction. Having just said, "You can read people like a book, by the fruit they manifest in action," Jesus now says, "Sometimes the loudest Jesus followers, who sound like disciples by what they say, are not truly mine" (see v. 46).

Jesus resolves the tension quickly by focusing on obedience beyond words, which is the fruit of discipleship. It turns out that like home-builders who choose good foundation stones, the better builders are not the people who talk a good game but, rather, the people who hear Jesus and do what he says.

Here Luke and Matthew are nearly the same. In each case, the parable closes a teaching unit. For Matthew, it properly closes the Sermon on the Mount; for Luke, it closes the briefer Sermon on the Plain. All hear (*akouō*) Jesus, but

---

The Distance between Feeling Right and Doing Right

Here I am reminded of another plausible form of the same error. It is a mistake concerning what is meant by faith. We know Scripture tells us that God accepts those who have faith in Him. Now the question is, What *is* faith, and how can a man tell that he *has* faith? Some persons answer at once and without hesitation, that "to have faith is to feel oneself to be nothing, and God every thing; it is to be convinced of sin, to be conscious one cannot save oneself, and to wish to be saved by Christ our Lord; and that it is, moreover, to have the love of Him warm in one's heart, and to rejoice in Him, to desire His glory, and resolve to live to Him and not to the world."

But I will answer, with all due seriousness, as speaking on a serious subject, that this is *not* faith. . . . Why? Because there is an immeasurable distance between feeling right and doing right. A man may have all these good thoughts and emotions, yet (if he has not yet hazarded them to the experiment of practice) he cannot promise himself that he has any sound and permanent principle at all. If he has not yet acted upon them, we have no voucher, barely on *account* of them, to believe that they are any thing but words.

Though a man spoke like an angel, I would not believe him, on the mere ground of his speaking. Nay, till he acts upon them, he has not even evidence to himself that he has true *living* faith. Do fervent thoughts make faith *living*? St. James tells us otherwise. He tells us *works*, deeds of obedience, are the life of faith. . . . So that those who think they really believe, because they have in word and thought surrendered themselves to God, are much too hasty in their judgement. They have done something, indeed, but not at all the most difficult part of their duty, which is to surrender themselves to God in deed and act. . . .

As far as we know any thing of the matter, justifying faith has no existence independent of its particular definite acts. . . . He who does one little deed of obedience, whether he denies himself some comfort to relieve the sick and needy, or curbs his temper, or forgives an enemy, or asks forgiveness for an offence committed by him, or resists the clamour or ridicule of the world—such a one . . . evinces more true faith than could be shown by the most fluent religious conversation, the most intimate knowledge of Scripture doctrine, or the most remarkable agitation and change of religious sentiments. Yet how many are there who sit still with folded hands, dreaming, doing nothing at all, thinking they have done every thing, or need do nothing, when they merely have had these good *thoughts*, which will save no one.

John Henry Newman (1801–1890), "Promising without Doing," in *Parochial and Plain Sermons* 1 (London: Longmans, Green, and Co., 1907), 165.

those who act on (*poieō*) what Jesus says, and so obey, are praised.

Connection in the Lectionary. The passages from Isaiah 55 and Psalm 92 connected to these verses from Luke similarly affirm the logic of blessing in faith. In Isaiah, God's word will have the power of integrity, healing the rift between the physical and spiritual by providing what is needed for the tree of discipleship to bear fruit. Practical metaphors, like rain or snow that feeds the ground (v. 10), evoke this sense of God's word. In Psalm 92, the righteous, like faithful disciples in Luke, exhibit joy, flourish, bear fruit, and bear witness to God's own righteousness (vv. 12–15).

WES AVRAM

Commentary 2: Connecting the Reading with the World

In the Eighth Sunday after Epiphany, Jesus concludes the Sermon on the Plain with a series of four of what are sometimes called parables, but could just as easily be called similes, each drawn from everyday life, the things that everyone in the crowd might see or experience. Luke may consider these passages to be a kind of foundational statement by Jesus. If so, verses 39–49, which serve as a conclusion of sorts to the Sermon on the Plain, are worthy of particular scrutiny.

The juxtaposition of blessings and woes that marked the earlier sections changes here to a short series of comparison stories: the blind being led by the blind, the speck and the plank, the good and bad fruit, and the good and bad houses. Each comparison revolves around the theme of discernment, knowing whom to listen to, what to choose, what to do. The preceding verses focused on enabling the hearer to envision (and build) the perfect community. The implication here is instruction for that community: that building must come from a "fully qualified" teacher. These verses, then, are meant to help the reader sift through competing claims and identify the qualities of the perfect teacher.

There is a certain irony implied in this passage. If a teacher teaches his or her own failings and if a student masters these flaws and failings, that student is a *success* by the teacher's standards. Perhaps what Jesus is implying is a series of unstated questions: What has taught, shaped, and influenced you? What has mastered you? Is it power? Fame? Glory? Comfort? The applause of others?

Assuming then that the teacher is worthy, the emphasis shifts to the application of what the student has heard and learned—the doing. The true followers of Jesus both hear *and* act on Jesus' words. When Jesus is not present, knowing whom to follow and listen to is no less important. There is a sense here that, beginning with verse 39, Jesus' words are aimed more at the disciples than the crowd. In verses 39–40, the pitfalls of following a blind teacher require discernment *and* action on the part of the listener/follower. Only the fully trained student, one immersed in the words of Jesus, can become a teacher worthy to be followed. It may be worth noting that in Matthew 23:16 Jesus calls the Pharisees "blind guides," but—as always—Jesus is likely casting the net much wider than merely the Pharisees. Perhaps Jesus is making a statement about all rulers. Whole nations have fallen when their leaders were bigoted, selfish, vain, and ambitious. Jesus may also be subtly letting his disciples know that, should they truly follow this path, there is only persecution and death.

The most famous comparison story—the speck in the brother's eye and the log in one's own—turns the narrative in a somewhat different direction. This is not the first time Jesus employs a humorous bit of hyperbole. Another such instance is in Matthew 23:24 with the equally vivid illustration of the Pharisees who strain out a gnat but swallow a camel. The underlying message, however, is deadly serious.

Jesus is shown as being angry only rarely, most notably in the cleansing of the temple and the harsh words aimed at hypocritical Pharisees. In those cases, what has stirred Jesus is judgment. To judge and condemn someone else when you are unable or unwilling to see your own serious moral failings is not a problem exclusive to Christians; it just seems worse when they do it. There is very little excuse or sympathy expressed for someone who has read the words in the previous verses—words that clearly outline what is expected of followers of the Way—and still decides not to embrace and apply those words.

Time and again, Jesus refuses to fall into the trap of judgment, instead choosing to follow the path of charity, love, and forgiveness. The mote/speck image is a wonderful one, easily and graphically memorable, an image that instantly encourages believers to think twice before judging others.

The theme of wood continues with the next verses, the illustration of the fruit trees that are recognized and given worth by what they produce. Good things—figs and grapes—do not come from thorns or brambles. Likewise, Jesus says, good people do and say good things. Bad people do and say bad things. On the surface, this seems obvious enough. However, as the context makes plain, many people who say they are good, are not. We can claim anything. It is our fruit—what we do—that distinguishes us. Jesus is the master, the good tree, and his words are the good fruit, the treasure. Those who will follow Jesus must also produce good fruit. In that sense, the word of God becomes grafted into our hearts.

This leads naturally into verses 46–49. Many people claim to follow Jesus. In some places, it is fashionable to do so. Again, saying it does not make it so. There is a hint of pathos in the words, "Why do you call me 'Lord, Lord,' and do not do what I tell you?" Jesus knows what is best. He knows that our lives would be so much easier, so much richer, so much more rewarding, if we would only do what he says, if only we would listen, if only we would *truly* follow him.

Saying something, but not really believing or living it, is sometimes called "lip service." Jesus closes the Sermon on the Plain with a wonderfully vivid illustration of the perils of lip service. Verses 47–48 describe the dwelling place of the homeowner who hears and acts on the words of Jesus. This home is built on bedrock: solid, unmoving, able to weather life's storms and floods. In verse 49, the hapless homeowner who hears the words of Jesus but does not act on them instead builds a house on sand, a home that is washed away by the first heavy rain.

The proof, once again, is in the action. The house built on sand is a form of Christianity built the easy way, lip service without conviction. The temptation to seek cheap grace and no-cost discipleship has dimmed little throughout Christian history. Perhaps we think that we "deserve" all of the good things we have received in life, because we are good. Perhaps we think these good things will continue flowing our way indefinitely. When hard times come—and they always do—we have neither the depth nor the experience to withstand them. Marriages, business, institutions of any kind must be built on a firm foundation in order to survive the tough days ahead. Beautiful, expensive clothes and facades cannot long hide the corruption beneath.

So the Sermon on the Plain comes to an end. Jesus has called his listeners to action—to feed the hungry and minister to the suffering. He has also called his listeners to ruthlessly examine their own hearts, to cast out judgment, vanity, and—in some cases—self-hatred. He has called his listeners to examine the words of others, particularly those who would be their leaders.

With wisdom comes responsibility. Jesus calls us to hear, to love, to act—not because we are supposed to, but because we want to, because we need to, joyfully. A good heart is a great treasure in the kingdom to come.

ROBERT F. DARDEN

Ninth Sunday after the Epiphany

1 Kings 8:22–23, 41–43   Galatians 1:1–12
Psalm 96:1–9   Luke 7:1–10

1 Kings 8:22–23, 41–43

22Then Solomon stood before the altar of the LORD in the presence of all the assembly of Israel, and spread out his hands to heaven. 23He said, "O LORD, God of Israel, there is no God like you in heaven above or on earth beneath, keeping covenant and steadfast love for your servants who walk before you with all their heart. . . .
41"Likewise when a foreigner, who is not of your people Israel, comes from a distant land because of your name 42—for they shall hear of your great name, your mighty hand, and your outstretched arm—when a foreigner comes and prays toward this house, 43then hear in heaven your dwelling place, and do according to all that the foreigner calls to you, so that all the peoples of the earth may know your name and fear you, as do your people Israel, and so that they may know that your name has been invoked on this house that I have built."

Commentary 1: Connecting the Reading with Scripture

This text is drawn from a larger narrative tradition of temple prayers. This traditional practice was not unique to Israel, as other groups often celebrated the conclusion of significant building projects with some act of adoration and thanksgiving. We find parallels in Sumerian, Babylonian, and Assyrian temple or palace building projects. These projects were not just material in nature but were material expressions of a higher spiritual dimension of reality. These projects were often described in great detail, perhaps as a testimony to the spiritual devotion of the architects and builders. These occasions were the basis for the emergence of narrative dedicatory prayer tradition with a specific literary structure. Solomon's prayer, as recorded in this text, in some ways shares that literary structure. This literary tradition is described in great detail in Victor Hurowitz's book *I Have Built You an Exalted House: Temple Building in the Bible in Light of Mesopotamian and North-West Semitic Writings* (1992). While this kind of comparative analysis can be extremely helpful, it is in the differences that the most fertile insights are to be found.

One of the central functions of such temples,

as the dwelling place of God, was to be the place where three important dimensions of life were encountered: the vertical, the horizontal, and the temporal. The temple was the place where heaven above met earth below. The temple was the place where God met God's people. The temple was the place where one could look back to the paradigm of Eden and forward to and through the reiterations of Eden of the first and second temples. Christians moved on, further, to seeing Jesus as the temple, looking through the people of God as the temple to the ultimate revelation of the temple of God in the New Jerusalem. The temple was the center of these cosmic continua and continually oriented and reoriented the lives of the people.

The verses that comprise this reading are important for several reasons. First, they are part of one of the longest prayers in the Old Testament. This prayer encompasses significant portions of chapter 8 and 9 and in its own way tells the story of the people and their historical experience with their God. However, the verses that have been selected for the lectionary reading for this Sunday provide us with an opportunity to examine more closely three themes that may be helpful for Bible study and sermon preparation.

The first theme has to do with the identity of Solomon. Solomon was wealthy, regal, and the last-born son of his father David, which is similar to how he is recognized in the Qur'an. Ultimately, his name means peaceful. He emerges as an important biblical figure largely in relation to his genealogy and his deeds. The circumstances surrounding his conception and birth situate him within the larger narrative of his father. However, we never really know Solomon in the way that we know his father and his siblings. Throughout the Old Testament, their identities are crafted before our eyes through adventure, love, hate, betrayal, reconciliation, tragedy, and so forth. Solomon stands under the long shadow of his father and his siblings. It would not be too much of a stretch to say that Solomon as a character recedes behind the figure of his father, and later behind his own historical deeds. This kind of recession of character is common in literary contexts where what a person accomplishes is more important that who that person is. This is the case with Solomon. We know who he is only through his deeds: deciding the case of the two mothers and the one live infant, negotiating a labor agreement with Hiram, exercising diplomacy among his neighbors.

Solomon is known primarily through his deeds, but this text provides an exception to this observation, and that brings us to our second point. In this text, Solomon offers the temple prayer. After all of the people and accoutrements are gathered, Solomon raises his arms and prays. This is a role that is normally assigned to the priest, but here Solomon, who is already king, adds this priestly dimension to his role. What does this tell us about Solomon? What is the significance of this development, in light of the priestly role that his father never fulfilled, and the dedication of the temple that his father could not build? The portions of the prayer referenced here, verses 22 and 23, are cultic in function. They are uttered to solidify the form and focus of religious reverence among the people. This portion of the prayer is directed toward adoration of God. Solomon emerges as the one who stands with the people before God to dedicate a house that belongs to God and this people.

Our third point focuses on our second set of verses for this reading. Here the tone and tenor of the prayer change radically. In these verses, Solomon petitions God on behalf of those who are not counted in the original covenant of God. Solomon sees this temple as more than a monument to the cultic solidarity of Israel. He affirms that "the foreigner," who is not ordinarily counted among the chosen ones, will come from a great distance, drawn by the name of the Almighty. Solomon begins to take on the role of the prophet who affirms that the reach and will of God transcend any narrow nationalistic interests. When the stranger comes to the temple, he or she will experience a God whose arms are outstretched, receptive, and embracing. They too will hear God's voice and experience God's presence. Most importantly, Solomon asks that God give the stranger the same privilege that the chosen ones enjoy: "Do whatever the foreigner asks of you, so that all the peoples of the earth may know your name and fear you, as do your own people Israel, and may know that this house I have built bears your name." Solomon pleads for their complete inclusion in God's covenantal grace.

In this prayer, two complementary, but sometimes competing, themes are evident. The particularity of God's choice of Israel is juxtaposed to the universality of God's embrace of all people. The figure of Solomon manages to hold these themes in a creative and revelatory tension. He is not the cultic hero that his father was, but he fully embodies the hopes, dreams, and aspirations of his people. At the same time, he prefigures that prophetic figure who would draw all people unto himself. Here we can, as noted above, connect this text with Jesus' identification of his own body with the temple, and with the *ekklēsia* as the temple. It points to the continual search of God's people for God's dwelling place.

A potential insight not to be missed here is the possibility that Solomon's chief trait, wisdom, is meant to be the center of the temple's attraction. We might ask whether worship in our own communities is centered on wisdom, or whether it is captive to predetermined conclusions about the great questions of life. This text can also be extremely illuminating in a context where reverence to social and political institutions is required but their inclusiveness is doubted. This text suggests a fundamental social truth. The authority of any institution is directly proportional to the degree that those to be governed are included in that institution.

JAMES H. EVANS JR.

Commentary 2: Connecting the Reading with the World

At only five verses, the reading from the Hebrew Bible for this Ninth Sunday after the Epiphany seems short. The astute interpreter, however, knows to approach this reading within the context of the chapter as a whole.

Our text depicts the dedication of the temple of Jerusalem, built by King Solomon (8:1–13). This dedication differs from any other in the ancient world. For neighboring peoples, the high point of the dedication of a sanctuary was the installation of a statue or image of the god or goddess in the newly constructed shrine. However, the God of Israel rejects such depictions. Therefore, Solomon's prayer takes center stage, as a verbal enthronement of God.

Solomon's prayer is an outstanding theological text, prefaced by an explanation of why he built the temple. Solomon invokes the prophecies in which God forbade David from building the temple and delegating the task to the great king's successor (8:14–21). The prayer begins in verse 22 and extends to verse 53; it is followed by a blessing of the assembly (vv. 54–61) and a series of inaugural sacrifices (vv. 62–66).

The first two verses of the prayer contain the main theological affirmation of the whole chapter: "O LORD, God of Israel, there is no God like you in heaven above or on earth beneath" (v. 23a). Through this affirmation, the text establishes yet another major difference from Israel's neighboring peoples. While other nations see the king as divine, Israel understands and affirms that only the Lord is God. Therefore, the king's authority does not derive from any personal divine nature but from the Lord's calling to serve the people of God. By the same token, the king has no innate power, for the only powerful one is the one true God. Any political power that the ruler may enjoy is delegated by the God of Israel.

This powerful God hears the prayers and pleas of the people. A series of supplications follow this bold theological declaration, affirming that God hears the people, particularly in times of suffering and distress (vv. 32–40). God hears even the prayers of those foreigners who may pray at the temple of Jerusalem (vv. 41–43). God's mercy toward the foreigner will be a witness to the reality of the presence of the Lord in the temple of Jerusalem.

The principal themes of the Old Testament reading echo in the Psalm, epistle, and Gospel readings for the Ninth Sunday after the Epiphany. Psalm 96 draws the worshiper's attention, as does Solomon's prayer, to the greatness of God's glory in comparison to the gods (who are no gods) of Israel's neighbors. In Galatians 1:1–12, Paul likewise contrasts the divine origin of the gospel he received to that of the "different" gospel the Galatians have adopted. Finally, Solomon's prayer that God would hear the prayer of the foreigner is fulfilled in Jesus' healing of the centurion's slave (Luke 7:1–10).

This Old Testament reading is part of a brief review within the lectionary of the "mighty acts of God." From Joseph's reunion with his brothers, to Moses' shining face after receiving the two tablets of the covenant, to Solomon's prayer in the temple, the lectionary recounts highpoints along Israel's journey with the Lord. The preacher might want to remind the congregation of this progression as they prepare to commence the journey of Lent on Ash Wednesday.

If one focuses on 1 Kings 8, hymns and anthems focusing on both prayer and wisdom may enhance the worship experience, preparing the audience to hear the word in a new light. Besides its use in the lectionary, 1 Kings 8 may also serve as the basis for special-events sermons, particularly on the dedication of a new or remodeled sanctuary.

A sermon based on this reading might caution the congregation not to equate their worship space with the temple. While we have myriad centers of worship in our respective communities, Israel had a central sanctuary. Not until the development of the synagogue did the Jewish people have worship centers close to home. Therefore, correlations between the temple of Jerusalem and our local church buildings are mostly unwarranted. Congregations that define their sacred spaces according to the temple's blueprint tend to establish false equivalences. They see their altar as the Holy of Holies, the sanctuary as the Holy Place, and the rest of the church building at the court of Israel. This false equivalence leads to unwarranted cautions about activities that may "defile" the sanctuary. For example, in case of a disaster, a congregation may house refugees in a classroom but may not allow them to sleep on a pew.

A sermon about 1 Kings 8—particularly if studied in tandem with Psalm 84—may recognize the tendency to equate one's church with the temple at Jerusalem, but it should also be an opportunity to remind our congregation that our particular church building is not the only legitimate place of worship in our midst.

Furthermore, a sermon on 1 Kings 8 can call our attention to the global implications of Christian worship. Whenever we gather for Sunday worship, we are worshiping alongside millions of fellow Christians around the world, transcending space and time, yet united by faith in the one and only God.

Solomon's prayer can also remind us that idolatry is alive and well in our day. People idolize their preferred politicians, political parties, and respective countries. Anyone who has lived in different cities around the world has heard people claiming that their particular country is "the greatest in the world." Even more dangerous is how people idolize political ideologies, such as capitalism or socialism. Once an ideology is sacralized, it is easy to justify the oppression of or violence toward those who do not submit to its precepts. Of course, money and the market can also become idols. The Bible warns against loving money (1 Tim. 6:10), and Adam Smith, the author of *The Wealth of the Nations,* described a market moved by "an invisible hand." This "hand" can cause money to become a fetish or an idol that can claim our loyalty.

Solomon's prayer reminds us that only the Lord is God. No ideological system or person should be idolized and claim divine authority. Rulers must see themselves as servants of God, submitted to divine authority, with no desire to usurp God's place.

For example, Hitler was not a Christian. He "worshiped" the Aryan race, the homeland, and the ideology of white supremacy. Empowered by this false, sacralized ideology, he launched a genocidal war to conquer, subjugate, and even rid the world of those he deemed "inferior." In the name of his false deity, he orchestrated the murder of millions of people. Sadly, his ideology still fuels hate toward "the other," even in the countries that went to war in order to defeat Hitler.

Finally, from a personal point of view, this text makes a strong claim on all believers. It asks people of faith to recognize God's authority and to submit to divine rule. This claim calls Christians to recognize Jesus Christ as God incarnate, submitting to his authority too. Jesus is "King of kings and Lord of lords" (Rev. 19:16).

Therefore, all Christians owe allegiance to Jesus Christ, who is the "prince" of the universe (Col. 1:15). To take such allegiance seriously, we must adhere to Jesus' teachings—transmitted by both word and deed. All Christians—especially those who reach positions of power in society—must be guided by the values of the kingdom of God, whose primary harbinger is Jesus Christ.

PABLO A. JIMENEZ

Psalm 96:1–9

¹O sing to the LORD a new song;
  sing to the LORD, all the earth.
²Sing to the LORD, bless his name;
  tell of his salvation from day to day.
³Declare his glory among the nations,
  his marvelous works among all the peoples.
⁴For great is the LORD, and greatly to be praised;
  he is to be revered above all gods.
⁵For all the gods of the peoples are idols,
  but the LORD made the heavens.
⁶Honor and majesty are before him;
  strength and beauty are in his sanctuary.

⁷Ascribe to the LORD, O families of the peoples,
  ascribe to the LORD glory and strength.
⁸Ascribe to the LORD the glory due his name;
  bring an offering, and come into his courts.
⁹Worship the LORD in holy splendor;
  tremble before him, all the earth.

Connecting the Psalm with Scripture and Worship

Psalm 96 is a song of expansive praise. "All the earth" is urged to join in the song of thanksgiving (vv. 1, 9), and all the nations are included in the audience. As God's glory is widely proclaimed and God's mighty works are broadly made known, God is rightly understood to be greater than all other gods. Indeed, they are revealed to be merely idols (v. 5). This psalm is lavish in its recognition of God's surpassing greatness. God's honor, majesty, strength, and beauty elicit praise from the whole creation. This call to worship is an inclusive summons: all people are beckoned to come into God's presence, offering themselves and their gifts and beholding God's holy splendor (vv. 7–9).

An expansive view of God's reach connects the psalm with today's first reading. The passage contains excerpts from Solomon's prayer at the dedication of the temple. The prayer is preceded in 1 Kings 8 by the procession of the ark of the covenant into the temple. The procession is accompanied by a liturgical rehearsal of God's saving work in the exodus and God's

faithfulness to the promise made to David (1 Kgs. 8:1–21). When Solomon lifts his arms in prayer. his opening words continue in this theme, noting God's steadfast love to Israel and God's covenant loyalty. These qualities, Solomon affirms, distinguish God from all other gods (vv. 22–23). The subsequent paragraphs of the prayer, not included in today's lection, continue in a similar way, extolling God's faithfulness to Israel and bidding God to hear the prayers of God's people (vv. 24–40).

The lection rejoins the prayer at a critical point, as Solomon expands his petitions to include "a foreigner, who is not of your people Israel" (v. 41). Solomon is confident that the greatness of God and the story of God's mighty deeds will come to be known in distant lands, drawing those from far away to come to Jerusalem and pray in the temple. Solomon asks God to hear these foreign prayers, so that "all the peoples of the earth" may come to know and revere God in the same manner that Israel does (v. 43). Solomon understands that what God has done for Israel is an indication of God's saving intent for the whole world. The God of Israel is not exclusive, but rather yearns to gather all people. The God "above all gods," as Psalm 96:4b puts it, is the God who will also receive and welcome the foreigner, the stranger, and the outsider.

The inclusive theme is continued in today's Gospel lesson. Jesus has come to Capernaum. There he meets a Roman centurion, a Gentile who is full of faith. The centurion, who has a slave who is gravely ill, believes that Jesus can heal him. With compassion for his slave and

Own That Love Is Heaven

Glory to God, and praise, and love
Be ever, ever given,
By saints below and saints above,
The Church in Earth and Heaven.

On this glad day the glorious sun
Of righteousness arose;
On my benighted soul he shone,
And fill'd it with repose.

Sudden expir'd the legal strife,
'Twas then I ceas'd to grieve;
My second, real, living life
I then began to live.

Then with my heart I first believ'd,
Believ'd with faith divine,
Power with the Holy Ghost receiv'd
To call the Savior mine.

I felt my Lord's atoning blood
Close to my soul applied;
Me, me he lov'd—the Son of God
For me, for me He died!

I found and own'd his promise true,
Ascertain'd of my part,
My pardon pass'd in Heaven I knew,
When written on my heart.

O for a thousand tongues to sing
My dear Redeemer's praise!
The glories of my God and King,
The triumphs of his grace.

My gracious Master and my God,
Assist me to proclaim,
To spread thro' all the Earth abroad
The honors of Thy name.

Jesus, the name that charms our fears,
That bids our sorrows cease!
'Tis music in the sinner's ears,
'Tis Life and Health and Peace.

He breaks the power of cancell'd sin,
He sets the prisoner free;
His blood can make the foulest clean;
His blood avail'd for me.

He speaks; and listening to his voice,
New life the dead receive,
The mournful broken hearts rejoice,
The humble poor believe.

Hear him, ye deaf; his praise ye dumb,
Your loosen'd tongues employ;
Ye blind, behold your Savior come;
And leap, ye lame, for joy.

Look unto him, ye nations; own
Your God, ye fallen race!
Look and be sav'd through faith alone;
Be justified by grace!

See all your sins on Jesus laid;
The Lamb of God was slain,
His soul was once an offering made
For every soul of man.

With me, your chief, you then shall know,
Shall feel your sins forgiv'n;
Anticipate your Heaven below,
And own that love is Heav'n.

Charles Wesley (1707–1788), "For the Anniversary Day of One's Conversion," in Frederic M. Bird, ed., *Charles Wesley Seen in His Finer and Less Familiar Poems* (New York: Hurd & Houghton, 1867), 8–10.

hope in Jesus, the centurion arranges for local Jewish elders to beseech Jesus on his behalf. Hearing good reports regarding this Gentile who has become friendly with his Jewish neighbors, even to the point of building their synagogue, Jesus grants the request.

As Jesus follows the elders to the centurion's house, there is a further message from the centurion: he is not worthy to have Jesus come under his roof; instead, he believes Jesus can heal the slave simply by speaking a word. The centurion, a man used to giving and receiving orders, understands well the power of the spoken word. The force of the centurion's faith is overwhelming. This is a Roman solider, a Gentile, an outsider; yet he has come to hear and believe the gospel. Even Jesus is amazed: "I tell you, not even in Israel have I found such faith" (Luke 7:9). The centurion becomes another example of "all the peoples" of the earth becoming aware of God's marvelous works and responding in faith.

All of these texts point homiletically to the width and breadth of the kingdom of heaven. Gods' saving work is not limited to a particular place or a particular people but, rather, is intended to spill over into all the world. People are welcome across all sorts of boundaries and divisions. Everyone with faith is included; no other qualification is necessary. Here is an opportunity to proclaim the relentless inclusiveness of the gospel, the love that keeps expanding, seeking out persons we might never expect. Perhaps this theme is further extended in the liturgy of the day by making particular effort to include a wide range of worship leaders: young and old, newcomers and long-standing members, women and men, persons of various ethnicities. The diversity of faces and voices could make vivid the expansive language of Psalm 96, representing the new song that includes all people and that attracts a hearing from all the families of the earth.

JOHN W. WURSTER

Galatians 1:1–12

¹Paul an apostle—sent neither by human commission nor from human authorities, but through Jesus Christ and God the Father, who raised him from the dead— ²and all the members of God's family who are with me,

To the churches of Galatia:

³Grace to you and peace from God our Father and the Lord Jesus Christ, ⁴who gave himself for our sins to set us free from the present evil age, according to the will of our God and Father, ⁵to whom be the glory forever and ever. Amen.

⁶I am astonished that you are so quickly deserting the one who called you in the grace of Christ and are turning to a different gospel— ⁷not that there is another gospel, but there are some who are confusing you and want to pervert the gospel of Christ. ⁸But even if we or an angel from heaven should proclaim to you a gospel contrary to what we proclaimed to you, let that one be accursed! ⁹As we have said before, so now I repeat, if anyone proclaims to you a gospel contrary to what you received, let that one be accursed!

¹⁰Am I now seeking human approval, or God's approval? Or am I trying to please people? If I were still pleasing people, I would not be a servant of Christ.

¹¹For I want you to know, brothers and sisters, that the gospel that was proclaimed by me is not of human origin; ¹²for I did not receive it from a human source, nor was I taught it, but I received it through a revelation of Jesus Christ.

Commentary 1: Connecting the Reading with Scripture

Galatians 1:1–12 sets the tone for and announces the principal topics of the whole of the letter. The tone is combative and somewhat defensive, reflecting the situation that called forth this response from the apostle. After Paul's departure from Galatia, Jewish Christian teachers had arrived among his congregations (1:7–9; 5:7–10, 12; 6:12–13). While they might have agreed with Paul on certain core teachings, they disagreed on the continuing force of the Torah's demands upon Christians—both Jews, who had been born into the covenant, and Gentiles, if they wished to be fully integrated into God's people (see the Antioch incident related in 2:11–14, introduced by Paul as an informative, analogous situation). These teachers may also have argued that observance of the Torah was required of *all* Christians who wished to fall in line with God's righteousness (5:2–4). For Gentile Christians, a decisive step forward along this road would involve submitting to circumcision (5:2–3, 12; 6:12–13).

In response to this challenge, Paul raises the topic of his own commissioning and authorization by God in 1:1, 11–12, which serves as a kind of thesis statement for the narrative found in 1:13–2:10. The authority and reliability of Paul's gospel—in which the Torah and Torah-maintained distinctions between Jew and Gentile play no ongoing role—are upheld by its divine origin and his divine commission. Like the centurion in the lection from Luke's Gospel, Paul is "one under authority," to whom *God* said, "Go," and he went; to whom God entrusted a verbal commission, and he proclaimed it faithfully. Paul will be clear, however, that what ultimately authenticated the gospel that he preached was not his insistence on his divine calling, but rather the results of his preaching—his hearers' firsthand encounter with God's Holy Spirit (3:1–5). His own authority is now just as fully subject to that message, once proclaimed, as is that of every other preacher (1:8–9).

In 1:6–9 Paul also raises the topic of discerning between the genuine good news and perversions of the same, which will lead to his demonstration of why the "other" gospel is "*no gospel,*" so as to prevent defection to the rival teachers' gospel on the part of any of Paul's converts (2:15–5:12). Paul can be generous when it comes to rivals who preach the genuine gospel (Phil. 1:15–18). He can be generous, and urge his addressees to be generous, in regard to some significant differences in Christian practice (see, e.g., Rom. 14:1–15:6). Here, however, Paul perceives that something essential to the gospel is at stake. These particular rival teachers have crossed an important line, moving from an "alternative" understanding of the truth of the gospel to a betrayal of that gospel (1:6–7).

For Paul, God's gifts and favor ("grace" itself, 1:6) and the value of Christ's self-giving death are ultimately at stake in Galatia (2:21; 5:4). Jesus' death was an act of selfless generosity, undertaken in order to effect rescue from the powers that dominate "the present evil age" (1:4; see 4:1–5) and to secure the gift of the Holy Spirit for all those who trust Jesus' mediation of God's favor (3:2, 5, 14). In Paul's experience of his mission, Jew and Gentile alike received God's Holy Spirit; this was proof positive of God's adoption of each into God's family on the basis of God's gift (4:6–7). This Spirit was also a power sufficient to lead each into that life of righteousness that the righteous God would approve (2:19–20; 3:3; 5:5–6, 16–25; 6:7–10). The Spirit would do this by bringing Christ to life within each of them (2:19–20; 4:19) without distinction.

If the Galatian Christians were to move now toward taking on the yoke of the Torah, the law of Moses, they would be acting as if God's Holy Spirit were an insufficient guide into and empowerment for righteousness—for lining oneself up with God's requirements of human beings. Such a move would be, in Paul's eyes, a vote of "no confidence" in Jesus and in the value of the gift of the Spirit secured at such cost to himself (2:21; 5:2–4). It would amount to the Galatian Christians putting themselves back under the powers of this age, from which Christ had redeemed them at the cost of his own blood (1:4), and honoring the old dividing lines of humanity that those powers imposed and that Christ had erased (3:26–29).

The Old Testament and Gospel readings focus on the positive encounter of foreigners—of *Gentiles*—with the God of Israel. In the first, Solomon prays that God will hear and answer the prayers of non-Jews offered at the newly built Jerusalem temple, to the increase of God's fame among the nations. In the second, acting through Jewish intermediaries, a Gentile centurion seeks and receives a divine favor from Jesus on behalf of a valued slave. The gospel that Paul preaches, and that he defends in Galatians against alternatives, represents the culmination of these earlier encounters. Paul's commission fulfills the psalmist's command to "declare his glory among the nations," calling "all the earth" to give God the honor due God's name (Ps. 96:3–9). Paul makes known "God's salvation" (Ps. 96:2), what God has wrought not on behalf of one nation (ancient Israel), but on behalf of all people in Jesus Christ.

The fame of the God of Israel increases exponentially among the Gentiles as the latter encounter this God and this God's favor in their reception of the Holy Spirit as a consequence of trusting Jesus. The trust that the centurion shows beyond what Jesus has encountered among his fellow Jews becomes the trust that attains God's promises, irrespective of whether one is Jew or Gentile. The scandal of the gospel Paul preaches is that the "foreigner" is no longer defined as the person "who is not of your people Israel" (1 Kgs. 8:41), for in Christ the categories "Jew" and "Gentile" no longer have definitional value for God's people (Gal. 3:26–29).

The themes of this lesson resonate throughout the biblical canon, particularly the New Testament. Other apostolic voices similarly contend that there is an inviolable essence of the gospel, departure from which represents a loss of the whole, rather than permissible variation or innovation (see 2 Tim. 2:16–19; Jude 3; 1–2 John). The theme of pleasing God rather than people, and the frequent incompatibility of the two, is prominent in Galatians. The rival teachers may have accused Paul of omitting mention of the requirements of circumcision and Torah-observance because he was a people pleaser and wanted to win over the Gentile Galatians more easily (1:10; 5:11). Paul, in turn, accuses the rival teachers of being motivated ultimately by a desire to please those more zealous Jews who put pressure on Jewish Christians when the latter rubbed shoulders too closely with Gentiles or seemed to play fast and loose with the covenant's demands (6:12–13)— Jews such as Paul himself once was (1:13–14).

This theme pervades the New Testament, from teachings attributed to Jesus (Luke 6:22–23, 26; John 5:41–44; 12:42–43) to explicit testimonies and instructions given throughout the epistolary literature (1 Thess. 2:4; 4:1; Heb. 10:32–36; 13:12–16; Jas. 4:4; 1 Pet. 4:1–6,

14–16). Finally, other New Testament authors also speak to the two principal threats to God's grace: not trusting it sufficiently (hence adding guardrails on the path to righteousness; see Acts 15:1–5; Col. 2:16–23; 1 Tim. 4:1–5), and not valuing it sufficiently (hence not allowing it to thoroughly redirect one's life toward a grateful, God-centered, God-serving response; see Rom. 2:4; 6:1–19; 1 Cor. 6:12–20; Eph. 4:17–24; Titus 2:11–14; Heb. 12:28–13:16; 2 Pet. 1:3–11; 3:13–15; Jude 4).

DAVID A. deSILVA

Commentary 2: Connecting the Reading with the World

The apostle Paul cannot finish his customary epistolary greeting to the churches in Galatia before he picks a fight with them. In what may seem like an innocuous greeting, Paul deliberately and proudly uses the title "apostle" to describe himself (v. 1). By so doing, he picks a theological and ecclesiological fight with Peter and many other early church leaders who reserved that term for those who were eyewitnesses to the life and ministry of Jesus. Clearly, by that definition, Paul does not qualify to be called an apostle. Even so, Paul begs to differ with anyone who would reject that he is an apostle of Jesus Christ, and he differs with them on a fundamental theological ground. He argues that the title "apostle" is not a title conferred "by human commission or human authorities" (v. 1), like the church council in Jerusalem, but only by God in Christ.

For Paul, apostle is less a title than a divine vocation. He does not need the authorities in Jerusalem to certify him ready to receive a call. God, through the risen Christ, has already extended a call to the newest of all the apostles. Paul's vocation then is to live into God's call to preach the transformational good news of the crucified and risen Christ. For those who preach the gospel centuries later, the apostle Paul is an important ally, one who was not a disciple of Jesus, but who was still called by God to be an apostle of the risen Christ. Paul is ready to pick a fight, a theological and ecclesiological fight, with anyone who would argue otherwise.

"Pick a fight" may seem like a particularly

poor preaching metaphor for the twenty-first century. The phrase has a violent tenor to it, in an age in which there is already far too much violence. The metaphor also seems to suggest an either-or position, insisting that one is either on the right side or on the wrong side of a fight. This is also an unhelpful dichotomy in a complex world and within a complex theological environment. Surely preachers can find a less combative and less binary metaphor to employ in a twenty-first-century sermon on Galatians 1:1–12.

Brian K. Blount, New Testament scholar, president of Union Presbyterian Seminary, and a contemporary prophetic preacher, begs to differ. In his powerful sermon "Pick a Fight," Blount employs this provocative metaphor to interpret a portion of John's Apocalypse. In his sermon, Blount gives this combative metaphor a fine apostolic thrust that intersects with Galatians 1:1–12, when he argues that followers of the risen Jesus are sometimes called by God to "pick a fight."

Blount preaches about contemporary inequalities in justice and challenges gospel people not to remain silent before such injustices:

> *You know* about a world where the two hundred richest persons hold roughly *eight* times as much money and assets as the populations of the *forty-three* poorest countries. What kind of *human* equation is that? *Pick a Fight!* In our own country, 1 percent of the people control 48 percent of this country's wealth. *Pick a Fight! You know* about a

world where domestic battering threatens the lives of more women than cancer, car accidents, and physical violence by strangers *combined. Pick a Fight! You know* that according to the US Census Bureau just a few years ago 41 percent of poor people in the US were living at 50 percent or less of the poverty line.[1]

Thank God the apostle Paul was not hesitant to pick a fight, a theological fight, a gospel fight, with those who followed him in the Galatian churches and reduced the gospel to pious platitudes and mindless aphorisms. What would happen if more preachers in the twenty-first-century church would listen to Paul's words to the churches in Galatia and "pick a fight" with those who preach a distorted Jesus? What if we called out those who preach a prosperity Jesus—a Jesus who wants all to be prosperous and comfortable—or preach a callous Jesus—a Jesus who wants people to pick themselves up by their bootstraps, even when they cannot afford a pair of boots? In an age in which the gospel of Jesus Christ is often diminished or obscured from pulpits, while a less challenging and more comfortable gospel is preached in its place, maybe preachers would do well to join the apostle Paul and pick a fight, a theological fight with those who preach pabulum at the cost of good and faithful theology.

Throughout the Galatians letter, the newest apostle can hardly contain his disgust at those in the churches of Galatia who have rejected Paul's preaching and have settled for gospel-lite. Before he can complete his customary epistle greeting, Paul rails, "I am astonished that you are so quickly deserting the one who called you in the grace of Christ and are turning to a different gospel—not that there is another gospel, but there are some who are confusing you and want to pervert the gospel of Christ" (vv. 6–7). If not indignant enough in these two verses, the apostle continues his words of indignation as he calls down the wrath of God upon any in Galatia who preach a gospel "contrary to what you received" (v. 9).

For preachers who doubt that preaching the gospel of Jesus Christ, after careful study, prayer, and preparation, makes any real difference in our secular age, Paul is ready to pick a fight. *Of course, preaching the gospel makes a difference in any age, especially in a secular age! Never forget it!* For this proud apostle, it makes all the difference in the health and well-being of the Christian community that the gospel is articulated and preached faithfully, clearly, and without simplification or being dumbed down. Paul's theological posture encourages preachers to recommit not only to careful exegetical study of the biblical witness, but to courageous homiletical proclamation of genuine gospel in a gospel-lite society.

Read the rest of Galatians before preaching Galatians 1:1–12. It will clarify why preaching the gospel of the risen Christ is absolutely critical in every age. Throughout Galatians, the apostle does not preach about minor matters of dispute in the church and the world. The gospel of Jesus Christ is a substantial gospel that calls for substantial preaching—in every age. The apostle loves this community of churches in Galatia enough to pick a fight, to rail against faith based on something less than the life, teaching, death, and resurrection of Jesus Christ. Therefore, throughout the epistle, Paul picks a fight with a form of Christianity being preached in Galatia that is contrary to the gospel revealed to him through the risen Christ.

Maybe on the Sunday when Galatians 1:1–12 appears in the lectionary, it is time for preachers across the land to pick a fight with preachers more concerned about the title before their names than calling the faithful to live into the gospel. Pick a fight with churches more concerned about the size of their endowment than the call of Christ to give to others extravagantly. Pick a fight with the "church police," more concerned with making sure the church does not change than to preach the One who makes all things new.

If you are a Gospel preacher and rarely preach from the Old Testament, the Psalms, or other books in the New Testament, maybe Galatians 1:1–12 will inspire in you the courage to pick a fight, and by so doing to trust in the words of Jesus penned in John's Gospel (8:32): "the truth will set you free."

GARY W. CHARLES

---

1. Brian K. Blount, unpublished sermon, used with permission of the author.

Luke 7:1–10

⁷After Jesus had finished all his sayings in the hearing of the people, he entered Capernaum. ²A centurion there had a slave whom he valued highly, and who was ill and close to death. ³When he heard about Jesus, he sent some Jewish elders to him, asking him to come and heal his slave. ⁴When they came to Jesus, they appealed to him earnestly, saying, "He is worthy of having you do this for him, ⁵for he loves our people, and it is he who built our synagogue for us." ⁶And Jesus went with them, but when he was not far from the house, the centurion sent friends to say to him, "Lord, do not trouble yourself, for I am not worthy to have you come under my roof; ⁷therefore I did not presume to come to you. But only speak the word, and let my servant be healed. ⁸For I also am a man set under authority, with soldiers under me; and I say to one, 'Go,' and he goes, and to another, 'Come,' and he comes, and to my slave, 'Do this,' and the slave does it." ⁹When Jesus heard this he was amazed at him, and turning to the crowd that followed him, he said, "I tell you, not even in Israel have I found such faith." ¹⁰When those who had been sent returned to the house, they found the slave in good health.

Commentary 1: Connecting the Reading with Scripture

The set of lectionary readings for the Ninth Sunday after the Epiphany (Year C) has to do with the revelation of God communicated through Israel to the entire world. Psalm 96 extols God's majesty over all other gods. Israel is commanded to proclaim God to all nations, because God is worthy of universal praise and worship. In 1 Kings 8, at the dedication of the Jerusalem temple, Solomon prays specifically that the supplication of a foreigner who seeks after the God of Israel be heard, in order for God's name to be made known and feared among all peoples. As an apostle commissioned by God and not by human authorities, Paul asserts in Galatians 1 the legitimacy and trustworthiness of the gospel that he brings to these Gentile converts in Asia Minor. The same "outward" trajectory—through Israel to the nations—is affirmed in Luke 7, where Jesus responds to the faith of a Roman centurion by restoring the man's slave from a life-threatening illness.

Luke unapologetically uses the world stage as the backdrop for his Gospel by naming the powers that be: Augustus and Quirinius at Jesus' birth (Luke 2:1), and Tiberius and Pilate at the start of John's and Jesus' public ministries

(3:1). Even as the author reaches back to God's promises in the Old Testament, it is emphasized that the coming of Israel's Messiah is "a light for revelation *to the Gentiles*" (Luke 2:32a; cf. Isa. 42:6), and that "*all flesh* shall see the salvation of God" (Luke 3:6; cf. Isa. 40:5 LXX). The references to Isaiah hearken back to God's call of Abram, through whom *the nations* will be blessed (Gen. 12:1–3). After delivering his inaugural sermon at Nazareth, Jesus goes on to identify himself with Elijah and Elisha, two of God's great prophets, one of whom was sent to minister to a Sidonian widow, whereas the other responded to the request of Naaman the Syrian for healing (Luke 4:25–27). By the time they get to chapter 7, in which Jesus is now confronted by a plea from a Gentile, Luke's readers are primed to expect God's salvific grace to extend to all the nations whom God has blessed through Israel. Here Jesus heals from a distance, recalling the aforementioned reference to Elisha in chapter 4, in which the prophet also healed Naaman's leprosy without ever setting eyes on the man.

The centurion is an ambiguous figure. Representing the oppressive power of Rome, his loyalty resides with Caesar, but he addresses Jesus as Lord. Here is a generous patron of the Jewish people of Capernaum and the builder of their synagogue, who as a foreigner is sufficiently sensitive to Jewish scruples to deem himself unworthy of having Jesus in his home, presumably on account of his Gentile status and therefore his ritual uncleanness. Yet at the end of the story the city's patron becomes Jesus' client, and Jesus turns shame to honor by commending the centurion for his exemplary faith. This story effectively breaks the stereotype that all Gentiles are enemies of Israel, demonstrating how the blessings of God are meant to include the nations, which, as in this case, is through the agency of Israel's Messiah.

Unlike the parallel passage in Matthew 8:5–10, Luke's account includes two sets of emissaries. The motive of the first group, the Jewish elders of Capernaum, is suspect. Appealing to the social practice of reciprocity, they talk up the benevolence of the centurion to have Jesus return the favor by helping the dying slave. Their words of persuasion expose an underlying Jewish ethnocentricity: "*our* people . . . *our* synagogue . . . for *us*" (Luke 7:5). The elders seem to have no qualms about sending Jesus to the home of a Gentile where he will surely contract uncleanness, let alone the risk of corpse impurity, should the invalid die. Perhaps they hope to maintain a symbiotic relationship with the centurion to mitigate the power differential between them and their Roman overlord. Regardless of their mixed message, Jesus shows no hesitation in going to the centurion's house, for ritual contamination is secondary when bringing a person to wholeness is at stake (cf. 5:13, 29–32; 7:14; 8:53–55).

A second group of envoys, made up of the centurion's friends, meets Jesus along the way. Refusing Jesus' entry to his home is not an act of rejection but the centurion's humble deference to Jesus' superior status. The message brought by his friends attributes all honor to Jesus. By addressing Jesus as the Lord, whose word alone has the authority to command all and any action, the centurion ignores the manipulative dynamics of reciprocity and submits to the power he believes Jesus possesses. Luke's readers expect no less, for they have seen the efficacy of Jesus' word—over demons (4:35, 41), illnesses (4:39), and disabilities (5:24–25; 6:10). Soon after this, Jesus will speak life to the dead (7:14; 8:54) and command the forces of nature (8:24). Jesus' authority is indisputable; he does what only God can do.

Divine compassion and human faith together put in motion a "virtuous cycle" that glorifies God and engenders more trusting responses. This positive cycle leads to an ever-deepening conviction of God's sovereignty over all things. Jesus' praise of the centurion's faith puts the Jewish elders to shame. Later in Luke, Jesus will recognize the repentance of Tyre and Sidon and indict the Jewish cities of Chorazin and Bethsaida for their unbelief (10:13–14). Toward the end of Luke, another centurion renders the final and true verdict: "Certainly this man was innocent" (23:47), exposing the complicity of the Jewish establishment that calls for Jesus' death. In Acts 10, the conversion of Cornelius, yet another centurion and a devout God-fearer, reiterates the point that God's gift of salvation moves in a universal trajectory. This has been the divine plan from the beginning.

That God's revelation and salvation are to be proclaimed to the whole world is a biblical mandate, introduced in the Old Testament and carried out in the New. The Matthean Jesus commissions the eleven to "make disciples of all nations" (Matt. 28:19). Before his ascension, the Lukan Jesus charges his disciples to preach repentance and forgiveness "in his name to all nations" (Luke 24:47) and to be his witnesses "in Jerusalem, in all Judea and Samaria, and to the ends of the earth" (Acts 1:8). Beginning with the disciples in Jerusalem and ending with Paul in Rome, Luke's second volume is replete with stories of the gospel being taken beyond the bounds of Israel. Gentiles come to faith in the book of Acts, ranging from an Ethiopian eunuch to a Philippian jailer and some Athenian philosophers, to name just a few. Notably, many of the letters of Paul are written to Christian believers in Gentile areas, from Galatia, Colossae, and Ephesus in Asia Minor to Philippi, Thessalonica, and Corinth in Macedonia and Achaia, and as far as Rome.

The collective testimony of the New Testament is but a foretaste of the grand scenario in eternity, in which "a great multitude that no one could count, from every nation, from all tribes and peoples and languages" gather to worship God and the Lamb upon the throne (Rev. 7:9–10). Only then is the call of Psalm 96 actualized in its fullest expression.

DIANE G. CHEN

Commentary 2: Connecting the Reading with the World

These ten verses in Luke invite us into the complex and surprisingly revelatory world of ancient Judah under Roman rule. Relationship, authority, religion, suffering, occupation, and affection are sewn together in such a way that we experience an epiphany related to faith and healing. After gathering his disciples and teaching primarily outside the towns and villages of Galilee, Jesus enters Capernaum, a small but important economic and social center on the Sea of Galilee. Here economic, religious, and social threads would have begun to connect Judah with Rome.

Although a small fishing village of approximately 1,500 people, archaeological evidence shows oil and grain mills, linking this village to the larger economic centers not far away. The presence of a Roman centurion suggests that maintaining a military presence in Capernaum was important in order to extend the influence of Rome. Despite the difficulties of occupation, the relationship between the centurion and the village seemed positive. The Jewish leaders felt free to serve as intermediaries between this military leader and Jesus. They even suggested that he "loves the people." Clearly he wielded some of his power to do good things. He provided funds to build a synagogue. To the religious leaders, he was "worthy."

Perhaps there are connections for us here. We live in worlds where dividing lines seem so clear. Elections turn around who should be in and who should be out. Religious intolerance tempts us to believe that other faiths cannot contain truth. Slogans on the protest line, clichés pasted to our bumpers, and fake news on the internet teach us to mistrust those who look or act differently from us. We reduce complex systems and complicated people to cardboard stereotypes.

Are we willing to find the worthiness in our adversaries? Are we willing to look for goodness in those who may be against us? Faith and healing were unleashed because this village and, of course, Jesus himself were able to find ways across the borders. We can only imagine the difficulty of nurturing relationships between Roman and Judean, Jew and Gentile, occupier and occupied, slave and free, wealthy and poor. Yet we catch a vision of cooperation across lines in this Gospel text that makes a way for God's reign to move and to take shape.

Of course, much of the possibility turns around the one with the most economic and social power: the centurion. He has both privilege and authority. Clearly he benefits from the system in the first-century Roman world. He owns a slave. He is a male. He has wealth, enough to be a benefactor to the community. Indeed, according to all standards in the ancient world, he is "worthy."

Yet he is not willing to accept the worthiness that is ascribed to him: "I am not worthy to have you come under my roof" (v. 6). In many ways, this is an extraordinary admission. Not willing to trade on his privilege or to assume that he should receive the benefits of his position, he acts with humility. What a concept: a leader who is shaped by humility, a leader who sets aside the benefits of position and office, a leader who is willing to recognize that there may be a greater authority than what the world gives to him. For so many of us who are leaders in society or in the church, there is such temptation to hide our vulnerabilities and to show only strength. This centurion in Luke is already pointing to the paradox of the cross, where power comes through weakness and life is raised out of vulnerable, sacrificial love.

Of course, this Gospel text overturns our notions of worthiness. It challenges the ways in which we ascribe privilege and status. In fact, it serves as an invitation for us to consider the ways that we acknowledge privilege. In North

America, the power of racism continues to move through patterns of white privilege, often unrecognized or denied. Perhaps this Gospel text invites predominantly white congregations to consider the ways in which individuals and institutions can recognize and begin to set aside patterns of ascribed worth that promote injustice and inequality. How might the world change if those with power could confess, "I am not worthy, but only say the word and I shall be healed,"—to use the liturgical form that often serves as an invitation to the Eucharist in the Roman Catholic Church?

The pinnacle of this Gospel narrative is the centurion's recognition of Jesus' authority. He does, indeed, understand how his own power works. He can give instructions, and they are followed. In Jesus, he sees a higher authority. He places himself "under" the authority of a Jewish street preacher from a rural community. He gives witness to the power of God in the person of Jesus. Jesus is amazed that this Roman military leader is able to see what others have not yet perceived. Does it surprise Jesus because this epiphany comes from an outsider? His own followers will refuse to see this truth until after the resurrection.

What can outsiders tell us about the truth? Can some outside our own traditions see things we cannot? Can we trust God's grace enough to let others teach us about how the church can witness to healing and saving power? Many mainline Protestant churches are experiencing despair at the decline of their institutions. The number of people who claim no religious tradition is growing (i.e., the "nones" or "none of the above"). Do the "nones" know something about how truth can be expressed? Do they know something about what makes for healing, something the church should hear? Can their wisdom help us proclaim the loving and saving power of Jesus Christ to heal the world?

One troubling dimension of this text is the assumption that slavery is a building block in society. The text tells us that the centurion values his slave highly. This may tell us of his affection for the person, or it may simply recognize that the slave has economic value to the centurion. Perhaps the centurion was moved by the slave's suffering to do whatever it might take to find healing. Either way, Jesus sees an opening, a possibility to reveal something of God's reign. The slave is found in good health. He is restored, returned back to life.

The story compels us to continue to marshal the power of God's reign to heal the world of slavery itself. We can hope that the centurion's slave was healed back into a generous and kind household, not returned to a brutal and arrogant master. Yet this healing by Jesus set into motion an arc of justice that moved forward into history, changing patterns for human relationships, ending slavery in many places, even as it finally did in the United States. The centurion and Jesus, by embracing God's reign across the boundaries, were able to set into motion waves of healing and justice that transcend the first century. Perhaps our own work for healing plants seeds that will change generations to come. Unfortunately the world has not yet been healed of all slavery. Human trafficking and the brutalization of young girls continue to recall the church to the divine work of healing and salvation.

The power of God that the centurion sees in Jesus is now present in the body of Christ. Our work in the world becomes a manifestation of God's power. On this last Sunday of the Epiphany season, we recognize once again the depth and grandeur of God's light that has been revealed to us: light that we hold in our hands and in our churches, a light that heals the world.

BRADLEY E. SCHMELING

Transfiguration Sunday

Exodus 34:29–35	2 Corinthians 3:12–4:2
Psalm 99	Luke 9:28–36 (37–43a)

Exodus 34:29–35

29Moses came down from Mount Sinai. As he came down from the mountain with the two tablets of the covenant in his hand, Moses did not know that the skin of his face shone because he had been talking with God. 30When Aaron and all the Israelites saw Moses, the skin of his face was shining, and they were afraid to come near him. 31But Moses called to them; and Aaron and all the leaders of the congregation returned to him, and Moses spoke with them. 32Afterward all the Israelites came near, and he gave them in commandment all that the LORD had spoken with him on Mount Sinai. 33When Moses had finished speaking with them, he put a veil on his face; 34but whenever Moses went in before the LORD to speak with him, he would take the veil off, until he came out; and when he came out, and told the Israelites what he had been commanded, 35the Israelites would see the face of Moses, that the skin of his face was shining; and Moses would put the veil on his face again, until he went in to speak with him.

Commentary 1: Connecting the Reading with Scripture

This text relates one of the more enigmatic stories of the manifestation of God to God's people. The setting is the conclusion of the second journey of Moses to Mount Sinai. The account of his first sojourn begins in chapter 24, in the context of the confirmation of the covenant between God and Israel. This lengthy account forms the legal and cultic basis for our understanding of the relationship between God and God's people. Moses is given specific instructions on the design and building of the ark of the covenant. He is given instructions on the Sabbath, and there is a lengthy section on the cultic responsibilities of the priests. Of particular interest is the section on the vestments of the priests, as the narrative states that the purpose of such vestments is to symbolize the dignity and honor of the priesthood. In chapter 24 and following, the holiness of God is emphasized. The people are warned through Moses of the dangers of allegiances to other gods and of adopting the customs of other people.

The story of the first sojourn is framed within the literary and theological context of forty days and forty nights. After this extended absence, Moses returns with the law of God written on two tablets, the fullness of which is pointed out by the detail that the tablets are inscribed on both sides. Aided by Aaron, the people have fallen into a kind of debauchery. Nearly all of the instructions that are given to Moses are violated before Moses can relate them to the people. Instead of building the ark of the covenant, the people have constructed an idolatrous golden calf. Instead of functioning as a priestly emissary for God, Aaron is a religious technocrat, fashioning a cultic practice based on the desires of the people.

What follows is a kind of cleansing of the camp that is carried out by the Levites. They are instructed to kill their brothers and their friends. The significance of this act is not primarily to remove all transgressors from the camp, but to identify and confirm the Levites as brutally obedient to God. This command emphasizes the requirement of loyalty to none other than God; this would become an identifying characteristic of the Levites. These intervening chapters also set the stage for the future of Israel by describing "the tent of meeting." This tent is the place where Moses' role as the emissary of God is confirmed. It is also the place where his young assistant, Joshua, begins his preparation for the assumption of leadership.

Moses' second journey to Mount Sinai, which is the focus of the text under consideration, shares with the first journey the temporal structure of forty days and forty nights. However, what happens in that time period is strikingly different in several ways. First, the content of the conversation between God and Moses is personal and conversational, rather than formal and technical. Second, God's instructions are now presented in a manner that is more easily committed to memory. In this way, the narrative could be used within the context of worship. Third, in the first sojourn, Moses is not allowed to see God's face. Indeed, God puts God's hand over the face of Moses, who is allowed to glimpse only the back of God. In this account, it is not the face of God that is the focus; it is Moses' shining face. The text under consideration suggests that the second journey to Mount Sinai was focused on the confirmation of Moses as a leader. While the people have in their experience seen God in the symbolic representation of the cloud or the pillar of fire, now they see God in the shining face of Moses. The text tells us that Moses did not know that his face was shining. The fact that he had been in the presence of God was obvious to others in a way that Moses did not immediately realize.

This text can function as an Old Testament foundation to the New Testament story of the transfiguration of Christ. However, its hermeneutical potential is not limited to this New Testament text. There are three features of this text that prefigure the New Testament narratives.

First, Moses went up to the mountain alone, while in the story of the transfiguration, the disciples are allowed to witness Jesus' encounter and the subsequent glowing of his raiment. Luke 9:28–36 describes this event in which Moses is present and the disciples are permitted to see the face of Jesus shine: "Jesus took with him Peter and John and James, and went up on the mountain to pray. And while he was praying, the appearance of his face changed, and his clothes became dazzling white. Suddenly they saw two men, Moses and Elijah, talking to him" (vv. 28–30; also see Matt. 17:1–3, where it says Jesus' face "shone like the sun").

Second, this text serves as the backdrop for understanding the account of the stoning of Stephen described in Acts 6 and 7. As Stephen is accused of blasphemy by the Sanhedrin court, the writer of Luke–Acts notes in Acts 6:15 (NIV) that "all who were sitting in the Sanhedrin looked intently at Stephen, and they saw that his face was like the face of an angel." Between this observation and the actual stoning of Stephen, he narrates a fairly lengthy account of Israel's story, with a particular focus on Moses and his encounter on Mount Sinai. It is this account that connects the shining face of Stephen with that of Moses. Moses' encounter with God, which resulted in his face shining, took place in the context of cultic worship, while Stephen's face shone in the midst of political, cultural, and religious conflict. The fact that his executors saw Stephen's face shining in the moment of his torture expands our understanding of where God may be encountered, especially in our own historical context.

Third, Moses covered his shining face with a veil when he moved among the people, but would remove that veil in the presence of God. The testimony of the early church is that this veil and all symbolic representations of the separation of God and God's people have been rent by the work of the cross: "If anyone builds on this foundation using gold, silver, costly stones, wood, hay or straw, their work will be shown for what it is, because the Day will bring it to light. It will be revealed with fire, and the fire will test the quality of each person's work. If what has been built survives, the builder will receive a reward" (1 Cor. 3:12–14 NIV).

Finally, this approach might lend a clue to the homiletical conundrum of the account of the empty tomb, in which the burial clothes of Jesus are found neatly folded, but the cloth that covered his face is found by itself neatly folded: "Then Simon Peter came along behind him and went straight into the tomb. He saw the strips of linen lying there, as well as the cloth that had been wrapped around Jesus' head. The cloth was still lying in its place, separate from the linen" (John 20:6–7 NIV). Perhaps the purpose of this narrative detail is to remind us that even death is not able to obscure a shining face or the afterglow of being in the presence of God.

JAMES H. EVANS JR.

Commentary 2: Connecting the Reading with the World

The reading from the Hebrew Bible for Transfiguration Sunday is Exodus 34:29–35, a very peculiar narrative that describes the impact of God's glory on Moses. After Moses goes up Mount Sinai to receive divine revelation (Exod. 24:9–18), a cloud covers the mountain and surrounds Moses with the glory of God for forty days (vv. 15–18). When Moses finally comes down from the sacred mountain with the two tablets of the covenant, he is not aware of the effect of the divine glory on his body. Now the skin of his face shines in such way that people are afraid of going near him (vv. 29–35).

This reading is perfect for Transfiguration Sunday, given that it is the subtext of the transfiguration narratives in the Gospels. In general, the New Testament assumes that its hearers and readers know the Hebrew Bible. Therefore, the Gospel narratives are chock-full of references, allusions, and echoes from the First Testament. In particular, the Gospel of Luke refers consistently to the Pentateuch.

Luke 9:28–36 should be understood as a theological elaboration of Exodus 34:29–35. Some points of contact between the narratives are:

- A mountain becomes the place for divine revelation (Exod. 34:2–3; Luke 9:28).
- The prophet goes up the mountain (Exod. 34:4; Luke 9:28).
- The prophet has an extraordinary spiritual experience (Exod. 34:8; Luke 9:29–31).
- A cloud represents God's presence and glory (Exod. 34:5; Luke 9:34).
- The encounter with the divine glory has a physical impact on the prophet, making him "shine" (Exod. 34:29; Luke 9:29).
- The experience manifests to the people of God that the prophet has a special relationship with God as the "chosen one" who will reveal the divine will to the new generation (Exod. 34:30; Luke 9:35).
- However, the experience is temporary and its effects are phased out as the prophet returns to dwell among the people of God (Exod. 34:34–35; Luke 9:36).

Of course, there are differences between the narratives as well. First, Jesus spent a relatively short time at the mountaintop. Second, Jesus was not alone; he meets two figures at the top of the mountain, one of whom is Moses. Therefore, for this day, one should consider the literary dependence and theological development between the readings from the Hebrew Bible and the Gospel of Luke.

However, the lectionary offers an interesting alternative to the preacher, which is to relate Exodus 24:29–35 with the reading from the epistle. In this case, the reading comes from 2 Corinthians 3:12–4:2. The difference is that this reading is critical of Moses' experience. Paul focuses on the veil worn by Moses, understanding it as a way of impeding full access to God's glory. Following rabbinical interpretative techniques, Paul understands that such a veil is still in place, hindering access to divine revelation. So Paul sees the veil as a representation of the "old covenant" that maintains the people of God bound to the law. The good news is that Jesus Christ has removed the "veil," allowing people full access to salvation. Now all believers can be transformed by God's grace! Of course, this message is consistent with Paul's exposition about the resurrection in 1 Corinthians 15, which affirms the future transformation of all believers (vv. 50–58).

It must be clear, then, that it is impossible to harmonize the three readings in a single sermon. The relationship between the readings from the Hebrew Bible and the Gospel is positive, while the reading of the epistle is critical of Exodus. In the first case, the Gospel builds upon Moses' experience while the epistle understands that such experience has been superseded.

The incompatibility between these two approaches has a direct impact on the liturgical context of the text. On the one hand, the liturgy can focus on the progression of divine revelation from the Hebrew Bible to the Gospel. In this case, the reading of Psalm 99 becomes critical, given that it affirms God's majesty and the revelation of divine glory through the motifs of the cloud and the mountain. In this case, hymns that make references to clouds, mountains, and glory may enhance the worship experience, preparing the audience to hear the sermon.

On the other hand, the liturgy can focus on the epistle's approach, stressing the discontinuity between an old covenant, where people's access to God's glory was impeded or "veiled," and the new covenant that grants all believers access to divine revelation. In such a case, hymns that celebrate the covenant, free access to divine revelation, and the transformation of all believers may enhance the worship experience, illustrating the topics that will be central to the sermon.

Local congregations may find it difficult to understand Exodus 34:29–35, given the "otherness" of the text. Most contemporary believers cannot relate to tablets of stone, shining faces, and veils that cover their leaders' faces. Furthermore, the text presents a dynamic that is utterly alien to most Christian churches: the affirmation that the leader or prophet enjoys a special relationship with God that manifests in a miraculous way. Although most parishioners expect their pastors to have a strong relationship with God, few view them with fear. Rather, most parishioners see them as empathetic, accessible, and friendly shepherds.

Another consideration is the social and ethical context of the text. Once I preached to a congregation that lost about two-thirds of its membership in five years. When I asked the minister about the situation, he told me that he patterned his leadership style on Moses' experience. He said, "Moses was the only one who received divine revelation; the children of Israel's responsibility was limited to obeying. I am 'Moses' here. God speaks to me, and the congregation must follow my lead."

Sadly, we are witnessing a rise in authoritarianism in both the church and the larger culture. For example, we have seen how new Christian movements—like the prosperity gospel and the new apostolic reformation—have abandoned the traditional views of church government in favor of a church polity centered on the authority of the pastor, who may be called "apostle." In secular politics, we have seen a turn to authoritarianism both in Europe and in the United States. In such an environment, biblical readings such as this one may be misused to legitimize authoritarian views of leadership. Of course, such approaches are unbiblical. Moses did not become a religious dictator, nor did Jesus wield power in an authoritarian way. Therefore, the church must denounce all authoritarian and autocratic views of leadership as both unbiblical and unethical.

From a cultural standpoint, this text is famous for its connection to Michelangelo's statue of Moses. The Hebrew word translated here as "shine" can also mean "horned." This explains why the celebrated Italian sculptor portrayed Moses with horns in this famous statue. However, this scene is not highlighted in contemporary films about Moses.

Regarding the relationship between this text and human knowledge, we may point to studies of how prayer, meditation, and other spiritual experiences affect positively the mind and the body, helping us to cope with suffering and disease.

Finally, from a personal point of view, a sermon relating Exodus 34 and Luke 9 can be significant for a contemporary audience that may thirst for life-transforming spiritual experiences. We cannot deny that spiritual experiences are extraordinary, leading an individual or a community of faith to experience a profound transformation. However, we should also acknowledge that spiritual experiences are also scary, given that they lead us to relate with God, who, as described by Rudolf Otto, is the "wholly other."

PABLO A. JIMENEZ

Psalm 99

¹The LORD is king; let the peoples tremble!
　　He sits enthroned upon the cherubim; let the earth quake!
²The LORD is great in Zion;
　　he is exalted over all the peoples.
³Let them praise your great and awesome name.
　　Holy is he!
⁴Mighty King, lover of justice,
　　you have established equity;
you have executed justice
　　and righteousness in Jacob.
⁵Extol the LORD our God;
　　worship at his footstool.
　　Holy is he!

⁶Moses and Aaron were among his priests,
　　Samuel also was among those who called on his name.
　　They cried to the LORD, and he answered them.
⁷He spoke to them in the pillar of cloud;
　　they kept his decrees,
　　and the statutes that he gave them.

⁸O LORD our God, you answered them;
　　you were a forgiving God to them,
　　but an avenger of their wrongdoings.
⁹Extol the LORD our God,
　　and worship at his holy mountain;
　　for the LORD our God is holy.

Connecting the Psalm with Scripture and Worship

Psalm 99 is one of several enthronement psalms that proclaim the sovereignty of God. According to the psalmist, God reigns by executing justice, establishing equity, and ensuring righteousness among God's people (vv. 4, 8). God is also characterized by holiness, an awe-inspiring, even fear-inducing, power over all peoples. People tremble before this God—even the earth shakes—for God's divine nature is overwhelming. Yet God need not be feared, for the Lord who is concerned with justice hears the cries of the people (v. 6) and forgives their sins (v. 8), even while setting things right. Such a God evokes the acclamations of the people, who continually sing out their praise.

Psalm 99 also hearkens back to the story of the exodus. Calling to mind the service of Moses and Aaron, the psalmist invites hearers to remember how God delivered the Hebrews from slavery and made them into God's own people. The psalmist also names Samuel, who, along with Moses and Aaron, called the people of Israel to repentance and interceded on their behalf. Psalm 99, therefore, not only evokes memories of liberation, but also elicits from the people songs of praise to the God who heard their prayers and forgave their transgressions. Furthermore, the psalm's mention of Moses in the context of proclaiming God's holiness brings to mind the patriarch's awesome and mysterious encounter on Mount Sinai with the Divine, the one who made the face of Moses shine.

For Christians, both the image of Moses' shining face and the sound of the psalmist's exhortations to praise anticipate the transfiguration of Jesus Christ, whose entire appearance is made to dazzle with the brightness of glory on yet another mountain. Before the gaze of the astonished disciples, Moses and Elijah appear with Jesus, the liberator of the people and the prophet who proclaims the coming reign of God. On this holy mountain, Peter, James, and John get a glimpse of Jesus' future glory before he takes the journey to the cross.

The holiness of Jesus then is akin to the holiness of God. The psalmist points to the willingness of the God of justice to meet the people where they are, forgiving them for their failures to live up to God's commands. Similarly, Luke offers a vision of Jesus as he will one day be—glorious, victorious, reigning eternally with God—just before he turns his face to Jerusalem, where he will suffer and die for all people, in order to reconcile them with the God who insists on justice yet shows mercy.[1]

Psalm 99 suggests two distinct but related approaches for preaching the texts for Transfiguration Sunday: a focus on the mysterious holiness of God, and a call for the people's uninhibited praise. In both Exodus and Luke, the divine presence appears as a cloud (Exod. 24:15; Luke 9:34–35). This image evokes a sense of mystery and awe, which is reflected in the language of the psalm. The psalmist speaks alternately to the people and to God, first describing God's sovereign nature (vv. 1–2), then inviting the people to give their praise; they respond by exclaiming, "Holy is he!" (v. 3). The psalmist then addresses God, recalling the divine ruler's love for justice and concern with equity. Again, the psalmist calls the people to praise: "Holy is he!" (v. 4–5). The psalmist continues to speak to the people, reminding them of their ancestors Moses, Aaron, and Samuel and their inability to fully keep the law of God. Because God forgives the people of their wrongs, the psalmist once

more calls for the people's praise (vv. 8–9). A preacher then may draw on the psalm to point to the unwavering faithfulness of the God who continually forgave the people of Israel and who, through Jesus Christ, reconciled all humankind to Godself. The psalm may also invite the preacher to highlight the unexplainable mystery of the divine presence, rather than try to explain away the phenomenon or blithely suggest that we can be transfigured too. (Beware confusing transfiguration with transformation.) A preacher may choose to focus on the pattern of praise that punctuates the psalm: we apprehend God's holy mystery and fall down before it in awe and praise, over and over again.

Psalm 99 suggests several liturgical uses. Worship planners might take a cue from the pattern mentioned above, where the psalmist alternately addresses the people and God, while the people break in with their shouts of praise. For instance, the psalm may be read at the opening of the worship service, using two voices: Voice 1 reads the verses that are addressed to the people, and Voice 2 reads the verses addressed to God, while the people respond with an expression of praise.

Voice 1: Verses 1–3
 People: *Holy is God!*

Voice 2: Verse 4
Voice 1: Verse 3a
 People: *Holy is God!*

Voice 1: Verses 6–7
Voice 2: Verses 8–9
 People: *Praise the Lord!*
     For the Lord our God is holy!

Such an opening could lead quite naturally into an exuberant singing of the hymn "Holy, Holy, Holy! Lord God Almighty!"

The psalm may also be sung after the first reading. Because of the repetition of the people's exclamation, "God is holy," a responsorial setting would work well. A cantor or choir would sing the verses, and the people would respond with a sung refrain. Alternatively, a reader could

---

1. J. Clinton McCann, "Psalms," in *New Interpreter's Bible* (Nashville: Abingdon Press, 1996), 4:1076.

read the verses while the people punctuate the psalm with a sung refrain.[2]

In summary, Psalm 99 calls the people to give praise to God, who not only demands righteousness but forgives the inability to live justly. The holiness of God is mysterious, but also imbued with mercy, and the people of God respond with grateful praise.

KIMBERLY BRACKEN LONG

---

2. John D. Witvliet, *The Biblical Psalms in Christian Worship: A Brief Introduction and Guide to Resources* (Grand Rapids: Eerdmans, 2007), 101.

2 Corinthians 3:12–4:2

[12]Since, then, we have such a hope, we act with great boldness, [13]not like Moses, who put a veil over his face to keep the people of Israel from gazing at the end of the glory that was being set aside. [14]But their minds were hardened. Indeed, to this very day, when they hear the reading of the old covenant, that same veil is still there, since only in Christ is it set aside. [15]Indeed, to this very day whenever Moses is read, a veil lies over their minds; [16]but when one turns to the Lord, the veil is removed. [17]Now the Lord is the Spirit, and where the Spirit of the Lord is, there is freedom. [18]And all of us, with unveiled faces, seeing the glory of the Lord as though reflected in a mirror, are being transformed into the same image from one degree of glory to another; for this comes from the Lord, the Spirit.

[4:1]Therefore, since it is by God's mercy that we are engaged in this ministry, we do not lose heart. [2]We have renounced the shameful things that one hides; we refuse to practice cunning or to falsify God's word; but by the open statement of the truth we commend ourselves to the conscience of everyone in the sight of God.

Commentary 1: Connecting the Reading with Scripture

This reading presents Paul's midrash specifically on the paired Old Testament lection. Second Corinthians 3:7–18 articulates a sustained contrast between the old covenant (the "ministry" of Moses engraved on stone plaques) and the new covenant (introduced as such in 3:6). In the paragraph preceding the lection (3:7–11), Paul acknowledges that the covenant that Moses administered possessed glory, such as was seen in Moses' face that shone radiantly after his encounters with God when receiving the commandments (Exod. 34:29; 2 Cor. 3:7). The reflected glory shining from Moses' face is the starting point for a "lesser to greater argument," in which Paul proposes the greater glory that accompanies the covenant administered by the Spirit, which brings righteousness and life, rather than condemnation and death (2 Cor. 3:7–9). Because the effects of the new covenant are more glorious (life in place of death), the ministry that brought this new covenant (e.g., Paul's apostolic ministry) must be more glorious as well.

In regard to Moses' veiling of his face, Paul attributes a motive to Moses that is not found in Exodus 34. Moses let his face show while it was still brightly reflecting God's glory,

addressing the people in this condition; he veiled his face only afterwards. Paul deduces that Moses' motive was to keep the Israelites from seeing this reflected glory fade away. In effect, he accuses Moses of masking the fading quality of the glory of the covenant of which Moses was the mediator.

As we will see shortly, this is less a statement about Moses' integrity or the quality of the Mosaic covenant, and more a statement about the way in which certain rival Jewish Christian teachers have been presenting themselves and seeking to establish themselves in Corinth. It is unlikely that the rival teachers here are promoting a Torah-observant gospel, as were others in Galatia, though they certainly are Jewish Christians like Paul (11:22–23). The rival teachers, however, were depending on and positively valuing their own abilities to impress and win over their hearers. In Paul's eyes, they built upon a far less lasting and glorious foundation than Paul himself did in his own dependence upon God's Spirit to show up and win over Paul's hearers. It is this contrast that seems to suggest to Paul the comparison here between the old covenant, which had a certain, if fading, glory, and the new covenant, which leads to the Christ followers' transformation and translation into glory.

Second Corinthians 3:1–6 anchors this passage in the challenges of the pastoral situation Paul addresses, namely, the ways in which certain rival teachers construct their authority and legitimacy as representatives of the gospel. These rivals rely upon ministerial credentials such as written testimonials from satisfied customers ("letters of recommendation," 3:1–3). This practice leads Paul to compare tablets of stone to tablets of living hearts and thence to compare the covenants. The rival teachers rely as well upon their own rhetorical power and impressive bearing, to which Paul compares unfavorably (10:10, 12; 11:5–6, 18–23a; 12:11). Paul will contend that this all exhibits a fading glory, rather than the basis for a lasting glory. Paul intentionally and steadfastly *refuses* to rely on such things.

For Paul it is essential that the exercise of his ministry not draw people's attention to the human strengths and charisma of a preacher, which are bound to fade, even as the physical body that generates them is bound to decay in the grave. Rather, everything about his ministerial persona and practice aims at being as transparent as possible to the power of God. Only an encounter with *this* power opens up the possibility for transcending the corruption of the grave (see 4:7–12).

The veil is a powerful image running throughout the lection and the paragraph that follows (4:3–6, which is a direct continuation of 4:1–2), where Paul continues to reflect upon his own ministry and responses to it. Paul contends that a veil lies over the Old Testament Scriptures when the majority of his fellow Jews read it and fail to see therein its testimonies to Jesus Christ (3:15–16). Similarly, a veil lies over his gospel as well, obscuring its glory from the many who do not embrace his message. When his hearers cannot see God's power breaking forth in the midst of weakness—whether that of Paul and his team or that of the crucified Messiah Paul proclaims—this veil is impeding their insight (4:7–18).

This is not a veil that Paul throws over his own face; if the power of God is veiled, this is the action of "the god of this age" and not Paul (4:4). Paul claims to be bolder than Moses, for Paul does not try to hide the fading, temporary glory of his life in the flesh. He does not hide from his audience the temporary quality and

---

Elevating Our Hearts toward God

Behold, O loving Lord, I offer you the talent that your condescending intimacy has revealed to me, unworthy as I am. I have used it to obtain the love of your love through what I have written or may yet write. With your grace I can boldly declare my only motive in saying or writing these things has been to obey your will, to promote your glory, and to show concern for the salvation of all. I desire that everyone should praise you and give you thanks that my unworthiness has not caused you to withdraw your mercy from me. I desire also that you should be praised for those who, reading these things, are charmed with the sweetness of your charity and are drawn to desire that love.

You alone are the almighty dispenser of all good things. Pasture us during our exile until, "Beholding the glory of the Lord with unveiled countenance, we are transformed into his image, from glory to glory by the power of the Spirit." In accord with your faithful promises and the humble desire of my heart, I beg you to give the peace of your love to all who read these writings with humility.

May they also have compassion for my miseries and a salutary compunction for their growth in perfection. By elevating their hearts toward you with burning love may they be like so many golden censers, whose sweet smells and colors shall abundantly supply for all my negligence and ingratitude. Amen.

Saint Gertrude the Great (1256–1302), *The Herald of Divine Love*, chap. 24, quoted in Shawn Madigan, CSJ, ed., *Mystics, Visionaries, and Prophets* (Minneapolis: Fortress Press, 1998), 163.

therefore secondary value of all human strengths by trying to cover it up with written testimonials, studied posturing, and charismatic preaching. Paul's transparency in this regard allows the power and light of God to break through upon his hearers, awakening them to the saving, life-giving power of God that transcends all human power and posturing.

While the connections between the Old Testament and epistle readings are explicit, Paul's interpretation of the former also resonates with the Gospel reading. The Gospel story suggests here at the transfiguration that the underlying message of the Hebrew Bible is the suffering, death, and resurrection of the Messiah. Paul expresses this as he writes that the veil that lies over his contemporary Jewish coreligionists' reading of the "old covenant" is removed "only in Christ," that is, from the standpoint of having come to faith in Jesus as that to which God has been leading God's people (2 Cor. 3:14–16).

This is presented more dramatically in the transfiguration narrative as Moses and Elijah, representatives of Law and Prophets, discuss with Jesus his "exodus," his going hence at his death (Luke 9:31). On the other side of the resurrection, the veil is removed from the disciples' own reading of "Moses, the prophets, and the psalms" by Jesus himself (Luke 24:44–47).

The preceding topic points to *the* focal question of the larger canonical context of these lessons, namely, the christocentric reading of the Jewish Scriptures that runs throughout the New Testament. Another canonical connection that would be too easily overshadowed by this is the theme of transformation in Paul's letters. The lection climaxes with Paul's reconfiguration of the scene of Moses' encountering God upon the mountain. Now it is the "we" of the Christ followers who look upon God's glory in the face of Christ (cf. 3:18 and 4:6) and are changed as a result, not just because God's glory radiates from our faces, but because we ourselves are becoming ever more closely and fully a reflection of Christ's own character.

The metamorphosis spoken of here ("we are being changed," *metamorphoumetha*, 3:18) is a significant focus of Paul's understanding of God's work in the believer throughout his letters. He uses a variety of expressions to name this single reality, whether that of being conformed to Christ (Phil. 3:8–11; Rom. 8:28–29), of the new person coming into being while the old person is laid aside (Eph. 4:22–24; Col. 3:5–17), or of Christ taking shape within and living through the believer (Gal. 2:19–20; 4:19). The idea here of being "changed from glory into glory" in ever greater degrees corresponds to Paul's larger conversation about becoming like Christ now in his other-centered humility, in order that one may also, in a future "then," become like Christ in his glory (see esp. Phil. 3:10–11, 20–21).

DAVID A. DESILVA

Commentary 2: Connecting the Reading with the World

For preachers who are reluctant to follow Jesus up the mountain of metamorphosis once again and are ready for something new on this mysterious day, the apostle Paul's words to the Corinthians in 3:12–4:2 offer a worthy homiletical challenge on Transfiguration Sunday in Year C.

Why is this a worthy challenge? It is difficult enough for twenty-first-century readers to sort through one half of the correspondence between the apostle Paul and the church in Corinth. Even when Paul's words seem clear and straightforward, such as in 5:7, "for we walk by faith, not by sight," they are not. Look carefully at the fifth chapter. This simple declarative phrase exists within an extremely complex argument over death and resurrection, embodied faith versus heavenly existence.

The specific Pauline epistle text under consideration for Transfiguration Sunday contains more than a few interpretive minefields, but also some powerful homiletical windows. Any text that begins "Since, then . . ." is begging for exploration of what precedes the transitional phrase. Second Corinthians 3:12 is no exception. Preachers would be wise to note that the lectionary limits of 3:12–4:2 are artificial and fit within a broader, literary context. One interpretive minefield that is relatively easy to avoid is to take seriously the broader literary context in which this text sits.

An interpretive minefield in this text for preachers is how Paul understands the relationship of Jews and Christians. Good preaching on this text requires careful articulation of 3:12–16, so that it does not become a holy harpoon to heave against Jews in Paul's day or Jews today. In this text, Paul, a Jew by birth, is having a theological family dispute with members of the family who do not agree that Jesus is the Anointed One of God. To miss the critical nuance of this internecine dispute means that preachers risk adding to the latent or blatant anti-Semitism that lives within society—and too often within the Christian community.

Another landmine is how to traverse the first-century concerns of Paul with the first-century concerns of the Christian church. The apostle Paul faced no shortage of disheartening realities in his missionary travels, many of which are reflected in his correspondence with churches in Asia Minor, including this text. Centuries later, there are different, but still numerous and disheartening, realities that the church faces today, from a decline in church attendance, a shortage of priests in the Roman Catholic tradition, a hardening of religious tendencies within the Christian family of faith, and an overall ignorance of the biblical witness, to mention but a few. For leaders, preachers, and people in the pews, our age is one in which hope is often veiled and the future is clouded.

So after so many cautionary words and with such dangerous interpretive landmines, amid the current social milieu of the church, why preach on this often maddening, always complex, text on Transfiguration Sunday? Why not walk up the mountain of transfiguration with Peter, James, and John and consign this thorny epistle text to lectionary litter?

In this epistle, Paul dares the Christians in Corinth to believe that they are being transformed in a way that gives glory to God in Christ. Paul's promise is that "we all, with unveiled face, beholding the glory of the Lord, are being transformed into the same image from one degree of glory to another. For this comes from the Lord who is the Spirit" (3:18 ESV). Just as Jesus was transformed, "metamorphosized" by God on the Mount of Transfiguration, so those with faith in Christ are being transformed by the Spirit of God; the veil of ignorance and bondage is being lifted.

Paul insists emphatically that the transformation of Christians and the transformation of the church are a gift of the Spirit. Faith transformation is not the final result of a carefully designed strategic plan or of exceptional personal piety. It is a gift. It is a gift from God. It is a gift from God that frees us from the law, no matter how invaluable the law once was to establishing identity and maintaining community.

Preach 2 Corinthians 3:12–4:2 on Transfiguration Sunday, and remember that our freedom is not a result of our ingenuity, our privileged place in society, our considerable intellect, or our substantial wealth. We are free from such illusions because God in Christ is freeing us from all that obstructs our vision from trusting in Christ and following him.

The great interpretive and homiletical questions, then, are these: Free from what? Free for what? If faith comes to us as divine gift, then those of us who trust in Christ are free from any convoluted understanding that requires us to earn our freedom by berating others into belief, as if we hold the secret to remove the veil of their unbelief, much less our own. The church's evangelical witness is to be done, but not in fear that unless we are "effective," others will be forever bound in sin and distant from the gospel. In Christ, argues Paul, believers are set free; they are free to witness to the freedom we know in Christ, free from worry whether our witness is "successful" or "effective." Our concern, rather, is whether it is free and faithful.

While this text looks back, sometimes in obscure ways, to Moses and the veil covering his face as he came down the mountain with the tablets of the law, ultimately the text points forward to the Spirit of God, who is engaged in transforming the world. In Christ, we "are being transformed into the same image from one degree of glory to another; for this comes from the Lord, the Spirit" (3:18). Simply put, God is not finished with us; in Christ, the Christian life is always a life of faith in progress.

Perhaps the most profound theological and homiletical thrust of this text is the opening sentence of chapter 4: "Therefore, since it is by God's mercy that we are engaged in this ministry, we do not lose heart" (4:1). Preachers, often more than lay leaders or congregational members, can easily mistake the source of their authority. They are ordained and commissioned by a church body to conduct their ministry, but according to Paul, such church orders are penultimate in authority. All of those who trust in Christ engage in Christian ministry "by God's mercy." Our goal then is to give glory to God, not necessarily to please church authorities or entertain congregations.

Preachers are also well acquainted with losing heart and caring for those who face life situations that cause them to lose heart. Martin Luther King Jr. often wove a variation of this admonition into his sermons: "Never lose heart." "Do not lose heart" is not an act of the will to "shape up" and "get over it." We do not lose heart, because God's mercy makes that possible, even in the most disheartening times. We do not lose heart, because Christ is Lord of the church, and our ministry is to invite people to walk with us into God-given freedom in Christ, free from the need to earn God's acceptance, free to live in hope as those who embrace God's acceptance that is already ours in Christ.

Maybe it is worth the homiletical lift to turn to the Corinthian correspondence on Transfiguration Sunday and to explore the profound and complex themes that Paul tackles in 3:12–4:2. Do so with trepidation, but confident that there is much of the glory of God yet to be revealed.

GARY W. CHARLES

Luke 9:28–36 (37–43a)

²⁸Now about eight days after these sayings Jesus took with him Peter and John and James, and went up on the mountain to pray. ²⁹And while he was praying, the appearance of his face changed, and his clothes became dazzling white. ³⁰Suddenly they saw two men, Moses and Elijah, talking to him. ³¹They appeared in glory and were speaking of his departure, which he was about to accomplish at Jerusalem. ³²Now Peter and his companions were weighed down with sleep; but since they had stayed awake, they saw his glory and the two men who stood with him. ³³Just as they were leaving him, Peter said to Jesus, "Master, it is good for us to be here; let us make three dwellings, one for you, one for Moses, and one for Elijah"—not knowing what he said. ³⁴While he was saying this, a cloud came and overshadowed them; and they were terrified as they entered the cloud. ³⁵Then from the cloud came a voice that said, "This is my Son, my Chosen; listen to him!" ³⁶When the voice had spoken, Jesus was found alone. And they kept silent and in those days told no one any of the things they had seen.

³⁷On the next day, when they had come down from the mountain, a great crowd met him. ³⁸Just then a man from the crowd shouted, "Teacher, I beg you to look at my son; he is my only child. ³⁹Suddenly a spirit seizes him, and all at once he shrieks. It convulses him until he foams at the mouth; it mauls him and will scarcely leave him. ⁴⁰I begged your disciples to cast it out, but they could not." ⁴¹Jesus answered, "You faithless and perverse generation, how much longer must I be with you and bear with you? Bring your son here." ⁴²While he was coming, the demon dashed him to the ground in convulsions. But Jesus rebuked the unclean spirit, healed the boy, and gave him back to his father. ⁴³And all were astounded at the greatness of God.

Commentary 1: Connecting the Reading with Scripture

Observed immediately before Ash Wednesday, Transfiguration Sunday (Year C) anticipates the season of Lent, when Christians prepare themselves for the events of Holy Week and Jesus' death. While it may seem strange to think of the glorification of Jesus ahead of his passion, the event of the transfiguration, found near the end of Jesus' Galilean ministry and not long before he "sets his face toward Jerusalem" (Luke 9:51), provides a much-needed preview of Jesus' future glory—a vision of assurance that will encourage the disciples through the dark, long hours between Good Friday and Easter Sunday that lie before them.

Chapter 9 plays a pivotal role in the third Gospel. The question of Jesus' identity comes to the foreground (9:18, 20), only to be followed by the prediction of his death and vindication (9:22), and the purposeful shift of Jesus' focus from Galilee to Jerusalem (9:51). Situated in the midst of these key moments of the Lukan narrative is the account of the transfiguration (9:28–36).

Speculations about who Jesus is have been brewing throughout his Galilean ministry. That Jesus is the Son of God and Davidic Messiah is a fact revealed to a select few in the infancy narratives (1:31–35; 2:11). Most people know Jesus as Joseph's son (3:23; 4:22), and they wonder if he is also a prophet (7:16; 9:7–9, 18–19), a teacher (4:32; 7:40; 9:38), or a healer exorcist (4:36, 40; 6:18). His detractors label him as a blasphemer (5:21) and a friend of sinners and tax collectors (7:34). Even John the Baptist has to ask if Jesus is the one who is to come (7:19–20). Therefore, when Jesus asks his disciples, "Who do you say that I am?" Peter's answer, "The Messiah of God," is perceptive (9:20). Even so, Jesus' disciples have yet to embrace the counterintuitive mission of God's Messiah.

Given this context, the event of the transfiguration authoritatively answers the question of Jesus' identity and mission. Having taken Peter, James, and John up to the mountain, Jesus, in appearance and garb, is transformed into a glorified state while he is praying (9:29). The text does not say exactly how Jesus' face changes, but his dazzling white garments suggest that his entire person is glowing in heavenly radiance. Then suddenly beside him appear Moses and Elijah, also in their glorified states (9:30–31a).

Among the Synoptic Gospels, Luke alone divulges the content of Jesus' conversation with Moses and Elijah. The three discuss Jesus' "departure [*exodos*], which he was about to accomplish at Jerusalem" (9:31b). The Greek word *exodos* carries multiple meanings. First, it recalls the first exodus, when God sent Moses to deliver the Israelites from bondage in Egypt. Second, *exodos* is a euphemism for death, anticipating the means by which the Messiah will save God's people this time. Third, Jesus will indeed depart after his resurrection by way of his ascension into glory. In these three meanings taken together, Jesus' "departure" (*exodos*) represents a salvific mission in which God's Messiah will suffer and die before he is raised and vindicated in glory. This follows exactly Jesus' prediction of his passion in response to Peter's correct identification of him as God's Messiah (9:20; cf. 9:44; 18:31–33; 24:26).

Flustered and unsettled by the supernatural happenings in front of him, Peter's suggestion to build three shelters, perhaps to prolong the experience, seems out of place (9:33). At any rate, the disciples become even more afraid when God's presence overshadows them in a cloud (9:34). Then God bears testimony to Jesus' identity and authority: "This is my Son, my Chosen; listen to him" (9:35; cf. 3:22). That Jesus is the Son of God points simultaneously to his divine identity by virtue of his supernatural conception, and to his royal status as the Messiah from the house of David (2 Sam. 7:14; Ps.

2:7). With God having the last word, the event ends as suddenly as it began (Luke 9:36).

The transfiguration is about Jesus' glory, and Jesus' glory is God's glory (9:26). In the lectionary readings for this Transfiguration Sunday, a comparison emerges between Jesus and Moses. The latter functions as a foil for Jesus, to underscore Jesus' superiority over even the greatest teacher and deliverer of Israel's past. Compared to that of Moses, Jesus' glory is of a totally different order.

Considering Exodus 34 and Luke 9, Moses was up on Mount Sinai, as Jesus is on a mountain. Moses' face shone from having been in God's presence, but Jesus' entire being turns a dazzling white in his glorified state. The Israelites were afraid when they saw Moses' face; so are Peter, James, and John watching the transcendent scene unfold before them. Moses taught the commandments he received from God to the people of Israel, and God commands the three disciples to listen to God's Son. Then, according to Psalm 99:6–7, God speaks to Moses in a cloud just as the heavenly voice addresses the disciples from within the cloud.

Beyond these similarities, it is the difference in the nature of that glory that points to Jesus' superiority over Moses. The glow on Moses' face did not originate from his own glory. It was derived from or reflected off the glory of God when Moses met with God; hence he hid his face behind a veil while the glow faded over time (2 Cor. 3:13; Exod. 34:33, 35). Jesus' glory is the heavenly glory inherent in his divine identity, now revealed to those who believe in him (2 Cor. 3:18a).

The glory of Jesus—so vividly depicted in the event of the transfiguration—is central to New Testament Christology. In the Old Testament, the glory of YHWH represented God's own presence among Israel, whether God appeared in a cloud (Exod. 16:10), at the tent of meeting (Num. 14:10), or when God filled the temple with divine glory (1 Kgs. 8:11). In the New Testament, as Son of God, Jesus embodies God's presence and glory in the world when "the Word became flesh and lived among us, and we have seen his glory, the glory as of a father's only son, full of grace and truth" (John 1:14). In Hebrews, Jesus is depicted as the "radiance of God's glory and the exact representation of [God's] being" (Heb. 1:3 NIV), "worthy of more glory than Moses" (Heb. 3:3). Then there is the grand vision in the book of Revelation, in which the glory attributed to the Lamb (Rev. 5:12–13) is on par with the glory of God (Rev. 4:9–11).

Eschatological and transcendent glory aside, Jesus' transfiguration has much to do with life on earth. For Peter, James, and John, the experience tests the resoluteness of their faith, because Jesus' path of suffering may be theirs to walk as well. As soon as they come down from the mountain, unbelief rears its ugly head when their fellow disciples fail to expel a demon from

a boy (Luke 9:37–43). However, if Jesus' disciples persevere to the end, not only will they behold Jesus' glory; they too will be transformed to share in that glory (2 Cor. 3:16–18).

Christians today have not witnessed Jesus' transfiguration, yet they believe that he is seated in his resplendent glory at the right hand of God. It is the promise and hope of joining Jesus in eternity that sustains believers of all generations through each Lenten and passion season on their own journeys of faith. The commemoration of Jesus' suffering and death is meaningful only because Christ, the vindicated Messiah and Lord, has already been glorified forever.

DIANE G. CHEN

Commentary 2: Connecting the Reading with the World

The juxtaposition of these two divergent pericopes, the transfiguration and the casting out of the demon, helps bring light to both stories. Most lectionaries make the healing story an optional extension of the transfiguration story. Perhaps there is revelation in holding them together, reading them not as disconnected narratives but as natural conversation partners. Can we truly understand the mystery of Christ's presence in our lives without engaging the work of healing and justice? Conversely, can we be sustained in our mission to be agents of liberation without being captured by the cloud of glory? Holding fast to this tensive relationship between mountain and valley allows us to be both restored and filled with renewed power, all without slipping into the clichés that often shape our off-the-mountain-into-the-valley, transfiguration-into-Lent approaches to this text. Our connections flow from mountain to valley for sure, but also from valley to mountain.

Let us start with the healing story for a change (Gk. *metamorphoomai*). Earlier in chapter 9, the disciples had been sent to preach and heal. They were also challenged by Jesus to "give them something to eat" when hungry crowds gathered, all before teaching them the mysterious koan of life with Christ: those who save their life will lose it, and those who lose their life

for the sake of Jesus will find it. We're not sure what happened while Jesus, Peter, John, and James were gone up the mountain, but clearly the disciples lost it. It was only a day, but when the four returned, the disciples were unable to access the healing power of God.

Many of us are all too familiar with this dynamic: filled with the power of the Spirit one day, only to come up empty the next. Churches are notorious at severing the transfiguring cord between work and spirit, making us the agents of a task list rather than missionaries with power. We are clear about what needs to be done—or worse, we are clear about what other people should be doing—yet we lose touch with *why*. Committee meetings seem sterile. Problems become overwhelming, and demons of injustice rage through our society while we watch in despair. These challenges seem particularly devastating as many preachers experience decline and an uncertain future in their denominations.

Sometimes we respond by throwing out process, remaking our structures, or streamlining ministries. We rail against old-fashioned ideas, and thinking outside the box becomes our holy grail. Perhaps our inability to be effective has less to do with process and more to do with our deeper connections to mystery, our experience of a living Christ. When Jesus rails against his followers for being a "faithless and perverse generation"—which demonstrates his true humanity with all its impatience and frustration—he notes their disconnection from the Spirit and their lack of generative power. One teacher reminds young church leaders to keep the connection alive between the living, breathing heart of the Christian faith and the work they do every day. He urges them to do what they need to do to keep the cord taut, expecting transfiguration, even in committee meetings. There is always glory in the quotidian ministry of the Christian church. Sometimes we just have a problem accessing it.

Luke is the only Gospel writer who says that Jesus, Peter, James, and John go up the mountain *to pray*. The experience of transfiguration happens when these four create an intentional space for an encounter with the Divine. It is likely no accident that they go up a mountain. In the ancient Near East, high places were often sites for altars and dreams. Centuries later, pagan Celts and eventually Christians would speak of *thin places*. "Heaven and earth," the Celtic saying goes, "are only three feet apart, but in thin places that distance is even shorter."[1]

In the twenty-first century, we are quick to see all places and all people as holy, but perhaps the transfiguration, despite its otherworldly cloud, invites us to reconsider how we create places for sacred encounter, places that can be deep with divinity. Where are our mountains of transfiguration? Where are the thin places for us, the places that invite us into the world between worlds? It is not likely at our desks or in front of our screens. It is a paradox that there is a connection between the ground under our feet and our spirit in the clouds. It would be an intriguing exploration to consider not only *how* we pray but *where* we pray. Does the transfiguration lead us to see mountains and valleys, the creation itself, as a witness to God's glory, a conversation between Christ and his followers? Is the voice from the cloud calling the followers of Jesus to listen to him in the sounds of bird and beast, wind and cloud?

Clearly heaven and earth come together in this experience. We do indeed learn something about prayer. The disciples are able to see the identity of Jesus, his face and his clothing transparent with glory, his person a thin place. It is grace to discover that the followers of Jesus, who so quickly fail, have an innate capacity to experience glory. Despite fighting sleep during their prayer time—something perhaps not uncommon in our own worship spaces—they are rewarded for their work to be awake to the moment. God rouses them to glimpse behind the curtain. Ironically, this teaches us something about liturgy. In our repetitive, sometimes even boring, ritual practice, we suddenly find ourselves catapulted into another world. In fact, it is precisely this week-in-and-week-out, regular practice that creates the potential for the mountaintop of transfiguration.

When the voice speaks from the cloud, it echoes the voice from the cloud at Jesus' baptism. However, this time, rather than addressing Jesus, it addresses the witnesses, those who have come to know Jesus: "Listen to him!" To the chattering, strategizing, negotiating, overwhelmed, terrified followers of Jesus: Listen. Just stop, and listen. Jesus will say what we need. He will teach us to see depth. He will speak to the demonic forces that throw us to the ground. He will speak even into suffering and death: "Today you will be with me in Paradise" (Luke 23:43). He will continue to speak with disciples on the road to Emmaus and beyond, up mountains and into valleys.

The image of Jesus speaking with Moses and Elijah is striking. Perhaps listening to Jesus comes through our engagement with other saints. Does the transfiguration point us to listen to those saints already involved in the ongoing conversation with God? Of course, it invites us to listen to the saints of the church for guidance and advice. Does it also invite us to create intentional spaces for listening to those who live in worlds different than our own? Are we transfigured when we listen to those most different than ourselves: those from different generations, cultures, neighborhoods, particularly those who live in society's thin and marginalized places? We are well acquainted with the notion that we

---

1. Eric Weiner, "Where Heaven and Earth Come Closer," *New York Times*, March 9, 2012, accessed Nov. 29, 2016, http://www.nytimes.com/2012/03/11/travel/thin-places-where-we-are-jolted-out-of-old-ways-of-seeing-the-world.html.

are to speak truth to power, but perhaps we are also called to listen to those far from the world's power, those being convulsed by injustice, as a key to accessing the Spirit's power.

Finally, we cannot preach the transfiguration without considering the cross, Jesus' "departure" (Gk. *exodos*), the mountain where the fullness of God's love is revealed, the temple curtain finally torn in two, heaven and earth flowing together, liberated, no longer a juxtaposition but a transcendent unity.

BRADLEY E. SCHMELING

Contributors

MARK ABBOTT, Director of Hispanic Distributed Learning, Asbury Theological Seminary, Florida Dunnam Campus, Orlando, FL

KLAUS-PETER ADAM, Associate Professor of Old Testament, Lutheran School of Theology at Chicago, Chicago, IL

RONALD J. ALLEN, Professor of Preaching and New Testament, Christian Theological Seminary, Indianapolis, IN

WES AVRAM, Senior Pastor, Pinnacle Presbyterian Church, Scottsdale, AZ

RHODORA E. BEATON, Associate Professor of Liturgical and Sacramental Theology, Aquinas Institute of Theology, St. Louis, MO

GLEN BELL, Pastor/Head of Staff, First Presbyterian Church of Sarasota, Sarasota, FL

MELISSA BROWNING, Assistant Professor of Contextual Ministry, McAfee School of Theology, Atlanta, GA

CYNTHIA M. CAMPBELL, President Emerita, McCormick Theological Seminary; Pastor, Highland Presbyterian Church, Louisville, KY

LEIGH CAMPBELL-TAYLOR, Interim Pastor, Oakhurst Presbyterian Church, Decatur, GA

WARREN CARTER, Professor of New Testament, Brite Divinity School at Texas Christian University, Fort Worth, TX

GARY W. CHARLES, Pastor, Cove Presbyterian Church, Covesville, VA

DIANE G. CHEN, Professor of New Testament, Palmer Theological Seminary of Eastern University, St. Davids, PA

KIMBERLY L. CLAYTON, Lecturer and Director of Contextual Education, Columbia Theological Seminary, Decatur, GA

SHANNON CRAIGO-SNELL, Professor of Theology, Louisville Presbyterian Theological Seminary, Louisville, KY

ROBERT F. DARDEN, Professor of Journalism, Public Relations, and New Media, Baylor University, Waco, TX

MARÍA TERESA DÁVILA, Associate Professor of Christian Ethics, Andover Newton Theological School, Newton Centre, MA

DAVID A. deSILVA, Trustees' Distinguished Professor of New Testament and Greek, Ashland Theological Seminary, Ashland, OH

PAUL SIMPSON DUKE, Co-Pastor, First Baptist Church of Ann Arbor, Ann Arbor, MI

STACEY SIMPSON DUKE, Co-Pastor, First Baptist Church of Ann Arbor, Ann Arbor, MI

JAMES H. EVANS JR., Robert K. Davies Professor Emeritus of Systematic Theology, Colgate Rochester Crozer Divinity School, Rochester, NY

JOEL B. GREEN, Professor of New Testament Interpretation, Fuller Theological Seminary, Pasadena, CA

ALAN GREGORY, Principal, St. Augustine's College of Theology, West Malling, Kent, UK

L. DANIEL HAWK, Professor of Old Testament and Hebrew, Ashland Theological Seminary, Ashland, OH

JOHN C. HOLBERT, Lois Craddock Perkins Professor Emeritus of Homiletics, Perkins School of Theology, Southern Methodist University, Dallas, TX

CYNTHIA A. JARVIS, Minister/Head of Staff, The Presbyterian Church of Chestnut Hill, Philadelphia, PA

WILLIE JAMES JENNINGS, Associate Professor of Systematic Theology and Africana Studies, Yale Divinity School, New Haven, CT

PABLO A. JIMENEZ, Associate Dean of Hispanic Ministries Program, Gordon Conwell Theological Seminary, South Hamilton, MA

E. ELIZABETH JOHNSON, J. Davison Philips Professor of New Testament, Columbia Theological Seminary, Decatur, GA

BETH FELKER JONES, Professor of Theology, Wheaton College, Wheaton, IL

STEVEN J. KRAFTCHICK, Professor of the Practice of New Testament Interpretation, Candler School of Theology, Emory University, Atlanta, GA

JOEL MARCUS LEMON, Associate Professor of Old Testament; Associate Director of the Graduate Division of Religion, Candler School of Theology, Emory University, Atlanta, GA

MICHAEL L. LINDVALL, Pastor Emeritus, The Brick Presbyterian Church in the City of New York, New York, NY

KIMBERLY BRACKEN LONG, Former Associate Professor of Worship, Columbia Theological Seminary, Decatur, GA

THOMAS G. LONG, Bandy Professor Emeritus of Preaching, Candler School of Theology, Emory University, Atlanta, GA

ELLEN OTT MARSHALL, Associate Professor of Christian Ethics and Conflict Transformation, Candler School of Theology, Emory University, Atlanta, GA

DONALD K. McKIM, Honorably Retired Presbyterian Church (U.S.A.), Germantown, TN

JAMES C. MILLER, Professor of Inductive Biblical Studies and New Testament, Asbury Theological Seminary, Florida Dunnam Campus, Orlando, FL

BLAIR R. MONIE, Professor in The Louis H. and Katherine S. Zbinden Distinguished Chair of Pastoral Ministry and Leadership, Austin Presbyterian Theological Seminary, Austin, TX

RODGER Y. NISHIOKA, Senior Associate Pastor; Director of Adult Educational Ministries, Village Presbyterian Church, Prairie Village, KS

JULIE FAITH PARKER, Assistant Professor of Old Testament, Trinity Lutheran Seminary, Columbus, OH

AMY PEELER, Associate Professor of New Testament, Wheaton College, Wheaton, IL; Associate Rector of St. Mark's Episcopal Church, Geneva, IL

EMERSON B. POWERY, Professor of Biblical Studies, Messiah College, Mechanicsburg, PA

DAVID J. SCHLAFER, Independent Consultant in Preaching and Assisting Priest, Episcopal Church of the Redeemer, Bethesda, MD

BRADLEY E. SCHMELING, Senior Pastor, Gloria Dei Lutheran Church, St. Paul, MN

MATTHEW L. SKINNER, Professor of New Testament, Luther Seminary, St. Paul, MN

DANIEL L. SMITH-CHRISTOPHER, Professor of Theological Studies (Old Testament), Director of New Zealand Study Programs, Loyola Marymount University, Los Angeles, CA

BRENT A. STRAWN, Professor of Old Testament, Candler School of Theology, Emory University, Atlanta, GA

JERRY L. SUMNEY, Professor of Biblical Studies, Lexington Theological Seminary, Lexington, KY

THEODORE J. WARDLAW, President, Austin Presbyterian Theological Seminary, Austin, TX

KHALIA J. WILLIAMS, Assistant Dean of Worship and Music, Assistant Professor in the Practice of Worship, Candler School of Theology, Emory University, Atlanta, GA

JOHN W. WURSTER, Pastor/Head of Staff, Saint Philip Presbyterian Church, Houston, TX

Author Index

Abbreviations

C1	Commentary 1	G	Gospel
C2	Commentary 2	OT	Old Testament
E	Epistle	PS	Psalm

Numerals indicate numbered Sundays of a season; for example, "Advent 1" represents the First Sunday of Advent, and "Christmas 1" the First Sunday after Christmas.

Contributors and entries

Mark Abbott	Epiphany 5 E C1, Epiphany 6 E C1
Klaus-Peter Adam	Christmas Day II OT C1, Christmas Day III OT C1, Epiphany 2 OT C1
Ronald J. Allen	Christmas Day III G C1, Christmas 1 G C1, Christmas 2 G C1
Wes Avram	Epiphany 6 G C1, Epiphany 7 G C1, Epiphany 8 G C1
Rhodora E. Beaton	Epiphany 4 PS, Epiphany 5 PS, Epiphany 6 PS
Glen Bell	Christmas 1 OT C1, Christmas 2 OT C1, Epiphany 3 OT C1
Melissa Browning	Christmas 1 OT C2, Christmas 2 OT C2, Epiphany 3 OT C2
Cynthia M. Campbell	Advent 1 E C1, Advent 2 E C1, Advent 3 E C1
Leigh Campbell-Taylor	Christmas Eve PS, Christmas Day II PS, Christmas Day III PS
Warren Carter	Epiphany 3 G C1, Epiphany 4 G C1, Epiphany 5 G C1
Gary W. Charles	Epiphany 9 E C2, Transfiguration E C2
Diane G. Chen	Epiphany 9 G C1, Transfiguration G C1
Kimberly L. Clayton	Advent 1 PS, Advent 2 PS, Advent 3 PS, Advent 4 PS
Shannon Craigo-Snell	Epiphany 2 E C1, Epiphany 3 E C1, Epiphany 4 E C1
Robert F. Darden	Epiphany 6 G C2, Epiphany 7 G C2, Epiphany 8 G C2
María Teresa Dávila	Epiphany 7 E C2, Epiphany 8 E C2
David A. deSilva	Epiphany 9 E C1, Transfiguration E C1
Paul Simpson Duke	Advent 4 G C2, Christmas Eve G C2, Christmas Day II G C2
Stacey Simpson Duke	Epiphany 5 OT C2, Epiphany 7 OT C2, Epiphany 8 OT C2

Scripture Index

Scripture citations that appear in boldface represent the assigned readings from the Revised Common Lectionary.

OLD TESTAMENT

Genesis

1	32
1–3	113
1:1–3	105
1:26–28	113
2:7	261–63
4:1–16	257
7:1	13
7:11	173
12:1–3	296
12:2	272
12:2–3	277
12:3	152, 219
14:18–24	105
15:1	92, 161
16:7–13	93
19	18
21–22	113
21:17	92, 161
22:12	92
25:22	131
26:24	92, 161
26:24–25	161
29:21–28	189
32:30	93
35:19	76
37–50	255, 257
37:3	255
37:3–11	260
37:6–7	255
37:7	256
37:9	255–56
37:33	258
37:33–35	255
37:35	258
39:1–23	255
39:23	258
40	255
41:1–57	256
41:16	256
41:38	255

41:51	258
42:1–8	256
42:4	258
42:6–9	260
42:7	256
42:9a	256
42:21	258
42:24	258
43:30	258
44:18–34	256
44:34	258
45	256
45:1–2	258
45:1–15	256–57
45:3–11	**255–58**, 260
45:4	258
45:5	258, 260
45:8	258
45:14–15	258
45:15	**255–58**
46:3	161
46:29	258
50:1	258
50:15–21	257
50:17	258
50:20	258, 260

Exodus

1:22	156
2:1–10	156
3:1–4:17	208, 211
3:2	93
3:5–6	225, 236
3:6	93
3:12	94
4:10	209
16	236
16:10	313
19:3–6	72
19:5	72
24–40	300
24:9–10	140
24:9–18	302

24:15	305
24:29–35	302
28:41	93
33:9	140
34	303, 307
34:29	307
34:29–35	**300–303**,305, 313
34:33	313
34:35	313
40:34	140

Leviticus

25	205
25:8–13	207

Numbers

6:24–25	53
6:24–26	40
12:6–8	156
14:10	313
22:22	93

Deuteronomy

4:19	93
6:1–9	129
6:4–9	112
7:6	72
13:2–6	156
15:2	205
17:3	93
18:9–14	158
18:15–22	208
28	251
30:1–5	192
32:10–14	113

Judges

6:11–12	208
13:22	93
14:10–12	189
19	76

Ruth

4:11–12	76